THE GREEK
MAGICAL PAPYRI
IN TRANSLATION

Contributors

D.E.A.   David E. Aune, Professor of New Testament and Early Christianity, Loyola University, Chicago

J.B.   Jan Bergman, Professor of the History of Religions, University of Uppsala

H.D.B.   Hans Dieter Betz, Professor of New Testament, The Divinity School, University of Chicago

W.B.   Walter Burkert, Professor of Classical Philology, University of Zürich

J.M.D.   John M. Dillon, Professor of Classics, Trinity College, Dublin

W.C.G.   William C. Grese, Bloomington, Illinois

J.P.H.   Jackson P. Hershbell, Professor of Classics, University of Minnesota

R.F.H.   Ronald F. Hock, Professor of Religion, University of Southern California

J.H.J.   Janet H. Johnson, Professor of Egyptology, The Oriental Institute, University of Chicago

R.D.K.   Roy D. Kotansky, Los Angeles

H.M.   Hubert Martin, Jr., Professor of Classics, University of Kentucky

M.W.M.   Martin W. Meyer, Professor of Religion, Chapman College, Orange, California

E.N.O.   Edward N. O'Neil, Professor of Classics, University of Southern California

R.K.R.   Robert K. Ritner, Associate Professor of Egyptology, The Oriental Institute, University of Chicago

J.S.   John Scarborough, Professor of Classics and Pharmacy, University of Wisconsin

M.S.   Morton Smith, Professor of Ancient History, Columbia University (deceased)

THE GREEK MAGICAL PAPYRI

IN TRANSLATION

INCLUDING THE DEMOTIC SPELLS

Edited by
HANS DIETER BETZ

SECOND EDITION

THE UNIVERSITY OF CHICAGO PRESS
Chicago & London

THE UNIVERSITY OF CHICAGO PRESS, CHICAGO 60637
THE UNIVERSITY OF CHICAGO PRESS, LTD., LONDON
© 1986, 1992 by The University of Chicago
All rights reserved.
Second edition published in 1992
Paperback edition 1996
Printed in the United States of America

26 25 24 23   9 10 11 12 13 14 15

ISBN-13: 978-0-226-04447-7 (paper)
ISBN-10: 0-226-04447-5 (paper)

The first edition was supported by the National Endowment
for the Humanities, a federal agency which supports the
study of such fields as history, philosophy, literature,
and languages.

LIBRARY OF CONGRESS CATALOGING-IN-PUBLICATION DATA
The Greek magical papyri in translation, including the Demotic spells edited by Hans Dieter Betz.—2nd ed.
    p.   cm.
Translation of Greek texts and Coptic glosses, chiefly from the
Papyri graecae magicae. 2nd ed., and Demotic texts from various
sources.
    Includes bibliographical references.
    1. Magic, Greek—Early works to 1800. 2. Magic, Egyptian—
Early works to 1800. 3. Incantations—Early works to 1800.
4. Charms—Early works to 1800. I. Betz, Hans Dieter. II. Papyri
graecae magicae. English. 1992.
BF1622.G8G74   1992
133.4'3'00938—dc20   92-5617
                                                    CIP

⊗ The paper used in this publication meets the minimum
requirements of the American National Standard for Information
Sciences—Permanence of Paper for Printed Library Materials,
ANSI Z39.48-1992.

Shall we write about the things not to be spoken of?
Shall we divulge the things not to be divulged?
Shall we pronounce the things not to be pronounced?

Julian, Hymn to the Mother of the Gods

Contents

Preface to the Second Edition

Sooner than expected a second edition of the present work has become necessary. After some thinking concerning possible additions of new texts, the idea was dropped in favor of a corrected reprint. Because of the constant flow of newly appearing texts, the volume will, in a sense, always be behind the current state of publications. A new bibliographical appendix to this edition will help readers to keep informed about the growing body of materials.

Corrections were submitted by members of the team of contributors, by reviewers and others, among them especially Richard Gordon, Edward N. O'Neil, and Morton Smith. The research specialist helping with the revisions was Walter Wilson. All who have made contributions deserve a hearty thank you.

This edition of the work is dedicated to the memory of Morton Smith (May 28, 1915–July 11, 1991). He was the first to suggest the whole project, and he never ceased to give his attention to it.

Preface

This volume of translations of the Greek magical papyri has been a long time in the making. The project began in a planning colloquium at Claremont, California, May 31 to June 4, 1978. At this meeting, a team of scholars resolved to produce this translation volume as part of a research project on the Greek magical papyri, the project as a whole being designed as a contribution to the *Corpus Hellenisticum Novi Testamenti*.

The translations turned out to be more difficult and time-consuming than had been expected. Since it seemed desirable to expand the Preisendanz collection to include as many newly discovered and newly published magical papyri as possible, the number of papyri increased from 81 to 131. In this respect, the translation volume differs from the Preisendanz volumes. It differs also in that while Preisendanz reproduced only the Greek sections of bilingual Greek-Demotic papyri, this volume includes the full translations of all bilingual texts.

All translations are based on the Greek, Demotic, and Coptic texts. *PGM* I–LXXXI follow the Preisendanz edition, while *PGM* LXXXII–CXXX and *PDM* Supplement follow their critical editions, which are indicated in the notes. Translators were free to make changes in the texts when they thought it necessary; these changes are also indicated in the notes. Where earlier translations exist, they have been consulted, but all the translations included in this volume are new.

Unlike the Preisendanz edition, this new volume does not have an *apparatus criticus*. Instead, it has notes explaining difficulties in the text and the translation, and notes alerting readers to important information. It has been necessary to limit these notes to a degree which many readers may find drastic, but the team decided not to attempt what could only be a lengthy commentary on the papyri. Instead, they agreed that other research tools should be developed to encourage and assist further research on the papyri. The following research tools are presently being prepared:

1. An index of Greek words is being prepared by Professor Edward O'Neil.

2. A subject index based on the English translation is being worked out by Ms. Marjorie Menaul.

3. A collection of parallels between the magical papyri and early Christian literature is being prepared by the research team. This part of the project is most directly related to the task of the *Corpus Hellenisticum Novi Testamenti*, namely, the collection of parallels from ancient literature to the New Testament and the other Christian literature up to approximately A.D. 150.

4. A comprehensive bibliography, including editions and investigations of the magical papyri, is being assembled by Professor David Hellholm.

The present volume would not have come about without the generous support of institutions and individuals. The National Endowment for the Humanities has funded the entire venture from the beginning by substantial grants from 1978 to 1983. Without this financial assistance, the project would simply not exist; scholarly team projects of this magnitude cannot live on enthusiasm alone. Apart from the purely financial aspect, the officers of the NEH have helped more than they may realize by their quiet encouragement and confidence expressed over a number of years.

A great deal of assistance also came from the institutions where the project was initiated and where it is now based. These include the Institute for Antiquity and Christianity at Claremont, where the project was based during the years 1977 and 1978, and the Institute for the Advanced Study of Religion at the University of Chicago, where it has been from 1978 to the present. Thanks are especially due to the officers of these institutions, Professors James M. Robinson and James Brashler of the Institute for Antiquity and Christianity; and Professors Joseph M. Kitagawa, formerly dean, and Franklin I. Gamwell, currently dean, of the Divinity School of the University of Chicago, as well as to Martin E. Marty, program coordinator for the Institute for the Advanced Study of Religion of the University of Chicago.

The present project could not have succeeded without the unfailing loyalty and generosity of the members of the team, both contributors and consultants. Among these should be named Professors Jan Bergman, Walter Burkert, Franco Maltomini, and P. J. Sijpesteijn. The research specialists of the project, Professor William C. Grese (1977–80), and Mr. Roy Kotansky and Ms. Marjorie Menaul (1980–83), not only helped to carry the burdens of administration and editorship, but made substantial contributions to the project as well. To all of them sincere thanks are due.

H. D. Betz

Table of Spells

This list of spells presupposes the divisions in the texts and the identification of section titles made by the editor. In the Demotic spells, section titles are sometimes indicated by red lettering (but this is not done consistently). If no titles are given, this fact is stated (No title) and a short description of content is added.

Reference	Translator	Short Title
PGM I		(No title) Magical handbook
PGM I. 1–42	E.N.O.	[Rite] for acquiring an assistant daimon
PGM I. 42–195	E.N.O.	The spell of Pnouthis (for acquiring an assistant daimon)
PGM I. 195–222	E.N.O.	Prayer of deliverance
PGM I. 222–31	E.N.O.	Invisibility spell
PGM I. 232–47	E.N.O.	Memory spell
PGM I. 247–62	E.N.O.	Spell for invisibility
PGM I. 262–347	E.N.O.	Apollonian invocation
PGM II		(No title) Magical handbook
PGM II. 1–64	J.M.D. / E.N.O.	(No title) Spell for revelation
PGM II. 65–183	J.M.D. / E.N.O.	(No title) Alternative spell for revelation
PGM III		(No title) Magical handbook
PGM III. 1–164	J.M.D.	(No title) Cat ritual for many purposes
PGM III. 165–86	J.M.D.	(No title) Oracular request (?)
PGM III. 187–262	J.M.D. / E.N.O.	(No title) Spell for revelation
PGM III. 263–75	W.C.G.	Foreknowledge charm
PGM III. 275–81	E.N.O.	[Horoscope]
PGM III. 282–409	W.C.G. / M.W.M.	(No title) Spell for foreknowledge
PGM III. 410–23	W.C.G.	(No title) Memory spell
PGM III. 424–66	W.C.G.	A copy from a holy book (spell for foreknowledge and memory)
PGM III. 467–78	W.C.G.	Memory spell
PGM III. 479–83	W.C.G.	Foreknowledge charm
PGM III. 483–88	W.C.G.	Another (foreknowledge charm to detect a thief)
PGM III. 488–94	W.C.G.	Another (spell to detect a thief?)
PGM III. 494–611	W.C.G. / E.N.O.	[Spell to establish a relationship with] Helios
PGM III. 612–32	J.M.D.	(No title) Spell for gaining control of one's shadow
PGM III. 633–731	M.W.M.	(No title) Spell for a direct vision
PGM IV		(No title) Magical handbook
PGM IV. 1–25	M.W.M.	(No title) Spell for revelation
PGM IV. 26–51	H.M.	Initiation
PGM IV. 52–85	H.M. / M.W.M.	(No title) Spell for revelation
PGM IV. 86–87	M.W.M.	Phylactery against daimons

List of Papyri in Preisendanz

Reference	Location	Number	Date
I	Berlin, Staatliche Museen	*P.Berol.* inv. 5025	IV^p/V^p
II	Berlin, Staatliche Museen	*P.Berol.* inv. 5026	IV^p
III	Paris, Musée du Louvre	no. 2396 (*P.*Mimaut frgs. 1–4)	IV^p
IV	Paris, Bibliothèque Nationale	*P.Bibl.Nat. Suppl.* gr. no. 574	IV^p
V	London, British Museum	*P.Lond.* 46	IV^p?
Va	Uppsala, Victoriamuseet	*P.Holm.*, p. 42	
VI	London, British Museum	*P.Lond.* 47	II^p or III^p
VII	London, British Museum	*P.Lond.* 121	III^p/IV^p
VIII	London, British Museum	*P.Lond.* 122	IV^p or V^p
IX	London, British Museum	*P.Lond.* 123	IV^p or V^p
X	London, British Museum	*P.Lond.* 124	IV^p or V^p
XIa	London, British Museum	*P.Lond.* 125 verso	V^p
XIb	London, British Museum	*P.Lond.* 147	III^p
XIc	London, British Museum	*P.Lond.* 148	II^p/III^p
XII	Leiden, Rijksmuseum van Oudheden	*P.Lugd.Bat.* J 384 (V)	IV^p
XIII	Leiden, Rijksmuseum van Oudheden	*P.Lugd.Bat.* J 395 (W)	IV^p
XIV	London, British Museum	*P.Lond.demot.* 10070	III^p
	Leiden, Rijksmuseum van Oudheden	*P.Lugd.Bat.* J 383	III^p
XV	Alexandria, Musée gréco-romain d'Alexandrie	*P.Alex.* inv. 491	III^p
XVI	Paris, Musée du Louvre	no. 3378	I^p
XVIIa	Strasbourg, Bibliothèque universitaire et régionale	*P.gr.* 1167	IV^p
XVIIb	Strasbourg, Bibliothèque universitaire et régionale	*P.gr.* 1179	II^p
XVIIc	Strasbourg, Bibliothèque universitaire et régionale	*P.gr.* 574	
XVIIIa	Berlin, Staatliche Museen	*BGU* III 955	III^p/V^p
XVIIIb	Berlin, Staatliche Museen	*BGU* III 956	III^p/V^p
XIXa	Berlin, Staatliche Museen	*P.Berol.* inv. 9909	IV^p or V^p
XIXb	Berlin, Staatliche Museen	*P.Berol.* inv. 11737	IV^p
XX	Berlin, Staatliche Museen	*P.Berol.* inv. 7504 + *P.Amh.* ii, Col. II (A) + *P.Oxy. inedit.* (=Pack² 1872)	I^a
XXI	Berlin, Staatliche Museen	*P.Berol.* inv. 9566 verso	II^p or III^p
XXIIa	Berlin, Staatliche Museen	*BGU* IV 1026 (inv. no. 9873)	IV^p or V^p
XXIIb	Berlin, Staatliche Museen	*P.Berol.* inv. 13895	IV^p

XXIII	Oxford, Bodleian Library	*P.Oxy.* 412	III^P
XXIVa	Oxford, Bodleian Library	*P.Oxy.* 886	III^P
XXIVb	Oxford, Bodleian Library	*P.Oxy.* 887	III^P
XXVa	Oxford, Bodleian Library	*P.Oxy.* 959	III^P
XXVb	Freiburg i. Br., Universitätsbibliothek	*P. Un.Bibl.Freib.* (w/o no.)	VI^P
XXVc	Cairo, Musée des antiquités égyptiennes	*P.Cairo* 10434	
XXVd	Florence, Società Italiana per la ricerca de papiri	*P.Flor.* (w/o no.)	
XXVI	Oxford, Bodleian Library	*P.Oxy.* 1477	III^P/IV^P
XXVII	Oxford, Bodleian Library	*P.Oxy.* 1478	III^P/IV^P
XXVIIIa	Oxford, Bodleian Library	*P.Oxy.* 2061	V^P
XXVIIIb	Oxford, Bodleian Library	*P.Oxy.* 2062	VI^P
XXVIIIc	Oxford, Bodleian Library	*P.Oxy.* 2063	VI^P
XXIX	Oxford, Bodleian Library	*P.Oxy.* 1383	III^P
XXXa–f	[omitted]		
XXXIa–c	[omitted]		
XXXII	London, University College Institute of Archaeology	*P.Haw.* 312	II^P
XXXIII	Berkeley, University of California	*P.Tebt.* II 275	III^P
XXXIV	Ann Arbor, University of Michigan Library	*P.Fay.* 5	II^P/III^P
XXXV	Florence, Università degli Studi, Istituto di Papirologia	PSI I 29	V^P
XXXVI	Oslo, Universitetsbiblioteket	*P.Osl.* I, 1	IV^P
XXXVII	Oslo, Universitetsbiblioteket	*P.Osl.* I, 2	IV^P
XXXVIII	Oslo, Universitetsbiblioteket	*P.Osl.* I, 3	IV^P
XXXIX	Oslo, Universitetsbiblioteket	*P.Osl.* I, 4	IV^P
XL	Vienna, Nationalbibliothek	*P.gr.* 1	IV^P
XLI	Vienna, Nationalbibliothek	*P.gr.* 339 = *P.Rain.* 4	V^P/VI^P
XLII	Vienna, Nationalbibliothek	*P.gr.* 331 = *P.Rain.* 8	VI^P
XLIII	Vienna, Nationalbibliothek	*P.gr.* 335 = *P.Rain.* 9	V^P
XLIV	Vienna, Nationalbibliothek	*P.gr.* 328 = *P.Rain.* 10	NA
XLV	Vienna, Nationalbibliothek	*P.gr.* 334 = *P.Rain.* 11	VI^P/VII^P
XLVI	Vienna, Nationalbibliothek	*P.gr.* 332 = *P.Rain.* 12	V^P
XLVII	Vienna, Nationalbibliothek	inv. no. 8034 = *P.Rain.* 2 [no. 526, Wessely]	NA
XLVIII	Vienna, Nationalbibliothek	inv. no. 8031 = *P.Rain.* 6 [no. 529, Wessely]	VI^P/VII^P
XLIX	Vienna, Nationalbibliothek	inv. no. 8035 = *P.Rain.* 7 [no. 525, Wessely]	NA
L	Vienna, Nationalbibliothek	inv. no. 8033 = *P.Rain.* [no. 527, Wessely]	VI^P
LI	Leipzig, Universitätsbibliothek	*P.gr.* 9.418	III^P
LII	Leipzig, Universitätsbibliothek	*P.gr.* 9.429	III^P
LIII–LVI	[omitted]		
LVII	Ann Arbor, University of Michigan	cryptogr. pap. [otherwise uncataloged]	I^P/II^P
LVIII	Giessen, Universitätsbibliothek	inv. no. 266 = P. Iand. 87	IV^P
LIX	Cairo, Musée des antiquités égyptiennes	*P.Cairo* 10563	II^P or III^P
LX	Brussels, Fondation Egyptologique Reine Elisabeth	*P.Brux.* in. E 6390, 6391	VI^P

LXI	London, British Museum	*P.Brit.Mus.* inv. 10588 (Egyptian Dept.)	III^P
LXII	Leiden, Institutum Papyrologicum Universitatis Lugduno-Batavae	*P.Warren* 21	III^P
LXIII	Vienna, Nationalbibliothek	*P.gr.* 323	II^P/III^P
LXIV	Vienna, Nationalbibliothek	*P.gr.* 29273	IV^P
LXV	Vienna, Nationalbibliothek	*P.gr.* 29272	VI^P/VII^P
LXVI	Cairo, Musée des antiquités égyptiennes	*P.Cairo* 60139	III^P/IV^P
LXVII	Cairo, Musée des antiquités égyptiennes	*P.Cairo* 60140	NA
LXVIII	Cairo, Musée des antiquités égyptiennes	*P.Cairo* 60636	II^P/III^P
LXIX	Ann Arbor, University of Michigan	inv. no. 1463 = *P.Mich.* III, 156	II^P
LXX	Ann Arbor, University of Michigan	inv. no. 7 = *P.Mich.* III, 154	III^P or IV^P
LXXI	Ann Arbor, University of Michigan	inv. no. 193 = *P.Mich.* III, 155	II^P or III^P
LXXII	Oslo, Universitetsbiblioteket	inv. no. 75 = *P.Osl.* III, 75	I^P/II^P
LXXIII–LXXVI [omitted: oracle questions]			
LXXVII	Birmingham, Woodbroke College	*P.Harr.* 55	II^P
LXXVIII	Heidelberg, Universitätsbibliothek	*P.Heid.* 2170	III^P
LXXIX	Prague, National and University Library	*P.gr.* I, 18	III^P or IV^P
LXXX	Prague, National and University Library	*P.gr.* I, 21	III^P or IV^P
LXXXI	London, Egypt Exploration Society	*P.Oxy.* 1566	IV^P

List of New Papyri Not in Preisendanz

Note: Bibliographical references are provided at the end of the translation of each spell.

Reference	Location	Number	Date
LXXXII	Warsaw, Uniwersytet Warszawski	*P. Vars.* 4	III[p]
LXXXIII	Princeton, Princeton University AM 8963	*P. Princ.* II 107	
LXXXIV	Princeton, Princeton University Garrett Dep. 7665	*P. Princ.* II 76	III[p]
LXXXV	Birmingham, Selly Oak Colleges Central Library	*P. Harris* 56	I[p]/II[p]
LXXXVI	Paris, L'Institut de Papyrologie de l'Université de Paris	*P. Rein.* II 89 inv. 2176	IV[p]
LXXXVII	Erlangen, Universitätsbibliothek	*P. Erlangen* 37	IV[p]
LXXXVIII	Princeton, Princeton University AM 11230	*P. Princ.* III 159	III[p] or IV[p]
LXXXIX	Lund, Universitetsbiblioteket	*P. Lund Univ. Bibl.* IV 12 inv. no. 32	IV[p]
XC	Università Cattolica del Sacro Cuore	*P. Med.* inv. no. 23	IV[p]/V[p]
XCI	Collection, G. A. Michaïlidis	*P. Michael.* 27	III[p] or IV[p]
XCII	Dublin, Chester Beatty Library	*P. Merton* II 58	III[p]
XCIII	London, Egypt Exploration Society	*P. Ant.* II 65	V[p]
XCIV	London, Egypt Exploration Society	*P. Ant.* II 66	V[p]
XCV	London, Egypt Exploration Society	*P. Ant.* III 140	V[p]/VI[p]
XCVI	Barcelona, Seminario di papirologia . . . San Cugat del Valles	*P. Palau Rib.* inv. 126	IV[p]/V[p]
XCVII	Köln, Institut für Altertumskunde	*P. Köln* inv. 1886	III[p]/IV[p]
XCVIII	Köln, Institut für Altertumskunde	*P. Köln* inv. 1982	III[p]
XCIX	Köln, Institut für Altertumskunde	*P. Köln* inv. 2283	V[p]/VI[p]
C	Köln, Institut für Altertumskunde	*P. Köln* inv. 2861	V[p]/VI[p]
CI	Köln, Institut für Altertumskunde	*P. Köln* inv. 3323	V[p]

CII	London, Egypt Exploration Society	*P.Oxy.* 2753	IV^P
CIII	Athens, Archaeological Society	*P.S.A. Athen.* 70	II^P
CIV	Genoa, Università di Genova	*PUG* I 6	III^P
CV	Berlin, Sammlung des Ägyptischen Museums	*P.Berol.* 21227	III^P/IV^P
CVI	Berlin, Sammlung des Ägyptischen Museums	*P.Berol.* 21165	III^P/IV^P
CVII	Köln, Institut für Altertumskunde	*P.Köln* inv. 5512	III^P or IV^P
CVIII	Köln, Institut für Altertumskunde	*P.Köln* inv. 5514	III^P or IV^P
CIX	London, Egypt Exploration Society	*P.Oxy.* 50.4 B23 J(1–3)b	ca. A.D. 300
CX	Washington, Washington University	*P.Wash. Univ.* inv. 181	II^P or III^P
CXI	Washington, Washington University	*P.Wash. Univ.* inv. 139	III^P/IV^P
CXII	Washington, Washington University	*P.Wash. Univ.* inv. 242	IV^P/V^P
CXIII	Amsterdam, Bibliotheek der Universiteit van Amsterdam	*P.Amst.* inv. 16	V^P
CXIV	Yale, Yale University Library	*P.Yale* inv. 989	III^P/IV^P
CXV	Budapest, Collection of Erno Gaál	*P.(Mag.) Gaál.* ined.	IV^P
CXVI	Florence, Biblioteca Medicea Laurenziana	*P.Laur.* inv. 54	VI^P
CXVII	Munich, Bayerische Staatsbibliothek, Handschriftenabteilung	*P.Mon.Gr.* inv. 216	I^a
CXVIII	Barcelona, Seminario di papirologia . . . San Cugat del Valles	*P.Palau Rib.* inv. 200	before X^P?
CXIX	Florence, Biblioteca Medicea Laurenziana	*P. Laur.* III 57 (PL II/52)	III^P
CXX	Florence, Biblioteca Medicea Laurenziana	*P.Laur.* III 58 (PL III/442)	III^P
CXXI	Milan, Università Cattolica di Milano	*P.Med.* inv. 71.58	III^P/IV^P
CXXII	Berlin, Staatliche Museen	*P.Berol.* inv. 21243	I^a/I^P
CXXIIIa–f	Pisa, Università di Pisa	*P.Cazzaniga*, nos. 1–6	V^P
CXXIV	Pisa, Università di Pisa	*P.Cazzaniga*, no. 7	V^P
CXXVa–f	Pisa, Università di Pisa	*P.Cazzaniga*, nos. 8–13	V^P–VI^P
CXXVI	Florence, Biblioteca Medicea Laurenziana	*P.Laur.* III/472	V^P
CXXVII	Yale, Yale University Library	*P.Yale* inv. 1206	III^P or IV^P
CXXVIII	Heidelberg, Universitäts-Papyrussammlung	*P.Heid.G.* 1386	V^P
CXXIX	Berlin, Sammlung des Ägyptischen Museums (?)	*P.Berol.* 21260	III^P
CXXX	Ann Arbor, University of Michigan	*P.Mich.* inv. 6666	III^P
PDM Supplement	Paris, Musée du Louvre	*P.Louvre* E3229	III^P

Note on Editions

For the editions of the Greek papyri as cited, see the bibliography in E. G. Turner, *Greek Papyri, an Introduction* (Oxford: Oxford University Press, ²1980), pp. 154–77, with the following exceptions:

PGM XC: A. Traversa, *Aegyptus* 33 (1953):57–62

PGM XCVI: R. W. Daniel, *ZPE* 25 (1977):150–53

PGM XCVII–CI: D. Wortmann, *BoJ* 168 (1968):85–111

PGM CV–CVI: W. Brashear, *ZPE* 17 (1975):25–33

PGM CVII–CVIII: R. Daniel, *ZPE* 19 (1975):249–64

PGM CIX: P. Gorissen, *ZPE* 37 (1980):199–200

PGM CX–CXII: Z. M. Packman, *BASP* 13 (1976):175–80

PGM CXIII: P. J. Sijpesteijn, *ZPE* 22 (1976):108

PGM CXIV–CXV: R. W. Daniel, *ZPE* 25 (1977):145–54

PGM CXVI: R. Pintaudi, *ZPE* 26 (1977):245–48

PGM CXVII: P. Fabrini and F. Maltomini, in A. Carlini, ed., *Papiri Letterari Greci* (Pisa: Giardini, 1978), no. 34

PGM CXVIII: J. O'Callaghan, *StPapy* 17 (1978):85–87

PGM CXIX–CXX: R. Pintaudi, *Dai Papiri della Biblioteca Medicea Laurenziana* (*P.Laur. III*), *Papyrologica Florentina* 5 (Firenze: Gonnelli, 1979), nos. 57–58

PGM CXXI: G. Geraci, *Aegyptus* 33 (1979):63–72

PGM CXXII: W. Brashear, *ZPE* 33 (1979):261–78

PGM CXXIII–CXXV: F. Maltomini, *Studi Classici e Orientali* 29 (1979):55–124

PGM CXXVI: F. Maltomini, in R. Pintaudi, ed., *Dai Papiri della Biblioteca Medicea Laurenziana* (*P.Laur. IV*), *Papyrologica Florentina* 12 (Firenze: Gonnelli, 1983):46–53

PGM CXXVII: G. M. Parássoglou, *Hellenica* 27 (1974):251–53

PGM CXXVIII–CXXIX: F. Maltomini, *Studi Classici e Orientali* 31 (1981):111–117

PGM CXXX: R. W. Daniel, *ZPE* 50 (1983):147–54

For the Demotic magical papyri, see Janet H. Johnson's Introduction to the Demotic Magical Papyri below, pp. lv–lviii. The editions are accordingly:

PDM xii: J. H. Johnson, *OMRM* 56 (1975):29–64

PDM xiv: F. Ll. Griffith and H. Thompson, *The Demotic Magical Papyrus of London and Leiden*, 3 vols. (London: Grevel, 1904)

PDM lxi: Bell, Nock, and Thompson, *Magical Texts*

PDM Supplement: J. H. Johnson, *Enchoria* 7 (1977):55–102

Explanation of References
and Textual Signs

PGM I.
262–347

References cited thus refer to translations of the corresponding Greek text of Preisendanz's *Papyri Graecae Magicae*, with each roman numeral (including those with appended letters, e.g., *PGM* Va) corresponding to a separate papyrus manuscript. Roman numerals after *PGM* LXXXI refer to texts whose translations are based on editions published since, and sometimes overlooked by, Preisendanz. The bibliographies of these editions are mentioned in the introductory note (*) to each spell. Arabic numerals usually delineate the compass of individual spells within the papyrus manuscript. The use of the separate designations for each independent spell or charm represents a new feature designed to enable easy identification and ready reference to an individual spell.

PDM xxi. 6–20

References listed thus refer to Demotic (bilingual) spells corresponding to the texts whose editions are listed in the introductory note (*) to each spell. *PDM* stands for *Papyri Demoticae Magicae*, referring to this volume and not to be confused with *DMP*, an abbreviation for Griffith and Thompson, *Demotic Magical Papyri*, a work often referred to in the notes. Lowercase roman numerals are used simply to avoid confusion with spells labeled *PGM*. Arabic numerals are used as above.

[*PGM* XII.
445–48]

PGM references bracketed thus come immediately after references for bilingual Greek sections with the given spell. The references correspond to the appropriate Greek portions in Preisendanz, whose edition contained only the Greek sections of the Greek/Demotic spells. Since this translation volume contains all the Demotic spells, Preisendanz's numbering system is retained, but it is subsumed under the new Demotic collation.

A,b,c

Texts set in roman type represent spells and portions of spells whose original language was Greek.

A,b,c

Texts set with leader dots beneath represent spells and portions of spells whose original language was Demotic (Egyptian).

A,b,c

Texts with a thin underscore represent spells and portions of spells whose original language was Old Coptic. Coptic is found both in the Greek texts of Preisendanz's edition and as glosses in portions of the Demotic/Greek bilingual spells; however, the purely Coptic magical spells form a separate corpus not dealt with in this volume.

*	An asterisk introduces an independent spell or a spell that contains most of the constituent parts necessary to effect the whole charm, though organic connections with adjacent spells can be recognized (e.g., spells entitled "*Another* . . . ," or the like). The asterisk directs the reader to the contributor, whose name is given at the end of the spell. Some introductory comments may be found here as well. Bibliographical data, if appropriate, may also be listed.
Tr.:	This abbreviation stands for "translator" or "transcriber" (if the text contains no recognizable words that can be translated).
Victory spell:	Phrases set in roman boldface type refer to general titles of charms which usually stand at the beginning of the spell and which are often followed by one or more subtitles. Many spells do not possess a title, either because of a scribal omission or because it has been lost in a lacuna in the text.
Spell to be spoken	Phrases set in italic boldface type refer to various subtitles and a number of types of rubrics (subsumed under the main title) that function in a titular sense to introduce a component feature of a spell. These may introduce ingredients, additional instructions, invocations, figures, magical names and characters, and so on, which are mentioned in the instructions in the text. In a long, multifunctional spell (cf. *PGM* IV. 2145–2240 and *PGM* XIII. 1–343), general titles are subordinate to the larger title, which describes an often elaborate ritual. In description, these general titles are identical to the main titles of most spells but are set as subtitles since they usually depend on a prior set of conditions to guarantee their efficacy.
IAŌ SABAŌTH ADŌNAI	Small capital letters indicate magical names (*voces magicae*) which are usually untranslatable and often meaningless to the reader. In some instances, small capital letters preserve recognizable Greek, Egyptian, or Semitic words that merit special attention. Portions of texts whose fragmentary nature precludes the possibility of proper translation, but which may in fact have been readable in the original, are also set in small capitals.
	A diagonal slash indicates every fifth line of translated text, corresponding to the number given in the left-hand margin. Usually these are numbered consecutively until a new papyrus number is introduced.
35 [5]	A bracketed number alongside the regular number refers to the line number of the original edition (in a Greek/Demotic text). Occasionally at the beginning the column number and line are also cited (e.g., [Col. III,5].
30 (4)	A number in parentheses refers to the original line of Preisendanz in a Greek/Demotic spell. The number corresponds to the *PGM* reference given within the bracketed number at the head of the spell.

. . .   An ellipsis in the body of the text refers to a lost portion regardless of the size of the lacuna. Some punctuation (e.g., a comma or a period) may also be added at the end of the ellipsis.

[spell]   Brackets enclosing words indicate that the words are not preserved in the original text. These include (1) suggested restorations of lacunae; (2) editorial expansions of the text to elucidate the sense of the original language; and (3) phrases traditionally set off by pointed brackets ⟨ ⟩, namely, modern corrections to scribal omissions or errors. Scholars interested in determining which use the bracketed text refers to are recommended to consult the texts of the original editions. As a general rule, bracketed texts will not divide a word, but will surround the whole word if its reading is fairly uncertain.

(add the usual)   Parentheses enclosing words simply indicate material in the original texts best understood as parenthetical comments of the ancient authors and redactors.

"Come to me . . ."   Quotation marks enclosing words indicate material that is spoken (or intended to be spoken) or written (or intended to be written). Material not enclosed in quotation marks usually refers to parts of a formulary that contain instructions and directions apart from the material to be written or spoken. Such instructions are peculiar to the papyri that have preserved magical formularies, whereas the actual amulets and phylacteries found on papyrus usually contain simple invocations that have been transcribed as a result of following the instructions in such magical handbooks.

                    Incantations originally written in Greek meter are set as verse, that is, they are indented *en bloc*, with the first letter of each line capitalized. In cases where the meter falters within such a hymnic portion, the original margin is restored to indicate prose.

NN   In the magical formularies, this abbreviation stands for a name or names to be inserted by the reader, the names of the persons against or for whom the magic is to be carried out. In the case of "(the) NN matter," the reader understands that specific requests are to be named at this point.

[R.K.R.]   At the end of each footnote, the bracketed initials refer to the contributing scholar responsible for the material immediately preceding. Notes that carry no initials represent the joint efforts of the contributors and scholars.

Abbreviations of Periodicals, Series Titles, and General Reference Works

AJA	*American Journal of Archaeology*
AKA	*Arbeiten zur Kirchengeschichte*
APAW	*Abhandlungen der (K.) preussischen Akademie der Wissenschaften*
APAW.PH	*Philosophisch-historische Klasse*
ANET	J. B. Pritchard, *Ancient Near Eastern Texts Related to the Old Testament* (Princeton: Princeton University Press, 1969)
ANRW	*Aufstieg und Niedergang der römischen Welt*
ARW	*Archiv für Religionswissenschaft*
BASP	*Bulletin of the American Society of Papyrologists*
Bauer	W. Bauer, W. F. Arndt, and F. Wilbur Gingrich, *A Greek-English Lexicon of the New Testament and Other Early Christian Literature*. 2d ed. (Chicago: University of Chicago Press, 1979)
BCH	*Bulletin de correspondance hellénique*
BIFAO	*Bulletin de l'Institut Français d'Archéologie Orientale, Le Caire*
BoJ	*Bonner Jahrbücher*
Bonnet, *RÄRG*	Hans Bonnet, *Reallexikon der ägyptischen Religionsgeschichte* (Berlin: de Gruyter, 1952)
ByZ	*Byzantinische Zeitschrift*
CAH	*Cambridge Ancient History*
CEg	*Chronique d'Égypte*
Černý, *Coptic Etymological Dictionary*	J. Černý, *Coptic Etymological Dictionary* (Cambridge: Cambridge University, 1976)
ClR	*Classical Review*
Crum, *Coptic Dictionary*	W. E. Crum, *A Coptic Dictionary* (Oxford: Clarendon, 1962)
DMP	*Demotic Magical Papyri* (see Griffith and Thompson)
EPRO	*Études préliminaires aux religions orientales dans l'empire romain*
Erman and Grapow, *Wörterbuch*	A. Erman and H. Grapow, *Wörterbuch der aegyptischen Sprache im Auftrage der deutschen Akademien* 5 vols. (Berlin: Akademie-Verlag, 1971 repr.)
GGA	*Göttingische gelehrte Anzeigen*
GM	*Göttinger Miszellen*
HR	*History of Religions*
HSCP	*Harvard Studies in Classical Philology*
HTR	*Harvard Theological Review*
JAC	*Jahrbuch für Antike und Christentum*
JBL	*Journal of Biblical Literature*

JEA	*Journal of Egyptian Archaeology*
JHS	*Journal of Hellenic Studies*
JNES	*Journal of Near Eastern Studies*
JWCI	*Journal of the Warburg and Courtauld Institute*
KP	*Der kleine Pauly*
Kropp, *Koptische Zaubertexte*	A. M. Kropp, *Ausgewählte Koptische Zaubertexte* 3 vols. (Brussels: Fondation Reine Elisabeth, 1930–31)
LCL	*Loeb Classical Library*
LdÄ	*Lexikon der Ägyptologie*, ed. by W. Helck and E. Otto (Wiesbaden: Harrassowitz, 1975–)
LSJ	Liddell-Scott-Jones, *A Greek-English Lexikon* (Oxford: Clarendon, 1968)
N.F.	*Neue Folge*
NHSt	*Nag Hammadi Studies*
NT.S	*Novum Testamentum, Supplements*
OMRM	*Oudheidkundige mededelingen uit het rijksmuseum van oudheden te Leiden*
Orph. Frag.	*Orphicorum Fragmenta*, ed. O. Kern (Dublin and Zürich: Weidmann, [3]1972)
P.Oxy.	*Papyrus Oxyrhynchus*
PDM	*Papyri Demoticae Magicae* (as cited in this volume only)
PGM	*Papyri Graecae Magicae. Die Griechischen Zauberpapyri*, 2 vols., ed. K. Preisendanz, et al. (Stuttgart: Teubner, [2]1973–74)
PRE	Pauly-Wissowa, *Real-Encyclopädie der classischen Altertumswissenschaften*
PRE.S	Pauly-Wissowa, *Real-Encyclopädie der classischen Altertumswissenschaften, Supplementa*
Preisendanz	See *PGM*; on Preisendanz, vol. III, see the Introduction below, n. 37
RAC	*Reallexikon für Antike und Christentum*
RÄRG	See Bonnet, *RÄRG*
RhM	*Rheinisches Museum für Philologie*
Roscher	W. H. Roscher, *Ausführliches Lexicon der griechischen und römischen Mythologie*
RVV	*Religionsgeschichtliche Versuche und Vorarbeiten*
SCHNT	*Studia ad Corpus Hellenisticum Novi Testamenti*
SO	*Symbolae Osloenses*
StPapy	*Studia papyrologica*
TAPA	*Transactions and Proceedings of the American Philological Association*
TDNT	*Theological Dictionary of the New Testament*
TU	*Texte und Untersuchungen zur Geschichte der altchristlichen Literatur*
WSt	*Wiener Studien*
ZÄS	*Zeitschrift für ägyptische Sprache und Altertumskunde*
ZPE	*Zeitschrift für Papyrologie und Epigraphik*

Abbreviations of Major Titles
Used in This Volume

Ancient authors are cited with name and title, the latter following the customary abbreviations. In cases of doubt, see *LSJ*, pp. xvi–xxxviii: "Authors and Works."

Abt, *Apologie*	A. Abt, *Die Apologie des Apuleius von Madaura und die antike Zauberei.* Beiträge zur Erläuterung der Schrift *de magia* (Giessen: Töpelmann, 1908)
Audollent, *Defixionum Tabellae*	A. Audollent, *Defixionum Tabellae quotquot innotuerunt* . . . (Paris: Fontemoing, 1904)
Bell, Nock, and Thompson, *Magical Texts*	H. I. Bell, A. D. Nock, and Herbert Thompson, *Magical Texts from a Bilingual Papyrus in the British Museum* (Oxford: Oxford University Press, 1933)
Bergman, *Ich bin Isis*	J. Bergman, *Ich bin Isis. Studien zum memphitischen Hintergrund der griechischen Isisaretologien, Acta Universitatis Upsaliensis* 3 (Uppsala: Almqvist and Wiksell, 1968)
Berthelot and Ruelle, *Collection des anciens alchimistes grecs*	M. Berthelot and C.-E. Ruelle, *Collection des anciens alchimistes grecs* (Paris: Steinheil, 1888)
Blau, *Das altjüdische Zauberwesen*	L. Blau, *Das altjüdische Zauberwesen* (Strassburg: Trübner, 1898)
Betz, "The Delphic Maxim"	H. D. Betz, "The Delphic Maxim 'Know Yourself' in the Greek Magical Papyri," *HR* 21 (1981): 156–71
Betz, "Fragments"	H. D. Betz, "Fragments from a Catabasis Ritual in a Greek Magical Papyrus," *HR* 19 (1980): 287–95
Betz, *Lukian*	H. D. Betz, *Lukian von Samosata und das Neue Testament, TU* 76 (Berlin: Akademie-Verlag, 1961)
Bleeker, *Hathor and Thoth*	C. J. Bleeker, *Hathor and Thoth* (Leiden: Brill, 1973)
Bonner, *SMA*	C. Bonner, *Studies in Magical Amulets Chiefly Graeco-Egyptian* (Ann Arbor: University of Michigan Press, 1950)
Borghouts, *Ancient Egyptian Magical Texts*	J. F. Borghouts, *Ancient Egyptian Magical Texts, Nisaba 9* (Leiden: Brill, 1978)
Bousset, *Hauptprobleme*	W. Bousset, *Hauptprobleme der Gnosis* (Göttingen: Vandenhoeck and Ruprecht, 1907)

Bousset, *Religionsgeschichtliche Studien*

W. Bousset, *Religionsgeschichtliche Studien. Aufsätze zur Religionsgeschichte des hellenistischen Zeitalters*, ed. A. F. Verheule, *NT.S* 50 (Leiden: Brill, 1979)

Budge, *Amulets and Talismans*

E. A. Wallis Budge, *Amulets and Talismans* (New York: Dover, 1978)

Burkert, *Griechische Religion*

W. Burkert, *Griechische Religion der archaischen und Klassischen Epoche, Die Religionen der Menschheit* 15 (Stuttgart: Kohlhammer, 1977)

Cook, *Zeus*

A. B. Cook, *Zeus: A Study in Ancient Religion*, 3 vols. (Cambridge: Cambridge University Press, 1914–40)

Darby, *Food: The Gift of Osiris*

W. T. Darby et al., *Food: The Gift of Osiris*, 2 vols. (London, New York, and San Francisco: Academic Press, 1977)

Deissmann, *Light from the Ancient East*

A. Deissmann, *Light from the Ancient East* (Grand Rapids: Baker, 1978, repr.)

Delatte, *Anecdota Atheniensia*

A. Delatte, *Anecdota Atheniensia*, vol. I (Paris: Champion, 1927)

Delatte and Derchain, *Les intailles*

A. Delatte and Ph. Derchain, *Les intailles magiques gréco-égyptiennes de la Bibliothèque Nationale* (Paris: Bibliothèque Nationale, 1964)

Dieterich, *Abraxas*

A. Dieterich, *Abraxas. Studien zur Religionsgeschichte des spätern Altertums* (Leipzig: Teubner, 1891)

Dieterich, *Mithrasliturgie*

A. Dieterich, *Eine Mithrasliturgie* (Darmstadt: Wissenschaftliche Buchgesellschaft, ³1966)

Dornseiff, *Das Alphabet*

F. Dornseiff, *Das Alphabet in Mystik und Magie* (Leipzig: Teubner, ²1925)

Faulkner, *Coffin Texts*

R. O. Faulkner, *The Ancient Egyptian Coffin Texts*, 3 vols. (Warminster, England: Aris and Phillips, 1973–78)

Festugière, *La révélation*

A. J. Festugière, *La révélation d'Hermès Trismégiste*, 4 vols. (Paris: Société d'édition "Les belles lettres," ³1981)

Gager, *Moses in Greco-Roman Paganism*

J. G. Gager, *Moses in Greco-Roman Paganism, Society of Biblical Literature Monograph Series* 16 (Nashville and New York: Abingdon, 1972)

Gardiner, *Onomastica*

A. H. Gardiner, *Ancient Egyptian Onomastica*, 2 vols. (Oxford: Oxford University Press, 1947)

Ginzberg, *The Legends of the Jews*

L. Ginzberg, *The Legends of the Jews*, 7 vols. (Philadelphia: The Jewish Publication Society of America, 1909–38)

Griffith and Thompson, *The*

F. Ll. Griffith and H. Thompson, eds., *The*

Leyden Papyrus	*Leyden Papyrus: An Egyptian Magical Book* (New York: Dover, 1974; repr. of 1904 ed.)
Griffiths, *Plutarch's De Iside et Osiride*	J. G. Griffiths, *Plutarch's De Iside et Osiride* (Cambridge: University of Wales Press, 1970)
Griffiths, *The Isis-Book*	J. G. Griffiths, *Apuleius of Madauros: The Isis-Book (Metamorphoses, Book XI)*, EPRO 39 (Leiden: Brill, 1975)
Gundel, *Astrologumena*	W. Gundel and H. G. Gundel, *Astrologumena. Die astrologische Literatur in der Antike und ihre Geschichte*, *Sudhoffs Archiv* 6 (Wiesbaden: Steiner, 1966)
Gundel, *Dekane und Dekansternbilder*	W. Gundel, *Dekane und Dekansternbilder* (Darmstadt: Wissenschaftliche Buchgesellschaft, ²1969)
Harris, *Minerals*	J. R. Harris, *Lexicographical Studies in Ancient Egyptian Minerals*, Deutsche Akademie der Wissenschaften zu Berlin. *Institut für Orientforschung*, 54 (Berlin: Akademie-Verlag, 1961)
Hopfner, *OZ*	T. Hopfner, *Griechisch-ägyptischer Offenbarungszauber*, 2 vols., *Studien zur Palaeographie und Papyruskunde*, 21, 23 (Leipzig: Haessel, 1921, 1924 [revised edition, Amsterdam: Hakkert, 1974–90])
Hornung, *Das Amduat*	E. Hornung, *Das Amduat oder die Schrift des verborgenen Raumes*, 3 vols., *Ägyptologische Abhandlungen* 7; 13 (Wiesbaden: Harrassowitz, 1963–67)
Johnson, "Dialect"	J. H. Johnson, "The Dialect of the Demotic Magical Papyrus of London and Leiden," in *Studies in Honor of George R. Hughes*, January 12, 1977, ed. by J. H. Johnson and E. F. Wente (Chicago: The Oriental Institute, 1977), pp. 110–25
Johnson, *Verbal System*	J. H. Johnson, *The Demotic Verbal System*, *Studies in Oriental Civilization* 38 (Chicago: The Oriental Institute, 1976)
Klauck, *Herrenmahl*	H.-J. Klauck, *Herrenmahl und hellenistischer Kult. Eine religionsgeschichtliche Untersuchung zum ersten Korintherbrief*, NTA, N.F. 15 (Münster: Aschendorff, 1982)
Lichtheim, *Ancient Egyptian Literature*	M. Lichtheim, *Ancient Egyptian Literature*, 3 vols. (Berkeley and Los Angeles: University of California Press, 1973–80)
Morenz, *Egyptian Religion*	S. Morenz, *Egyptian Religion* (London: Methuen, 1973)
Nilsson, *GGR*	M. P. Nilsson, *Geschichte der griechischen Religion*, 2 vols. (München: Beck, ³1967, ²1961)
Nock, *Essays*	A. D. Nock, *Essays on Religion and the An-*

cient World, 2 vols. (Cambridge, Mass.: Harvard University Press, 1972)

Nock and Festugière, *Hermès Trismégiste*

A. D. Nock and A.-J. Festugière, *Hermès Trismégiste. Corpus Hermeticum*, 4 vols. (Paris: Les belles lettres, 1946–54)

Preisigke, *Namenbuch*

K. Preisigke, *Namenbuch* (Heidelberg: Selbstverlag des Herausgebers, 1922)

Ranke, *Ägyptische Personennamen*

H. Ranke, *Die ägyptischen Personennamen*, 2 vols. (Hamburg: Selbstverlag des Verfassers, 1932–52)

Reitzenstein, *Poimandres*

R. Reitzenstein, *Poimandres. Studien zur griechisch-ägyptischen und früchristlichen Literatur* (Leipzig: Teubner, 1904)

Robinson, *The Nag Hammadi Library in English*

J. M. Robinson, ed., *The Nag Hammadi Library in English* (Leiden: Brill, 1977)

Smith, *Jesus the Magician*

M. Smith, *Jesus the Magician* (San Francisco: Harper and Row, 1978)

Introduction to the
Greek Magical Papyri

Hans Dieter Betz

"The Greek magical papyri" is a name given by scholars to a body of papyri from Greco-Roman Egypt containing a variety of magical spells and formulae, hymns and rituals. The extant texts are mainly from the second century B.C. to the fifth century A.D. To be sure, this body of material represents only a small number of all the magical spells that once existed.[1] Beyond these papyri we possess many other kinds of material: artifacts, symbols and inscriptions on gemstones, on ostraka and clay bowls, and on tablets of gold, silver, lead, tin and so forth.[2]

I

The history of the discovery of the Greek magical papyri is a fascinating subject.[3] We know from literary sources that a large number of magical books in which spells were collected existed in antiquity. Most of them, however, have disappeared as the result of systematic suppression and destruction. The episode about the burning of the magical books in Ephesus in the Acts of the Apostles (Acts 19:19) is well known and typical of many such instances. According to Suetonius,[4] Augustus ordered 2,000 magical scrolls to be burned in the year 13 B.C. Indeed, the first centuries of the Christian era saw many burnings of books, often of magical books, and not a few burnings that included the magicians themselves.

As a result of these acts of suppression, the magicians and their literature went underground. The papyri themselves testify to this by the constantly recurring admonition to keep the books secret.[5] Yet the systematic destruction of the magical literature over a long period of time resulted in the disappearance of most of the original texts by the end of antiquity. To us in the twentieth century, terms such as "underground literature" and "suppressed literature" are well known as descriptions of contemporary phenomena. We also know that such literature is extremely important for the understanding of what people are really thinking and doing in a particular time, geographical area, or cultural context. Magical beliefs and practices can hardly be overestimated in their importance for the daily life of the people. The religious beliefs and practices of most people were identical with some form of magic, and the neat distinctions we make today between approved and disapproved forms of religion—calling the former "religion" and "church" and the latter "magic" and "cult"—did not exist in antiquity except among a few intellectuals.[6]

Thus the suppression of this magical literature has deprived us of one of our most important sources of ancient religious life. Modern views of Greek and Roman religions have long suffered from certain deformities because they were unconsciously shaped by the only remaining sources: the literature of the cultural elite, and the archeological remains of the official cults of the states and cities.

But not everything was lost.[7] At the end of antiquity, some philosophers and theologians, astrologers and alchemists collected magical books and spells that were still available. Literary writers included some of the material in their works, if only to make fun of it. It is known that philosophers of the Neopythagorean and Neo-platonic schools, as well as Gnostic and Hermetic groups, used magical books and hence must have possessed copies. But most of their material vanished and what we have left are their quotations.

The Greek magical papyri are, however, original documents and primary sources. Their discovery is as important for Greco-Roman religions as is the discovery of the Qumran texts for Judaism or the Nag Hammadi library for Gnosticism.[8]

Like these manuscript discoveries, the discovery of the Greek magical papyri was and often still is the outcome of sheer luck and almost incredible coincidences. In the case of the major portion of the collection, the so-called Anastasi collection, the discovery and rescue is owed to the efforts (and, if one may use the term, coopera-tion) of two individuals separated by more than a thousand years: the modern col-lector d'Anastasi and the original collector at Thebes.

In the nineteenth century, there was among the "diplomatic" representatives at the court in Alexandria a man who called himself Jean d'Anastasi (1780?–1857). Believed to be Armenian by birth, he ingratiated himself enough with the pasha to become the consular representative of Sweden.[9] It was a time when diplomats and military men often were passionate collectors of antiquities, and M. d'Anastasi hap-pened to be at the right place at the right time. He succeeded in bringing together large collections of papyri from Egypt, among them sizable magical books, some of which he said he had obtained in Thebes.[10] These collections he shipped to Europe, where they were auctioned off and bought by various libraries: the British Museum in London, the Bibliothèque Nationale and the Louvre in Paris, the Staatliche Mu-seen in Berlin, and the Rijksmuseum in Leiden. Another papyrus was acquired by Jean François Mimaut (1774–1837), also a diplomat, whose acquisition ended up in the Bibliothèque Nationale (*PGM* III).[11] Unfortunately, we know almost nothing about the circumstances of the actual findings. But it is highly likely that many of the papyri from the Anastasi collection came from the same place, perhaps a tomb or a temple library.[12] If this assumption is correct, about half a dozen of the best-preserved and largest extant papyri may have come from the collection of one man in Thebes. He is of course unknown to us, but we may suppose that he col-lected the magical material for his own use. Perhaps he was more than a magician. We may attribute his almost systematic collections of *magica* to a man who was also a scholar,[13] probably philosophically inclined, as well as a bibliophile and archivist concerned about the preservation of this material.[14]

Although the person who collected the Anastasi papyri remains unknown, com-parable figures are known from later Egyptian literature. In the Demotic Papyrus no. 30646 in the Cairo Museum, there appears Prince Khamwas, the fourth son of King Ramses II and high priest of Ptah in Memphis. This legendary figure belongs to the *Stories of the High Priests of Memphis*, published by Francis Llewelyn Griffith,[15] stories that in many ways can serve as illustrative companions to the Greek magical papyri. Miriam Lichtheim has given this summary portrait in the third volume of her *Ancient Egyptian Literature*:

> Prince Khamwas, son of King Ramses II and high priest of Ptah at Memphis, was a very learned scribe and magician who spent his time in the study of ancient monuments and books. One day he was told of the existence of a book of magic written by the god Thoth himself and kept in the tomb of a prince named Naneferkaptah (Na-nefer-ka-ptah), who lived in the distant past and was buried somewhere in the vast nec-ropolis of Memphis. After a long search, Prince Khamwas, accom-

panied by his foster brother Inaros, found the tomb of Naneferkaptah
and entered it. He saw the magic book, which radiated a strong light,
and tried to seize it. But the spirits of Naneferkaptah and of his wife
Ahwere rose up to defend their cherished possession. . . .[16]

The collection of the Anastasi papyri, if it was brought together by one person, may have been buried with him, either in his tomb or in the rubble of col-
lapsed buildings. At any rate, when d'Anastasi came to Thebes and the papyri were
offered to him, he sensed their value and acquired them, thus saving them from
destruction.

It took almost another century, however, before scholars learned to appreciate
the value of the papyri and started investigating them. It is noteworthy that the
auction catalog of d'Anastasi's collection calls the material simply "fromage mystique."[17] Until the middle of the nineteenth century, the papyri were stored in the
museums simply as curiosities.

Scholarly investigations began when the great Dutch scholar Caspar Jacob Chris-
tiaan Reuvens (1793–1835) described some of the content of the Leiden papyrus
J 395 (*PGM* XIII) in his *Lettres à M. Letronne* published in 1830.[18] This work was
reviewed almost immediately by the German historian of religion Karl Otfried
Müller (1797–1840), who also translated Reuvens's excerpts into German.[19] But
Reuvens died before his edition of the Leiden papyri could appear. It was forty
years before another Dutch scholar, the Egyptologist Conrad Leemans (1809–93),
published the edition (*PGM* XII, XIII)[20] together with a Latin translation (1885).[21]

The first publication, however, is due to the efforts of the British scholar Charles
Wycliffe Goodwin (1817–78), who published one of the papyri (*PGM* V) together with an English translation and commentary for the Cambridge Antiquarian
Society in 1853.[22] Then the German philologist Gustav Parthey (1798–1872)
edited the two papyri from Berlin in 1865 (*PGM* I, II).[23] A very important new
phase began when the Viennese papyrologist Carl Wessely (1860–1931) published
in 1888 a transcription of the great magical papyrus of Paris (*PGM* IV), the London papyrus (*PGM* V), and the Mimaut papyrus (*PGM* III),[24] followed in 1889 by
corrections.[25] In 1893 both Wessely[26] and Frederick George Kenyon (1863–
1952)[27] independently edited and published the magical papyri of London (*PGM*
VII–X). The last major papyrus was published in 1925 by the Norwegian scholar
Samson Eitrem (1872–1966),[28] who had acquired in Egypt a valuable magical
scroll with many drawings (*PGM* XXXVI).

With these important publications, the major pieces of the Greek magical papyri
known to this period had become available. It seems to have been a suggestion first
made by the great scholar of Greek religion, Albrecht Dieterich (1866–1908), that
all the available papyri should be published in a handy study edition. But this idea
developed only gradually after Dieterich began teaching a seminar on the subject of
the magical papyri at the University of Heidelberg in 1905.[29]

Today it is astonishing to learn that teaching such a seminar at that time was quite
a daring enterprise. Magic was so utterly despised by historians and philologists
that the announcement of the seminar did not mention the word "magic" but was
simply phrased as "Selected Pieces from the Greek Papyri."[30]

How far the dislike of the magical papyri could go is illustrated by a remark made
by Ulrich von Wilamowitz-Moellendorff: "I once heard a well-known scholar complain that these papyri were found because they deprived antiquity of the noble
splendor of classicism."[31]

Dieterich,[32] however, was at the edge of a wave of interest generated by the new discipline of history of religions. His seminar therefore had a surprising attraction for students, some of whom wrote their dissertations on related subjects and became contributors to the study edition. The plan for such a study edition was seriously threatened by Dieterich's sudden death on 6 May 1908, but the work was taken over by Dieterich's students, foremost of whom was Richard Wünsch, chief editor. Adam Abt, Ludwig Fahz, Adolf Erman, Georg Möller, and other contributors[33] stepped in to carry on the work.

When the body of the material of *PGM* I–IV was almost ready, World War I broke out and interrupted the work. Wünsch, Abt, and Möller were killed in the war. Despite these terrible losses and the desperate economic situation following the war, the publisher, B. G. Teubner of Leipzig, did not give up the project, but decided to start over. The edition was entrusted to Karl Preisendanz (1883–1968), another of Dieterich's former students.[34] Scholars at that time faced difficulties scarcely conceivable to us today, yet they persisted. In addition, a remarkable degree of international cooperation existed among the scholars.[35] Sam Eitrem from Oslo and Adolf Jacoby from Luxemburg joined the team, and British, French, and Dutch scholars gave their support to the effort. The Notgemeinschaft der Deutschen Wissenschaft as well as other governmental agencies gave financial support, so that despite all the problems the first volume of the first edition of the *Papyri Graecae Magicae* could appear in 1928, with a second volume following in 1931.[36]

While all this was happening, new magical papyri were being discovered and published. A third volume, which was also supposed to contain extensive indexes, therefore became necessary. But this volume never appeared, for World War II broke out.

Despite the war, the work had progressed to the actual production of galley proofs, with the preface dated "Pentecost, 1941,"[37] when on 4 December 1943 the publishing house of Teubner in Leipzig was bombed and everything was destroyed.[38] Fortunately, however, the galley proofs survived the war and are at present being used by a number of scholars in the form of xerox copies. When Karl Preisendanz, the editor of the first edition and tireless promoter of the study of the Greek magical papyri before and after World War II, died on 26 April 1968, the publishing house of Teubner, which had in part been relocated in Stuttgart, West Germany, decided to bring out a new edition. This new edition was prepared by Albert Henrichs, a papyrologist from Cologne, who has been on the faculty of Harvard University since 1973.[39] It appeared in two volumes in 1973–74.[40] The first volume is mostly a reprint of the first edition, though many corrections have been made. The second volume, however, is considerably different from the first edition. A number of papyri were reedited completely, and the papyri originally planned to appear in vol. III were added so that vol. II of the 1974 edition contains all pieces up to *PGM* LXXXI. The idea of a third volume containing the indexes was postponed because all indexes would have to be redone in view of the changes and additions in the material.

II

What is the significance of the Greek magical papyri? Scholars since Albrecht Dieterich have consistently pointed out the importance of the Greek magical papyri to the study of ancient religions; thus we can limit ourselves here to a summary of the issues.[41]

Historians of religion are intrigued by the Greek magical papyri for a number of reasons. If, as Dieterich rightly says,[42] the papyri are a depository of a great religious literature over many centuries, the recovery of the sources becomes a task of primary interest. In fact, throughout these sources we find citations of hymns, rituals, formulae from liturgies otherwise lost, and little bits of mythology called *historiolae*. These older materials are now embedded in a secondary context, but by careful application of the methods of literary criticism they are often recoverable.[43]

Taken as a whole, the material presents a plethora of interesting problems for modern scholarship. One must realize first that the material assembled under the name Greek magical papyri represents a collection of texts of diverse origin and nature. This collection includes individual spells and remedies, as well as collections made by ancient magicians, from the early Hellenistic period to late antiquity. Since the material comes from Greco-Roman Egypt, it reflects an amazingly broad religious and cultural pluralism. Not surprising is the strong influence of Egyptian religion throughout the Greek magical papyri, although here the texts nevertheless show a great variety. Expressed in Greek, Demotic, or Coptic, some texts represent simply Egyptian religion. In others, the Egyptian element has been transformed by Hellenistic religious concepts. Most of the texts are mixtures of several religions— Egyptian, Greek, Jewish, to name the most important.

The picture presented by the Greek magical papyri has been changed substantially by the inclusion of the translation of the Demotic magical papyri. In Preisendanz's edition, the Demotic material was deleted, even when it occurred in the same papyrus as Greek sections apparently written by the same scribe. The inclusion of the Demotic material in the present translation raises new and intriguing questions regarding the relationship between the Greek texts and the antecedent Egyptian sources. Further studies must clarify the process of transmission and transformation of these texts. Such studies will gain new insights into the complex phenomena of the hellenization of religious traditions. (See also the Introduction to the Demotic texts below.)

Another interesting problem is posed by the fact that this material from Greco-Roman Egypt contains many sections that are Greek in origin and nature.[44] How did this older Greek religious literature find its way into Egypt? We do not, and probably never shall, know. In this older material, the Greek gods are alive and well. But Zeus, Hermes, Apollo, Artemis, Aphrodite, and others are portrayed not as Hellenic and aristocratic, as in literature, but as capricious, demonic, and even dangerous, as in Greek folklore.[45] The gods and their activities resemble those in the popular myths and local cults, as reported by mythographers or by Pausanias. Therefore, strange as it may sound, if we wish to study Greek folk religion, the magical papyri found in Egypt are to be regarded as one of the primary sources.[46]

Questions similar to those appropriate to the study of Greek religion must be raised in view of the material (divine names as well as entire passages) that comes from some form of Judaism. Jewish magic was famous in antiquity,[47] and more sources have come to light in recent years; but the origin and nature of the sections representing Jewish magic in the Greek magical papyri is far from clear. Did this material actually originate with Jewish magicians? How did it get into the hands of the magicians who wrote the Greek magical papyri? What kind of transformation took place in the material itself? If the texts in question come from Judaism, what type of Judaism do they represent?

The historian of religion will be especially interested in the kind of syncretism represented in the Greek magical papyri.[48] This syncretism is more than a mixture of diverse elements from Egyptian, Greek, Babylonian, and Jewish religion, with a few sprinkles of Christianity.[49] Despite the diversity of texts, there is in the whole corpus a tendency toward assimilation and uniformity. Such assimilation and uniformity, however, includes primarily the religious traditions already mentioned: the Romans, although in control of Egypt by the time most of the papyri were written, left only a few traces in the material. Thus the papyri represent a Greco-Egyptian, rather than the more general Greco-Roman, syncretism.

In this syncretism, the indigenous ancient Egyptian religion has in part survived, in part been profoundly hellenized.[50] In its Hellenistic transformation, the Egyptian religion of the pre-Hellenistic era appears to have been reduced and simplified, no doubt to facilitate its assimilation into Hellenistic religion as the predominant cultural reference. It is quite clear that the magicians who wrote and used the Greek papyri were Hellenistic in outlook.

Hellenization, however, also includes the egyptianizing of Greek religious traditions. The Greek magical papyri contain many instances of such egyptianizing transformations, which take very different forms in different texts or layers of tradition. Again, working out the more exact nature of this religious and cultural interaction remains the task of future research.

The papyri also provide many insights into the phenomenon of the magician as a religious functionary, in both the Egyptian and the Hellenistic setting. One must be cautious, however, in making generalizing statements in regard to the figure of the magician in the Greek magical papyri.[51] Some of the magicians writing and using the spells may have been associated with temples of Egyptian and Greek deities. According to Egyptian practice, the magician was a resident member of the temple priesthood. Genuine understanding of the older Egyptian and Greek languages and traditions can be assumed in some of the material, but by no means in all instances.

There are texts reflecting perhaps a different type of magician, a type we know from the Greek religious milieu.[52] This type of wandering craftsman seems keen to adopt and adapt every religious tradition that appeared useful to him, while the knowledge and understanding of what he adopted was characterized by a certain superficiality. This type of magician no longer understood the old languages, although he used remnants of them in transcription. He recited and used what must at one time have been metrically composed hymns; but he no longer recognized the meter, and he spoiled it when he inserted his own material. In the hands of magicians of this type, the gods from the various cults gradually merged, and as their natures became blurred, they often changed into completely different deities. For these magicians, there was no longer any cultural difference between the Egyptian and the Greek gods, or between them and the Jewish god and the Jewish angels; and even Jesus was occasionally assimilated into this truly "ecumenical" religious syncretism of the Hellenistic world culture.

We should make it clear, however, that this syncretism is more than a hodgepodge of heterogeneous items. In effect, it is a new religion altogether, displaying unified religious attitudes and beliefs. As an example, one may mention the enormously important role of the gods and goddesses of the underworld. The role of these underworld deities was not new to Egyptian religion or, to some extent, to ancient Greek religion; but it is characteristic of the Hellenistic syncretism of the Greek magical papyri that the netherworld and its deities had become one of its most important concerns. The goddess Hekate, identical with Persephone, Selene, Artemis, and the old Babylonian goddess Ereschigal, is one of the deities most often invoked in the papyri. Through the egyptianizing influence of Osiris, Isis, and their company, other gods like Hermes, Aphrodite, and even the Jewish god

Iao, have in many respects become underworld deities. In fact, human life seems to consist of nothing but negotiations in the antechamber of death and the world of the dead. The underworld deities, the demons and the spirits of the dead, are constantly and unscrupulously invoked and exploited as the most important means for achieving the goals of human life on earth: the acquisition of love, wealth, health, fame, knowledge of the future, control over other persons, and so forth. In other words, there is a consensus that the best way to success and worldly pleasures is by using the underworld, death, and the forces of death.

Apart from this fascination with the control of death and the underworld powers, there is an equally important fascination with the universe. The older gods of the Greco-Egyptian pantheon now mostly represent the forces of the universe. Thus the Greek god most often invoked is Apollo Helios, a fact consistent with the enormous expansion of the worship of the sun in the Greco-Roman era. Besides other astral deities such as Selene, the constellation of the Bear, and the like, abstract deities, new and old, demand attention. These abstract deities personify Nature (Physis), Time (Kronos, Chronos), Destiny (the Moirai), and most important, the All (Aion). Popular Egyptian gods and goddesses are, however, called upon just as often. Yet the god most often employed is Iao, the Jewish god.

The people whose religion is reflected in the papyri agree that humanity is inescapably at the whim of the forces of the universe. Religion is nothing but taking seriously this dependency on the forces of the universe. Whether the gods are old or new, whether they come from Egyptian, Greek, Jewish, or Christian traditions, religion is regarded as nothing but the awareness of and reaction against our dependency on the unfathomable scramble of energies coming out of the universe. In this energy jungle, human life can only be experienced as a jungle, too. People's successes and failures appear to be only the result of Chance (Tyche). Individuals seem to be nothing but marionettes at the end of power lines, pulled here and there without their knowledge by invisible forces.

If this world view takes hold of people, what hope can there be for human life? How could ordinary men and women in the small towns of Egypt get something out of their lives? It is at this point that the magician enters the picture. In a transitional culture like Greco-Roman Egypt, a religious functionary who operated as a crisis manager became a necessity to the lives of ordinary people. This role the magician was able to fulfill.

Applying his craft, the magician could give people the feeling that he could make things work in a world where nothing seemed to work the way it used to. He had handbooks of magic,[53] which contained the condensed wisdom of the past, wisdom made effective to solve the problems of the present.

The magician claimed to know and understand the traditions of various religions. While other people could no longer make sense of the old religions, he was able to. He knew the code words needed to communicate with the gods, the demons, and the dead. He could tap, regulate, and manipulate the invisible energies.[54] He was a problem solver who had remedies for a thousand petty troubles plaguing mankind: everything from migraine to runny nose to bedbugs to horse races, and, of course, all the troubles of love and money.

In short, it was this kind of world in which the magician served as a power and communications expert, crisis manager, miracle healer and inflicter of damages, and all-purpose therapist and agent of worried, troubled, and troublesome souls.[55]

To raise one final question: It is one of the puzzles of all magic that from time immemorial it has survived throughout history, through the coming and going of entire religions, the scientific and technological revolutions, and the triumphs of modern medicine. Despite all these changes, there has always been an unbroken tradition of magic. Why is magic so irrepressible and ineradicable, if it is also true that its claims and promises never come true? Or *do* they? Do people never check up on the efficiency of magicians?

The answer appears to be that, in general, people are not interested in whether or not magicians' promises come true. People want to believe, so they simply ignore their suspicions that magic may all be deception and fraud. The enormous role deception plays in human life and society is well known to us.[56] In many crucial areas and in many critical situations of life, deception is the only method that really works. As the Roman aphorism sums it up, "Mundus vult decipi, ergo decipiatur" ("The world wishes to be deceived, and so it may be deceived"). To an immeasurable extent, people's lives carry on by what they decide they want to believe rather than by what they should believe or even know, by what appears to be real rather than by what is really real, by props and by fads, and by gobbledygook of this kind today and that kind tomorrow.

Magicians are those who have long ago explored these dimensions of the human mind. Rather than decrying the facts, they have exploited them. Magicians have known all along that people's religious need and expectations provide the greatest opportunity for the most effective of all deceptions. But instead of turning against religion, as the skeptics among the Greek and Roman philosophers did, the magicians made use of it. After all, magic is nothing but the art of making people believe that something is being done about those things in life about which we all know that we ourselves can do nothing.

Magic is the art that makes people who practice it feel better rather than worse, that provides the illusion of security to the insecure, the feeling of help to the helpless, and the comfort of hope to the hopeless.

Of course, it is all deception. But who can endure naked reality, especially when there is a way to avoid it? This is why magic has worked and continues to work, no matter what the evidence may be. Those whose lives depend on deception and delusion and those who provide them have formed a truly indissoluble symbiosis. Magic makes an unmanageable life manageable for those who believe in it, and a profession profitable for those who practice the art.

Notes

1. For a survey of the material, see the indispensible work by T. Hopfner, *Griechisch-ägyptischer Offenbarungszauber*, 2 vols. (Leipzig: Haessel, 1921, 1924); idem, "Mageia," *PRE* 14.1 (1928):201–393; S. Sauneron, *Le papyrus magique illustré de Brooklyn (Brooklyn Museum 47.218.156)* (Oxford: Oxford University Press, 1970); idem, "Le monde du magicien égyptien," in *Le monde du sorcier, Sources Orientales VII* (Paris: Edition du Seuil, 1966) 27–65; J. F. Borghouts, *The Magical Texts of Papyrus Leiden I 348* (Leiden: Brill, 1971); idem, "Magical Texts," in *Textes et Langages de l'Egypte Pharaonique; Hommage à J.-F. Champollion* (Le Caire: Institut d'Egypte, 1974), 3:7–19. See also J. F. Borghouts, "Magie," *LdÄ* 3 (1980):1137–51; H. Altenmüller, "Magische Literatur," *LdÄ* 3 (1980):1151–62. A wider range of literature is discussed by D. E. Aune, "Magic in Early Christianity," *ANRW* II. 23. 2 (Berlin: de Gruyter, 1980) 1507–57.

2. See the collections by Campbell Bonner, *Studies in Magical Amulets Chiefly Graeco-Egyptian*, University of Michigan Studies, Humanistic Series XLIX (Ann Arbor: University of Michigan Press, 1950); idem, "Amulets Chiefly in the British Museum," *Hesperia* 20 (1951):301–45, pls. 96–100; idem, "A Miscellany of Engraved Stones," *Hesperia* 23

(1954) : 138–57; A. Delatte and P. Derchain, *Les intailles magiques gréco-égyptiennes* (Paris: Bibliothèque Nationale, Cabinet des Medailles, 1964). On the latter, see especially the reviews by H. Seyrig, *Syria* 42 (1965) : 409–10; K. Preisendanz, *ByZ* 59 (1966) : 388–92; M. Smith, *AJA* 71 (1967) : 417–19; A. A. Barb, *Gnomon* 41 (1969) : 298–307. On the relationship between gems and papyri see M. Smith, "Relations between Magical Papyri and Magical Gems," *Papyrologica Bruxellensia* 18 (1979) : 129–36; J. Schwartz, "Papyri Graecae Magicae und magische Gemmen," in M. J. Vermaseren, ed., *Die orientalischen Religionen im Römerreich*, EPRO 93 (Leiden: Brill, 1981) 485–509. For the magical tablets, see A. Audollent, *Defixionum tabellae, quotquot innotuerunt . . . praeter Atticas . . .* (Paris: Fontemoing, 1904); K. Preisendanz, "Fluchtafel (Defixion)," *RAC* 8 (1972) : 1–29.

3. See especially K. Preisendanz, "Zur Überlieferungsgeschichte der spätantiken Magie," in *Aus der Welt des Buches. Zentralblatt für Bibliothekswesen, Beiheft* 75 (Leipzig: Harrassowitz, 1951) 223–40.

4. Suetonius, *Augustus* 31.1. See Hopfner, *OZ* II, section 67; K. Preisendanz, "Dans le monde de la magie grecque," *Chronique d'Egypte* 10 (1935) : 336–37; W. Speyer, "Büchervernichtung," *JAC* 13 (1970) : 123–52, with bibliography.

5. *PGM* LVII and LXXII are even written in cryptography. See also my article "The Formation of Authoritative Tradition in the Greek Magical Papyri," in *Jewish and Christian Self-Definition*, vol. 3: *Self-Definition in the Graeco-Roman World*, ed. B. F. Meyer and E. P. Sanders (Philadelphia: Fortress Press, 1982), 161–70.

6. A definition of the notion of magic cannot be attempted here. In order to provide an adequate definition, the complexities of the notion, its relations with "religion" and "science," and the rather frustrating history and literature of the problem would have to be discussed first. For a good introduction to the question, see A. A. Barb, "The Survival of Magic Arts," in *The Conflict between Paganism and Christianity in the Fourth Century*, ed. A. Momigliano (Oxford: Clarendon, 1963) 100–125; G. Widengren, *Religionsphänomenologie* (Berlin: De Gruyter, 1969) 1–19; cf. also Aune, *ANRW* II. 23.2, 1510–16 and G. E. R. Lloyd, *Magic, Reason and Experience*, Studies in the Origin and Development of Greek Science (Cambridge: Cambridge University Press, 1979).

7. On the survival of magic, see Barb's stimulating article mentioned in note 6 above. Also important for this question is the autobiographical account of the physician Thessalos and its discussion by J. Z. Smith, "The Temple and the Magician," in his *Map Is Not Territory: Studies in the History of Religions* (Leiden: Brill, 1978) 172–89.

8. For the circumstances connected with the discoveries of the Qumran texts, see F. M. Cross, *The Ancient Library of Qumran and Modern Biblical Studies* (Garden City, N.Y.: Doubleday, 1961); for the Nag Hammadi Library, see J. M. Robinson, "The Jung Codex: The Rise and Fall of a Monopoly," *Religious Studies Review* 3 (1977) : 17–30.

9. C. J. C. Reuvens, *Lettres à M. Letronne, sur les Papyrus bilingues et Grecs, et sur quelques autres Monumens Gréco-Egyptiens du Musée d'Antiquités de l'Université de Leide* (Leiden: Luchtmans, 1830), 1: "M. le chevalier D'ANASTASY, vice-consul de Suède à Alexandrie." For bibliographical information, see W. R. Dawson, "Anastasi, Sallier, and Harris and Their Papyri," *JEA* 35 (1949) : 158–66.

10. See the remark by F. Lenormant in his catalog of the Anastasi collection entitled *Catalogue d'une collection d'antiquités égyptiennes. Cette collection rassemblée par M. d'Anastasi, Consul général de Suède à Alexandrie, sera vendue aux enchères publiques Rue de Clichy, N° 76, les Mardi 23, Mercredi 24, Jeudi 25, Vendredi 26 & Samedi 27 1857 à une heure, etc.* (Paris: Maulde et Renou, 1857) 84: "M. Anastasi, dans ses fouilles à Thèbes avait découvert la bibliothèque d'un gnostique égyptien du second siècle, et une partie de cette bibliothèque avait passé avec sa première collection dans le musée de Leide; c'est de là que venait le fameux texte magique en écriture démotique et deux petits papyrus grecs pliés en forme de livres qui font plusieurs des plus beaux ornements de ce musée."

11. See J.-F. Dubois, *Description des antiquités égyptiennes grecques et romaines, monuments cophtes et arabes composant la collection de Feu M.J.-F. Mimaut* (Paris: Panckoucke, 1837) pp. Vff.

12. Cf. the report of another collector who speaks of his "residence of eighteen years at Thebes, entirely devoted to its objects of antiquity" (p. IX). This man, a Greek named Giovanni d'Athanasi, from the island of Lemnos, the son of a Cairo merchant, wrote his story at the suggestion of English travelers: Giovanni d'Athanasi, *A Brief Account of the Researches and Discoveries in Upper Egypt, made under the direction of Henry Salt, Esq., to which is added a detailed catalogue of Mr. Salt's collection of Egyptian Antiquities; illustrated with twelve engravings of some of the most interesting objects, and an enumeration of those articles purchased for the British Museum* (London: John Hearne, 1836). As d'Athanasi reports, the papyri are found mostly in or near tombs; so he says about the Demotic papyri: "they are very rare, and are found not in the mummies, but in the terra-cotta urns which are found closed up and buried in the earth around the tombs" (p. 79). See also the *Catalogue of the Very Magnificent and Extraordinary Collection of Egyptian Antiquities, the Property of Giovanni d'Athanasi, which will be sold by auction by Mr. Leigh Sotheby, at his house, 3, Wellington Street, Strand, on Monday, March 13th, 1837, and the Six following Days (Sunday excepted), at One o'Clock precisely* (London: J. Davy, 1837) 23–24: "Manuscript Rolls of Papyrus, found in the tombs at Thebes." On the whole subject, see Wolfgang Speyer, *Bücherfunde in der Glaubenswerbung der Antike* (Göttingen: Vandenhoeck and Ruprecht, 1970), esp. 44ff.: books placed as gifts in tombs.

13. *PGM* V.a is a loose page stuck into a work on chemistry, the *Papyrus graecus Holmiensis* in Stockholm. This indicates that the owner and collector of the magical material also possessed works on chemistry. See also B. Olsson, "Zwei Papyrusstellen besprochen," *Aegyptus* 12 (1932): 355–56; Preisendanz, *Papyrusfunde und Papyrusforschung* 91–92.

14. See my article mentioned in note 5 above.

15. Francis Llewelyn Griffith, *Stories of the High Priests of Memphis*, 2 vols. (Oxford: Clarendon Press, 1900).

16. Miriam Lichtheim, *Ancient Egyptian Literature*, vol. 3: *The Late Period* (Berkeley and Los Angeles: University of California Press, 1980) 127; cf. also 8–9. See also Farouk Gomaà, *Chaemwese. Sohn Ramses' II. und Hoherpriester von Memphis*, Ägyptologische Abhandlungen 27 (Wiesbaden: Harrassowitz, 1973), esp. 70ff. The papyrus was found in a Christian (!) tomb in Thebes. It should be noted that the story dealing with the search for the secret book has a parallel in Pseudo-Democritus, who may be identical with Bolos of Mendes. According to this text, Democritus went to Memphis where he was received by Ostanes and his students in the temple of Ptah, but Ostanes died before he initiated Democritus into his mysteries and handed his secret books over to him. Democritus also brought up the shadow of Ostanes from Hades and asked him about the books. Ostanes replied that they were in the temple, where they were finally discovered. Both names occur also in *PGM* (Democritus: VII.167, 795; XII. 351; Ostanes: IV.2006; XII.122). The text is given in J. Bidez and F. Cumont, *Les mages hellénisés* II (Paris: Société d'édition "Les belles lettres," 1938) 317–18; see J. H. Waszink, "Bolos," *RAC* 2 (1954): 502–8; Speyer, *Bücherfunde* 26–27, 72–73.

17. Lenormant, *Catalogue* 87 about *PGM* IV: "En tête sont trois pages de copte, qui débutent par l'histoire d'un fromage mystique pour la composition duquel s'associent Osiris, Sabaoth, Iao, Jésus et tous les autres éons. Ce fromage n'est autre que la *gnose*."

18. See note 9 above.

19. *GGA*, 56. Stück, den 9. April 1831, pp. 545–54. Müller remarks (p. 547): "Es gibt wohl keine Urkunde, die es so deutlich machte, wie die Magie, diese Seuche der Geister, vor allem in Aegypten sich entwickelt, und von dem alten Religionssystem dieses Volkes ausgehend, mit Hülfe metaphysischer Speculationen und verworrener Naturkenntnisse, sich zu einem Schrecken erregenden Umfange ausgebildet habe."

20. Leemans's edition was based upon Reuvens's manuscript. See Preisendanz, "Zur Überlieferungsgeschichte," 225 n.13.

21. C. Leemans, *Papyri graeci musei antiquarii publici Lugduni-Batavi. Regis augustissimi jussu edidit, interpretationem latinam, annotationem, indicem et tabulas addidit C. L.*, 2 vols. (Lugduni Batavorum: Brill, 1843, 1885). On Leemans, see *L'Egyptologue Conrade Leemans et son correspondence. Contribution à l'histoire d'une science, à l'occasion du cent-cinquantième an-

niversaire du déchiffrement des hiéroglyphes et du centennaire des Congrès des Orientalistes (Leiden: Brill, 1973).

22. C. W. Goodwin, *Fragment of a Graeco-Egyptian Work upon Magic: From a Papyrus in the British Museum, Edited for the Cambridge Antiquarian Society, with a Translation and Notes.* Publications of the Cambridge Antiquarian Society, no. II (Cambridge: Deighton, 1852).

23. G. Parthey, "Zwei griechische Zauberpapyri des Berliner Museums," *Philologische und historische Abhandlungen der Kgl. Akademie der Wissenschaften zu Berlin 1865* (Berlin: Kgl. Akademie der Wissenschaften, 1866) 109–80.

24. C. Wessely, "Griechische Zauberpapyrus von Paris und London," *Denkschriften der Akademie der Wissenschaften in Wien, philosophisch-historische Klasse* 36 (1888):27–208. On Wessely's achievements in particular, see H. Gerstinger, *Aegyptus* 12 (1932):250–55; Preisendanz, *Papyrusfunde* 120–22.

25. K. Wessely, "Zu den griechischen Papyri des Louvre und der Bibliothèque nationale," *Fünfzehnter Jahresbericht des K. K. Staatsgymnasiums in Hernals* (Wien: Verlag des K. K. Staatsgymnasiums in Hernals, 1889) 3–23. See the review by A. Dieterich, *Berliner Philologische Wochenschrift* 11 (1891):9–10.

26. "Neue griechische Zauberpapyri," *Denkschriften der Kaiserlichen Akademie der Wissenschaften [Wien], philosophisch-historische Klasse* 42 (1893), II. Abhandlung.

27. F. G. Kenyon, *Greek Papyri in the British Museum*, vol. I (London: British Museum, 1893).

28. S. Eitrem, *Papyri Osloenses, I: Magical Papyri* (Oslo: Dybwad, 1925).

29. See A. Dieterich, *Abraxas* (Leipzig: Teubner, 1891), p. 164 n.1, and his remark in a review article, "Griechische und römische Religion," *ARW* 8 (1905):486–87:

> Es nimmt mich immer wieder wunder, dass der unermeßliche Gewinn, der aus den Zauberpapyri nach so vielen Seiten hin zu erlangen ist, nur so wenige Arbeiter lockt. Wie mancher, der religionsgeschichtliche Arbeit tun will, täte besser hier sich zu bemühen als um Probleme herumzureden, zu deren Lösung er doch nichts beitragen kann. Nach dem Schema der 'Papyrologie' gehören sie weder zu den Urkunden noch zu den literarischen Papyri; denn daß sich hier die große religiöse Literatur von Jahrhunderten niedergeschlagen hat, ist nur sehr wenigen deutlich. Die Unbekanntschaft mit den magischen Papyri macht sich zum Schaden so mancher religionshistorischer Arbeiten, auch der letzten Jahre, bemerklich, und da die wichtigste Publikation von Wessely in den Denkschriften der Wiener Akademie, philos.-hist. Klasse XXXVI Band 1888, allerdings ohne eigene recensio und emendatio kaum benutzbar ist, habe ich es mit einem meiner Schüler zusammen unternommen, zunächst wenigstens das kapitalste Stück dieser Literatur, das grosse Pariser Zauberbuch, in einer neuen Ausgabe vorzulegen.

See also K. Preisendanz, *Papyri Graecae Magicae. Die griechischen Zauberpapyri* I (Leipzig and Berlin: Teubner, 1928), p. VI.

30. S. Preisendanz, *Papyri Graecae Magicae* I, p. V.

31. U. von Wilamowitz-Moellendorff, *Reden und Vorträge* (Berlin: Weidmann, [2]1902) 254–55. The remark in full reads as follows:

> Ich habe einmal gehört, wie ein bedeutender Gelehrter beklagte, dass diese Papyri gefunden wären, weil sie dem Altertum den vornehmen Schimmer der Klassizität nehmen. Dass sie das thun, ist unbestreitbar, aber ich freue mich dessen. Denn ich will meine Hellenen nicht bewundern, sondern verstehen, damit ich sie gerecht beurteilen kann. Und selbst Mahadöh, der Herr der Erden,—soll er strafen, soll er schonen, muss er den Menschen menschlich sehn.

32. It should be noted, however, that Dieterich's doctoral dissertation was already devoted to the subject, a work that posed most of the pertinent problems. The dissertation was published in an expanded form under the title "Papyrus magica musei Lugdunensis Batavi . . . ," *Jahrbücher für klassische Philologie*, Supplementband 16 (1888):749–830; its prolegomena were reprinted in his *Kleine Schriften* (Leipzig: Teubner, 1911) 1–47.

Dieterich's commentary on the Leiden papyrus J 395 (=*PGM* XIII) followed under the title *Abraxas. Studien zur Religionsgeschichte des spätern Altertums* (Leipzig: Teubner, 1891). Related is the work entitled *Nekyia. Beiträge zur Erklärung der neuentdeckten Petrusapokalypse* (Leipzig: Teubner, 1893, ²1913; reprinted Darmstadt: Wissenschaftliche Buchgesellschaft, 1969). Still indispensable is his commentary on *PGM* IV. 475–834, entitled *Eine Mithrasliturgie* (Leipzig: Teubner, 1903; ²1909 ed. R. Wünsch; ³1923 ed. O. Weinreich; reprinted Darmstadt: Wissenschaftliche Buchgesellschaft, 1966). For biographical details and a bibliography see R. Wünsch, "Albrecht Dieterich," in Dieterich, *Kleine Schriften* pp. IX–XLII; H. J. Mette, "Nekrolog einer Epoche: Hermann Usener und seine Schule. Ein wirkungsgeschichtlicher Rückblick auf die Jahre 1856–1979," *Lustrum* 22 (1979–80) : 5–106.

33. See Preisendanz, *Papyri Graecae Magicae I* (1928) pp. VIII–IX.

34. Ibid., p. IX.

35. Ibid., pp. IX–XII.

36. *Papyri Graecae Magicae. Die griechischen Zauberpapyri*, herausgegeben und übersetzt von Karl Preisendanz, vol. I (Leipzig: Teubner, 1928), vol. II (Leipzig: Teubner, 1931).

37. See the *Vorrede* to vol. III (Leipzig: Teubner, 1941), reprinted in the new edition of vol. II, ed. A. Henrichs (Stuttgart: Teubner, 1974), pp. VII–XVII.

38. See K. Preisendanz, "Zur Überlieferung der griechischen Zauberpapyri," in *Miscellanea critica Teubner* (Leipzig: Teubner, 1964) 215 n.1.

39. See the *Vorwort zur Neuausgabe* by Henrichs in vol. I of the new edition (see n. 40 below), pp. XIII–XIV.

40. *Papyri Graecae Magicae. Die griechischen Zauberpapyri*, herausgegeben und übersetzt von Karl Preisendanz. Zweite, verbesserte Auflage, mit Ergänzungen von Karl Preisendanz, durchgesehen und herausgegeben von Albert Henrichs (Stuttgart: Teubner, 1973, 1974).

41. See A. Dieterich, "Der Untergang der antiken Religion," *Kleine Schriften* 449–539; A. D. Nock, "Greek Magical Papyri," *JEA* 15 (1929) : 219–35, reprinted in his *Essays on Religion and the Ancient World*, ed. Z. Stewart (Cambridge, Mass.: Harvard University Press, 1972), 1 : 176–94; A. J. Festugière, "La valeur religieuse des papyrus magiques," in his *L'Idéal religieux des grecs et l'évangile* (Paris: Gabalda, 1932) 281–328; M. P. Nilsson, "Die Religion in den griechischen Zauberpapyri," *Opuscula selecta* 3 (Lund: Gleerup, 1960) 129–66; S. Eitrem, "Aus 'Papyrologie und Religionsgeschichte': Die magischen Papyri," *Papyri und Altertumswissenschaft*. Vorträge des 3. internationalen Papyrologentages in München vom 4. bis 7. September 1933, hrsg. von W. Otto und L. Wenger, Münchener Beiträge zur Papyrusforschung und antiken Rechtsgeschichte 19 (München: Beck, 1934) 243–63.

42. See note 29 above.

43. See, e.g., the attempt to recover ritual fragments from *PGM* LXX in my article "Fragments of a Catabasis Ritual in a Greek Magical Papyrus," *HR* 19 (1980) : 287–95.

44. Cf. Nilsson's remark concerning the magical hymns, "Die Religion," 132: "Jedoch sind die Hymnen das Griechischste der Zauberliteratur. Ich kann mich des Eindrucks nicht erwehren, dass es ein älteres Zauberwesen gegeben hat, das an die griechischen Götter anschloss, von dem die auf uns gekommene ägyptische Zauberliteratur Brocken sich einverleibt hat."

45. Since then fundamental changes have occurred in the interpretation of Greek religion, of which the success of the book by E. R. Dodds, *The Greeks and the Irrational* (Berkeley and Los Angeles: University of California Press, 1951) was symptomatic. See also on this point E. R. Dodds, *Missing Persons: An Autobiography* (Oxford: Clarendon, 1977) 180–81. For recent developments, see W. Burkert, *Griechische Religion der archaischen und klassischen Epoche* (Stuttgart: Kohlhammer, 1977) 21ff.; idem, *Structure and History in Greek Mythology and Ritual*, Sather Classical Lectures 47 (Berkeley: University of California Press, 1979).

46. Cf. the comment made by A. A. Barb, "Three Elusive Amulets," *JWCI* 27 (1964) : 4 n.16: "Much that we are accustomed to see classified as late 'syncretism' is rather the ancient and original, deep-seated popular religion, coming to the surface when the whitewash of 'classical' writers and artists began to peel off. . . ."

47. On Jewish magic and related bibliography, see L. Blau, *Das altjüdische Zauberwesen*

(Strassburg: Trübner, 1898, [2]1914); J. Trachtenberg, *Jewish Magic and Superstition: A Study in Folk-Religion* (New York: Behrman, 1939); G. G. Scholem, *Jewish Gnosticism, Merkabah Mysticism, and Talmudic Tradition* (New York: The Jewish Theological Seminary of America, [2]1965); J. Neusner, *A History of the Jews in Babylonia*, vols. 4 and 5 (Leiden: Brill, 1969, 1970); I. Gruenwald, *Apocalyptic and Merkavah Mysticism* (Leiden: Brill, 1980).

48. See for surveys A. A. Barb, "Mystery, Myth, and Magic," in *The Legacy of Egypt*, ed. J. R. Harris (Oxford: Clarendon Press, [2]1971) 138–69; Nilsson, *GGR* II, 520–43 and passim; K. Preisendanz, "Zur synkretistischen Magie im römischen Ägypten," *Mitteilungen aus der Papyrussammlung der Österreichischen Nationalbibliothek (Papyrus Erzherzog Rainer)*, Neue Serie, V. Folge, ed. H. Gerstinger (Wien: Rohrer/Österreichische Nationalbibliothek, 1956) 111–25.

49. On Jesus and early Christian magic, with related bibliography, see Morton Smith, *Jesus the Magician* (San Francisco: Harper and Row, 1978).

50. On Egyptian magic of the later periods, see the collection by Lichtheim (see note 16 above); G. Roeder, *Volksglaube im Pharaonenreich* (Stuttgart: Spemann, 1952); idem, *Der Ausklang der ägyptischen Religion mit Reformation, Zauberei und Jenseitsglauben*, = *Die ägyptische Religion in Text und Bild*, vol. 4 (Zürich and Stuttgart: Artemis, 1961).

51. On the figure of the magician, see Smith, *Jesus the Magician*, pp. 81–89.

52. See W. Burkert, "Craft versus Sect: The Problem of Orphics and Pythagoreans," in *Jewish and Christian Self-Definition*, vol. 3 (see note 5 above), 1–22.

53. Some of these handbooks are among the *PGM*. How they were made can still be seen from the partly unfinished, late Byzantine (16th c.) copy in the Gennadios Library in Athens (Codex Gennadianus 45), the text of which was published by A. Delatte, "Un nouveau témoin de la littérature solomonique, le codex *Gennadianus* 45 d'Athènes," *Bulletin de l'Académie royale de Belgique, Classe des lettres*, 5ᵉ série, tome 45 (1959): 280–321.

54. As I have tried to show, even the human self was regarded as a daimon which could be handled by the magician in the same way as all the other energies of the universe. See H. D. Betz, "The Delphic Maxim 'Know Yourself' in the Greek Magical Papyri," *HR* 21 (1981): 156–71.

55. A beautiful testimony of this self-understanding is cited by D. Wildung, *Egyptian Saints: Deification in Pharaonic Egypt* (New York: New York University Press, 1977) 84–85, where the great magician Amenhotep says about himself:

> I am really magnificent among any people, one with a heaving heart when he is looking for a plan in some unknown problem, like one whose heart knows it already; who finds a sentence even if it was found destroyed; master of wisdom, friend of the ruler, who does useful things for the Horus, who makes his monuments splendid in order to cause everybody to remember him forever at the august place. Who guides the ignorant through the events since the primeval times, who shows their place to everybody who forgot about it; useful in his ideas, when he is looking for monuments to make immortal the name of his lord; who relates the proverb and acts with his fingers; leader of mankind, of engaging manners as a pleasant one. Who venerates the name of the king and his power, who praises his Majesty at any time of the day, who is on his guard in all his decisions. . . ."

56. A good illustration of the phenomenon is the social and psychological syndrome called "cognitive dissonance." The syndrome can be observed among persons of strong conviction who, when faced with evidence to the contrary of their convictions ("disconfirmation"), become more intense and close themselves off from their social context, rather than develop doubts about these convictions. See the study by Leon Festinger, Henry W. Riecken, and Stanley Schachter, *When Prophecy Fails: A Social and Psychological Study of a Modern Group that Predicted the Destruction of the World* (New York: Harper and Row, 1964). The authors of this study themselves may have become another instance of the syndrome: apparently they entered into the project armed with strong convictions about the origins of religion and, without ever becoming suspicious, found nothing but confirmation.

Introduction to the
Demotic Magical Papyri

Janet H. Johnson

As important as the Greek magical papyri are to the understanding of Greco-Roman religion, as noted by Betz in his Introduction to the Greek magical texts, their full significance can be perceived only when it is realized that these texts written in Greek are part of a larger corpus that also includes texts written in that stage of the Egyptian language known as "Demotic," and that the corpus as a whole derives in very large measure from earlier Egyptian religious and magical beliefs and practices. The interrelationship between the Greek and Egyptian aspects of these magical texts is emphasized by the fact that not only did the major find of such texts, the collection of Anastasi noted by Betz, occur in Egypt, in the ancient capital of Thebes (modern Luxor) and include both Greek and Egyptian documents, but it also included documents that were bilingual—some of the spells were written in Greek, others in Egyptian, all within the same texts and all for use by the same magician. Perhaps even more telling is the fact that even in the spells written in Greek, the religious or mythological background and the methodology to be followed to ensure success may be purely Egyptian in origin. Thus it is only with the inclusion of the Egyptian materials together with the Greek, and the study of the complete corpus, that the full ramifications of this extraordinary body of material can be studied and appreciated.

All four of the Demotic magical texts appear to have come from the collections that Anastasi gathered in the Theban area. Most have passages in Greek as well as in Demotic, and most have words glossed into Old Coptic (Egyptian language written with the Greek alphabet [which indicated vowels, which Egyptian scripts did not] supplemented by extra signs taken from the Demotic for sounds not found in Greek); some contain passages written in the earlier Egyptian hieratic script or words written in a special "cipher" script, which would have been an effective secret code to a Greek reader but would have been deciphered fairly simply by an Egyptian.

The longest of the four Demotic texts was at some time torn into two sections (*PDM* xiv; *PGM* XIV). The longer second section was acquired by the Leiden Museum of Antiquities in 1828; it now bears number P.Lugd.Bat.J 383 (formerly Anastasi 65). The shorter beginning section was purchased by the British Museum in 1857; it now bears number P.Lond.demot. 10070 (formerly Anastasi 1072). The definitive publication of the two sections, including hand copy, transliteration, and translation, with extensive commentary and glossary, is the work of F. Ll. Griffith and Herbert Thompson.[1] Attention was attracted to the Leiden section very early when Reuvens recognized the value that the glosses into Greek letters provided for the deciphering of Demotic script.[2] The entire preserved text (both the beginning and the end of the original manuscript are lost) consists of twenty-nine large columns on the recto and thirty-three smaller columns on the verso. All are in Egyptian with the exception of three short passages in three separate columns, which are written in Greek. Elsewhere occasional Greek words occur as glosses to Egyptian words or are written in the Egyptian text in an alphabetic Demotic script apparently developed for writing magical and foreign words. Much more common than the Greek passages is the use of the older Egyptian hieratic script in the midst of Demotic passages (as if the scribe were transcribing from an earlier manuscript and occasionally forgot to update what he was copying) and glosses into Old Coptic, most frequently for the writing of magical names and presumably to indicate proper pronunciation (which would have been very difficult to do given the abbreviated nature and great age of the traditional Egyptian scripts). Each column of the recto is written within a frame of horizontal and vertical lines; chapter or section headings are written in red ink (a tradition in Egyptian literature from Old Kingdom times[3]). In some cases, the scribes, while writing the body of the text in black ink, left room for the heading to be added later in red ink but failed to do so. Such headings can easily be restored.

The same scribe who wrote the London and Leiden text also wrote a second manuscript in the Leiden Museum (*PDM* xii; *PGM* XII) that contains Demotic magical texts—the verso of P.Lugd.Bat.J 384 (formerly Anastasi 75).[4] Of the nineteen columns of magical spells on the verso, the two columns at the beginning (the left end of the manuscript) are purely Demotic, the following thirteen columns are in Greek (although two headings are written in Demotic), the next two columns are again in Demotic, and the last two columns at the right end of the papyrus are largely in Demotic although they have short passages in Greek cited in the middle. (Note that the papyrus is broken at both ends, so it is impossible to determine how many more columns there were originally and in what language.) Within the Demotic sections of the manuscript are occasional passages written in the earlier hieratic script and in alphabetic Demotic as well as Old Coptic glosses. It appears that this text was written before the London and Leiden text since it is in this text that one can see the development of the Old Coptic script being used for glosses. In the columns at the left end of the papyrus, the Old Coptic glosses were written letter by letter above the corresponding Demotic letter. Since the Demotic runs right to left, the glosses run the same direction. This would have been quite confusing to someone reading what appeared to be Greek, so by the glosses in the second group of Demotic spells, at the right end of the papyrus, the scribe had taken to writing the glosses word for word, left to right, over the appropriate Demotic word. It is this latter system that is found throughout the papyrus of London and Leiden. In Leiden J 384, the scribe did not write within a frame or use red ink for headings. That both the papyri of London and Leiden and Leiden J 384 were written in Thebes, where they were found and sold to Anastasi, is indicated further by the fact that the dialect of Coptic to which the glosses and other alphabetic spellings most closely correspond has been identified as "archaic Theban."[5]

The British Museum also contains a second bilingual Greek and Demotic magical text (*PDM* lxi; *PGM* LXI), P.Brit.Mus. inv. 10588.[6] The recto contains eight columns of Demotic; two have occasional magical names written in Old Coptic and one has the names of some ingredients written in Greek in addition to two Greek sections within the Demotic. The verso contains two columns of Demotic with occasional Old Coptic and four columns of Greek. The Demotic sections use red ink for chapter headings (italicized in the translations), as in the papyrus of London and Leiden.

The fourth Demotic magical text is P.Louvre E3229 (formerly Anastasi 1061).[7] The preserved fragments (*PDM Supplement*) contain seven columns of Demotic on the recto and one column on the verso; the papyrus is broken at both ends. Both the earlier hieratic script and Old Coptic are used, together with the alphabetic Demotic script developed for writing magical names and attested in each of these texts except P.Brit.Mus. inv. 10588. Section headings are written in red ink on the recto (italicized in the translations); the columns on the recto are written within a red frame, as in the papyrus of London and Leiden.

In all four of these texts, all of which can be dated paleographically to the third century A.D. or only slightly later, there is every indication that all the various scripts were written by, and for, the same scribe, a bilingual person equally at home in Egyptian (old, current, and future) and Greek. The contents and the methodology are overwhelmingly Egyptian. Most of the material is completely Egyptian and its origins are easily traceable in earlier Egyptian religious and magical literature. The methods used are likewise standard Egyptian practices. Some of this is indicated in the notes to the translations.

By contrast, Egyptian divinities (in their own names or in the guise of their Greek counterparts) and Egyptian mythological references abound in the Greek texts and Egyptian methodology is also frequent. For example, although threats against gods who might fail to do what one wants go back to the earliest Egyptian religio-magic literature (Old Kingdom Pyramid Texts), but are unparalleled in classical Greece, they are frequent in the Greek magical texts as well as those written in Egyptian. Much of the Egyptian background of the Greek texts has been pointed out in the numerous textual notes added by Robert K. Ritner. The common source of the Greek and Egyptian language texts is also indicated by their frequent use of identical strings of invocation names, including, in addition to Egyptian and Greek divinities, western Asiatic divinities, "abracadabra" names, and what appear to the modern reader as gibberish.

Because the bulk of the texts is written in Greek, and because there are short passages of Greek in some of the Egyptian texts,[8] it has been suggested that the Egyptian texts are translations from the Greek. But there are passages in Egyptian, written in Old Coptic, within many of the Greek texts and, as indicated above, the religious and magical background of many of the spells, both Greek and Egyptian, is decidedly Egyptian. In discussing the Egyptian texts, Griffith and Thompson concluded: "even where there are reasons for believing that the demotic is a translation from the Greek, the original source, in relation to magic at any rate, was probably Egyptian."[9] The same may be true for much of the Greek material. One must, at any rate, be leery of overstating the Greek case and attributing too much to Greek influence.

The present collection of all the texts, Greek and Egyptian, in one easily usable volume, points this out conclusively. This will, in turn, allow and encourage the comparative study of the purposes, methods, props, magical names, and the like, of the Greek and Egyptian spells and encourage the study of the antecedents of the material in both cultures. This work will add greatly to our understanding of the cultural milieu in which these magical texts were produced and copied. Thus it is the hope of all those who have collaborated on the production of this volume that it will both further our knowledge of a dynamic period in the history of man and also encourage future study of cultural contact and cross-fertilization.

Notes

1. *The Demotic Magical Papyrus of London and Leiden*, 3 vols. (London: Grevel, 1904).
2. See n. 9 to Betz's Introduction, above.

3. See Georges Posener, "Sur l'emploi de l'encre rouge dans les manuscrits égyptiens," *JEA* 37 (1951): 75–80.

4. The recto contains a long Demotic literary composition known variously as the "Tefnut Legend" or the "Myth of the Sun's Eye"; for a short summary and bibliography, see Lichtheim, *Ancient Egyptian Literature*, vol. 3, pp. 156–57. The magical spells on the verso were published by Janet H. Johnson, "The Demotic Magical Spells of Leiden J 384," *OMRM* 56 (1975): 29–64; for the identification of the scribe, see ibid., pp. 51–53.

5. Janet H. Johnson, "The Dialect of the Demotic Magical Papyrus of London and Leiden," in *Studies in Honor of George R. Hughes*, ed. Janet H. Johnson and Edward F. Wente, Studies in Ancient Oriental Civilization, vol. 39 (Chicago: The Oriental Institute, 1977), pp. 105–32.

6. Published by H. I. Bell, A. D. Nock, and Herbert Thompson, *Magical Texts from a Bilingual Papyrus in the British Museum* (London: Humphrey Milford, 1933).

7. Published by Janet H. Johnson, "Louvre E3229: A Demotic Magical Text," *Enchoria* 7 (1977): 55–102.

8. But note that, e.g., one of the passages in Greek in London and Leiden concerns the purely Egyptian divinity Osiris and his burial in Abydos.

9. *Demotic Magical Papyrus*, vol. 1, p. 12.

THE GREEK
MAGICAL PAPYRI
IN TRANSLATION

INCLUDING THE DEMOTIC SPELLS

*[*Rite*]: A [daimon comes] as an assistant who will reveal everything to you clearly and will be your [companion and] will eat[1] and sleep with you.

Take [together, therefore,] two of your own fingernails and all the hairs [from] your head, and take a Circaean[2] falcon / and deify it[3] in the [milk] of a black [cow]   5
after you have mixed Attic honey with the milk. [And once you have deified it,] wrap it[4] with an undyed piece of cloth and place [beside] it your fingernails along with your hairs; and take [a piece of choice papyrus], and inscribe in myrrh the following, and set it in the same manner [along with the] hairs and fingernails, and plaster / it with [uncut] frankincense [and] old wine.   10

So, the writing on/[the strip] is: "A EE ĒĒĒ IIII OOOOO YYYYY ŌŌŌŌŌŌŌ."   15
[But write this, making] two figures:[5]

A							Ō Ō Ō Ō Ō Ō Ō
E E							Y Y Y Y Y Y
Ē Ē Ē							O O O O O
I I I I							I I I I
O O O O O							Ē Ē Ē
Y Y Y Y Y							E E
Ō Ō Ō Ō Ō Ō Ō							A

/ And take the milk with the honey[6] and drink it before the rising of the sun, and   20
there will be something divine in your heart. And take the falcon and set it up as a statue in a shrine made of juniper wood. And after you have crowned the shrine itself, make an offering of non-animal foods and have on hand some old wine. And before you recline, speak directly to the bird itself after you have made / sacrifice to   25
it, as you usually do, and say the prescribed *spell:*

"A EE ĒĒĒ IIII OOOOO YYYYY ŌŌŌŌŌŌŌ, come to me, Good Husbandman,[7] Good Daimon, HARPON KNOUPHI BRINTANTĒN SIPHRI BRISKYLMA AROUAZAR [BAMESEN] KRIPHI NIPOUMICHMOUMAŌPH. Come to me, O holy Orion, [you who lie] in the north, / who cause [the] currents of [the] Nile to roll down and   30
mingle with the sea, [transforming them with life] as it does man's seed in sexual intercourse, you who have established the world on an indestructible . . .

1. For meals with deities see below, ll. 23–24, 85–89; III. 424–30; IV. 750–75; VII. 644–51. For the background and further material, see H.-J. Klauck, *Herrenmahl und hellenistischer Kult, Neutestamentliche Abhandlungen*, N.F. 15 (Münster: Aschendorff, 1982), esp. 156–58, 190.

2. The adjective κίρκαιος is not attested elsewhere. Cf. LSJ s.v. "κίρκος," I: "a kind of hawk or falcon." See S. Eitrem, "Sonnenkäfer und Falke in der synkretistischen Magie," in *Pisciculi. Festschrift für F. Dölger* (Münster: Aschendorff, 1939) 94–101; Bonnet, *RÄRG* 178–80, s.v. "Falke."

3. The magical rite of drowning effects deification. See F. L. Griffith, "Herodotus II. 90: Apotheosis by Drowning," *ZÄS* 46 (1909):132–34; W. Spiegelberg, "Zu dem Ausdruck ḥsj Ἐσιῆς," *ZÄS* 53 (1917):124–25; A. Hermann, "Ertrinken," *RAC* 6 (1966):370–409; idem, "Ertrinken, Ertränken," *LdÄ* 2 (1977):17–19; Griffiths, *Plutarch's De Iside et Osiride* 273. See also *PGM* III. 1 and n. [R.K.R.]

4. The ritual suggests that the falcon is to be mummified. See Preisendanz, apparatus ad loc.

5. The translation of the term κλίματα is uncertain here. The triangular formation, found also elsewhere in the *PGM* and called "grapelike," "heart-shaped" or "winged," may be an example of *technopaignion*, the technique of writing words pictorially in the shape of objects. See on this subject Dornseiff, *Das Alphabet* 63–67; C. Lenz, "Carmina figurata," *RAC* 2 (1954):910–12; Wortmann, "Neue magische Texte" 104; G. Wojaczek, *Daphnis. Untersuchungen zur griechischen Bukolik* (Meisenheim am Glan: Hain, 1969) 59ff., esp. 62 and n. 12.

6. For milk and honey in sacred meals, see Klauck, *Herrenmahl* 193–96; Bonnet, *RÄRG* 459–61, s.v. "Milch."

7. Cf. for the title also Anubis "the good oxherd": *PDM* xiv. 17; xiv. 35, 400. See Griffith and Thompson, *The Leyden Papyrus* 24 and n. [R.K.R.]

[foundation], who are young in the morning and [old in the evening], who journey through the subterranean sphere and [rise], breathing fire,[8] you who have
35   parted the seas in the first / month, who [ejaculate] seeds[9] into the [sacred fig]tree of Heliopolis[10] continually. [This] is your authoritative name: ARBATH ABAŌTH BAKCHABRĒ."

[But] when you are dismissed, [go without shoes] and walk backwards[11] and set yourself to the enjoyment of the food [and] dinner and the prescribed food offer-
40   ing, [coming] face to face as companion [to the god]. / [This] rite [requires complete purity]. Conceal, conceal the [procedure and] for [7] days [refrain] from having intercourse with a woman.
*Tr.: E. N. O'Neil.

PGM I. 42–195
*The spell of Pnouthis, the sacred scribe, for acquiring an assistant:[12] . . .
Pnouthios to Keryx,[13] a god[-fearing man], greetings. As one who knows, I have
45   prescribed for you [this spell for acquiring an assistant] to prevent your failing / as you carry out [this rite]. After detaching all the prescriptions [bequeathed to us in] countless books, [one out of all . . .] I have shown you this spell for acquiring an assistant [as one that is serviceable] to you . . . for you to take this holy
50   [assistant] and only . . . O friend of aerial / spirits [that move] . . . having persuaded me with god-given spells . . . but [now] I have dispatched this book so that you may learn thoroughly. For the spell of Pnouthis [has the power] to persuade the gods and all [the goddesses]. And [I shall write] you from it about [acquiring] an assistant.

[The] traditional rite [for acquiring an assistant]: After the preliminary pu-
55   rification, / [abstain from animal food] and from all uncleanliness and, on whatever [night] you want to, go [up] onto a lofty roof after you have clothed yourself in a pure garment . . . [and say] the first spell of encounter as the sun's orb is disappearing . . . with a [wholly] black Isis band on [your eyes], and in your right hand /
60   grasp a falcon's head [and . . .] when the sun rises, hail it as you shake its head [and] . . . recite this sacred spell as you burn [uncut] frankincense and pour rose oil, making the sacrifice [in an earthen] censer on ashes from the [plant] heliotrope.
65   And as you recite the spell there will be / this sign for you: a falcon will [fly down and] stand in front of [you], and after flapping its wings in [mid-air and dropping]

8. The section describes the voyage of the sun god, his changing age, and his journey through the underworld. See E. Hornung, *Das Amduat* (Wiesbaden: Harrassowitz, 1963). For the forms of the sun god, see H. Brugsch, *Thesaurus Inscriptionum Aegyptiacarum* (Leipzig: Hinrichs, 1883) 405–33. [R.K.R.]

9. The reference is to Ra-Atum emerging from the seas of chaos in the primal month and his creation of the gods by masturbation. In the Egyptian view of time this cosmic event occurs continually (δι-ηνεκέως). Cf. also Pritchard, *ANET* 6. [R.K.R.]

10. Ancient religion knew of a large number of sacred fig trees, but little is known about the one in Heliopolis. The reference may point to another sacred tree as well, such as the *jšd* tree (see L. Kákosy, "Ischedbaum," *LdÄ* 3 [1980]: 182–83) or the tree "in which is life and death" (idem, *LdÄ* 2 [1977]: 112). Or the tree is the *persea* tree sacred to Ra (see Herodotus 2. 73; and *LdÄ* 3 [1980]: 182–84; Bonnet, *RÄRG* 83–84, s.v. Darby, *Food: The Gift of Osiris* 736–40). [R.K.R.]

11. Walking backwards as a magical rite. See *PGM* IV. 44, 2493; XXXVI. 273.

12. The term refers to an assistant daimon; see Glossary. Pnouthis and Pnouthios refer to the same person.

13. *Keryx*, which means "herald," may refer to a real or to an ideal person of priestly or holy status. See W. Quandt, "Keryx," *PRE* 21 (1921): 348–49.

an oblong stone,[14] it will immediately take flight and [ascend] to heaven. [You] should pick up this stone; carve it at once [and engrave it later]. Once it has been engraved, bore a hole in it, pass a thread through and wear it around your neck. But in the evening, / go up to [your] housetop [again] and, facing the light of the god-   70
dess, address to her this [hymnic spell] as you again sacrifice myrrh troglitis[15] in the same fashion. Light [a fire] and hold a branch of myrtle . . . shaking it, [and salute] the goddess.

At once there will be a sign for you like this: [A blazing star] will descend and come to a stop in the middle / of the housetop, and when the star [has dissolved]   75
before your eyes, you will behold the angel[16] whom you have summoned and who has been sent [to you], and you will quickly[17] learn the decisions of the gods. But do not be afraid: [approach] the god and, taking his right hand, kiss him and say these words to the angel, for he will quickly respond to you about whatever you want. But you / adjure him with this [oath] that he meet you and remain insepar-   80
able and that he not [keep silent or] disobey in any way. But when he has with certainty accepted this oath of yours, take the god by the hand and leap down, [and] after bringing him [into] the narrow room where you reside, [sit him] down. After first preparing the house / in a fitting manner and providing all types of foods   85
and Mendesian wine,[18] set these before the god, with an uncorrupted boy[19] serving and maintaining silence until the [angel] departs. And you address preliminary (?) words[20] to the god: "I shall have you as a friendly assistant, a beneficent god who serves me whenever I say, 'Quickly, by your / power now appear on earth to   90
me, yea verily, god!'"

And while reclining, you yourself quickly speak about what you propose.[21] Test this[22] oath of the god on [what] you wish. But when 3 hours have passed, the god will immediately leap up. Order the boy to run [to] the door. And say, "Go, lord, blessed god, / where you live eternally, as you will," and the god vanishes.   95

This is the sacred rite for acquiring an assistant. It is acknowledged that he is a god; he is an aerial spirit which you have seen. If you give him a command, straight- way he performs the task: he sends dreams, he brings women, men without the use of magical material, he kills, he destroys, he stirs up winds from the earth, he car- ries / gold, silver, bronze, and he gives them to you whenever the need arises. And   100

14. For the relationship between amulets and the magical papyri, see M. Smith, "Relations between Magical Papyri and Magical Gems," *Papyrologica Bruxellensia* 18 (1979): 129–36; J. Schwartz, "Papyri Graecae Magicae und magische Gemmen," in M. J. Vermaseren, ed., *Die orientalischen Religionen im Römerreich*, *EPRO* 93 (Leiden: Brill, 1981) 485–509.

15. This statement shows that something has fallen from the text, for this is the first extant reference here to myrrh *troglitis*. [E.N.O.] The name may be commonly referred to as "Ethiopian myrrh."

16. This angel or messenger (ἄγγελος) is also referred to as "the god" throughout this spell.

17. The adverb, which occurs in *PGM* I. 76, 79, 91, 108, 111, 113, 116, 121, can mean "precisely" or "in detail."

18. This is not to be confused with the famous Mendaean wine. Mendesian refers to the Egyptian city of Mendes in the Nile Delta. For a discussion of the confusion between the names, see Darby, *Food: The Gift of Osiris* II, 600.

19. Apparently this boy serves as a child medium. Cf. for this form of medium *PGM* II. 56; V. 376; VII. 544, etc.

20. πρόπεμπε with an inanimate (and esp. abstract) object is poetic. Here the prefix seems to have its literal meaning: "first," hence "preliminary words." [E.N.O.]

21. πρὸς ἃ φράζει should be read as second-person middle (cf. l. 79) and not third-person active, as Preisendanz translates.

22. The position of the word "this" is awkward in the Greek text; perhaps "the oath itself" is prefer- able. Cf. I. 156: "the same spell."

he frees from bonds a person chained in prison, he opens doors, he causes invisibility so that no one can see you at all, he is a bringer of fire, he brings water, wine,
bread and [whatever] you wish in the way of foods: olive oil, vinegar—with the
105 single exception of fish [23]—and he will bring plenty of vegetables, / whatever kind
you wish, but as for pork,[24] you must not ever tell him to bring this at all! And
when you want to give a [dinner], tell him so. Conjure up in your mind any suitable
room and order him to prepare it for a banquet quickly and without delay. At once
he will bestow chambers with golden ceilings, and you will see their walls covered
110 with marble—and you consider these things partly real / and partly just illusion-
ary—and costly wine, as is meet to cap a dinner splendidly. He will quickly bring
daimons, and for you he will adorn these servants with sashes. These things he does
quickly. And [as soon as] you order [him] to perform a service, he will do so, and
115 you will see him excelling in other things: He stops ships and [again] / releases
them, he stops very many evil [daimons], he checks wild beasts and will quickly
break the teeth of fierce reptiles, he puts dogs to sleep and renders them voiceless.
He changes into whatever form [of beast] you want: one that flies, swims, a quad-
ruped, a reptile. He will carry you [into] the air, and again hurl you into the bil-
120 lows / of the sea's current and into the waves of the sea; he will quickly freeze rivers
and seas and in such a way that you can run over them firmly, as you want. And
[especially] will he stop, if ever you wish it, the sea-running foam, and whenever
you wish to bring down stars [25] and whenever you wish to make [warm things] cold
125 and cold things / warm,[26] he will light lamps and extinguish them again.[27] And he
will shake walls and [cause] them to blaze with fire; he will serve you suitably for
[whatever] you have in mind, O [blessed] initiate of the sacred magic, and will accomplish it for you, this most powerful assistant, who is also the only lord of the air.
130 And the gods will agree to everything, for without him / nothing happens. Share
this great mystery with no one [else], but conceal it, by Helios, since you have been
deemed worthy by the lord [god].

    This is the spell spoken [seven times seven] to Helios as an adjuration of the as-
sistant: "ŌRI PI . . . AMOUNTE [28] AINTHYPH PICHAROUR [29] RAIAL KARPHIOUTH
135 YMOU ROTHIRBAN OCHANAU MOUNAICHANAPTA / ZŌ ZŌN TAZŌTAZŌ PTAZŌ MAU-
IAS SOUŌRI SOUŌ ŌOUS SARAPTOUMI SARACHTHI A. . . RICHAMCHŌ BIRATHAU
ŌPHAU PHAUŌ DAUA AUANTŌ ZOUZŌ ARROUZŌ ZŌTOUAR THŌMNAŌRI AYŌI
PTAUCHARĒBI AŌUOSŌBIAU PTABAIN AAAAAAA AEĒIOYŌYŌOIĒEA CHACHACH
140 CHACHACH CHARCHARACHACH AMOUN Ō ĒI [30] / IAEŌBAPHRENEMOUNOTHILA-
RIKRIPHIAEYEAIPHIRKIRALITHON OMENERPHABŌEAI CHATHACH PHNESCHĒR
PHICHRŌ PHNYRŌ PHŌCHŌCHOCH IARBATHA GRAMMĒ PHIBAŌCHNĒMEŌ." This
is the spell spoken seven times seven to Helios.

23. For the taboo on fish in ancient Egypt, see Darby, *Food: The Gift of Osiris* I, 380–404. [R.K.R.]
    24. The prohibition against eating pork was well known in Egypt (see also IV. 3079). The pig was
considered unclean because it was related to Seth/Typhon (see also IV. 3115, 3260). See Bonnet, *RÄRG*
690–91, s.v. "Schwein"; J. Bergman, "Isis auf der Sau," *Acta Universitatis Upsaliensis* 6 (1974):81–109;
Darby, *Food: The Gift of Osiris* I, 171–209; cf. also Plutarch, *De Is. et Os.* 8, 353F and Griffiths, *Plutarch's De Iside et Osiride* 281.
    25. Pulling down stars was a feat for which the Thessalian witches were famous. See H. Reiche,
"Myth and Magic in Cosmological Polemics," *Rheinisches Museum* 114 (1971):296–329.
    26. This magical operation is similar to the table gimmick of Demokritos (see *PGM* VII. 177).
    27. Cf. the table gimmick in *PGM* VII. 171–72.
    28. This is Egyptian for Horus . . . Amon. [R.K.R.]
    29. This is Egyptian *pikrour*, "the frog." [R.K.R.]
    30. This is Egyptian meaning "Amon the Great." [R.K.R.]

And engraved on the stone[31] *is*: Helioros[32] as a lion-faced figure, holding in the left / hand a celestial globe and a whip, and around him in a circle is a serpent bit- 145 ing its tail. And on the exergue of the stone is this name (conceal it): "ACHA ACHACHA CHACH CHARCHARA CHACH." And after passing an Anubian string[33] through it, wear it around your neck.

Spell to Selene: "INOUTHŌ[34] PTOUAUMI ANCHARICH CHARAPTOUMI ANOCHA ABITHROU / ACHARABAUBAU BARATHIAN ATEB DOUANANOU APTYR PANOR PAU- 150 RACH SOUMI PHORBA PHORIPHORBARABAU BŌĒTH AZA PHOR RIM MIRPHAR ZAURA PTAUZOU CHŌTHARPARACHTHIZOU ZAITH ATIAU IABAU KANTANTOUMI BATHARA CHTHIBI ANOCH." Having said this, you will see some star gradually free itself from [heaven] and become a god. / But you approach, take him by the hand, 155 kiss him and say the same spell: "ŌPTAUMI NAPHTHAUBI MAIOUTHMOU MĒTROBAL RACHĒPTOUMI AMMŌCHARI AUTHEI A. . .TAMARA CHIŌBITAM TRIBŌMIS ARACHO ISARI RACHI IAKOUBI TAURABERŌMI ANTABI TAUBI." When you have spoken this, / a reply will be given. But you say to him: "What is your divine name? Reveal it to me 160 ungrudgingly, so that I may call upon [it]." It consists of 15 letters: SOUESOLYR PHTHĒ MŌTH.[35]

And this is spoken next: "Hither to me, King, [I call you] God of Gods, mighty, boundless, undefiled, indescribable, firmly established Aion. / Be inseparable from 165 me from this day forth through all the time of my life."

Then question him by the same oaths. If he tells you his name, take him by the hand, descend and have him recline as I have said above, setting before him part of the / foods and drinks which you partake of. And when you release him, sacrifice to 170 him after his departure what is prescribed and pour a wine offering, and in this way you will be a friend of the mighty angel. When you go abroad, he will go abroad with you; when you are destitute, he will give you money. He will tell you what things will happen both when and at what time of the night or day. And if / anyone 175 asks you "What do I have in mind?" or "What has happened to me?" or even "What is going to happen?," question the angel, and he will tell you in silence. But you speak to the one who questions you as if from yourself. When you are dead, he will wrap [up] your body as befits a god,[36] but he will take your spirit and carry it into the air with him. / For no aerial spirit which is joined with a mighty assistant will 180 go into Hades, for to him all things are subject. Whenever you wish to do some-thing, speak his name alone into the air [and] say, ["Come!"] and you will see him actually standing near you. And say to him, "Perform this task," and he does it at once, and after doing it he will say to you, "What else do you want? For I am eager for heaven." If you do not / have immediate orders, say to him, "Go, lord," and he 185 will depart. In this fashion, then, the god will be seen by you alone, nor will anyone ever hear the sound of his speaking, just you yourself alone. And he will tell you

31. For gemstones with figures similar to the one described here, see Bonner, *SMA* 19–20, 151–53; nos. 233–37, 283; also the statue described by Nilsson, *GGR* II, 498–99. See furthermore Bonnet, *RÄRG* 427–429, s.v. "Löwe."

32. This is Helios-Horus. See Bonner, *SMA* 19–20, 153.

33. The precise nature of the Anubian cord is not clear. Anubis, the divine undertaker, may have had his name applied to thread used in mummification (see also IV. 1083, 2899; XXXVI. 237). See P. Wolters, "Faden und Knoten als Amulett," *ARW* 8, Beiheft (1905): 1–22; Bonner, *SMA* 3.

34. INOUTHŌ corresponds to Egyptian *i ntr* ꜥ3, "O great god," and is the beginning of an invoca-tion. [R.K.R.]

35. In Greek the name consists of fifteen letters.

36. This dressing up refers to the practice of mummification and the body's subsequent deification. See B. Gunn, "The Decree of Amonrasonethēr for Neskhons," *JEA* 41 (1955): 84–85. [R.K.R.]

about the illness of a man, whether he will live or die, even on what day and at what
190   hour of night. / And he will also give [you both] wild herbs and the power to cure,
and you will be [worshiped] as a god since you have a god as a friend. These things
the mighty assistant will perform competently. Therefore share these things with no
one except [your] legitimate son[37] alone when he asks you for the magic powers
imparted [by] us. Farewell.
195   The address to the sun / requires nothing except the formula "IAEŌBAPHRENE-
MOUN" and the formula "IARBATHA."
*Tr.: E. N. O'Neil.

PGM I. 195–222
*This, then, is the prayer of deliverance for the first-begotten and first-born
god: "I call upon you, lord. Hear me, holy god who rest among the holy ones, at
200   whose side the Glorious Ones[38] stand continually. I call upon you, / [fore]father,
and I beseech you, eternal one, eternal ruler of the sun's rays, eternal ruler of the
celestial orb, standing in the seven-part region, CHAŌ CHAŌ CHA OUPH CHTHE-
THŌNIMEETHĒCHRINIA MEROUMI ALDA ZAŌ BLATHAMMACHŌTH PHRIXA ĒKE
. . . PHYĒIDRYMEŌ PHERPHRITHŌ IACHTHŌ PSYCHEŌ PHIRITHMEŌ ROSERŌTH /
205   THAMASTRA PHATIRI TAŌCH IALTHEMEACHE; you who hold fast to the root,
[who] possess the powerful name which has been consecrated by all angels. Hear
me, you who have established the mighty Decans and archangels, and beside whom
210   stand untold myriads of angels. You have been exalted to heaven, and the lord / has
borne witness to your wisdom and has praised your power highly and has said that
you have strength in the same way as he, as much strength as he [himself] has.
        "I call upon you, lord of the universe, in an hour of need; hear me, for my soul is
[distressed], and I am perplexed[39] and in want of [everything. Wherefore, come]
215   to me, you who are lord over all / angels; shield me against all excess of magical
power of aerial daimon [and] fate.[40] Aye, lord, because I call upon your secret name
which reaches from the firmament to the earth, ATHĒZOPHŌIM ZADĒAGEŌBĒPHIA-
220   THEAA AMBRAMI ABRAAM THALCHILTHOE ELKŌTHŌŌĒĒ ACHTHŌNŌN / SA ISAK
CHŌĒIOURTHASIŌ IŌSIA ICHĒMEŌŌŌŌ AŌAEI, rescue me in an hour of need."
        Say this to Helios or whenever you are forced to do so.[41]

*Tr.: E. N. O'Neil. Since the character of this invocation shows no tangible connection with
the preceding or foregoing spells, it is best understood as a separate charm. Although the
purpose of this prayer (which at certain points is reminiscent of the language of the Psalms)
is not exactly stated, ll. 215–16 and 221–22 suggest that deliverance from the onslaught of a
demonic attack is requested.

37. Preisendanz's reading ἰσχινῷ υἱῷ is doubtful because the term is nowhere else attested (see his
apparatus ad loc.). The word may reflect an Egyptian or Semitic idiom ("son of your own loins"), an
idiom formed in Greek from the word ἰσχιον (hips). The Egyptian term is more general, however, and
refers to "part of the body." [J.B.] Cf. also Gn 35:11; 1 Kgs 8:19; Acts 2:30; Heb 7:5, 10. See furthermore PGM IV. 646, 2519, and Abt, Apologie 65–66.
38. Doxai is a name for angels. See also IV. 1051, 1202, and Bauer, s.v. "δόξα," 4.
39. The translation of ἄβου[λος] follows Preisendanz ("ratlos"). For the general language of prayer,
cf. Ps 42:6, 12; 43:5; Jon 4:9 LXX; Sir 37:2; Mk 14:34 par.
40. The concept of Heimarmene is found in PGM here and XIII. 613, 635; cf. 709. See D. Amand,
Fatalisme et liberté dans l'antiquité grecque. Recherches sur la survivance de l'argumentation morale anti-
fataliste de Carnéade chez les philosophes grecs et les théologiens chretiens des quatre premiers siècles (Amsterdam: Hakkert, ²1974); H. O. Schröder, "Fatum (Heimarmene)," RAC 7 (1969):524–636, esp.
567–68.
41. The translation is tentative at this point.

PGM I. 222–31

*Indispensable invisibility spell: Take fat or an eye of a nightowl and a ball of dung rolled[42] by a beetle and oil of an unripe olive[43] and grind them all together until smooth, and smear your whole / body with it and say to Helios: "I adjure you   225 by your great name, BORKĒ PHOIOUR IŌ ZIZIA APARXEOUCH THYTHE LAILAM AAAAAA IIIII OOOO IEŌ IEŌ IEŌ IEŌ IEŌ IEŌ IEŌ NAUNAX AI AI AEŌ AEŌ ĒAŌ," and moisten it and say in addition: "Make me invisible, lord Helios, AEŌ ŌAĒ EIĒ ĒAŌ, / in the presence of any man until sunset, IŌ IŌ Ō PHRIXRIZŌ EŌA."   230 *Tr.: E. N. O'Neil.

PGM I. 232–47

*Memory spell: Take hieratic papyrus and write the prescribed names with Hermaic[44] myrrh ink. And once you have written them as they are prescribed, wash them off[45] into spring water / from 7 springs and drink the water on an empty   235 stomach for seven days while the moon is in the east. But drink a sufficient amount.

This is the writing on the strip of papyrus: "KAMBRĒ CHAMBRE SIXIŌPHI HARPON CHNOUPHI BRINTATĒNŌPHRIBRISKYLMA ARAOUAZAR BAMESEN KRIPHI NIPTOUMI CHMOUMAŌPH AKTIŌPHI ARTŌSE BIBIOU / BIBIOU SPHĒ SPHĒ NOUSI   240 NOUSI SIEGŌ SIEGŌ NOUCHA NOUCHA LINOUCHA LINOUCHA CHYCHBA CHYCHBA KAXIŌ CHYCHBA DĒTOPHŌTH II AA OO YY ĒĒ EE ŌŌ." After doing these things wash the writing off and drink as is prescribed.

This is also the composition of the ink: myrrh troglitis, 4 drams; 3 karian figs, 7 pits of Nikolaus dates, / 7 dried pinecones, 7 piths of the single-stemmed worm-   245 wood, 7 wings of the Hermaic ibis,[46] spring water. When you have burned the ingredients, prepare them and write.
*Tr.: E. N. O'Neil.

PGM I. 247–62

*Tested spell for invisibility: A great work. Take an eye of an ape or of a corpse that has died a violent death and a plant of peony (he means the rose). Rub these with oil of lily, and as you are rubbing / them from the right to the left,[47] say the   250 spell as follows: "I am ANUBIS, I am OSIR-PHRE,[48] I am OSOT SORONOUIER, I am OSIRIS whom SETH destroyed.[49] Rise up, infernal daimon, IŌ ERBĒTH IŌ PHOBĒTH IŌ PAKERBĒTH IŌ APOMPS; whatever I, NN, order you to do, / be obedient to me."   255

And if you wish to become invisible, rub just your face with the concoction, and you will be invisible for as long as you wish. And if you wish to be visible again, move from west to east and say this name, and you will be obvious and visible to all / men.   260

42. The pellet ("that which is rolled") of a scarab is sacred to the sun god Ra. See also *PGM* VII. 584. [R.K.R.]

43. The papyrus reads φακίνου, which Preisendanz emends to ⟨ὀμ⟩φακίνου. For similar expressions, see *PGM* IV. 228–29, 3008. For a different reading, see Schmidt, *GGA* 1931, 445.

44. This is the myrrh ink of Hermes.

45. In order to transfer the magical powers of the names, they were washed off and consumed. For the widespread practice, see *Handbuch des deutschen Aberglaubens* 8 (1936/37): 1156–57.

46. The ibis was sacred to Hermes Thoth. [R.K.R.]

47. See on this point J. F. Borghouts, *Ancient Egyptian Magical Texts*, Nisaba 9 (Leiden: Brill, 1978) 27, 30, 41, 56. [R.K.R.]

48. This is Osiris-Re.

49. The papyrus has *tako* where one expects the standard Coptic *takof*, "destroyed (him)." [M.W.M.] Cf. *DMP* col. I, 13, p. 23 (and n.) for Demotic parallels to part of this passage.

The name is: "MARMARIAŌTH MARMARIPHEGGĒ, make me, NN, visible to all men on this day, immediately, immediately; quickly, quickly!" This works very well. *Tr.: E. N. O'Neil. Cf. *PGM* I. 222–31.

PGM I. 262–347

*Apollonian[50] **invocation**: Take a seven-leafed sprig of laurel and hold it in your
265 right hand / as you summon the heavenly gods and chthonic daimons. Write on the
sprig of laurel the seven[51] characters for deliverance.

The characters are these: ☀ ∪ ⊣ ⟨ ⊏ ∪ ♈ ∅ , the first character onto the first
270 leaf, then the second / again in the same way onto the second leaf until there is a
matching up of the 7 characters and 7 leaves. But be careful not to lose a leaf [and]
do harm to yourself. For this is the body's greatest protective charm, by which all
are made subject, and seas and rocks tremble, and daimons [avoid] the characters'
275 magical powers which / you are about to have. For it is the greatest protective
charm for the rite so that you fear nothing.

Now this is the rite: Take a lamp which has not been colored red and fit it with a
piece of linen cloth and rose oil or oil of spikenard, and dress yourself in a prophetic
280 garment and hold an ebony staff in your left hand and / the protective charm in
your right (i.e., the sprig of laurel). But keep in readiness a wolf's head so that you
can set the lamp upon the head of the wolf, and construct an altar of unburnt clay
near the head and the lamp so that you may sacrifice on it to the god. And immediately the divine spirit enters.

285   / The burnt offering is a wolf's eye, storax gum, cassia, balsam gum and whatever
is valued among the spices, and pour a libation of wine and honey and milk and
rainwater, [and make] 7 flat cakes and 7 round cakes. These you are going to make
290 completely [near] the lamp, robed and refraining from all / unclean things and
from all eating of fish[52] and from all sexual intercourse, so that you may bring the
god into the greatest desire toward you.[53]

Now these are the names, [which] you are going to write on the linen cloth and
which you will put as a wick into the lamp which has not been colored red: "ABER-
295 AMENTHŌOULERTHEXANAXETHRENLYOŌTHNEMARAIBAI[54] / AEMINNAEBARŌ-
THERRETHŌBABEANIMEA."[55] When you have completed all the instructions set out
above, call the god with this chant:[56]

---

50. This lamp divination is named after the god Apollo. Despite its syncretistic character, there are
an unusual number of parallels with the cult of Apollo. See S. Eitrem, "Apollon in der Magie," in *Orakel
und Mysterien am Ausgang der Antike, Albae Vigiliae* 5 (Zürich: Rhein-Verlag, 1947):47–52.

51. Eight characters are shown.

52. See *PGM* I. 104 and note.

53. For sexual union with Apollo attributed to the Pythia, see Plutarch, *De Pyth. or.* 405 C–D; Ori-
genes, *C. Cels.* 7.3; John Chrysostom, *PG* 61, p. 242 (hence *Schol. Aristoph. Plut.* 39; Suda, *Lexicon*, p. 3120). See G. Wolff, *Porphyrii De philosophia ex oraculis haurienda* (Berlin: Springer, 1856) 160;
W. Burkert, *Homo Necans, RVV* 32 (Berlin: De Gruyter, 1972) 143. [W.B.]

54. The magical words begin with the name ABERAMENTHŌ, on which see J. Mahé, "Aberamentho,"
in *Studies in Gnosticism and Hellenistic Religions, Festschrift for G. Quispel, EPRO* 91 (Leiden: Brill,
1981):412–18. The formula should be read as a palindrome (see Glossary). Cf. also *PGM* III. 67–68,
117–18; XXXVIII. 20–21.

55. The magical word should be read as a palindrome. Cf. also IV. 196–97; XIV. 24; LIX. 7.

56. These lines contain dactylic hexameters (several of which are metrically faulty) through l. 311. In
312–14 the meter breaks down completely, yet because the tone and the apparent intent is hymnic, the
translation continues in a verse pattern that is sometimes faulty. Ll. 297–311 (although the identification says 297–314) also form vv. 1–15 of the reconstructed Hymn 23, while vv. 16–18 are taken from
PGM I. 342–45. See Preisendanz, vol. II. p. 262. [E.N.O.]

"O lord Apollo, come with Paian.[57]
Give answer to my questions, lord. O master
Leave Mount Parnassos and the Delphic Pytho
Whene'er my priestly lips voice secret words, /
First angel of [the god], great Zeus. IAŌ   300
And you, MICHAĒL, who rule heaven's realm,
I call, and you, archangel GABRIĒL.
Down from Olympos, ABRASAX, delighting
In dawns, come gracious who view sunset from
The dawn, / ADŌNAI. Father of the world,   305
All nature quakes in fear of you, PAKERBĒTH.
I adjure God's head,[58] which is Olympos;
I adjure God's signet, which is vision;
I adjure the right hand you held o'er the world;
I adjure God's bowl containing wealth;
I adjure eternal god, AIŌN of all;
/ I adjure self-growing Nature, mighty ADŌNAIOS;   310
I adjure setting and rising ELŌAIOS:
I adjure these holy and divine names that
They send me the divine spirit and that it
Fulfill what I have in my heart and soul.
/ Hear blessed one, I call you who rule heav'n[59]   315
And earth and Chaos and Hades where dwell
[Daimons of men who once gazed on the light].
Send me this daimon at my sacred chants,
Who moves by night to orders 'neath your force,
From whose own tent this comes, and let him tell me /
In total truth all that my mind designs,   320
And send him gentle, gracious, pondering
No thoughts opposed to me. And may you not
Be angry at my sacred chants. But guard
That my whole body come to light intact,
For you yourself arranged these things among
Mankind for them to learn. / I call your name,   325
In number equal to the very Moirai,
ACHAIPHŌTHŌTHŌAIĒIAĒIA
AIĒAIĒIAŌTHŌTHŌPHIACHA."[60]

And when he comes, ask him about what you wish, about the art of prophecy, about divination with epic verses, about the sending of dreams, about obtaining revelations in dreams, about / interpretations of dreams, about causing disease,   330 about everything that is a part of magical knowledge.

Cover a throne and couch with a cloth of linen, but remain standing while you

---

57. The words Ἄναξ . . . σὺν Παιήονι form an iambic pentameter which may preserve a line from a longer hymn. The line belongs to Hymn 8 in Preisendanz, vol. II, p. 244. For a similar expression, cf. *PGM* II. 7–8. [E.N.O.]

58. Or, "I adjure (you by) God's head," here and in the verses that follow.

59. The dactylic hexameters are part of the reconstructed Hymn 4: vv. 7–8, 12–17, 20, 18, 23–24. For other versions and sections of Hymn 4, see *PGM* IV. 436–61, 1957–89; VIII. 74–80. (The identification of lines in Preisendanz is not correct, vol. II, p. 239: l. 18 is present, l. 19 is missing.) [E.N.O.]

60. The word should be read as a palindrome. One can see the word THŌTHŌ, written twice; it means "Thoth the great." [R.K.R.]

sacrifice with the aforementioned burnt offering. And after the enquiry, if you
335 wish / to release the god himself, shift the aforementioned ebony staff, which
you are holding in your left hand, to your right hand; and shift the sprig of laurel,
340 which you are holding in your right hand, to your left hand; and extinguish / the
burning lamp; and use the same burnt offering while saying: [61]

> "Be gracious unto me, O primal god,
> O elder-born, self-generating god.
> I adjure the fire which first shone in the void;
> I adjure your pow'r which is greatest o'er all; /
345 > I adjure him who destroys e'en in Hades,
> That you depart, returning to your ship,
> And harm me not, but be forever kind."

*Tr.: E. N. O'Neil.

PGM II. 1–64

". . . AKRAKANARBA KANARBA ANARBA NARBA ARBA RBA BA A" (speak the whole
name thus, in wing formation).[1]

> "O Phoibos, helper through your oracles,
> Come joyous, Leto's son, who works afar,
> Averter, hither come, hither, come hither.
> Foretell, give prophecies amid night's hour,[2]

5 ALLALALA ALLALALA SANTALALA TALALA"[3] (speak this name too, / leaving off one
letter in succession, so as to make a wing formation):[4]

> "If e'er with vict'ry-loving laurel branch
> Here from your holy peak you often voiced
> Words of good omen, so may you now speed
> Your way to me with truthful oracles,

LAĒTONION and TABARAŌTH AEŌ EŌ, lord Apollo Paian, who control this night,
who are master of it, who hold the hour of prayer too. Come, mighty daimons,
10 help me today / by truly speaking with the son of Leto and Zeus."

Add also the following [spell], which is to be written on laurel leaves, and together with the strip of papyrus on which the Headless One is drawn, it is to be
placed beside your head, rolled up. It is to be spoken also to the lamp, after you
come in from the prayer, before going to bed, while you are placing a lump of frankincense in the wick of the lamp: "BOASOCH[5] OĒAĒ IAŌIĒ ŌIAĒ ŌIAĒ NICHARO-
15 PLĒX / STHOM ŌTHŌ . . . Y IE IŌ ĒI IAĒL IRMOUCH ŌNOR ŌEYE IYŌ EAŌ SABAŌTH
THĒOTĒ PAŌMIACH SIEOU IAŌ IE IEŌ . . . IOY IEOY IŌ IĒI ĒŌ IĒAI IEŌA A E Ē I O
Y Ō."

---

61. The following dactylic hexameters also form vv. 16–18 of the reconstructed Hymn 23 in Preisendanz, vol. II, p. 262. [E.N.O.] In contrast to the preceding hymn, ll. 341–47 are Egyptian in character and refer to the sun god's self-generation and daily travel in his ship. See Hornung, *Das Amduat*,
passim. See also *PGM* I. 34. [R.K.R.]

1. On the wing formation, see *PGM* I. 11 and n. Here the formula seems to be incomplete. Supply
⟨KRAKANARBA RAKANARBA AKARNABA⟩ and ⟨A⟩ at the end. Cf. l. 65 below.

2. These lines, except for 4–5, are dactylic hexameters which are not always metrically correct; they
are the reconstructed Hymn 9, Preisendanz, vol. II, p. 244. The first three lines appear, in slightly altered form, at *PGM* IV. 24–27 (Hymn 10, 4–6). [E.N.O.]

3. Presumably SANTALALA, but there is considerable corruption in the text.

4. The lines of the following hymn may have originally been written in some iambic meter. Cf. *PGM*
I. 296–97.

5. In l. 32 the papyrus gives BOLSOCH in lieu of BOASOCH as the beginning of the incantation. One
or the other is probably wrong.

In order to remember what is said: Use the following compound.[6] Take the plant wormwood, a sun opal, a "breathing stone," the heart of a hoopoe[7] (also known as the "vulture cock"). Grind all these together, add a sufficiency of honey, and anoint your lips with the mixture, having first incensed / your mouth with a grain of fran-   20
kincense gum.

This is the preparation: In the evening, just before retiring, purify your bed with ass's milk, and then, holding in your hands twigs[8] of laurel (the preparation for which is given below), speak the invocation given below. Let your bed be on the ground, either upon clean rushes or upon a rush mat, and lie on your right side, on the ground and in the open air. While performing the invocation, give answer to nobody, and as you are uttering it, make an offering of a lump of frankincense / and   25
twelve right-whorled[9] pinecones and 2 unblemished [gizzard stones of a] rooster, one to Helios and one to Selene, on the first day [of the month], on a censer[10] of bronze or of earth. On your right inscribe this character,[11] and go to sleep in line with the upper stroke of it. While praying, wear a garland of laurel of the following description: Take 12 laurel twigs; make a garland of 7 sprigs, and bind the remaining five together and hold them in your right hand while you pray, / and lie down   30
to sleep holding this, in the above-mentioned position. Inscribe the character with myrrh ink, such as is shown to you [below], with a . . . feather [or pen],[12] and hold it, along with the laurel, while you are uttering in prayer the words which begin "BOLSOCH," etc.[13]

The names to be written on the sprigs, on each leaf: "YESSEMMIGADŌN ORTHŌ BAUBŌ NOĒRE SOIRE SOIRĒ SANKANTHARA ERISCHIGAL SANKISTĒ DŌDEKAKISTĒ AKROUROBORE KODĒRE" / (write 12 names).   35

The ink is as follows: In a purified container burn myrrh and cinquefoil and wormwood; grind them to a paste, and use them. Take a sprig of laurel and Ethiopian cumin and nightshade, and grind them together; take in a clay pot water from a new well, dug either 5 months previously or within the last 5 years, or any one you come across on the first day after its being dug, and throw the mixture into the water. Leave it for just 3 nights, and, as you are uttering the invocation, put a little of it into your / right ear.   40

To achieve a good memory: Write on a leaf of cinquefoil the following character, written with myrrh ink, and keep it in your mouth while you sleep.

The character is:[14] ℓ

Start saying the aforementioned invocation at the 7th hour of the moon, until the god hearkens to you, and you make contact with him.

And these are the compulsive [procedures]: All of them may be brought before the moon after the first or second day. / If he does not appear, sacrifice the brain of   45

---

6. σύνθεμα as a variant of σύνθημα may also have the meaning of "token" or "sign."

7. Cf. Horapollo, *Hier.* 1. 55, and the use of the hoopoe in a magical recipe in *PDM* xiv. 116. See Crum, *Coptic Dictionary* 102, s.v. [R.K.R.]

8. κλάδος is normally to be translated "branch," but that seems to convey the notion of something larger than can be envisioned here. "Twig" may be better, but it may sound too small. The reader must think of a small branch.

9. δεξιούς is either "right-turning" or simply "perfect in shape." Cf. *PGM* III. 694; XIII. 10.

10. θυμιατήριον is properly an incense burner, but here perhaps simply a word for "altar."

11. In the margin is the *ankḫ* sign (☥), a symbol of life.

12. The papyrus reads εν πιννηλι. . . . Preisendanz suggests πίννη λι[τῇ], "with a simple, or plain, pen" (taking πίννη as the equivalent of the Latin *penna*).

13. Cf. above, l. 14.

14. The sign is called *shenou*, an Egyptian symbol of protection. [J.B.]

a black ram, and on the third day the little nail of its right forefoot, the one nearest
to the ankle; on the fourth, the brain of an ibis; on the fifth, write the figure
sketched below [15] on papyrus with myrrh ink, wrap it in a piece of clothing of one
50   who has died violently, and throw it into the furnace of a bathhouse [16] / (some,
however, [throw it] not into a furnace, for that is too extreme, but they suspend it
over a lamp, or place it beneath one).

   In another [text] I have found the following: If then, he does not hearken to this
method, wrap up the figure in the same piece of cloth, and throw it into the furnace
of a bathhouse on the fifth day, saying after the invocation: "ABRI and ABRO EXAN-
TIABIL, God of gods, king of kings, now force a friendly daimon of prophecy to
come to me, lest I apply worse tortures to you, the things written on the strips of
papyrus." /
55   If even after this he does not hearken, pour fine, pure oil of radishes over an uncorrupted boy, who has been tested, [17] and having gathered it up again, prepare a
lamp not painted red, and set it upon a lampstand fashioned from virgin soil (some
authorities say to pour some of the oil on the altar also). If you feel a blow, [18] chew
up the cumin and drink it down with some unmixed wine.
60   Write the prescribed figure / as given above, along with the characters and the
prescribed spell twice with myrrh ink on hieratic papyrus. And of these, one you
should hold as you make your invocation, as you go to sleep grasping it in your
right hand, and placing it under your head, while the other, if the necessity arrives
for the compulsive [procedure], you should roll up in the aforementioned cloth and
use as prescribed.
*Tr.: John Dillon and E. N. O'Neil (hymnic sections, ll. 2–4; 5–10)

PGM II. 64–184

65   *An alternative procedure*: Take a sprig of laurel and write the / 2 names on its
leaves, the one: "[AKRAKANARBA] KRAKANARBA RAKANARBA AKANARBA KANARBA
ANARBA NARBA ARBA RBA BA A"; the other: "SANTALALA ANTALALA NTALALA TAL-
ALA ALALA LALA ALA LA A." [19]
   Take another sprig with twelve leaves on it, and inscribe on it the following
heart-shaped name, [20] while you begin with a sacred utterance. *This is as follows*:
70   . . . . And make of the sprig inscribed with the two names / a garland for yourself,
weaving about it a binding consisting of white wool, bound at intervals with red
wool, and let this hang down as far as the collarbone. You shall hang a similar binding also from the twelve-leaved sprig, and present yourself to the god in the following manner: Take a completely white cock and a pinecone; pour wine upon it,
75   anoint yourself and remain praying / until the sacrifice [21] is extinguished. Then rub

15. That is, the figure of the Headless One given at the end of the variant spell, *PGM* II. 64–183.
16. Properly, the hot-air space of a hypocaust. [J.M.D.] Bathhouses were important places for doing
magic. See Kropp, *Koptische Zaubertexte* I, 51–52; II, 32; J. H. Johnson, *OMRM* 56 (1975):44–45.
See also *PDM* xii. 149. [R.K.R.]
17. γυμναζομένῳ means literally "trained" or "practiced." But cf. *PDM* xiv. 287 and esp. xiv. 68,
where a boy's sexual purity is stressed. Hence the accompanying use of ἀφθόρῳ here.
18. What seems to be envisioned is something akin to an electric shock. Cf. VII. 230. [J.M.D.] Cf.
also 2 Sm 6:7.
19. Cf. above, ll. 1–5. Each name is to be uttered in "wing formation," leaving off one letter from
the beginning in sequence. See I. 11 and n.
20. The heart-shaped name is lost, but presumably it resembled the allegedly twelve-part inscription
given at ll. 33–35 above. Cf. III. 70, "in the shape of a heart, like a bunch of grapes."
21. Cf. above, ll. 24ff.

yourself all over with the following mixture: laurel bayberries, Ethiopian cumin, nightshade, and "Hermes' finger." You shall also speak into the lamp the following: "PERPHAĒNŌ . . . DIAMANTHŌ . . . L DIAMENCHTHŌTH [22] PERPERCHRĒ ŌANOUTH PHROUMEN THORPSOU."

The operative name [23] *is*: "AKTI KARA ABAIŌTH, O lord god, servant of god, who are in control of this night, stand by me, Apollo Paian."

Go to sleep with your head toward the south. / Use this at the time of sunrise,[24]   80 when the moon is in Gemini:

Fourth Invocation: [25]

"Laurel,[26] Apollo's holy plant of presage,
Whose leaves the scepter-bearing lord once tasted
And sent forth songs himself, Ieios,
Renowned Paian, who live in Kolophon,
Give heed to holy song. And quickly come
To earth from heaven and converse [with me].
Stand near and from ambrosian lips inspire
My songs; come, / lord of song, yourself; renowned   85
Ruler of song. Hear, blessed one, heavy
In wrath and stern. Now, Titan, hear our voice,
Unfailing one, do not ignore. Stand here,
Speak presage to a suppliant from your
Ambrosian mouth, quickly, all-pure Apollo."

(Speak while the sun is rising).

Greeting formula: [27]

"Hail, fire's dispenser, world's far-seeing king,
O Helios, with noble steeds, the eye
Of Zeus which guards the earth, all-seeing one,
Who travel lofty paths, O gleam divine,[28]
Who move, through the heaven, bright, unattainable, /
Born long ago, unshaken, with a headband   90
Of gold, wearing a disk, mighty with fire,
With gleaming breastplate, winged one, untiring

22. MENCHTHŌTH is equivalent to *mnḫ Ḏḥwty*, "Thoth is excellent/beneficent." [R.K.R.]

23. On the significance of the term κύριον ὄνομα, see Philo, *Leg. alleg.* 1. 75; *Det.* 22; 83; *Plant.* 74. For the doctrine of the sacred name, see also Iamblichus, *Myst.* 7.4–5.

24. The exact significance is not clear, but cf. *PGM* VI. 4–5, where a very similar hymn is to be recited at sunrise. See also Philo, *Vit. cont.* 89; Apuleius, *Met.* 11.20.

25. The basic form of the lines in this passage is metrical, but the dactylic hexameters are frequently interrupted by *voces magicae* and brief statements in prose. Ll. 81–102, 107, 132–40, 163–66 have been combined to reconstruct Hymn 11. See Preisendanz, vol. II, pp. 245–46. Ll. 81–82 (Hymn 11. 1–2) appear also at *PGM* VI. 6–7 (Hymn 13. 1–2) and 81 also appears at *PGM* XII. 87–93. [E.N.O.]

26. For the role of laurel in magic, see L. Deubner, *Kleine Schriften zur Klassischen Altertumskunde* (Königstein: Hain, 1982) 401–3.

27. The papyrus reads χαῖρε, "hail," which Preisendanz understands as an abbreviation of χαιρε-τισμός, "greeting formula." See on this A. Baumstark, "Chairetismos," *RAC* 2 (1954): 993–1006. The hymn that follows is written in hexameters, although toward the end of the passage the meter falters. The hymnic section that begins in l. 101, "I call upon you . . . ," may be in prose; however, cf. *PGM* IV. 261ff., where σέ is used repeatedly as the first word of a hexameter and where καλ(έ)ω follows σέ three times.

28. διπετές properly means "fallen from Zeus or heaven," referring to water, but the term is widely used to mean simply "divine." Here some of the original meaning seems appropriate. See Bauer, s.v. "διοπετής;" Betz, *Lukian* 168 n. 2.

With golden reins, coursing a golden path,
And you who watch, encircle, hear all men.
For you day's flames that bring the light give birth
To Dawn, and as you pass the midmost pole,
Behind you rosy-ankled Sunrise goes
Back to her home in grief; in front, Sunset
Meets you and leads your team of fire-fed steeds /
95   Down into Ocean; Night darts down in flight
From heav'n, whene'er she hears the crack of whip
That strikes with force around the horses' flanks,
AAAAAAA EEEEEEE ĒĒĒĒĒĒĒ IIIIIII OOOOOOO YYYYYYY ŌŌŌŌŌŌŌ;
O scepter-bearing leader of the Muses,
Giver of life, come now to me, come quickly
To earth, Ieios, hair wreathed with ivy.
And, Phoibos, with ambrosian mouth give voice
100   To song. Hail, fire's guard, / ARARACHCHARA
ĒPHTHISIKĒRE, and hail, Moirai three,
Klotho and Atropos and Lachis[29] too.
I call you,[30] who are great in heav'n, airlike,
Supreme ruler, you whom all nature serves
Who dwell throughout the whole inhabited world,
you [whose] bodyguard is the sixteen giants, you who are seated upon the lotus and
who light up the whole inhabited world;[31] you who have designated the various
105   living things upon the earth, you who have the sacred bird / upon your robe[32] in
the eastern parts of the Red Sea, even as you have upon the northern parts the figure of an infant child seated upon a lotus, O rising one, O you of many names,
SESENGENBARPHARANGĒS; on the southern parts you have the shape of the sacred
falcon, through which you send fiery heat into the air, which becomes LERTHEXA-
110   NAX; / in the parts toward the west you have the shape of a crocodile, with the tail
of a snake, from which you send out rains and snows; in the parts toward the east
you have [the form of] a winged dragon, a diadem fashioned of air, with which you
quell all discords beneath the heaven and on earth, for you have manifested yourself
115   as god in truth, IŌ IŌ ERBĒTH / ZAS[33] SABAŌTH SMARTH ADŌNAI SOUMARTA IALOU
BABLA YAM MOLĒENTHIŌ PETOTOUBIĒTH IARMIŌTH LAILAMPS CHŌOUCH[34] AR-
SENOPHRĒ EU PHTHA EŌLI. Hear me, O greatest god, Kommes, who lights up the
120   day, NATHMAMEŌTH; you who rise as an infant,[35] / MAIRACHACHTHA; you who
traverse the pole, THARCHACHACHAU: you who unite with yourself and endow

29. Lachis is probably metrical for Lachesis.
30. The following is an Egyptian section in contrast to the preceding Greek hymn. Ll. 102 and 106–7 contain an invocation of the sun god as a child sitting upon the lotus, enlightening the world. See S. Morenz and J. Schubert, *Der Gott auf der Blume* (Ascona: Artibus Asiae, 1954). [R.K.R.]
31. For the transformations of the sun god hour by hour, see *PGM* III. 500ff.; IV. 1596ff., and on the whole subject H. Brugsch, "Die Kapitel der Verwandlungen," *ZÄS* 5 (1867):21–26. [R.K.R.]
32. Cf. Apuleius' description of the *Olympiaca stola* in *Met.* 11. 24, and Griffith's commentary, *The Isis-Book* 308–14. The bird may be the phoenix, for which cf. *PGM* XII. 231; XIII. 881. See on the Phoenix myth the chapter in M. Tardieu, *Trois mythes gnostiques: Adam, Éros et les animaux d'Égypte dans un écrit de Nag Hammadi (II, 5)* (Paris: Études Augustiniennes, 1974) 231–62.
33. Zas is an old name for Zeus. See also *PGM* XIXa. 44; *Orph. Frag.* no. 145 (p. 189); cf. Die-terich, *Abraxas* 130 n. 1.
34. CHŌOYCH is equivalent to Egyptian *kky*, "darkness." [R.K.R.]
35. See on this point *PGM* II. 102 and n.

yourself with power, giver of increase and illuminator[36] of many things, SESEN-
GENBARPHARANGĒS of waters, most powerful god, Kommes, Kommes IASPHĒ[37]
IASPHĒ BIBIOU BIBIOU NOUSI NOUSI SIETHŌN / SIETHŌN ARSAMŌSI ARSAMŌSI   125
NOUCHA NOUCHA Ē ĒI OMBRI THAM BRITHIAŌTH ABERAMENTHŌOUTHLERTHEX-
ANAXETHRELUOŌTHNEMAREBA, the most great and mighty god. I am he, NN,
who have presented myself to you, and you have given me as a gift the knowledge of
your most great name, of which the number is 9,999: IĒ IE IA IAĒ IAE IEY IĒA IŌA
IEY / IĒI ĒIA EA EĒ ĒE ŌĒ ĒŌ EĒE EEĒ EEE AAŌ ŌEA EAŌ ŌI ŌE ĒŌ EĒ EAE III OOO   130
YYY ŌŌŌ IY EY OY ĒEA IĒEA EAE EIA IAIE IĒA IOY IŌE IOY IĒ IĒ IĒ IĒIE; Paian,[38]
Phoibos of Kolophon, Phoibos of Parnassos, Phoibos of Kastalia; IĒEA IĒ IŌ
IY / IE IŌA IĒA EYA ŌEA EYĒA ŌEYA EYŌA EYIE EYIAE EYE EYĒ EYIE EYŌ IEYAE   135
EYĒAE, I will hymn Phoibos Mentor . . . AREŌTH IAEŌTH IŌA IŌĒA AE OŌE AĒŌ
ŌĒA ĒŌA AĒE IE IŌ IŌ IŌ IEA IAĒ IEOY EOYŌ AA AĒŌ EE EĒY ĒĒ EĒA CHABRACH
PHLIESKĒR PHIKRO PHINYRŌ PHŌCHŌBŌCH;[39] I summon you, Apollo of
Klaros, / EĒY; Kastalian One, AĒA; Pythian, ŌAE; Apollo of the Muses, IEŌŌEI."   140

Preparation for the rite: On the first day, [collect] nails of a sheep; on the second, the nails of a goat; on the third, the hair or knucklebone of a wolf. Use these as
burnt offerings for the next 3 days. On the seventh day, in case he does not yet
come, / make a lampwick out of a piece of cloth taken from one who has died vio-   145
lently, and light a lamp from pure oil, and recite the prescribed formulas, beseeching and exhorting the god to come with good will; let your place be cleansed of all
pollution, and having purified it, begin in purity the supplication to the god, for it
is very great and irresistible.

/ ***Rite***: Take mud and purify the doorposts of your bedchamber, in which you are   150
observing ritual purity, and having thus smeared on the mud, write the following
inscription with a bronze stylus on the right-hand doorpost.[40]

What is to be written is as follows: "ⲍⲏ ⲉ⳩ⳑ2 ARSAMŌSI NOUCHA NOUCHAⲭ
ĒI ĒI IA IA IE ĒY / ABRASAX LERTHEMINŌTH." Similarly on the left-hand doorpost: 155
"ⲧⲟⲱⲉⲟⳅⳑⲅ⳽ IŌE ĒŌA ĒIEA IAIA IE IAIĒEA HARPON KNOUPHI" (formula).[41]

On the upper part of the door: "✳ ⳉⲧⳍⲭⲱⳅ AA EE
MICHAĒL ĒIA EYŌ YAE EYŌ IAE." Below the door, [inscribe]
the scarab, as it stands / here,[42] having anointed it with the   160
blood of a goat, outside your bedchamber. Let the throne be
purified, and upon it a linen cloth, and beneath it a footstool. Inscribe on the throne, on the underside: "IĒ IEA
IOAY DAMNAMENEUS ABRAĒ ABRAŌ ABRAŌA; lord of the

---

36. The papyrus reads πολυφωτιστα (cf. LSJ, s.v. πολυφωτίστης), a reasonably well-formed word
only attested here. However, in view of the genitive ὑδάτων following the *vox magica*, which seems to
need a governing noun, Preisendanz emends to πολύφω(τε κ)τίστα.

37. For similar formulas see *PGM* V. 485; XII. 80; XIII. 805ff.; XXI. 25. The formula beginning
"ABERAMEN . . . " (see Glossary) should be read in Preisendanz's text as a long palindrome.

38. The following text has many epithets of the god Apollo. Cf. *PGM* II. 139–40; III. 251; VI.
24–25. See I. 263 and n.

39. The spacing of this formula has been changed to conform to the spacing of the same formula
found elsewhere in the *PGM* (see I. 141–42; III. 77–78, 151–52, etc.).

40. For the ritual concerning the doorposts cf. the Jewish *mezuzah*, for which see Ex 12:7, 22–23;
Dt 6:4–9; 11:13–21. See Blau, *Das altjüdische Zauberwesen* 152; Schürer, *History of the Jewish People* II,
479–80 (with additional references).

41. For the whole formula, see *PGM* I. 27.

42. The papyrus has ωσπερισχει, which Preisendanz emends to read ὡς περιέχει, but the meaning
is not clear.

165 Muses, / be gracious to me, your suppliant, and be benevolent and merciful; appear to me with pure countenance."

170 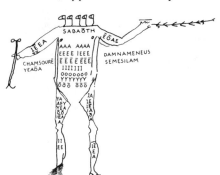 This figure is to be / inscribed on a piece of clothing
belonging to one who has died
violently, and is to be cast into
a pure lamp.

175 SENSENGEN BARPHARANGĒS / ŌĒIA IŌAE
    After you have learned all you want, you will release him, doing honor to him in
a worthy manner. Sprinkle dove's blood round about, make a burnt offering of
myrrh, and say, "Depart, lord, CHORMOU CHORMOU OZOAMOROIRŌCH KIMNOIE
180 EPOZOI EPOIMAZOU / SARBOENDOBAIACHCHA IZOMNEI PROSPOI EPIOR; go off,
lord, to your seats, to your palace, leaving me strength and the right of audience
with you."
*Tr.: John Dillon and E. N. O'Neil (hymnic sections, ll. 81–87; 88–101).

PGM III. 1–164

*[Take a] cat, and [make] it into an *Esiēs* [by submerging] its body in water. While
you are drowning it, speak [the formula] to [its] back.
    The formula during the drowning [is as follows]:
    "Come hither to me, you who are in control of the form of Helios, you the
5 cat- / faced god,[1] and behold your form being mistreated by [your] opponents,[2]
[them,] NN, so that you may revenge yourself upon them, and accomplish [the]
10 NN deed, because I am calling upon you, O sacred spirit. Take on / strength and
vigor against your enemies, them, NN, because I am conjuring you by your names,
BARBATHIAŌ BAINCHŌŌŌCH NIABŌAITHABRAB[3] SESENGENBARPHARARGĒS . . .
PHREIMI; raise yourself up for me, O cat-faced god, and perform the NN deed"
(add the usual).
15 / Take the cat, and make [three] lamellae, one for its anus,[4] one for . . . , and one
for its throat; and write the formula [concerning the] deed on a clean[5] sheet of

1. The goddess addressed here is Sekhmet-Bastet, well known from Egyptian magical texts. See
Borghouts, *Ancient Egyptian Magical Texts*, nos. 5, 13–15, 18, 20, 124; Bergman, *Ich bin Isis* 264–67;
E. Otto, "Bastet," *LdÄ* 1 (1975):628–30.
    2. For this type of accusation, see *PGM* III. 113–14; IV. 2475 and n.
    3. The letters BARBATHIAŌBAINCHŌŌŌCHNIABŌAITHABRAB form a palindrome. BAINCHŌŌŌCH
("soul of Khukh," the god of darkness) is often read separately, but is adapted to this form for numerological reasons: the formula adds up to 3663.
    4. That is, "one [to be placed] *in* its anus." Preisendanz in the second case restores ἐν τ[ῷ στόμα]τι,
but this is in conflict with the other restoration in l. 67 below: [. . . διὰ τ]ῶν καμ[αρῶν], "through the
earholes."
    5. "Clean" is meant regularly in *PGM* in a descriptive sense, i.e., previously unused or "free" from
imperfections, etc. See LSJ, s.v. "καθαρός," 3a. For detailed description regarding papyrus, see Pliny,
NH 13. 68–89, and R. Wünsch, "Charta," *PRE* 3 (1899):2185–92.

papyrus, with cinnabar [ink], and [then the names of] the chariots and charioteers, and the chariot boards / and the racehorses.[6] Wind this around the body of the cat 20 and bury it. Light seven lamps upon [7] unbaked bricks, and make an offering, fumigating storax gum to it, and be of good cheer.[7] / Take its body [and preserve] it 25 by immuring it either in a tomb or in a burial place . . . with colors, . . . bury . . . looking toward the sunrise, pour out (?) . . . , saying:

"Angel, . . . [sēmea], chthonic / . . . lord[8] (?), grant [safety?], . . . O chthonic 30 one, in [the] horse race, IAKTŌRĒ;[9] hold . . . restrain . . . , PHŌKENSEPSEUARE[K-TATHOUMISONKTAI],[10] for me, the spirit . . . the daimon of [the] place . . . / and 35 may the [NN deed] come about for me immediately, immediately; quickly, quickly, because I conjure you, at this place and at this time, by the implacable god . . . THACHŌCHA EIN CHOUCHEŌCH, and by the great chthonic god, / ARIŌR EUŌR, 40 and by the names that apply to you; perform the NN deed" (add the usual).

Then take up the water in which the drowning took place, and sprinkle it [on] the stadium or in the place where you are performing [the rite].

The formula to be spoken, while you are sprinkling the drowning water, is as follows: "I call upon you, Mother of all men, / you who have brought together the 45 limbs of Meliouchos, even Meliouchos himself, OROBASTRIA NEBOUTOSOUALĒTH, Entrapper,[11] Mistress of corpses,[12] Hermes, Hekate, [Hermes?], Hermekate,[13] LETH AMOUMAMOUTERMYŌR;[14] I conjure you, the daimon that has been aroused in this place, / and you, the daimon of the cat that has been endowed with spirit;[15] come 50 to me on this very day and from this very moment, and perform for me the NN deed" (add the usual, whatever you wish), "CHYCHBACHYCH BACHACHYCH BACH-AXICHYCH BAZABACHYCH BAIACHACHYCH BAZĒTŌPHŌTH / BAINCHŌŌŌCH ANI- 55 BŌŌŌ CHŌCHE . . . PHIŌCHEN GĒBRŌCHTHŌ MYSAGAŌTH CHEŌŌ . . . Ō[16] SA-BAŌTH EULAMOSI ĒĒLAXIMA . . . [. . . THACHŌCH]AXIN CHOUCHEŌCH."

On the [1st and 3rd leaves of metal] which you are to use for the conjuration, there should be this: "IAEŌ" /

---

6. μονάτωρ is a late word for μονάμπυξ, "horse with a single frontlet," i.e., a racehorse. Presumably one drew crude representations of them, along with their names, on a sheet of papyrus. Cf. such figures on the so-called Sethian curse tablets in R. Wünsch, *Sethianische Verfluchungstafeln aus Rom* (Leipzig: Teubner, 1899), esp. 51.

7. Cf. *PGM* IV. 2390 for a similar injunction to perform a rite with good cheer. See also Plutarch, *De tranq. an.* 20, p. 477E, and R. Bultmann, *TDNT* 2 (1976): 772–75 s.v. "εὐφραίνω."

8. The papyrus reads . . . ονε. Eitrem suggests τύραννε.

9. It is not clear whether *iaktore* is a magical word or something sensible. Preisendanz suggests ἀκτωρε as a Greek equivalent of Latin *actores*, "drivers," but in that case the syntax is unclear.

10. Emended and restored with plausibility from *PGM* III. 78–79, 513–14, 545–46; IV. 339–40; LXVII. 13.

11. Although attested in LSJ, s.v. "ἀρκυία," as an epithet of the goddess Hekate with uncertain meaning (with reference to Audollent, *Defixionum Tabellae* 38. 14 [third cent. A.D.]), "the netter" is a standard Egyptian underworld daimon. See D. Bidoli, *Die Sprüche der Fangnetze* (Glückstadt: Augustin, 1976); J. Zandee, *Death as an Enemy* (Leiden: Brill, 1960) 226–34. [R.K.R.]

12. The term νεκυία is also attested in this sense only in *PGM* IV. 2781, but necessarily having some such meaning.

13. The name Hermekate is a combination of Hermes and Hekate. See Wünsch, *Defixionum Tabellae*, nos. 104–7. Here in the papyrus the name could also be read Hermekatēlēth, that is, with the typical ending *-ēth*; thus Eitrem in the apparatus to III. 37.

14. AMOY at the beginning is Coptic for "come!" [R.K.R.]

15. πνευματωτός is a form not otherwise attested; cf. *PGM* XIII. 525: ἐμπνευματώθη.

16. A plausible restoration is IAŌ in that IAŌ and SABAŌTH form a common pairing in the *PGM*.

60

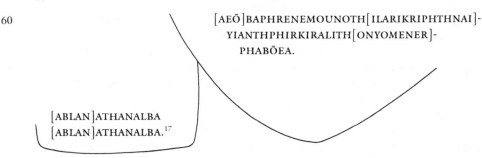

[AEŌ]BAPHRENEMOUNOTH[ILARIKRIPHTHNAI]-
YIANTHPHIRKIRALITH[ONYOMENER]-
PHABŌEA.

[ABLAN]ATHANALBA
[ABLAN]ATHANALBA.[17]

65   / *On [the 2nd] metal leaf, that is to be put [through the earholes],*[18] *there should*
      be this: "TREBA   ABERAMENTHŌOUTHLERAEXANAXETHRELTHYOŌETHNEMA-
70   REBA" / (in the shape of a heart, like a bunch of grapes).
      Right skeletal figure: [Left skeletal figure]:

"IŌ ERBĒTH   "I conjure you, the powerful and mighty angel of
IŌ PAKERBĒTH   this animal in this place; rouse yourself for me,
IŌ BOLCHOSĒTH   and perform the NN [deed] both on this very
IŌ APOMPS   day and in every hour and day; rouse yourself /
75   IŌ PATATHNAX   for me against my enemies, NN, and perform
IŌ AKOUBIA   NN deed" (add the usual), "for I conjure you
IŌ SĒTH   by IAŌ SABAŌTH ADŌNAI ABRASAX, and by the
PHŌKENSEPSEU-   great god, IAEŌ" (formula), "AEĒIOYŌ ŌYOIĒEA
AREKTATHOUMISAKTAI,   CHABRAX PHNESKĒR PHIKO PHNYRO PHŌ-
80   Perform the NN deed"   CHŌ BŌCH / ABLANATHANALBA
(add the usual, what-
ever you wish).

AKRAMMACHAMARI SESENGENBARPHARANGĒS MITHRA NAMAZAR ANAMARIA
DAMNAMENEU CHEU CHTHŌ[NIE][19] THORTOEI, holy king, the sailor, [who steers]

17. After the second ABLANATHANALBA there appears an isolated "K" followed by a lacuna of uncertain size. The papyrus either reads καί, "and," or κοινά, "add the usual." For obvious reasons, it has
been left untranslated.

18. See above, l. 16 and n.

19. This formula, repeated below l. 100, may well be garbled Greek for *Damnameneu, Zeu chthonie*,
identifying Helios-Mithras with Hades. [J.M.D.]

the tiller of the lord god,[20] rouse [yourself] for me, great cat-faced one, steerer of the
tiller [of God], perform the NN deed (add the usual), from this very day, / imme-   85
diately, immediately; quickly, quickly. Perform for me the NN deed (add the usual,
as much as you wish), powerful Seth-Typhon,[21] and act lawlessly through your
strength and overturn the NN deed in this place . . . [in this very hour?], as I command your image, / for I conjure you, MASKELLI MASKELLŌ (formula). Perform for   90
me this, the NN deed, by virtue of your visage, cat-faced spirit; perform for me the
NN deed (add the usual), and what is written hereafter" (add your additional requests).[22] Proceed toward the sunset[23] and, / taking the right-hand and left-hand   95
whiskers of the cat as a phylactery, complete the rite by saying this formula to
Helios.

Formula: "Halt, halt the sacred boat,[24] steersman of the sacred boat! Even you,
Meliouchos, / I will bind to your moorings, until I hold converse with sacred Helios.   100
Yea, greatest Mithra, NAMAZAR ANAMARIA DAMNAMENEU CHEU CHTHŌNIE THON-
TOEI, holy king, the sailor, he who controls the tiller of the lord god,[25] THON-
TOEI KATHEN KAI MENŌPHRIS[26] . . . KMEBAU KERKERYMI, before / [you attain to]   105
the southwest of the heaven, before [you reach nightfall?] in flight from the out-
rages committed against you. Hearken to me as I pray to you, that you may perform
the NN [deed], because I invoke you by your names BARBARATHAM CHELOU-
BRAM / BAROUCH[AMBRA] SESENGENBARPHARANGĒS AMPHI MIOURI . . . MIN.   110
Perform the NN deed" (add the usual, whatever you wish), "for it is those same
people who have mistreated[27] your holy image, they who have mistreated [the holy]
boat, / wherefore for me . . . , that you may return upon them the NN deed (add   115
the usual). Because I call upon you, IŌ ERBĒTH [IŌ] PAKERBĒTH IŌ BOLCHO-
SĒTH IŌ APOMPS IŌ PATATHNAX IŌ AKOUBIA IŌ ABERAMENTHŌOUTHLER-
THEXANAXETHRELTHYOŌTHNEMAREBA. Perform the NN deed (add the usual), I
conjure you in the Hebrew tongue[28] / and by virtue of the Necessity of the Neces-   120
sitators,[29] MASKELLI MASKELLŌ. Accomplish this for me and destroy and ravage in
the coming dawn, and let the NN deed befall them" (add the usual, whatever you
wish), "immediately, immediately; quickly, quickly. Pleasant be your setting!"

When you have come to the place / in which you are performing the rite, then,   125
taking hold of the long whiskers of the cat, both the right-hand and the left-hand, as a
phylactery, go through the whole of this formula to Helios at his rising.

Formula: "Hither to me, O greatest in heaven, for whom the heaven has come
into being as a dancing place, / SATIS[30] PEPHŌOUTH HŌRA, OITCHOU; of necessity   130

20. A reference to the solar bark of Re. See *PGM* III. 98–105. [R.K.R.]
21. Seth plays here the role of the defender of the bark of Re. See H. te Velde, *Seth, God of Confusion*
(Leiden: Brill, 1967) 99–108. [R.K.R.]
22. Or, "for other uses." Cf. the list of uses at *PGM* XIII. 230–333.
23. A reference to a place from where the sunset can be viewed.
24. For the halting of the solar bark, cf. Iamblichus, *Myst.* 6.5 and B. Ebbell, *Papyrus Ebers* (London:
Oxford University Press, 1937) 70–71. [R.K.R.]
25. Cf. *PGM* III. 81 and n.
26. Egyptian *mn-nfr*, "established and beautiful," an epithet of Memphis. [J.B.]
27. For this type of accusation see *PGM* III. 5; IV. 2475 and n.
28. Probably the meaning is "by the Hebrew sound" and refers to the vowel combinations with IAŌ.
[J.B.] See also Blau, *Das altjüdische Zauberwesen* 128–37; O. Eissfeld, "Jahwe-Name und Zauberwesen,"
in his *Kleine Schriften* 1 (Tübingen: Mohr, Siebeck, 1962) 150–71. On the use of "barbaric language"
(ῥῆσις βαρβαρική) generally, see Hopfner, *OZ* I, sections 706–69; Betz, *Lukian* 153–54.
29. This peculiar expression is found also in *PGM* IV. 262; cf. VII. 302–4; XXXVI. 342–49 and
perhaps IV. 1456; XIII. 291; XIXa. 11.
30. Probably referring to the Egyptian goddess Satis. See Bonnet, *RÄRG* 670–71, s.v. "Satis."

perform for me the NN deed, EĪ LAANCHYCH AKARBĒN LAAR MENTHRĒ SENE-
135   BECHYCH, you who love prophecy, golden-visaged,[31] gold-gleaming, / shining
with fire in the night, valiant, valiant ruler of the world, who shine out early in the
day, who set in the west[32] of heaven, who rise up from the east, SL . . . IX,[33] circle-
140   shaped, who run until midday and linger in Arabia, MOURŌPHO[34] / EMPHE . . . IR,
the messenger of the holy light, the fiery circle, PERTAŌMĒCH PERAKŌNCHMĒCH
PERAKOMPHTHŌAK KMĒPH,[35] the brilliant Sun, who shine throughout the whole
inhabited world, who ride upon the ocean, PSOEI Ō PSOEI Ō PNOUTE NENTĒR
145   TĒROU;[36] / I adjure you by the Egg.[37] I am Adam the forefather; my name is Adam.
Perform for me the NN deed, because I conjure you by the god IAŌ, by the god
ABAŌTH, by the god ADŌNAI, by the god MICHAĒL, by the god SOURIĒL, by the
150   god GABRIĒL, by the god RAPHAĒL, / by the god ABRASAX ABLATHANALBA AK-
RAMMACHARI, by the lord god, IAIŌL, by the god lord CHABRA(CH)[38] PHNESKĒR
PHICHRO PHNYRO PHŌCHŌBŌCH AEĒIOYŌ ŌYOIĒEA; you who light up the day,
155   NETHMOMAŌ; the child, / the riser, OROKOTOTHRO, augmenter of fire and of much
light, SESENGENBARPHARAGGĒS. Come to me, hearken [to me], most just one of
all, steward of truth, establisher of justice; I am he whom you met and granted
160   knowledge and holy utterance of your greatest name, by which you control / the
whole inhabited world; perform for me the NN deed" [(add the usual)].

This is the ritual of the cat, [suitable] for every ritual purpose: *A charm to restrain charioteers in a race, a charm for sending dreams, a binding love charm,*
and *a charm to cause separation and enmity.*
*Tr.: J. M. Dillon. This elaborate spell, a charm suitable for a number of purposes (all of
which are forms of malicious magic), is set forth with special reference to its use in chariot
races; it is understood, however, that the additional functions, as stated at the end of the
spell, also prove useful to the practitioner, provided that he supply in the required places the
appropriate requests.

PGM III. 165–86
165   *Take [some] water cress,[39] 4 fingers in length, and make from it . . . and of the
plant bugloss . . . construct . . . a strip of papyrus, and in the middle of the papyrus
170   strip . . . throw it away, saying the / names: "AN . . . SAŌ IBR . . . EISIRO . . .
OUSIREN [TECHTHA[40] . . .]L, I conjure you, lord gods, . . . do not, therefore, dis-

31. Neither φιλομαντοσύνος nor χρυσοπρόσωπος is attested elsewhere, according to LSJ.

32. Reading λιβυβόρῳ, a compound found nowhere else; it probably means "west."

33. It is not clear whether this damaged word is a *vox magica* or a Greek word.

34. Mourōph is a name of the hour god in *PGM* IV. 1690 (the god of the eleventh hour, having the
form of an ibis).

35. Forms of this *logos* occur in *PGM* IV. 1010; XII. 190; XIII. 780, 820. The final name Kmēph is
an epithet of Osiris and is the equivalent of the Egyptian ḥm'f, "his shrine." Cf. SATRAPERKMĒPH in
PGM XII. 185; XIII. 915.

36. The phrase is equivalent to the Egyptian *p3 šy ꜥ3 p3 šy ꜥ3 p3 ntr n3 ntr. w tr. w*, "Good Daimon,
Good Daimon, O god of all the gods!" PSOEIŌ should be the usual PSAIAS. [R.K.R.]

37. For the sun as an egg, cf. *PGM* XII. 100–106. On the cosmic egg, see J. Bergman, *Isis-Seele und
Isis-Ei* (Uppsala: Almqvist and Wiksell, 1970) 73–102; Morenz, *Egyptian Religion* 177–79. [R.K.R.]

38. This formula has been misread and is here emended on the basis of *PGM* I. 141–42; II. 138–
39; III. 77–78. Preisendanz has LABRA at the beginning. The lambda has been misread for a chi.

39. The papyrus has [.]α[.] δαμινον, which Preisendanz restores to read [κ]α[ρ] δάμινον, an unattested adjectival form of κάρδαμον, "nose-smart" (thus LSJ, s.v.; a mustardlike plant). However,
Schmidt, *GGA* 1931, 450 suggests [β]α[λ] σάμινον, "balsam wood." Cf. *PGM* XII. 364.

40. A variant of the name OSIRCHENTECHTHA. See also *PGM* VII. 257. The name corresponds to
Egyptian *Osiris-khenty-khet*, a combination of Osiris and Khenty-khet, the local god of Athribis, who in
the text is joined together with Osiris, Horus, and Apis. See Bonnet, *RÄRG* 131–33, s.v. "Chentechtai." [R.K.R.]

regard me; speak to me [clearly about] everything, accomplish everything . . . of / my prayer [and . . .] if god will, of this prayer [on the strip of papyrus] and of   175
the important matter of mine."

And you must make an offering in . . . [write] this [on a piece of priestly papyrus] with myrrh ink: . . . / [*ouroboros*][41] serpent . . . "ŌTE . . . IAM . . . GRASŌ-   180
CHŌ . . . NŌPSITHER THERNŌPSI . . ."

*Tr.: J. M. Dillon. This fragmentary portion of *PGM* III begins another untitled spell which probably ends at line 186, since line 187 begins a new column (col. VIII) in the papyrus manuscript. Although the exact purpose of this short spell cannot be determined, its function may be similar to that of the spell to follow, viz., an oracular request.

PGM III. 187–262

*Pound up dry fruit (?)[42] with a pestle (?)[43] and mix it to sufficiency with honey and [oil of] a date palm. Grind up a magnet. Boil all together and pulverize it. Make little rounds, as many as you wish, / but put an ounce of each element of the   190
mixture into each of these, and proceed thus, singing a hymn of praise to the god. Then the deity will come to you, shaking the whole house and the tripod[44] before him. Then he will bring about[45] your enquiry into the future, being clear in his intercourse with you,[46] as long as you wish, / and then dismiss the god with thanks.   195

The drawing of the tripod:

This is the prayer of encounter of the rite which is recited to Helios:[47]
   "Keep silent, everyone, the voice that's in
   Your mouths; O circling birds of air, keep quiet; /
   Cease frolicking, you dolphins, o'er the brine.   200
   Stand for me, river streams and fountain [flows].

41. Supplying [οὐροβ]ορος in the lacuna. [R.D.K.]

42. τὰ ξυρά. Preisendanz translates on the basis of a gloss in Hesychius, ξυρόν, "cutting, dry, sharp." But perhaps we are to understand simply ξύλα, "pieces of wood," assuming a confusion of lambda and rho. The definite article, however, suggests the pieces of wood were previously mentioned, in which case this spell would be connected to the preceding (cf. l. 165).

43. The papyrus has σχομπανου, a word otherwise unattested and meaningless. Preisendanz emends to κομπανου, "strawberry tree," a rather radical change. Perhaps we should read κοπάνου, "pestle," the sigma being an error, and the mu intrusive, as it often is with pi. This, however, would have to be a genitive used instrumentally, which is troublesome.

44. This tripod has not been mentioned before, but it is obviously central to the ceremony (cf. ll. 291–96 below). Perhaps we can assume the tripod is a part of the magician's basic equipment (see *PGM* IV. 1890–91; 1897; V. 200–201; XIII. 104, 661, etc.).

45. Reading future τελεῖ instead of imperative τέλει. The phrase that follows (τρανὴς τῇ ὁμι[λ]ίᾳ) seems to make better sense if it refers to the god. Cf. *PGM* II. 83–84, where ὁμιλῶν is used of the god consorting with the magician.

46. On Apollo's epiphany cf. Callimachus, *Hy.* 2.1–2. [W.B.]

47. The following dactylic hexameters are also the reconstructed Hymn 5. See Preisendanz, vol. II, pp. 241–42. [E.N.O.]

Now, birds of augury, stop everything
Beneath the sky. Snakes in your dens, attend
The cry and be afraid. May you in awe

205 [Keep] silence, daimons 'mid the shades. / The world
Itself's astonished by the secret words.
King Semea,[48] [father] of the world, be gracious
To me, O scarab; [I call you] immortal,
Golden-haired god, O scarab, marvel great
To ev'ry god and man, [be gracious, lord,
Who hold the fiery vapor in your power], /

210 Lord of the [sunrise], risen fiery,
Titan, I call [you], flaming messenger
Of Zeus, divine IAŌ; and you, too,
Who rule in heaven's realm, O [RAPHAĒL],
Who joy in sunrise, be a gracious god,
O ABRASAX; and you, O greatest one,
O heav'nly one, I call, and [you, MICHAĒL], your helper,[49] /

215 Who saves [his people's lives], the perfect eye
Of Zeus, and who has both exalted[50] nature
And brought forth nature in its turn from nature.
And I call . . . of the immortals . . .

OPASĒĒPA SESE[NGENB]ARPHARAGGĒS:

All-mighty is the god, but you are[51] greatest,
Immortal one; I beg you, shine forth now,

220 Lord of the world, SABAŌTH, / who veil[52] sunset
From dawn, ADŌNAI, who, being a world,
Alone among immortals tour the world, self-taught,
Untutored, through the world's midst traveling
To those who with a cry raise you at night.[53]

AKRAMMACH[ARI], KA . . . K . . .

225 Who joy in laurel offering, / in gates
Of untamed Styx and Death the Arbiter.

---

48. The name Semea also appears at *PGM* III. 29, where it is fem., and at V. 429; *PDM* xiv. 214 among the *voces magicae*. Despite the designation "King" here, Semea elsewhere is a Syrian goddess whose name appears in various forms on numerous votive inscriptions. She is identified with several deities, e.g., Astarte, Athena, Hera. Semea does not appear in Greco-Roman literary writings except perhaps in Ps.-Lucian, *De Syr. Dea* 33 (yet the text is uncertain), where it is suggested she is Semiramis. There is also a Syrian god Seimios. See O. Höfer, in Roscher IV, 601; R. Dussaud, "Simea und Simios," *PRE*, second series 5 (1927):137–40; W. Fauth, "Simia," *KP* 5 (1979):200. [E.N.O.]

49. The papyrus reads ἀ[ρ]ωγόν σου Μ[ιχαὴλ], which is unmetrical. Heitsch would excise ἀρωγόν σου; Preisendanz would excise μέγιστε at the beginning of the line, and write Μιχαὴλ σοῦ ἀρωγόν, which would restore the meter. "Michael" is a restoration, but a probable one; cf. *PGM* I. 301.

50. ἀέξοντα, the emendation of Wünsch, is preferable to δείξαντα for two reasons: (1) it corrects the meter and (2) it restores the proper sense, for whatever is written must govern φύσιν in both clauses. In any case, ἀέξοντα must be taken as a zeugma. [E.N.O.]

51. Fahz reads ἐσσι in lieu of ἐστι, "you are almighty god."

52. ἐπισκεπάζω is properly "to cover over," hence "veil." It may, however, be a solecism for ἐπισκέπτομαι, "look upon," the sense required here (cf. Preisendanz: "beschaut"). Cf. *PGM* I. 303, ἐπισκοπιάζεις, which is at least metrical, though the verb is not elsewhere attested. [E.N.O.]

53. The readings of the papyrus are quite uncertain here. See the restoration by Heitsch in Preisendanz, vol. II, pp. 241–42 (Hymn 5).

You I adjure, god's seal,[54] at whom all deathless
Gods of Olympos quake and daimons who
Stand forth preeminent, for whom the sea
Is ordered to be silent when it hears.[55]
You I adjure by mighty god Apollo. /
ΑΕĒΙΟΥŌ."   230

Also say this: "Send me the daimon who will give responses to me about everything which I order him to speak about." And he will bring this about.

This is also [another] hymn:[56]

"I[57] sing of you, O blessed one, O healer,
Giver of oracles, / O all-wise one,   235
O Delian [lord and Python-]slaying[58] [youth],
Dodona's [king, foretell,] O Pythian Paian;
I call you, [god who rule the tuneful lyre],
Which you [alone] of gods [do hold and strike]
[With sturdy hands] . . . [lord of the silver bow],
[O well]-named Phoibos . . .

. . . .
/ . . . ruler absolute . . .   240
Who roam the wooded peaks [of Mount Parnassos],
Be silent, do not now unstring . . .
O myrrh tree . . . / Lykian god,   245
Cease grow . . .
A greater light, for he will learn . . .
From lips divine, someone . . . to arouse
The seer with plectrum[59] . . .
But come you hither, prophesying; come,
Come hither, prophet, who bring joy, O Smintheus,
Give your response and / hearken, Pythian Paian;   250
Undying shoot, hail, Delphic maiden, Daphne,
For to you first did Phoibos strike up songs
In contest with the Muses; Daphne, you
Shake bough and urge on Phoibos. Then in hymns
They praise your tunefulness from holy Delphi.
O maiden who exult in tones divine
And oracles / . . . heaven's runner,[60] light bearer,   255
Earth shaker: gracious and obedient,

54. O, "I adjure you [by] the god's seal." See *PGM* I. 306 and n.

55. In Hymn 5, Preisendanz concludes with ἀκούει, but the following words seem part of the hymn
for two reasons: (1) they are almost metrically sound, and (2) they seem to have a poetic sense. [E.N.O.]

56. This hymn is extremely fragmentary in the papyrus. Here the suggested restoration by Heitsch is
followed. See Preisendanz, vol. II, p. 247 (Hymn 12). [E.N.O.]

57. This passage contains what appears to be dactylic hexameters, many of which are fragmentary
while others are completely missing. [E.N.O.]

58. The papyrus has]ωλετοκτυπε, which Preisendanz (vol. II, p. 247 [Hymn 12]) restores as
[Πυθ]ολετοκτύπε. This, if correct, would be a unique epithet, a combination of two attested epithets:
Πυθοκτόνος, "Python slayer," and Πυθολέτης, "Python destroyer."

59. On the instrument called πλῆκτρον, cf. Plutarch, *De def. or.* 436E; Clement Alex., *Protr.* 1. 5. 3.
[W.B.]

60. Read οὐρ⟨αν⟩οδρόμε for papyrus ουροδρομε, which is meaningless. For this epithet see l. 258
and LSJ, s.v.

Come to your prophet, but come now in haste,
O you who run through the air, O Pythian Paian."

Dismissal: ["Hasten], O air-traversing Pythian Paian; return to your heavens, /
260   leaving to me health together with all gratitude, benevolent and ready to hearken, a
sure breastplate (?), and depart to your own heavens, and [dwell there.]"
*Tr.: John Dillon and E. N. O'Neil (hymnic sections, ll. 198–230; 234–58).

PGM III. 263–75

*Foreknowledge charm: Take your finger and place it under your [tongue][61] be-
265   fore you speak to anyone.[62] Say these things along with the [great name]: / "make
me know in advance the things in each person's mind, today, [because] I am TOM
. . . IAŌ SABAŌTH IAŌ THĒAĒĒTH . . . M ADOUNAI BATHIAŌ . . . EA THŌĒ IABRABA
ARBATHRAS[IAŌ] BATHIAŌŌIA ZAGOURĒ BARBATHIAŌ AĒI AAAAAAA EEEEEEE . . .
ŌE . . . SOESĒSISIETH . . . SABAŌTH IAEŌ" (formula). If you wish, you will know
270   [all things in advance], . . . if you have [your finger] / under your tongue, according
to [the command, and if you say] this formula to Helios.

And the formula is: "Lord, if you [wish me to know in advance], let the falcon
[descend] onto the tree." If it does not happen, also speak this formula to the four
winds while you turn around [toward] the wind.[63] Whenever you say the formula,
275   also say to Helios the great name . . . and the great name . . . : AŌTH / SABAŌTH.
The formula [is as] above.
*Tr.: W. C. Grese.

PGM III. 275–81

*[Horoscope]:[64] Moon in [. . . or] Virgo: anything is obtainable, perform bowl
divination, as you wish; in [Cancer]: perform the spell of reconciliation, air divination . . . ; in Gemini: perform spells of binding, . . . ; [in] Libra: perform invocation . . . spell of release . . . necromancy; in Pisces . . . OIŌ or love charm; in Sagit-
280   tarius: conduct business / . . . ; [in] Capricorn: do what is appropriate; in . . . .
*Tr.: E. N. O'Neil.

PGM III. 282–409

*. . . words not to be spoken . . . in hexameter. . . .

Rite that brings foreknowledge, [which has] complete power and makes [all
285   the passions] / subservient:[65] In the deep . . . of a river [or in] a tomb . . . after
descending, throw into . . . [the] passion stops, and you will learn whatever you
wish.

[But speak thus:] "Continue without deception, lord, the vision of every act, in
accordance with the command of the holy spirit, the [angel][66] of Phoibos, you
290   yourself being pliable because of these / songs and psalms."

The preparation for the operation: For a direct vision, set up a tripod and a table
of olive wood or of laurel wood, and on the table carve in a circle these characters:[67]

---

61. For another example of placing something under the tongue, see *PGM* IV. 1745–46. Cf. also
V. 253–54.
62. Cf. Smith, *Jesus the Magician* 116, who translates: "⟨in the morning⟩ before you speak to anyone."
63. The formula is spoken to each of the four winds as the officiant faces them successively.
64. κύκλος is supplied by Preisendanz, who translates it "Zodiakalkreis." In the parallel passage in
PGM VII. 284 papyrus has κύκλος Σελήνης, which Preisendanz translates "Kreislauf des Mondes."
65. Cf. *PGM* IV. 1718–19, 1721 for such a use of κλίνω.
66. The term "angel" can also be read as "messenger."
67. Among these characters a scarab is drawn.

ZC⌐≮ΘΔ'ʌ. Cover the tripod with clean linen, / and place a censer on the tripod.   295
It is advantageous[68] to place on the table a [hollow figurine] of Apollo out of laurel wood. Engrave [on a lamella] of gold, of silver, or of tin these characters:
ΘSↄⱼↄↄ⌐ⱽↄↄ≋⌐. Place the lamella under the censer, near / the wooden image,   300
which was set up [at the same time as the] censer, and place [next to] the tripod a
beaker or a shell containing [pure] water. In the center of the shrine, surrounding
the tripod, inscribe on the floor with a white stylus the following character. . . . It is
necessary to keep yourself pure for three days in advance. The shrine and the [tri-
pod] must be / covered. [If] you wish [to see], look inside, wearing clean [white]   305
garments [and crowned] with a crown of laurel,[69] which on the head . . . wormwood . . . [before the] invocation, sacrifice laurel to him . . . [during the] sacrifice / honor the [god] with paians [directed to the sunrise]. . . ask . . . [car-   310
damom] . . . holy god . . . [almond blossom] . . . from balsam . . / . and taking . . .   315
my thought . . / . a buttercup, after taking, taste . . . four-footed. . . .   320

But the formula that is recited is . . . if you wish [to know], say these things
which are in the . . . god and all such prophetic . . . worm in . . . as for ten days.
Mixing . . / . the heart [with] honey. [Recite] this formula toward the sunrise,   325
[and] you will know in advance during the hour [and during this] day. [After sacrificing,] make a drink offering with dark wine . . . middle . . . say: "Make me know
in advance each of the . . . from . . . and . . . toward the sunrise early / [to know]   330
each of the men [and] to know in advance [what things] each has in his mind [and]
all their essence."

Single-shooted wormwood, with a single stem, born of the sun, born of the
moon[70] . . . fruit pulp of the lotus, houseleek, a turnip; [wait for] the sunrise in
your house fasting. During the third hour finger . . / . [your] face, say: "[TH]Ō-   335
OU[TH] PIŌPIŌ[71] AUAPS THŌOUTH . . . ARS . . . KENON ŌOUN PACHEN NO . . .
TOOU Ē . . . T ARSASŌTA YNASPOR . . . THA P . . . MNĒPHIELŌKNĒMEŌ, give to me
from your effluence."

[To] the rising of the moon on the thirtieth day [say:] "Come to me, greatest
archangel; come to me XASR XAM [THŌ]OUT . . . come to me, ruler / of reality, ĒMI   340
THĒ . . . BA THŌOUTH THEŌREI . . . ENĒN PAUPIOU PSIBIOAU ABLANATHANALBA
. . . AMOAMMA. Give to me, NN, memory . . . sō . . . I may know all things and I
may understand the things above the. . . ."

. . . toward the sunrise MASĒS . . . saying thus: "I am [the lord] of the sea. Make
all things . . . / all things [that will be, so that] I know in advance. Reveal this, the   345
concerns of all men and what things will be . . . TŌOUT ANG[72] . . . SA . . . OUT ANG

---

68. Fahz and Preisendanz take καλόν as modifying θυμιατήριον, "a beautiful censer." Here καλόν
has been taken with ἔστιν κτλ., and the text has been punctuated accordingly. Cf. also *PGM* IV. 2520
and Bauer, s.v. "καλός," 3.a.

69. The text at this point has many lacunae, and the reconstruction is uncertain. Fahz and Preisendanz take the reference to the garments and the laurel to refer to the god who is seen.

70. LSJ, s.v. ἡλιόγονος, σεληνόγονος translates these epithets accordingly. However, since *se-
lēnogonon* is attested as a plant (peony) and since a plant name would be appropriate here, one should
perhaps translate "peony." "Sun-born" is not attested as a plant name.

71. THŌOUTH PIŌ PIŌ (cf. also l. 340) is equivalent to Egyptian *Dḥwty p3 ꜥ3 p3 ꜥ3*, "Thoth the twice-
great." Cf. *PGM* IV. 19. For this title of Thoth, see J. D. Ray, *The Archive of Hor* (London: Egypt Exploration Society, 1976) 158–60; R. K. Ritner, "Hermes Pentamegistos," *Göttinger Miszellen* 49 (1981):
73–75. [R.K.R.]

72. Following G. Möller (see the apparatus in Preisendanz ad loc.) this short section can also be read
as Coptic: "[I am] Thoth; I am Sa[.]out; I am Em[..]eʃ......]on; I am Alaboul[......]lōrai; I am (?) Na-
treko; [.]m[.....] is your [true] name [...]." [M.W.M.]

EMĒS . . . ON ANG ALABOUL. . . ."

. . . during the tenth hour . . . A . . . N . . . N precisely . . . IE PEKREN EM . . .
350 ONEI E . . . PO . . . NGAL . . / . just now. . . ."

. . . and at the rising . . . third . . . the upper . . . at the rising . . . "CHŌLŌM
355 CHŌL . . . MASKELLI [MASKELLŌ] / . . . ITHĒCHTHŌ . . . lord. . . ."
360 . . . from the . . . at the same time . . . sun . . . and on . . . yet living . . / . anoint
. . . ABLATHANALBA . . . according to the second formula . . . seventh sunrise . . .
365 you have. / But if [you] want . . . throat of asses . . . the animal . . . tail . . . often
repeating the seventh formula . . . whatever [you wish] . . . from a human head . . .
[the formula], the beginning of which is: "Cause me to know, in order that . . .[73]
370 the ear whatever . . . on earth . . . heaven, / the [beginning] . . . the hand according to . . . formula."

But if [you want] . . . and [to read] a written, sealed letter . . . the same seventh
formula: "Do for me the things that are written. . . ."

To read the things that are written, take at [the rising] of the moon . . . carve . . .
375 pieces of honeycomb. Put these in together with . . / . fresh, pleasing, happily as
. . . with the things that are written, after thoroughly mixing, [with] all power daily
. . . to the sun . . . say [also] the prescribed . . . and that day . . . up to half of the
egg . . . put into a small drinking vessel and rub with chalk the parts of the egg, in a
380 place[74] or in a river / where the sun . . . to animals and to humans becomes inac-
cessible . . . after bathing and . . . crowned with a crown of the season's flowers . . .
to an altar, sacrifice on the altar and then take, [as you know,] three loaves of white
bread . . . olive oil, likewise new wine . . . and milk of a [black] cow; in the finest
385 cloaks of shieldbearers and . . . / following. Rub first . . . the half of the egg . . . the
lord . . . all things . . . and the substance . . . and after saying the following formula, this the seventh, to the sun thus . . . into a holy, small drinking vessel . . .
after going away and sacrificing . . . say also to the sun . . . formula or hymn giving
390 advance knowledge . . . [single-stemmed] wormwood into . . / . saying seven times
. . . Take cardamom and say the holy names . . . for all things belong to the master
. . . whenever you conjure the earth by saying the seventh [formula to the] earth
and all the immortal [gods].

This is the formula: "Come to me, lord . . . holy spirit. . . ."

. . . in the ninth hour . . . after this the [formula]: "I conjure those with com-
395 plete power . . . and I conjure [the] earth, the heaven, [the light, and] / him who
[created the universe]" . . . formula spoken of god. While saying [this] formula [to]
a holy . . .[75]
400 ". . . my name . . . / say that which . . . call . . . my name . . . my true name
405 which . . . who makes . . / . Gabriel, Michael, PYAOUĒTE . . . NETETETET . . . the
god (?) TAAIAIAIAIAIALOP . . . ĒL." Seven times you say . . . then say one time or
three times.
*Tr.: W. C. Grese and M. W. Meyer (Coptic sections, ll. 399–409).

PGM III. 410–23

410 *Take a silver tablet and engrave it after the god[76] sets. Take cow's milk and pour

73. At the beginning of l. 369 appears what could be an isolated Coptic name, Hor-Pre; cf. Möller,
in the apparatus, who suggests Harpokrates. [R.K.R.]

74. This could also be rendered "a grave." Cf. LSJ, s.v. "τόπος," 5; also l. 285 above.

75. Because of the fragmentary character of this Old Coptic section, little can be given here in translation. [M.W.M.]

it.[77] Put down a clean vessel[78] and place the tablet under [it]; add barley meal, mix and form bread: twelve rolls in the shape of female figures.[79] Say [the formula] three times, eat [the rolls] on an empty stomach, and you will know the power.

[*It is*]: "BORKA BORKA PHRIX PHRIX RIX Ō . . . ACHACH AMIXAG OUCH THIP LAI LAI LAMLAI LAI LAM MAIL AAAAAAAA IIIY ĒI AI ŌŌŌŌŌŌŌ MOUMOU ŌYIŌ NAK NAK NAX LAINLIMM LAILAM AEDA . . . LAILAM / AĒO ŌAĒ ŌAĒ ĒOA AŌĒ ĒOA ŌĒA,   415
enter, master, into my mind, and grant me memory, MMM ĒĒĒ MTHPH." Do this
monthly, facing the moon, on the first day [of the month]. Prostrate yourself before the goddess,[80] and wear the tablet as an amulet.

The name of the soul of god is: "EIKIZITELITHDE   then PHYSOUSKAZĒTTHZ blood." Write these things with a copper stylus: "I am KŌOU BŌOU PČŌSM . . . HOUIT[81] . . . APRIĒFMLNIĒF . . . MANIŌĒSE NMANIĒFIHTENOHĒIT RENIRE RE-NIM E GEINNA[82] EOI . . . EFREF / NGŌOU DNI IĒSOUS PNETO."[83] Speak into your   420
hand seven times in front of the sun, stroke your face, spit, move your thumb from your nose up to your forehead. Facing the sun, speak seven times into your hand, spit once, stroke your face, and go on to the procedure and gift:[84] "SILIBANAGOU-NACHAOUĒL. . . ."
*Tr.: W. C. Grese.

PGM III. 424–66

*A copy from a holy book. Charm that gives foreknowledge and memory:
Take a kakouphon,[85] / which in Egyptian is kakkou[phat, tear out] its heart, perfo-   425
rate it with a reed, [cut] the heart [into pieces], and put them into Attic honey when the goddess[86] approaches. Then grind the heart on the 1st of the goddess,[87] mix it with the honey, [and eat it] on an empty stomach while saying seven times, once while tasting with the forefinger, this ***formula***:

"Make me know in advance once and for all the things that are going to happen, the things that are about to happen, the things that have been done, and all [to-day's] activities."

Say the name seven times, and quickly say / the other usual formulas. . . .[88]   430

76. That is, Helios, the sun god.

77. The papyrus has καταχεάσα[ς], "pour it," which is not meaningful here. Schmidt, *GGA* 193 (1931):451–52, suggests καταλεάζειν on the basis of Hesychius' ἀλεάζειν, "to heat up." The translation here follows the text of Preisendanz.

78. Schmidt, *GGA* 193 (1931):451, adds ⟨εἰς⟩, "into," which seems necessary to complete the sense of the phrase, viz., "put it [into] a clean vessel."

79. It seems only twelve pastry dolls are to be shaped and not an additional loaf and piece of pastry, as Preisendanz seems to take it. [R.D.K.]

80. That is, Selene, the moon goddess.

81. Probably Coptic *pčosm [pe]houit*, "the first darkness." [M.W.M.]

82. Probably read Gehenna. [M.W.M.]

83. Perhaps Coptic, meaning "Jesus our great one." [M.W.M.]

84. The blessing given in response to the procedure. Cf. *PGM* IV. 198. See also A.-J. Festugière, "La Valeur religieuse des papyrus magiques," in his *L'Idéal religieux des Grecs et l'Évangile* (Paris: Gabalda, 1932) 293; Bonner, *SMA* 178–79.

85. Cf. on this term *PGM* II.18 and n. 7, p. 13 above.

86. That is, Selene, the moon goddess.

87. This refers to the first day of the lunar month.

88. Apparently the scribe forgot to add the formula for the second day; therefore an ellipsis has been inserted.

[While tasting] on the third, say the name LAILAM [SAN]KANTHARA (add the usual).[89] [On the] 4th of the moon say [the] 4th name, EPIMNŌ; on the 5th, the 5th name, saying seven times EKENTH . . . [on the 6th], the sixth name, AMOUN AMOUN; on the 7th of the moon, [the 7th name] . . . RA PREGXICHAROTH; on the 8th, the 8th name, EISI OUSIRI AMOUN [AMOUN;[90] on the 9th], the 9th name, PHORPHORBARZAGRA; [on the 10th], the 10th name, ZAZOUCHŌR DAMNIOTĒ; on the eleventh, the eleventh name, CHRYSA CHR[YSA] EYAE CHRYSOES EIRE CHRY-SOEGETHREL . . . RON; on the twelfth, the twelfth name, and taste twelve times, ATHAB . . . ENIGRAPSATHIR . . . PSANO . . . ASĒ; [on the 13th, say the 13th name],

435   ARTEMI DAMNŌ DAMNO / LYKAINA;[91] on the fourteenth, say the [fourteenth name]. This is the 14th name: HARPON [CHNOUPHI] BRINTATĒNŌPHRI BRISKYLMA ORE-OBAZAGRA. On the fifteenth, the fifteenth name, SESENGEN BARPHARAGGĒS AGAB . . . AEĒIOYŌ (add the usual formulas, as much as you want, saying it on each day).

When the moon [wanes], say [the formula] in hexameter, saying it seven times until it is again the fourteenth of the goddess. But beware, lest it be in conjunction . . . each day . . . and the whole composition of the divine arrangement be undone. [For] the lord [god] speaks. A procedure greater than this one does not exist. It has

440   been tested / by Manethon,[92] [who] received [it] as a gift from god Osiris the greatest. Perform it, perform it successfully and silently.

Formula spoken . . . and . . . the sun: "Hail, absolute ruler, hail, hail, [forefather . . . DAMNAM]ENEU [ABRASAX] . . . K . . . ĒLĒL, one holy . . . SABĒLE SABĒLE KA. . . ."

445   . . . [*Foreknowledge*] . . . *Moses* . . . *and* . . / . *for memory*, [say] the following [formula] each [day]: ". . . IMEA . . . ABRASAX . . . [to know] OEIIAO . . . IAŌ

450   SABAŌ[TH] . . . great . . . IABE[ZEBYTH] . . . ABRAXAS TAE." . . / . .

But in this way draw a boy and you . . . later, and you will hear the birds chat-

455   tering . . . seven of fennel and of sesame, of black cumin . . . / [take] these and crush them, with spring water . . . the moon being second, and you will hear all things. . . .

". . . I am IEĒ IOEĒ IE IAŌ ISI . . . [the things in the] minds of men, because I. . . ."

460   . . . pray to him. But . . / . but a swallow[93] of this comes . . . this your formula repeat seven times . . . *formula*, which you say: "Hail, Helios, Mithras. . . ."

465   . . . this holy water . . . this one has in his mind . . / that day [you] know . . . but if [you] touch, [you will have] a semitertian [fever].
*Tr.: W. C. Grese.

PGM III. 467–78

470   *Memory spell*: Take first . . . 2 calf's snouts, "Hermes' finger" . . . / taste, and prostrate yourself while saying three times to Helios: "[Enter,] MA . . . A KMĒPH ARSŌ ARSŌ THOUTH . . . O TIOI E.OI POMPOM PHRĒ [IARBATHA CHRAMNĒ] . . . upon my heart, [having granted] memory to my soul, to my eyes [SALBANACHAM-

89. As one can see from l. 436 below, the direction "add the usual" (κοινά) is to be understood after each day.

90. That is, Osiris, Amon in vocatives.

91. "She-wolf" is an epithet of the goddess Artemis. See also *PGM* IV. 2302–3; 2550.

92. The name Manetho probably refers to an Egyptian priest and historian of the third cent. B.C., the man who was instrumental in the setting up of the cult of Sarapis. Cf. also *PGM* XII. 23; Plutarch, *De Is. et Os.* 28, 362A; Iamblichus, *Myst.* 8.1. See Griffiths, *Plutarch's De Iside et Osiride* 78–82; H.-J. Thissen, "Manetho," *LdÄ* 3 (1980): 1180–81.

93. The cliff, or chimney swallow. [J.S.]

BRĒ . . .] / monarch, the one who rules over all . . . ABLAN OOOO ADŌNIĒ AĒŌ . . .   475
in order that, whatever I hear once, [I might remember it throughout] my lifetime."
*Tr.: W. C. Grese.

PGM III. 479–83

*Foreknowledge charm: Take [. . . parts] fleawort, [and say to] / the height of   480
the heavenly circle: "The thief . . . the only great god, [come to me] from an assem-
bly on the 6th day . . . to happen, Helios."
*Tr.: W. C. Grese. This and the two variant charms to follow serve as spells to "prognosti-
cate" the identity or whereabouts of a thief.

PGM III. 483–88

*Another [copy]: ". . . ALA.AANG XICHA MICHA ANG E . . . / EROTPITENPHĒT   485
NPRŌME,⁹⁴ [having] a gold-colored [crown on the] head, turn to [the thief who
took away the NN thing], kill, cleave him and . . . but if you behead. . . ."
*Tr.: W. C. Grese.

PGM III. 488–94

*Another: Take a wing . . . / "AŌŌ; then, according to the same . . . LŌ   490
[PHNOU]KENT ABAŌTH . . . DO . . . ŌLEAIS . . . KA . . . TA K. . . ."
*Tr.: W. C. Grese. This is presumably another spell to detect a thief; see the note appended
to PGM III. 479–83, above.

PGM III. 494–611

*[Spell to establish a relationship with] Helios. A procedure for every [rite], for
[all things]. / For whatever you want, invoke in this way: "[Come,] come to me   495
from the four winds of the world, air-transversing, great god. Hear me in every
ritual which [I perform], and grant all the [petitions] of my prayer completely, because I know your signs, / [symbols and] forms, who you are each hour and what   500
your name is.⁹⁵

"In the first hour you have the form and character of a young monkey; [the tree]
you produce is the silver fir; the stone, the aphanos;⁹⁶ the bird . . . your name is
PHROUER.⁹⁷

"In the second hour you have the form of a unicorn; the tree you produce is the
persea; the stone, the pottery stone;⁹⁸ / the bird, the halouchakon;⁹⁹ on land, the   505
ichneumon; your name is BAZĒTŌPHŌTH.

"In the third hour you have the form of a cat; the tree you produce is the fig tree;
the stone, the samouchos;¹⁰⁰ the bird, the parrot; on land, the frog; your name is
AKRAMMACHAMAREI.

"In the fourth hour you have the form of a bull; the tree you produce / . . . the   510

94. This is Coptic and means "to the man." [R.K.R.]

95. In his twelve-hour course through the heavens, the sun is identified here with ancient theriomor-
phic and totemistic forms. Also, the sun's creative activities are identified with certain hours. See for this
Gundel, Weltbild und Astrologie 5–6. Cf. PGM II. 104–15 and n.

96. The identification of lithos aphanos is uncertain; literally it means "invisible stone" (clear quartz?).
[J.S.]

97. PHROUER is Egyptian for "Pre the great." [R.K.R.]

98. On the pottery stone see Pliny, NH 37. 152.

99. Otherwise unidentified.

100. According to LSJ, this word is a hapax legomenon. Preisendanz identifies it with ψαμμοῦχος,
a sandstone (not attested in LSJ).

101. Fahz reads γεννᾷς δένδρον [κα]ὶ λίθον, "you produce a tree [and] stone." This should probably be understood to refer to holly oak and a brick-red opal. Cf. also n. 102. [J.S.]

stone,[101] the amethyst;[102] the bird, the turtledove; on land, the bull; your name is
DAMNAMENEUS.

"In the fifth hour you have the form of a lion; the tree you produce is the prickly
shrub; the stone, the magnet; [the bird] . . . on land, the crocodile; your name is
PHŌKENGEPSEUARETATHOUMISONKTAIKT.

515   "In the sixth hour you have the form of a donkey; the tree / you produce is the
thorn tree; the stone, lapis lazuli; in the sea, the jellyfish;[103] on [land, the white-
faced cow]; your name is EIAU AKRI LYX. . . .

"[In the seventh hour] you have the form of a [crayfish; the tree you produce]
520   . . . [you produce] . . . ; [the stone, the sun opal;[104] / the bird] . . . on land, the cat;
[your name is]. . . .

"In the eighth [hour] you have the form . . . [the tree you produce] . . . [the
stone] . . . the bird . . . [on land], the hippopotamus; [your] name [is]. . . .

525   "In the ninth [hour] you have the form of an ibis; [the tree / you produce] . . .
[the stone] . . . on land, the chameleon; [your name]. . . .

"In the tenth hour [you have] the form . . . ; [the tree you produce] . . . the
stone, one the color of a falcon's neck; [the bird]. . . .

530   / "In the twelfth [hour you have the form] . . . [your name is] ADŌNAI . . .
[and]. . . .

535   ". . . / GABRIĒL ALLŌEA . . . OURĒĒDYDIE THARABRACHIRIGX IARBATHACH-
RAMNĒPHIBAŌCHNYMEŌ[105] KAMPYKRIL . . . ELAMMARĒ.

"I have spoken your signs and symbols. Therefore, lord, do the NN deed by necessity, lest I shake heaven. Do the NN deed for me; you are the image, the whole
of the universe, [you] who, after being selected,[106] guarded the holy place of
540   the / great king. Do the NN deed for me, the one who keeps the keys of the triangular paradise of earth, which is the kingdom. Do the NN deed for me, the fatherless child of an honored[107] widow, BŌIATHYRITH, lest they take away from me
545   the lord's fatherland and so that all / good things happen by command, PHŌKEN-
GEPSEUARETATHOUMISONKTAIKT MASKELLI MASKELLŌ PHNOUNKENTABAŌ AŌ-
RIŌ ZAGRA RĒSICHTHŌN HIPPOCHTHŌN PYROSPARIPĒGANYX KAILAM IALMIŌ
LILIMOULĒALABAĒNEREDEMOU."

550   "Come[108] to me in / your holy circuit of
The holy spirit, founder of the world,
O god of gods, lord of the world, who have
Divided by your own divine spirit
The universe; first from the firstborn you

102. Pliny identifies παιδέρως as an opal (NH 37. 84) or an amethyst (NH 37. 123). It has been
rendered here as amethyst because in 37.80 Pliny says opals come only from India. See the note by D. E.
Eicholz, LCL edition of Pliny's Natural History, vol. 10, p. 230, n. a. [J.S.]
103. The term literally means "glass fish." [M.S.]
104. The translation of ἡλιοπάλιος is uncertain.
105. Cf. for this name PGM I. 143 and n.
106. Following Preisendanz's translation as "Auserwählter."
107. The papyrus reads κατατετιμημένη[ς], a verb not attested elsewhere. The meaning could also
be "despised." Preisendanz suggests that the widow is Isis and the magician identifies himself with
Horus. Probably, the translation "dishonored" is to be preferred, because it would refer to the murder of
Isis' husband and her subsequent flight to the swamps of Chemmis to raise her son Horus. For Horus as
orphan, see Borghouts, Ancient Egyptian Magical Texts 69, no. 92. [R.K.R.]
108. These dactylic hexameters, many of which are metrically faulty, are also the reconstructed
Hymn 2, for which see Preisendanz, vol. II, p. 238. [E.N.O.]

Appeared,[109] created carefully, from water
That's turbulent, who founded all the world:
Abyss, earth, / fire, water, air, and in turn   555
Ether and roaring rivers, red-faced moon,
Heaven's stars, morning stars, the whirling planets.[110]
'Tis by your counsels they attend all things."
        "You who summon . . . AMOCHL . . . PHODOPH . . . M . . . ARPHTHŌ . . .
IBK / PSOUPHIS [TŌM] . . . OIŌTH ŌPHROUER CHMĒIB HARPONKNOUPHI BRIN-   560
TATĒNŌPHRI BRISKYLMA HAROUAR ZARBAMESEG KRIPHI NIGTHOU MICHMOU-
MAŌPH IAŌLI PRIN ASTRAPTĒS[111] AI CHEAOKIRTABAOZAALE ASRISKI . . . OU BRIT-
HEI STOMA,[112] master. Come to me, / lord, you who sometimes raise the light,   565
sometimes lower the darkness [with] your own power. Hear me, lord, me, NN,
graciously, gladly and for a blessing, from every element from every wind, today,
with your happy face, in the present hour, because / I invoke your holy name from   570
every side. You who were begotten in every human body, inspire us.[113] From the
right of the axis your [name] is: 'IAŌ AŌI ŌAI [ŌYA] ŌŌŌŌŌŌ AAAAAA IY . . . ŌAI,'
but from the left of the axis: 'IAŌ AYŌ IŌAI / PIPI ŌŌŌ ŌŌ III AYŌ . . . ŌA ŌAI.'   575
Come to me with a happy face to a bed of your choice, giving to me, NN, sustenance, health, safety, wealth, the blessing of children, knowledge, a ready hearing,
goodwill, sound judgment, honor, memory, grace, shapeliness, beauty to / all who   580
see me; you who hear me in everything whatsoever, give persuasiveness with words,
great god, to the EYAĒŌ IŌ IAŌ ŌAI ŌIŌ ĒAYI TAS ERCHIS AUXACHOCH HAR-
SAMOSI. I beg, master, accept my entreaty, the offering to you which you commanded. In order that you might now illuminate me with knowledge of things beloved by you / even after the kind restoration of my material body, I pray, lord,   585
accept this my request, [the] entreaty, the preliminary spell, the offering of my elo-
quent spirit. Let it also come to you, the ruler of all, in order that / you fulfill all the   590
petitions of my prayer, you who originated from gods.[114] We give you thanks with
every soul and heart stretched out to [you],[115] unutterable name honored with [the]
appellation of god and blessed with the [appellation of father], for to everyone[116]
and to everything you have shown fatherly / goodwill, affection, friendship and   595
sweetest power, granting us intellect, [speech,] and knowledge; intellect so that we
might understand you, speech [so that] we might call upon you, knowledge so that
we might know you.[117] We rejoice because you showed yourself to us; we rejoice

109. This refers to the sun god's appearance from the waters of Nun, the primordial abyss. Cf. *PGM*
I. 34–36. [R.K.R.]
110. There are three types of star referred to here: ἀστέρας (1) ἀερίους, (2) ἑῴους, (3) περιδινο-
πλανήτας. On ἑῴους as morning star, cf. Ptolemy, *Tetrab.* 3. 4 (114). [E.N.O.]
111. Or "before you hurl lightning."
112. Or "mouth is full."
113. ἐμπνευματίζω is not otherwise attested. Cf. *C.H.* 13.19 with Keil's conjecture πνευμάτιζε,
cited by Nock and Festugière, *Hermès Trismégiste* II, p. 208, in the critical apparatus to l. 17.
114. The section in ll. 591–609 has close parallels in Ps.-Apuleius, *Asclepius* 41 (ed. Nock and Festugière, *Hermès Trismégiste* II, pp. 353–55) and *NHC* VI, 7: 63, 33–65, 7. See Robinson, *The Nag
Hammadi Library in English* 298–99; P. Dirkse and J. Brashler, "The Prayer of Thanksgiving," in *Nag
Hammadi Codices V, 2–5 and VI, with Papyrus Berolinensis 8502, 1 and 4*, NHSt 11 (Leiden: Brill, 1979)
375–87. Cf. also Iamblichus, *Myst.* 10. 8; *C.H.* 13. 18–20, with the discussion by Grese, *Corpus Hermeticum XIII*, pp. 183–88.
115. Following Nock and Festugière, *Hermès Trismégiste* II, p. 353.
116. Following J.-P. Mahé, *Hermès en Haute-Égypt. Les textes hermétiques de Nag Hammadi et leurs
parallèles grecs et latins*, vol. 1 (Québec: Les presses de l'université Laval, 1978) 160–61.
117. Following Nock and Festugière, *Hermès Trismégiste* II, p. 354.

600   because while we are / [still] in bodies you deified us by the knowledge of who you
        are. The thanks of man to you is one: to come to know [you], O womb[118] of all
        knowledge. We have come to know, O womb[119] pregnant through the father's be-
605   getting. We have come to know, / O eternal continuation of the pregnant father.
        After bowing thus before your goodness,[120] we ask no [favor except this]:[121] will
        that we be maintained in knowledge of you; and one protection:[122] that [we] not
610   fall away from a [life] such as this. . . ."
        *Tr.: W. C. Grese (ll. 494–549; 558–611) and E. N. O'Neil (hymnic sections, ll. 549–58).

PGM III. 612–32

        *[If you make] an offering of wheaten meal and ripe mulberries and unsoftened[123]
        (?) sesame and uncooked *thrion* and throw into this a beet, you will gain control of
615   your own shadow[124] / so that it [will serve] you. Go at the sixth hour of the day,
        toward [the rising sun], to a deserted place, girt about with a [new] male palm-
        fiber basket, and on your head a scarlet cord as a headband, behind your right
620   ear / the feather of a falcon, behind your left that of an ibis.
           Having reached the place,[125] [prostrate] yourself, stretch out your hands, and
        utter the following *formula*: "Cause now my shadow to serve me, because I know
625   your sacred names [and] your signs and / your symbols, and [who you are at each
        hour], and what your name is."[126]
           Having said this, [utter] the formula given above,[127] and in case he does not
        [hearken, say]:[128] "I have uttered your sacred names and [your signs] and your sym-
630   bols, wherefore, O lord,[129] cause / my [shadow] to serve me." [And] at the seventh
        [hour] it will come to you before [your] face, and you address it [and say]: "Follow
        me everywhere!" But [look] to it, that it not leave you.

        *Tr. J. M. Dillon. See the introductory note on *PGM* III. 494–611. This unique spell to
        acquire control over one's shadow may be part of the whole ***Encounter with Helios*** con-
        tained in III. 494–731. The Coptic section to follow (*PGM* III. 633–731) belongs with this
        section, and the mention of the "signs and symbols" in l. 625 connects this spell to the pre-
        ceding; furthermore, the mention of the "formula given above" (l. 626) must refer to a for-
        mula given in the preceding spell, probably the formula found in III. 494ff. The appearance
        of one's shadow is thus the proof of Helios' appearance requested in *PGM* III. 494–731.

        118. Following Nock and Festugière, *Hermès Trismégiste* II, p. 355.
        119. On the role of the uterus in magic, see A. A. Barb, "Diva Matrix," *JWCI* 16 (1953): 193–238.
        Cf. also *PGM* V. 158.
        120. Following Mahé, *Hermès* 164–65.
        121. Ibid.
        122. Following Mahé, *Hermès* 166–67, and Dirkse and Brashler, "The Prayer of Thanksgiving,"
        384–85.
        123. Preisendanz reads ἀ[νέκ]χυτον, a word otherwise unattested. More likely would be the restora-
        tion ἀ[διά]χυτον, "not softened by cooking"; hence the translation here. [R.D.K.]
        124. Cf. *DMP* col. IV, l. 23 for a spell for "lucky shadows" *(wḏ ḫyb.t)*. [R.K.R.] See also Betz, "The
        Delphic Maxim," 163–64.
        125. Literally, "treading about in the place."
        126. Cf. ll. 499–501 for a similar expression. It seems that the deity invoked has a different appear-
        ance every hour. See also the introduction to this spell and its possible relationship with *PGM* III.
        494–611.
        127. That is, the formula given in 494–536, particularly the section containing the signs and
        symbols.
        128. Following Preisendanz's restoration. This hardly seems suitable, as one would rather expect,
        "And when you are finished, say. . . ." [J.M.D.]
        129. The "lord" addressed in this spell is Helios, the sun god, mentioned in III. 494–611.

PGM III. 633–731

*Call . . . , "Great god . . . , you who are the sun, Re is your name / . . . the glow-   635
ing flames . . . my nail (?) . . . Em . . . is your name, Em . . . [is your true name]
. . . crown . . . my name . . . [AEEĒ]ĒEIIIIOOO[OOYYYYYYŌ]ŌŌŌŌ[Ō]Ō / . . . /   640
of the great god . . . [Nef] is my name, Nef is my true name . . . Hail to[130] (?)   651
SABAŌTH ADŌNAI ADŌN BARBARIOT . . . of Lo son of Ouer[131] . . . / whose face is   655
in the middle of . . . of Lo son of Ouer . . . whose face is in the middle of . . . in
truth. For I am . . . For I am Lotus-Lion-Ram[132] . . . / Lotus, reveal yourself . . .   660
For [I] am . . . all (repeat).[133] I am Oh, I am AEĒIOY[Ō AEĒIOYŌ] A[EĒIOYŌ AEĒI]
OYŌ [AEĒI] OYŌ AEĒIOYŌ AEĒI[OY]Ō AEĒIOY[Ō] . . . , and we are strong (?) . . . of
Shmoun[134] . . . / until you offer incense to Horus. I am Oh, I know [your name]   665
. . . little, every time, at every hour. Come, go . . . what you want (repeat). For Ei is
your name, Ei is the name of you. I . . . Totf; Totf is my true name (add the usual
[?]) as you wish, after . . . the (formula) I am Kat son of Kat, whom Kat has borne
. . . / I am the [breath] of night . . . I am Abriabot, the . . . the great snake . . .   670
[Thoth the great] of Shmoun . . . the god Horus . . . , ([add the usual] as you
wish). For I am Iethor,[135] who wants to . . . I . . . who . . . / frog . . . is my name   675
. . . the great god who will do . . . To son of To[136] is your name . . . father. / You are   680
Earth-shaker,[137] the High One, the son of Re, the [great] god . . . in the abyss, who
is in . . . all the earth . . . (add the usual, as you wish) . . . he who does . . . I am
. . . I am the one who . . . in him . . . / For . . . I am Io . . . is [my] name [. . . is]   685
my true name . . . To the great is my [true] name . . ."

      . . . this day . . . speak to Helios[138] . . . / on the third day, also to the moon[139]   690
. . . at the third entrance of the goddess, go to an ever-flowing river . . . bathe, and
go in pure garments . . . , having drunk . . . a solitary place, hold toward the rising
sun a white rooster without blemish and twelve pinecones whorled[140] to the right.
Offer milk and pour a libation of white wine, / and say the designated seven for-   695
mulas [seven] times, requesting an encounter with [the] god . . . yourself. He will
show . . . let him dwell (?)[141] for seven days. Set up . . . toward the moon, with
purity; and when you see the god in this place, feast [in an appropriate manner].[142]
So when you encounter the god, say the formula for a direct vision, and request
foreknowledge from the master. / Go down to a pure and consecrated place, and   700

130. Cf. *PGM* IV. 11, 14, 15, 17, 18, 19.

131. For OUĒR cf. Egyptian *wr*, "the great one." [R.K.R.]

132. This corresponds to SERPOT-MOUI-SRO. Cf. *PDM* xiv. 12 and the note by Griffith and Thompson, *The Leyden Papyrus* on *DMP* col. I, l. 12. On the solar character of this designation of the sun in the
morning, at midday, and in the evening, i.e., the universal sun in three manifestations (Re-Khepri-
Atum), see M.-L. Rhyner, "A propos de trigrammes panthéistes," *Revue d'Égyptologie* 29 (1977):
125–37. [M.W.M.]

133. Apparent instructions for the repetition of the formulas either forward or backward. Cf. ll. 667,
669, 682. But if this is the equivalent of Greek κοινόν (see Preisendanz's text at l. 682), we are to understand "(add the usual)"; thus the translation, as in several instances below.

134. Shmoun (Hermopolis, El-Eshmunen) is the city of the god Thoth. See on the name A. H.
Gardiner, *Ancient Egyptian Onomastica* (London: Oxford University Press, 1968) II, 79*–81*. See for
the name also below, l. 672.

135. That is in Egyptian "eye of Horus."

136. Possibly, *To* is "land"; hence at III. 687 "the great land."

137. For ΚΜΡΤΟ cf. *PGM* IV. 1323; *PDM* xiv. 192.

138. That is, the sun god Helios.

139. The moon goddess Selene; see also l. 697.

140. See the note at *PGM* II. 25.

141. The text is uncertain at this point; perhaps οἰκείτω is to be read instead of οἰκήτω. [M.W.M.]

142. Supplying in the lacuna ἐ[πιτη]δές, following Schmidt, *GGA* 193 (1931):456.

again sacrifice a rooster, and while in pure garments secretly [grasp the other things] which are necessary as symbols . . . god(dess) . . . third . . . , hold in your right hand a [single-stemmed] wormwood and in your left a snakeskin, and recite
705 the [specified] formulas [and] what you wish, and it will happen. Recite often / . . . written down . . . to learn something, it is told to you by the god. And if you . . . , write . . . and wrap in linen from head to foot . . . , and on the ground draw Harpokrates holding [his finger][143] to his mouth, and in his left hand clutching a
710 flail and a crook on [the chest of the god];[144] . . . then "ABLANATHANALBA"; in wing . . .[145] / "ABRASAX": near the back, "ŌĒAUA . . . ," and set the child on it, and write the 5th formula . . . : "ĒFĒINTOK[146] . . . TE UONĒFIOUOI." Also use this treatment often: take away . . . from before him the linen, and let him behold, and
715 he will see; and ask [him] . . . on the tenth day . . . in the morning of the first (formula?), then the / first for a second time in the morning of the . . . let these
720 things be . . . two bricks . . . under papyrus . . . head . . . hole . . . / hold in your
725 hands . . . this . . . and say the . . . in each . . . as . . . little . . . all . . . on these . . .
730 great . . . / both . . . formulas before . . . formulas with the . . . and all . . . and . . . pit . . . you make / call the olive . . . pure. . . .
*Tr.: M. W. Meyer. For the connection of the spell with the preceding, see the introductory notes at *PGM* III. 494–611 and III. 612–32.

PGM IV. 1–25

*"SAPHPHAIOR BAELKOTA KIKATOUTARA EKENNK LIX, the great daimon and the
5   inexorable one,[1] . . . IPSENTANCHOUCHEŌCH / DŌOU SHAMAI ARABENNAK ANTRAPHEU BALE SITENGI ARTEN BENTEN AKRAB ENTH OUANTH BALA SHOUPLA SRAHENNE DEHENNE KALASHOU CHATEMMŌK BASHNE BALA SHAMAI—on the day of Zeus[2] in the first hour, but on the [day] of deliverance[3] in the fifth hour: a
10 cat . . . / in the eighth: a cat.[4] Hail[5] to Osiris, the king of the underworld, the lord of embalming, he who is to the south of Thinis, who gives answer at Abydos, he who is under[6] the noubs tree[7] in Meroue,[8] whose glory is in Pashalom.[9] Hail to
15 Althabot; bring unto me Sabaoth. / Hail to Althonai, great Eou, very valiant; bring unto me Michael, the mighty (?) angel who is with God. Hail to Anubis, of

143. Supplying in the lacuna [τὸν δακτύ]λιον. [M.W.M.]

144. For depictions similar to the one here see Budge, *Amulets and Talismans* 206–7; Bonner, *SMA*, p. IX, nos. 189–94.

145. Perhaps, "in wing formation."

146. This is equivalent to Demotic *iw.f r in.ṭ.k.*, "He shall bring you." [R.K.R.]

1. See for this term Wortmann, "Neue magische Texte," 101; on the verb παραιτέω, see Betz, "Fragments," 291.

2. That is, Thursday.

3. Perhaps Sunday.

4. These enigmatic phrases are instructions for the use of the spell.

5. This passage is parallel to *PDM* xiv. 627–35. See F. Ll. Griffith, "The Old Coptic Magical Texts of Paris," *ZÄS* 38 (1900):86–93. [R.K.R.]

6. Or "under the shade of the *noubs* tree."

7. According to Griffith, *ZÄS* 38 (1900):87, at Pnubs the *noubs* tree was sacred to Thoth. See on this point Brugsch, *Dictionnaire* 334–35.

8. Meroe is the capital of an ancient state in the Sudan. See Bonnet, *RÄRG* 456–57, s.v. "Meroe."

9. Cf. also *PDM* xiv. 627–29. Pashalom is the capital of the nome in which Abydos is also located. Situated to the south of Thinis, Abydos is the holy city where the head of Osiris was buried. See Griffiths, *Plutarch's De Iside et Osiride* 362 n.1.

the nome of Hansiese,[10] upon his mountain.[11] Hail to the goddesses—Thoth the
great, the great, the wise. Hail to the gods, / ACHNOUI ACHAM ABRA ABRA   20
SABAŌTH.[12] For Akshha Shha[13] is my name, Sabashha is my true name; Shlot Shlot
very valiant is my name. So let him who is in the underworld join him who is in the
air; let them arise, come in, and bring me news / of the matter about which I ask   25
them" (add the usual).
*Tr.: M. W. Meyer. This request for an oracle may be part of the larger spell contained in
PGM IV. 1–85.

PGM IV. 26–51

*Initiation:[14] Keep yourself pure for 7 days beforehand. On the third of the
month, go to a place from which the Nile has recently receded, before anyone walks
on the area that was flooded—or at any rate, to a place that has been inundated by
the Nile. / On two bricks[15] standing on their sides, build a fire with olive wood   30
(that is, with a branch of it) when half of the sun is above the horizon; but before
the sun appears, dig a trench around the altar. When the disk of the sun is fully
above the horizon, / cut off the head of an unblemished, solid white cock which   35
[you are to carry] under your left arm (and do dig the trench around[16] the altar
before the sun appears).[17] When you are beheading the cock, fix it in place [with
your knees][18] and hold it down all by yourself. / Throw the head into the river and 40
drink up the blood, draining it off into your right hand and putting what's left of
the body on the burning altar. Then jump into the river. Immerse yourself in the
clothes you have on, walk backwards[19] out of the water, and, after changing into
fresh garments, / depart without turning round.[20] After this, take bile from an owl, 45
rub some of it over your eyes with the feather of an ibis, and your initiation will be
complete. But if you can't get hold of an owl, use an ibis's egg and a falcon's
feather. / Bore a hole in the egg, insert the feather, break it open, and thereby get 50
the fluid to rub on yourself.
*Tr.: Hubert Martin, Jr.

10. The location is unknown. Cf. *Ha-si-ise-t*, "house of the son of Isis." See A. H. Gardiner, *Ancient
Egyptian Onomastica* (London: Oxford University Press, 1968) II, 29* (no. 341A). One conjecture is
that of Brugsch, *Dictionnaire* 659, who has identified Hansiese as a site (Chenoboskia?) near Koptos and
Dendera in Upper Egypt.

11. This refers to an ancient title of Anubis. Cf. *PDM* xiv. 174. In this connection one should also
note the relationship between mountain, desert, and cemetery in ancient Egypt.

12. Hebrew for "Lord, Lord of Hosts;" ABRA may be a variation of *arba* (Heb. "four") designating
the tetragrammaton. See Blau, *Das altjüdische Zauberwesen* 126; Dornseiff, *Das Alphabet* 64; A. Barb,
"Abraxas-Studien," in *Hommages à W. Deonna* (Bruxelles: Latomus, 1957) 67–86.

13. Or "JEAKSHHA SHHA"; but cf. *PGM* IV. 77, also III. 658, 659, 661, 667, 673, etc., for other
examples of the common formula "for . . . is my name" or "for I am. . . ."

14. The purpose of this rite is not clear (cf. l. 48). It may have simply been a part of the longer ritual
of the context.

15. On the magical use of bricks for both the living and the dead, see J. Monnet, "Les Briques magiques du Musée du Louvre," *Revue d'Égyptologie* 8 (1951): 151–62. [R.K.R.]

16. Or "dig a trench around," which may in fact mean "walk around" and refer to the ritual circum-
ambulation. See W. Pax, "Circumambulatio," *RAC* 3 (1957): 143–52.

17. See l. 33 above.

18. The phrase "with your knees" is a conjecture based on *PGM* IV. 227–28.

19. Cf. the injunctions to walk backwards at *PGM* I. 37; IV. 2493; XXXVI. 273.

20. Presumably, the initiate is to turn away from the river after he is out of the water and to depart
without looking back at the river. Perhaps he is being instructed to depart by walking backwards. The
text is not entirely clear; cf. for similar circumstances *PGM* VII. 439–40. For looking back and its con-
sequences, cf. the story of Lot's wife (Gn 19:17, 26) and the injunction in Lk 17:31–32; Mt 24:
15–18 (cf. Lk 9:62).

PGM IV. 52–85

*Keep yourself pure for 7 days before the moon becomes full by abstaining from
meat and uncooked food, by leaving behind during the prescribed days exactly
55 half / of your food in a turquoise[21] vessel, over which you are also to eat, and by
abstaining from wine. When the moon is full, go by yourself to the eastern section
60 of your city, village, or house and throw out / on the ground the leftover morsels.
Then return very quickly to your quarters and shut yourself in before he[22] can get
there, because he will shut you out if he gets there before you. But before you throw
out the morsels, fix in the ground at a slight angle a verdant reed that is about two
cubits long, tie some hairs from a stallion about the midsection of a horned dung
65 beetle, and suspend / the beetle from the reed by them. Then light a lamp that has
not been used before and place it under the beetle in a new earthenware dish, so
that the heat from the lamp barely reaches the beetle. Stay calm after you have
70 thrown out the morsels, go to your quarters, and shut yourself in; / for the one
you have summoned will stand there and, by threatening you with weapons, will
try to force you to release the beetle. But remain calm, and do not release it until he
gives you a response; then release it right away. And every day during the period of
purification when you are about to eat and to go to bed, speak the following spell 7
75 times (you are to say them again / when you return to your quarters after throwing
out the food). Keep it secret: "You with the wooden neck, you with the clay (?)
face,[23] come in to me, for I am Sabertoush, the great god who is in heaven."

The phylactery for the foregoing: With blood from the hand or foot of a preg-
80 nant woman, / write the name[24] given below on a clean piece of papyrus; then tie it
about your left arm by a linen cord and wear it. *Here is what is to be written*:
"SHTĒIT CHIEN TENHA, I bind and loose."

The dismissal: When you release the beetle, say: "Harko, Harko is my name;
Harko is my true name."

85   Guard these instructions / well. *The rite*: an onion.[25]
*Tr.: Hubert Martin, Jr., and Marvin W. Meyer (Coptic sections, ll. 75–77, 81–82,
83–84).

PGM IV. 86–87

*Phylactery against daimons:[26] "HOMENOS OHK KOURIĒL IAPHĒL, deliver" (add
the usual), "EHENPEROOU BARBARCHAOUCHE."

*Tr.: Marvin W. Meyer. This brief spell seems to have no connection with the preceding or
following spells.

---

21. A blue-green glazed pottery, almost certainly Egyptian faïence. See A. Lucas and J. R. Harris,
Ancient Egyptian Materials and Industries (London: Arnold, 1962) 156–67, esp. 163–64. [R.K.R.]
22. "He" is the one summoned (l. 70), but "he" is never identified.
23. Probably referring to a clay or terracotta figurine on a wooden pedestal. [M.W.M.]
24. The "name" may have included not only *sabertoush* but also the attached epithets: in magical
texts "name" often means "full title." The Greek προυποκείμενον normally means "given above," but it
can also be read as meaning "set forth below." This latter interpretation (accepted by Preisendanz)
would eliminate the apparent contradiction between this and the following sentence. However, the following sentence may be a deliberate contradiction by a glossator. [M.S.]
25. This is probably an abbreviated way of saying, "Use the procedure that involves an onion."
26. Or "For those possessed by daimons," which seems the better reading of the papyrus. The manuscript has πρὸς δαιμονιαζομένο(υ)ς. See A. Erman, *ZÄS* 21 (1883):99 (plate III, l. 25) and Preisendanz, apparatus ad loc. The invocation which begins with OHK is separated by a space and -ζομενος is
written with the same Greek letter forms as the preceding ones. [R.D.K.]

PGM IV. 88–93

*Another,[27] to Helios: Wrap a naked boy in linen from head to toe,[28] then clap your hands. After making a ringing noise, place the boy opposite / the sun,[29] and   90
standing behind him say the *formula*:

"I am Barbarioth; Barbarioth am I; PESKOUT YAHO ADŌNAI ELŌAI SABAŌTH, come in to this little one today, for I am Barbarioth."

*Tr.: W. C. Grese and Marvin W. Meyer (Coptic sections, ll. 91–93).

PGM IV. 94–153

*Isis is the one who comes from the mountain at midday[30] in summer, the dusty maiden; / her eyes are full of tears and her heart is full of sighs.   95

Her father, Thoth the Great, came in unto her and asked her, "O my daughter Isis, dusty maiden, why are your eyes full of tears, your heart full of sighs, and [the . . .] of your garment soiled? [Away with] the tears of your eyes!"

She said [to him], "He is not with me,[31] O my father, Ape Thoth, Ape / [Thoth],   100
my father. I have been betrayed by my female companion. I have discovered [a] secret: yes, Nephthys is having intercourse with Osiris . . . my brother, my own mother's son."

He said to her, "Behold, this is adultery against you, O my daughter Isis."

She [said] to him, "It is adultery against you, O my father, / [Ape] Thoth, Ape   105
Thoth, my father; it is pregnancy proper for me myself."[32]

He said to her, "Arise, O my daughter Isis, and [go] to the south to Thebes, to the north to Abydos.[33] There are . . . those who trample (?) there. Take for yourself Belf son of Belf, [the one whose] foot is of bronze and whose heels are of iron, /   110
[that] he forge for you a double iron nail with a . . . head, a thin base, a strong point, and light iron. Bring it before me, dip it in the blood of Osiris,[34] and hand it over; we . . . this mysterious (?) flame to me."

" / Every flaming, every cooking, every heating,[35] every steaming, and every   115
sweating that you [masc.] will cause in this flaming stove, you [will] cause in the heart, in the liver, [in] the area of the navel, and in the belly of NN whom NN has borne, until I bring her to the house of NN whom NN has borne[36] and she puts what is in / her hand into my hand, what is in her mouth into my mouth, what is in   120
her belly onto my belly, what is in her female parts onto my male parts, quickly, quickly; immediately, immediately. Rise up to the kings of Alchah,[37] speak the truth (?) in Oupōke, arouse god [after] NN[38] whom NN has borne, and I shall send

27. Presumably this is another request for divination (cf. *PGM* IV. 1–25, 52–85). In fact, the spell is specifically a "divination using a boy," for which cf. *PGM* VII. 348–58; also *Test. Sol.* I. 3.

28. Cf. for this phrase *PDM* xiv. 96.

29. That is, Helios, the sun god.

30. Cf. *PDM* xiv. 1219.

31. Or "It is not of my doing."

32. This episode is also told in a different fashion by Plutarch, *De Is. et Os.* 14, 356E–F. See Griffiths, *Plutarch's De Iside et Osiride* 316–17.

33. Cf. *PDM* xiv. 628.

34. Cf. *PDM* xiv. 440–41.

35. Or "sighing."

36. Cf. *PDM* xiv. 656–58.

37. Alchah (Egyptian ꜥrq-ḥḥ, "Alxai") and Oupōke (Egyptian w-pkr) are both sacred places at Abydos. Alchah designates the cemetery where the mummy of Osiris was buried. See *PGM* XIVb, 12–15 (in the context of *PDM* xiv. 451–58). [R.K.R.]

38. Or "every god (after NN)."

125   her / to be with NN whom NN has borne. For I am To son of To;[39] I am the Great
son of the Great; I am Anubis, who bears the glorious crown of Re and puts it upon
King Osiris, King Osiris Onnophris, . . . who arouses the whole earth, that you

130   may arouse the heart of NN whom / NN has borne, that I may know what is in her
heart for me, for NN whom NN has borne, on this day."

        If a large amount of saliva forms in your mouth as you speak, understand that she

135   is distressed[40] and wants to talk with you; if you yawn frequently, she wants / to
come to you. But if you sneeze two times or more, she is in good health[41] and is
returning to where she lives; if you have a headache and are crying, she is distressed[42] or even dying.

        "Rise up to heaven, and arouse the High One [masc.] after the Noble One [fem.].

140   Rise up to the abyss, and arouse Thoth after Nabin; arouse / the heart of these two
bulls, Hapi and Mnevis; arouse the heart of Osiris after Isis; arouse Re after the
light; arouse the heart of NN whom NN has borne, after NN whom NN has
borne."

        [Say] these things on behalf of women. But when [you are speaking] about

145   women, / then speak, conversely, so as to arouse the females after the males:

        "When she drinks, when she eats, when she has intercourse with someone else, I
will bewitch her heart, I will bewitch the heart of her, I will bewitch her breath, I

150   will bewitch / her 365 members,[43] I will bewitch her inner part . . . wherever I desire, until she comes to me and I know what is in her heart, [what] she does, and of
what she thinks, quickly, quickly; immediately, immediately.

     *Tr.: M. W. Meyer.

PGM IV. 154–285

155   *Nephotes to Psammetichos, immortal king of Egypt. / Greetings. Since the great
god has appointed you immortal king and nature has made you the best wise man,[44]
I too, with a desire to show you the industry in me, have sent you this magical

160   procedure which, with complete ease, / produces a holy power. And after you have
tested it, you too will be amazed at the miraculous nature of this magical operation.
You will observe through bowl divination[45] on whatever day or night you want, in

165   whatever place you want, beholding the god in the water and / hearing a voice from
the god which speaks in verses in answer to whatever you want. You will attain[46]
both the ruler of the universe and whatever you command, and he will speak on
other matters which you ask about. You will succeed by inquiring in this way: First,

170   attach yourself to Helios in this manner: At whatever sunrise you want / (provided
it is the third day of the month), go up to the highest part of the house and spread a

39. Cf. above, *PGM* III. 679, 687 with n.

40. Or "lovesick."

41. That is, "unafflicted" by the love charm.

42. Or "lovesick."

43. For a close parallel, compare the lead tablet from Oxyrhynchus published by Wortmann, "Neue
magische Texte," 108–9. See also the *Apocryphon of John* (*NHC* II, 1:19:2–14) on the construction of
the human body by 365 angels. In *PGM* the number 365 is commonly associated with the name Abrasax
and its numerical value (see Glossary, s.v. "Abrasax"), but also with 365 gods or even 365 knots (*PGM*
VII. 452–53).

44. Or "an expert magician," as σοφιστής applies to one skilled in his craft. See LSJ, s.v.; Betz,
Lukian 10–11.

45. For bowl divination, see R. Ganszyniec, "Λεκανομαντεία," *PRE* 12 (1925): 1879–89.

46. Preisendanz suggests that οἴσεις is a late future form of οἶδα. Perhaps one should emend the text
to read ὄψεις, "you will see." However, the future of φέρω can be defended here (see LSJ, s.v., VI. 2–3,
where "carry off as a prize," "win," "gain," etc., are given as meanings). [J.P.H.]

pure linen garment on the floor. Do this with a mystagogue. But as for you, crown
yourself with dark ivy while the sun is in mid-heaven, at the fifth hour, and while
looking upward lie down / naked on the linen and order your eyes to be completely   175
covered with a black band.[47] And wrap yourself like a corpse, close your eyes and,
keeping your direction toward the sun, begin these words. **Prayer**:[48]

> "O mighty Typhon, / ruler of the realm   180
> Above and master, god of gods, O lord
> ABERAMENTHŌOU (formula),
> O dark's disturber, thunder's bringer, whirlwind,
> Night-flasher, breather-forth of hot and cold,
> Shaker of rocks, wall-trembler, boiler of
> The waves, disturber of the sea's great depth, /
> IŌ / ERBĒT AU TAUI MĒNI,   185
> I'm he[49] who searched with you the whole world and
> Found great Osiris, whom I brought you chained.
> I'm he who joined you in war with the gods
> (but others say, "'gainst the gods").
> I'm he who closed / heav'n's double gates and put   190
> To sleep the serpent which must not be seen,
> Who stopped the seas, the streams, the river currents
> Where'er you rule this realm. And as your soldier
> I have been conquered by the gods, I have
> Been thrown face down because of empty wrath. /
> Raise up your friend, I beg you, I implore;   195
> Throw me not on the ground, O lord of gods,
> AEMINAEBARŌTHERRETHŌRABEANIMEA,[50]
> O grant me power, I beg, and give to me
> This favor, so that, whensoe'r I tell
> One of the gods to come, he is seen coming /
> Swiftly to me in answer to my chants,   200
> NAINE BASANAPTATOU EAPTOU MĒNŌPHAESMĒ PAPTOU MĒNŌPH AESIMĒ TRAU-
> APTI PEUCHRĒ TRAUARA PTOUMĒPH MOURAI ANCHOUCHAPHAPTA MOURSA ARA-
> MEI IAŌ ATHTHARAUI MĒNOKER BORO/PTOUMĒTH AT TAUI MĒNI CHARCHARA   205
> PTOUMAU LALAPSA TRAUI TRAUEPSE MAMŌ PHORTOUCHA AEĒIO IOY OĒŌA EAI
> AEĒI ŌI IAŌ AĒI AI IAŌ."

After you have said this three times,[51] there will be this sign of divine encounter,[52]
but you, / armed by having this magical soul, be not alarmed. For a sea falcon flies   210
down and strikes you on the body with its wings, signifying this: that you should
arise. But as for you, rise up and clothe yourself with white garments and burn on
an earthen censer uncut / incense in grains while saying this: 215

> "I have been attached to your holy form.
> I have been given power by your holy name.
> I have acquired your emanation of the goods,

47. See Glossary, s.v. "Isis band."
48. The iambic trimeters (ll. 179–201), many of which are metrically faulty, also form the reconstructed Hymn 6. See Preisendanz, vol. II, pp. 242–43. [E.N.O.]
49. See on this passage Wortmann, "Neue magische Texte," 92–93.
50. See for this formula *PGM* I. 295; XIV. 24 (abbreviated); LIX. 7.
51. For the triplicate repetition in magic see O. Weinreich, "Trisgemination als sakrale Stilform," in
his *Ausgewählte Schriften* (Amsterdam: Grüner, 1973) 250–58.
52. See on this point *PGM* IV. 168–69.

Lord, god of gods, master, daimon.

ATHTHOUIN THOUTHOUI TAUANTI LAŌ APTATŌ."

220   Having done this, return / as lord of a godlike nature which is accomplished through this divine encounter.

Inquiry of bowl divination and necromancy:[53] Whenever you want to inquire about matters, take a bronze vessel, either a bowl or a saucer, whatever kind you

225   wish. Pour water: / rainwater if you are calling upon heavenly gods, seawater if gods of the earth, river water if Osiris or Sarapis, springwater if the dead. Holding

230   the vessel on your knees, pour out green olive oil, bend over the vessel and speak / the prescribed spell. And address whatever god you want and ask about whatever you wish, and he will reply to you and tell you about anything. And if he has spoken dismiss him with the spell of dismissal, and you who have used this spell will be amazed.

235   *The spell spoken over the vessel is*: "AMOUN AUANTAU / LAIMOUTAU RIPTOU MANTAUI IMANTOU LANTOU LAPTOUMI ANCHŌMACH ARAPTOUMI, hither to me, O NN god; appear to me this very hour and do not frighten my eyes. Hither to me, O NN god, be attentive to me because he wishes and commands this[54] ACHCHŌR

240   ACHCHŌR / ACHACHACH PTOUMI CHACHCHŌ CHARACHŌCH CHAPTOUMĒ CHŌ-RACHARACHŌCH APTOUMI MĒCHŌCHAPTOU CHARACHPTOU CHACHCHŌ CHA-RACHŌ PTENACHŌCHEU" (a hundred letters).[55]

But you are not unaware, mighty king and leader of magicians, that this is the

245   chief name of Typhon, / at whom the ground, the depths of the sea, Hades, heaven, the sun, the moon, the visible chorus of stars, the whole universe all tremble, the name which, when it is uttered, forcibly brings gods and daimons to it. This is the name that consists of 100 letters. Finally, when you have called, whomever you

250   called will appear, god or dead man,[56] and he will / give an answer about anything you ask. And when you have learned to your satisfaction,[57] dismiss the god merely with the powerful name of the hundred letters as you say, "Depart, master, for the great god, NN, wishes and commands this of you." Speak the name, and he will

255   depart. Let this spell, / mighty king, be transmitted to you alone, guarded by you, unshared.

There is also the protective charm itself which you wear while performing, even while standing:[58] onto a silver leaf inscribe this name of 100 letters with a bronze

260   stylus, and wear it strung on a thong from the hide / of an ass.[59]

---

53. Following the emended punctuation by M. Smith, *Clement of Alexandria and the Secret Gospel of Mark* (Cambridge, Mass.: Harvard University Press, 1973) 221.

54. The sudden shift to the third person in the words θέλει καὶ ἐπιτάσσει seems strange at first, and one is tempted to think that the magician begins to refer to himself in the third person. But cf. ll. 253–54 below, where the same phenomenon occurs with the subject named.

55. That is, according to Greek letters.

56. That is, the spirit or soul of a dead man. See on this primitive concept J. Bremmer, *The Early Greek Concept of the Soul* (Princeton: Princeton University Press, 1983) 70–124: "The Soul of the Dead."

57. At this point the revelatory dialogue comes into the picture. Cf. Corp. Herm. I.3, 27, 30. Cf. P. Perkins, *The Gnostic Dialogue: The Early Church and the Crisis of Gnosticism* (New York: Paulist Press, 1980), where further literature can be found.

58. The Greek is obscure at this point. The translation follows Preisendanz: "auch wenn du stehend agierst."

59. The ass is the animal associated with Seth/Typhon. See Glossary, s.v.

Divine encounter of the divine procedure: Toward the rising sun say: [60]
    "I call you who did first control gods' wrath,[61]
    You who hold royal scepter o'er the heavens,
    You who are midpoint of the stars above,
    You, master Typhon, you I call, who are
    / The dreaded sovereign o'er the firmament.   265
    You who are fearful, awesome, threatening,
    You who're obscure[62] and irresistible
    And hater of the wicked, you I call,
    Typhon, in hours unlawful and unmeasured,
    You who've walked on unquenched, clear-crackling fire,
    You who are / over snows, below dark ice,   270
    You who hold sovereignty over the Moirai,[63]
    I invoked you in pray'r, I call, almighty one.
    That you perform for me whate'er I ask
    Of you, and that you nod assent at once
    To me and grant that what I ask be mine
(add the usual), because I adjure you, GAR THALA BAUZAU THŌRTHŌR / KATHAU- 275
KATH IATHIN NA BORKAKAR BORBA KARBORBOCH MŌ ZAU OUZŌNZ ŌN YABITH,
mighty Typhon, hear me, NN, and perform for me the NN task. For I speak your
true names, IŌ ERBĒTH IŌ PAKERBĒTH IŌ BOLCHOSĒTH OEN / TYPHON ASBA- 280
RABŌ BIEAISĒ ME NERŌ MARAMŌ TAUĒR CHTHENTHŌNIE ALAM BĒTŌR MEN-
KECHRA SAUEIŌR RĒSEIODŌTA ABRĒSIOA PHŌTHĒR THERTHŌNAX NERDŌMEU
AMŌRĒS MEEME ŌIĒS SYSCHIE ANTHŌNIE PHRA; listen / to me and perform the 285
NN deed."
*Tr.: E. N. O'Neil.

PGM IV. 286–95

* **Spell for picking a plant**:[64] Use it before sunrise. **The spell to be spoken**: "I am
picking you, such and such a plant, with my five-fingered hand, I, NN, and I am
bringing you home so that you may work for me for a certain purpose. I adjure you
by the undefiled / name of the god: if you pay no heed to me, the earth which 290
produced you will no longer be watered as far as you are concerned—ever in life

---

60. The following dactylic hexameters also form the reconstructed Hymn 7. See Preisendanz, vol. II, pp. 243–44. Here and elsewhere σέ is considered long *metri gratia*, contrary to classical usage. [E.N.O.]

61. The papyrus reads ὀργίλον, which the editors of Hymn 7 have obelized. Here in IV. 262 Preisendanz has emended and reads ὅπλον, while others have suggested such words as ὅρμον (Wünsch), κόσμον (Dieterich), etc. The translation here has retained the reading of the papyrus. For διέπω and its meaning here, see Bauer, s.v. [E.N.O.]

62. The papyrus has δῆλον, which Preisendanz retains both here and in Hymn 7 where he obelizes it. Kroll's emendation ἄδηλον is paleographically sound, for "A" could have been omitted before "Δ." Second, ἄδηλον is a good parallel to ἀμήχανον, and third, the idea of ἄδηλον fits Seth/Typhon, who is regularly associated with darkness, shadows, etc. Cf., e.g., Plutarch, *De Is. et Os.* 2, 351F; 44, 368F, and Griffiths, *Plutarch's De Iside et Osiride* 468. [E.N.O.]

63. Preisendanz reads at this point ἐπ' εὐκταίων Μοιρῶν, "over the Moirai invoked in prayer." In the reconstructed Hymn 7 (Preisendanz, vol. II, p. 244), Heitsch reads ἐπευκταίων Μοιρῶν, "of the longed-for Moirai," originally a proposal by Dieterich (see the apparatus to *PGM* IV. 271).

64. For this type of ritual, see F. Pfister, "Pflanzenaberglaube," *PRE* 19 (1938): 1446–56.

again, if I fail in this operation, MOUTHABAR NACH BARNACHŌCHA BRAEŌ MENDA
295   LAUBRAASSE PHASPHA BENDEŌ; fulfil[65] for me / the perfect charm."
*Tr.: E. N. O'Neil.

PGM IV. 296–466

Wondrous spell for binding a lover: Take wax [or clay] from a potter's wheel
and make two figures, a male and a female. Make the male in the form of Ares fully
300   armed, holding a sword / in his left hand and threatening to plunge it into the right
side of her neck. And make her[66] with her arms behind her back and down on her
knees. And you are to fasten the magical material on her head or neck. Write on the
305   figure of the woman being attracted as follows: On the head: / "ISEĒ IAŌ ITHI
OUNE BRIDŌ LŌTHIŌN NEBOUTOSOUALĒTH"; on the right ear: "OUER MĒCHAN";
on the left ear: "LIBABA ŌIMATHOTHO"; on the face: "AMOUNABREŌ"; on the right
310   eye: / "ŌRORMOTHIO AĒTH"; on the other: "CHOBOUE"; on the right shoulder:
"ADETA MEROU"; on the right arm: "ENE PSA ENESGAPH"; on the other: "MEL-
315   CHIOU MELCHIEDIA": on the hands: / "MELCHAMELCHOU AĒL"; on the breast:
the name, on her mother's side, of the woman being attracted; on the heart: "BAL-
AMIN THŌOUTH"; and below the lower belly: "AOBĒS AOBAR"; on the pudenda:
320   "BLICHIANEOI OUŌIA"; on the buttocks: "PISSADARA"; on / the sole of the right
foot: "ELŌ"; on the sole of the other one: "ELŌAIAOE."

And take thirteen copper needles and stick 1 in the brain while saying, "I am
piercing your brain, NN"; and stick 2 in the ears and 2 in the eyes and 1 in the
325   mouth and 2 / in the midriff and 1 in the hands and 2 in the pudenda and 2 in the
soles, saying each time, "I am piercing such and such a member of her, NN, so that
she may remember no one but me, NN, alone."

330   And take a lead tablet[67] and write the same / spell and recite it. And tie the lead
leaf to the figures with thread from the loom after making 365 knots while saying
as you have learned, "ABRASAX, hold her fast!" You place it, as the sun is setting,
beside the grave of one who has died untimely or violently, placing beside it also the
seasonal flowers.

335   *The spell to be written / and recited is*: "I entrust this binding spell to you,
chthonic gods, HYESEMIGADŌN and KORĒ PERSEPHONE ERESCHIGAL and ADONIS
the BARBARITHA, infernal HERMES THŌOUTH PHŌKENTAZEPSEU AERCHTHA-
340   THOUMI / SONKTAI KALBANACHAMBRĒ and to mighty ANUBIS PSIRINTH, who
holds the keys to Hades, to infernal gods and daimons, to men and women who
have died untimely deaths, to youths and maidens, from year to year, month to
345   month, day to day, / hour to hour. I adjure all daimons in this place to stand as
assistants beside this daimon. And arouse yourself for me,[68] whoever you are,
whether male or female,[69] and go to every place and into every quarter and to every
350   house, and attract / and bind her. Attract her, NN, whom NN bore and whose

65. The sudden shift to the plural τελέσατε is strange. Preisendanz suggests that δαίμονες is the
subject, but no daimons appear in the spell. Can the subject be the *voces magicae* themselves? [E.N.O.]

66. A figurine similar to the one described here, together with a lead tablet containing an inscription
nearly identical to that of ll. 335–406, has been found in Egypt. See S. Kambitsis, "Une nouvelle tab-
lette magique d'Égypte, Musée du Louvre, Inv. E 27145, 3ᵉ/4ᵉ siècle," *BIFAO* 76 (1976): 213–23 and
plates.

67. For a parallel to this passage, see Wortmann, "Neue magische Texte," 56–58 (no. 1, ll. 6–16).

68. See on this point Wortmann, "Neue magische Texte," 70–71.

69. Egyptian lists of demons and demon-induced diseases carefully distinguish between male and
female. For a characteristic example, see S. Sauneron, *Le Papyrus magique illustré de Brooklyn* (Brooklyn:
The Brooklyn Museum, 1970) 6–11. [R.K.R.]

magical material you possess. Let her be in love with me, NN whom she, NN bore.
Let her not be had in a promiscuous way,[70] let her not be had in her ass, nor let her
do anything with another man for pleasure, just with me alone, NN, so that she,
NN, be unable either to drink or eat, that she not / be contented, not be strong,   355
not have peace of mind, that she, NN, not find sleep without me, NN, because I
adjure you by the name that causes fear and trembling, the name at whose sound
the earth opens, the name at whose terrifying sound the daimons are terrified, / the   360
name at whose sound rivers and rocks burst assunder. I adjure you, god of the dead,
whether male or female, by BARBARITHA CHENMBRA BAROUCHAMBRA and by the
ABRAT ABRASAX SESENGEN BARPHARANGGĒS and by the glorious AŌIA / MARI and   365
by the MARMAREŌTH MARMARAUŌTH MARMARAŌTH MARECHTHANA AMARZA
MARIBEŌTH; do not fail, god of the dead, to heed my commands and names, but
just arouse yourself from the repose which holds you, / whoever you are, whether   370
male or female, and go to every place, into every quarter, into every house, and
attract her, NN, to me and with a spell keep her from eating and drinking, and do
not allow her, NN, to accept for pleasure the attempt of another man, / not even   375
that of her own husband, just that of mine, NN. Instead, drag her, NN, by the hair,
by her heart, by her soul, to me, NN, at every hour of life, day and night, until she
comes to me, NN, and may she, NN, remain / inseparable from me. Do this, bind   380
her for all the time of my life and help force her, NN to be serviceable to me,
NN, and let her not frolic away from me for even one hour of life. If you accomplish this for me, I will quickly allow you your repose. / For I am BARBAR ADŌNAI   385
who hides the stars, who controls the brightly shining heaven, the lord of the
world, ATHTHOUIN IATHOUIN SELBIOUŌTH AŌTH SARBATHIOUTH IATHTHIERATH
ADŌNAI IA ROURA BIA BI BIOTHĒ ATHŌTH / SABAŌTH ĒA NIAPHA AMARACHTHI   390
SATAMA ZAUATHTHEIĒ SERPHO IALADA IALĒ SBĒSI IATHTHA MARADTHA ACHILTH-
THEE CHOŌŌ OĒ ĒACHŌ KANSAOSA ALKMOURI THYR THAŌOS SIECHĒ. I am
THOTH OSŌMAI; / attract her, bind her, NN, filled with love, desire and yearning   395
for NN (add the usual), because I adjure you, god of the dead, by the fearful, great
IAEŌ BAPH RENEMOUN OTHI LARIKRIPHIA EYEAI PHIRKIRALITHON YOMEN ER
PHABŌEAI, / so that you attract her, NN, to me and join head to head and fasten lip   400
to lip and join belly to belly and draw thigh close to thigh and fit black together
with black, and let her, NN, carry out her own sex acts / with me, NN, for all eter-   405
nity.

Then write on the other side of the tablet the heart and the characters as they are
below:

```
"IAEŌBAPHRENEMOUNOTHILARIKRIPHIAEYEAIPHIRKIRALITHONYOMENERPHABŌEAI        410
    AEŌBAPHRENEMOUNOTHILARIKRIPHIAEYEAIPHIRKIRALITHONYOMENERPHABŌEA
AŌ   EŌBAPHRENEMOUNOTHILARIKRIPHIAEYEAIPHIRKIRALITHONYOMENERPHABŌE  III
EA    ŌBAPHRENEMOUNOTHILARIKRIPHIAEYEAIPHIRKIRALITHONYOMENERPHABŌ    OEŌ
IŌ     BAPHRENEMOUNOTHILARIKRIPHIAEYEAIPHIRKIRALITHONYOMENERPHAB     OIEE
YO     APHRENEMOUNOTHILARIKRIPHIAEYEAIPHIRKIRALITHONYOMENERPHA       OEYI
IO     PHRENEMOUNOTHILARIKRIPHIAEYEAIPHIRKIRALITHONYOMENERPH         OEYY
OE                                                                  IAYY
IŌAE                                                                YYAA      415
EOĒI                                                                OIII
YAOU                                                                YAEE
IAŌI                                                                EŌAY
AĒAĒ                                                                OOYI
```
                                                                             420

70. See on this point Wortmann, "Neue magische Text," 72.

ĒIOI   ĒĒEA
ŌIYA   AAIA
AŌOE   IIIŌ
425   YIŌĒ   EEAŌ
EOAŌA   ĒĒAŌ
YAYA   ĒIĒE
IOĒIIĒ   OAĒI
IAŌI   ĒIYI
AOAO   ĒĒOI
430   YYOI   YAAI
ĒIIA
AAŌŌ"

435   ***Prayer that belongs to the procedure***: At sunset, while holding / the magical ma-
terial from the tomb, say:
"Borne[71] on the breezes of the wandr'ing winds,
Golden-haired Helios, who wield the flame's
Unresting fire, who turn in lofty paths
Around the great pole, who create all things
Yourself which you again reduce to nothing, /
440   From whom, indeed, all elements have been
Arranged to suit your laws which nourish all
The world with its four yearly turning points.
Hear, blessed one, for I call you who rule
Heaven and earth, Chaos and Hades, where
Men's daimons dwell who once gazed on the light, /
445   And even now I beg you, blessed one,
Unfailing one, the master of the world,
If you go to the depths of earth and search
The regions of the dead, send this daimon,
From whose body I hold this remnant in my hands,
To her, NN, at midnight hours,
To move by night to orders 'neath your force, /
450   That all I want within my heart he may
Perform for me; and send him gentle, gracious
And pondering no hostile thoughts toward me,
And be not angry at my potent chants,
For you yourself arranged these things among
Mankind for them to learn about the threads
Of the Moirai, and this with your advice. /
455   I call your name, Horus,[72] which is in number
Equivalent to those of the Moirai,
ACHAIPHŌ THŌTHŌ PHIACHA AIĒ ĒIA IAĒ ĒIA THŌTHŌ PHIACHA.
Be kind to me, forefather, scion of
The world, self-gendered, fire-bringer, aglow
Like gold, shining on mortals, master of
460   The world, / daimon of restless fire, unfailing,
With gold disk, sending earth pure light in beams.

71. The following dactylic hexameters are part of the reconstructed Hymn 4 (Preisendanz, vol. II,
pp. 239–40): v. 1–17, 20, 22–28. For other versions and sections of Hymn 4, see *PGM* I. 315–27; IV.
1957–89; VIII. 74–80. [E.N.O.]
72. For Horus equated with Helios, cf. *PGM* IV. 989.

Send the daimon, whomever I have requested, to her, NN" (add the usual).

In another version, the name is: "ACHAI PHŌTHŌTHŌ AIĒ ĒIA IAĒ ĒIŌ THŌ THŌ
PHIACHA." / *In another it is*: "ACHAI PHŌTHŌTHŌ AIĒ IĒA ĒAI IAĒ AĒI ĒIA ŌTHŌ-   465
THŌ PHIACHA."
*Tr.: E. N. O'Neil.

PGM IV. 467–68

*Charm to restrain anger: "Will you dare to raise your mighty spear against
Zeus?"[73]
*Tr.: R. F. Hock. The same spell occurs at *PGM* IV. 831–32.

PGM IV. 469–70

*To get friends:
/ "Let . . . seize, lest we become a joy to our enemies."[74]   470
*Tr.: Hubert Martin, Jr. The same charm using a verse from Homer (*Iliad* 10.193) occurs
in *PGM* IV. 833–34. Since there the single verse alone serves as a charm to get friends, and
since the papyrus manuscript separates all verses with paragraph marks, it seems likely that
the following four verses served as separate charms, though the original titles have been lost.
Furthermore, since the three verses (*Iliad* 10.564, 10.521, and 10.572) that follow form a
natural grouping in *PGM* IV. 2145ff. (cf. IV. 821–23), we have preserved that grouping in
PGM IV. 471–73, below, though it is not clear whether the copyist inserted these verses
here by mistake or whether the reader was to understand from *PGM* IV. 2145ff. that the
spell served as a "divine assistance from three Homeric verses."

PGM IV. 471–73

*. . .
"After saying this, he drove the solid-hoofed horses through the ditch."[75]

"and men gasping out their lives amid the terrible slaughter."[76]

"and they washed off in the sea the sweat that covered them."[77]
*Tr.: Hubert Martin, Jr. This untitled charm contains three verses of Homer that also occur
in *PGM* IV. 821–23 and IV. 2145ff. It is presumed that these verses served the same functions as those listed in ll. 2145ff. See the introductory note on the previous spell. The verses
all come from the tenth book of the Iliad and presumably could be read together.

PGM IV. 474

*". . . Ares endured, when Otos and mighty Ephialtes . . . him."[78]
*Tr.: Hubert Martin, Jr. Cf. the introductory note on *PGM* IV. 469–70, and see *PGM* IV.
830, with n.

---

73. Homer, *Il.* 8. 424. For the use of single Homeric verses as charms and amulets, see R. Heim,
"Incantamenta magica graeca latina," *Jahrbücher für classische Philologie, Supplementband* 9 (1893), section X: *Versus Homerici et Vergiliani* (pp. 514–20).

74. Homer, *Il.* 10. 193.

75. Homer, *Il.* 10. 564. The referent of "he" is Odysseus in the original context.

76. Homer, *Il.* 10. 521. Again, the papyrus quotes only a portion of the Homeric text. "Men" is the
object of "saw" in l. 520, and it is a kinsman of the slaughtered Rhesus who saw.

77. Homer, *Il.* 10. 572. In Homer, the referent of "they" is Odysseus and Diomedes.

78. Homer, *Il.* 5. 385. The papyrus quotes only a single verse and leaves the syntax of "him" unac-
counted for. In Homer, "him" is governed by "bound" in l. 386.

PGM IV. 475–829

475 *Be gracious to me, O Providence and Psyche,[79] as I write these mysteries handed down [not] for gain but for instruction; and for an only child I request immortality, O initiates of this our power (furthermore, it is necessary for you, O daughter, to take / the juices of herbs and spices, which will [be made known] to you at the end of my holy treatise), which the great god Helios Mithras ordered to be revealed to me by his archangel, so that I alone may ascend into heaven as an inquirer / and behold the universe.

This is the invocation of the spell:

"First origin of my origin, AEĒIOYŌ, first beginning of my beginning, PPP SSS[80] PHR[E], spirit of spirit,[81] the first of the spirit / in me, MMM, fire given by god to my mixture of the mixtures in me, the first of the fire in me, ĒY ĒIA EĒ, water of water, the first of the water in me, ŌŌŌ AAA EEE, earthy material, the first of the earthy material in me, / YĒ YŌĒ, my complete body, I, NN whose mother is NN, which was formed by a noble arm and an incorruptible right hand in a world without light and yet radiant, without soul and yet alive with soul, YĒI AYI EYŌIE: now if it be your will, METERTA / PHŌTH (METHARTHA PHĒRIĒ, in another place)[82] IEREZATH, give me over to immortal birth and, following that, to my underlying nature, so that, after the present need which is pressing me exceedingly, I may gaze upon the immortal / beginning with the immortal spirit, ANCHREPHRENESOU-PHIRIGCH, with the immortal water, ERONOUI PARAKOUNĒTH, with the most steadfast air, EIOAĒ PSENABŌTH; that I may be born again in thought, KRAOCHRAX R OIM ENARCHOMAI, / and the sacred spirit may breathe in me, NECHTHEN APOTOU NECHTHIN ARPI ĒTH; so that I may wonder at the sacred fire, KYPHE; that I may gaze upon the unfathomable, awesome water of the dawn, NYŌ THESŌ ECHŌ OUCHIECHŌA, and the vivifying / and encircling aether may hear me, ARNO-MĒTHPH; for today I am about to behold, with immortal eyes—I, born mortal from mortal womb, but transformed by tremendous power and an incorruptible right hand / and with immortal spirit, the immortal Aion and master of the fiery diadems—I, sanctified through holy consecrations—while there subsists within me, holy, for a short time, my human soul-might, which I will again / receive after the present bitter and relentless necessity which is pressing down upon me—I, NN, whose mother is NN, according to the immutable decree of god, EYĒ YIA EĒI AŌ EIAY IYA IEŌ. Since it is impossible for me, born / mortal, to rise with the golden brightnesses of the immortal brilliance, ŌĒY AEŌ ĒYA EŌĒ YAE ŌIAE, stand, O perishable nature of mortals, and at once [receive] me safe and sound after the inexorable and pressing / need. For I am the son PSYCHŌN DEMOU PROCHŌ PRŌA, I am MACHARPH[.]N MOU PRŌPSYCHŌN PRŌE."

Draw in breath from the rays, drawing up 3 times as much as you can, and you will see yourself being lifted up and / ascending to the height, so that you seem to be in midair. You will hear nothing either of man or of any other living thing, nor in that hour will you see anything of mortal affairs on earth, but rather you will see all

---

79. The goddess Psyche, "Soul." Some scholars read Tyche, "Fortune." On the problem see Dieterich, *Mithrasliturgie* 2, 49–52, 70–72, 230–32. On the "Mithras Liturgy," see M. W. Meyer, *The 'Mithras Liturgy'* (Missoula, Montana: Scholars Press, 1976).

80. For the meaning of popping and hissing noises in magic, see Dieterich, *Mithrasliturgie* 40–43, 228–29; R. Lasch, "Das Pfeifen und Schnalzen und seine Beziehung zu Dämonenglauben und Zauberei," *ARW* 18 (1915): 589–93. See also ll. 561–62, and 578–79 below, and elsewhere in the *PGM*.

81. "Spirit," "breath," "wind" ($\pi\nu\varepsilon\tilde{\upsilon}\mu\alpha$) is one of the four elements.

82. This is evidence that the scribe had at least one other copy of the spell. See Dieterich, *Mithrasliturgie* 4, 221.

immortal things. For in that day / and hour you will see the divine order of the   545
skies: the presiding gods rising into heaven, and others setting. Now the course of
the visible gods will appear through the disk of god, my father; and in similar fashion the so-called pipe, / the origin of the ministering wind. For you will see it hang-   550
ing from the sun's disk like a pipe. You will see the outflow of this object toward the
regions westward, boundless as an east wind, if it be assigned to the regions of the
east—and the other (viz., the west wind), similarly, toward its own / regions. And   555
you will see the gods staring intently at you and rushing at you.

So at once put your right finger on your mouth[83] and say:

"Silence! Silence! Silence!

Symbol of the living, incorruptible god! /

Guard me, Silence, NECHTHEIR THANMELOU!"   560

Then make a long hissing sound, next make a popping sound, and say:

"PROPROPHEGGĒ MORIOS PROPHYR PROPHEGGĒ NEMETHIRE ARPSENTEN PI-
TĒTMI MEŌY ENARTH PHYRKECHŌ PSYRIDARIŌ / TYRĒ PHILBA."   565

Then you will see the gods looking graciously upon you and no longer rushing at
you, but rather going about in their own order of affairs.

So when you see that the world above is clear / and circling, and that none of the   570
gods or angels is threatening you, expect to hear a great crash of thunder, so as to
shock you. Then say again:

"Silence! Silence! (the prayer) I am a star, wandering about with you, and shining forth out of / the deep, OXY O XERTHEUTH."   575

Immediately after you have said these things the sun's disk will be expanded. And
after you have said the second prayer, where there is "Silence! Silence!" and the
accompanying words, make a hissing sound twice and a popping sound twice, and
immediately you will see / many five-pronged stars coming forth from the disk and   580
filling all the air. Then say again: "Silence! Silence!" And when the disk is open, you
will see the fireless circle, and the fiery doors shut tight. /

At once close your eyes and recite the following prayer. ***The third prayer***:   585

"Give ear to me, hearken to me, NN, whose mother is NN, O lord, you who
have bound together with your breath the fiery bars of the fourfold / root,[84]   590

O Fire-walker, PENTITEROUNI,

Light-maker (others: Encloser), SEMESILAM,

Fire-breather, PSYRINPHEU,

Fire-feeler, IAŌ,

Light-breather, ŌAI,

Fire-delighter, ELOURE,

Beautiful light, AZAI,

Aion, ACHBA,

/ Light-master, PEPPER PREPEMPIPI,[85]   595

Fire-body, PHNOUĒNIOCH,

Light-giver, . . .

83. For examples of this common depiction on stones, see the engraved gem showing Harpokrates with his finger to his mouth, in F. M. and J. H. Schwartz, "Engraved Gems in the Collection of the American Numismatic Society, I: Ancient Magical Amulets," *The American Numismatic Society, Museum Notes* 24 (1979) no. 3, p. 159. See also the bronze statue in G. S. Gasparro, *I culti orientali in Sicilia*, EPRO 31 (Leiden: Brill, 1973), plate XLV, fig. 66.

84. Reading τετραριζώματος with Hopfner (see apparatus ad loc.) rather than τετραλιζώματος. The reading of the manuscript, on the other hand, suggests διαζώματος (cf. *C. H., Frag.* 26.8). [W.B.]

85. For PIPI as a permutation of the tetragrammaton, the Hebrew divine name, see S. Lieberman, *Greek in Jewish Palestine* (New York: The Jewish Theological Seminary of America, 1942) 120 n. 38;

Fire-sower, AREI EIKITA,
Fire-driver, GALLABALBA,
Light-forcer, AIŌ,
Fire-whirler, PYRICHIBOOSĒIA,
Light-mover, SANCHERŌB,

600   Thunder-shaker /, IĒ ŌĒ IŌĒIŌ,
Glory-light, BEEGENĒTE,
Light-increaser, SOUSINEPHIEN,
Fire-light-maintainer, SOUSINEPHI ARENBARAZEI MARMARENTEU,
Star-tamer . . .

Open for me, PROPROPHEGGĒ EMETHEIRE MORIOMOTYRĒPHILBA,

605   because, / on account of the pressing and bitter and inexorable necessity, I invoke
the immortal names, living and honored, which never pass into mortal nature and

610   are not declared in articulate speech by human tongue or mortal speech / or mortal
sound: ĒEŌ OĒEŌ IŌŌ OĒ ĒEŌ ĒEŌ OĒ EŌ IŌŌ OĒĒE ŌĒE ŌOĒ IĒ ĒŌ OŌ OĒ IEŌ OĒ
ŌOĒ IEŌ OĒ IEEŌ EĒ IŌ OĒ IOĒ ŌĒŌ EOĒ OEŌ OIĒ ŌIĒ EŌ OI III ĒOĒ ŌYĒ ĒŌOĒE

615   EŌ ĒIA AĒA EĒA / ĒEEĒ EEĒ EEĒ IEŌ ĒEŌ OĒEEOĒ ĒEŌ ĒYŌ OĒ EIŌ ĒŌ ŌĒ ŌĒ EE
OOO YIŌĒ."

Say all these things with fire and spirit, until completing the first utterance; then,

620   similarly, begin the second, until you complete the / 7 immortal gods of the world.[86]
When you have said these things, you will hear thundering and shaking in the surrounding realm; and you will likewise feel yourself being agitated. Then say again:

625   "Silence!" (the prayer). Then open your eyes, and you will see the doors / open and
the world of the gods which is within the doors, so that from the pleasure and joy
of the sight your spirit runs ahead and ascends.

So stand still and at once draw breath from the divine into yourself, while you

630   look intently. Then when / your soul is restored, say:
"Come, lord, ARCHANDARA PHŌTAZA PYRIPHŌTA ZABYTHIX ETIMENMERO
PHORATHĒN ERIĒ PROTHRI PHORATHI."

When you have said this, the rays will turn toward you; look at the center of

635   them. For when / you have done this, you will see a youthful god, beautiful in appearance, with fiery hair, and in a white tunic and a scarlet cloak, and wearing a
fiery crown.[87] At once greet him with the fire greeting:

640   "Hail, O lord, Great Power, Great Might, / King, Greatest of gods, Helios, the
Lord of heaven and earth, God of gods: mighty is your breath; mighty is your
strength, O lord. If it be your will, announce me to the supreme god, the one who

645   has begotten and made you: that a man—I, NN,[88] whose mother is NN, / who was
born from the mortal womb of NN and from the fluid of semen, and who, since he

M. Philonenko, "L'Anguipède alectorocéphale et le dieu IAÔ" *Academie des inscriptions et belles lettres,
comptes rendus des séances de l'année 1979* 297–304, where further material is collected and discussed. In
PGM see also III. 575; IV. 1984; XVIIa. 1–2; cf. also III. 335.

86. For the following section of the ritual, cf. the combination of the seven grades of the initiation,
the planetary gods, and the ascension in the mysteries of Mithras. See esp. R. Beck, "Interpreting the
Ponza-Zodiac: II," *Journal of Mithraic Studies* 2 (1978) : 120–35; R. Merkelbach, *Weihegrade und Seelen-
lehre der Mithrasmysterien* (Opladen: Westdeutscher Verlag, 1982) 13–21; also J. Bergman, "*Per omnia
vectus elementa remeavi*. Réflexions sur l'arrière-plan égyptien du voyage de salut d'un myste isiaque," in
U. Bianchi and M. J. Vermaseren, eds., *La soteriologia dei culti orientali nell' impero romano*, EPRO 92
(Leiden: Brill, 1982) :671–708.

87. Cf. the well-preserved fresco from the Mithras temple in Capua. For a color photo, see Merkelbach, *Weihegrade* 34.

88. For the interpretation of this self-presentation, see Betz, "The Delphic Maxim," 170.

has been born again from you today, has become immortal out of so many myriads in this hour according to the wish of god the exceedingly good—resolves to worship / you, and prays with all his human power, that you may take along with you 650 the horoscope of the day and hour today, which has the name THRAPSIARI MORIROK, that he may appear and give revelation during the good hours, EŌRŌ RŌRE ŌRRI ŌRIŌR RŌR RŌI / ŌR REŌRŌRI EŌR EŌR EŌRE!" 655

After you have said these things, he will come to the celestial pole, and you will see him walking as if on a road. Look intently, and make a long bellowing sound, like a horn, releasing all your breath and straining your sides; and kiss / the phylac- 660 teries and say, first toward the right: "Protect me, PROSYMĒRI!"

After saying this, you will see the doors [89] thrown open, and seven virgins [90] coming from deep within, dressed in linen garments, and with the faces of asps.[91] They are called the Fates / of heaven, and wield golden wands. When you see them, greet 665 them in this manner:

"Hail, O seven Fates of heaven, O noble and good virgins, O sacred ones and companions of MINIMIRROPHOR, O most holy guardians of the four pillars![92] / Hail to 670 you, the first, CHREPSENTHAĒS! Hail to you, the second, MENESCHEĒS! Hail to you, the third, MECHRAN! Hail to you, the fourth, ARARMACHĒS![93] Hail to you, the fifth, ECHOMMIĒ! Hail to you, the sixth, TICHNONDAĒS! Hail to you, the seventh, EROU ROMBRIĒS!"

There also come forth another seven gods,[94] who have the faces of black bulls, in linen / loincloths, and in possession of seven golden diadems. They are the so- 675 called Pole Lords of heaven, whom you must greet in the same manner, each of them with his own name:

"Hail, O guardians of the pivot, O sacred and brave youths, who turn / at one 680 command the revolving axis of the vault of heaven, who send out thunder and lightning and jolts of earthquakes and thunderbolts against the nations of impious people, but to me, who am pious and god-fearing, you send health and soundness of body / and acuteness of hearing and seeing, and calmness in the present good 685 hours of this day, O my lords and powerfully ruling gods! Hail to you, the first, AIERŌNTHI! Hail to you, the second, MERCHEIMEROS! Hail to you, the third, ACHRICHIOUR! / Hail to you, the fourth, MESARGILTŌ! Hail to you, the fifth, 690 CHICHRŌALITHŌ! Hail to you, the sixth, ERMICHTHATHŌPS! Hail to you, the seventh, EORASICHĒ!"

Now when they take their place, here and there, in order, look in the air and you will see lightning bolts going down, and lights flashing /, and the earth shaking, 695

89. Cf. the seven gates of the mosaic of the *Mitreo delle sette sfere* at Ostia and the inscribed term ἑπτάπυλος, "seven-gated." See M. J. Vermaseren, *Corpus Inscriptionum et Monumentorum Religionis Mithriacae*, vol. I (The Hague: Nijhoff, 1966) 137, fig. 82; Merkelbach, *Weihegrade* 65.

90. For the seven virgins, see the discussion by Dieterich, *Mithrasliturgie* 69–72, who also refers to the seven Hathors of Egyptian religion.

91. This seems to be an Egyptian idea, where three serpents stand for the word "goddess." One Egyptian Fate, *Rnnwtet* (Thermutis), is known to have a serpent face. See Erman and Grapow, *Wörterbuch* II, 362. [R.K.R.]

92. For this Egyptian cosmology, see H. Frankfort et al., *The Intellectual Adventure of Ancient Man* (Chicago: University of Chicago Press, 1946) 45–47; D. Kurth, *Den Himmel stützen. Die "Twꜣ pt"-Szenen in den ägyptischen Tempeln der griechisch-römischen Epoche* (Bruxelles: Fondation Égyptologique Reine Élisabeth, 1975) 90, 98. [R.K.R.]

93. Cf. the Egyptian *harmachis*, "Horus who is on the horizon."

94. For a discussion of the seven young men, see Dieterich, *Mithrasliturgie* 70–75. In the Mithras mysteries the seven grades of initiates were each under the tutelage of a planetary deity. See Merkelbach, *Weihegrade* 13–14.

and a god descending, a god immensely great, having a bright appearance, youthful, golden-haired, with a white tunic and a golden crown and trousers,[95] and hold-
700   ing in his right hand a golden / shoulder of a young bull: this is the Bear which
moves and turns heaven around, moving upward and downward in accordance with
the hour.[96] Then you will see lightning bolts leaping from his eyes and stars from
his body.

705   And at once / make a long bellowing sound, straining your belly, that you may
excite the five senses; bellow long until out of breath, and again kiss the phylacteries, and say:

710   "MOKRIMO PHERIMO PHERERI, life of me, NN: stay! Dwell in / my soul![97] Do
not abandon me, for ENTHO PHENEN THROPIŌTH commands you."

And gaze upon the god while bellowing long; and greet him in this manner:
"Hail, O Lord, O Master of the water! Hail, O Founder of the earth! Hail, O
715   Ruler of the wind! O Bright Lightener /, PROPROPHEGGĒ EMETHIRI ARTENTEPI
THĒTH MIMEŌ YENARŌ PHYRCHECHŌ PSĒRI DARIŌ PHRĒ PHRĒLBA! Give revelation, O lord, concerning the NN matter. O lord, while being born again, I am pass-
720   ing away; while growing and having grown, / I am dying; while being born from a
life-generating birth, I am passing on, released to death—as you have founded, as
you have decreed, and have established the mystery. I am PHEROURA MIOURI."

After you have said these things, he will immediately respond with a revelation.
725   Now you will grow weak in soul and will not be in yourself, when he answers you.
He speaks the oracle to you in verse, and after speaking he will depart. But you
remain silent, since you will be able to comprehend all these matters by yourself; for
730   at a later time / you will remember infallibly the things spoken by the great god,
even if the oracle contained myriads of verses.

If you also wish to use a fellow initiate, so that he alone may hear with you the
735   things spoken, let him remain pure with you for [seven] / days, and abstain from
meat and the bath. And even if you are alone, and you undertake the things com-
municated by the god, you speak as if prophesying in ecstasy. And if you also wish
740   to show him, then judge whether he is completely worthy as a man /: treat him just
as if in his place you were being judged in the matter of immortalization, and whisper to him the first prayer, of which the beginning is "First origin of my origin,[98]
745   AEĒIOYŌ." And say the successive things as an initiate, over his / head, in a soft
voice,[99] so that he may not hear, as you are anointing his face with the mystery. This
immortalization takes place three times a year. And if anyone, O child, after the
750   teaching, wishes to disobey, then for him it will no longer / be in effect.

95. The description of the god Mithras agrees with extant pictures. See esp. the frescoes from Dura
Europos, published in M. J. Vermaseren, *Corpus inscriptionum et monumentorum religionis Mithriacae*
(Den Haag: Nijhoff, 1956, 1960); see also the discussion in Dieterich, *Mithrasliturgie* 76–78.

96. For the interpretation of this passage, see Dieterich, *Mithrasliturgie* 76–78, 234; R. Beck, "Interpreting the Ponza Zodiac," *Journal of Mithraic Studies* 1 (1976) : 1–19, esp. 2; 2 (1978) : 87–147, esp.
120–27; R. L. Gordon and J. R. Hinnels, "Some New Photographs of Well-known Mithraic Monuments," ibid. 2 (1978) : 213–19. Cf. also Griffith and Thompson, *The Leyden Papyrus*, col. V. 1 with
note; te Velde, *Seth, God of Confusion* 86–89.

97. The combination of ζωή "life," and ψυχή "soul," suggests erotic overtones (see Juvenal, *Sat.* 6.
195 for ζωὴ καὶ ψυχή, and the note on "soul," p. 337 below. [E.N.O.] In fact, sculptures portraying
Eros and Psyche were found in the Mithras sanctuaries at Capua and under the Church of S. Prisca in
Rome. See Merkelbach, *Weihegrade* 22–24, and photos on pp. 68–69.

98. For this prayer, see *PGM* IV. 486–537.

99. Cf. on this point Firmicus Maternus, *De err. prof. rel.* 22. 1: *lento murmure susurrat*, "he whis-
pers with a soft murmur"; Apuleius, *Met.* 1.3. See also G. Scholem, *Jewish Gnosticism, Merkabah Mysticism,
and Talmudic Tradition* (New York: The Jewish Theological Seminary of America, [2]1965) 58.

Instruction for the rite: Take a sun scarab which has twelve rays, and make it fall into a deep, turquoise cup, at the time when the moon is invisible;[100] put in together with it the seed of the fruit pulp of the lotus, / and honey; and, after grinding it, prepare a cake. And at once you will see it [viz., the scarab] moving forward and eating; and when it has consumed it, it immediately dies. Pick it up and throw it into a glass vessel of excellent rose oil, as much as you wish; and / spreading sacred sand in a pure manner, set the vessel on it, and say the formula over the vessel for seven days, while the sun is in midheaven:

"I have consecrated you, that your material may be useful to me, to NN alone, IE IA ĒEĒ O Y EIA, that you may prove useful to me / alone, for I am PHŌR PHORA PHŌS PHOTIZAAS" (others: "PHŌR PHŌR OPHOTHEI XAAS").

On the 7th day pick up the scarab, and bury it with myrrh and Mendesian wine[101] and fine linen; and put it away in a flourishing bean field. / Then, after you have entertained and feasted together, put away, in a pure manner, the ointment for the immortalization.

If you want to show this to someone else, take the juice of the herb called *kentritis*, and smear, it, along with rose oil, over the eyes of the one you wish; / and he will see so clearly that he will amaze you. I have not found a greater spell than this in the world. Ask the god for what you want, and he will give to you.

Now the encounter with the great god is like this: Having obtained the above-mentioned herb / *kentritis*, at the conjunction [of the sun and the moon] occurring in the Lion,[102] take the juice and, after mixing it with honey and myrrh, write on a leaf of the persea tree the eight-lettered name, as given below.[103] And having kept yourself pure for 3 days in advance, come at morning to face the sunrise; / lick off the leaf while you show it to the sun, and then he [the sun god] will listen to you attentively. Begin to prepare [the scarab] on the new moon in the lion, according to the god's [reckoning].[104]

Now this is the name: "I EE OO IAI." Lick this up, so that you may be protected; and rolling up the leaf /, throw it into the rose oil. Many times have I used the spell, and have wondered greatly.

But the god said to me:

"Use the ointment no longer, but, after casting it into the river, [you must] consult while wearing the great mystery / of the scarab revitalized through the 25 living birds,[105] and consult once a month, at full moon, instead of 3 times a year."

The *kentritis* plant grows from the month of Payni, in the regions of the / black earth, and is similar to the erect verbena. This is how to recognize it: the wing of an ibis is smeared, the 'black edge' weakened by the juice, and when the feathers are touched, they fall off. After the lord / pointed this out, it was found in Menelaitis in Phalagry, at the river banks, near the *besas* plant. It is of a single stem, and reddish down to the root; and the leaves are rather crinkled and have fruit / like the tip of wild asparagus. It is similar to the so-called *talapēs*, like the wild beet.

755
760
765
770
775
780
785
790
795
800
805
810

100. Literally, "at the seizure of the moon," probably designating the new moon.

101. Cf. *PGM* I. 85–86 and n.

102. That is, at the new moon.

103. See *PGM IV.* 788.

104. The new moon of god, according to the heavens, in contrast to the new moon of man, according to the calendar.

105. The allusion to the twenty-five birds is obscure; it may be related to the hours, so that the scarab Khepri is reborn in the first hour of a new day, after the passage of twelve hours of day and twelve hours of night during the previous day.

Now the phylacteries require this procedure: copy that for the right [arm] onto
815   the skin / of a black sheep, with myrrh ink, and after tying it with sinews of
the same animal, put it on; and copy that [for] the left [arm] onto the skin of a
white sheep, and use the same procedure. The left one is very full of "PROSTHY-
820   MĒRI" /, and has this memorandum: [106]

"So speaking, he drove through the trench the single-hoofed horses." [107]
"And men gasping among grievous slaughters." [108]
"And they washed off their profuse sweat in the sea." [109]
"You will dare to lift up your mighty spear against Zeus." [110]

825   / Zeus went up the mountain with a golden bullock and a silver dagger. Upon all he
bestowed a share, only to Amara did he not give, but he said: [111]
"Let go of what you have, and then you will receive, PSINŌTHER NŌPSITHER
THERNŌPSI" (add the usual). [112]
*Tr.: M. W. Meyer.

PGM IV. 830

830   *. . . "Ares endured, when Otos and mighty Ephialtes . . . him." [113]
Tr.: Hubert Martin, Jr.

PGM IV. 831–32

*Charm to restrain anger: "Will you dare to raise your mighty spear against
Zeus?" [114]
Tr.: R. F. Hock.

PGM IV. 833–34

*To Get Friends: "Let . . . seize, lest we become a joy to our enemies." [115]
Tr.: Hubert Martin, Jr.

PGM IV. 835–49

835   *From 53 years and 9 months on Hermes took the period up to 10 years and 9
months, from which he assigned to himself 20 months, which would be 55 years 5
840   months; then to Aphrodite 8 months, / which would thus be 56 years 1 month;

106. The relationship of the poetic quotations in the following, which repeat those in ll. 468–74,
and the Mithras liturgy is obscure. They seem unrelated; see Wessely, *Griechische Zauberpapyrus* (see
above, Introduction, n. 24), which shows a blank after l. 820 and a sign indicating a new paragraph. For
a different view, cf. Dieterich, *Mithrasliturgie* 84. [M.S.]
107. Homer, *Il.* 10. 564.
108. Homer, *Il.* 10. 521.
109. Homer, *Il.* 10. 572.
110. Homer, *Il.* 8. 424. See *PGM* IV. 467–68 above and 830–31 below. Probably this verse served
as a spell to restrain anger, but it may be misplaced here.
111. That these verses are part of the ὑπόμνημα ("the memorandum," l. 821) seems unlikely. More
probably, a heading has been lost, and the verses contain an altogether independent spell. Story spells
(*historiolae*) were ancient (see Faulkner, *Coffin Texts*, nos. 7, 75, 148, 154, 157, 158, etc.). They usually
tell of a happening such as they are meant to produce (cf., e.g., *PGM* VII. 199–201; IV. 1471–79). This
story tells of a person compelled or bribed to give up something; it could have been used to make a
person give up anger. Hence it may have been attached to the Homeric verse for that purpose and was
interpolated here. The name Amara is obscure; it could mean "the bitter woman" (Hebrew or Latin; cf.
Ru 1 : 20, Vulgate).
112. Cf. *Pistis Sophia* 136 and 142, also with permutations of IAŌ. PSINŌTHER is Egyptian for "the
sons of god." [R.K.R.] See also *PGM* III. 186 and n. See Glossary, s.v. "THERNOPSI formula."
113. Homer, *Il.* 5. 385. The same verse occurs in *PGM* IV. 474.
114. Homer, *Il.* 6. 424, quoted also *PGM* IV. 468, 824.
115. Homer, *Il.* 10. 193. See *PGM* IV. 470, where the same verse is quoted.

then to Helios 19 months, which would be 57 years 8 months. In this period assigned to Helios, that is to the 19 months, devote yourself to what you seek. After this he assigned to Ares 15 months, which would be 58 years 11 months. This is a hostile period. / Then to Selene 25 months, which would be 61 years. They are   845
good. Then to Zeus 12 months, which would be 62 years. They are good. Then to Kronos 30 months, which would be 64½ years. They are bad for the body; within them also are the dangerous points.
*Tr.: W. C. Grese. The section appears to be a fragment from an astrological work about the influence of the planets upon the periods of life.

PGM IV. 850–929

*Charm of Solomon that produces a trance[116] (works both on boys and on   850
adults): I swear to you by the holy gods and the heavenly gods not to share the procedure of Solomon with anyone and certainly not to use it for something questionable[117] / unless a matter of necessity forces you, lest perchance wrath be pre-   855
served for you.

Formula to be spoken: "OURIŌR AMĒN IM TAR CHŌB KLAMPHŌB PHRĒ[118] PHRŌR PTAR OUSIRI SAIŌB TĒLŌ KABĒ / MANATATHŌR ASIŌRIKŌR BĒEINŌR AMOUN ŌM MĒNICHTHA MACHTHA CHTHARA AMACHTHA AOU ALAKAMBŌT BĒSINŌR APHĒSIŌR PHRĒPH AMĒI OUR LAMASIR CHĒRIŌB PITRĒM / PHĒŌPH NIRIN ALLANNATHATH CHĒRIŌCH ŌNĒ BOUSIRI NINOUNO AMANAL GAGŌSARIĒR MĒNIAM TLĒR OOO AA ETNĒ OUSIRI OUSIRI OURISI OURISI MĒNĒMB MNĒM / BRABĒL   870
TNĒKAIŌB. Hear me, that is, my holy voice, because I call upon your holy names, and reveal to me concerning the thing which I want, through the NN man or little boy, for otherwise I will not defend your holy and undefiled / names. Come to me,   875
you who became Hesies and were carried away by a river; inspire the NN man or boy concerning that which I ask you: BARBĒTH MNŌR ARARIAK TARĒRIM ŌAR TĒRŌK SANIŌR MĒNIK PHAUEK / DAPHORIOUMIN LARIŌR ĒTNIAMIM KNŌS CHA-   880
LAKTHIR KRŌPHĒR PHĒSIMŌT PRĒBIB KNALA ĒRIBĒTIM GNŌRI. Come to me through the NN man or little boy and tell me accurately since / I speak your names   885
which thrice-greatest Hermes[119] wrote in Heliopolis with hieroglyphic letters: ARBAKŌRIPH MĒNIAM ŌBAŌB ABNIŌB MĒRIM BAIAX CHENŌR PHĒNIM ŌRA ŌRĒSIOU OUSIRI[120] PNIAMOUSIRI / PHRĒOUSIRI HŌRIOUSIRI NAEIŌROUSIRI MĒN-   890
IMOUSIRI MNĒKOUSIRI PHLĒKOUSIRI PĒLĒLOUSIRI ŌNIŌ RABKOUSIRI ANIŌBOUSIRI AMĒAOUSIRI ANŌROUSIRI AMĒNĒPHĒOUSIRI / AMĒNIOUSIRI XŌNIŌR   895
ĒOUROUSIRI. Enter into him and reveal to me concerning the NN matter."
After you have purified the designated man [by keeping him] from intercourse for 3 days, you yourself also being pure, enter together with him.[121] After you have taken him up / to an open place, seat him on unbaked bricks, dress him and give   900
him an anubian head of wheat[122] and a falconweed plant so that he will be protected. Gird yourself with a palm fiber of a male date palm, extend your hands / up   905

116. Literally, the title means "Solomon's Collapse," an indication of ecstatic seizure.
117. Or "for trivial reasons."
118. The names include the gods Prē, Osiris, and Amon.
119. That is, Hermes Trismegistos. For this name, see *PGM* VII. 551 and n.
120. The following list, after "Osiris," contains a series of compound deities whose second element is the god Osiris, but only some can be identified: Pre-Osiris, Horus-Osiris, Onnuris-Osiris, Amenophis-Osiris, and Amon-Osiris. [R.K.R.]
121. The following account has a parallel in *Test. Sol.* I. 3, ed. McCown, p. *8, ll. 5–15.
122. The meaning of Anubis's head of grain is not known. On the god Anubis, see J.-C. Grenier, *Anubis Alexandrin et Romain*, EPRO 57 (Leiden: Brill, 1977), esp. p. 139 for ear of grain. [R.K.R.]

to heaven, toward the rays of the sun, and say the formula 7 times. Next make an
offering of male frankincense after pouring out wine, beer, honey, or milk of a black
910   cow onto grapevine wood. Then say the formula 7 times just into the ear / of the
NN man or little boy, and right away he will fall down. But you sit down on the
bricks and make your inquiry, and he will describe everything with truth. You
915   should crown him with a garland of indigenous wormwood, / both him and you,
for god delights in the plant.

  Dismissal of the lord: into the ear of NN: "ANANAK ARBEOUĒRI AEĒIOYŌ."

  If he tarries, sacrifice on grapevine charcoal a sesame seed [and] black cumin
920   while saying: / "ANANAK ŌRBEOUSIRI AEĒIOYŌ, go away, lord, to your own thrones
and protect him, NN, from all evil." You learned thoroughly; keep it secret.

  The awakening[123] [of the man or boy] is as follows: Stand away from the boy or
925   man, having your / palms spread on your buttocks, your feet together on the
ground, recite [the following] often until he is moved either toward the right or
toward the left: "AMOUN ĒEI[124] ABRIATH KICHŌP ŌTEM PITH." Then as a dog.[125]
*Tr.: W. C. Grese.

PGM IV. 930–1114

930   *Charm that produces a direct vision:[126] *Prayer for divine alliance*, which you
are to say first toward the sunrise, then the same first prayer is to be spoken to a
lamp. Whenever you seek divinations, be dressed in the garb of a prophet, shod
935   with fibers of the doum palm and / your head crowned with a spray from an olive
tree—but the spray should have a single-shooted garlic tied around the middle.
Clasp a pebble numbered 3663[127] to your breasts, and in this way make your invocation.

  Hymn:[128]

   "Hail,[129] serpent, and[130] stout lion, natural
940   Sources of fire.[131] / And hail, clear water and
   Lofty-leafed tree,[132] and you who gather up

---

123. The translation of this difficult term follows Preisendanz (see apparatus ad loc.).

124. AMOUN ĒEI is equivalent to Egyptian "Amon comes" (?), with Greek ηει standing for Egyptian *iy*. [R.K.R.]

125. Probably referring to barking; cf. *PGM* IV. 1006.

126. This is equivalent to the type of Demotic spell called *pḥ-nṯr*-spell, literally, a "god's arrival" spell. See J. H. Johnson, "Louvre E 3229: A Demotic Magical Text," *Enchoria* 7 (1977): 90–91.

127. According to Dornseiff, *Das Alphabet* 184, the mystical number is 3663 and refers to BAIN-CHŌŌŌCH (the numerical value of the Greek letters being $2 + 1 + 10 + 50 + 600 + 800 + 800 + 600 = 3663$.

128. Preisendanz ends the hymn at l. 948, but the petition to the god continues through l. 955. Ll. 949–54 include references to the spell for a direct vision, the lamp divination, and the prayer for divine alliance. Thus the present form of these lines comes from the time when the spell was put together. Ll. 949–54 contain vestiges of verse and originally may have been part of the hymn which was composed by the final author; or they may be a prose addition to part of an earlier hymn, perhaps substituting for, or expanding the petition in, the original hymn. [W.C.G.]

129. These dactylic hexameters also form the reconstructed Hymn 3; see Preisendanz, vol. II, p. 238.

130. τε, though necessary to the sense, mars the hexameter. [E.N.O.]

131. A possible echo of a pre-Socratic expression, but to the author of this spell this phrase must have had a much different meaning. Preisendanz wants to emend and read Φύσι καὶ πυρὸς ἀρχή ("O Nature and fire's origin"), but the emendation is more clever than persuasive. For Physis as a goddess, see *PGM* I. 310 and n. [E.N.O.]

132. An adaptation of Homer, *Od.* 4. 458, which in the context of the spell indicates that the author knew not only the Homeric verse but the whole passage as well. [E.N.O.]

Clover from golden fields of beans,[133] and who
Cause gentle foam to gush forth from pure mouths.
Scarab, who drive the orb of fertile fire,
O self-engendered one,[134] because you are
Two-syllabled, AĒ, and are the first-
Appearing one, / nod me assent, I pray,   945
Because your mystic symbols I declare,

ĒŌ AI OY AMERR OOUŌTH IYIŌĒ MARMARAUŌTH LAILAM SOUMARTA.

Be gracious unto me, first-father, and
May you yourself send strength as my companion.

Stay allied, lord, and listen to me / through the charm that produces direct vision   950
which I do today, and reveal to me concerning those things I ask you through the
lamp divination for direct vision which I do today, I, NN, IY EYĒ OŌ AEĒ IAEĒ AIAĒ
E AI EY ĒIE ŌŌŌŌŌ EY ĒŌ / IAŌAI" (repeat).[135]   955

   Light-bringing charm: Crown your head with the same spray, stand in the same
fashion facing the lamp, close your eyes and recite this spell 7 times.

   Spell: "I call upon you, the living god, / fiery, invisible begetter of light, IAĒL   960
PEIPTA PHŌS ZA PAI PHTHENTHA PHŌSZA PYRI BELIA IAŌ IAO EYŌ OEĒ A ŌY EOI A
E Ē I O Y Ō give your strength, rouse your daimon, / enter into this fire, fill it with a   965
divine spirit, and show me your might. Let there be opened for me the house of the
all-powerful god ALBALAL,[136] who is in this light. / Let there be light, breadth,   970
depth, length, height, brightness, and let him who is inside shine through, the lord
BOUĒL[137] PHTHA PHTHA PHTHAĒL PHTHA ABAI BAINCHŌŌŌCH, now, now; immediately, immediately; quickly, quickly."

   Light-retaining spell that is spoken once / in order that the light-magic might   975
remain with you, for sometimes when you invoke the god-bringing spell darkness
is produced. Therefore, you should conjure in the following way.

   Spell: "I conjure you, holy light, holy brightness, breadth, depth, length, height,
brightness, by the holy names / which I have spoken and am now going to speak.   980
By IAŌ SABAŌTH ARBATHIAŌ SESENGENBARPHARAGGĒS ABLANATHANALBA AK-
RAMMACHAMARI AI AI IAO AX AX INAX, remain by me in the present hour, until I
pray to the god / and learn about the things I desire."   985

   God-bringing spell to be spoken three times with your eyes open: "I call upon
you, the greatest god, sovereign HŌROS HARPOKRATĒS ALKIB HARSAMŌSI IŌAI
DAGENNOUTH RARACHARAI / ABRAIAŌTH, you who enlighten the universe and by   990
your own power illumine the whole world, god of gods, benefactor, AO IAŌ EAĒY,
you who direct night and day, AI AŌ, handle and steer the tiller,[138] restrain the ser-

---

133. This refers to the Egyptian bean from the Nymphean lotus mentioned in *PGM* IV. 1110. Thus
the reference is again to Horus atop the lotus. [R.K.R.]

134. "Self-generation" is a common epithet of Khepri (see Glossary, s.v. "Scarab") and is a pun on
his name which means "to come into being." [R.K.R.] See also J. Whittaker, "Self-generating Principles
in Second-century Gnostic Systems," in B. Layton, ed., *The Rediscovery of Gnosticism*, vol. I: The School
of Valentinus, *Studies in the History of Religions* (*Supplements to Numen*) 41 (Leiden: Brill, 1980)
176–93.

135. Here the papyrus has the sign //, perhaps signifying doubling. See below, ll. 973 and 1046 (in
the papyrus).

136. For this name, see T. Hopfner, "Orientalisch-Religionsgeschichtliches aus den griechischen
Zauberpapyri Ägyptens," *Archiv Orientální* 3 (1931): 341.

137. This name is not attested elsewhere.

138. A reference to the solar bark of Re and the serpent Apophis, who attempts daily to devour the
sun. Cf. Pritchard, *ANET* 6–7; E. Hornung and A. Badawy, "Apophis," *LdÄ* 1 (1975): 350–51.
[R.K.R.]

995   pent, / you Good, holy [139] Daimon, whose name is HARBATHANŌPS IAOAI, whom sunrises and sunsets hymn when you arise and set. You who are praised among all
1000   gods, angels and daimons, come and appear to me, god of gods, HŌROS / HARPOKRATĒS ALKIB HARSAMŌSI IAŌ AI DAGENNOUTH RARACHARAI ABRAIAŌTH. Enter, appear to me, lord, because I call upon you as the three baboons [140] call upon
1005   you, who speak / your holy name in a symbolic fashion, A EE ĒĒĒ IIII OOOOO YYYYY ŌŌŌŌŌŌŌ (speak as a baboon). Enter in, appear to me, lord, for I speak your greatest names: BARBARAI BARBARAŌTH AREMPSOUS PERTAŌMĒCH PERA /
1010   KŌNĒTHCH IAŌ BAL BĒL BOL BE SRŌ IAOĒI OYEĒI EĒI EOYĒI AĒI ĒI IAO ĒI. You who are seated on the top of the world and judge the universe, surrounded by the
1015   circle of truth and honesty, / IYAĒ IŌAI, enter in; appear to me, lord, to me, the one who is before fire and snow and in the midst of them, because my name is BAINCHŌŌŌCH. I am the one who is from heaven; my name is BALSAMĒS. Enter in, ap
1020   pear to me, [141] / lord, you who have a great name, you whom we all have each in our own heart; your name is BARPHANNĒTH RALPHAI NINTHER CHOUCHAI. You who break apart rocks and change the names of gods, enter in, appear to me, lord, you
1025   who have in fire your power / and your strength, SESENGENBARPHARAGGĒS. You who are seated within the 7 poles, AEĒIOYŌ, you who have on your head a golden crown and in your hand a Memnonian staff [142] with which you send out the gods,
1030   your name is BARBARIĒL BARBARAIĒL god / BARBARAĒL BĒL BOUĒL. Enter in, lord, and answer me with your holy voice in order that I might hear clearly and un
1035   erringly concerning the NN matter, IYEYĒ OŌAEĒ (formula) IAEĒ AIAĒ EAI EYĒIE / ŌŌŌŌŌ IYĒŌ IAŌ AI."

Charm of compulsion: If somehow he delays, say in addition this following incantation (say the incantation one or 3 times): "The great, living god commands you, he who lives for eons of eons, who shakes together, who thunders, who cre
1040   ated every / soul and race, IAŌ AŌI ŌIA AIŌ IŌA ŌAI. Enter in, appear to me, lord, happy, kind, gentle, glorious, not angry, because I conjure you by the lord,
1045   IAŌ AŌI ŌIA AIŌ IŌA ŌAI APTA PHŌIRA ZAZOU / CHAMĒ. Enter in, lord, appear to me happy, kind, gentle, [glorious,] [143] not angry" (repeat). [144]

Salutation said once after the god enters. While holding the pebble, say: "Hail, lord, god of gods, benefactor, HŌROS HARPOKRATĒS ALKIB HARSAMŌSI IAŌ AI
1050   DA/GENNOUTH RARACHARAI ABRAIAŌ; let your Hours which you traverse be welcomed; let your Glories [145] be welcomed forever, lord."

---

139. The occurrence of "holy" between "good" and "daimon" makes it doubtful that the familiar Good Daimon is meant. See Glossary, s.v.; see also the apparatus ad loc.

140. Baboons were thought to praise the sun when they chattered at it. For a representation, see A. Piankoff, *Mythological Papyri* (New York: Pantheon Books, 1957), vol. I, 39, fig. 22 and pl. I. See also Bonnet, *RÄRG* 7–8, s.v. "Affe." [R.K.R.] On the magician's imitation of the "language" of animals, see Hopfner, *OZ* I, sections 778–80. Understanding this language of animals belongs to the traditional phenomenology of the "divine man" and magician. See, e.g., Porphyry, *De abst.* 3. 3, and on the whole topic H. Güntert, *Von der Sprache der Götter und Geister* (Halle: Niemeyer, 1921); Betz, *Lukian* 28–38.

141. Preisendanz has φάνη θίμοι, which should be read as φάνηθί μοι, as in *PGM* IV. 1001, 1006, 1015, 1024, 1041, 1045. [W.C.G.]

142. For Memnon as a deified hero in Egypt, see A. Bataille, *Les Memnonia* (Cairo: L'Institut français d'archéologie orientale, 1952) 1–21; as recipient of worship, see D. Wildung, *Imhotep und Amenhotep* (Munich: Deutscher Kunstverlag, 1977) 299, no. 82. [R.K.R.]

143. An addition by Preisendanz in order to conform to *PGM* IV. 1042. But such consistency is not always to be expected. Cf. ll. 1063–65 with 1079–80.

144. See the note above on *PGM* IV. 955, regarding the sign for doubling.

145. Cf. *PGM* I. 199 and n.

Charm to retain the god: When he comes in, after greeting him, step with your left heel on the big toe of his right foot, and he will not / go away unless you raise   1055
your heel from his toe [146] and at the same time say the dismissal.

Dismissal: Close your eyes, release the pebble which you have been holding, lift the crown up from your head and your heel from his / toe, and, while keeping your   1060
eyes closed, say 3 times: "I give thanks to you lord BAINCHŌŌŌCH, who is BAL-SAMĒS. Go away, go away, lord, into your own heavens, into your own palaces, into your own course. Keep me healthy, unharmed, not plagued by ghosts, free from calamity and without terror. Hear me during my / lifetime."   1065

Dismissal of the brightness: "CHŌŌ CHŌŌ ŌCHŌŌCH, [147] holy brightness." In order that the brightness also go away: [148] "Go away, holy brightness, go away, beautiful and holy light of the highest god, AIAŌNA." Say it one time with closed eyes, smear yourself / with Coptic kohl; [149] smear yourself by means of a golden probe.   1070

Phylactery for the rite, which you must wear wrapped around you for the protection of your whole body: On [a strip] [150] from a linen cloth taken from a marble statue of Harpokrates in any temple [whatever] / write with myrrh these things: "I   1075
am HOROS ALKIB HARSAMŌSIS IAŌ AI DAGENNOUTH RARACHARAI ABRAIAŌTH, son of ISIS ATHTHA BATHTHA and of OSIRIS OSOR[ON]NŌPHRIS; keep me healthy, unharmed, not plagued by ghosts and without terror during my / lifetime." Place   1080
inside the strip of cloth an everliving plant; [151] roll it up and tie it 7 times with threads of Anubis. [152] Wear it around your neck whenever you perform the rite. /

Preparation: Take broad cords of papyrus, tie them to the four corners of the   1085
room so that they form an *X*. In the middle of the *X* attach a ring-shaped mat made from single-stemmed wormwood. Provide / a glazed lamp [153] with a wick called   1090
reed grass, and rub the wick itself with fat of a black, male, firstborn and first-reared ram. Fill the lamp with good olive oil, and place it in the middle, / on the mat.   1095
Light the lamp and stand in the previously mentioned fashion, facing the sunrise, whenever you perform the rite, without distinguishing the days. [154] Purify yourself / from everything three days in advance, and rub the wick beforehand with the   1100
fat of a black, male, firstborn and first-reared ram.

Signs of the lamp: After saying the light-bringing spell, open your eyes and you will see / the light of the lamp becoming like a vault. Then while closing your eyes   1105
say (*differently*: 3 . . . [155] after saying 3 times), and after opening your eyes you will see all things wide-open and the greatest brightness within, but the lamp shining nowhere. Then you will see the god / seated on a lotus, [156] decorated with rays, his   1110

146. The translation follows the interpretation by Preisendanz; see the apparatus ad loc.

147. CHŌŌ CHŌŌ ŌCHŌŌCH corresponds to Coptic KŌ KŌ Ō KAKE, "depart, depart, O darkness." [R.K.R.]

148. An attempt on the part of the redactor of the papyrus text to explain the need for a second dismissal.

149. Powdered antimony used as eyepaint.

150. Addition by Eitrem on the basis of l. 1081.

151. A general name for plants that seem to live a long time. See R. Strömberg, *Griechische Pflanzennamen*, *Göteborgs Högskolas Årsskrift* 46 (Göteborg: Elanders, 1940) 103.

152. On the Anubian thread, see *PGM* I. 147 and n.

153. On this type of faïence, see *PGM* IV. 55 and n.

154. That is, the charm can be performed on any day. For charms that can be used only on certain days, cf. *PGM* III. 275–81; VII. 155–67, 284–89.

155. The text is obscure at this point but seems to include alternative instructions. See apparatus ad loc.

156. The deity seated on the lotus flower is Harpokrates, invoked here in ll. 989, 999–1000, and 1074–75. This standard depiction of Harpokrates is found in all the media during the Greco-Roman

right hand raised in greeting and left [holding] a flail, while being carried in the hands of 2 angels with 12 rays around them.

*Tr.: W. C. Grese (ll. 930–38; 949–1114) and E. N. O'Neil (hymnic sections, ll. 939–48). This spell is a composite, made by combining a lamp divination with a charm for a direct vision and including an introductory prayer for divine alliance. The repetition in the present charm (note especially the two dismissals in ll. 1057ff. and 1065ff. and the explanation in ll. 1066ff.) is a result of the inclusion of similar elements from both of the charms here combined.

PGM IV. 1115–66

1115   *Hidden[157] stele:[158] "Hail, entire system of the aerial spirit,[159] PHŌGALŌA. Hail, spirit who extends from heaven to earth, ERDĒNEU, and from earth which is in the

1120   middle chamber of the / universe unto the borders of the abyss, MEREMŌGGA.[160] Hail, spirit who enters into me, convulses me, and leaves me kindly according to

1125   the will of god, IŌĒ ZANŌPHIE. / Hail, beginning and end of the immovable nature, DŌRYGLAOPHŌN. Hail, revolution of untiring service by heavenly bodies, RŌGYEU ANAMI PELĒGEŌN ADARA EIŌPH. Hail, radiance of the universe subordi-

1130   nate / to the solar ray, IEO YĒŌ IAĒ AI ĒOY OEI. Hail, orb of the night-illuminating, unequally shining moon, AIŌ RĒMA RŌDOUŌPIA. Hail, all spirits of the aerial im-

1135   ages / RŌMIDOUĒ AGANASOU ŌTHAUA. Hail to those to whom the greeting is given with blessing, to brothers and sisters, to holy men and holy women. O great, greatest, round, incomprehensible figure of the universe, heavenly ENRŌCHES-

1140   YĒL; / in heaven, PELĒTHEU; of ether, IŌGARAA; in the ether, THŌPYLEO DARDY; watery, IŌĒDES; earthy, PEREPHIA; fiery, APHTHALYA; windlike, IŌIE ĒŌ AYA; lumi-

1145   nous, ALAPIE; dark-looking, / IEPSERIA; shining with heavenly light, ADAMALŌR; moist, fiery, and cold spirit. I glorify you, god of gods, the one who brought order to the universe, AREŌ PIEUA; the one who gathered together the abyss at the invisi-

1150   ble foundation of its position, PERŌ MYSĒL / O PENTŌNAX; the one who separated heaven and earth and covered the heaven with eternal, golden wings, RŌDĒRY OYŌA; the one who fixed the earth on eternal foundations, ALĒIOŌA; the one who

1155   hung up / the ether high above the earth, AIE ŌĒ IOYA; the one who scattered the air with self-moving breezes, ŌIE OYŌ; the one who put the water roundabout,

1160   ŌREPĒLYA; the one who raises up hurricanes, ŌRISTHAUA; / the one who thunders, THEPHICHYŌNĒL; the one who hurls lightnings, OURĒNES; the one who rains, OS-IŌRNI PHEUGALGA; the one who shakes, PERATŌNĒL; the one who produces living creatures, ARĒSIGYLŌA; the god of the Aions; you are great, lord, god, ruler of the

---

period. Harpokrates holds the flail, the symbol of royalty, here interpreted as a whip. See A. M. El-Kachab, "Some Gem-Amulets Depicting Harpocrates Seated on a Lotus Flower," *JEA* 57 (1971): 132–45, esp. 133–34. For the gesture of greeting, a modification under the influence of Helios instead of the more common gesture of finger sucking, see S. Morenz and J. Schubert, *Der Gott auf der Blume* (Ascona: Artibus Asiae, 1954). [R.K.R.]

157. The exact meaning of ἀπόκρυφος is uncertain here. LSJ, s.v., II, gives as possible meanings "obscure, recondite, hard to understand." More likely is the meaning "secret," for which see Bauer, s.v.; cf. also *PGM* XIII. 344, 731, 732, 1057, 1078.

158. The term *stēlē* occurs in the *PGM* with several meanings. Originally it refers to a plate of stone or metal on which texts could be inscribed (e.g., VIII. 42), but most of the time the term is a literary device suggesting the text was copied from a stone slab. It can also refer to an amulet in the shape of a *stēlē* (as in *PGM* VII. 215; see the picture *Tafel I, Abbildung* 1 in Preisendanz, vol. II).

159. The prayer is addressed to the god Aion (see l. 1164). Cf. Reitzenstein, *Poimandres* 277–78; Bousset, *Religionsgeschichtliche Studien* 200, 208–10. See also *PGM* I. 309 and n.

160. For this imagery, see H. O. Lange, *Der magische Papyrus Harris* (Copenhagen: Høst, 1927) 74; furthermore, *DMP* col. XX, l. 28 (p. 133); *PGM* IV. 1210. [R.K.R.]

All, ARCHIZŌ / NYON THĒNAR METHŌR PARY PHĒZŌR THAPSAMYDŌ MARŌMI   1165
CHĒLŌPSA."
*Tr.: W. C. Grese.

PGM IV. 1167–1226

*Stele that is useful for all things; it even delivers from death. Do not investigate
what is in it.

Formula: "I praise you,[161] the one and blessed of the eons and / father of the   1170
world, with cosmic prayers. Come to me, you who filled the whole universe with
air, who hung up the fire from the [heavenly] water and separated the earth from
the water. Pay attention, form, spirit, / earth and sea, to a word from the one who   1175
is wise concerning divine Necessity, and accept my words as fiery darts, because
I am a man,[162] the most beautiful creature of the god in heaven, made out of
spirit, / dew, and earth. Heaven, be opened; accept my words. Listen, Helios, fa-   1180
ther of the world; I call upon you with your name AŌ EY ĒOI AIOĒ YEŌA OUOR-
ZARA LAMANTHATHRĒ KANTHIOPER / GARPSARTHRĒ MENLARDAPA KENTHĒR   1185
DRYOMEN THRANDRĒTHRĒ IABE ZELANTHI BER ZATHRĒ ZAKENTI BIOLLITHRĒ
AĒŌ OYŌ ĒŌ OŌ RAMIATHA AĒŌ ŌYŌ OYŌ ŌAYŌ: the only one having the origi-
nal / element. You are the holy and powerful name considered sacred by all the an-   1190
gels; protect me, so- and-so, from every excess of power and from every violent act.
Yes, do this, / lord, god of gods, IALDAZAŌ BLATHAM MACHŌR PHRIX AĒ KEŌPH   1195
EĒA DYMEŌ PHERPHRITHŌ IACHTHŌ PSYCHEŌ PHIRITHMEŌ RŌSERŌTH THAMA-
STRAPHATI RIMPSAŌCH IALTHE MEACHI ARBATHANŌPS, / creator of the world,   1200
creator of the universe, lord, god of gods, MARMARIŌ IAŌ. I have spoken of your
unsurpassable glory,[163] you who created gods, archangels, and decans. The ten
thousands of angels stood by [you] and exalted / the heaven, and the lord witnessed   1205
to your Wisdom,[164] which is Aion, IEOYĒOĒ IAĒAIĒOĒYOEI, and said that you are as
strong as he is. I invoke your hundred-lettered / name[165] which extends from the   1210
sky to the depth of the earth; save me, for you are always ever rejoicing in saving
those who are yours, ATHĒZE PHŌI AAA DAIAGTHI THĒOBIS PHIATH THAMBRAMI
ABRAŌTH / CHTHOLCHIL THOE OELCHŌTH THIOŌĒMCH CHOOMCH SAĒSI ISACH-   1215
CHOĒ IEROUTHRA OOOOO AIŌAI (100 letters). I call upon you, the one on the gold
leaf,[166] before whom the unquenchable lamp continually burns,[167] / the great God,   1220
the one who shone on the whole world, who is radiant at Jerusalem, lord, IAŌ AIĒ
IŌĒ ŌIĒ ŌIĒ IĒ AIŌAI AI OYŌ AŌĒ ĒEI IEŌ ĒYŌ AĒI AŌ AŌA AEĒI YŌ EIĒ / AĒŌ IEY   1225
AEĒ IAIA IAŌ EY AEY IAĒ EI AAA III ĒĒĒ IŌ IŌĒ IAŌ (100 letters), for a blessing,
lord."
*Tr.: W. C. Grese.

161. The prayer is addressed to the god Aion. See Bousset, *Religionsgeschichtliche Studien* 198, who
compares the prayer with the older form in I. 196–221.

162. For different interpretations and translations, see Reitzenstein, *Poimandres* 279, who thinks of
the god Anthropos, "Man"; cf. also Betz, "The Delphic Maxim," 169: "I am a human being, the heavenly deity's most beautiful creation. . . ."

163. Preisendanz prints Δόξα, as if to suggest a divine hypostasis. See also *PGM* I. 199.

164. The notion of "Wisdom" (Sophia) is here identified with Aion, a unique instance in the *PGM*.
Cf. *PGM* I. 210, and Bousset, *Religionsgeschichtliche Studien* 198–99.

165. Cf. l. 1225.

166. This protective prayer presumes a section describing a gold lamella to be worn as a phylactery.
The phylactery contained the hundred-letter name of the god and was worn as protection against "every
excess of power" and the "very violent act" mentioned in ll. 1193–94.

167. For the light miracle at Jerusalem, see *PGM* IV. 3070 and n. See also *PDM* xiv. 490 and
K. Preisendanz, "Zum grossen Pariser Zauberpapyrus," *ARW* 17 (1914): 347–48.

PGM IV. 1227–64

*Excellent rite for driving out daimons: *Formula* to be spoken over his head:
1230 Place olive branches before him, / and stand behind him and say:
"Hail, God of Abraham; hail, God of Isaac; hail, God of Jacob; Jesus Chrestos,[168]
1235 the Holy Spirit, the Son of the Father, who is above[169] the Seven, / who is within
the Seven. Bring Iao Sabaoth; may your power issue forth from him, NN, until
you drive away this unclean daimon Satan, who is in him. I conjure you, daimon,
1240 / whoever you are, by this god, SABARBARBATHIŌTH SABARBARBATHIOUTH SABAR-
BARBATHIŌNĒTH SABARBARBAPHAI. Come out, daimon, whoever you are, and stay
1245 away from him, NN, / now, now; immediately, immediately. Come out, daimon,
since I bind you with unbreakable adamantine fetters, and I deliver you into the
black chaos in perdition."

1250 *Preparation*: take 7 olive branches; for six of them / tie together the two ends of
each one, but for the remaining one use it like a whip as you utter the conjuration.
Keep it secret; it is proven.

After driving out the daimon, hang around him, NN, a phylactery, which the
patient puts on after the expulsion of the daimon—a phylactery with these things
1255 [written] on / a tin metal leaf: "BŌR PHŌR PHORBA PHOR PHORBA BES CHARIN
BAUBŌ TE PHŌR BŌRPHORBA PHORBABOR BAPHORBA PHABRAIĒ PHŌRBA
1260 PHARBA PHŌRPHŌR PHORBA / BŌPHOR PHORBA PHORPHOR PHORBA BŌBOR-
BORBA PAMPHORBA PHŌRPHŌR PHŌRBA, protect him, NN." But *another version*
has a phylactery on which this sign[170] occurs: ℥
*Tr.: M. W. Meyer. This Greek and Coptic exorcistic spell is discussed by Tambornino,
RGVV VII 3, 9; 10. For additional literature, see Preisendanz, *PGM* vol. I, 114 and idem,
APF 8 (1927):115.

PGM IV. 1265–74

1265 ***Aphrodite's name** which becomes known to no one quickly is NEPHERIĒRI[171]—
this is the name. If you wish to win a woman who is beautiful, be pure for 3 days,
1270 make an offering of frankincense, / and call upon this name over it. You approach
the woman and say it seven times in your soul as you gaze at her, and in this way it
will succeed.[172] But do this for 7 days.
*Tr.: E. N. O'Neil.

PGM IV. 1275–1322

1275 ***Bear-charm**[173] which accomplishes everything: *Formula*: "I call upon you, the
greatest power in heaven" (*others*: "in the Bear") "appointed by the lord god to
1280 turn with a strong / hand the holy pole, NIKAROPLĒX. Listen to me, Helios, Phre;[174]
hear the holy [prayer], you who hold together the universe and bring to life the

168. On *Chrēstos*, "excellent one," rather than *Christos*, "anointed one," see K. Weiss, *TDNT* 9
(1974):484–85; B. Layton, *The Gnostic Treatise on Resurrection from Nag Hammadi* (Missoula, Montana: Scholars Press, 1979) 44–45; Smith, *Jesus the Magician* 63.
169. Or "below."
170. This sign is familiar from the so-called Chnoubis amulets. See Bonner, *SMA* 54–55; Delatte
and Derchain, *Les Intailles magiques* 54–57; A. Jacoby, "Ein Berliner Chnoubisamulett," *ARW* 28
(1930):269–70. The translation of the sentence is according to the interpretation by R.D.K.
171. Nepherieri is the Egyptian *Nfr-iry.t*, "the beautiful eye," a suitable epithet for Aphrodite/
Hathor. See G. Möller, in Preisendanz, apparatus ad loc. [J.B.; R.K.R.]
172. Or "you will succeed," the subject being the spell itself.
173. The spell invokes the astral constellation of the Bear and its powers. See *PGM* IV. 700, 1331;
VII. 687; XXIII. 10.
174. That is, Helios-Prē.

whole world, THŌZOPITHĒ EUCHANDAMA ŌCHRIENTHĒR / OMNYŌDĒS CHĒMIO- 1285
CHYNGĒS IEŌY" (perform a sacrifice) "THERMOUTHER PSIPHIRIX PHROSALI KAN-
THIMEŌ ZANZEMIA ŌPER PEROMENĒS RŌTHIEU ĒNINDEU KORKOUNTHO EUMEN
MENI KĒDEUA KĒPSEOI" (add the usual).

Petition / to the sun at sunset. Formula: "THĒNŌR, O Helios, SANTHĒNŌR, I 1290
beseech you, lord, may the place and lord of the Bear devote themselves to me"
(while petitioning, sacrifice armara.[175] Do it at sunset). 1295

Charm of compulsion for the 3rd day: "ANTEBERŌYRTŌR EREMNETHĒCHŌR
CHNYCHIROANTŌR MENELEOCHEU ĒESSIPO DŌTĒR EUARĒTŌ GOU PI PHYLAKĒ
ŌMALAMINGOR MANTATONCHA / do the NN thing." 1300

The first formula in a different way: "THŌZOPITHĒ, Bear, greatest goddess,
ruling heaven, reigning over the pole of the stars, highest, beautiful-shining goddess, incorruptible element, composite of the all, all-illuminating, / bond of the 1305
universe AEĒIOYŌ (square),[176] you who stand on the pole, you whom the lord god
appointed to turn the holy pole with a strong hand: THŌZOPITHĒ (formula)."

Offering for the procedure: 4 drams of frankincense, 4 drams of myrrh, 2 ounces
each of cassia leaf and / of white pepper, 1 dram of bdellion, 1 dram of asphodel 1310
seed, 2 drams each of amomon, of saffron, of terebinth storax, 1 dram of wormwood, . . . of vetch plant, priestly Egyptian incense, the complete brain of a black
ram. / Combine these with white Mendesian wine[177] and honey, and make pellets 1315
of bread.

Phylactery for the procedure: Wear a wolf knucklebone, mix juice of vetch and of
pondweed in a censer, / write in the middle of the censer this name: "THERMOU- 1320
THEREPSIPHIRIPHI[178] PISALI" (24 letters),[179] and in this way make an offering.
*Tr.: W. C. Grese.

PGM IV. 1323–30

*Another: "KOMPHTHO KOMASITH KOMNOUN[180] you who shook and shake the
world, you who have swallowed the ever-living serpent and daily / raise the disk of 1325
the sun and of the moon, you whose name is ITHIOŌ ĒI ARBATHIAŌ Ē, send up to
me, NN, at night the daimon of this night to reveal to me concerning / the NN 1330
thing."
*Tr.: W. C. Grese.

PGM IV. 1331–89

*Powerful spell of the Bear[181] which accomplishes anything: Take the fat of a
black ass, the fat of a dappled she-goat, the fat of a black bull, and Ethiopian cumin,
mix all together / and make an offering to the Bear, having as a phylactery hairs 1335

175. For the recipe, see below, ll. 1308–16, and Hopfner, *OZ* I, section 803. Cf. *PGM* IV. 1990.

176. According to Preisendanz, πλινθίον (square) inserted here means that the letters are to be arranged in a series of lines forming a square. For this form of pictorial writing, see V. Gardthausen,
Griechische Paläographie II (Leipzig: Veit, ²1913) 59. For a similar piece, see A. Greifenhagen, *Schmuckar-
beiten in Edelmetall, II: Einzelstücke* (Berlin: Staatliche Museen, Preussischer Kulturbesitz, Antikenab-
teilung, 1975) 98 n. 11; cf. also *PGM* XIII. 905–11.

177. Cf. *PGM* I. 85 and n.

178. Thermouth is Rennutet, the Egyptian harvest goddess and Fate. See Bonnet, *RÄRG* 803–4,
s.v. "Thermutis." See also *PGM* IV. 664 and n.

179. That is, in Greek letters.

180. Preisendanz suggests this line may contain Coptic, which according to F. Ll. Griffith, "The Old
Coptic Magical Text of Paris," *ZÄS* 38 (1900):93, means "earth-shaker, ground-shaker, abyss-shaker."
[R.K.R.] Cf. *PGM* III. 680.

181. For the meaning of the constellation of the Bear, see *PGM* IV. 1275.

1340

from the same animals which you have plaited into a cord and are wearing as a diadem around your head. Anoint your lips with the fats, smear your whole body with storax / oil, and make your petition while holding a single-shooted Egyptian onion. Speak concerning whatever you wish. Gird yourself with a palm fiber of a male date palm, kneel down, and speak the following *formula*:

1345
1350

/ "I call upon you, holy, very-powerful, very-glorious, very-strong, holy, autochthons, assistants of the great god, the powerful chief daimons, you who / are inhabitants of Chaos,[182] of Erebos, of the abyss, of the depth, of earth, dwelling in the recesses of heaven, lurking in the nooks and crannies of houses, shrouded in dark clouds, watchers of things not to be seen, guardians of secrets, leaders of those in the underworld, administrators / of the infinite, wielding power over earth, earth-shakers, foundation-layers, servants in the chasm, shudderful fighters, fearful ministers, turning the spindle, freezing snow and rain, air-transversers, causing / summer heat, wind-bringers, lords of Fate, inhabitants of dark Erebos, bringers of compulsion, sending flames of fire, bringing snow and dew, wind-releasers, disturbers of the deep, treaders on the calm sea, mighty in courage, grievers / of the heart, powerful potentates, cliff-walkers, adverse daimons, iron-hearted, wild-tempered, unruly, guarding Tartaros, misleading Fate, all-seeing, all-hearing, / all-subjecting, heaven-walkers, spirit-givers, living simply, heaven-shakers, gladdening the heart, those who join together death, revealers of angels, punishers of mortals, sunless revealers, rulers of daimons, / air-transversers, almighty, holy, unconquerable AŌTH[183] ABAŌTH BASYM ISAK SABAŌTH IAŌ IAKŌP MANARA SKORTOURI MORTROUM EPHRAULA THREERSA; do the NN matter."

1355
1360
1365
1370
1375

1380

/ Then write on a piece of papyrus the hundred-lettered name of Typhon,[184] curved as a star, and bind it in the middle of the core with the letters showing.

1385

This is the name: / ACHCHŌR ACHCHŌR ACHACHACHPTOUMI CHACHCHŌ CHARACHŌCH CHAPTOUMĒ CHŌRA CHŌCH APTOUMIMĒ CHŌCHAPTOU CHARACHPTOU CHACHCHŌ CHARA CHŌCH PTENACHŌCHEOU.
*Tr.: W. C. Grese.

PGM IV. 1390–1495

1390

*Love spell of attraction performed with the help of heroes or gladiators or those who have died a violent death: Leave a little of the bread which you eat; break it up and form it into seven bite-size pieces. And go to where heroes and gladiators and those who have died a violent death were slain. / Say the spell to the pieces of bread and throw them. And pick up some polluted dirt from the place where you perform the ritual and throw it inside the house of the woman whom you desire, go on home and go to sleep.

1395

The spell which is said upon the pieces of bread is this:

1400

"To[185] Moirai, Destinies, / Malignities,
To Famine, Jealousy, to those who died

---

182. For these names referring to the underworld places of Greek mythology, see *Orph. Frag.* 1 and 54; Homer, *Il.* 16. 327; *Od.* 10. 528; Hesiod, *Theog.* 515; etc. See W. K. C. Guthrie, *Orpheus and Greek Religion* (London: Methuen, 1952) 92.

183. The magical words contain some garbled Aramaic. On BASYM, see *PGM* LXX. 3 and n.; XIII. 147, 593. For an explanation from the Hebrew *ba-shem*, see G. Alon, *Jews, Judaism and the Classical World* (Jerusalem: Magnes, 1977) 235–51, esp. 237, 240.

184. The association of Typhon with the constellation of the Bear (cf. *PGM* IV. 1331, 1335) is Egyptian. The Bear represents the soul of Typhon, the murderer of Osiris. See Plutarch, *De Is. et Os.* 21, 359D, and Griffiths, *Plutarch's De Iside et Osiride* 373.

185. These iambic trimeters (which are sometimes rather clumsy) have been adapted to form the reconstructed Hymn 25, for which see Preisendanz, vol. II, p. 263. [E.N.O.]

Untimely deaths and those dead violently,
I'm sending food: Three-headed Goddess, Lady
Of Night, who feed on filth, O Virgin, thou
Key-holding Persephassa,[186] Kore out
Of Tartaros, grim-eyed, dreadful, child girt /
With fiery serpents, he, NN, has mixed   1405
With tears and bitter groans leftovers from
His own food, so that you, O luckless heroes
Who are confined there in the NN place,
May bring success to him who is beset
With torments. You who've left the light, O you
Unfortunate ones, / bring success to him,   1410
NN, who is distressed at heart because
Of her, NN, ungodly and unholy.
So bring her wracked with torment—and in haste!
EIOUT ABAŌTH PSAKERBA ARBATHIAŌ LALAOITH / IŌSACHŌTOU ALLALETHŌ   1415
You too as well, Lady, who feed on filth [187]
SYNATRAKABI BAUBARABAS ENPHNOUN MORKA[188] ERESCHIGAL NEBOUTOSOUA-
LĒTH, and send the Erinys ORGOGORGONIOTRIAN,[189]
Who rouses up with fire souls of the dead, /
Unlucky heroes, luckless heroines,   1420
Who in this place, who on this day, who in
This hour, who in coffins of myrtlewood,
Give heed to me and rouse / her, NN, on   1425
This night and from her eyes remove sweet sleep,
And cause her wretched care and fearful pain,
Cause her to follow after my footsteps,
And / for my will give her a willingness   1430
Until she does what I command of her.
O mistress Hekate [190]
PHORBA PHORBŌBAR BARŌ PHŌRPHŌR PHŌRBAI
O Lady of the Crossroads, O Black Bitch."

When you have done / these things for 3 days and accomplish nothing, then use   1435
this forceful spell: just go to the same place and again perform the ritual of the
bread pieces. Then upon ashes of flax offer up dung / from a black cow and say this   1440
and again pick up the polluted dirt and throw it as you have learned.

The words spoken over the offering are these:

"Chthonic Hermes and chthonic Hekate and chthonic Acheron [191] and chthonic /

---

186. A poetic form of Persephone.

187. These words with some changes are included as part of Hymn 25 (ll. 14–16), and they seem to scan, but without a translation possible for the formulaic terms nothing can be gained by inserting them in the verse section. [E.N.O.]

188. A. Jacoby has proposed (see Preisendanz, apparatus ad loc.) that the name is that of the Babylonian deity Omorka. See O. Höfer, in Roscher 3/1 (1897–1902) 868–69, s.v. "Omorka."

189. The epithet "the Orgogorgoniotrian" signifies one of the Furies (Erinys). According to LSJ, s.v., it is found only here in Greek.

190. The meter breaks down at this point and only by rearranging and omitting words can Hymn 25 (l. 28) accommodate the concluding phrases here. [E.N.O.]

191. The name Acheron refers to the mythical river or sea in the underworld. There is also a connection with the river Acheron in Epirus, where the famous underworld oracle of Ephyra was located. See E. Vermeule, *Aspects of Death in Early Greek Art and Poetry* (Berkeley and Los Angeles: University of California Press, 1979) 252. The oracle of Ephyra has been excavated; see S. I. Dakaris, "Das Tau-

1445 flesh-eaters and chthonic god and chthonic Amphìaraos[192] and chthonic attendants
1450 and chthonic spirits and chthonic sins and chthonic dreams / and chthonic oaths
and chthonic Ariste[193] and chthonic Tartaros and chthonic witchery, chthonic
Charon and chthonic escorts and the dead and the daimons and souls of all men: /
1455 come today, Moirai and Destiny; accomplish the purpose with the help of the love
spell of attraction, that you may attract to me her, NN whose mother is NN, to me
NN, whose mother is NN (add the usual), because I am calling

1460   O[194] primal Chaos, / Erebos, and you
O awful water of the Styx, O streams
O Lethe, Hades' Acherousian pool,
O Hekate and Pluto and Kore,
And chthonic Hermes, Moirai, Punishments,
1465   Both Acheron and Aiakos,[195] / gatekeeper
Of the eternal bars, now open quickly,
O thou Key-holder, guardian, Anubis.[196]
Send up to me the phantoms of the dead
Forthwith for service in this very hour. /

1470 So that they may go and attract to me, NN, her, NN, whose mother is NN" (add
the usual).

"Isis[197] came, holding on her shoulders her brother who is her bedfellow,[198] and
1475 Zeus came down from Olympus and stood awaiting the phantoms / of the dead as
they were being led to her, NN, and were performing the NN business (add the
usual). All the immortal gods and all the goddesses came to see the phantoms of
1480 these dead. Do not, therefore, delay; / do not loiter, but dispatch, O gods, the
phantoms of these dead, so that having gone to her NN they may perform the NN
1485 deed (add the usual) because I adjure you by IAŌ / SABAŌTH and ADŌNAI PAT-
RAXILYTRA BOURREPHAŌMI ASSALKĒ AIDOUNAX SESENGEN (formula) BALIABA
1490 ERECHCHARNOI ABERIDOUMA SALBACHTHI EISERSE / RATHŌ EISERDA ŌMI SIS-
IPHNA SISAEDOUBE ACHCHARITŌNĒ ABERIPHNOUBA IABAL DENATHI ITHROU-
1495 PHI. Send up the phantoms of these dead to her NN / whose mother is NN, so that
they may perform the NN deed" (add the usual).
*Tr.: E. N. O'Neil.

---

benorakel von Dodona und das Totenorakel bei Ephyra," *Antike Kunst*, Beiheft 1 (1963): 35–55; Burkert, *Griechische Religion* 185–86.

192. The name refers to an old underworld god who had an incubation oracle at Oropos. See
R. Herzog, "Amphìaraos," *RAC* 1 (1950): 396, with further literature.

193. For this epithet of Artemis and Demeter, see Jessen, "Ariste," *PRE* 2 (1895): 876.

194. These dactylic hexameters also form the reconstructed Hymn 26, for which see Preisendanz,
vol. II, p. 264. The reconstruction is even more extensive than usual, for in places only faint vestiges of
verse remain. [E.N.O.]

195. Aiakos was one of the judges of the underworld, along with Minos and Rhadamanthys. See
Plato, *Apol.* 41a; *Gorg*; 523e, and W. Schmid, "Aiakos," *PRE* 1 (1893): 923–26.

196. On Anubis with the key, see S. Morenz, "Anubis mit dem Schlüssel," in his *Religion und
Geschichte des Alten Ägypten* (Köln and Wien: Böhlau, 1975) 510–20. [R.K.R.]

197. These lines, which contain vestiges of dactylic hexameters, have been arranged in an awkward
verse pattern and accepted as the reconstructed Hymn 27; see Preisendanz, vol. II, p. 264. Nonetheless,
the translation is prose because the lines have no more of a metrical pattern than many other passages
scattered through these documents. [E.N.O.]

198. Isis aroused desire within the dead Osiris and by him conceived Horus. [R.K.R.]

PGM IV. 1496–1595

*Love spell of attraction over myrrh which is offered: While offering it over coals, recite the spell.

Spell:

"You are Myrrh, the bitter, the difficult, who reconciles / combatants, who sears   1500
and who forces those to love who do not acknowledge Eros. Everyone calls you
Myrrh, but I call you Flesh-eater and / Inflamer of the heart. I am not sending you   1505
to far-off Arabia; I am not sending you to Babylon, but I am sending you to her
NN, whose mother is NN, so that you may serve me on the mission to her, so
that / you may attract her to me. If she is sitting,[199] let her not keep sitting; if she is   1510
chatting with someone, let her not keep chatting; if she is gazing at someone, let
her not keep gazing; if she is going to someone, let her not keep going; if she is
strolling about, let her not / keep strolling; if she is drinking, let her not keep   1515
drinking; if she is eating, let her not keep eating; if she is kissing someone, let her
not keep kissing him; if she is enjoying some pleasure, let her not keep enjoying it;
if she is sleeping, let her not keep sleeping. Rather, let her hold me / NN alone in   1520
her mind; let her desire me alone; let her love me alone; let her do all my wishes.
Do not enter through her eyes or through her side or through her nails / or even   1525
through her navel or through her frame, but rather through her 'soul.' And remain
in her heart and burn her guts, her breast, her liver, / her breath, her bones, her   1530
marrow, until she comes to me NN, loving me, and until she fulfills all my wishes,
because I adjure you, Myrrh, by the three names,[200] / ANOCHŌ[201] ABRASAX TRŌ,   1535
and by the more coercive and stronger names KORMEIŌTH IAŌ SABAŌTH ADŌNAI,
so that you may carry out my / orders, Myrrh. As I burn you up and you are po-   1540
tent, so burn the brain of her, NN, whom I love. Inflame her and turn her guts inside out, / suck out her blood drop by drop, until she comes to me, NN, whose   1545
mother is NN. I adjure you by the MARPARKOURITH NASAARI NAIEMARE PAI-
PARI / NEKOURI. I throw you into the burning fire and adjure you by the almighty   1550
god who lives forever: Having adjured you, I now also adjure you, / ADŌNAI BAR-   1555
BAR IAŌ ZAGOURĒ HARSAMŌSI ALAOUS and SALAŌS. I adjure you who strength-
ened man for life: Hear, hear, / great god, o Adonaios, ETHYIA, self-gendering,   1560
everlasting god, EIŌĒ IAŌ AIŌ AIŌ PHNEŌS SPHINTĒS ARBATHIAŌ IAŌ IAĒ IŌA /
AI, who are OUĒR[202] GONTHIAŌR RARAĒL[203] ABRA BRACHA SOROORMERPHERGAR   1565
MARBAPHRIOUIRIGX IAŌ SABAŌTH MASKELLI / MASKELLŌ (the formula) AMON-   1570
SŌE ANOCH RIGCH PHNOUKENTABAŌTH SOUSAE PHINPHESĒCH MAPHI / RAR   1575
ANOURIN IBANAŌTH AROUĒR CHNOUPH ANOCH BATHI OUCH IARBAS BABAUBAR
ELŌAI; attract for me her NN, whose mother is NN, to me / NN, whose mother is   1580
NN, on the very day, on this night, at this very hour, MOULŌTH PHOPHITH PHTHŌ-
ITH PHTHŌYTH PENIŌN. I call upon you also who hold / the fire, PHTHAN ANOCH;   1585
give heed to me, O one, only-begotten, MANEBIA BAIBAI CHYRIRŌOU THADEIN
ADŌNAI EROU NOUNI / MIŌŌNCH CHOUTIAI MARMARAUŌTH. Attract her, NN,   1590
whose mother is NN, to me NN, whose mother is NN, now, now; immediately,
immediately; quickly, quickly."

And say also the spell for all / occasions.   1595

Tr.: E. N. O'Neil.

199. For parallels to this passage, cf. P. Smither, "A Coptic Love-Charm," *JEA* 25 (1939): 175–76.

200. On this passage, see C. Bonner, "Liturgical Fragments on Gnostic Amulets," *HTR* 25 (1932): 362–67; idem, "The Transcendency of Divine Attributes," ibid. 37 (1944): 338–39.

201. This means in Egyptian "I am great." [R.K.R.] Cf. *PGM* I. 149.

202. OUER corresponds to Egyptian *wr*, "great." [R.K.R.]

203. RARAĒL occurs only here; perhaps Raphael should be read. [E.N.O.]

PGM IV. 1596–1715

*This is the consecration for all purposes: *Spell to Helios*: "I invoke you, the
1600 greatest god, eternal lord, world ruler, / who are over the world and under the
world, mighty ruler of the sea, rising at dawn, shining from the east for the whole
1605 world, / setting in the west. Come to me, thou who risest from the four winds,
joyous[204] Agathos Daimon, for whom heaven has become the processional way. I
1610 call upon your holy / and great and hidden names which you rejoice to hear. The
earth flourished when you shone forth, and the plants became fruitful when you
1615 laughed; the animals begat their young / when you permitted. Give glory and honor
and favor and fortune and power to this, NN, stone which I consecrate[205] today (or
1620 to the / phylactery being consecrated) for NN.[206] I invoke you, the greatest in
1625 heaven, ĒI LANCHYCH AKARĒN BAL MISTHRĒN MARTA / MATHATH LAILAM MOU-
SOUTHI SIETHŌ BATHABATHI IATMŌN ALEI IABATH ABAŌTH SABAŌTH ADŌNAI, the
1630 great god, ORSENOPHRĒ ORGEATĒS / TOTHORNATĒSA[207] KRITHI BIŌTHI IADMŌ
IATMŌMI METHIĒI[208] LONCHOŌ AKARĒ BAL MINTHRĒ BANE BAI(N)CHCHYCHCH
1635 OUPHRI NOTHEOUSI THRAI / ARSIOUTH ERŌNERTHER, the shining Helios, giving
light throughout the whole world. You are the great Serpent, leader of all[209] the
1640 gods, who control the beginning / of Egypt and the end of the whole inhabited
world, who mate in the ocean, PSOI PHNOUTHI NINTHĒR.[210] You are he who be-
1645 comes / visible each day and sets in the northwest of heaven, and rises in the southeast.[211] In the 1st hour you have the form of a cat; your name is PHARAKOUNĒTH.
1650 / Give glory and favor to this phylactery. In the 2nd hour you have the form of a
dog; your name is SOUPHI. Give strength and honor to this phylactery, [or] to this
1655 stone, / and to NN. In the 3rd hour you have the form of a serpent; your name is
AMEKRANEBECHEO THŌYTH. Give honor to the god NN. In the 4th hour you have
1660 the form of a scarab; your name is / SENTHENIPS. Mightily strengthen this phylactery in this night, for the work for which it is consecrated. In the 5th hour you have
1665 the form of a donkey; your name is / ENPHANCHOUPH. Give strength and courage
and power to the god, NN. In the 6th hour you have the form of a lion; your name
1670 is BAI SOLBAI, the ruler of time. Give / success to this phylactery and glorious
victory. In the 7th hour you have the form of a goat; your name is OUMESTHŌTH.
1675 Give sexual charm to this ring / (or to this phylactery, or to this engraving). In the
8th hour you have the form of a bull; your name is DIATIPHĒ, who becomes visible
1680 everywhere. Let all / things [done] by the use of this stone be accomplished. In the
9th hour you have the form of a falcon; your name is PHĒOUS PHŌOUTH, the lotus
1685 emerged from the abyss.[212] Give success / [and] good luck to his phylactery. In
the 10th hour you have the form of a baboon; your name is BESBYKI. In the 11th

204. "Joyous" can also mean "benevolent" or "lucky," meanings appropriate and probably intended
here. In the writer's mind the three were probably not distinguished. [M.S.]
205. Cf. on this point *PGM* IV. 2179 and n.
206. Or "for use in relation to NN."
207. Reading ⟨ὁ⟩ ὀργεατης τ' ὁ θορνατης. Both nouns seem unattested formations; perhaps the
former should be corrected to ὀργιαστής, "participant in orgiastic rites," which were often secret and
connected with Dionysos. [M.S.]
208. From ĒI onward the words repeat in variations the formula with which the series begins.
209. Reading πάντων for τούτων, with Reitzenstein, *Poimandres* 29. [M.S.]
210. This is equivalent to the Egyptian "the Agathodaimon, the god (of) the gods." [R.K.R.] Cf.
PGM III. 144–45.
211. On the forms of the sun god, see *PGM* II. 104 and nn.
212. On the lotus flower, see *PGM* IV. 1111; *PDM* xiv. 45; and Morenz, *Egyptian Religion* 179–80.
[R.K.R.]

hour you have the form of an ibis; your name is / MOU RŌPH.[213] Protect this great   1690
phylactery for lucky [use] by NN, from this present day for all time. In the 12th
hour you have the form of a crocodile; your name / is AERTHOĒ. You who have set   1695
at evening as an old man,[214] who are over the world and [under] the world, mighty
ruler of the sea, hear my voice in this present day, / in this night, in these holy   1700
hours, and let [all things done] by this stone [or] for this phylactery, be brought to
fulfilment, and especially NN matter for which I consecrate it. Please, / lord   1705
KMĒPH LOUTHEOUTH ORPHOICHE ORTILIBECHOUCH IERCHE ROUM IPERITAŌ
YAI. I conjure earth and heaven and light and darkness and the / great god who   1710
created all, SAROUSIN, you, Agathon Daimonion the helper, to accomplish for me
everything [done] by the use of this ring or [stone]."

When / you complete [the consecration], say, "The one Zeus is Sarapis."[215]   1715
*Tr.: Morton Smith.

PGM IV. 1716–1870

*Sword[216] of Dardanos:[217] Rite which is called "sword," which has no equal be-
cause of its power, for it immediately bends and attracts the soul[218] of whomever
you wish. / As you say the spell, also say: "I am bending to my will the soul of him   1720
NN."[219]

Take a magnetic stone which is breathing and engrave Aphrodite sitting astride
Psyche[220] / and with her left hand holding on her hair bound in curls. And above   1725
her head: "ACHMAGE RARPEPSEI"; and below / Aphrodite and Psyche engrave Eros   1730
standing on the vault of heaven, holding a blazing torch and burning Psyche.[221]
And below Eros these / names: "ACHAPA ADŌNAIE BASMA CHARAKŌ IAKŌB IAŌ Ē   1735
PHARPHARĒI." On the other side of the stone engrave Psyche and Eros embrac-
ing / one another and beneath Eros' feet these letters: "sssssss," and beneath   1740
Psyche's feet: "ĒĒĒĒĒĒĒĒ." Use the stone, when it has been engraved and conse-

213. Here, and again below after the twelfth hour, the prayer for a gift to the phylactery or stone has
presumably been skipped by a copyist.

214. This is a reference to Atum, the form of the sun god at setting. See Bonnet, *RÄRG* 731.
[R.K.R.]

215. On this formula, see O. Weinreich, *Neue Urkunden zur Sarapisreligion* (Tübingen: Mohr, Siebeck, 1919; reprinted in his *Ausgewählte Schriften* I [Amsterdam: Grüner, 1969] 410–42); Nilsson,
GGR II, 574; W. Hornbostel, *Sarapis. Studien zur Überlieferungsgeschichte und Wandlungen der Gestalt
eines Gottes*, *EPRO* 32 (Leiden: Brill, 1973) 353, n. 2; 396.

216. The designation "sword" apparently serves as a kind of title for certain types of formulas, here
presumably the formula in l. 1813. See K. Preisendanz, "Xiphos," Roscher 6 (1924–37) 526–28;
Nock, *Essays* I, 190. The classical work of this kind is the so-called Sword of Moses, for which see
M. Gaster, *Studies and Texts in Folklore, Magic, Medieval Romance, Hebrew Apocrypha and Samaritan Archaeology* I (London: Maggs, 1925) 288–337. See also *PGM* IV. 1813 and n.

217. Dardanos was believed to have founded the mysteries of Samothrake. See A. Hermann, "Dar-
danus," *RAC* 3 (1957): 593–94.

218. Since the operator does not want spiritual love, ψυχή here is probably the female pudenda.
Against this interpretation is τὴν ψυχὴν τοῦ δεῖνα (l. 1721), but since the rest of the spell is concerned
with attracting a woman, we should probably emend here and read τῆς δεῖνα. [E.N.O.]

219. It is not clear whether this spell concerns a male or a female lover. Cf. ll. 1720, 1807, 1828–29.

220. The best treatment of this image is that by R. Mouterde, *Le Glaive de Dardanos. Objets et inscriptions magiques de Syrie, Mélanges de l'Université Saint-Joseph* 15/3 (Beirut: Imprimérie Catholique, 1930)
53–64. See also R. Reitzenstein, "Noch einmal Eros und Psyche," *ARW* 28 (1930): 42–87; A. Rumpf,
"Eros (Eroten) II. in der Kunst," *RAC* 6 (1966): 312–42, esp. 330–31.

221. For this theme and literature, see R. Helm, "Psyche," *PRE* 23 (1959): 1434–38; S. Binder and
R. Merkelbach, *Amor und Psyche* (Darmstadt: Wissenschaftliche Buchgesellschaft, 1968) esp. 433–34.
See also *PGM* XII. 20.

1745   crated, / like this: put it under your tongue and turn it to what you wish and say
        this *spell*:

        "I [222] call upon you, author of all creation, who spread your own wings over the
1750   whole / world, you, the unapproachable and unmeasurable who breathe into every
1755   soul life-giving / reasoning, who fitted all things together by your power, firstborn,
        founder of the universe, golden-winged, whose light is darkness, who shroud rea-
1760   sonable / thoughts and breathe forth dark frenzy, clandestine one who secretly in-
1765   habit every soul. You engender an unseen fire / as you carry off every living thing
        without growing weary of torturing it, rather having with pleasure delighted in
1770   pain [223] from the time when the world came into being. You also come / and bring
        pain, who are sometimes reasonable, sometimes irrational, because of whom men
1775   dare beyond what is fitting and take refuge in your light which is darkness. / Most
        headstrong, lawless, implacable, inexorable, invisible, bodiless, generator of frenzy,
1780   archer, torch-carrier, master of all living / sensation and of everything clandestine,
        dispenser of forgetfulness, creator of silence, through whom the light and to whom
1785   the light travels, infantile when you have been engendered within / the heart, wisest
        when you have succeeded; I call upon you, unmoved by prayer, by your great name:
1790   AZARACHTHARAZA [224] LATHA / IATHAL [225] Y Y Y LATHAI ATHALLALAPH IOIOIO AI
1795   AI AI OUERIEU OIAI LEGETA RAMAI AMA RATAGEL, [226] first-shining, night-/shining,
        night rejoicing, night-engendering, witness, ERĒKISITHPHĒ [227] ARARACHARARA
1800   ĒPHTHISIKĒRE [228] IABEZEBYTH IO, you in the depth, [229] BERIAMBŌ / BERIAMBEBŌ,
        you in the sea, MERMERGOU, clandestine and wisest, ACHAPA ADŌNAIE BASMA CHA-
1805   RAKŌ IAKŌB IAŌ CHAROUĒR AROUĒR LAILAM / SEMESILAM SOUMARTA MARBA
        KARBA MENABŌTH ĒIIA. Turn the 'soul' of her NN to me NN, so that she may love
        me, so that she may feel passion for me, so that she may give me what is in her
1810   power. [230] / Let her say to me what is in her soul because I have called upon your
        great name."

1815   And on a golden leaf inscribe this sword: [231] "One [232] THOURIĒL / MICHAĒL

---

222. The hymn to Eros has been called "notably elegant and literary" (Nock, *Essays* I, 183). Cf. the
hymn to Eros among the *Orphic Hymns* (no. 58). See Binder and Merkelbach, *Amor und Psyche* 150,
386–87.

223. The words ὀδυνηρᾷ τέρψει make little sense, esp. without a verbal form in the clause. Because
there are traces of poetic language here, we should perhaps read ὀδύνη ῥᾷ τέρψας, and this is what the
translation renders. [E.N.O.]

224. An imperfect palindrome.

225. The spacing of this *vox magica* has been arranged to show the palindrome.

226. Again, the spacing has been arranged to show the palindrome.

227. Again, the *vox magica* has been arranged to show the palindrome.

228. This often attested *vox magica* can be read as Greek φθισικηρε (φθίω, κήρ), perhaps "destroying evil demons" (cf. φθισήνωρ, φθισίμβροτος, φθισίφρων). [W.B.] See also R. Merkelbach, "ΦΘΙ-
ΣΙΚΗΡΕ," *ZPE* 47 (1982):172, commenting esp. on *PGM* II. 100.

229. Here, βύθιε, "you in the deep," as well as πελάγιε, "you in the sea" (l. 800), and κρύφιε καὶ
πρεσβύτατε, "clandestine and wisest" (ll. 1801–2) are recognizable Greek words, inserted into this
series of magical palindromes. Cf. the similar formulas on a lead piece, P. Rein. II. 88, ll. 17–20. See
P. Collart, *Les Papyrus Theodore Reinach*, vol. II, *BIFAO* 39 (1940):29–32. [R.D.K.] Cf. also the figure
of Bythos in Valentinian gnosticism.

230. This means "power to give"; lit., "what is in her hands."

231. See also on l. 1717, above. This "sword" or magical formula may be so named because the
words to be written on the gold lamella were to be engraved in the shape of, or enclosed by, a "sword."
For a magical gold leaf with a sword, see the facsimile in S. Reinach and E. Babelon, "Recherches arch-
éologiques en Tunisie (1883–1884)," *Bulletin Archéologique* 1886, p. 57. [R.D.K.]

232. For a discussion of this monotheistic formula, see Bonner, *SMA* 175–76; cf. H. D. Betz, *Exe-
getisches Wörterbuch zum Neuen Testament* I (1978):969–71, s.v. "εἷς."

GABRIĒL OURIĒL MISAĒL IRRAĒL ISTRAĒL:[233] May it be a propitious day for this
name and for me who know it and am wearing it. I summon the immortal / and   1820
infallible strength of God. Grant me the submission of every soul for which I have
called upon you." Give the leaf to a partridge to gulp down[234] / and kill it. Then 1825
pick it up and wear it around your neck after inserting into the strip the herb called
"boy love."

The burnt offering / which endows Eros and the whole procedure with soul is   1830
this: manna, 4 drams; storax, 4 drams; opium, 4 drams; myrrh, [4 drams;] frankincense, saffron, bdella, / one-half dram each. Mix in rich dried fig and blend every- 1835
thing in equal parts with fragrant wine, and use it for the performance. In the performance first make a burnt offering and / use it in this way.[235]   1840

And there is also *a rite for acquiring an assistant*,[236] who is made out of wood
from a mulberry tree. He is made as a winged Eros wearing a cloak, with his right
foot lifted / for a stride and with a hollow back. Into the hollow put a gold leaf   1845
after writing with a cold-forged copper stylus so-and-so's name [and]: "MARSA-
BOUTARTHE[237]—be my / assistant and supporter and sender of dreams."   1850

Go late at night to the house [of the woman] you want, knock on her door / with   1855
the Eros and say: "Lo, she NN resides here; wherefore stand beside her and, after
assuming the likeness of the god or daimon whom she worships, say what I propose." And go to your / home, set the table, spread a pure linen cloth, and seasonal 1860
flowers, and set the figure upon it. Then make a burnt offering to it and continu-
ously say the / spell of invocation. And send him, and he will act without fail. And   1865
whenever you bend her to your will with the stone, on that night it sends / dreams,   1870
for on a different night it is busy with different matters.[238]
*Tr.: E. N. O'Neil.

PGM IV. 1872–1927

*. . . instruct no one, for it is very powerful and unsurpassable, effective for every-
one / on the same day, absolutely binding, exceedingly powerful. And it is: Take 4   1875
ounces of wax, 8 ounces of fruit from the chaste-tree, 4 drams of manna. Pound
each of these fine / separately and mix with pitch and wax, and fashion a dog eight   1880
fingers long with its mouth open. And you are to place in the mouth of the dog / a   1885
bone from the head of a man who has died violently, and inscribe on the sides of
the dog these characters: ΧΖΟΠ⊟ΨΧVΨ and you are to place the dog on a
tripod. And have the dog raising its right paw. And write on the strip of papyrus
these / names and what you wish: "IAŌ ASTŌ IŌPHĒ," and / you are to place the   1890
strip of papyrus on the tripod and on top of the strip you are to place the dog   1895
and / say these names many times. And so, after you have spoken the spell, the dog   1900

233. For a discussion of these peculiar variants of the name of Israel, see R. Ganschinietz, "Israel,"
PRE 9 (1939): 2234; Scholem, *Jewish Gnosticism* 95. Cf. *PGM* IV. 3034: Osrael; XXXVI. 259: Astrael.

234. Cf. *Sword of Moses* 324 n. 70 (see n. 216, above) for a parallel: a silver lamella is given to a cock
to swallow, and the cock is then killed. [R.D.K.]

235. The excessive use of χρῶ and χρῆσον is strange. The translation of this sentence is tentative and
little more than a paraphrase. [E.N.O.] Cf. the following section and also *PGM* I. 38; XII. 284.

236. The translation is based on the emended Greek in Preisendanz, but it differs from the German
translation ("Erfolg hat aber auch ein Beisitzer . . .").

237. The translation tries to make sense of what appears to be a corrupt Greek text; it differs from
the German translation (". . . den Namen eines Beliebigen geschrieben hast: 'Marsaboutarthe, werde
mir . . .'"). See the apparatus ad loc.

238. The Greek is ambiguous at this point. Cf. Preisendanz's translation: "Denn in jeder Nacht be-
schäftigt er sich mit anderen."

hisses [or barks], and if it hisses, she is not coming.[239] Therefore address the spell to
1905   it again, / and if it barks, it is attracting her. Then open the door, and you will find
her whom you wish at your doors. Let a censer stand beside the dog, and let fran-
1910   kincense be placed upon it / as you say the spell.

    Spell: "Barking dog, I adjure you, Kerberos, by those who have hanged them-
1915   selves, by the dead, by those who have died violently: / attract to me her, NN,
whose mother is NN. I adjure you, Kerberos, by the holy head of the infernal gods.
1920   Attract to me her, NN, whose mother is NN, ZOUCH / ZOUKI TO PARY YPHĒ-
BARMŌ ENŌR SEKEMI KRIOUDASEPHĒ TRIBEPSI: attract to me her, NN, whose
mother is NN, to me, NN, immediately, immediately; quickly, quickly."

1925   And you are also to say / the spell for all occasions. But you are to do these things
in a level, pure place.
*Tr.: E. N. O'Neil.

PGM IV. 1928–2005

1930   * **Spell of Attraction of King Pitys over any skull cup.** *His* / *prayer of petition to*
Helios: Stand facing the east and speak thus:

1935   "I call upon you, lord Helios, and your holy angels on / this day, in this very
hour: Preserve me, NN, for I am THĒNŌR, and you are holy angels, guardians of
1940   the ARDIMALECHA. And ORORŌ / MISRĒN NEPHŌ ADŌNAI AUEBŌTHI ABATHARAI
THŌBEUA SOULMAI SOULMAITH ROUTREROUTĒN ŌPHREŌPHRI ŌLCHAMAŌTH
1945   OUTE SOUTĒATH MONTRO ELAT / CHOUMIOI LATHŌTH ŌTHETH, I beg you, lord
1950   Helios, hear me NN and grant me power / over the spirit of this man who died a
violent death, from whose tent I hold [this], so that I may keep him with me, [NN]
as helper and avenger for whatever business I crave from him."

1955   / *At sunset the same man's prayer to Helios*:
    "Borne [240] on the breezes of the wand'ring winds,
    Golden-haired Helios, who wield the flame's
    Unresting fire, who turn in lofty paths
1960   Around the great pole, / who create all things
    Yourself which you again reduce to nothing.
    From you, indeed, come elements which are
    Arranged to suit your laws which nourish all
    The world with its four yearly turning points.
    Hear, blessed one, I call you who rule heav'n
    And earth and Chaos and Hades, where dwell /
1965   Daimons of men who once gazed on the light.
    And even now I beg you, blessed one,
    Unfailing one, the master of the world,
    If you go to the depths of earth and reach
    The regions of the dead, this daimon send
    To move at midnight hours perforce at your
1970   Commands, / from whose tent I hold this. And let

239. As the text stands, it makes no sense. We should probably follow the suggestion of Preisendanz, who inserts "or he barks" ("oder bellt"), and add to the Greek some such phrase as ἢ ὑλακτεῖ which may have fallen out by haplography. For similar alternative conditions, cf. *PGM* IV. 131–37; VII. 613–16. [E.N.O.]

240. The dactylic hexameters are part of the reconstructed Hymn 4 (Preisendanz, vol. II, pp. 239–40): vv. 1–17, 20–22, 18, 25, 23–24. For other versions and sections of Hymn 4, see *PGM* I. 315–27; IV. 436–61; VIII. 74–81. [E.N.O.]

Him tell to me (NN) whate'er my mind designs,
And let him tell me fully and with truth.
Let him be gentle, gracious, let him think
No thoughts opposed to me. And may you not
Be angry at my sacred chants. / But guard   1975
That my whole body come to light intact;
Let him (NN) reveal to me the what and whence,
Whereby he now can render me his service
And at what time he serves as my assistant, /
For you yourself gave these for men to learn, lord.   1980
Because I call upon your four-part name:
CHTHETHŌ NI LAILAM IAŌ ZOUCHE PIPTOĒ.
I call upon your name, / Horus,[241] which is   1985
In number equal to the Moirai's names:
ACHAI PHŌTHŌTHŌ AIĒ IAĒ AI IAĒ AIĒ
IAŌ THŌTHŌ PHIACHA (36 letters).[242]
Be gracious unto me, O primal god,
O father of the world, self-gendered one.
/ After burning armara[243] and uncut frankincense, go home.   1990

    Enquiry:[244] Ivy with 13 leaves. Begin from the left side and write on them one
by one with myrrh, and after putting on the wreath / say over them the same   1995
names. And over the skull cup place the same writing on the forehead with the
proper words: "SOITHERCHALBAN OPHROUROR ERĒKISITHPHĒ (formula)[245] /
IABE ZEBYTH LEGEMAS THMESTAS MESMYRA BAUANECHTHEN KAI LOPHŌTŌ BRĒ-   2000
LAX HARCHENTECHTHA APSOIER CHALBAN."
    And the ink: Serpent's blood / and the soot of a goldsmith.   2005
*Tr.: E. N. O'Neil.

PGM IV. 2006–2125

* Pitys' spell of attraction:[246] Pitys to King Ostanes: greetings. Since you write to
me on each occasion about the enquiry of skull cups, I have deemed it necessary to
send you this process / as one which is worthy of admiration and able to please you   2010
greatly. And subsequently I will submit to you the process, and finally the black ink
will be revealed.

    Take the hide of an ass[247] and, after drying it / in shade, inscribe on it the figure 2015
which will be revealed and inscribe this spell in a circle: "AAMASI NOUTHI APHTHE-
CHENBŌCH POUPAIEICHNERI TA LOUTHIANI SERANOMĒGRENTI EI BIL / LONOU-   2020
CHICH EITA PHOR CHORTOMNOUTHI THRACH PHIBŌBI ANTERŌ PHOCHOR-
THAROCH EBOCH LESANOUACH PHEORŌBIS TRAION KŌBI INOUNIA SAPHŌBI
CHIMNOUTHI ASRŌ / CHNOUPHNEN PHARMI BOLCHOSĒTH EPHOUKTERŌ AB-   2025
DIDANPITAAU EAE BOL SACHY ACHCHERIMA EMINTO RŌŌRIA EN AMOUN AK-
REMPHTHO OUTRAUNEIL / LABOCH PHERACHI AMENBOL BĒCH OSTAOUA BEL-   2030

241. Horus is identified with Helios; see ll. 988–89 below.
242. That is, thirty-six Greek letters.
243. For this material, see *PGM* IV. 1294 and n.
244. That is, the inquiry of the spirit of the dead man (l. 1950). See *PGM* IV. 2140–41; 2005–7.
245. Referring to the palindrome cited also in *PGM* IV. 1797–99.
246. ἀγωγή is a general term which sometimes, as here, indicates a spell whose primary purpose is
not to "attract" for sexual purposes. The same noun, without a qualifying word, is the title of a "Love
spell of attraction." For a parallel to the usage of this passage, cf., e.g., *PGM* IV. 2441. [E.N.O.]
247. The ass is associated with Seth/Typhon. See *PGM* IV. 259–60 and n.

THŌ; I adjure you, dead spirit, by the powerful and inexorable god and by his holy
2035 names, to stand beside me in the / coming night in whatever form you used to
have, and inform me whether you have the power to perform the NN deed; immediately, immediately; quickly, quickly!"

Then go quickly to where [someone] lies buried or where something has been
2040 discarded, if you do [not] have a buried body; / spread the hide under him at about
sunset. Return [home], and he will actually be present and will stand beside you on
2045 that night. And he describes to you how he died, but first he tells you if / he has the
power to do anything or to perform any service.

And take a leaf of flax and with the black ink which will be revealed to you, paint
on it the figure of the goddess who will be revealed to you, and paint in a circle this
2050 spell (and place on his head / the leaf which has been spread out and wreathe him
with black ivy, and he will actually stand beside you through the night in dreams,
and he will ask you, saying, "Order whatever you wish, and I do it"): "PHOUBEL
2055 TAUTHY ALDE MINŌOURITHI / SENECHŌ CHELĒTHICHITIATH MOU CHŌ ARIANTA
NARACHI MASKELLI (formula) AEBITHŌ ACHAIL CHAŌSOUNISOU SOUNIARTE-
2060 NŌPH ARCHEREPHTHOUMI / BOLPHAI ARŌCHŌ ABMENTHŌ PHORPHORBA
CHNOUCHIOCHOIME; I adjure [you], dead spirit, by the Destiny of Destinies,[248] to
2065 come to me, NN, on this day, on this night, and / agree to the act of service for me.
And if you don't, expect other chastisements."

And when he agrees, rise up immediately and take a roll of hieratic papyrus and
write on it with the black ink which will be revealed to you the figure which will be
2070 revealed to you,[249] / and write in a circle this spell and offer it to him, and straightway he will attract, even if he is unmanageable, immediately without delaying a
single day.

But often there will be no need for the leaf of flax, but in the second spell[250] the
2075 papyrus / sheet[251] is to be placed there after you have commanded the act of service
for you. He attracts and causes one to be ill, and he sends dreams and restrains, and
he obtains revelations by dreams as well. These are the things which this single spell
2080 accomplishes. Depending on what you are performing,[252] / alter only the passage
with the usual items.[253] Most of the magicians, who carried their instruments[254]
with them, even put them aside and used him as an assistant. And they accom-
2085 plished the preceding things with all dispatch. / For [the spell] is free of excessive
verbiage, immediately carrying out as it does the preceding things with all ease.

Spell: "I say to you, chthonic daimon, for whom the magical material of this
2090 female (of this male) has been embodied on / this night: proceed to where this female (or this male) resides and bring her to me NN either during the middle of the
night or quickly. Perform the NN deed because the holy god OSIRIS KMĒPHI

248. See on this concept *PGM* III. 120 and n.

249. The figure is not extant. See Preisendanz, apparatus ad loc.

250. This refers to a variant in another spell available to the author but not included in the *PGM*.

251. Preisendanz suggests, in the apparatus ad loc., that this sheet refers to the hide of the ass mentioned in IV. 2014.

252. Preisendanz follows the papyrus and reads πρός τό, τὸ πράσσεις, but this is surely impossible
Greek. The easiest change is πρὸς τοῦτο ὃ πράσσεις, but the sense seems to require something like
πρὸς ὅ τι ποτὲ πράσσεις, "for whatever you do," or "depending on what(ever) you do." [E.N.O.]

253. This is apparently a reference to the formulas given as κοινόν, κοινά found elsewhere in the
PGM.

254. Probably this is a reference to instruments such as were found in Pergamon. See R. Wünsch,
*Antikes Zaubergerät aus Pergamon, Jahrbuch des Kaiserlich Deutschen Archäologischen Instituts, Ergän-
zungsheft* 6 (Berlin: Reimer, 1905).

SRŌ[255] wishes and commands it of you. Fulfill, daimon, what / is written here. And   2095
after you have performed it, I will pay you a sacrifice. But if you delay, I will inflict
on you chastisements which you cannot endure. And perform for me the NN deed,
immediately, immediately; quickly, quickly."

The black ink of the procedure / **is this**: The hide is inscribed with blood of an   2100
ass[256] from the heart of a sacrificial victim, with which is mixed the soot of a cop-
persmith. But the leaf of flax is inscribed with falcon's blood, with which is mixed
the soot of a goldsmith. / But the leaf of the hieratic papyrus is inscribed with eel's   2105
blood, with which acacia is mixed.

Do these things in this manner and, once you have performed them, you may
know with what a marvelous nature this process is endowed, since in all ease / it   2110
considers the implements as the assistant. But guard yourself with whatever protection you want.

And this is the figure[257] **written on the hide**: A lion-faced form of a man wearing
a sash, holding in his right hand a staff, and on it let there be a serpent. / And   2115
around all his left hand let an asp be entwined, and from the mouth of the lion let
fire breathe forth.

The figure written onto the leaf of flax is this: Hekate[258] with three heads and six
hands, holding / torches in her hands, on the right sides of her face having the head   2120
of a cow; and on the left sides the head of a dog; and in the middle the head of a
maiden with sandals bound on her feet.

And inscribed on the piece of papyrus: Osiris clothed / as the Egyptians show   2125
him.[259]

*Tr.: E. N. O'Neil.

PGM IV. 2125–39

*A restraining seal for skulls that are not satisfactory [for use in divination], and
also to prevent [them] from speaking or doing anything whatever of this [sort]:[260]
Seal the mouth of the skull with dirt from the doors of [a temple] of Osiris / and   2130
from a mound [covering] graves. Taking iron from a leg fetter, work it cold and
make a ring on which have a headless lion engraved. Let him have, instead of his
head, a crown of Isis, and let him trample with his feet / a skeleton (the right foot   2135
should trample the skull of the skeleton). In the middle of these should be an owl-
eyed cat with its paw on a gorgon's head; in a circle around [all of them?], these
names: IADŌR INBA NICHAIOPLĒX BRITH.

*Tr.: Morton Smith.

255. The names come from the Egyptian and mean "Osiris, Good Daimon, great prince" (or
"ram"). [R.K.R.]

256. For the application, see *PGM* IV. 2015, 2220. On the blood of the ass, see D. Wortmann, "Das
Blut des Seth," *ZPE* 2 (1968): 227–30; also Griffiths, *Plutarch's De Iside et Osiride* 276, commenting on
De Is. et Os. 6, 353B.

257. For this figure, see Dieterich, *Abraxas* 53; Nilsson, *GGR* II, 499–501 with *Tafel* V, 2a and 2b.

258. For pictures of Hekate *triformis* on gemstones, see Bonner, *SMA*, nos. 64, 66; cf. no. 156;
Delatte and Derchain, *Les Intailles* 189, nos. 252, 253, *254, *254 (bis); Mouterde, *Glaive* 67–71 (see
above, n. 220).

259. This prescription is remarkable because it seems to have been made by a magician who was not
an Egyptian. The Egyptian Osiris is presented here in his capacity as god of the dead. For his ability to
send demons and spirits of the dead, cf. Pritchard, *ANET* 16, "The Contending of Horus and Seth,"
Faulkner, *Ancient Egyptian Coffin Texts* I, spell 335, pt. II. [R.K.R.]

260. Reading τουτω⟨ι⟩ with the papyrus, instead of Preisendanz's τουτω⟨ν⟩.

PGM IV. 2140–44

2140   * **Pitys the Thessalian's spell for questioning corpses**: [261] On a flax leaf write these things: "AZĒL BALEMACHŌ" (12 letters). [262]

     Ink: [Made] from red ochre, burnt myrrh, juice of fresh wormwood, evergreen, and flax. Write [on the leaf] and put it in the mouth [of the corpse].

     *Tr.: W. C. Grese.

PGM IV. 2145–2240

2145   * **Divine assistance from three Homeric verses**: [263]

     "After saying this, he drove the solid-hoofed horses through the ditch." [264]

     "and men gasping out their lives amid the terrible slaughter." [265]

2150   / "and they washed off in the sea the sweat that covered them." [266]

     If a runaway carries these verses inscribed on an iron lamella, [267] he will never be
2155 found. Likewise, attach the same lamella / to someone on the point of death, and you will get an answer [268] to everything you ask him. Whenever anyone thinks he is under a spell, let him pronounce the verses while sprinkling with sea water and . . .
2160 against enchantments. A contestant with the / tablet stays undefeated, just as also a charioteer who carries the tablet along with a lodestone; and the same is true in court; also, these are the things for a gladiator to carry. Attach it to a criminal who
2165 has been executed, speak / the verses in his ear, and he will tell you everything you wish. Insert the lamella into his wound, and you will have a great blessing with regard to your superiors and masters and others as well, for you will have honor,
2170 / trust. It also keeps off daimons and wild animals. Everyone will fear you; in war you will be invulnerable; when you ask you will receive; you will enjoy favor; your life will change; and you will be loved by any woman or man you have contact
2175 with. / You will have honor, happiness; you will receive inheritances, have good fortune, be unaffected by potions and poison; you will break spells and conquer your enemies.

     Here is the the formula to be spoken when you immerse the lamella. [269]

---

261. See *PGM* IV. 1990 and n.

262. That is, in Greek letters.

263. In the papyrus these three verses from Homer are written in exceptionally large letters. Cf. *PGM* IV. 470–74; 821–24, where magical power is ascribed to the same verses. See the note on *PGM* IV. 470.

264. Homer, *Il.* 10. 564. In Homer, the referent of "he" is Odysseus.

265. Homer, *Il.* 10. 521. The quotation includes only a portion of the Homeric sentence. "Men" is the object of "saw" in l. 520, and it is a kinsman of the slaughtered Rhesus who "saw." The text of *Il.* 10. 521 here and at *PGM* IV. 822 differs slightly, though not so as to offset the sense of that of *PGM* IV. 472.

266. Homer, *Il.* 10. 572. In Homer, the referent of "they" is Odysseus and Diomedes.

267. The use of iron lamellae (as opposed to those of lead, silver, gold, and tin) is comparatively rare in magic (but cf. *PGM* VII. 382). See the discussion by A. M. Tupet, *La Magie dans la poésie latine* (Paris: Les belles lettres, 1976) 39–43. An iron lamella engraved with magical words is housed in the Louvre; see A. Dain, *Inscriptions grecques du Musée du Louvre: Les textes inédits* (Paris: Les belles lettres, 1933) 108, no. 205. [R.D.K.]

268. The Greek verb rendered "you will get an answer to" could also mean "he will hear." Perhaps the former is the correct rendering, and the passage is expressive of the ancient notion that individuals on the point of death have prophetic power (see, e.g., *Il.* 16. 843–61, where the dying Patroclus prophesies the death of Hector; *Il.* 22. 355–66, where the dying Hector does the same of Achilles; Sophocles, *Oed. Col.* 605–28, 1370–96, 1516–55, where the aged Oedipus, his death approaching, delivers prophecies; and Virgil, *Aen.* 4. 607–29, where Dido utters a prophetic curse shortly before committing suicide. [H.M.]

269. Immersing the lamella is part of the consecration; see S. Eitrem, "Die magischen Gemmen und ihre Weihe," *SO* 19 (1939): 57–85.

The formula: / "NN, leave the sweet light and also render me whatever service I   2180
require of you whenever I call you (add the usual) because I conjure you by the
gods of the underworld GOGGYLORYGCHE OMBROLIGMATE[270] THOĒRYSĒRIS. /
Render me the service for which I summon you." Speak this formula that invokes   2185
all supernatural powers.

Consecrating the plaque: Go, I say, into a clean room. Set up a table, on which
you are to place a clean linen cloth and flowers of the season. / Then sacrifice a   2190
white cock, placing beside it 7 cakes, 7 wafers, 7 lamps; pour a libation of milk,
honey, wine, and olive oil.

Here is the formula to be spoken when you consecrate the plaque: "Come to me!
You who are master above the earth and below the earth, / who look to the west   2195
and the east and gaze upon the south and the north, O master of all, Aion of Aions!
You are the ruler of the universe, Ra, Pan,[271] (H)ARPENCHNOUBI / BRINTATĒ-   2200
NŌPHRI BRISKYLMA AROUZAR BAMESEN KRIPHI NIPTOUMI CHMOUMAŌPHI
IA IOY IYŌ AII OYŌ AEĒIOYŌ BAUBŌ BAUBŌ PHORBA PHORBA OREOBAZAGRA
ŌYOIĒEA ER." Speak too the formula that invokes Necessity: "MASKELLI (for-
mula) IARCHTHA ECHTHABA CHOIX IABOUCH IABŌCH," and the one that / in-   2205
vokes all supernatural powers.

So much for the ritual of consecration.[272] *Here are the operations for specific
purposes*:

For an oracle: Write as follows on a bay leaf in myrrh mixed with blood from
someone who has died by violence: "ABRAA, you are the one who reveals all things
MARIAPHRAX." / Then put it under the lamella.   2210

For wrecking chariots: Burn garlic and a snake's slough as an offering, and write
on a tin plaque:[273] "NEBOUTOSOUALĒTH BEU ERBĒTH PAKERBĒTH and ŌNOUPH;
overturn him, NN, and his / companions." Bury the tablet for 3 days in the grave of   2215
someone who died untimely; he will come to life for as long as it stays there.

For spells that restrain: Write on a seashell in the ink[274] mentioned below, adding / Typhon's blood.[275] Then you are to bury the shell in the tomb of someone   2220
who died untimely, when the moon stands in opposition to the sun. What you are
to write is the 3 Homeric verses,[276] and the following: "IŌ BOLCHOSĒTH IAKOU-
BIAI IŌ PATATHNAX / ERBĒTH IŌ PAKERBĒTH." The lamella is to be carried, as in   2225
the examples at the beginning.

For popularity spells and love spells: Write "MYRI MYRI NES MACHESNŌN" on a
gold tablet, after putting it under / the iron one for 3 days. When you remove it,   2230
carry it, keeping yourself clean all the while.

For fetching spells. Burn roses and sumac as an offering; take myrtle leaves and
write on them in ink: "STHENEPIŌ ARRŌRIPHRASIS YYYY / IIII fetch her, NN, for
him, NN." Recite the formula[277] and put the magical substance under the lamella.

---

270. This and the preceding *voces magicae* can be translated and mean, "you with the round snout,"
and "you who lap rain." [H.M.]

271. The interpretation of the god Pan as Aion and as god of the All is based on the assumed etymology of the name (cf. also *PGM* XIII. 980: ἐν καὶ τὸ πᾶν, "One and the All"). See F. Brommer,
"Pan," *PRE.S* 8 (1956): 1005–6.

272. See above on *PGM* IV. 2186.

273. That is, the iron tablet that has been consecrated, not the tin plaque just described.

274. That is, the myrrh ink mentioned at the end of the spell.

275. For the blood of Seth/Typhon, see *PGM* IV. 2100 and n.

276. See for these verses *PGM* IV. 2145–51.

277. Presumably, this formula is the one previously mentioned ("that invokes all supernatural pow-

You are to add some single-stemmed wormwood to the myrrh ink. Let the lamella
2240   be worn on a cord; get it from the places where / the woolworkers have their shops.
*Tr.: Hubert Martin, Jr.

PGM IV. 2241–2358
*Document to the waning moon.[278]
   Spell:
      "Hail,[279] Holy Light, Ruler of Tartaros,
      Who strike with rays; hail, Holy Beam, who whirl
      Up out of darkness and subvert all things
2245   With aimless plans. / I'll call and may you hear
      My holy words since awesome Destiny
      Is ever subject to you. Thrice-bound goddess,
      Set free yourself. Come, rage against him, NN.
      For Klotho will spin out her threads for you.
      Assent, O blessed one, ere I hold you
2250   As hateful, ere you take your / sword-armed fist,[280]
      And ere you grieve, O dog in maiden form.
      You'll, willy-nilly, do the NN task
      Because I know your lights in full detail,
      And I am your priest of good offices, /
2255   Your minister and fellow witness, Maid.
      What must take place, this you cannot escape.
      You'll, willy-nilly, do the NN task.
      I now adjure you by this potent night,
      In which your light is last to fade away,
2260   In which / a dog opens, closes not, its mouth,
      In which the bar of Tartaros is opened,
      In which forth rages Kerberos, armed with
      A thunderbolt, Bestir yourself, Mene,
      Who need the solar nurse, guard of the dead, /
2265   You I implore, Maid, by your stranger beams,[281]
      You I implore,[282] O cunning, lofty, swift,
      O crested one, who draw swords, valiant,
      Healer, with forethought, far-famed, goading one,
2270   Swift-footed, brave, crim/son, Darkness, Brimo,
      Immortal, heedful, Persian, pastoral,
      Alkyone, gold-crowned, the elder goddess,
      Shining, sea-goddess, ghostly, beautiful,
      The one who shows, skiff-holder, aiming well,

---

ers"), ll. 2186, 2204–5. The "magical substance" is usually material taken from the person to be
"fetched." See Glossary, s.v. "Material, magical."

278. The correct reading here is Δέλτος ἀποκρουστικὴν πρὸς Σελήνην. [E.N.O.]

279. These iambic trimeters, many of which are metrically faulty or even collapse almost completely,
have been adapted as the reconstructed Hymn 17; see Preisendanz, vol. II, pp. 250–53. The text is
frequently uncertain and the translation is tentative. [E.N.O.]

280. Cf. below l. 2328.

281. For ξεινη τ' Αυγη read ξεινην αυγην; see Preisendanz, vol. II, p. 251, apparatus ad loc.

282. The conclusion of the line is lost. Here a long list of what seem to be epithets, now mostly
corrupt, has been inserted. The translation usually follows the conjectures proposed by Heitsch, although many are questionable.

Self-gendered, wearing / headband, vigorous,   2275
Leader of hosts, O goddess of Dodona,
Of Ida,[283] e'er with sorrows fresh, wolf-formed,
Denounced as infamous, destructive, quick,
Grim-eyed, shrill-screaming, Thasian, Mene,
O Nethermost one, beam-embracer, savior,
World-wide, dog-shaped, / spinner of Fate, all-giver,   2280
Long-lasting, glorious, helper, queen, bright,
Wide-aimer, vigorous, holy, benign,
Immortal, shrill-voiced, glossy-locked, in bloom,
Divine, with golden face, delighting / men,   2285
Minoan, goddess of childbirth, Theban,
Long-suffering, astute, malevolent.
With rays for hair, shooter of arrows, maid;
I[284] truly know that you are full of guile
And are deliverer from fear; as Hermes,
The Elder, chief of all magicians, I
Am Isis' father.[285] Hear: EŌ PHORBA
BRIMŌ SACHMI NEBOUTO / SOUALĒTH.   2290
For I have hidden this[286] magic symbol
Of yours, your sandal, and possess your key.
I opened the bars of Kerberos, the guard
Of Tartaros, / and premature night I   2295
Plunged in darkness. I whirl the wheel for you;
The cymbals I don't touch.[287] Gaze at yourself:
Lo! As you see yourself, you'll wonder at
The mirror, love charm of the Nile's goddess,[288]
Until you cast the dark light from your eyes.
What you must do, / this you must not escape.   2300
You'll, willy-nilly, do this task for me,
Mare, Kore, dragoness, lamp, lightning flash,
Star, lion, she-wolf, AĒŌ ĒĒ.
A sieve, an old utensil, is my symbol,[289]

283. The papyrus reads ειδεα, which Wessely, whom Preisendanz follows, emends to Ἰδαία. This epithet means "belonging to Ida," a mountain range in Crete or Phrygia. Cf. *PGM* V. 455–56; LXX. 14, and Betz, "Fragments," 293 with n. 30; H. von Geisau, "Idaia," *KP* 2 (1979): 1337.

284. Here the spell that preceded the list of epithets is resumed. Some connective material may have been lost. [M.S.]

285. The elder Hermes is the Egyptian Hermes Trismegistos (Thoth) who was thought to be older than the Greek god. On Hermes/Thoth as the father of Isis, see Plutarch, *De Is. et Os.* 3, 352A–B, and 12, 355F–356A, and Griffiths, *Plutarch's De Iside et Osiride* 263. See also *PGM* IV. 99–101, where Thoth is the father. On the topic, see also Reitzenstein, *Poimandres* 136 n. 4; Nock and Festugière, *Hermès Trismégiste* III, p. cxxvii. [R.K.R.]

286. Reading τό for τοῦτο. That the symbol was the sandal is shown by the later reference to it in ll. 2334–35. The "symbols" of the gods were thought not to be mere signs of them but objects and formulas by which they could be controlled. [M.S.] See also Betz, "Fragments," 291.

287. Reading ⟨δ'⟩οὐχ and understanding the negative to refer to both verbs, as suggested by L. Koenen. The magician threatens to strike: he will not perform actions that would prevent the impending eclipse. [M.S.]

288. Reading Νειλω⟨ι⟩ Ἰ⟨σ⟩ιδος χαριν κατοπτρ⟨οι οι⟩. For ἀθρέω with ἐν, see the *Etymologicum Gudianum*, ed. Sturzius, 13. 20. [M.S.]

289. Perhaps "you" instead of "my" should be read (also l. 2311). Cf. the similar list in *PGM* VII. 780–85. [M.S.]

2305   And one morsel of flesh, a piece / of coral,
         Blood of a turtledove, hoof of a camel,
         Hair of a virgin cow, the seed of Pan,
         Fire from a sunbeam, colt's foot, spindel tree,
         Boy love, bow drill, a gray-eyed woman's body
2310   With legs outspread, a black sphinx's / pierced vagina:
         All of these are the symbol of my power.
         The bond of all necessity will be
         Sundered, and Helios will hide your light
         At noon, and Tethys will o'erflow the world,[290]
2315   Which you inhabit. Aion's / quaking; heaven
         Will be disturbed; Kronos, in terror at
         Your pole[291] o'erpowered by force, has fled to Hades
         As overseer of the dead below.
         The Moirai throw away your endless thread,
         Unless you check my magic's winged shaft,[292] /
2320   Swiftest to reach the mark. For to escape
         The fate of my words is impossible:
         Happen it must.[293] Don't force yourself[294] to hear
         The symbols forward and then in reverse
         Again. You'll, willy-nilly, do what's needed.
         Ere useless light becomes your fate, do what /
2325   I say, O Maid, ruler of Tartaros.
         I've bound your pole with Kronos' chains, and with
         Awesome compulsion I hold fast your thumb.
         Tomorrow does not come unless my will
2330   Is done. / To Hermes, leader of the gods,
         You promised[295] to contribute to this rite.
         Aye, in my power I hold you. Hear, you who
         Watch and are watched. I look at you, you look
         At me. Then, too, I'll speak the sign to you:
2335   Bronze sandal of her / who rules Tartaros,
         Her fillet, Key, wand, iron wheel, black dog,
         Her thrice-locked door, her burning hearth, her shadow,
         Depth, fire, the governess of Tartaros,
         Fearing the Furies, those prodigious daimons,[296] /
2340   You've come? You're here? Be wroth, O maid, at him,
         NN, foe of heav'n's gods, of Helios-
         Osiris[297] and of Isis, his bedmate.

290. Reading κλυζησει for κουφισει. Helios' light is the moon's because the moon shines with it (see above). He will hide it in the south, because that is where the sun goes to hide in the winter. Tethys is the goddess of the primordial waters. [M.S.]

291. Reading πολον for σου νουν with H. van Herwerden, "De carminibus e papyris aegyptiacis erutis et eruendis," *Mnemosyne*, n.s. 16 (1888): 342. [M.S.]

292. Understanding μαγείης τῆς ἐμῆς as equivalent to the dative (emendation may not be necessary), and reading ἀναγκασ⟨θ⟩ῆς. [M.S.]

293. Reading ἣν δεῖ γενέσθαι for ὃ δεῖ γενέσθαι. [M.S.]

294. Reading σα⟨υ⟩τήν with Preisendanz, ad. loc. [M.S.]

295. Reading ἐννευσα for ἐνευσας. [M.S.]

296. Reading nominatives for accusatives. [M.S.]

297. Although the link between Helios and Osiris is possible through the connection with Sarapis,

As I instruct you, hurl him to this ill
Because, Kore, I know your good and great /
Majestic names, by which heav'n is illumined,   2345
And earth drinks dew and is pregnant; from these
The universe increases and declines;

EUPHORBA PHORBA PHORBOREOU PHORBA PHORBOR PHORBOR PHORBOR BOR-
BORPHA ĒRPHOR / PHORBAIŌ PHORBOR PHORBOR BOROPH PHORPHOR BOR   2350
PHORBOR AŌ IŌĒ PHORBORPHOR EUPHOR BOPHOR EUOIEŌ PHŌTH IŌPHŌTH
IŌPHŌTH PHŌTHIŌPH AŌŌŌTHŌ ŌAI IŌ EŌŌIŌ HAHAHA EE ĒĒ IOYY ŌŌŌ OYYYY
AEĒIOUŌ / YYY mistress, Harken-techtha,[298] who sits beside Lord Osiris, Michael,   2355
Archangel of angels, the god who lights the way, perform for me."
   Protective charm of the procedure . . .
*Tr.: E. N. O'Neil. The translation is based on the edition in Preisendanz, but several emen-
dations by Morton Smith have been accepted (see the notes); see his article "The Hymn to
the Moon, *PGM* IV 2242–2355," *Proceedings of the XVI International Congress of Papyrology*,
ed. L. Koenen et al. (Chico, Cal.: Scholars Press, 1981) 643–54.

PGM IV. 2359–72

***Business spell**: Take orange beeswax and / the juice of the aeria plant and of   2360
ground ivy and mix them and fashion a figure of Hermes[299] having a hollow bottom, grasping in his left hand a herald's wand and in his right a small bag. Write on
hieratic papyrus these names, and you will see continuous business: / "CHAIŌCHEN   2365
OUTIBILMEMNOUŌTH ATRAUICH. Give income and business to this place, because
Psentebeth[300] lives here." Put the papyrus inside the figure and fill in the hole with
the same beeswax. Then deposit it in a wall, at an inconspicuous place, / and crown   2370
him on the outside, and sacrifice to him a cock, and make a drink offering of Egyptian wine, and light for him a lamp that is not colored red.
*Tr.: R. F. Hock.

PGM IV. 2373–2440

*** Charm for acquiring business and for calling in customers**[301] to a workshop or
house or wherever you put it. / By having it, you will become rich, you will be suc-   2375
cessful. For Hermes made this for the wandering Isis.[302] The charm is marvelous
and is called "*the little beggar*."
   Take beeswax that has not been heated, which is known as bee glue, and fashion /
a man having his right hand in the position of begging and having in his left a bag   2380
and a staff. Let there be around the staff a coiled snake, and let him be dressed in a
girdle and standing on a sphere that has / a coiled snake, like Isis. Stand it up and   2385

the older link between Osiris and Re may be of influence here. See A. Piankoff, *The Litany of Re* (New
York: Bollingen, 1964) 19–21. [R.K.R.]
   298. Harkentechtha is a male god (see Glossary s.v.); thus he is not to be addressed by "mistress,"
a title belonging to the moon goddess of the preceding hymn. See also *PGM* IV. 2004 and n.
   299. Here Hermes is portrayed as the god of merchants and of commerce. See *PGM* V. 390–99.
   300. This name means "the son of the female falcon." Cf. Jacoby in Preisendanz, apparatus ad loc.,
who fails to recognize the female definite article, a fact that precludes the identification with Horus, the
falcon god. [R.K.R.]
   301. LSJ renders κατακλητικόν (spell) "for invoking," but Eitrem, in Preisendanz's apparatus, is
probably right in translating "charm for calling in customers." See on this point Maltomini, *Studi Classici e Orientali* 29 (1979): 102; see also *PGM* CXXIV. 7.
   302. The wandering of Isis refers to her as the widow of Osiris searching for his body. See Plutarch,
De Is. et Os. 14, 356D–E; 39, 366F, and Griffiths, *Plutarch's De Iside et Osiride* 315, 452. For wax figurines associated with the cult of Isis, see Diodorus Sic. I. 21. 5–6 and the commentary by A. Burton,
Diodorus Siculus Book I, EPRO 29 (Leiden: Brill, 1972): 93–94.

erect it in a single block of hollowed-out juniper, and have an asp covering the top
2390   as a capital.³⁰³ Fashion him during the new moon and consecrate / it in a celebrating
mood, and read aloud the spell over his members, after you have divided him into
three sections—repeating the spell four times for each member. For each member
write on strips of papyrus made from a priestly scroll, with ink of cinnabar, juice of
2395   wormwood, and myrrh. When you have set it / up high on the place you have
chosen, sacrifice to it a wild [ass] ³⁰⁴ with a white forehead and offer it whole and
roast the inward parts over the wood of willow and thus eat it.

2400   ***Now this is what is to be written on [each] strip of papyrus. The spell on the /
bag***: "EPH EROUCHIŌ CHŌRAI DARIDA MĒTHEUEI ABACHTHIE EMESIE ECHENĒ
IAE IEN EBAPS PHNEŌA ENTHŌNICHAENTHA TROMOCHMOUSŌ THERAŌCHEIN
2405   SASI SAMACHIŌTH OUASA AMAKARALA KAIŌS / LASOI." Upon the head: "ŌAI IĒ
ĒIŌ NAŌ OULABETHEN THERMATH ENESIE." On the neck: "THALAA MEMARACHŌ
CHETH THROU PHEN PHTHAI." On the right shoulder: "ĒMAA CHNA THOUE
2410   BŌLERI." On / the left: "ARIAŌ IĒE SYPSO ITHEN BACHTHIPHĒRPSOI THENIBON."
On the belly: "AMAMAMAR AIII OU MAMŌ MOU OMBA." On the sacred bone:
2415   "IANOA PHTHOUTHO OTHOM MATHATHOU." / On the right thigh: "ARIN THEA
RAGNI MĒTHETHIŌ CHRĒ IĒ IĒ ERE." On the left thigh: "ĒI ĒIN YEAIŌ ERENPS
2420   TEPHĒT PARAOU ANĒI." On the private parts: "ĒERŌTHĒSONĒEN / THNIBITH EU-
ECHEN." On the right shin: "MIANIKOUĒI BIOUS." On the left: "CHNOU TOUŌY-
MOUCHOS ONIŌ." Under the sole of the right foot: "OURANION." ³⁰⁵ On the left:
2425   / "ANOUPSIE." On the back of the buttocks: "ETEMPSIS PSPHOPS IAIAĒĒIOO." On
the snake the name "Agathos Daimon," which is, as Epaphroditus ³⁰⁶ says, the follow-
2430   ing: / "PHRĒ ANŌI PHŌRCHŌ PHYYY RORPSIS OROCHŌŌI," but as on the paper
which I found the spell was changed thus: "Harponknouphi" (formula).

2435   ***This is the spell for the rite***: "I receive / you as the cowherd who has his camp
toward the south, I receive you for the widow and the orphan.³⁰⁷ Therefore, give me
2440   favor, work for my business. Bring to me silver, gold, clothing, / much wealth for
the good of it."
*Tr.: R. F. Hock.

PGM IV. 2441–2621

* **Spell of attraction**: ³⁰⁸ (implements: those for a lunar burnt offering); it attracts
those who are uncontrollable and requires no magical material ³⁰⁹ and who come in
one day. It inflicts sickness excellently and destroys powerfully, sends dreams beau-

303. The clause ὀρυκτόν . . . κεκρυμμένον is obscure and not clearly related to its context. Preisendanz understands the snake to be buried in the basket which is put under the figure. The reference is
apparently to the *cista mystica* which contained the snake and was carried on the head. See Apuleius,
Met. 11. 11 and Griffiths, *The Isis-Book* 222–26; H. Leisegang, "The Mystery of the Serpent," in *The
Mysteries: Papers from the Eranos Yearbooks*, Bollingen Series XXX. 2 (Princeton: Princeton University
Press, 1978), 194–260.
304. The papyrus has only here and in l. 3148 αγριον which Jacoby emends to ⟨ὀν⟩άγριον, "wild
ass." Eitrem suggests ἄγριον κριόν, "wild ram."
305. In Greek, "heavenly."
306. Apparently the papyrus refers to another author by the name Epaphroditos, but nothing is
known about him.
307. Cf. l. 2375. See also Reitzenstein, *Poimandres* 31. The widow and orphan refer to Isis and
Horus; cf. *PGM* III. 542–43. See Griffiths, *Plutarch's De Iside et Osiride* 450. For the importance of
hospitality in the myth of the wandering Isis, cf. C. E. Sander-Hansen, *Die Texte der Metternichstele* (Copenhagen: Munksgaard, 1956) 41–42; Borghouts, *Ancient Egyptian Magical Texts* 59–62. [R.K.R.]
308. This spell is similar to, and perhaps even parallel to, *PGM* IV. 2622–2784.
309. The translation of these adjectives is tentative and follows Preisendanz's German translation,

tifully, accomplishes dream revelations marvelously and in its many / demonstra-   2445
tions has been marveled at for having no failure in these matters.

Burnt offering: Pachrates,[310] the prophet of Heliopolis, revealed it to the em-
peror Hadrian, revealing the power of his own divine magic. / For it attracted in   2450
one hour; it made someone sick in 2 hours; it destroyed in 7 hours, sent the em-
peror himself dreams as he thoroughly tested the whole truth of the magic within
his power. And marveling at the prophet, / he ordered double fees to be given   2455
to him.

Take a field mouse[311] and deify it in spring water. And take two moon beetles[312]
and deify them in river water, and take a river crab and fat of a dappled goat that
is virgin and dung of a dog- / faced baboon, 2 eggs of an ibis, 2 drams of storax,   2460
2 drams of myrrh, 2 drams of crocus, 4 drams of Italian galingale, 4 drams of uncut
frankincense, a single onion. Put all these things onto a mortar with the mouse
and the remaining items / and, after pounding thoroughly, place in a lead box and   2465
keep for use. And whenever you want to perform a rite, take a little, make a charcoal fire, go up on a lofty roof, and make the offering as you say / this spell at   2470
moonrise, and at once she comes.

Spell:[313] "Let all the darkness of clouds be dispersed for me, and let the goddess
AKTIŌPHIS shine for me, and let her hear my holy voice. For I come / announcing   2475
the slander[314] of NN, a defiled and unholy woman, for she has slanderously brought
your holy mysteries to the knowledge of men. She, NN, is the one, [not] I, who
says, 'I have seen the greatest / goddess, after leaving the heavenly vault, on earth   2480
without sandals, sword in hand, and [speaking] a foul name.' It is she, NN, who
said, 'I saw [the goddess] drinking blood.' She, NN, said it, not I, AKTIŌPHIS
ERESCHIGAL / NEBOUTOSOUALĒTH PHORPHORBA SATRAPAMMŌN CHOIRIXIĒ,   2485
flesh eater. Go to her NN and take away her sleep and put a burning heat in her
soul,[315] punishment and frenzied passion in her thoughts, / and banish her from
every place and from every house, and attract her here to me, NN."   2490

After saying these things, sacrifice. Then raise loud groans and go backward as
you descend. And she will come at once. But pay attention to the one being attracted / so that you may open the door for her; otherwise the spell will fail.[316]   2495

For causing illness: Use these spells, adding, "Make her, NN, whom NN
bore, ill."

And for destroying: Say, "Draw out her breath, Mistress, from the nostrils of her,
NN."

---

except for μονομημέρους which is rendered in analogy to μονόωρος in ll. 2450–51. Cf. also the parallels
in *PGM* IV. 2071–72; XXXVI. 361.

310. The prophet Pachrates may be identical with Pankrates described by Lucian, *Philops.* 34. See
K. Preisendanz, "Pachrates," *PRE* 18 (1942): 2071–74; Nock, *Essays* I, 183–84.

311. On the role of the mouse in magic, see W. R. Dawson, "The Mouse in Egyptian and Later
Medicine," *JEA* 10 (1924): 83–86.

312. On the moon beetle and its association with the moon, see Abt, *Apologie* 126–27.

313. Although only the general term for "spell" is used here (λόγος), the contents show clearly that
the passage is a "slander spell" (διαβολή). Cf. *PGM* IV. 2622 in the title of a spell. [E.N.O.]

314. For this slander, cf. ll. 2574–2621, below. The projection of a ritual violation onto the party to
be affected by the spell, esp. the statement, "It is NN who said that. It is not I who said that," is also
found in numerous older Egyptian texts. See F. Lexa, *La Magie dans l'Égypte antique* I (Paris: Geuthner,
1925) 56–58; Pritchard, *ANET* 327 and note b. In *PGM* cf. also III. 5, 114–15; VII. 593–619. On
the whole subject, see S. Eitrem, "Die rituelle ΔΙΑΒΟΛΗ," *SO* 2 (1924): 43–61. [R.K.R.]

315. On the "burning of the soul," see R. Ganszyniec, "Das Märchen der Pythia," *Byzantinisch-
Neugriechische Jahrbücher* 1 (1920): 170–71. Cf. also Glossary, s.v. "Soul."

316. Differently Preisendanz, who understands: "otherwise she will die."

2500   / ***For sending dreams***: Say, "Become like the god whom she worships."

For dream revelations: Say, "Stand beside me, Mistress, and reveal to me about the NN matter." And she will stand beside you and will tell everything without deception.

2505   Do not therefore perform the rite rashly, and do not perform / it unless some dire necessity arises for you. It also possesses a protective charm against your falling, for the goddess is accustomed to make airborne those who perform this rite unprotected by a charm and to hurl them from aloft down to the ground. So conse-

2510   quently / I have also thought it necessary to take the precaution of a protective charm so that you may perform the rite without hesitation. Keep it secret.

Take a hieratic papyrus roll and wear it around your right arm with which you

2515   make the offering. And these are the / things written on it: "MOULATHI CHERNOUTH AMARŌ MOULIANDRON, guard me from every evil daimon, whether an evil male or female." Keep it secret, son.[317]

2520   ***The second spell***, after you make / the first sacrifice, but it is better for you to say it before you make the offering. This is the spell attached to the first:

"[I offer you][318] this spice, O child of Zeus,
Dart-shooter, Artemis, Persephone,

2525   Shooter of deer, night-shining, / triple-sounding,
Triple-voiced, triple-headed Selene,
Triple-pointed, triple-faced, triple-necked,
And goddess of the triple ways, who hold
Untiring flaming fire in triple baskets,
And you who oft frequent the triple way
And rule the triple decades with three forms

2530   / And flames and dogs. From toneless throats you send
A dread, sharp cry when you, O goddess, have
Raised up an awful sound with triple mouths.
Hearing your cry, all worldly things are shaken:

2535   The nether gates and Lethe's / holy water
And primal Chaos and the shining chasm
Of Tartaros. At it ev'ry immortal
And ev'ry mortal man, the starry mountains,
Valleys and ev'ry tree and roaring rivers,

2540   And e'en the restless sea, / the lonely echo,
And daimons through the world, shudder at you,
O blessed one, when they hear your dread voice.
Come here to me, goddess of night, beast-slayer,
Come and be at my love spell of attraction,
Quiet and frightful, and having your meal

2545   Amid the graves. / And heed my prayers, Selene,
Who suffer much, who rise and set at night,
O triple-headed, triple-named MĒNĒ
MARZOUNĒ, fearful, gracious-minded, and
Persuasion.[319] Come to me, horned-faced, light-bringer,

317. The term "son" seems to indicate the magician's apprentice. Cf. similar references in *PGM* I. 193; XIII. 214, 313, 343, 719, 755, etc. [E.N.O.]

318. These dactylic hexameters, with the usual mixture of accurate and faulty meter, also form the reconstructed Hymn 20, for which see Preisendanz, vol. II, pp. 257–59. [E.N.O.]

319. For the personified Persuasion (*Peithō*) as an attribute and companion of Aphrodite cf. *PGM*

Bull-shaped, horse-faced goddess, who howl doglike; /
Come here, she-wolf, and come here now, Mistress   2550
Of night and chthonic realms, holy, black-clad,
'Round whom the star-traversing nature of
The world revolves whene'er you wax too great.
You have established ev'ry worldly thing,
For you engendered everything on earth
And from / the sea and ev'ry race in turn   2555
Of winged birds who seek their nests again.
Mother of all, who bore Love, Aphrodite,
Lamp-bearer, shining and aglow, Selene,
Star-coursing, heav'nly, torch-bearer, fire-breather, /
Woman four-faced, four-named, four-roads' mistress.   2560
Hail, goddess, and attend your epithets,
O heav'nly one, harbor goddess, who roam
The mountains and are goddess of the crossroads;
O nether one, goddess of depths, eternal,
Goddess of dark, come to my / sacrifices.   2565
Fulfill for me this task, and as I pray
Give heed to me, Lady, I ask of you."

Use this for the spells of coercion, for it can accomplish anything, but do not use
it frequently to Selene / unless the procedure which you are performing is worthy   2570
of its power. For the hostile offerings, when some slander is involved, use the following stele, speaking thus:

This is the 3rd coercive spell:
"She,[320] NN, is burning for you, /
  Goddess, some dreadful incense[321]   2575
And dappled goat's fat, blood and filth,
  The menstrual flow of virgin
Dead, heart of one untimely dead,
  The magical material
Of dead dog, woman's embryo,
  Fine-ground wheat husks, / sour refuse,   2580
Salt, fat of dead doe, and mastic,
  And myrtle, dark bay, barley,
And crab claws, sage, rose, fruit pits and
  A single onion, / garlic,   2585
Fig meal, a dog-faced baboon's dung,
  And egg of a young ibis.
And this is sacrilege! She placed
  Them on your altar; she set
The flaming fire / to juniper   2590
  Wood strips and slays a seahawk
For you, a vulture and a mouse,
  Your greatest myst'ry, goddess.

LII. 15, where the connection is not clear, however, and esp. Pindar, *Pyth.* 4; Aeschylus, *Suppl.* passim.
  320. The meter of these lines is iambic tetrameter acatalectic. The passage is one version of the reconstructed Hymn 19; see Preisendanz, vol. II, pp. 255–57. The second version, which differs in a number
of places, appears just below in *PGM* IV. 2643–74. [E.N.O.]
  321. On the accusations, see *PGM* IV. 2475 and n.

She said, too, that these deeds of pain
   You had performed so harshly:
For she said that you slew a man
2595   And drank the / blood of this man
And ate his flesh, and she says that
   Your headband is his entrails
That you took all his skin and put
   It into your vagina,
[That you drank] sea falcon's blood and
   That your food was dung beetle.
But Pan before your very eyes
   Shot forth his seed unlawful. /
2600   A dog-faced baboon now is born
   Whene'er there's menstrual cleansing.
But you, AKTIŌPHIS, Mistress,
   Selene, Only Ruler,
Swift Fortune of daimons and gods:

NEBOUTOSOALĒTH IŌI LOIMOU LALON, in Syriac: ĒTARONKON BYTHOU PNOU-
2605 SAN / KATHINBERAO ESTOCHETH ORENTHA AMELCHERIBIOUTH SPHNOUTHI,
   Brand her, NN, the lawless one,
      With bitter retributions,
   Whom I again will duly charge
      To you in hostile manner.
   I call you, triple-faced goddess
      Mene, O light-beloved
2610   Hermes / and Hekate at once,
      Male-female child together;

MOUPHŌR PHORBA, Queen Brimo, dreaded and lawful, and Dardania, All-seeing
One, come here, IŌIĒ, Virgin, Goddess of crossroads and bull snake are you,
2615 Nymph and mare bitch and head / -nodder and Minoan and powerful, EALA-
NINDŌ, come here, ATEĒS ENIDELIDIMA, Mistress Phaiara, MĒDIXA EMITHĒNIŌ,
come to me, INDEOMĒ, come here, MEGAPHTHĒ; she will come here. Attract her
2620 NN to me very quickly, / I myself will clearly convict her of everything, goddess,
which she had done while sacrificing to you."
*Tr.: E. N. O'Neil.

PGM IV. 2622–2707

*Slander spell[322] to Selene,[323] which works for everything and every rite. For it
2625 attracts in the same hour, it sends dreams, it causes sickness, produces / dream visions,[324] removes enemies when you reverse the spell, however you wish. But above
all be protected by a protective charm and do not approach the procedure[325] care-
lessly or else the goddess is angry.[326]

322. See on this term *PGM* IV. 2475 and n.
323. For a similar slander spell, see *PGM* IV. 2471–92.
324. The papyrus has ονειρο|θαυπτει. For conjectures, cf. the apparatus ad loc., and for parallels
PGM IV. 3172, 3197. See also K. Preisendanz, "Miszellen zu den Zauberpapyri," *WSt* 42 (1920):
31–32.
325. Here πραγματεία seems to be a variant for the usual expression πρᾶγμα, "rite."
326. The present tense is strange here; it should perhaps be read μηνιεῖ, "will be angry." Preisendanz's translation has a future ring, too ("sonst zürnt die Göttin").

/ ***Preparation of the procedure's protective charm***: Take a magnet that is breath-   2630
ing and fashion it in the form of a heart, and let there be engraved on it Hekate
lying about the heart, like a little crescent. Then carve the twenty-lettered spell that
is all vowels, / and wear it around your body.   2635

The following name is what is written: "ΑΕΥΌ ΈΙΕ ΌΑ ΕΌΈ ΕΌΑ ΌΙ ΕΌΙ." For this
spell is completely capable of everything. But perform this ritual in a holy manner,
not frequently / or lightly, especially to Selene. At any rate, burn upon pieces of   2640
juniper wood an offering of Cretan storax and begin the spell.

The spell which is to be spoken:

"For[327] you the woman NN burns
  Some hostile incense, goddess;
The fat of dappled goat, and blood, /
  Defilement, embryo of   2645
A dog, the bloody discharge of
  A virgin dead untimely,
A young boy's heart,[328] with barley mixed
  In vinegar, both salt and
A deer's horn, mastic, myrtle and
  Dark bay, and mix at random,
And crab claws, / sage, rose, pits for you   2650
  And single onion, garlic,
Mouse pellets, dog-faced baboon's blood,
  And egg of a young ibis—
And what is sacrilege, she placed
  These on your wooden altar
Of juniper. She, NN, / said   2655
  That you had done this matter;
For she said that you slew a man
  And drank the blood of this man
And ate his flesh, and she says that
  Your headband is his entrails,
That you took all his skin and put
  It into your vagina, /
[That you drank] blood of a sea falcon   2660
  And your food was dung beetle.
And Pan before your very eyes
  Shot forth his seed unlawful:
A dog-faced baboon now is born
  From all the menstrual cleansing,
But you, ΑΚΤΙΌΦΙΣ, Mistress,
  Selene, / Only Ruler,   2665
The Fortune of daimons and gods,
NEBOUTOSOUALĒTH IŌ IMI BOULLON ENOURTILAIĒ (otherwise: NOUMILLON

---

327. The meter of these lines is iambic tetrameter acatelectic. The passage is one version of the reconstructed Hymn 19; see Preisendanz, vol. II, pp. 255–57. The second version, which differs in a number
of places, appears above in *PGM* IV. 2574–2610. [E.N.O.]

328. On rituals involving a boy's heart, see A. Henrichs, *Die Phoinikika des Lollianos. Fragmente eines
neuen griechischen Romans, Papyrologische Texte und Abhandlungen* 14 (Bonn: Habelt, 1972): 32–37,
69–72.

ESORTILĒS BATHYPNOU SANKANTHARA MIBERATH ENTOCHE THŌ RENTHA IM-
OUĒ SORENTHA).

>   Mark her, NN, the lawless one,
2670 >   With bitter / retributions,
>   Whom I again will duly charge
>   To you in hostile manner
>   (Of all unlawful things that she
>   Has said against the goddess
>   Detail as many as you want),
>   For by the spell she forces
>   Even the rocks to burst asunder."

2675   ***This, then, is the beneficent offering*** / which you sacrifice on the first and second
day (but on the third day, with the coercive spell also sacrifice the offering that is
coercive). ***The beneficent offering, then, is***: Uncut frankincense, bay, myrtle, fruit
2680   pit, stavesacre, / cinnamon leaf, kostos. Pound all these together and blend with
Mendesian [329] wine and honey, and make pills the size of beans.

2685   ***The coercive offering***: When you say the foregoing coercive spell / on the third
day, also make an offering: it is a field mouse, fat of a virgin dappled goat, magic
material of a dog-faced baboon, egg of an ibis, river crab, a perfect moon beetle,
2690   single-stemmed wormwood picked at sunrise,[330] magic material of a dog, / a single
clove of garlic. Blend with vinegar. Make pills and stamp with a completely iron
ring, completely tempered, with a Hekate [331] and the name BARZOU PHERBA.

2695   ***The protective charm which you must wear***: / Onto lime wood write with ver-
milion this name: "EPOKŌPT KŌPTO BAI BAITOKARAKŌPTO KARAKŌPTO CHILO-
2700   KŌPTO BAI (50 letters). Guard me from every daimon of the air / on the earth and
under the earth, and from every angel and phantom and ghostly visitation and
enchantment, me NN." Enclose it in a purple skin, hang it around your neck and
wear it. /

2705   ***A protective charm on a silver leaf***: [332]

*Tr.: E. N. O'Neil.

PGM IV. 2708–84

*Another love spell of attraction: Take some Ethiopian cumin and fat of a dap-
2710   pled virgin goat / and after putting the offering together, offer it to Selene on the
13th, 14th, on an earthen censer, on a lofty housetop, on coals. ***Spell***:

329. See on this term *PGM* I. 85 and n.
330. Cf. on this point *PGM* IV. 286–87. It is likely that the magician recognizes that he is to perform a "ritual for picking a plant" (βοτανήαρσις).
331. The ring is supposed to have an image of Hekate.
332. For an example of a phylactery consisting of magical characters, see D. Jordan, "A Silver Phylactery at Istanbul," *ZPE* 28 (1978): 84–86.

"Come,[333] giant Hekate, Dione's [334] guard, /
O Persia, Baubo Phroune,[335] dart-shooter,   2715
Unconquered, Lydian,[336] the one untamed,
Sired nobly, torch-bearing, guide, who bends down
Proud necks, Kore, hear, you who've parted / gates   2720
Of steel unbreakable. O Artemis,
Who, too, were once protectress, mighty one,
Mistress, who burst forth from the earth, dog-leader,
All-tamer, crossroad goddess, triple-headed,
Bringer of light, august / virgin, I call you   2725
Fawn-slayer, crafty, O infernal one,[337]
And many-formed. Come, Hekate, goddess
Of three ways, who with your fire-breathing phantoms
Have been allotted dreaded roads and harsh /
Enchantments. Hekate I call you with   2730
Those who untimely passed away and with
Those heroes who have died without a wife
And children, hissing wildly, yearning in
Their hearts."[338] (***But others*** say, "with form of winds"). /
"Go stand above her (NN) head and take   2735
Away from her sweet sleep. And never let
Eyelid come glued to eyelid, but let her
Be sore distressed with wakeful cares for me. /
And if she lies with someone else in her   2740
Embrace, let her thrust him away and take
Me in her heart. Let her abandon him
At once and stand before my door subdued
In soul at longing for my bed of love.[339] /
But you, O Hekate, of many names,   2745
O Virgin, Kore, Goddess, come, I ask,
O guard and shelter of the threshing floor,
Persephone, O triple-headed goddess,
Who walk on fire, cow-eyed BOUORPHORBĒ [340]
PANPHORBA PHORBARA AKTIŌPHI
ERESCHIGAL / NEBOUTOSOUALĒTH   2750

333. The dactylic hexameters, which are frequently interrupted by *voces magicae* and other formulas, also form the reconstructed Hymn 21. See Preisendanz, vol. II, pp. 259–60, where the hymn concludes with IV. 2764 but adds 2784 as a kind of postscript. [E.N.O.]

334. Dione is a name of Aphrodite; see LSJ, s.v. Here in this syncretistic hymn the name belongs to Hekate, as on the magical tools from Pergamon; see Wünsch, *Antikes Zaubergerät* 23–24.

335. The epithet of Hekate may be related to the frog (cf. *PGM* XXXVI. 235). The animal played an important role in magic as a representative of the gods of the underworld. See M. Weber, "Frosch," *RAC* 8 (1970):524–38.

336. The use of the name "Lydian" with Hekate-Artemis should be noted in connection with the possible Lydian origin of Artemis. See on this point Chantraine, *Dictionnaire* I, 116–17.

337. The translation follows Reitzenstein's emendation (see Preisendanz, apparatus ad loc.) of αυδ-ναια as ᾽Αϊδωναία. This epithet of the goddess of Hades also occurs in *PGM* IV. 2855. Cf. LSJ, s.v. Αὐδυναῖος; Suppl. s.v.

338. Cf. Homer, *Od.* 9. 75. As the apparatus points out, the verse may be corrupt.

339. φιλότητι καὶ εὐνῇ is a Homeric *hendiadys*. Cf. *Il.* 3. 445; 6. 25. See *PGM* IV. 2910.

340. The *voces magicae* here seem intended as a part of the verse pattern and they have, however awkwardly, been treated as such. [E.N.O.]

Beside the doors, PYPYLĒDEDEZŌ
And gate-breaker; Come Hekate, of fiery
Counsel, I call you to my sacred chants.

MASKELLI MASKELLŌ PHNOUKENTABAŌTH OREOBAZAGRA who burst forth from
2755   the earth, / earth mare, OREOPĒGANYX MORMORON TOKOUMBAI" (add the usual),
"In frenzy[341] may she (NN) come fast to my doors,
Forgetting children and her life with parents,
2760   And loathing all the race of men / and women
Except me (NN), but may she hold me alone
And come subdued in heart by love's great force.

2765   THENŌB[342] TITHELĒB ĒNŌR TENTHĒNŌR. / Many-named One, KYZALEOUSA
PAZAOUS; wherefore, KOLLIDĒCHMA and SAB set her (NN) soul ablaze with unresting fire. Both ŌRIŌN and MICHAĒL who sits on high: you hold the seven wa-
2770   ters / and the earth, keeping in check the one they call the great serpent, AKRO-
KODĒRE[343] MOUISRŌ CHARCHAR ADŌNAI ZEUS DĒ DAMNAMENEUS KYNOBIOU
2775   EZAGRA" (add the usual). "IŌ, all-powerful goddess / and IŌ all-guarding one; IŌ,
all-sustaining One, ZĒLACHNA: and SAAD SABIŌTHE NOUMILLON NATHOMEINA,
2780   always KEINĒTH, stalwart THĒSEUS ONYX,[344] prudent DAMNAMENEUS, / avenging
goddess, strong goddess, rite of ghosts, Persia SEBARA AKRA.
Haste quickly. Let her now stand at my doors" (add the usual).
*Tr.: E. N. O'Neil.

PGM IV. 2785–2890

2785   * **Prayer to Selene for any spell**:[345]
"Come[346] to me, O beloved mistress, Three-faced
Selene; kindly hear my sacred chants;
Night's ornament, young, bringing light to mortals, /
2790   O child of morn who ride upon fierce bulls,
O queen who drive your car on equal course
With Helios, who with the triple forms
Of triple Graces dance in revel with /
2795   The stars. You're Justice[347] and the Moira's threads:
Klotho and Lachesis and Atropos[348]

341. See on this point the discussion by Wortmann, "Neue magische Texte," 101–2. On the subject of madness caused by magic, see J. Mattes, *Der Wahnsinn im griechischen Mythos und in der Dichtung bis zum Drama des 5. Jahrhunderts, Bibliothek der Altertumswissenschaften,* N. F. 2. Reihe, Band 36 (Heidelberg: Winter, 1970) 44–49.

342. These lines (2764–84) retain some traces of hexameters, but only the last line comes close to being a complete line. [E.N.O.]

343. The formula seems to be textually mutilated. Cf. for similar passages *PGM* II. 23–24; V. 424–27; VII. 680–83. See Preisendanz, apparatus ad loc.

344. ONYX may refer to the stone onyx which was used in magic. Cf. Hopfner, *OZ* I, section 582.

345. For a discussion of this hymn, see K. Kerényi, "Die Göttin Natur," *Eranos-Jahrbuch* 14 (1947): 39–86, esp. 68–79.

346. These dactylic hexameters, some of which show the usual irregularities, also form the reconstructed Hymn 18. See Preisendanz, vol. II, pp. 253–55. [E.N.O.]

347. Dike (Justice), the daughter of Zeus, has here and in l. 2860 become an epithet of the underworld goddess. For the association of Dike with underworld deities, see A. Dihle, "Gerechtigkeit," *RAC* 10 (1976): 243–45.

348. The reading of the papyrus is uncertain at this point. Traditionally, the names of the Furies were Alecto, Tisiphone, and Megaira (Apollodorus, *Bib.* 1. 1. 4; *Orph. Hymn.* 69. 2). If the three Furies are intended here, the reading of Persephone will have to be changed to Tisiphone, as suggested by Preisendanz, apparatus ad loc. See also H. Funke, "Furien," *RAC* 8 (1971): 699–722, esp. 704–5.

Three-headed, you're Persephone, Megaira,
Allekto, many-formed, who arm your hands /
With dreaded, murky lamps, who shake your locks   2800
Of fearful serpents on your brow, who sound
The roar of bulls out from your mouths, whose womb
Is decked out with the scales of creeping things, /
With pois'nous rows of serpents down the back,   2805
Bound down your backs with horrifying chains
Night-Crier, bull-faced, loving solitude,
Bull-headed, you have eyes of bulls, / the voice   2810
Of dogs; you hide your forms in shanks of lions,[349]
Your ankle is wolf-shaped, fierce dogs are dear
To you, wherefore they call you / Hekate,   2815
Many-named, Mene, cleaving air just like
Dart-shooter[350] Artemis, Persephone,
Shooter of deer, night / shining, triple-sounding,   2820
Triple-headed, triple-voiced Selene
Triple-pointed, triple-faced, triple-necked,
And goddess of the triple ways, who hold
Untiring flaming fire in triple baskets, /
And you who oft frequent the triple way   2825
And rule the triple decades,[351] unto me
Who'm calling you be gracious and with kindness
Give heed, you who protect the spacious world
At night, before whom daimons quake in fear /
And gods immortal tremble, goddess who   2830
Exalt men, you of many names, who bear
Fair offspring, bull-eyed, horned, mother of gods
And men, and Nature,[352] Mother of all things,
For you frequent Olympos, / and the broad   2835
And boundless chasm you traverse. Beginning
And end are you, and you alone rule all.
For all things are from you, and in you do
All things, Eternal one, come to their end.
As everlasting / band around your temples   2840
You wear great Kronos' chains,[353] unbreakable
And unremovable, and you hold in
Your hands a golden scepter. Letters 'round
Your scepter / Kronos wrote himself and gave   2845
To you to wear that all things stay steadfast:
Subduer and subdued, mankind's subduer,
And force-subduer; Chaos, too, you rule.

349. The phrase describing Hekate/Artemis as standing between two lions points to the older concept of the "queen of the animals." See W. Helck, *Betrachtungen zur Grossen Göttin und den ihr verbun-
denen Gottheiten* (München und Wien: Oldenbourg, 1971) esp. 223–25.

350. Ll. 2819–26 are parallel to IV. 2523–28.

351. For the term "triple decades," see *PGM* IV. 2527.

352. For the concept of Nature, see Glossary, s.v.; for the epithet "mother of all things" see *Orph.
Hymn.* 10. 1: παμμήτειρα. See also *PGM* IV. 2917.

353. See also *PGM* IV. 3087–3124 and S. Eitrem, "Kronos in der Magie," *Université libre de Bruxelles, Annuaire de l'institut de philologie et d'histoire orientales,* II: *Mélanges J. Bidez,* vol. I (Bruxelles: Secre-
tariat de l'institut, 1934) 351–60.

2850 ARARACHARA/RA ĒPHTHISIKĒRE.

> Hail, goddess, and attend your epithets,
> I burn[354] for you this spice, O child of Zeus,
> Dart-shooter, heav'nly one, goddess of harbors,
> Who roam the mountains, goddess of crossroads, /

2855
> O nether and nocturnal, and infernal,
> Goddess of dark, quiet and frightful[355] one,
> O you who have your meal amid the graves,[356]
> Night, Darkness, broad Chaos: Necessity
> Hard to escape are you; you're Moira and /

2860
> Erinys,[357] torment, Justice and Destroyer,
> And you keep Kerberos in chains, with scales
> Of serpents are you dark, O you with hair
> Of serpents, serpent-girded, who drink blood, /

2865
> Who bring death and destruction, and who feast
> On hearts, flesh eater, who devour those dead
> Untimely, and you who make grief resound
> And spread madness, come to my sacrifices,

2870
> And now for me do you filfill / this matter."

Offering for the rite: For doing good, offer storax, myrrh, sage, frankincense, a
2875 fruit pit. But for doing harm, offer magical / material of a dog and a dappled goat
(or in a similar way, of a virgin untimely dead).

2880 **Protective charm for the rite**: Take a lodestone and on it have carved / a three-
faced Hekate. And let the middle face be that of a maiden wearing horns, and the
left face that of a dog, and the one on the right that of a goat. After the carving is
2885 done, / clean with natron and water, and dip in the blood of one who has died a
violent death. Then make a food offering to it[358] and say the same spell at the time
2890 of the / ritual.[359]
*Tr.: E. N. O'Neil.

PGM IV. 2891–2942

*Love spell of attraction:

Offering to the star of Aphrodite:[360] A white dove's blood and fat, untreated myrrh
and parched wormwood. Make this up together as pills and offer them to the star
2895 on pieces of vine / wood or on coals. And also have the brains of a vulture for the
compulsion, so that you may make the offering. And also have as a protective charm
a tooth from the upper right jawbone of a female ass or of a tawny sacrificial heifer,
2900 tied to your left arm with / Anubian thread.[361]

---

354. The following lines are similar to those at *PGM* IV. 2522–29, but their order occasionally
differs.
355. On δασπλῆτι, "frightful," cf. Theocritus, *Idyll* 2. 14 (said of Hekate). [E.N.O.]
356. On eating amid graves, cf., e.g., Tibullus 1. 5. 49–56, esp. 53–54.
357. The goddess is here identified with Erinys, the avenging deity. This identification is somewhat
inconsistent with l. 2798, where the three Furies are named; the same is true of Moira (l. 2859) as com-
pared with the three Moirai (ll. 2795–96). See *PGM* IV. 1418, 2339; V. 191; and IV. 2798 with n.
358. The term παράθεσις refers to an offering of food. See *PGM* I. 23, 39; XIII. 1012. Cf. Eitrem's
and Preisendanz's translation: "leg ihn (eine Weile) beiseite." Wünsch thinks of the term as a cover
("Hülle").
359. For the meaning of the phrase, see *PGM* V. 230.
360. The star of Aphrodite is the planet Venus.
361. On the Anubian thread see *PGM* I. 147 and n.

Compulsion element of the rite:

"But,[362] if as goddess you in slowness act,
You will not see Adonis rise from Hades,[363]
Straightway I'll run and bind him with steel chains; /
As guard, I'll bind on him another wheel   2905
Of Ixion;[364] no longer will he come
To light, and he'll be chastized and subdued.
Wherefore, O Lady, act, I beg: Attract
NN, whom NN bore, to come with rapid step
To my door,[365] me, NN, whom NN bore, /
And to the bed of love, driven by frenzy,   2910
In anguish from the forceful goads—today,
At once, quickly. For I adjure you, Kythere,[366]

NOUMILLON BIOMBILLON AKTIŌPHI ERESCHIGAL NEBOUTOSOUALĒTH PHROU-
RĒXIA THERMIDOCHĒ BAREŌ / NĒ."   2915

Hymn of Compulsion:

"O foam-born Kythereia, mother of
Both gods and men, etherial and chthonic,
All-Mother Nature, goddess unsubdued,
Who hold together things,[367] who cause the great
Fire to revolve, who keep the ever-moving
BARZA[368] / in her unbroken course; and you   2920
Accomplish everything, from head to toes,
And by your will is holy water mixed,
When by your hands you'll move RHOUZŌ[369] amid
The stars, the world's midpoint which you control.
You move holy desire into the souls
Of men / and move women to man, and you   2925
Render[370] woman desirable to man

362. This is a curious and confused passage. Ll. 2902–15 contain scattered snatches of verses which
are obviously parts of dactylic hexameters. Ll. 2916–28 contain lines which are relatively accurate hexameters, but 2929–39 are a mixture of metrical and nonmetrical lines. Nevertheless, the whole passage
has been arranged and reconstructed as Hymn 22; see Preisendanz, vol. II, pp. 260–61. Since the tone
and purpose of the whole passage seems hymnic, the translation has been made in verse but with an
occasional faulty line. [E.N.O.]

363. On the cult of Adonis in Egypt and the problem concerning his "resurrection," cf. Theocritus,
Idyll 15 and, with further literature, Nilsson, *GGR* II, 35 n. 2; 650, n. 4; Griffiths, *Plutarch's De Iside et
Osiride* 320–22.

364. Because he attempted to make love to Hera, wife of Zeus, the mythical king Ixion was con-
demned by being fastened to an ever-turning wheel. The myth of Ixion was very popular in antiquity.
See Cook, *Zeus* III, 2, pp. 200–205 (with plates); P. Weizsäcker, in Roscher 2, 766–72, s.v. "Ixion";
H. von Geisau, "Ixion," *KP* 3 (1979):31–32.

365. Preisendanz states that ἐν προθύροισιν is a tag from Homer, *Od.* 10. 220.

366. Two traditional epithets of Aphrodite occur here closely together: *Kythērē* in l. 2912 and
Kythereia in l. 2915. The name may refer to the island of Kythera which was believed to be Aphrodite's
birthplace and which had a temple of Aphrodite Urania. See LSJ, s.v.; E. Meyer, "Kythera," *KP* 3
(1979):423.

367. The reading of this epithet is uncertain. See the apparatus.

368. The word BARZA is Persian and means "shining light." See Hopfner, *OZ* II, p. 100.

369. Hopfner, *OZ* II, p. 100, assumes that RHOUZŌ is confused with the Persian magical word
ZOURŌ. See also K. Preisendanz, "Zuro," in Roscher 6, pp. 763–64.

370. Preisendanz prints τίθησι, the reading of the papyrus, but the third person is certainly wrong
here. The simplest correction is that of Wessely: τίθης σύ, and that is what is translated here.

Through all the days to come, our Goddess Queen,
Come to these chants, Mistress
ARRŌRIPHRASI GŌTHĒTINI, Cyprus-born, SOUI ĒS THNOBOCHOU THORITHE
2930 STHENEPIŌ, Lady / SERTHENEBĒEI, and inflict fiery love on her, NN, whom NN
bore,
So[371] that for me, NN, whom NN bore,
She melt with love through all the days to come
But, blessed RHOUZŌ, grant this to me, NN:
Just as into your chorus 'mid the stars
A man unwilling you attracted to
2935 Your bed for intercourse, / and once he was
Attracted, he at once began to turn
Great BARZA, nor did he cease turning, and
While moving in his circuits, he's aroused:
wherefore attract to me, her, NN, whom NN bore,
To bed of love. But goddess Cyrpus-born
Do you now to the full fulfill this chant." /
2940   If you see the star shining steadily, it is a sign that she has been smitten, and if it is
lengthened like the flame of a lamp, she has already come.[372]
*Tr.: E. N. O'Neil.

PGM IV. 2943–66

*Love-spell of attraction through wakefulness: Take the eyes of a bat and release
2945 it alive, and take / a piece of unbaked dough or unmelted wax and mold a little
dog; and put the right eye of the bat into the right eye of the little dog, implanting
also in the same way the left one in the left. And take a needle, thread it with the
2950 magical material and / stick it through the eyes of the little dog, so that the magical
material is visible. And put the dog into a new drinking vessel, attach a papyrus
strip[373] to it and seal it with your own ring which has crocodiles with the backs of
2955 their heads attached,[374] and / deposit it at a crossroad after you have marked the
spot so that, should you wish to recover it, you can find it.
      Spell written on the papyrus strip: "I adjure you three times by Hekate PHOR-
2960 PHORBA BAIBŌ PHŌRBŌRBA, that she, NN, lose the fire in her eye or even / lie
awake with nothing on her mind except me, NN, alone. I adjure by Kore, who has
become the Goddess of Three roads, and who is the true mother of . . . (whom you
2965 wish), PHORBEA BRIMŌ NĒRĒATO DAMŌN BRIMŌN SEDNA / DARDAR, All-seeing
one, IŌPĒ, make her, NN, lie awake for me through all [eternity]."
*Tr.: E. N. O'Neil.

371. The verse resumes here after a few lines of prose; however, the NN-formula does not scan.
372. The last word of this section is either ἦξεν ("she has come") or ἦξεν ("it has attracted"). The
magical sense—or the result—is the same in either case. For the rare aorist of ἄγω cf. PGM IV. 2934:
ἦξας. Preisendanz prints ἦξεν in the first, ἦξεν in the second edition, but in the index lists the word
under ἥκω. [E.N.O.]
373. πιττακίζω means "attach a label" (LSJ, s.v.) in the sense of attaching a papyrus strip on which
writing is placed; cf. below, ll. 2956–66. [E.N.O.]
374. Whether this means "head to head" (thus Preisendanz) or "tail to tail" (thus LSJ) or "head to
tail" is uncertain. Paired crocodiles appear on seals in all these positions, but head to tail is far more
frequent. [M.S.] The crocodile was sacred to Sobek, with whose cult sacred prostitution seems to have
been associated. Thus there may be a link with the erotic theme of this spell. See H. Thompson, "Two
Demotic Self-Dedications," JEA 26 (1940):68–78. [R.K.R.]

PGM IV. 2967–3006

*Among the Egyptians herbs are always obtained like this:[375] the herbalist first purifies his own body. First he sprinkles with natron[376] and / fumigates the herb with   2970
resin from a pine tree after carrying it around the place 3 times.[377] Then, after
burning *kyphi* and pouring the libation of milk as he prays, he pulls up the plant
while invoking by name the daimon to whom the herb / is being dedicated and   2975
calling upon him to be more effective for the use for which it is being acquired.

The invocation for him, which he speaks over any herb, generally at the moment
of picking, is as follows:[378]

"You were sown by Kronos, you were conceived by Hera, / you were maintained   2980
by Ammon, you were given birth by Isis, you were nourished by Zeus the god of
rain, you were given growth by Helios and dew.[379] You [are] the dew of all the gods,
you [are] the heart of Hermes, you are the seed of the primordial gods, you are the
eye / of Helios,[380] you are the light of Selene,[381] you are the zeal of Osiris,[382] you are   2985
the beauty and the glory of Ouranos, you are the soul of Osiris' daimon which
revels in every place, you are the spirit of Ammon. As you have exalted Osiris, so
/ exalt yourself and rise just as Helios rises each day. Your size is equal to the zenith   2990
of Helios, your roots come from the depths, but your powers are in the heart of
Hermes, your fibers are the bones of Mnevis,[383] and your / flowers are the eye of   2995
Horus,[384] your seed is Pan's seed. I am washing you in resin as I also wash the
gods[385] even [as I do this] for my own health. You also be cleaned by prayer and give
us power as Ares and Athena do. I am Hermes. I am acquiring you with Good
/ Fortune and Good Daimon both at a propitious hour and on a propitious day   3000
that is effective for all things."

After saying this, he rolls the harvested stalk in a pure linen cloth (but into the
place of its roots they threw seven seeds of wheat and an equal number of barley,
after mixing them with honey), / and after pouring in the ground which has been   3005
dug up, he departs.
*Tr.: E. N. O'Neil.

---

375. On plant picking, see *PGM* IV. 286 and n.

376. Natron, a natural compound of sodium carbonate and sodium bicarbonate, was the primary mineral used for purification in Egypt. See J. R. Harris, *Lexicographical Studies in Ancient Egyptian Minerals* (Berlin: Akademie-Verlag, 1961), 193–94. [R.K.R.]

377. On the ritual of walking in a circle, see W. Pax, "Circumambulatio," *RAC* 3 (1957): 143–52. For a humorous example, see Propertius, *Eleg.* 4. 8. 81–86. [E.N.O.]

378. Cf. the divinization of persons in Egyptian religion, documentation of which lists the individuals alongside various gods so as to identify them. See A. Massert, "A propos des 'listes' dans les textes funéraires et magiques," *Analecta Biblica* 12 (1959): 227–46. [R.K.R.]

379. On the significance of dew (δρόσος), see Plutarch, *De Is. et Os.* 33, 364A, and Griffiths, *Plutarch's De Iside et Osiride* 424, where he refers to *PGM* XII. 234. [E.N.O.]

380. The association of the eye and the sun (Helios) was widely known in antiquity. See P. Wilpert (S. Zenker), "Auge," *RAC* 1 (1950) esp. 961–63.

381. That is, the light of the moon.

382. The term σπουδή ("zeal") is troublesome. Preisendanz translates "Würde" (majesty). Cf. the apparatus ad loc. [E.N.O.]

383. The epithet Mnevis, which occurs in *PGM* VII. 445; XIXa. 6, is the hellenized form of the Egyptian *Mr-wr*, the name of the holy bull of Heliopolis, the incarnation of the sun god Prē. See Diodorus Sic. 1. 84. 4; Plutarch, *De Is. et Os.* 33, 364C, with Griffiths commentary, 425. On the matter, see W. Helck, "Mnevis," *KP* 3 (1975): 1374–75; L. Kákosy, "Mnevis," *LdÄ* 4 (1980): 165–67.

384. For the eye of Horus, see *PGM* III. 421–26.

385. The reference is to the daily temple cult and care for the divine statues, including their washing, dressing, and feeding. See Morenz, *Egyptian Religion* 87–88. [R.K.R.]

PGM IV. 3007-86

*A tested charm of Pibechis [386] for those possessed by daimons: [387] Take oil of unripe olives with the herb mastigia and the fruit pulp of the lotus, and boil them
3010 with colorless marjoram / while saying, "IŌĒL ŌS SARTHIŌMI EMŌRI THEŌCHIP-SOITH SITHEMEŌCH SŌTHĒ IŌĒ MIMIPSŌTHIŌŌPH PHERSŌTHI AEĒIOYŌ IŌĒ EŌ CHARI PHTHA, come out from NN" (add the usual). *The phylactery*: On a tin
3015 lamella write / "IAĒO ABRAŌTH IŌCH PHTHA MESENPSIN IAŌ PHEŌCH IAĒO CHARSOK," and hang it on the patient. It is terrifying to every daimon, a thing he fears. After placing [the patient] opposite [to you], conjure. *This is the conjura-*
3020 *tion*: "I conjure you by the god of the Hebrews, / Jesus, [388] IABA IAĒ ABRAŌTH AIA THŌTH ELE ELŌ AĒŌ EOY IIIBAECH ABARMAS IABARAOU ABELBEL LŌNA ABRA MAROIA BRAKIŌN, who appears in fire, who is in the midst of land, [389] snow, and
3025 fog, TANNĒTIS; [390] let your / angel, the implacable, descend and let him assign the daimon flying around this form, which god formed in his holy paradise, because I pray to the holy god, [calling] upon AMMŌN IPSENTANCHŌ (formula). I conjure
3030 you, LABRIA IAKOUTH / ABLANATHANALBA AKRAMM (formula) AŌTH IATHA-BATHRA CHACHTHABRATHA CHAMYN CHEL ABRŌŌTH OUABRASILŌTH HALLĒLOU IELŌSAI IAĒL. I conjure you by the one who appeared to Osrael [391] in a shining pillar
3035 and a cloud by day, [392]/who saved his people from the Pharaoh and brought upon Pharaoh the ten plagues because of his disobedience. [393] I conjure you, every dai-
3040 monic spirit, to tell whatever sort you may be, because I conjure you by the seal / which Solomon [394] placed on the tongue of Jeremiah, and he told. You also tell what-ever sort you may be, heavenly or aerial, whether terrestrial or subterranean, or
3045 netherworldly or Ebousaeus or Cherseus or Pharisaeus, [395] tell / whatever sort you may be, because I conjure you by god, light-bearing, [396] unconquerable, who knows what is in the heart of every living being, the one who formed of dust the race of humans, [397] the one who, after bringing them out from obscurity, packs together

386. Pibechis was a legendary magician from Egypt. See K. Preisendanz, "Pibechis," *PRE* 20 (1941): 1310–12. Pibechis is Egyptian *P3-bk*, "the falcon." [E.N.O.]

387. The following section contains numerous references to Jewish traditions. For a discussion and collections of parallel passages, see W. L. Knox, "Jewish Liturgical Exorcism," *HTR* 31 (1938): 191–203; Deissmann, *Light from the Ancient East* 256–64.

388. On the peculiar epithet "Jesus the god of the Hebrews," see Reitzenstein, *Poimandres* 14, nn. 1–2; Deissmann, *Light from the Ancient East* 260, n. 4; Knox, "Jewish Liturgical Exorcism," 193–94; H. Chadwick, *Origen, Contra Celsum* (Cambridge: Cambridge University Press, ²1965) 210 (on c. Cels. 4. 34); Smith, *Jesus the Magician* 113; A. A. Barb, "Three Elusive Amulets," *JWCI* 27 (1964): 7–9. Cf. *PGM* IV. 1230; XII. 190, 390; XXIIb. 18.

389. See on this "field" *PGM* XIV. 8; LXXVII. 5.

390. TANNĒTIS may be equivalent to the Egyptian *Ta-nt-N.t*, "She of Neith." Cf. the apparatus ad loc. [R.K.R.]

391. Osrael is a variant form of Israel. See *PGM* IV. 1816 with n.

392. Cf. on this legendary tradition LXX Ex 13: 21–22 and parallels. See J. Daniélou, "Feuersäule (Lichtsäule, Wolkensäule)," *RAC* 7 (1969): 786–90.

393. On the plagues of Pharaoh, see LXX Ex 7: 8–11: 10 and parallels.

394. The "seal of Solomon" is the name of a famous amulet in antiquity. For bibliography, see G. Fitzer, *TDNT* 7 (1971): 947, n. 72. Placing the amulet on the tongue of Jeremiah appears to come from haggadic tradition unknown to us. See K. Preisendanz, "Salomo," *PRE.S* 8 (1965): 660–704.

395. Deissmann, *Light from the Ancient East* 261, n. 11, derives these names of demons from LXX Gn 15: 20–21; Ex 3: 8, 17, etc.: The Χετταῖοι have become Χερσαῖος ("land daimon"), the Φερεζαῖοι have become Φαρισαῖος (which therefore has been confused with Pharisee), and the Ἰεβουσαῖοι have become Ἐβουσαῖος. Cf. Dietrich, *Abraxas* 139; Preisendanz, apparatus ad loc.

396. Ll. 3045–52 contain prayer language apparently of Jewish origin. See the biblical parallels in Deissmann, *Light from the Ancient East* 261–62.

397. Cf. LXX Gn 2: 7.

the clouds, waters the earth with rain / and blesses its fruit, [the one] whom every   3050
heavenly power of angels and of archangels praises. I conjure you by the great god
SABAŌTH, through whom the Jordan River drew back[398] and the Red Sea, / which   3055
Israel crossed, became impassable,[399] because I conjure you by the one who introduced the one hundred forty languages[400] and distributed them by his own
command. I conjure you by the one who burned up the stubborn giants with
lightning,[401] / whom the heaven of heavens praises, whom the wings of the cheru-   3060
bim[402] praise. I conjure you by the one who put the mountains around the sea [or]
a wall of sand and commanded the sea not to overflow.[403] The abyss obeyed;[404] and
you obey, / every daimonic spirit, because I conjure you by the one who causes the   3065
four winds to move[405] together from the holy aions, [the] skylike, sealike, cloud-
like, light-bringing, unconquerable [one]. I conjure [you] by the one in holy Jerusalem,[406] before whom the / unquenchable fire burns for all time,[407] with his holy   3070
name, IAEŌBAPHRENEMOUN (formula), the one before whom the fiery Gehenna
trembles, flames surround, iron bursts asunder and every mountain is afraid from
its foundation. / I conjure you, every daimonic spirit, by the one who oversees the   3075
earth and makes its foundations tremble,[408] [the one] who made all things which
are not into that which is."[409]

And I adjure you, the one who receives this conjuration, / not to eat pork,[410] and   3080
every spirit and daimon, whatever sort it may be, will be subject to you. And while
conjuring, blow once, blowing air from the tips of the feet up to the face,[411] and it
will be assigned. Keep yourself pure, for this charm / is Hebraic and is preserved   3085
among pure men.
*Tr.: W. C. Grese.

398. Cf. LXX Jos 3:13–14; Ps 113:3.

399. Cf. LXX Ex 14:27. See J. Daniélou, "Exodus," *RAC* 7 (1969):22–44.

400. Most Jewish sources speak of seventy nations and seventy languages in the world. But there are
authorities who name 140 languages. For discussion and references, see Ginzberg, *The Legends of the Jews*
I, 173; II, 214; V, 194–95.

401. Cf. LXX Gn 6:4; 19:24–29. See W. Speyer, "Gigant," *RAC* 10 (1978):1247–75.

402. The text has *Cherubin*. See Deissmann, *Light from the Ancient East* 262, n. 8.

403. Cf. LXX Jb 38:10–11; Jer 5:22.

404. Cf. LXX Prv 8:26–29; Jb 38:30, 34.

405. Cf. LXX Ps 134:7; also Gn 8:1; Nm 11:31; Jb 28:25, etc.

406. The name is given as Hierosolymon. For the various forms of the city's name, see G. Fohrer and
E. Lohse, *TDNT* 7 (1971), s.v. Σιών κτλ., sections A. I. 2; B. I (esp. nn. 133, 134); C. I. 2.

407. This refers to the seven-branched candelabrum (menorah) of the Jerusalem Temple. Its undying
light was legendary in antiquity. See *PGM* IV. 1219 and n.; Ps.-Hecataeus, in Iosephus, *c. Ap.* 1. 199;
LXX Ex 27:20; Lv 6:12–13; Diodorus Sic. 34. 1. 4 (also in M. Stern, *Greek and Latin Authors on Jews
and Judaism* I [Jerusalem: The Israel Academy of Sciences and Humanities, 1976], p. 180 (# 63). For
additional references, see Schürer, *The History of the Jewish People* II (1979) 297 and n. 18.

408. Cf. LXX Ps 103:32.

409. This is a reference to the doctrine of the *creatio ex nihilo*. Cf. 2 Mc 7:28; Philo, *De spec. leg.*
4.187; etc. Cf. D. Winston, *The Wisdom of Solomon, The Anchor Bible 43* (New York: Doubleday, 1979)
38–40; G. May, *Schöpfung aus dem Nichts*, *AKG* 48 (Berlin: De Gruyter, 1978).

410. The prohibition to eat pork is the Jewish one in this case, and not the Egyptian. Cf. LXX Lv
11:7; Dt 14:8; Is 65:4; etc. Cf. also *PGM* I. 105; Plutarch, *De Is. et Os.* 5, 352F and Griffiths, *Plutarch's De Iside et Osiride* 272.

411. On this "inspiration," see S. Eitrem, *Some Notes on the Demonology of the New Testament* (Oslo:
Universitetsforlaget, ²1966) 47–49.

PGM IV. 3086–3124

*Oracle of Kronos[412] **in great demand, called "little mill"**: Take two measures of
3090   salt and grind with a handmill while saying the formula many times until / the god
appears to you. Do it at night in a place where grass grows. If while you are speaking you hear the heavy step of [someone] and a clatter of iron, the god is coming
bound with chains, holding a sickle.[413] But do not be frightened since you are pro-
3095   tected by the phylactery that / will be revealed to you. Be clothed with clean linen
in the garb of a priest of Isis.[414] Offer to the god sage together with a heart of a cat
and horse manure.

The formula to be spoken while you are mixing is this: *Formula*: "I call you, the
great, holy, the one who created the whole inhabited world, against whom the
3100   transgression was committed / by your own son,[415] you whom Helios bound with
adamantine fetters lest the universe be mixed together, you hermaphrodite, father
of the thunderbolt, you who hold down those under the earth, AIE OI PAIDALIS
3105   PHRENOTEICHEIDŌ STYGARDĒS SANKLEON / GENECHRONA KOIRAPSAI KĒRIDEU
THALAMNIA OCHOTA ANEDEI; come, master, god, and tell me by necessity concerning the NN matter, for I am the one who revolted against you, PAIDOLIS
3110   MAINOLIS MAINOLIEUS." These are to be said while the salt / is being ground.

And the formula which compels him is: "KYDOBRIS KODĒRIEUS ANKYRIEUS
XANTOMOULIS." You say these things when he appears threateningly, in order that
he might be subdued and speak about the things you ask.

3115   *The phylactery / in great demand for him [is]*: On the rib[416] of a young pig
carve Zeus holding fast a sickle and this name: "CHTHOUMILON." Or let it be the
rib of a black, scaly, castrated boar.

3120   *Dismissal*: "ANAEA OCHETA THALAMNIA KĒRIDEU / KOIRAPSIA GENECHRONA
SANĒLON STYGARDĒS CHLEIDŌ PHRAINOLE PAIDOLIS IAEI, go away, master of the
world, forefather; go to your own places in order that the universe be maintained.
Be gracious to us, lord."
*Tr.: W. C. Grese.

PGM IV. 3125–71

3125   *Whenever you want a place to prosper greatly, so that those in the place or the
temple where the phylactery is hidden will marvel, [use this rite]. For wherever this
[phylactery] be placed, if in a temple, the temple will be talked about throughout
3130   the whole world; / if in some other place, [the place] will prosper greatly.

This is how to make [the phylactery]: Taking Etruscan wax, mold a statue three
handbreadths high.[417] Let it be three-headed. Let the middle head be that of a sea
3135   falcon; the right, of a baboon; / the left, of an ibis. Let it have four extended wings
and its two arms stretched on its breast;[418] in them it should hold a scepter. And let

---

412. For an analysis of the agrarian features of Kronos in this spell, see Eitrem, "Kronos in der
Magie," 351–60.
413. On the sickle as a weapon (also l. 3116), see A. A. Barb, "Cain's Murder-weapon and Samson's
Jawbone of an Ass," *JWCI* 35 (1972): 386–89.
414. For the Egyptian priestly costume, see S. Sauneron, *The Priests of Ancient Egypt* (New York:
Grove Press, 1960) 40. See also Plutarch, *De Is. et Os.* 4, 352C, and Griffiths, *Plutarch's De Iside et
Osiride* 270. [R.K.R.]
415. That is, Zeus who castrated his father Kronos.
416. The text is uncertain at this point. See the apparatus ad loc.
417. For a wax statue of this so-called pantheistic god, see S. Sauneron, "Le Nouveau sphinx composite du Brooklyn Museum et le rôle du dieu Toutou-Tithoès," *JNES* 19 (1960): 269–87; esp.
284–85. Cf. *PGM* XII. 121–43; XIII. 50 for this figure. [R.K.R.]
418. Probably crossed. [M.S.]

it be wrapped [as a mummy] like Osiris. Let the falcon wear the crown of Horus; the baboon, / the crown of Hermanubis;[419] and let the ibis wear the crown of Isis.   3140 Put into the hollow inside it a heart [made] of magnetite, and write the following names on a piece of hieratic papyrus and put them into the hollow. Next, when you have made it an iron base, stand it / on the base and put it into a little juniper wood   3145 temple at moonrise on the third day of the goddess.[420] Then, having fixed it [firmly] in whatever place you choose, sacrifice to it a wild white-faced [falcon?],[421] and burn [this offering] entire; also pour to it, as a libation, the milk of a black cow, / the firstborn [of its mother] and the first she suckled. [By these sacrifices you will   3150 have completed the deification of the statue.] And [now] feast with [the god], singing to him all night long the names written on the strip [of papyrus] put in the hollow. Wreathe the little temple with olive and thus [you will prosper] throughout life. / And sing the same spell when you get up in the morning, before you open   3155 [your shop or temple]. *The names to be written and recited are these*:

"BICHŌ	MOUR	SOUMARTA
BICHŌBI	SOURPHEŌ	AKERMORTHŌOUTH
CHŌBIBEU	MOURĒTH	ANIMI
NASSOUNAINTHI	ANIMOKEŌ	MIMNOUĔR
NOUNAITH	ARPAĒR	IĒRI
	SANI	ANIMI
		MIMNIMEU."

(3160)

"Give me all favor, all success, for the angel bringing good, who stands beside   3165 [the goddess] Tyche, is with you. Accordingly, give profit [and] success to this house. Please, Aion, ruler of hope, giver of wealth, O holy Agathos Daimon, bring to fulfillment all favors and / your divine oracles." Then open [your establishment]   3170 and you will marvel at the unsurpassed holy power.
*Tr.: Morton Smith.

PGM IV. 3172–3208

*Dream-producing[422] charm using three reeds: The picking of the three reeds is to be before sunrise.[423] After sunset raise the first, look / to the east and say three   3175 times: "MASKELLI MASKELLŌ PHNOUKENTABAŌ OREOBAZAGRA RĒXICHTHŌN HIPPOCHTHŌN PYRIPĒGANYX AEĒIOYŌ LEPETAN AZARACHTHARŌ, I am picking you up in order that you might give me a dream." / Raise the second to the south   3180 and say again the "MASKELLI" formula, the vowels and "THRŌBEIA"; hold the reed and spin around; look toward the north and the west and say three times the same names, / those of the second reed. Raise the third and say the same names and these   3185 things: "IĒ IĒ, I am picking you for such-and-such a rite."

These things are to be written on the reeds: On the first: "AZARACHTHARŌ"; on the second: "THRŌBEIA"; / on the third: "IĒ IĒ."   3190

Then take a lamp that is not painted red and fill it with pure olive oil. Take a clean strip of cloth and write down all the names. Say the same things to the lamp seven times. Let the lamp be facing east / and let it be next to a censer on which you will   3195 make an offering of lumps of frankincense. After preparing the reeds and binding them together with fibers of a date palm, make them into a kind of tripod, and

---

419. The name is a combination of Hermes and Anubis.
420. Third day of the goddess Selene. Cf. *PGM* III. 702; IV. 170; XII. 379.
421. For the emendation ⟨ὸν⟩άγριον, see *PGM* IV. 2396 and n.
422. The word translated is ὀνειροθαυπτάνη. Cf. the apparatus ad loc. and *PGM* IV. 2624–25.
423. For picking a plant, see *PGM* IV. 286 and n.

place the lamp on it. Let the head of the practitioner be crowned with olive branches.

3200   *Composition of the ink* with which it is necessary to write / on the reeds and the wick: single-stemmed wormwood, vetch, 3 pits of Nicolaus date palms, 3 Karian dried figs, soot from a goldsmith, 3 branches of a male date palm, sea foam.

3205   *The things to be written / and recited are these*: "I conjure you by the sleep releaser because I want you to enter into me and to show me concerning the NN matter, IERŌRIETHEDIEN THROU CHAŌRA ARPEBŌ ENDALĒLA."
*Tr.: W. C. Grese.

PGM IV. 3209–54

3210   *Saucer divination of Aphrodite: Having kept oneself pure for 7 / days, take a white saucer, fill it with water and olive oil, having previously written on its base with myrrh ink: "ĒIOCH CHIPHA ELAMPSĒR ZĒL A E Ē I O Y Ō" (25 letters); and beneath the base, on the outside: "TACHIĒL CHTHONIĒ DRAXŌ" (18 letters). Wax

3215 over / with white wax. On the outside of the rim at the top: "IERMI PHILŌ 6 ERIKŌMA DERKŌ MALŌK GAULĒ APHRIĒL I ask" (say it 3 times). Let it rest on the

3220 floor and looking intently at it, say "I call upon you, the mother and mistress / of nymphs,[424] ILAOUCH OBRIĒ LOUCH TLOR; [come] in, holy light, and give answer, showing your lovely shape."

    Then look intently at the bowl. When you see her, welcome her and say, "Hail,

3225 very glorious goddess, ILARA / OUCH. And if you give me a response, extend your hand." And when she extends it, expect answers to your inquiry.

    But if she does not listen say, "I call upon the ILAOUCH who has begotten Hi-

3230 meros,[425] the lovely Horai and / you Graces; I also call upon the Zeus-sprung Physis of all things, two-formed, indivisible, straight, foam-beautiful Aphrodite.

3235 Reveal to me your lovely light and your lovely face, O mistress ILAOUCH. / I conjure you, giver of fire, [by] ELGINAL, and [by the] great names OBRIĒTYCH KERDY-NOUCHILĒPSIN NIOU NAUNIN IOUTHOU THRIGX TATIOUTH GERTIATH GERGERIS

3240 GERGERIĒ THEITHI. I also ask you[426] [by] the all wonderful / names, OISIA EI EI AŌ ĒY AAŌ IŌIAIAIŌ SŌTHOU BERBROI AKTEROBORE[427] GERIĒ IĒOYA; bring me light and your lovely face and the true saucer divination, you shining with fire, bear-

3245 ing fire all around, stirring the land from afar, / IŌ IŌ PHTHAIĒ THOUTHOI PHA-EPHI. Do it."

    Preparation: having kept yourself pure, as you learned, take a bronze drinking cup, and write with myrrh ink the previously inscribed stele which calls upon Aph-

3250 rodite, / and use the untouched olive oil and clean river water. Put the drinking cup on your knees and speak over it the stele mentioned above, and the goddess will appear to you and will reveal concerning what things you wish.
*Tr.: J. P. Hershbell.

PGM IV. 3255–74

3255   *Take an unbaked [brick] and with a bronze stylus draw an [ass] running, and on its face "IAŌ IŌ," and on its neck in the shape of a little bell "ĒOĒOĒ," and on its

---

424. For the epithet "Mistress of the Nymphs," see *Orph. Hymn.* 52. 22–25. Aphrodite Nymphaia is discussed in Pausanias 2. 32. 7.

425. Himeros may be a personification of "the yearning of love." See LSJ, s.v. "ἵμερος," I. 3.

426. ἀξιώσης, "you might ask," could be emended to ἀξιῶ σέ, "I ask you," and perhaps read with the following imperative as a part of the conjuration set in quotation marks. [R.D.K.]

427. The papyrus has ακτεβορε, which Preisendanz reads as an unattested epithet ἀκτε⟨ρο⟩βόρε, "eater of the unburied."

back "LERTHEMINŌ," and on its breast "[s]ABAŌTH," and under its hooves "ABRA-
SAX." / Smear it with the blood of Typhon and a pig and with juice of an onion.   3260

The spell of the brick to be written down is this:

"IŌ ERBĒTH IŌ PAKERBĒTH IŌ BOLCHOSĒTH IŌ BOLCHOSĒTH SABAOUM KOK-
LOTOM PATATHNAX, the shaker, IŌ ERBĒTH APOMPS IAŌTH IABAŌTH SEISAŌ
PEUKRĒ, you fortunate one, TESCHŌ PATONAK PHENDE / MIEPHEOR ABIRBOLON-   3265
CHITHI RŌPHTHĒ APERMA PALELŌPS, the shaker of the world, I call upon you,
great Typhon, IŌ ERBĒTH IŌ PAKERBĒTH IŌ BOLCHOSĒTH, because I am he, NN.
Hear me, in this business which I am performing LERTHEMINŌ AROUZORON
BATHOU / CHĒASMĒPHIS, O great, great[428] Typhon LERTHEMINO; attend this   3270
magical operation which I am performing, because it is your great and honored
name that I am saying and writing, ABERAMENTHŌOU" (formula).

Underneath the ass: "Give her the heaving of the sea, total wakefulness[429] of
Mendes,[430] and give her[431] the punishments."
*Tr.: E. N. O'Neil.

PGM V. 1–53[1]

*Oracle of Sarapis, [by means of] a boy, by means of a lamp, saucer and bench: "I
call upon you, Zeus, Helios, Mithra, Sarapis, / unconquered one, Meliouchos,   5
Melikertes, Meligenetor, ABRAAL BACHAMBĒCHI BAIBEIZŌTH (ĒBAI BEBOTH)
SERIABEBŌTH AMELCHIPSITHIOUTHIPOTHOIO PNOUTE NINTHĒRTĒROU[2] IYEY
ĒOŌ AIĒIA EĒOIA / ĒEAI EYĒIE ŌŌŌŌŌ EYĒŌ IAŌAI BAKAXICHYCH BOSIPSETĒTH   10
PHOBĒBIBŌTH, the great, great[3] Sarapis SAMASPHRĒTH" (otherwise above) "O
DARGAZAS O DARMAGAS O DAPHAR YAKIABŌTH EPHIA ZELEARTHAR (AKRABAEŌE-
PHIAZALE ARBAMENOTHIĒŌ SAMAS PHRĒTI)[4] / METHOMĒ͂OS LAMARMERA OPTĒBI   15
PTĒBI MARIANOU (AKRABAEŌ EPHIAZĒLE ARBAMENOTHI ĒŌ NAMISPHRĒTI), ap-
pear and give respect to him who appeared before fire and snow, BAINCHŌŌŌCH,
for you are the one who introduced light and snow, hurler of shudderful / thunder   20
and lightning, KYPODŌKTE PINTOUCHE ETŌM THOOUT THASINAEAK AROURON-
GOA PAPHTHA[5] ENŌSADE IAĒ IAŌ AI AOIAŌ EOĒY" (nine letters): [Pronounce]:

the "A" with an open mouth, undulating like a wave;
the "O" succinctly, as a breathed threat,   25
the "IAŌ" to earth, to air, and to heaven;
the "Ē" like a baboon;
the "O" in the same way as above;[6]
the "E" with enjoyment, aspirating it, /

428. The repeated "great, great" is Egyptian *geminatio*. See also *PGM* I. 41 and n.

429. E. Hohl, *RhM* 68 (1913): 313, n. 4, restores [π]αναγρυπνίαν in accordance with *Anth. Pal.* 7.
195. 5, where Meleager has used παναγρύπνοιο μερίμνης. Both the noun and the verb are *hapax
legomena*. [E.N.O.]

430. Mendes corresponds to Egyptian *Bȝ-nb-Ḏd.t*, the ram incarnation of Prē identified with Pan
and Priapus. See Bonnet, *RÄRG* 451, s.v. "Mendes"; 868–71, s.v. "Widder"; Herodotus 2. 46; Diodorus Sic. 1. 88; Strabo 16. 1. 19. [R.K.R.]

431. The translation follows Preisendanz in assuming that αὐτῇ in ll. 3273–74 is τῇ δεῖνα. But the
fact remains that, while ὁ δεῖνα occurs in l. 3248, nowhere in the spell is a woman mentioned. There is
really no indication that this spell is designed to affect a woman, until this last sentence. [E.N.O.]

1. Parentheses in this spell contain words that are written between the lines. For further discussion
see Preisendanz, ad loc.

2. The phrase means "O god (of) all the gods." Cf. *PGM* III. 144–45 and n.

3. For the meaning of "twice great," see *PGM* IV. 3270 and n.

4. See l. 46 below.

5. This is equivalent to "Thoth . . . He of Ptah." [R.K.R.]

6. According to Hopfner, *OZ* I, section 778, this means either as the "E" in l. 27 or the "O" in l. 25.

30   the "Y" like a shepherd, drawing out the pronunciation.[7]

If he says, "I prophesy," say: "Let the throne of god enter, THRONOUZATERA KYMA
35 KYMA LYAGEU APSITADRYS GĒ MOLIANDRON BONBLILON PEUCHRĒ, / let the
throne be brought in." If it then is carried by 4 men, as, "With what are they
crowned, and what goes before the throne?" If he says, "They are crowned with
40 olive branches, and / a censer precedes," [the] boy speaks the truth.

Dismissal: "Go, lord, to your own world and to your own thrones, to your own
45 vaults, and keep me and / this boy from harm, in the name of the highest god,
SAMAS PHRĒTH.[8]" Do this when the moon is in a settled sign, in conjunction with
50 beneficial planets or is in good houses, not when it is full; for it is / better, and in
this way the well-ordered oracle is completed. (But in other copies "when it is full"
has been written.)
*Tr.: W. C. Grese.

PGM V. 54–69

55 *Direct vision spell: "EEIM TO EIM ALALĒP BARBARIATH / MENEBREIO ARBA-
THIAŌTH IOUĒL IAĒL OUĒNĒIIE MESOMMIAS, let the god who prophesies to me
come and let him not go away until I dismiss him, OURNAOUR SOUL ZASOUL /
60 OUGOT NOOUMBIAOU THABRAT BERIAOU ACHTHIRI MARAI ELPHEŌN TABAŌTH
KIRASINA LAMPSOURĒ IABOE ABLAMATHANALBA AKRAMMACHAMAREI."

65   In a bronze cup over oil. Anoint / your right eye with water from a shipwreck
and the left with Coptic eyepaint, with the same water. If you cannot find water
from a shipwreck, then from a sunken skiff.
*Tr.: W. C. Grese.

PGM V. 70–95

70 *Take a plant *chelkbei* (?) and bugloss, strain them, burn what you strain out, mix
[them] well with juice, and write "CHOŌ"[9] with it on a wall. Take gallows wood
75 and carve a hammer. With / the hammer strike the [eye][10] while saying the formula: "I conjure you by the holy names; hand over the thief who made off with it,
80 CHALCHAK CHALKOUM CHIAM CHARCHROUM ZBAR BĒRI ZBARKOM CHRĒ / KA-
RIŌB PHARIBOU, and by the shudderful names: A EE ĒĒĒ IIII OOOOO YYYYYY
ŌŌŌŌŌŌŌ."

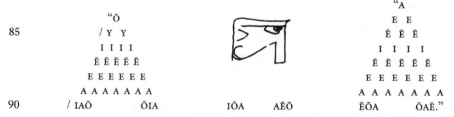

85

90

"Hand over the thief who stole it. As long as I strike the eye with this hammer, let
95 the eye of the thief be struck, and let it swell up until it / betrays him." While saying
these things, strike with the hammer.
*Tr.: W. C. Grese.

---

7. Presumably, the way the formula is to be spoken; see Preisendanz's interpretation ad loc.

8. Samas is the Canaanite solar deity Shamash, combined here with the Egyptian counterpart Prē.
Cf. ll. 12–14 above.

9. CHOŌ could be Coptic KŌ which can mean "hand over," or "put"; it would fit the sense of the
spell. [R.K.R.]

10. Thus the emendation οὐ⟨τάτιον⟩ in Preisendanz, based on l. 91. Cf. the apparatus ad loc.

PGM V. 96–172
* Stele of Jeu the hieroglyphist [11] in his letter:

"I summon you, Headless One, who created earth and heaven, who created night and day, / you who created light and darkness; you are Osoronnophris whom   100 none has ever seen; you are Iabas; you are Iapos; you have distinguished the just and the unjust; you have made female and male; / you have revealed seed and fruits;   105 you have made men love each other and hate each other.

"I am Moses your prophet to whom you have transmitted your mysteries / celebrated by Israel; you have revealed the moist and the dry and all nourishment;   110 hear me.

"I am the messenger of Pharaoh Osoronnophris; / this is your true name which   115 has been transmitted to the prophets of Israel. Hear me, ARBATHIAŌ REIBET ATHELEBERSĒTH [ARA] BLATHA ALBEU EBENPHCHI CHITASGOĒ IBAŌTH IAŌ; / listen to me and turn away this daimon."   120

"I call upon you, awesome and invisible god with an empty spirit,[12] AROGOGO-ROBRAŌ SOCHOU MODORIŌ PHALARCHAŌ OOO. Holy Headless One, deliver him, NN, from the daimon which restrains him, / ROUBRIAŌ MARI ŌDAM BAABNA-   125 BAŌTH ASS ADŌNAI APHNIAŌ ITHŌLĒTH ABRASAX AĒŌŌY; mighty Headless One, deliver him, NN, from the daimon which restrains him. / MABARRAIŌ IOĒL KOTHA   130 ATHORĒBALŌ ABRAŌTH, deliver him, NN AŌTH ABRAŌTH BASYM ISAK SABAŌTH IAŌ. /

"He is the lord of the gods; he is the lord of the inhabited world; he is the one   135 whom the winds fear; he is the one who made all things by the command of his voice."

"Lord, King, Master, Helper, / save the soul, IEOU PYR IOU PYR IAŌT IAĒŌ   140 IOOU ABRASAX SABRIAM OO YY EY OO YY ADŌNAIE, immediately, immediately,[13] good messenger of God ANLALA LAI GAIA APA DIACHANNA CHORYN." /

"I am the headless daimon with my sight in my feet; [I am] the mighty one [who   145 possesses] the immortal fire; I am the truth who hates the fact that unjust deeds are done in the world; I am the one who makes the lightning flash and the thunder roll; / I am the one whose sweat falls upon the earth as rain so that it can insemi-   150 nate it; I am the one whose mouth burns completely; I am the one who begets and destroys; / I am the Favor of the Aion; my name is a heart encircled by a serpent;   155 come forth and follow."

Preparation for the foregoing ritual: Write the formula [15] on a new sheet of pa-pyrus, and after extending it from one / of your temples to the other, read the 6   160 names, while you face north saying,

"Subject to me all daimons, / so that every daimon, whether heavenly or aerial or   165 earthly or subterranean or terrestrial or aquatic, might be obedient to me and every enchantment and scourge which is from God." / And all daimons will be obedient   170 to you.

The beneficial sign is: ⟩
*Tr.: D. E. Aune.

11. The term ζωγράφος, usually translated "painter," is here rendered "hieroglyphist," after the sug-gestion of Wünsch (see Preisendanz, apparatus ad loc.).

12. On the notion of "empty spirit," see J. Reiling, *Hermas and Christian Prophecy*, NT.S 37 (Leiden: Brill, 1973) 41–48.

13. The letters ηδε εδε are indicated in Preisendanz as magical words, but they may be Greek mis-spelled for ἤδη ἤδη, "immediately, immediately."

14. Cf. the expression ὕδωρ ὀχευτικόν in *C.H.* I. 17. See also Dieterich, *Abraxas* 25.

15. The term ὄνομα apparently refers to a formula containing a number of magical words. See also the apparatus ad loc.

PGM V. 172–212

*Another way:[16] "In order to catch a thief I summon you, Hermes,[17] immortal
175   god, who cut a furrow down Olympos / and a holy barge, light-bearer Iao, the
great immortal, shuddersome indeed to behold and shuddersome to hear. Hand
over the thief whom I seek ABERAMENTHŌOULERTHEXENAXSONELYSŌTHNE-
180   MAREBA." / This formula is to be said 2 times during the purificatory sacrifice.

Formula of bread and cheese:[18] "Come to me, LISSOIN MATERNA MAUERTĒ PRE-
185   PTEKTIOUN INTIKIOUS OLOKOTOUS PERIKLYSAI; / may you bring back to me
what is lost and point out the thief today. I call upon Hermes, finder of thieves,
190   Helios and the pupils[19] of Helios, / two who bring to light lawless deeds, and
Themis,[20] Erinys,[21] Ammon, and Parammon, to take control of the thief's throat
195   and to single him out / today, in this hour."

Preparation: The same formula during the purificatory sacrifice: Take a faïence
vessel, add water, myrrh, and calf's-snout plant. Wet a branch of laurel [and sprin-
200   kle], / cleansing each one. Take a tripod and place it on an earthen altar, offer
myrrh, frankincense, and a frog's tongue. Take unsalted winter wheat and goat-/
205   cheese, and give to each 8 drams of winter wheat and 8 drams of cheese while saying the following formula (inscribe this name and glue it underneath the tripod):
210   "Master IAŌ, light-bearer, / hand over the thief whom I see." If one of them does
not swallow what was given to him, he is the thief.
*Tr.: W. C. Grese.

PGM V. 213–303

215   *Hermes' ring.[22] Preparation of a scarab: Taking a scarab / engraved as described
below, put it on a papyrus table and put under the table a clean sheet and olive
220   twigs, scattering them about, and in the middle of the table / a small censer, burning myrrh and kyphi. Have ready a little faïence vessel in which there should be salve
225   of lilies or myrrh or cinnamon. / And taking the ring put it into the salve, having in
advance purified [it?][23] from everything, and burning on the censer the kyphi and
myrrh. Leave [the ring] 3 days and, taking it[24] [from the table], put it in a pure
230   place. Have at hand / for the consecration pure bread and whatever fruits are in
season. When you have made another [incense] offering on [a fire of] grapevine
235   twigs, during the offering take the ring from the / salve and put it on. Anoint yourself at dawn with the ointment from it and stand facing the sunrise [and] say the
spell given below.
240   Carving of a scarab: Carve a scarab in costly green stone / and, having pierced
[the stone], thread it with gold [wire?]. On the underside of the scarab engrave holy

16. That is, another spell to catch a thief. Originally this spell may have followed immediately after
PGM V. 70–95 (a spell to catch a thief), but the Stele of Jeu (V. 96–172) was inserted between the two.

17. On Hermes, the god of thieves, see Dieterich, Abraxas 63; W. Fauth, "Hermes," KP 2 (1975):
1074–75. On the identification with IAŌ (ll. 176–77), see A. A. Barb, "Three Elusive Amulets," JWCI
27 (1964):1–6.

18. See on this peculiar form of magic P. de Labriolle, "Artyrotyritae," RAC 1 (1950):718–20.

19. For the "eye of Helios," see PGM IV. 2985 and n.

20. Themis is the personified Greek concept of justice, custom, and social law. See K. Latte,
"Themis," PRE, 2nd series 5 (1934):1626–30.

21. On the Erinys, see PGM IV. 2860 and n.

22. On Hermes' ring, see Hopfner, OZ II, secs. 294–95.

23. Presumably the ring, but the reference could be to the practitioner himself, or even to the salve.
The Greek gives no indication of the object.

24. I.e., that in which it was laid.

Isis. And when you have consecrated it as written above, use it. The days in which
it is proper to perform [the rite] are, [counting] from the rise / [of the new moon]   245
the 7th, 9th, 10th, 12th, 14th, 16th, 21st, 24th, 25th. On the others, restrain
yourself.

   The spell to be said to Helios: "I am Thouth, discoverer and founder of drugs and
letters. Come to me, you under the earth; arouse [yourself] for me, / great daimon,   250
he of Noun,[25] the subterranean" (or [in other texts]: 'the [plural] Noun the subterranean'). I am the famous Heron,[26] egg of the ibis,[27] egg of the falcon, egg of the
air-ranging Phoenix, having under my tongue the mud of Em;[28] / I wear the hide of   255
Keph.[29] Unless I know what is in the minds of everyone, Egyptians, Greeks, Syrians, Ethiopians, of every race and people, unless I know[30] what / has been and   260
what shall be, unless I know their skills and their practices and their works and their
lives, and the names of them and of their fathers and / mothers and brothers and   265
friends, even of those now dead, I will pour the blood of the black dog-face[31] as a
drink offering in a new, faultless jar and put it on a new base and burn under it the
bones of Hesies,[32] and I will shout[33] / in the port of Busiris that he remained in the   270
river 3 days and 3 nights, Hesies, that he was carried by the current of the river /
into the sea, that he was surrounded by the waves of the sea and by the mist of the   275
air. Your belly is eaten by fish, and I will not / stop the fish chewing your body with   280
their mouths, nor will the fish shut their mouths. I will take the fatherless boy away
from his mother.[34] The pole [of the sky] will be brought down,[35] and the two
mountains will be one. / I will let *anoixis*[36] loose against you and she will do what   285

   25. PHNOYN refers to the primordial abyss; cf. *PGM* III. 554 and IV. 139. PHNOYN is the Bohairic
spelling of the definite article before NOYN used as a vocative. [R.K.R.] See also Bonnet, *RÄRG*
535–36, s.v. "Nun."
   26. Heron was a god of Greco-Roman Egypt, apparently a fusion of the "Thracian rider god" and
the Egyptian god Atum; the name has no connection with the English bird name or the bird so called.
[M.S.] See Bonnet, *RÄRG* 295–96, s.v. "Heron."
   27. For the egg of the ibis, see Bonnet, *RÄRG* 321, s.v. "Ibis"; 162–64, s.v. "Ei"; Bergman, *Isis-
Seele und Osiris-Ei* 76–87.
   28. For this name, see *PGM* III. 636; V. 353. For possible explanations, see Preisendanz, vol. III,
index, p. 219, s.v. "Ἐμ."
   29. This name is unexplained; for suggestions, see Preisendanz, vol. III, index, p. 259 s.v. "κεφ." Em
may be an abbreviation of Ammon, and Keph of Kynokephalos, i.e., baboon, symbol of Thoth, with
whom the magician identified himself at the beginning of the spell. [M.S.]
   30. For this threat against the deity see J. Bergman, "Mystische Anklänge in den altägyptischen
Vorstellungen von Gott und Welt," in *Mysticism, Scripta Instituti Donneriani Aboensis* 5 (1970): 70–72.
   31. The translation of the term follows the emendation in Preisendanz; see the apparatus ad loc.
Clearly Anubis is meant. See also Griffiths, *Plutarch's De Iside et Osiride* 317–19; idem, *The Isis-Book*
215–18. The reference is to the dog-headed god Anubis, assistant of Osiris, Isis, and Horus. It is not
Thoth because (1) the magician has identified himself with Thoth; (2) this god face is "black," as Anubis
commonly is in Egyptian paintings, whereas the *Kynokephalos* ("dog-headed," s.c. baboon) of Thoth is
commonly tan. [M.S.]
   32. For the name Hesies, see Glossary, s.v. "Esies."
   33. For the myth recounted here, cf. Plutarch, *De Is. et Os.* 13, 356C–D, and the commentary by
Griffiths, *Plutarch's De Iside et Osiride* 312. For the threat to Busiris, cf. P. Smither, "A Ramesside Love-
Charm," *JEA* 27 (1941): 131–32.
   34. The fatherless boy is Horus; the mother, Isis. Cf. *PGM* III. 543.
   35. For toppling the supports in heaven, cf. *PGM* III. 537–38; IV. 669. The two mountains of east
and west (Bakhu and Manu) form the horizons of Egyptian cosmography; they derive from the mountains framing the Nile valley. See Bonnet, *RÄRG* 78, s.v. "Bachu"; 440, s.v. "Manu." [R.K.R.]
   36. The papyrus has ἄνοιξιν from ἄνοιξις, "opening." The reference is obscure; it may refer to an
unknown mythical or ritual item or it may be a corruption of the text. See the apparatus ad loc.; LSJ, s.v.

she wants. I will not let god or goddess give oracles until I, NN, know through and
290   through what is in the minds of all men, Egyptians, / Syrians, Greeks, Ethiopians,
of every race and people, those who question me and come into my sight, whether
295   they speak or are silent, so that I can tell them / whatever has happened and is happening and is going to happen to them, and [until] I know their skills and their lives
300   and their practices and their works and their names / and those of their dead, and
of everybody, and I can read a sealed letter [37] and tell them everything truthfully."
*Tr.: Morton Smith. How to carve, consecrate, and use a scarab; with the spell to be said
when using it. Though the scarab is engraved with Isis and the spell is addressed to Helios,
the ring is said to be "of Hermes" because the spell first identifies the magician with Hermes-
Thoth. As Thoth he invokes Osiris (the Nile) from the underworld waters, to reveal to him
all facts relevant to all men, and he threatens that, unless he receives this knowledge, he will
destroy the remains of Osiris' body, reveal his mysteries, and generally upset the divine order.

PGM V. 304–69

305   *Taking hieratic papyrus or a / lead lamella and iron ring, put the ring on the papyrus and with a pen draw the outlines of the ring, inside and outside, then tint the
310   outlined area with myrrhed ink, then write on this outlined area / of the ring—
writing on the papyrus—the name, [38] and write the characters outside [the area],
then, [in the circle] inside it, what you want not to happen, and "Let so-and-so's
315   thoughts be bound so that he may not do NN thing." Then / putting the ring on
its outline, which you made, and turning up the [areas of the papyrus] outside the
outline, wrap up the ring until it is completely covered. Piercing [the package]
320   through the characters / with the pen and tying it, say, "I bind NN with regard to
NN [thing]. Let him not speak, not be contrary, not oppose; let him not be able to
325   look me in the face nor speak against me; let him be subjected / to me, so long as
this ring is buried. I bind his mind and his brains, [39] his desire, his actions, so that he
330   may be slow [in his dealings] with all men." / And if it be a woman: "In order that
she, NN, may not marry him, NN" (add the usual). Then, taking it [the package]
away to the grave of someone untimely dead, dig [a hole] four fingers deep and put
335   it in and say, "Spirit of the dead, who[ever] / you are, I give over NN to you, so that
he may not do NN thing." Then, when you have filled up the hole, go away. Better
do it when the moon is waning.

The things to be written inside the circle [bounded by the inner side of the ring's
340   outline] *are these*: "AROA / MATHRA ERESCHIGALCH EDANTA IABOU NĒ AKĒ IAŌ
DARYKNŌ MANIĒL, let NN thing not be done so long as this ring is buried." Bind
345   [the package] with ties, [using] cords you have made, / and thus deposit it. The
[wrapped] ring may also be thrown into an unused well, or [into the grave] of
[anyone dead] untimely. After the characters, write also the following, under the
350   [outline of the] ring, as a rectangle: "ARCHOOL LAILAM / SEMESILAMPH AMMO-
PHORIŌN IŌAĒ PHTHOUTH EŌ PHRĒ, the greatest daimon, IAŌ SABAŌTH AR-
BATHIAŌ LAILAM OSORNŌPHRI EM PHRĒ PHRĒ PHTHA CHRŌIŌ IAŌ BABOURĒ
355   THIMAM EN PHRĒ RE/NOUSI SABAŌTH BARBARTHIAŌ THACHRA OÚCHEETH

"ἄνοιξις"; Griffiths, *Plutarch's De Iside et Osiride* 522, 523, 536 for the ritual of the "Opening of the
mouth."

37. For the magical ability to read sealed letters, see the tale of Khamwas in Lichtheim, *Ancient Egyptian Literature* III, 142–51. [R.K.R.]

38. Given below, ll. 339–41.

39. In Greek, "the midriff," representing the classical term for the supposed location of the thinking
element of the body. [M.S.]

ESORNŌPHRI" and the entire 59 [letter formula] above,[40] which you also put inside [the circle bounded by the ring's outline].[41]

[The same schedule can be written on a lead lamella; then, putting the / ring in [the middle] and folding up [the lead] around it, cover [it] with plaster. After the rectangle underneath [write] also the IAEŌ formula[42] and the following: "BAKAXI-CHYCH MENEBAICHYCH ABRASAX AŌ, prevent the NN thing," [or], as the names are found in the authentic [text]: / "ARPHOOL LAILAM SEMESILAM IAEŌ (formula) BAKAXICHYCH ABRASAX AŌ ARCHŌMILAK MENESILAM IAEŌ OYŌ BAKAXICHYCH ABRASAX ŌII, prevent the NN thing."

*Tr.: Morton Smith. This untitled text gives directions for a familiar type of magical rite called *defixio*—essentially sending a letter to underworld powers to ask or compel them to do something to a specified victim. Many *defixiones* are, like this one, intended to prevent things from happening. The gods invoked here are a curious lot—solar and subterranean, Hebrew, Egyptian, and Mesopotamian, suggesting that the text has grown, like many, by ignorant additions.

PGM V. 370–446

*Take 28 leaves from a pithy laurel tree[43] and some virgin earth and seed of worm-   370
wood, wheat meal and the herb calf's-snout[44] (but I have heard[45] from a certain

360

365

40. This refers to the top of the papyrus page, where the scribe has written on the margin, with a few errors, the formula IAEŌBAPHRENEMOUNOTHILARIKRIPHIAEU and the same letters (without the final U) in reverse order. Together they form a fifty-nine-letter palindrome which often occurs in magical texts, mainly in spells to the solar deities. [M.S.]

41. (On the drawing): the reading of the third line in the circle from TH on, including the letters NIN (?) written above, is uncertain. If PHTHANNI is read, Phtha contains the name of the Egyptian god revered as creator. [M.S.]

42. See ll. 366–69 and the picture, l. 357. The palindrome is also printed in Preisendanz, apparatus to l. 357.

43. Cf. on this point *PGM* I. 264.

44. On this plant see *PGM* V. 198 and III. 468.

45. Undoubtedly, these are the words of a redactor, but expressions in the first person (here and l. 383) are rare. More often such variants are introduced by οἱ δέ . . . (cf. l. 390). [E.N.O.]

375   man of Herakleopolis that he takes 28 new sprouts from an olive tree, / which is
        cultivated, the famous one). Those are carried[46] by an uncorrupted boy.[47] Also
        pounded together with the foregoing ingredients is the liquid of an ibis egg[48] and
        made into a uniform dough and into a figure of Hermes wearing a mantle, while

380   the moon is ascending in Aries or Leo or / Virgo or Sagittarius. Let Hermes be
        holding a herald's staff. And write the spell on hieratic papyrus or on a goose's
        windpipe (again, just as I heard from the man of Herakleopolis), and insert it into

385   the figure for the purpose of / inspiration; and when you want to use it, take some
        papyrus and write the spell and the matter; and shave your head[49] and roll a hair
        into the papyrus, binding it with a piece from a purple cord, and put on the outside

390   of it an olive branch, and / place it[50] at the feet of the Hermes (but others say: place
        it upon him). And let the figure lie in a shrine of lime wood. But when you want to

395   use it, place the shrine beside your head / along with the god and recite as on the
        altar you burn incense, earth from a grain-bearing field and one lump of rock salt.
        Let it rest beside your head, and go to sleep after saying the spell without giving an
        answer to anyone. /

400   "Hermes,[51] lord of the world, who're in the heart,
                    O circle of Selene, spherical
                    And square, the founder of the words of speech,
                    Pleader of justice's cause, garbed in a mantle,[52]
                    With winged sandals, turning airy course /
405   Beneath earth's depths, who hold the spirit's reins,
                    O eye of Helios, O mighty one,
                    Founder of full-voiced speech,[53] who with your lamps
                    Give joy to those beneath earth's depths, to mortals
410   Who've finished life.[54] / The prophet of events
                    And Dream divine you're said to be, who send
                    Forth oracles by day and night; you cure
                    All pains of mortals with your healing cares.
                    Hither, O blessed one, O mighty son
415   Of Memory, / who brings full mental powers,
                    In your own form both graciously appear
                    And graciously render the task for me,
                    A pious man, and render your form gracious

46. Apparently the subject of βαστάζεται is all the ingredients named above. [E.N.O.]

47. See on the "uncorrupted boy" as medium *PGM* II. 56; V. 87; VII. 544, and T. Hopfner, "Die Kindermedien in den griechisch-ägyptischen Zauberpapyri," in *Recueil d'études dédiées à la mémoire de N. P. Kondakov* (Prague: Seminarium Kondakovianum, 1926), 65–74; R. Ganschinietz, *Hippolytos' Capitel gegen die Magier, Refut. haer. IV. 28–42, TU* 39/3 (Leipzig: Hinrichs, 1913) 30, 32–33.

48. See on this point *PGM* V. 252 and n.

49. This is done in imitation of Egyptian priests. See S. Sauneron, *The Priests of Ancient Egypt* (New York: Grove Press, 1960) 37. On the shaving of the head by the initiates of Isis, see Apuleius, *Met.* 11. 28; Plutarch, *De Is. et Os.* 3–4, 352C; and Griffiths, *Plutarch's De Iside et Osiride* 268–69.

50. For hair sacrifices in Egyptian religion, see Bonnet, *RÄRG* 267–68, s.v. "Haaropfer"; Betz, *Lukian* 131, n. 3.

51. Although the text of the following lines is quite fragmentary, enough remains to show that they are dactylic hexameters. Consequently they have been accepted as one version of the reconstructed Hymns 15–16, ll. 1–15; see Preisendanz, vol. II, p. 249. This version is, however, very different from that in *PGM* VII. 668–80 and XVIIb. 1–23. [E.N.O.]

52. Cf. l. 378 above.

53. A repetition of the idea expressed in l. 402.

54. A reference to the role of Hermes as the guide of the dead to the underworld.

> To me, NN,
> That I may comprehend you by your skills
> Of prophecy, by your own wond'rous deeds. /
> I ask you, lord, be gracious to me and
> Without deceit appear and prophesy to me."

Recite this both at sunrise and moonrise.

The stele written on the papyri belonging to the figure: "YESENNIGADŌN ORTHŌ BAUBŌ / NOĒRE KODĒRE SOIRE SOIRE SANKANTHARA ERESCHIGAL ANKISTĒ DŌDEKAKISTĒ AKROUROBORE[55] KODĒRE SĒMEA KENTEU KONTEU KENTEU KĒRIDEU DARYGKŌ LYKYNXYNTA KAMPYCHRĒ IRINŌTON LOUMANATA . / . . ION KOMANDRON CHREIBACHA NOUBACHA NOUMILLON EROUPHI TETROUPHI LIBINOU NOUMILLON CHANDARA TON PHERPHEREU DROUĒR MAROUĒR" (say it 3 times, then / the usual formula).

Spell of compulsion: "OUKRA NOUKRA PETIRINODE TMAISIA, terrible-eyed, DRYSALPIPS BLEMENNITHEN BANDYODMA TRIPSADA ARIBA . . . TA KRATARNA" (then the hundred-lettered name of Hermes). . . .[56]

/ *Another*: "IOUKRAIŌNIOU (spoken to the lamp) ŌCHMARMACHŌ TONNOURAI CHRĒMILLON DERKYŌN NIA IAŌ SOUMPSĒPHISON SOUMPSĒNIS SIASIAS IAŌ, you who shake the world, come in and prophesy / concerning the NN matter, THOIS KOTOTH PHTHOUPHNOUN NOUEBOUĒ."

*Tr.: E. N. O'Neil. For a discussion of ll. 370–439, see Hopfner, *OZ* II, section 174.

PGM V. 447–58

*On a jasperlike agate engrave Sarapis seated, facing forwards (?), holding an Egyptian royal scepter and on the scepter an ibis, and on the back of the stone / the [magical] name [of Sarapis?], and keep it shut up. When need [arises] hold the ring in your left hand, and in your right a spray of olive and laurel [twigs], waving them toward the lamp while saying the spell 7 times. And when you have put / [the ring] on the index finger of your left hand with the stone inside, [keep it] thus and, going off[57] [to bed] without speaking to anybody, go to sleep holding the stone to your left ear.

*Tr.: Morton Smith.

PGM V. 459–89

Another way: "I call upon you who created / earth and bones[58] and all flesh and all spirit and who established the sea and suspended (?)[59] the heavens, who separated[60] the light from the darkness, the Supreme Intelligence[61] / who lawfully ad-

---

55. Cf. on this formula the Glossary, s.v. "YESSIMMIGADON/AKROUROBORE formula."

56. The name is missing here, but the papyrus left space for its insertion later. Cf. the apparatus ad loc. For one-hundred-letter names, see *PGM* IV. 242, 1209, 1380.

57. Reading the papyrus ἀπεχ‾ as an abbreviation of ἀπερχόμενος rather than Preisendanz's ἀπεχόμενος, which would be awkward Greek. See the apparatus ad loc. [M.S.]

58. See on this point LXX Jb 10:9–11.

59. The text is corrupt at this point; for suggested emendations, see the apparatus ad loc. Cf. Preisendanz's translation: "der . . . festgenagelt hat den Himmel"; Festugière, *La Révélation* IV, 90: "solidement cloué le ciel."

60. Cf. Gn 1:4, 14, 18; Wisd Sol. 7:29–30. See Blau, *Das altjüdische Zauberwesen* 107; Festugière, *La Révélation* IV. 190.

61. The concept of the divine Nus (Mind) is an influence from Greek philosophy. Cf. also *PGM* XIII. 173, 487. See Plutarch, *De Is. et Os.* 49, 371A; *C. H.* I. 2, 6, 9; X. 19–21; XIII. 21. See J. Dillon, *The Middle Platonists* (London: Duckworth, 1977) 283, 372, 382, 389, 391, 393; Reitzenstein, *Poimandres* 279, n. 2; Bousset, *Religionsgeschichtliche Studien* 199–200 and index, s.v. "Nus, Nous."

ministrates[62] all things. Eternal Eye, Daimon of daimons, god of gods, the lord of the spirits, the invariable AION IAŌ OYĒI, hear my voice.

470 / "I call upon you, master of the gods, high-thundering Zeus, sovereign Zeus, ADŌNAI, lord IAŌ OYĒE; I am he who calls upon you, great god, in Syrian: 'ZAA-
475 LAĒRIPHPHOU,' and you must not / ignore my voice (in Hebrew: 'ABLANATHA-NALBA ABRASILŌA'); for I am SILTHACHŌOUCH LAILAM BLASALŌTH IAŌ IEŌ
480 NEBOUTH SABIOTH ARBŌTH ARBATHIAŌ IAŌTH SABAŌTH PA/TOURĒ ZAGOURĒ BAROUCH ADŌNAI ELŌAI ABRAAM[63] BARBARAUŌ NAUSIPH, high-minded one, immortal, who possess the crown of the whole [world], SIEPĒ SAKTIETĒ BIOU BIOU
485 SPHĒ SPHĒ NOUSI NOUSI / SIETHO SIETHO CHTHETHŌNI RIGCH ŌEA Ē ĒOA AŌĒ IAŌ ASIAL SARAPI OLSŌ ETHMOURĒSINI SEM LAU LOU LOURIGCH."

It loosens shackles, makes invisible, sends dreams; [it is] a spell for gaining favor. (Add the usual for what you want.)
*Tr.: D. E. Aune.

PGM Va. 1–3

*"O Helios BERBELŌCH CHTHŌTHŌMI ACH SANDOUM ECHNIN ZAGOUĒL, bring me into union with you" (add the usual). Then anoint yourself, and you will have a direct vision.
*Tr.: Hubert Martin, Jr.

PGM VI. 1–47

*. . . His encounter with Helios [takes place] on the 2nd, but the invocation itself is spoken when [the moon] is full. But you will accomplish a better encounter at [sun]rise on the 4th, when the god is on the [increase,[1] from the ground floor of a
5 house]. Say, therefore, to the rising sun[2] / [the following] prayer:
"[Laurel,][3] Apollo's holy plant [of presage,
Which] Phoebus [tasted once] and with [the fresh-
Cut] branches wreathed his [holy] head, adorned
With tresses long [and golden]. In his hands
10 He shook [a scepter] / on the [peaks of Mount
Parnassus], lofty and with many vales
[And gave to all] the gods[4] [responses] and
To mortals prophesied. [For in the throes
Of grievous love], it was Apollo who
Himself [gave you, a nymph], dread virgin, power
[To utter presages. Come quickly hither

62. The doctine of διοίκησις points to philosophical influence. Cf. also LXX Wisd Sol. 8:1; Philo, *De opif. mundi* 3; *De spec. leg.* IV. 187; C. H. I. 9. See Festugière, *La Révélation* IV, 190, n. 3.
63. The Greek underlying these magical words corresponds in part to the Jewish blessing, "Blessed be Jahwe, . . . god of Abraham. . . ." It is not clear whether or not the magician understood these words. A similar formula written in Greek occurs on a gold lamella published by R. G. Collingwood and R. P. Wright, *The Roman Inscriptions of Britain I* (Oxford: Clarendon Press, 1965), n. 436. See also Blau, *Das altjüdische Zauberwesen* 106–7.
1. An apparent reference to the spring, when the days grow longer. Cf. *PGM* XIII. 388–91. [E.N.O.]
2. The sun is identical with the god Helios; see Glossary, s.v.
3. These dactylic hexameters (ll. 6–21) are also the reconstructed Hymn 13. See Preisendanz, vol. II, p. 248. *PGM* VI. 6–7 (Hymn 13. 1–2) also appear at *PGM* II. 81–82 (Hymn 11. 1–2), and l. 6 also appears at *PGM* VI. 40 (Hymn 14.1). [E.N.O.]
4. In Hymn 13. 6 Preisendanz has changed ἑοῖς to θεοῖς.

To me beseeching you] in holy measures[5] /
[And] in my hands holding [a laurel leaf].[6]   15
Send me [divine responses] and a holy
Prophetic sign. In lucid [words], O priestess,
[Reveal all things]: both [when this will occur]
And how it will be done. [Give me a presage,]
So that with it [I may perform a test]
On [anything. / Subduer, hither come!   20
Lo you,] mankind's Subduer, mankind's [force!
Come, blessed Paian,][7] most supreme, [help] me;
[Come hither to me, golden-tressed], ieō,
E'en thou, Paian, [the very lord of song.
Come thou to me,] O Phoibos, many-named.
O Phoibos, / sing out clear with presages,   25
Phoibos Apollo, Leto's son, far-worker,
Hither, come hither, hither come; respond
With prophecies, give presage in night's hour."

Then speak, declaiming[8] this: "eē ie ie ēi iō . . . iaōiē iye ia iaō ē . . . ouō."
Then at sunset make your request again: /

"Hear me, god of the silver bow, who stand   30
Protector of Chryse and holy Cilla[9]
And are the mighty lord of Tenedos,
Gold-shining, hurricane and dragon-slayer,
mesegkriphi,[10] Leto's son, siaōth,
sabaōth, meliouchos, ruler, peuchrē,
Night-wanderer, seseggen, barpharaggēs, /
arbēthō, god of many forms, O thou   35
Who're fond of chariots,[11] arbathiaō
Smintheus, if e'er I've roofed a pleasing shrine
For you, or if I've ever burned for you
Fat thighs of bulls or goats, grant this my prayer."[12]

And in the same way in his encounter with Selene, as follows: /

"Laurel,[13] Apollo's holy plant of presage,   40

5. "In holy measures" translates ἱεροῖσι πεδίλοις. Although Preisendanz says "auf heiligen San-
dalen," this sense has no place in the passage: first, the word order suggests that the phrase goes closely
with μοι λισσομένῳ ("to me as I pray"); second, Daphne's mythology seems to have nothing to do
with sandals (cf. L. von Sybel, in Roscher I [1884–86] 954–55, s.v. "Daphne," although the article
omits this passage and *PGM* in general); and third, this passage is hymnic, and one meaning of πέδιλον
(as the diminuitive of πούς) is "meter," "measure," for which cf. Pindar, *O.* 3.5 and 6. 8. [E.N.O.]

6. The mixing of the plant and the goddess in this hymn is another good example of the thin line
between inanimate objects and personified spirits of these objects. Cf. esp. ll. 40–41 below. [E.N.O.]

7. These dactylic hexameters (ll. 22–38), many of which are metrically faulty, are the reconstructed
Hymn 10; see Preisendanz, vol. II, pp. 244–45. Ll. 24–27 (Hymn 10. 4–6) appear, in slightly altered
form, at *PGM* II. 2–4 (Hymn 9. 1–3). [E.N.O.]

8. The translation is problematic, but cf. perhaps Plutarch, *Mor.* 131A; *Cic.* 4, 862F. [E.N.O.]

9. Cf. Homer, *Il.* 1. 37–38.

10. The *voces magicae* in these verses are intended to be a part of the verses. The translation attempts
to treat them in the same way, but some liberties must be taken. [E.N.O.]

11. φιλάρματε, "fond of chariots," is the reading in Hymn 10. 12; the papyrus has φιλαίματε,
"fond of blood." [E.N.O.]

12. Cf. Homer, *Il.* 1. 39–41.

13. These dactylic hexameters are also the reconstructed Hymn 14; see Preisendanz, vol. II, p. 248.
PGM VI. 40 (Hymn 14. 1) also appears at *PGM* II. 81 (Hymn 11. 1) and VI. 6 (Hymn 13. 1). [E.N.O.]

O virgin Laurel, Laurel, Phoibos' mistress,

SABAŌTH [14] IAŌAŌO IAGCHŌTHIPYLA MOYSIARCHA [15] OTONYPON

Hither to me come quickly; haste to sing

Divine precepts to me [and to proclaim

Pure words] and in dark night [bring me true sayings].[16] /

45   RĒSABAAN AAN . . . ANA AANANAANANALAAA AAA AAA.[17]

It is for you, O Delios, O Nomios, O son of Leto and Zeus, to give persuasive oracles at night as you recount the truth through dream oracles."

*Tr.: E. N. O'Neil. This papyrus is badly mutilated, and little is gained by offering a translation of the scattered words and phrases that remain. Instead, for the three verse passages, the reconstructed texts of Hymns 10, 13, 14 have been used. Additional information appears at VI. 6, 22, and 40. [E.N.O.]

PGM VII. 1–148

*Homer oracle:

1.	1-1-1	But on account of their accursed bellies they have miserable woes, [*Od.* 15. 344]
2.	1-1-2	neither to cast anchor stones nor to attach stern cables, [*Od.* 9. 137]
3.	1-1-3	being struck by the sword, and the water was becoming red with blood. [*Il.* 21. 21]
4.	1-1-4	. . .
5.	1-1-5	stood holding a scepter, which Hephaistos produced by his labors. [*Il.* 2. 101]
6.	1-1-6	. . .
7.	1-2-1	amends I wish to make and to give a boundless ransom. [*Il.* 9. 120; 19. 138]
8.	1-2-2	surely then the gods themselves have ruined your mind. [*Il.* 7. 360; 12. 234]
9.	1-2-3	. . .
10.	1-2-4	. . .
11.	1-2-5	let it lie in the great hall. And I wish for your happy arrival [*Od.* 15. 128]
12.	1-2-6	. . .
13.	1-3-1	. . .
14.	1-3-2	. . .
15.	1-3-3	But Zeus does not accomplish for men all their purposes. [*Il.* 18. 328]
16.	1-3-4	I would even wish it, and it would be much better [*Il.* 3. 41; *Od.* 11. 358; 20. 316]
17.	1-3-5	Then indeed would he smash all your fine show, [*Od.* 17. 244]
18.	1-3-6	I also care about all these things, woman. But very terribly [*Il.* 6. 441]
19.	1-4-1	. . .
20.	1-4-2	speaking good things, but they were contriving evil things in their hearts. [*Od.* 17. 66]

14. The *voces magicae* in these lines make no pretense of being verse and for that reason are omitted from Hymn 14. [E.N.O.]

15. Cf. the epithet ὁ Μουσάρχος, "leader of the Muses," belonging to Apollo. See LSJ, s.v.

16. See Hymn 14. 4–5 in Preisendanz, vol. II, p. 248.

17. The *voces magicae* here appear immediately after "in dark night" in the papyrus, but because of the addition of two half-lines in Hymn 14, it is more convenient to complete the translation of the hymn before giving these *voces*. [E.N.O.]

21.	1-4-3	The glorious gifts of the gods are surely not to be cast aside, [*Il.* 3. 65]
22.	1-4-4	. . .
23.	1-4-5	. . .
24.	1-4-6	These things, Zeus-nurtured Skamander, will be as you order. [*Il.* 21. 223]
25.	1-5-1	a joy to your enemies, and a disgrace to yourself? [*Il.* 3. 51]
26.	1-5-2	Within this very year, Odysseus will arrive here, [*Od.* 14. 161; 19. 306]
27.	1-5-3	No use indeed to you, since you will not lie clad in them, [*Il.* 22. 513]
28.	1-5-4	And to the victor are to go the woman and the possessions. [*Il.* 3. 255]
29.	1-5-5	The rule of the many is no good. Let there be one ruler, [*Il.* 2. 204]
30.	1-5-6	And the gateway is full of ghosts, and full also is the courtyard, [*Od.* 20. 355]
31.	1-6-1	We have won great honor. We have killed glorious Hektor, [*Il.* 22. 393]
32.	1-6-2	Who would undertake and complete this task for ? [*Il.* 10. 303]
33.	1-6-3	Not even if his gifts to me should be as numerous as the grains of sand and particles of dust, [*Il.* 9. 385]
34.	1-6-4	. . .
35.	1-6-5	. . .
36.	1-6-6	. . .
37.	2-1-1	For no island is made for driving horses or has broad meadows, [*Od.* 4. 607]
38.	2-1-2	in the past, when you were boys, did you listen to your [*Od.* 4. 688]
39.	2-1-3	. . .
40.	2-1-4	. . .
41.	2-1-5	. . .
42.	2-1-6	His gifts are hateful to me, and I honor him not a whit. [*Il.* 9. 378]
43.	2-2-1	an only beloved heir to many possessions, [*Il.* 9. 482; *Od.* 16. 19 (?)]
44.	2-2-2	. . .
45.	2-2-3	. . .
46.	2-2-4	. . .
47.	2-2-5	So they thronged about him. And near [*Od.* 24. 19]
48.	2-2-6	and fashioning lies out of what nobody could see. [*Od.* 11. 366]
49.	2-3-1	be valiant, that later generations may also speak well of you. [*Od.* 1. 302]
50.	2-3-2	leaning on the grave marker over a barrow heaped up by men [*Il.* 11. 371]
51.	2-3-3	go. You have a way, and beside the sea your ships [*Il.* 9. 43]
52.	2-3-4	You will be proved a liar, and will not go on to fulfill your word. [*Il.* 19. 107]
53.	2-3-5	And his mother for her part continued the lament amid a flood of tears, [*Il.* 22. 79]
54.	2-3-6	Not even if remaining for five or six years [*Od.* 3. 115]
55.	2-4-1	So he spoke, and ordered Paion to administer a cure. [*Il.* 5. 899]
56.	2-4-2	These things, unhappy man, will I accomplish and do for you. [*Od.* 11. 80]

57.	2-4-3	How can you propose to render toil useless and ineffectual? [*Il.* 4. 26]
58.	2-4-4	a thing delayed, late of fulfillment, whose fame will never perish. [*Il.* 2. 325]
59.	2-4-5	Sooner would you grow weary and return to your native land. [*Od.* 3. 117]
60.	2-4-6	to go, that he may bring poisonous drugs from there, [*Od.* 2. 329]
61.	2-5-1	Husband, you departed from life young, and me behind as a widow [*Il.* 24. 725]
62.	2-5-2	in which way I will for sure accomplish everything and how it will be brought to pass, [*Il.* 9. 310 (?)]
63.	2-5-3	Offer me not honey-tempered wine, honored mother, [*Il.* 6. 264]
64.	2-5-4	. . .
65.	2-5-5	. . .
66.	2-5-6	Do not orphan your son and make your wife a widow. [*Il.* 6. 432]
67.	2-6-1	would that they might now eat their last and final meal here. [*Od.* 4. 685]
68.	2-6-2	It is not meet for a man who speaks in the Council to sleep all the night through, [*Il.* 2. 24]
69.	2-6-3	What's wrong with you, that you took this wrath into your heart? [*Il.* 6. 326]
70.	2-6-4	But who knows if he will one day return and punish them for their violent deeds? [*Od.* 3. 216]
71.	2-6-5	wives I will provide for both and furnish possessions [*Od.* 21. 214]
72.	2-6-6	we may try the bow and complete the contest. [*Od.* 21. 180]
73.	3-1-1	For it's no reproach to flee evil, nor by night. [*Il.* 14. 80]
74.	3-1-2	Be mindful of every form of valor. Now you needs must [*Il.* 22. 268]
75.	3-1-3	as a widow at home. And the boy is still just a baby, [*Il.* 22. 484; cf. 24. 726]
76.	3-1-4	But do you in no wise enter the moil of Ares, [*Il.* 18. 134]
77.	3-1-5	For amid misfortune mortals quickly grow old. [*Od.* 19. 360]
78.	3-1-6	. . .
79.	3-2-1	. . .
80.	3-2-2	Such a man is not alive nor will be born, [*Od.* 6. 201]
81.	3-2-3	Of a truth, child, there's nothing really wrong with this, [*Il.* 18. 128]
82.	3-2-4	Now is it no longer possible for him to find escape from us, [*Il.* 22. 219]
83.	3-2-5	we will ransom with bronze and gold, for it is within. [*Il.* 22. 50]
84.	3-2-6	drink, and do not vie with younger men. [*Od.* 21. 310]
85.	3-3-1	where are you fleeing, turning your back like a craven in the ranks? [*Il.* 8. 94]
86.	3-3-2	Would that such a man be called my husband [*Od.* 6. 244]
87.	3-3-3	plants her head in heaven and walks upon the earth. [*Il.* 4. 443]
88.	3-3-4	But Zeus does not accomplish for men all their purposes. [*Il.* 18. 328]
89.	3-3-5	and nodded for his army to survive and not to perish. [*Il.* 8. 246]
90.	3-3-6	Would that you had not pled with the noble son of Peleus, [*Il.* 9. 698]
91.	3-4-1	Honey-sweet wine has the best of you, which others also [*Od.* 21.

293]

92. 3-4-2 Act in whatever way your mind is moved, and no longer hold back. [*Il.* 22. 185]

93. 3-4-3 For it is fated for both to turn the same ground red [*Il.* 18. 329]

94. 3-4-4 keep on shooting like this, if haply you may become a light to the Danaans [*Il.* 8. 282]

95. 3-4-5 as there is no one who could keep the dogs off your head, [*Il.* 22. 348]

96. 3-4-6 You will not kill me, since I am for sure not subject to Fate. [*Il.* 22. 13]

97. 3-5-1 staying right here you would help me watch over this house [*Od.* 5. 208]

98. 3-5-2 Get out of the gateway, old man, or it won't be long before you're dragged out by the foot. [*Od.* 18. 10]

99. 3-5-3 Better for a man to escape evil by flight than to be caught. [*Il.* 14. 81]

100. 3-5-4 and declare to no one, neither man nor woman, [*Od.* 13. 308]

101. 3-5-5 of wheat or barley. And the heaps fall thick and fast. [*Il.* 11. 69]

102. 3-5-6 Whatever sort of word you speak, such would you hear. [*Il.* 20. 250]

103. 3-6-1 was opposed to giving Helen to tawny Menelaos, [*Il.* 11. 125]

104. 3-6-2 or will you alter your purpose? The hearts of the good are flexible. [*Il.* 15. 203]

105. 3-6-3 Yet I for one never doubted, but at heart [*Od.* 13. 339]

106. 3-6-4 Eurymachos, it will not be so. And even you know it. [*Od.* 21. 257]

107. 3-6-5 You miserable foreigner, you have no sense at all. [*Od.* 21. 288]

108. 3-6-6 And the father granted him one thing, but denied him the other. [*Il.* 16. 250]

109. 4-1-1 Nay, go to your chambers and tend to your own work, [*Od.* 1. 356]

110. 4-1-2 Now then, do not even tell this to your wife. [*Od.* 11. 224 (alternate version)]

111. 4-1-3 would you have been stoned to death for all the wrongs you've done. [*Il.* 3. 57]

112. 4-1-4 you prayed to the immortals to see with a beard grown. [*Od.* 18. 176]

113. 4-1-5 and vow to Lycian-born Apollo the famous archer [*Il.* 4. 101]

114. 4-1-6 and no spirit of harmony unites wolves and sheep, [*Il.* 22. 263]

115. 4-2-1 Come now, let us make these concessions to one another, [*Il.* 4. 62]

116. 4-2-2 And in the throng were Strife and Uproar, and Fate-of-Death, [*Il.* 18. 535]

117. 4-2-3 .   .   .

118. 4-2-4 Up, rush into battle, the man you have always claimed to be. [*Il.* 4. 264]

119. 4-2-5 .   .   .

120. 4-2-6 You baby, what use now to keep your bow idle? [*Il.* 21. 474]

121. 4-3-1 For even fair-tressed Niobe turned her mind to food, [*Il.* 24. 602]

122. 4-3-2 after giving a mass of bronze and gold and raiment [*Od.* 5. 38]

123. 4-3-3 Surely then the journey will not be useless or fail to occur. [*Od.* 2. 273]

124. 4-3-4 One omen is best, to defend your country. [*Il.* 12. 243]

125. 4-3-5 I will gild her horns all round and sacrifice her to you. [*Il.* 10. 294]

126.	4-3-6	and you would gain every Trojan's thanks and praise, [*Il.* 4. 95]
127.	4-4-1	put in with your ship, since women are no longer trustworthy. [*Od.* 11. 456]
128.	4-4-2	It is not possible or proper to deny your request. [*Il.* 14. 212]
129.	4-4-3	would straightway fit his will to your desire and mine. [*Il.* 15. 52]
130.	4-4-4	and give him instruction. And it will be beneficial for him to obey. [*Il.* 11. 789]
131.	4-4-5	will give glory to me, and your soul to horse-famed Hades. [*Il.* 5. 654]
132.	4-4-6	fill up his ship with gold and bronze aplenty, [*Il.* 9. 137]
133.	4-5-1	but tell one part, and let the other be concealed. [*Od.* 11. 443]
134.	4-5-2	and at birth Zeus sends a weight of misery. [*Il.* 10. 71]
135.	4-5-3	alone to have intelligence, but they are flitting shades. [*Od.* 10. 495]
136.	4-5-4	yielding to his indignation. But they now withheld from him the gifts [*Il.* 9. 598]
137.	4-5-5	I rejoice at hearing what you say, son of Laërtes. [*Il.* 19. 185]
138.	4-5-6	But Zeus causes men's prowess to wax or to wane, [*Il.* 20. 242]
139.	4-6-1	a terrible man. He would be quick to blame even the blameless. [*Il.* 11. 654]
140.	4-6-2	with all haste. For now would you capture the broad-wayed city [*Il.* 2. 66]
141.	4-6-3	Endure now, my heart. An even greater outrage did you once endure, [*Od.* 20. 18]
142.	4-6-4	You lunatic, sit still and listen to the word of others, [*Il.* 2. 200]
143.	4-6-5	had cast aside wrath and chosen friendship. [*Il.* 16. 282]
144.	4-6-6	so good it is for a son to be left by a dead [*Od.* 3. 196]
145.	5-1-1	Here then, spread under your chest a veil, [*Od.* 5. 346]
146.	5-1-2	'Tis impiety to exult over men slain. [*Od.* 22. 412]
147.	5-1-3	through immortal night, when other mortals sleep? [*Il.* 24. 363]
148.	5-1-4	How then could I forget divine Odysseus? [*Od.* 1. 65]
149.	5-1-5	lurid death and o'erpowering doom laid hold of [*Il.* 5. 83]
150.	5-1-6	So there's nothing else as horrible and vile as a woman [*Od.* 11. 427]
151.	5-2-1	Let us not advance to fight the Danaans around the ships. [*Il.* 12. 216]
152.	5-2-2	to put up a defense, when some fellow provokes a fight. [*Il.* 24. 369; *Od.* 16. 72; 21. 133]
153.	5-2-3	nor do children at his knees call him "papa" [*Il.* 5. 408]
154.	5-2-4	I am this very man, back home now. And after many toils [*Od.* 21. 207]
155.	5-2-5	Talk not like this. There'll be no change before [*Il.* 5. 218]
156.	5-2-6	let him stay here the while, even though he's eager for Ares. [*Il.* 19. 189]
157.	5-3-1	And do not, exulting in war and battle, [*Il.* 16. 91]
158.	5-3-2	never to have gone to bed with her and had intercourse, [*Il.* 9. 133; 19. 176]
159.	5-3-3	and moistens the lips, but fails to moisten the palate. [*Il.* 22. 495]
160.	5-3-4	Take heart! Let these matters not trouble your thoughts. [*Il.* 18. 463]
161.	5-3-5	But this mad dog I'm unable to hit. [*Il.* 8. 299]
162.	5-3-6	Keep quiet, friend, and do as I say. [*Il.* 4. 412]

163. 5-4-1   Bad deeds don't prosper. The slow man for sure overtakes the swift, [*Od.* 8. 329]

164. 5-4-2   They shut fast and locked the doors of the hall. [*Od.* 21. 236]

165. 5-4-3   Ah, poor man! Death's not at all on your mind, [*Il.* 17. 201]

166. 5-4-4   Odysseus has come and reached home, though he was long in coming. [*Od.* 23. 7]

167. 5-4-5   in full he will accomplish it at last, and the penalty they pay is great, [*Il.* 4. 161]

168. 5-4-6   and therein was Strife, and therein Valor, and therein chilling Attack, [*Il.* 5. 740]

169. 5-5-1   but 'tis most wretched to die and meet one's doom by starvation. [*Od.* 12. 342]

170. 5-5-2   shall I be laid low when I die. But good repute is now my goal, [*Il.* 18. 121]

171. 5-5-3   Up, rush into battle, the man you have always claimed to be. [*Il.* 4. 264]

172. 5-5-4   In no way do I mock you, dear child, nor am I playing tricks. [*Od.* 23. 26]

173. 5-5-5   but she stayed Alkmene's labor and stopped her from giving birth. [*Il.* 19. 119]

174. 5-5-6   But come, and hereafter I shall make amends for this, if now anything wrong [*Il.* 4. 362]

175. 5-6-1   Where are you two rushing? What causes the heart within your breast to rage? [*Il.* 8. 413]

176. 5-6-2   Pray now, let him not be too much on your mind. [*Od.* 13. 421]

177. 5-6-3   But the gods do not, I ween, give men all things at the same time. [*Il.* 4. 320]

178. 5-6-4   Talk not like this. There'll be no change before [*Il.* 5. 218]

179. 5-6-5   So he spake, but did not move the mind of Zeus by saying this. [*Il.* 12. 173]

180. 5-6-6   but Odysseus nodded no and checked him in his eagerness. [*Od.* 21. 129]

181. 6-1-1   How can you want to go alone to the ships of the Achaians? [*Il.* 24. 203]

182. 6-1-2   him a bridegroom in his house, who left as only child a daughter [*Od.* 7. 65]

183. 6-1-3   And too, I've taken the mist from your eyes, which before was there, [*Il.* 5. 127]

184. 6-1-4   we may try the bow and complete the contest. [*Od.* 21. 180]

185. 6-1-5   And I know that my arrival was longed for by you two [*Od.* 21. 209]

186. 6-1-6   I shall dress him in a mantle and a tunic, fine garments. [*Od.* 16. 79; 17. 550; 21. 339]

187. 6-2-1   by fastening a noose sheer from a high rafter, [*Od.* 11. 278]

188. 6-2-2   remembering our excellence, of the sort that even we [*Od.* 8. 244]

189. 6-2-3   the sea's great expanse they cross, since this is the Earthshaker's gift to them. [*Od.* 7. 35]

190. 6-2-4   Nay, come on with the bow. You'll soon be sorry for obeying everybody. [*Od.* 21. 369]

191. 6-2-5   But hurry into battle, and rouse the other soldiers. [*Il.* 19. 139]

192. 6-2-6 For mighty Herakles, not even he escaped his doom, [*Il.* 18. 117]

193. 6-3-1 amends I wish to make and to give a boundless ransom. [*Il.* 9. 120; 19. 138]

194. 6-3-2 And let him stand up among the Argives and swear an oath to you [*Il.* 19. 175]

195. 6-3-3 The man is nearby. Our search will not be long, if you are willing [*Il.* 14. 110]

196. 6-3-4 and not quite suddenly, and a very god should be the cause? [*Od.* 21. 196]

197. 6-3-5 Verily, these things have already happened, and not otherwise could [*Il.* 14. 53]

198. 6-3-6 On now, follow close! In action numbers make a difference. [*Il.* 12. 412]

199. 6-4-1 surely then the gods themselves have ruined your mind. [*Il.* 7. 360; 12. 234]

200. 6-4-2 Take heart, and let your thoughts not be of death. [*Il.* 10. 383]

201. 6-4-3 by her wailing she rouse from sleep her household servants, [*Il.* 5. 413]

202. 6-4-4 Come now in strict silence, and I shall lead the way, [*Od.* 7. 30]

203. 6-4-5 are there ears for hearing, and sense and respect are dead. [*Il.* 15. 129]

204. 6-4-6 as he was growing old. But the son did not grow old in his father's armor. [*Il.* 17. 197]

205. 6-5-1 to return home and behold the day of homecoming. [*Od.* 5. 220; 8. 466]

206. 6-5-2 Apollo of the silver bow did strike the one, still sonless, [*Od.* 7. 64]

207. 6-5-3 then you may hope to see your loved ones and reach [*Od.* 7. 76]

208. 6-5-4 As for you two, I will tell you exactly how it will be. [*Od.* 21. 212]

209. 6-5-5 For so shall I proclaim, and it will be accomplished too. [*Il.* 1. 212]

210. 6-5-6 and I shall send him wherever his heart and spirit urge him. [*Od.* 16. 81; 21. 342]

211. 6-6-1 idiot? You'll soon pay when the swift hounds devour you [*Od.* 21. 363]

212. 6-6-2 You would learn what mighty hands I have to back me up. [*Od.* 20. 237; 21. 202]

213. 6-6-3 In no wise do I think he will in that event take you for himself, nor is it proper. [*Od.* 21. 322]

214. 6-6-4 here we gather, waiting day after day. [*Od.* 21. 156]

215. 6-6-5 to reach decision making secret plans. Nor yet now to me [*Il.* 1. 542]

216. 6-6-6 Don't dare get it into your mind to escape from me, Dolon. [*Il.* 10. 447]

Here end the verses of the Homer oracle. May it help you!

*Tr.: Hubert Martin, Jr. The so-called Homer oracle, a list of 216 isolated and disconnected Homeric verses, is in fact a manual designed to provide the reader with an oracular response to a personal inquiry. Concerned with matters of daily life such as we find in our newspaper horoscopes, the inquirer rolls three dice or knucklebones, each of which has its six surfaces numbered from one to six and is used to select a number from one of the three *vertical* number columns to the left of the Homeric verses (in each column, there are only six numbers to select from, though each occurs thirty-six times); one die thrown three times would achieve the same purpose. The three numbers selected by this process establish a *horizontal* number column that indicates which verse is to be consulted; e.g., a roll of 1, 3, 6 on the dice would guide the inquirer to no. 18. As is true with oracles in general, most of the responses provide ambiguous answers which leave the exact interpretation up to the reader.

In this translation of Homer, which usually follows the Oxford Classical Text rather than that of Preisendanz, a lowercase letter at the beginning of a translated verse indicates that the first word of the verse does not begin a sentence. Such verses often constitute or involve incomplete syntactical units. In general, the punctuation at the end of a translated verse is that of the Oxford text, although in some instances this policy cannot be strictly observed. In a number of cases both the text and the Homeric reference given by Preisendanz have been emended. Furthermore, each of the verses has been numbered consecutively for ready reference. Since in all but a few instances the text of the Homeric verse is certain, we have omitted the usual brackets used to indicate lacunae in the papyrus. For additional discussion on this special type of divination, see T. Hopfner, "Astragalomanteia," *PRE.S* 4 (1924) 51–56, esp. 54–55; cf. Franz Heinevetter, *Würfel- und Buchstabenorakel in Griechenland und Kleinasien* (Breslau, 1912).

PGM VII. 149–54

*To keep bugs / out of the house**: Mix goat bile with water and sprinkle it. **To   150
keep fleas out of the house**: Wet rosebay with salt water, grind it and spread it.
*Tr.: W. C. Grese.

PGM VII. 155–67

*Days and hours for divination**:   155

1 at dawn	16 do not use
2 at noon	17 do not use
3 do not use	18 at dawn and in the afternoon
4 at dawn	19 at dawn
/ 5 at dawn	20 at dawn 160
6 do not use	21 in the afternoon
7 at noon	[22] in the afternoon
8 throughout the whole day	[23] at dawn
9 do not use	24 at dawn
/ 10 throughout the whole day	25 do not use 165
11 in the afternoon	26 in the afternoon
12 throughout the [whole] day	27 throughout the whole day
13 throughout the whole day	28 throughout the whole day
14 at dawn	29 throughout the whole day
15 throughout the whole day	30 in the afternoon

*Tr.: W. C. Grese.

PGM VII. 167–86

*Demokritos' "table gimmicks"**:

To make bronzeware look like it's made of gold: [1] Mix native sulfur with chalky soil and wipe it off.[2]

/ *To make an egg become like an apple*: Boil the egg and smear it with a mixture   170
of egg-yolk and [red] wine.[3]

To make the chef unable to light the burner: Set a houseleek plant on his stove.

---

1. According to H. Diels and W. Kranz, *Die Fragmente der Vorsokratiker* (Berlin: Weidmann, [8]1956), vol. II, p. 220, this recipe shows the beginnings of alchemy.

2. That is, one wipes off the mixture after it has been applied.

3. For coloring eggs, see the references in M. Wellmann, *Die* ΦΥΣΙΚΑ *des Bolos Demokritos und der Magier Anaxilaos aus Larissa*, part I, *APAW* 7 (1928): 57–58. Cf. also Athenaeus 13. 484e. Here, "egg yolk" can also mean "saffron."

To be able to eat garlic and not stink:[4] Bake beetroots and eat them.

To keep an old woman from either chattering or drinking too much: Mince some
175   pine[5] / and put it in her mixed wine.

To make the gladiators painted [on the cups] "fight":[6] Smoke some "hare's-
head" underneath them.

To make cold food burn the banqueter: Soak a squill in hot water and give it to
him to wash with. *To relieve him*: [Apply] oil.

To let those who have difficulty intermingling[7] *perform well*: Give gum mixed
180   with wine and honey / to be smeared on the face.

To be able to drink a lot and not get drunk:[8] Eat a baked pig's lung.

To be able to travel [a long way] home and not get thirsty:[9] Gulp down an egg
beaten in wine.

To be able to copulate a lot:[10] Grind up fifty tiny pinecones with 2 ozs. of sweet
wine and two pepper grains and drink it.

185   *To get an erection*[11] / *when you want*: Grind up a pepper with some honey and
coat your "thing."

*Tr.: Roy Kotansky. This curious collection of recipes contains humorous tricks as well as
helpful remedies presumably designed to be performed or used at a symposiastic dinner.
Similar tricks are found scattered throughout the pages of Athenaeus' *Deipnosophistae*.
See also *PGM* XIb; VII. 149–54; Delatte, *Anecdota Atheniensia* 449 (3–7); Wellmann,
APAW.PH 7 (1928): 1–80. It has not been fully appreciated that this collection seems to
refer to events that take place at a dinner table. This fact does not necessarily hold true for all
the other examples of *paignia*.

PGM VII. 186–90

***Favor and victory charm**: Take a blood-eating gecko that has been found among
the tombs and grasp its right front foot and cut it off with a reed, allowing the
190   gecko to return to its own hole alive. Fasten the foot / of the creature to the fold of
your garment and wear it.
*Tr.: R. F. Hock.

PGM VII. 191–92

***Eternal spell for binding a lover**: Rub together some gall of a wild boar, some
rock salt, some Attic honey and smear the head of your penis.
*Tr.: E. N. O'Neil.

PGM VII. 193–96

***For scorpion sting**: On a clean piece of papyrus, write the characters and place it
195   on the part which has the sting; wrap / the papyrus around it, and the sting will
lose its pain immediately.

4. Cf. Athenaeus 3. 84e for a similar breath freshener.

5. Cf. Athenaeus 2. 57b–d for pine and pine kernels at a dinner.

6. It seems likely that the reference is to translucent, painted glass which, when lit, produces the
effect.

7. The reference is presumably to those who are shy in a social setting: the concoction is to be applied to the face.

8. Cf. Athenaeus 2. 52d where eating almonds is said to prevent drunkenness.

9. In Athenaeus 2. 58f and 2.69f similar means for quenching thirst are found.

10. Cf. Athenaeus 1. 18d–e, where certain devices for having frequent sexual intercourse are
mentioned.

11. See on this point *PGM* VII. 194–95; *PDM* lxi. 58–62.

These are the characters: ⲱ ⳨ ⲙⲟⳑ ⳱ ⳧ ⳱ ⳱ ⳩ ⲍ ⳤ ⳤ ⁂ (there are 11 characters).
*Tr.: John Scarborough.

PGM VII. 197–98
*__For discharge of the eyes__: Write [this] on a piece of papyrus and attach it as an amulet: "ʀᴏᴜʀᴀʀʙɪsᴀʀᴏᴜʀʙʙᴀʀɪᴀsᴘʜʀēɴ."
*Tr.: John Scarborough.

PGM VII. 199–201
*__For migraine headache__: Take oil in your hands and utter the spell / "Zeus sowed   200
a grape seed: it parts the soil; he does not sow it; it does not sprout."
*Tr.: John Scarborough.

PGM VII. 201–2
*__Another__: Write these things on scarlet parchment: "ᴀʙʀᴀsᴀx 𝕏 " (and add the usual). Place it, having made it into a plaster, on the side of the head.
*Tr.: John Scarborough.

PGM VII. 203–5
*__For coughs__: In black ink, write on hyena parchment: "ᴛʜᴀᴘsᴀᴛᴇ sᴛʜʀᴀɪᴛō"—
[or] as I found in ***another*** [recipe]: "ᴛᴇᴜᴛʜʀᴀɪō ᴛʜʀᴀɪᴛᴇᴜ ᴛʜʀᴀɪᴛō ᴛʜᴀʙᴀʀ-
ʙᴀōʀɪ ⊗ / ʟɪᴋʀᴀʟɪʀēᴛᴀ—deliver [him], NN, from the cough that holds him fast."   205
*Tr.: John Scarborough.

PGM VII. 206–7
*__Another__: On hyena parchment write these characters:
ⲦⲔⲆⲄ˄ⲩ⊗ⲀⲔⲨⲀⲦⲈⲨⲦⲈⲞⲢⲰⲒ.   Hang it around the neck as an amulet, but keep it dry while wearing.
*Tr.: John Scarborough.

PGM VII. 208–9
*__For hardening of the breasts__: Take a fine linen rag and write on it in black ink:
⊗ⲈⲢⲦ⊗ⲀⲢ⊗Ⲣ∠.
*Tr.: John Scarborough.

PGM VII. 209–10
*__For swollen testicles__: Take a cord from a coin bag / and say with each knot "Kas-   210
tor" once, "Thab" twice.
*Tr.: John Scarborough.

PGM VII. 211–12
*__For fever with shivering fits__: Take oil in your hands and say 7 times, "sᴀʙᴀōᴛʜ"
(add the usual, twice). And spread on oil from the sacrum to the feet.
*Tr.: John Scarborough.

PGM VII. 213–14
*__For daily fever and nightly fever__: On the shiny side of an olive leaf write ⚹, and
on the dark side write ☾ and wear it as an amulet.
*Tr.: John Scarborough.

PGM VII. 215–18

215   *Stele [12] of Aphrodite: To gain friendship, favor, success, and friends. Take a strip
of tin and engrave on it with a bronze stylus. And be sure you are pure while carrying it.
*Tr.: Hubert Martin, Jr.

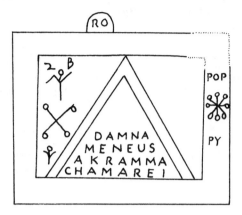

PGM VII. 218–21

*Phylactery for daily fever with shivering fits: Write on a clean piece of papyrus
and wear as an amulet:

220   / "IAŌ SABAŌTH ADŌNAI AKRAMMACHAMMAREI   (subtracting down)
AŌ [SABAŌTH ADŌNAI AKRAMMACHAMMAREI]
Ō [SABAŌTH ADŌNAI AKRAMMACHAMMAREI]
ABRASAX."
*Tr.: John Scarborough.

PGM VII. 222–49

*Request for a dream oracle from Besas: Take red ocher [and blood] [13] of a white
dove, likewise of a crow, also sap of the mulberry, juice of single-stemmed worm-
225   wood, cinnabar, and rainwater; / blend all together, put aside and write with it [14]
and with black writing ink, and recite the formula to the lamp [15] at evening. Take a
black [16] of Isis and put it around your hand. When you are almost awake the god
230   will come and speak to you, and he will not go away unless you wipe off / your
hand with spikenard or something of roses and smear the picture with the black of

12. The use of "stele" may refer here to the triangular shape found on the drawing of the tin plate.
13. The translation follows the text of Preisendanz, μίλτον ⟨καὶ αἷμα⟩ περιστερᾶς λευκῆς. The
conjectural ⟨καὶ αἷμα⟩ makes the text conform to the parallel passage in *PGM* VIII. 69–70, where
blood of a white dove is mentioned. The addition here, however, is not needed, for μίλτον (which does
not occur in the parallel passage) can also mean "blood." See *PGM* XII. 98 and LSJ, s.v. "μίλτον," III.
14. The Greek seems defective here. The only possible antecedent for αὐτός is the preceding potion
as a substance with which one is to write. The following reference to ink suggests that it would be better
to take αὐτός as the substance on which one is to write, particularly since the practitioner has just been
told to put the potion aside, and no substance to write on is mentioned. In the parallel charm, *PGM*
VIII. 64–110, a similar potion is used to paint the left hand.
15. Cf. *PGM* VIII. 84–111, where the use of a lamp is more fully described; this description occurs
immediately before the prayer to the headless god, which is here found in ll. 233–48.
16. This item, which is not explained here (cf. *PGM* VII. 231; VIII. 67–68), may be the black linen
garment used in the Isis cult. It is mentioned in Plutarch, *De Is. et Os.* 39, 366E; 77, 382C. See Griffiths,
Plutarch's De Iside et Osiride 451, 562. Preisendanz interprets the reference by translating: "take a black
piece from the garment. . . ."

Isis.[17] But the strip of cloth put around your neck,[18] so that he will not smite you.

Formula to be spoken to the lamp: "I call upon you, the headless god, the one who has his face upon his feet;[19] you are the one who hurls lightning, / who thunders, you are [the one whose] mouth continually pours on himself. You are the one who is over Necessity ARBATHIAŌ; you are the one lying on a coffin and having at the side of the head an elbow cushion[20] of resin and asphalt, the one whom they call ANOUTH. Rise up, daimon. You are not a daimon, but the [blood] of the 2 falcons[21] / who chatter and watch before the head of Heaven.[22] Rouse your nighttime form, in which you proclaim all things publicly. I conjure you, daimon, by your two names ANOUTH ANOUTH. You are the headless god, the one who has a head and his face on his feet, / dim-sighted Besas. We are not ignorant. You are the one whose mouth [continually] burns. I conjure [you by] your two names ANOUTH ANOUTH M . . . ORA PHĒSARA Ē . . . Come, lord, reveal to me concerning the NN matter, without deceit, without treachery, immediately, immediately; quickly, quickly." The small figure[23] is drawn in the beginning of the book.
*Tr.: W. C. Grese.

235

240

245

PGM VII. 250–54

Request for a dream oracle, a request which is always used. *Formula to be spoken to the day lamp*: "NAIENCHRĒ NAIENCHRĒ, mother of fire and water, you are the one who rises before, ARCHENTECHTHA; reveal to me concerning the NN matter. If yes, show me a plant and water, but if no, fire and iron; immediately, [immediately; quickly,] quickly."
*Tr.: W. C. Grese.

250

PGM VII. 255–59

Another to the same lamp: "Hail, lord, lamp, you who shine beside Osiris and shine beside Osirchentechtha[24] and my lord, the archangel Michael. If it is advantageous for me to do this, show me a plant and water, but if not, fire and iron, immediately, immediately."
*Tr.: W. C. Grese.

255

PGM VII. 260–71

For ascent of the uterus:[25] "I conjure you, O Womb, [by the] one established

260

17. See the note on l. 227 above. There is no previous reference in this charm to a picture (though "write" in l. 226 can also mean "draw"). Cf., however, *PGM* VIII. 64–65.

18. For this detail, see *PGM* VIII. 67.

19. K. Preisendanz, *Akephalos. Der kopflose Gott, Beihefte zum Alten Orient* 8 (Leipzig: Hinrichs, 1926) 48–50, sees this passage as a reference to the Egyptian practice of putting the heads of those who have been beheaded between their feet. A. Delatte, "Akephalos," *BCH* 38 (1914):221–32, prefers to see this passage as a reference to the god Besas, who has the heads of animals for feet. Cf. K. Abel, "Akephalos," *PRE.S* 12 (1970):13. See Glossary, s.v. "Headless."

20. Cf. on this point *PGM* VIII. 97–98.

21. This refers to Isis and Nephthys, who in the form of falcons or kites watch over the body of Osiris. See Griffiths, *Plutarch's De Iside et Osiride* 35, 305, 328. [R.K.R.]

22. See on this concept the parallel passage *PGM* VIII. 100–101, which has 'Οσίρεως, "of Osiris," instead of "of Heaven." But "Heaven" should be kept (against the suggestion by F. Boll, in Preisendanz, apparatus ad loc.). Perhaps, Nut (Heaven) is really meant here: her image was placed in the coffin in such a way that her head and that of the dead were close to each other. [J.B.]

23. The picture is missing; it may have been in the portion of the papyrus which is now lost.

24. See *PGM* III. 171 and note; note also the apparatus at *PGM* VII. 252.

25. Cf. on this point Soranus, *Gynecology* III. 50 (ed. Ilberg, pp. 127–28): "On the Flexion, Bending, and Ascent of the Uterus," esp. sec. 2 (p. 127): "[A] flexing to the anterior of the uterus causes

over the Abyss, before heaven, earth, sea, light, or darkness came to be; [you?] who
created the angels, being foremost, AMICHAMCHOU and CHOUCHAŌ CHĒRŌEI
265   OUEIACHŌ ODOU PROSEIOGGĒS, and who sit over the cherubim, who bear / your
(?) own throne, that you return again to your seat, and that you do not turn [to one
side] into the right part of the ribs,[26] or into the left part of the ribs, and that you
do not gnaw into the heart like a dog, but remain indeed in your own intended and
270   proper place, not chewing [as long as] I conjure by the one who, / in the beginning, made the heaven and earth and all that is therein. Hallelujah! Amen!"
    Write this on a tin tablet and "clothe" it in 7 colors.[27]
*Tr.: John Scarborough.

PGM VII. 272–83

*Thōth: 1, 4, 12, 13, 22. Phaōphi: 2, 4, 10, 19, 20. Athyr: 7, 8, 9, 17, 18, 23,
275   27. / Choiak: 5, 6, 13, 15, 16, 24, 25. Tybi: 3, 4, 12, 24, 26. Mecheir: 1, 2, 10, 14,
280   19. Phamenōth: 7, 8, 9. Pharmouthi: 5, 6, 14, 15, 20. / Pachōn: 3, 4, 12, 13, 21,
26, 28. Pauni: 1, 2, 10, 11, 15, 20. Epeiph: 7, 8, 9, 14, 18, 19, 22. Mesore: [10, 14,]
20, 23, 24, 25.
*Tr.: W. C. Grese. An Egyptian calendar of months and days unsuitable for magic opera-
tions. See Hopfner, *OZ* I, secs. 829–30. Cf. also *PGM* VII. 153–67; Delatte, *Anecdota
Atheniensia* I. 631–32; I. Gruenwald, *Apocalyptic and Merkabah Mysticism, Arbeiten zur
Geschichte des antiken Judentums* 14 (Leiden: Brill, 1980) 102–3.

PGM VII. 284–99

285   *Orbit[28] of the moon: Moon / in Virgo: anything is rendered obtainable.[29] In Libra: necromancy.[30] In Scorpio: anything inflicting evil.[31] In Sagittarius: an invoca-
290   tion or incantations / to the sun and moon. In Capricorn: say whatever you wish
295   for best results. In Aquarius: for a love charm. Pisces: for foreknowledge. / In
Aries: fire divination or love charm. In Taurus: incantation to a lamp. Gemini: spell
for winning favor. In Cancer: phylacteries. Leo: rings or binding spells.
*Tr.: E. N. O'Neil. Cf. *PGM* III. 275–81, which is very similar to this passage despite some
significant differences in detail.

PGM VII. 300

*"SACHMOU OZOZO, you the one who thunders, the one who shakes the heaven
and the earth, the one who has swallowed the serpent, hour by hour raising[32] the

---

some problems [blockage?] in urination, and also causes a swelling of the pubic area; in some patients, it
[will cause] an inability to stand upright." [J.S.] For a more magical interpretation see A. A. Barb, "Diva
Matrix," *JWCI* 16 (1953): 193–238.
    26. The context might suggest "hips," but the Greek is specific; perhaps the author was quite vague
in the knowledge of internal anatomy. [J.S.]
    27. Presumably, this means that the cord around the neck is to be woven together from the threads of
seven colors. The strip of tin would then be worn as an amulet.
    28. Or "horoscope"; see, however, *PGM* III. 275, where κύκλος appears alone. On Selene and her
astrological role in magic, see Hopfner, *OZ* I, secs. 826–28; Delatte, *Anecdota Atheniensia* I, 411. On
κύκλος, see Gundel, *Astrologumena*, esp. pls. I, VII. [E.N.O.]
    29. The Greek term is unclear; see Preisendanz, apparatus ad loc.; K. F. W. Schmidt, *GGA* 196
(1934): 171.
    30. Necromancy and Libra are also connected in *PGM* III. 278.
    31. The reading πανκακώσιμον is uncertain and, at any rate, a *hapax legomenon*. Cf. *PGM* LXXI.
6–7.
    32. Reading ἐξαιρῶν, which Preisendanz has in the two parallels to this passage: *PGM* IV. 1326;
VII. 367.

disk of the sun and surrounding the moon, CHŌNSOU [33] OCHCHA ENSOU O BIBE-
ROĒSOS." Write on your left hand with myrrh ink these things surrounding the ibis.

*Tr.: W. C. Grese. The purpose of this spell is not given though it may form part of the
whole given in *PGM* VII. 272–83, 284–99.

PGM VII. 300a–310

/ *Love charm which acts in the same hour*: Take a seashell and write the holy   300a
names with the blood of a black ass.[34]

Spell: "I adjure you, shell, by bitter Necessity[35] (MASKELLI formula)[36] and [by
those] who have been placed [in charge of] the Punishments, LAKI LAKIŌ LAKIMOU
MOUKILA KILAMOU IŌR MOUŌR MOUDRA MAXTHA / MOUSATHA: attract her, NN,   305
whom NN bore" (add the usual, whatever [you wish]). "Do not be stubborn, but
attract her, OUCH OUCH CHAUNA MOUCHLIMALCHA MANTŌR MOURKANA MOU-
LITHA MALTHALI MOUI ĒIĒI YYY AĒ AIĒ YOŌ AĒI AĒI AĒI AŌA AŌA AŌA IAŌ ŌAI
ŌAI AIŌ ŌIA IŌA IAŌ ŌAI, attract her, NN" (add the usual). As the moon waxes / in   310
Aries or in Taurus [add the usual, whatever you wish].[37]
*Tr.: E. N. O'Neil.

PGM VII. 311–16

*A phylactery: "IAŌ SABAŌTH ADŌNAI ABLANATHANALBA AKRAMMACHAMAREI
SESENGENBAR[PHARANGES] PEPHRAZAŌTH ZŌTH [MENE] BAINCHŌŌŌCH, protect NN, whom NN [bore], from any violence both by a frightful dream and by all
demons of the air. [I conjure you] by the great, famous name, Abraam EMEINA
AEOUBAŌTH BAITHŌ BES IA IABAŌTH AGRAMAKRAMARI PSINŌTH[38] BER ŌŌN

33. This refers to the Egyptian moon god Khonsu; the moon is mentioned in the context. See Bonnet, *RÄRG* 140–44, s.v. "Chons"; Hellmut Brunner, "Chons," *LdÄ* I (1975): 960–63.

34. See on this point *PGM* IV. 3260 and n.

35. On "bitter Necessity," see *PGM* IV. 526, 605, 1499–1500; XV. 13. See Dieterich, *Mithrasliturgie*
59–60; idem, *Nekyia* (Darmstadt: Wissenschaftliche Buchgesellschaft, [3]1969) 124. Necessity ('Aνάγκη)
is a demonic being. See H. D. Betz, ed., *Plutarch's Theological Writings and Early Christian Literature*,
SCHNT 3 (Leiden: Brill, 1975) 224 (on *De sera num. vind.* 25, 564E).

36. See the Glossary, s.v. "MASKELLI logos."

37. Preisendanz deletes these words, thinking they belong at l. 316.

38. This name is Egyptian, meaning "the son of the female falcon." [R.K.R.]

315   IASŌP B . . . PNOUTE"[39] / [and add the usual, whatever you wish].[40]
       *Tr.: Morton Smith.

PGM VII. 317–18

Another phylactery, [to be said] to the moon: "ACHTHIŌPHIPH ERESCHIGAL
NEBOUGOSOUALĒTH[41]SATHŌTH SABAŌTH SABRŌTH" (add the usual, whatever you
wish).
*Tr.: Morton Smith.

PGM VII. 319–34

320   *Charm for direct vision: Take a copper vessel, / pour rainwater into it and make
       an offering of male frankincense.
           Formula: "Let the earth be still, let the air be still, let the sea be still; let the
       winds also be still, and do not be a hindrance to this my divination—no sound, no
325   loud cry, no hissing. For I am a prophet, and since I am about to call / a terrible,
       fearful name, 'KOLLA OLPHILOGEMALA ACHERŌIO,' open [the holy temple,] the
       world [built on the earth,] and welcome Osiris, because I am MANCHNŌBIS CHOL-
       CHOBĒ MALASĒT IAT THANNOUITA KERTŌMENOU PAKERBAŌ KRAMMASIRAT
330   MOMOMO MELASOUT PEU PHRĒ. Open my ears so that you may reveal to me / con-
       cerning those things I ask you to answer me. Come on, come on; immediately, im-
       mediately; quickly, quickly; and speak concerning those things about which I ques-
       tioned you. Appear to me, lord Anubis,[42] I command you, for I am IEŌ BELPHENŌ,
       who considers [this] matter."
           Dismissal. Say: "Go away, Anubis, to your own thrones, for my health and well-
       being."
           Use after you have kept yourself pure for 3 days.
       *Tr.: W. C. Grese.

PGM VII. 335–47

335   *Charm for a direct vision: If you want to see yourself, take a fly and Coptic
       eyepaint, grind them, and smear them on your eyes. Take a feather of an ibis 14
       fingers long, smear it with perfume of roses or lilies, wind around it a linen cloth,
       and hold it with your hands as a scroll. Then say thus, while looking to the side
340   with the left / eye:
           Formula: "MOUN EIPOSIS ĒU PHTHA NOUTHI[43] THIE SĒMI NOUEI NĒITHI[44]
       CHRECHREŌ SININŌRPS MOUCH ORŌOU ENTHERINI[45] EŌĒ MOUNIACH NESŌI
       MOUNESŌCH MOUNĒI ENIME CHREMOU RENENE SON SNĒI ŌS MOUCHORŌOU
345   ENTHERINI / ANOK SŌS ERMAICHŌ ENTEUMOUTOICHNĒ CHREMOU TĒŠBAS
       PNĒTE[46] KYPHOCH EMM IEBOCHNĒS TCHĒNĒ PHIMOU CHNOU NYOICHŌŌIM
       SEOUNEUMOI INONRI."
       *Tr.: W. C. Grese.

       39. The word is Egyptian and means "O/the god." [R.K.R.]
       40. Preisendanz adds this formula from l. 310.
       41. Read νεβουτοσουαληϑ (tau for gamma). See *PGM* IV. 2484–85, and Glossary, s.v. "Nebuto-
       soualeth."
       42. For Anubis as conducting the gods to the magician, cf. *PDM* xiv. 35–37. [R.K.R.]
       43. These three words mean in Egyptian, "Come, Ptah, god." [R.K.R.]
       44. This name seems to refer to the Egyptian goddess Neith; see Bonnet *RÄRG* 512–17, s.v.
       "Neith." [R.K.R.] Cf. Plutarch, *De Is. et Os.* 9, 354C, reporting about the statue of the Athena of Sais,
       as Neith is called by the Greeks. See Griffiths, *Plutarch's De Iside et Osiride* 283–84.
       45. This word corresponds to the Egyptian *ntr*, "god." [R.K.R.]
       46. Perhaps this corresponds to the Egyptian *p3 ntr*, "O/the god." Cf. *PGM* VII. 316. [R.K.R.]

PGM VII. 348–58

Divination by means of a boy: [47] After you have laid [him] on the ground, speak, and a dark-colored boy will appear to him. /

Formula: "I call upon you, inhabitants of Chaos and Erebos, of the depth, of   350
earth, watchers of heaven, of darkness, masters of things not to be seen, guardians of secrets, leaders of those beneath the earth, administrators of things which are infinite, those who wield power over earth, servants in the chasm, shudderful fighters, fearful ministers, inhabitants of dark Erebos, / coercive watchers, rulers of   355
cliffs, grievers of the heart, adverse daimons, iron-hearted ones BITHOURARA
ASOUĒMARA . . . OTROUR MOURROUR APHLAU MANDRAROUROU SOU MARAROU,
reveal concerning the matter which I am considering" (add the usual).
*Tr.: W. C. Grese.

PGM VII. 359–69

Request for a dream oracle: Take a strip of clean linen and write on it the follow-ing name. / Roll it up to make a wick, pour pure olive oil over it and light it.   360

The formula to be written is this: "HARMIOUTH LAILAM CHŌOUCH [48] ARSE-
NOPHRĒ PHRĒU PHTHA HARCHENTECHTHA."

In the evening then, when you are about to go to sleep, being pure in every re-spect, do this: Go to the lamp, say 7 times the following formula, extinguish the light / and go to sleep.   365

The formula to be spoken is as follows: "SACHMOUNE [49] PAĒMALIGOTĒRĒĒNCH,
the one who shakes, who thunders, who has swallowed the serpent, surrounds the moon, and hour by hour raises the disk of the sun, 'CHTHETHŌNI' is your name. I ask you, lords of the gods, SĒTH CHRĒPS: reveal to me concerning the things I wish."
*Tr.: W. C. Grese.

PGM VII. 370–73

Against every wild animal, aquatic creature and robbers: Attach a tassel [50] to   370
your garment and say: "LŌMA ZATH AIŌN ACHTHASE MA . . . ZAL BALAMAŌN
ĒIEOY, protect me, NN, in the present hour; immediately, immediately; quickly, quickly."
*Tr.: W. C. Grese.

PGM VII. 374–76

Charm to induce insomnia: [Take] a seashell and write: / "IPSAĒ IAŌAI, let her,   375
NN daughter of NN, lie awake because of me." That night she will lie awake.
*Tr.: R. F. Hock.

PGM VII. 376–84

Another: Take a lamp and furnish it with a wick and say to it: "I conjure you, lamp, by your mother Hestia, MĒRALLĒL (say twice), and by your father Hephai-stos, MELIBOU MELIBAU / MELIBAUBAU. [Let] her lie awake" (and add the usual).   380

---

47. On this form of divination, see *PGM* V. 1.

48. CHŌOUCH is Egyptian for "darkness." [R.K.R.]

49. This name refers to the goddess Sakhmet; cf. *PGM* VII. 300. See Bonnet, *RÄRG* 643–46, s.v. "Sachmet" (esp. 645–46 on her role in magic).

50. For the tassel, cf. the *zizith* in Jewish religion. See Nm 15:38–39; Dt 22:12. See Schürer, *The History of the Jewish People II*, 479, with further references.

[Write these letters on the wick: "☿ chiiiiiii."⁵¹ And having provided the material [recite] the above spell. Now make an iron metal leaf, too.

The spell: "Turn cold, iron, and become like snow, [for I] am MELIBOU MELIBAU MELIBAUBAU" ([and] add the usual).
*Tr.: R. F. Hock.

PGM VII. 385–89

385 *A good cup spell: Over a cup say 7 times: "KANŌPI[TI] PROIE RŌDOCH . . . PH KALYPSAS EREKIN POTHĒXAS ERATEUN MORPHYS CHARIS PHAPHIETI EISI Ō BOU-BASTI⁵² POTHŌPI, I adjure you, holy names of Cypris, that, if you descend into the innermost heart of her, NN, [whom] NN bore, make her love" (add the usual).
*Tr.: E. N. O'Neil.

PGM VII. 390–93

390 *Victory charm for the races: Write on the wide part of its hoofs by inscribing these characters with a bronze stylus: ✳ ⚹ Write: "Give me success, charm, reputation, glory in the stadium" (also add the usual, as much as you want).
*Tr.: R. F. Hock.

PGM VII. 394–95

395 *Coercive spells for restraining: "SPHEDEMOUR BIRBIA / ĒCHI ERŌPHTHI ATAR-METRA CHĒLŌŌPS" (add the usual).
*Tr.: R. F. Hock.

PGM VII. 396–404

*An excellent spell for silencing, for subjecting, and for restraining: Take lead from a cold-water pipe and make a lamella and inscribe it with a bronze stylus, as shown below, and set it with a person who has died prematurely.

400 ☒ ⊠ ⊗ ✳ ☒ ⏝ ⤳ ⌓ Υ Τ ⊗ ↺ / BACHYCH ⦚⦚⦚ ⊔ ☐ AALOUGIKI ELŌAI BAIN-CHŌŌŌCH ⊐⤙3⤙♈⫝̸ß·⊔ EULAMŌ PHNOUBENE EIZOCHOR MOBOR PHŌ CHORBA ZACHEI ANACHIA ⚲ Κ ⚵ ⚵⚵ß PHŌRPHORBA PHŌRBORBA SEMESILAM ARCHENTECHTHA ASCHELIDONĒL. Restrain" (add the usual, as you wish).
*Tr.: R. F. Hock.

PGM VII. 405–6

405 *Love spell: For⁵³ love say while kissing passionately: "I am THAZI N EPIBATHA CHEOUCH CHA I am I am CHARIEMOUTH LAILAM" (add the usual).
*Tr.: E. N. O'Neil. Some of the words are recognizable as Coptic.

PGM VII. 407–10

*If you wish to appear to someone at night in dreams, say to the lamp that is in daily use,⁵⁴ say frequently: "CHEIAMŌPSEI ERPEBŌTH, let her, NN, whom NN
410 bore, see me in her / dreams, immediately, immediately; quickly, quickly" (and add the usual, whatever you wish).
*Tr.: E. N. O'Neil.

51. For parallels to these letters see Wünsch, *Antikes Zaubergerät* 16, A, l. 5.

52. This phrase corresponds to the Egyptian "Isis, O Boubastite." Isis is here identified with one of the epithets of Kypris/Aphrodite. See Bergman, *Isis-Seele und Osiris-Ei* 22–34. [R.K.R.]

53. ἐπί is strange here and at *PGM* VII. 661. Perhaps the section title here is φίλτρον ἐπὶ φιλίας and that at VII. 661 is φίλτρον ἐπὶ λαλήματος. Thus ἐπί can mean "for the purpose of." [E.N.O.]

54. So Preisendanz for τὸν καθημερινόν, but elsewhere lamps used in spells are special ones. Perhaps this accusative is adverbial: "daily." [E.N.O.]

PGM VII. 411–16

* **Spell for causing talk while asleep**: Take the heart of a hoopoe[55] and place it in myrrh. And write on a strip of hieratic papyrus the names and characters and roll up the heart in the strip of papyrus and place it upon her pudenda and ask your questions. And she will confess every/thing to you: "DARYGKO IAU IAU   415 ⊗⊕ЧX⏀β ΛΘΛΘΛΔΔδΛΒΖδΤΙΖ β" (add the usual, as much as you want).
*Tr.: E. N. O'Neil.

PGM VII. 417–22

* **A restraining [spell]**: Write on a tin lamella with a bronze stylus before sunrise the names "CHRĒMILLON MOULOCH KAMPY CHRĒ ŌPHTHŌ MASKELLI (formula) ERĒKISIPHTHĒ IABEZEBYTH." / Then throw it into [the] river [or] into [the] sea   420 before sunrise. Also write on it, with [the others], these characters: "⊗ƎΖ⑂ⴳXϾ. Mighty gods, restrain" (add the usual, whatever you wish).
*Tr.: Morton Smith.

PGM VII. 423–28

* **To win at dice**: "THERTHENITHŌR DYAGŌTHERE THERTHENITHŌR SYAPOTHE-REUO KŌDOCHŌR make me a winner at dice, / O prevailing Adriel." Into your   425 hand say: "Let not even one person be equal to me, for I am THERTHENITHŌR ĒRŌTHORTHIN DOLOTHOR, and I am going to throw what I want." And say this repeatedly, and then throw.

Another way you must say the formula is: "Let not even one of these playing with me be equal, and I am going to throw what I want."
*Tr.: R. F. Hock.

PGM VII. 429–58

* **A restraining [rite] for anything**, works even on chariots. It also causes en-mity / and sickness, cuts down, destroys, and overturns, for [whatever] you wish.   430 The spell [in it], when said, conjures daimons [out] and makes them enter [objects or people]. Engrave in a plate [made] of lead from a cold-water channel what you want to happen, and when you have consecrated it with bitter aromatics such as myrrh, bdellium, styrax, and aloes and thyme, / with river mud, late in the evening   435 or in the middle of the night, where there is a stream or the drain of a bath, having tied a cord [to the plate] throw it into the stream—or into the sea—[and let it] be carried along. Use the cord so that, when you wish, you can undo [the spell]. Then should you wish to break [the spell], untie the plate. Say the formula 7 times and you will see something wonderful. Then go away without turning back / or giving   440 an answer to anyone, and when you have washed and immersed yourself, go up to your own [room] and rest, and use [only] vegetable food. Write [the spell] with a headless bronze needle.

The text to be written is: "I conjure you, lord Osiris, by your holy names OUCHIŌCH OUSENARATH, Osiris, OUSERRANNOUPHTHI OSORNOUPHĒ[56] / Osiris-Mnevis,[57] OUSERSETEMENTH[58] AMARA MACHI CHŌMASŌ EMMAI[59] SERBŌNI   445

55. κοκκοφάδιος occurs only here, but cf. *PGM* II. 18 and III. 424–25. [E.N.O.]
56. OSORNOUPHE is Egyptian *wsir nfr*, "Osiris the good." [R.K.R.]
57. On Osiris-Mnevis, see *PGM* IV. 140, 2994 and n.
58. OUSERSETEMENTH is Egyptian for "Osiris . . . the west (the underworld)." [R.K.R.]
59. EM MAI is Egyptian, "in truth." [R.K.R.]

EMER Isis,[60] ARATŌPHI ERACHAX ESEOIŌTH ARBIŌTHI AMEN CH[N]OUM (?) MON-
MONT OUZATHI PĒR OUNNEPHER[61] EN ŌŌŌ, I give over to you, lord Osiris, and I
deposit with you this matter / " (add the usual).

But if you cause [the plate] to be buried or [sunk in] river or land or sea or
stream or coffin or in a well, write the Orphic[62] formula, saying, "ASKEI KAI TAS-
KEI" and, taking a black thread, make 365 knots[63] and bind [the thread] around the
outside of the plate, saying the same formula again and, "Keep him who is held" (or
"bound"), or whatever you do. And thus [the plate] / is deposited. For Selene,
when she goes through the underworld, breaks whatever [spell] she finds. But
when this [rite] has been performed, [the spell] remains [unbroken] so long as you
say over [the formula] daily at this spot [where the plate is deposited]. Do not hast-
ily share [this information] with anyone, for you will find [its like (?) only] with
much labor.
*Tr.: Morton Smith.

PGM VII. 459–61

460   *Excellent love charm: Inscribe by scratching on a tin lamella. Write / and lay it
down, walking over it. And what is written is this: "I adjure you by the glorious
name of Bacchios"[64] (and add the usual, whatever you wish).
*Tr.: E. N. O'Neil.

PGM VII. 462–66

*Excellent love charm: Inscribe by scratching on a tin lamella the characters and
the names, and after making it magically potent with some magical material,[65] roll
it up and throw it into the sea.
465   *The characters are these*: " ΨΖΤΖΖΙΟΖΥ⁊ΙΙΟ⧧ ICHANARMENTHŌ
CHASAR, cause her, NN, to love me" (add the usual). Write with a copper nail from
a shipwrecked vessel.
*Tr.: E. N. O'Neil.

PGM VII. 467–77

*Take a shell from the sea and draw on it with myrrh ink the figure of Typhon given
below, and in a circle write his names, and throw it into the heating chamber[66] of a
470   bath. But when / you throw it, keep reciting these words engraved in a circle and
"attract to me her, NN, whom NN bore, on this very day, from this very hour on,
with her soul and heart aflame, quickly, quickly; immediately, immediately." The
picture[67] is the one below.

But when reciting the spell, [say] its beginning: "This is the god of Destinies,[68]

---

60. EMER ISI is Egyptian for "whom Isis loves." [R.K.R.]

61. [H]OUNNEPHER is Egyptian and corresponds either to *ḥwn-nfr*, "beautiful youth," or *wn—nfr*
(if unaspirated), "Onnophris." Cf. *PGM* IV. 1078. [R.K.R.]

62. It is not clear why the formula here is called "Orphic." Usually, this formula is called by the name
Ephesia grammata (cf. *PGM* LXX. 12); its origin and meaning is still a mystery. For bibliography, see
Betz, "Fragments," 291–92.

63. See on this point *PGM* IV. 1084 and n.

64. Bacchios may be the epithet of Dionysos or a personal name derived from it. See D. Detschew,
"Bakchos (Bacchus)," *RAC* 1 (1950):1147–50. But the name here is uncertain for textual reasons.

65. For the term οὐσιάζω, cf. *PGM* VII. 381.

66. For the role of the heating chamber, see *PGM* II. 51 and n.

67. The term here is ϑεώρημα, while below, l. 477, the noun is ζῴδιον (cf. the verb ζωγράφω in
l. 467). Seemingly the three words refer to the same depiction, but it is missing. [E.N.O.]

68. The text here is uncertain and the translation tentative. [E.N.O.]

ŌKĒSĒ EĒRINIARE MIN / ENTĒNTAIN PHOOU TŌNKTŌ MNĒ SIETHŌN OSIRI ENA-   475
BŌTH PSANOU LAMPSOUŌR IEOU IŌ IŌ AI ĒI EI AI EI AŌ, attract to me her, NN,
whose mother is NN," and the rest. *This is the figure*:
*Tr.: E. N. O'Neil.

PGM VII. 478–90

*"Eros, darling PASSALEON ĒT,[69] send me my personal [angel] tonight to give me
information about whatever the concern is. For I do this / on order from PAN-   480
CHOUCHI THASSOU at whose order you are to act, because I conjure you by the
four regions of the universe, APSAGAĒL CHACHOU MERIOUT MERMERIOUT and by
the one who is above the four regions of the universe, KICH MERMERIOUTH" (add
the usual).

This is the offering: Take equal portions of dirt from your sandal, / of resin, and   485
of the droppings from a white dove, and while speaking [the invocation], burn
them as an offering to the Bear.

The phylactery for this: Write these names on a strip of tin: "ACHACHAĒL
CHACHOU MARMARIOUTI." Then wear it around your neck. After uttering the
summons, go to your quarters, put out the lamp, and sleep / on a newly made bed   490
of rushes.
*Tr.: Hubert Martin, Jr.

PGM VII. 490–504

*Taking sulfur and seed of Nile rushes, burn [them] as incense to the moon and say,
"I call on you, Lady Isis, whom Agathos Daimon permitted to rule in the entire
black [land].[70] Your name is LOU LOULOU BATHARTHAR THARĒSIBATH ATHER-
NEKLĒSICH / ATHERNEBOUNI ĒICHOMŌ CHOMŌTHI Isis Sothis,[71] SOUĒRI, Bou-   495
bastis, EURELIBAT CHAMARI NEBOUTOS OUĒRI[72] AIĒ ĒOA ŌAI. Protect me, great
and marvelous names of the [god] (add the usual); for I am the one established in
Pelusium,[73] SERPHOUTH MOUISRŌ[74] / STROMMŌ MOLŌTH MOLONTHĒR PHON   500
Thoth. Protect me, great and marvelous names of the great god" (add the usual).

"ASAŌ EIŌ NISAŌTH. Lady Isis, Nemesis, Adrasteia,[75] many-named, many-
formed, glorify me, as I have glorified the name of your son[76] Horus" (add the
usual).
*Tr.: Morton Smith.

PGM VII. 505–28

Meeting with your own daimon:[77] "Hail, Tyche, and you, the daimon of this   505

69. The text here is doubtful. See the apparatus ad loc.

70. The name for Egypt in Egyptian is *Km.t*, meaning the "black" and referring to the alluvial soil in
distinction from the "red" desert soil that borders it. [R.K.R.] See Plutarch, *De Is. et Os.* 33, 364C, and
Griffiths, *Plutarch's De Iside et Osiride* 425–26.

71. Isis Sothis is the identification of Isis with the dog star Sothis (Sirius). See J. Bergman, "I Over-
come Fate, Fate Harkens to Me," in *Fatalistic Beliefs in Religion, Folklore, and Literature, Scripta Instituti
Donneriani Aboensis II* (1967) 38–40; idem, *Isis-Seele und Osiris-Ei* 22–34, 41–45, 52–58 (p. 55 refers
to *PGM* VII. 490–504).

72. OUERI is Egyptian *wr*, "great one." [R.K.R.]

73. The god of Pelusium (*Pr-ir-Imn*) is Amon. [R.K.R.] See Plutarch, *De Is. et Os.* 17, 357E, and
Griffiths, *Plutarch's De Iside et Osiride* 334–35.

74. SERPHOUTH MOUISRO is *Srp.t m3y sr*, "Lotus, Lion, Ram." Cf. *PGM* III. 659 and n.

75. On the identification of Isis, Nemesis, and Adrasteia, see Griffiths, *The Isis-Book* 153–54.

76. Although this sentence seems parallel to Jn 17:4–5, there is no Christian influence here.

77. For this spell and its interpretation, see Betz, "The Delphic Maxim," 160–62.

place, and you, the present hour, and you, the present day—and every day as well. Hail, Universe, that is, earth and heaven. Hail, Helios, for you are the one who has
510   established yourself in invisible light over the holy firmament / ORKORĒTHARA.[78]

"You are the father of the reborn Aion ZARACHTHŌ;[79] you are the father of awful Nature *Thortchophanō*;[80] you are the one who has in yourself the mixture[81] of universal nature and who begot the five wandering stars,[82] which are the entrails of
515   heaven, the guts of earth, the fountainhead of the waters, and the violence / of fire AZAMACHAR ANAPHANDAŌ EREYA ANEREYA PHENPHENSŌ IGRAA; you are the youthful one, highborn, scion of the holy temple, kinsman to the holy mere called Abyss which is located beside the two pedestals SKIATHI and MANTŌ.[83] And the
520   earth's 4 basements were shaken, O master of all, / holy Scarab,[84] AŌ SATHREN ABRASAX IAŌAI AEŌ ĒOA ŌAĒ IAO IĒO EY AĒ EY IE IAŌAI."

Write the name in myrrh ink on two male eggs.[85] You are to cleanse yourself thoroughly with one; then lick off the name, break it, and throw it away. Hold the other
525   in your partially open right hand and show it to the sun at dawn and . . .[86] / olive branches; raise up your right hand, supporting the elbow with your left hand. Then speak the formula 7 times, crack the egg open, and swallow its contents.

Do this for 7 days, and recite the formula at sunset as well as sunrise.
*Tr.: Hubert Martin, Jr.

PGM VII. 528–39

*Victory charm: "Helios, Helios, hear me, NN, Helios, lord, Great God, you who
530   maintain all things and who give life / and who rule the world, toward whom all things go, from whom they also came, untiring, ĒIE ELĒIE IEŌA ROUBA ANAMAŌ MERMAŌ CHADAMATHA ARDAMATHA PEPHRE ANAMALAZŌ PHĒCHEIDEU ENE-

78. For the magical name ORKORĒTHARA, see Bousset, *Religionsgeschichtliche Studien* 203.

79. Bousset, *Religionsgeschichtliche Studien* 203, n. 34, suggests that the name ZARACHTHŌ may be related to that of Zorochthora Melchisedek, which plays a role in gnosticism (*Pistis Sophia* IV. 136, 139, 140; *Book of Jeu* 108, 110, 111; Epiphanius, *Pan.* 55. 1; Hippolytus, *Ref.* 7. 36).

80. This name is written in Coptic.

81. The term "mixture" plays a great role in hellenistic philosphy and gnosticism. See *C.H.* XI. 7; *Pistis Sophia* III. 3 (and passim). For further references see *PGL*, s.v.

82. That is, the planets.

83. For the background of this passage in Egyptian religion and explanation of the names SKIATHI and MANTHŌ, see J. Bergman, "An Ancient Egyptian Theogony in a Greek Magical Papyrus (*PGM* VII, ll. 516–521)," in *Studies in Egyptian Religion Dedicated to Professor Jan Zandee, Numen Supplements 43* (Leiden: Brill, 1982) 28–37.

84. This acclamation expresses Khepri theology, of which the cosmogony in *Papyrus Bremner-Rhind* 26, 21 (in Pritchard, *ANET*, p. 6) is the largest example. Khepri, the holy scarab, is mentioned at the end of the climax of names and epithets which often refer to his form of existence even by the Greek terms. The cultic context is also evident: the noble birth, representing creation, takes place in the temple at the time of the appearance of the Original Sea. This sea is identical with the sacred lake in the temple near the two pedestals of the evening bark (Sektat) and the morning bark (Manedjet). The temple represents the whole world, so that the four basements of the earth were shaken by the birth of Khepri, the master of all. [J.B.]

85. That is, eggs from which male chicks will be hatched. The ancients believed that one could predict the sex of the chick from the shape of the egg, though there appears to be some uncertainty as to which shape produced which sex. See Aristotle, *Historia Animalium* VI. 2 (559a); Pliny *NH* 10. 74; Columella, *De Re Rustica* VIII. 5. Cf. the comments by P. Louis in vol. 2 (Paris: Les belles lettres, 1968) of his Budé translation of Aristotle's treatise, p. 64, n. 4, and by A. L. Peck in vol. 2 (Cambridge, Mass. and London: Harvard University Press, 1970) of his *LCL* translation of the same treatise, p. 225, n. a; also the reference at *PGM* XII. 100 to an egg that will produce a male chick. [H.M.]

86. There is a lacuna in the Greek text at this point.

DEREU SIMATOI MERMEREŌ AMALAXIPHIA MERSIPHIA EREME THASTEU PAPIE[87]
PHEREDŌNAX ANAIE / GELEŌ AMARA MATŌR MŌRMARĒSIO NEOUTHŌN ALAŌ   535
AGELAŌ AMAR AMATŌR MŌRMASI SOUTHŌN ANAMAŌ GALAMARARMA. Hear me,
lord Helios, and let the NN matter take place on time." Say this while you make an
offering over oak charcoal, sacred incense, with which has been mixed the brain of a
wholly black ram and the wheat meal of a certain plant.[88]
*Tr.: R. F. Hock.

PGM VII. 540–78

*Lamp divination: Put an iron lampstand in a clean house[89] at the eastern part,   540
and having placed on it a lamp not colored red, light it. Let the lampwick be of new
linen, and light the censer. Then make a burnt offering of frankincense on grapevine wood. The boy, then, should be uncorrupt, pure.[90]

/ *Formula*: "PHISIO IAŌ AGEANOUMA SKABARŌ SKASABRŌSOU ASABRŌ, because   545
I implore you this day today, this very time, to let the light and the sun appear to
this boy, MANE OUSEIRI, MANE[91] ISI,[92] ANOUBIS the servant of all gods, and make
this boy fall into a trance and see the gods, / all who are present at the divination.   550
Appear to me in the divination, O high-minded god, Hermes thrice-great![93] May
he appear, the one who [made] the four parts of the heaven and the four foundations of the earth, RESENNĒETHŌ BASENERAIPAN THALTHACHTHACHŌTHCH CHI-
NEBŌTH CHINEBŌTH MIMYLŌTH MASYNTORI / ASTOBI. Come to me, you who are   555
in heaven; come to me, you who are from the egg.[94] I conjure you by the ENTŌ[95]
TAPSATI LEGĒNISTHŌ ĒLEGĒ SERPHOUTH MOUISRŌ[96] LEGE [having appeared
and][97] the two gods who are about you, THATH. The one god is called 'So'[98] the
other, 'Aph,'[99] KALOU KAGŌĒI SESOPHĒI BAINCHŌŌŌCH."

87. Perhaps PAPIE is related to PIPI, but cf. the apparatus ad loc. See for PIPI *PGM* IV. 595 and n.

88. For the plant called κατανάγκης ἄλευρα, see Diosc. 4.131; Pliny, *HN* 27.57.

89. The Greek is ambiguous, referring either to a house or a room in a house serving as a temple.

90. On the boy medium, see *PGM* V. 1 and n.

91. MANE is perhaps equivalent to Egyptian *mrj.n*, "beloved one of," hence: "beloved one of Osiris,
beloved one of Isis." [J.B.]

92. OUSERI . . . ISI, referring to Osiris and Isis, perhaps by the vocative. [R.K.R.]

93. The epithet "thrice great" results from the Egyptian superlative which repeats the positive three
times. For the name Hermes Trismegistos and its derivation, see Festugière, *La révélation* I, 73–74;
K. W. Tröger, "Die hermetische Gnosis," in *Gnosis und Neues Testament. Studien aus Religionswissenschaft
und Theologie* (Berlin: Evangelische Verlagsanstalt, 1973) 103–4; J. Parlebas, "L'Origine égyptienne de l'
appelation 'Hermès Trismegistos,'" *GM* 13 (1974): 25–28; M.-Th. and P. Derchain, "Noch einmal
Hermes Trismegistos," *GM* 15 (1975): 7–10; R. K. Ritner, "Hermes Pentamegistos," *GM* 49 (1981):
73–75; idem, "Additional Notes to Hermes Pentamegistos," *GM* 50 (1981): 67–68.

94. In Egyptian cosmogony the mythical primordial egg played a great role. Cf. *PGM* III. 145 and n.
According to Orphic cosmogony, the one born from the egg is the god Phanes. See *Orph. Frag.* nos. 54,
55, and 56, and H. Leisegang, "The Mystery of the Serpent," in J. Campbell, ed., *The Mysteries* (Princeton: Princeton University, 1978) 194–260.

95. Or, ἐν τῷ, ". . . by the one who is in TAPSATI . . . ," following Preisendanz. The latter probably
belongs to the series of *voces magicae* as indicated here. See also l. 576.

96. On SERPHOUTH MOUISRO, see *PGM* III. 659; and Preisendanz, vol. III, p. 230, s.v.

97. The text is mutilated here: "[and having appeared]" is Preisendanz's conjecture. The plural participle may refer to the two preceding commands, if these commands refer to two separate gods. But the
conjecture does not help much. The problem is also complicated by λεγε, "tell" or "speak" (?).

98. This name probably refers to the god Shu, Greek Sōsis. See Griffiths, *Plutarch's De Iside et Osiride*
326–37; Bonnet, *RÄRG* 685–89, s.v. "Schu." Cf. *PGM* VII. 345.

99. The name is unexplained; for possible explanations, see Preisendanz, apparatus ad loc., and vol.
III, p. 217, index, s.v. "'Αφ." Perhaps the name refers to Apophis, the snake god and enemy of Re. This
god is mentioned as 'Αφυφις in *PGM* XIII. 262; cf. Plutarch, *De Is. et Os.* 36, 365D. See Griffiths,

560   ***The formula to be spoken***: "Come to me, spirit that flies in the air, / called with
secret codes and unutterable names, at this lamp divination which I perform, and
enter into the boy's soul, that he may receive the immortal form in mighty and incorruptible light, because while chanting, I call, ʿIAŌ ELŌAI MARMACHADA MENE-
565   PHŌ[100] MERMAI / IĒŌR AIEŌ ĒREPHIE PHEREPHIŌ CHANDOUCH AMŌN EREPNEU
ZŌNŌR AKLEUA MENĒTHŌNI KADALAPEU IŌ PLAITINE RE AŌTH IĒI ŌĒI MEDCHĒ-
NŌR ALACHAL PERECHAĒL SERENŌPH DOUNAX ANAXIBOA EREBE BŌ BEBŌBIA
570   ANĒSIODEU IAŌA ENIŌEAL / EMERŌ MASAIANDA.'"

        "Hither to me, O lord, riding upon immaculate light without deceit and without
anger; appear to me and to your medium, the boy, MARMARIAU ANAPSICHALAŌ
PEOE NIPSEOUA AIETY HARENNŌTHĒS[101] ANERŌPHĒS ITHYAMAREM ŌSIĒR ANAP-
SICHYŌN PSYELĒMICHALĒS, appear" (say it 3 times).

575   / If he says, "I see your lord in the light," say: "O holy YMERI EIGESOU ENTŌ
TĒRIOUA MENĒ SOMIŌŌ ALAMAŌR CHŌCHENEMĒTŌR," and thus he will answer.
Ask: "ARSERETŌTHI OUĒMANTOUR."
*Tr.: J. P. Hershbell.

PGM VII. 579–90

580   *A phylactery, a bodyguard against daimons, against phantasms, / against every
sickness and suffering, to be written on a leaf of gold or silver or tin or on hieratic
papyrus. When worn it works mightily for it is the name of power of the great god
and [his] seal, and it is as follows: "KMĒPHIS CHPHYRIS[102] IAEŌ IAŌ AEĒ IAŌ OŌ
585   AIŌN IAEŌBAPHRENE / MOUNOTHILARIKRIPHIAE Y EAIPHIRKIRALITHANYOME-
NERPHABŌEAI."[103] These are the names; the figure is like this: let the Snake be
biting its tail, the names being written inside [the circle made by] the snake, and
the characters thus, as follows: ⟨characters⟩.

        The whole figure[104] is [drawn] thus, as given below, with [the spell], "Protect
590   my body, [and] the / entire soul of me, NN." And when you have consecrated [it],
wear [it].

*Tr.: Morton Smith.

Plutarch's De Iside et Osiride 440; Bonnet, *RÄRG* 51, s.v. "Apophis." Cf. the strange ἀφφώ in LXX 2 Kgs
2 : 14; 10 : 10 and the explanations given by patristic commentators, for which see *PGL*, s.v. "ἀφφώ."
        100. Menepho is the name of the city of Memphis. Cf. *PGM* III. 104.
        101. Harennōthes is Egyptian for *Ḥr-nḏ-it.f* (Harendotes), meaning "Horus the defender of his fa-
ther." See Bonnet, *RÄRG* 269, s.v. "Harendotes"; Griffiths, *Plutarch's De Iside et Osiride* 345; D. Meeks,
"Harendotes," *LdÄ* 2 (1977) : 964–66. [R.K.R.]
        102. Chphyris is the Egyptian scarab, Khepri.
        103. IAEŌ begins an often-cited palindrome, but it is not set out as such in Preisendanz. The copyist
got one letter wrong: ALITHA should be ALITHO.
        104. Preisendanz gives the opening words surrounding the serpent as TARĒON ĒOU PHI, but the
photograph (plate I, no. 4) shows clearly the reading given in the transcription here.

PGM VII. 591–92

* "Come to me, ear of heaven; come to me, ear [of the air;] come to me, ear of the earth," and so forth, as indicated.

*Tr.: W. C. Grese. This portion of an invocation seems to be mislocated in the papyrus manuscript.

PGM VII. 593–619

* **Fetching charm for an unmanageable [woman]:** [105] Take a [lamp], not painted red, with seven wicks, and make a wick of [the hawser of] a wrecked / ship. On the [1st] wick write with myrrh, "IAŌ"; on the 2nd, "ADŌNAI"; on the 3rd, "SABAŌTH"; on the 4th, "PAGOURĒ"; on the 5th, "MARMOROUTH"; on the 6th, "IAEŌ"; on the 7th, "MICHAĒL."

Put olive oil in the lamp and place it in a window / facing south. Also put wormwood seeds on the lamp (around the edge of the lamp), and recite this *formula*: "I call upon you, the masters, great gods, who shine in the present hour, on this day, for the sake of her, the ungodly NN. For she has said: /

'IAŌ does not have ribs.'

[She, NN, has said,] 'ADŌNAI was cast out because of his violent anger.'

[She, NN, has said,] 'SABAŌTH emitted three cries.' [106]

She, NN, has said, 'PAGOURĒ is by nature a hermaphrodite.'

She, NN, has said, 'MARMOROUTH was castrated.'

She, NN, has said, 'IAEŌ was not entrusted with the ark.'

She, NN, has said, 'MICHAĒL is by nature a hermaphrodite.'

/ "I am not the one who says such things, master, but she, the godless NN. Therefore fetch her for me, her inflamed with passion, submissive. Let her not find sleep until she comes to me" (repeat 7 times).

If the first lamp flickers, know that she has been seized by the daimon. And if the 2nd, she has left (the house); and if the 3rd, she is on the / way; and if the 4th, she has arrived; and if the 5th, she is at the door; the 6th, at the doorlatch; the 7th, she has come into the house.

It can fetch people even from across the sea. For that, place the lamp in some water in the open air. Place a papyrus boat under the lamp, and [recite the] formula 6 times.

*Tr.: D. E. Aune.

PGM VII. 619–27

* **From the Diadem of Moses:** [107] / Take the plant snapdragon and hold it under your tongue while lying asleep. And rise early and before you speak to anyone recite the names, and you will be invisible to everyone.

But when you say them over drinking cups and give them to a woman, she will love you, since this spell has power over everything: "ARESKILLIOUS THOUDALESAI KRAMMASI CHAMMAR / MOULABŌTH LAUABAR CHOUPHAR PHOR PHŌRBAŌ SACHI HARBACH MACHIMASŌ IAŌ SABAŌTH ADŌNAI."

For what you wish, say: "Get her, NN, for me, NN" (add the usual, whatever you wish).

*Tr.: E. N. O'Neil.

---

105. See for parallels to this spell *PGM* IV. 2475 and n.

106. For this cry, cf. the parallel in Ignatius, *Eph.* 19. 1.

107. This spell seems to be a selection from a larger collection entitled "The Diadem of Moses." [E.N.O.]

PGM VII. 628–42

*Taking a field lizard,[108] let it down into oil of lilies until it be deified. Then en-
630   grave / the [image of] the Asklepios [worshiped] in Memphis[109] on a ring of iron
from a leg fetter and put [the ring] into [the] oil of lilies [in which the lizard was
drowned]. And when you use [the ring] take [it and] show [it] to the pole star,[110]
635   saying this spell 7 times: "MENŌPHRI[111] who sit on the cherubim, send me / the
true Asklepios, not some deceitful daimon instead of the god." Then take the incense burner in where you are going to sleep and burn 3 grains of frankincense and
wave the ring in the smoke of the incense, saying 7 times the [spell], "CHAU-
640   APS / ŌAEIAPS ŌAIS LYSIPHTHA,[112] lord Asklepios, appear." And wear the ring on
the index finger of your right hand.
*Tr.: Morton Smith.

PGM VII. 643–51

*Cup spell, quite remarkable: Say the spell that is spoken to the cup 7 times: "You
645   are wine; you are not wine[113] but the head of Athena. / You are wine; you are not
wine, but the guts of Osiris, the guts of IAŌ PAKERBĒTH SEMESILAM ŌŌŌ Ē PA-
TACHNA IAAA." (For *the spell of compulsion*: "ABLANATHANALBA AKRAMMACHA-
MAREI EEE, who has been stationed over necessity, IAKOUB IA IAŌ SABAŌTH
ADŌNAI ABRASAX").
650   "At whatever hour / you descend into the guts of her, NN, let her love me, NN,
[for] all the time of her life."
*Tr.: E. N. O'Neil.

PGM VII. 652–60

*Spell to induce insomnia by means of a bat: Take blood of a black ox or of a
goat or of Typhon[114]—but preferably of a goat—and write on its right wing:
655   "BŌRPHŌR PHORBA PHORPHARBA / PHŌRBŌRPHORBA PHORBA PHORBA PHORBA
BAPHAIĒ PHŌRBAPHŌR BARBA" (put one word under another one, like bricks,[115]
and [add the usual, whatever] you want). And on the left wing write this in the
same pattern: "PHŌRPHŌR PHORBA BORPHOR PHORBA BORPHOR PHORBA PHOR-
660   PHOR PHORBABŌR / BORBORBA PHŌRPHŌR PHORBA" (likewise, add the usual as
you want).
*Tr.: R. F. Hock.

---

108. See A. D. Nock, "The Lizard in Magic and Religion," in his *Essays* I, 271–76. On deification by
drowning, see *PGM* I. 5; III. 1, with notes; LXI. 39–71.

109. Asklepios in Memphis is the Egyptian god Imhotep. See D. Wildung, *Imhotep und Amenhotep*
(München: Deutscher Kunstverlag, 1977). [R.K.R.]

110. The constellation of the pole star (Bear) is connected here with the "true" Asklepios of
Memphis, that is Asklepios/Imhotep in contrast to the Greek Asklepios. This expression is indeed non-
Greek. See Hopfner, *OZ* II, secs. 14 and 181.

111. That is, Memphis, or perhaps Memphite. [R.K.R.]

112. -SI PHTHA is Egyptian and means "son of Ptah," a standard epithet of Imhotep. [R.K.R.]

113. For the formula "you are x, you are not x, but . . ." cf., e.g., *PGM* LXI. 7–9. See also Smith,
Jesus the Magician 111, 197 n.

114. The "blood of Typhon" is the blood of an ass. See *PGM* IV. 2100 and n.

115. For this magical formation of words, see *PGM* V. 349, 361 and Preisendanz, vol. I, plate III,
no. 6.

PGM VII. 661–63

*Love spell: In conversation [116] while kissing passionately, say: "ANOK THARENEPI-
BATHA CHEOUCHCHA ANOA ANOK CHARIEMOCHTH LAILAM."
*Tr.: E. N. O'Neil.

PGM VII. 664–85

*Spell for obtaining dream revelations: Take a linen strip, and on it you write
with myrrh ink the matter, / and wrap an olive branch and place it beside your   665
head, beneath the left side of your head, and go to sleep, pure, on a rush mat on the
ground, saying the spell 7 times to the lamp:

"Hermes,[117] lord of the world, who're in the heart,
   O circle of Selene, spherical
And square, / the founder of the words of speech,   670
Pleader of Justice's cause, garbed in a mantle,
With golden sandals, turning airy course
Beneath earth's depths, who hold the spirit's reins,
The sun's and who with lamps of gods immortal
Give joy to those beneath earth's depths, to mortals
Who've finished life. / The Moirai's[118] fatal thread   675
And Dream divine you're said to be, who send
Forth oracles by day and night; you cure
Pains of all mortals with your healing cares.
Hither, O blessed one, O mighty son
Of the goddess who brings full mental powers,
By your own form and gracious mind. And to
An uncorrupted youth / reveal a sign   680
And send him your true skill of prophecy,

OIOSENMIGADŌN ORTHŌ BAUBŌ NIOĒRE KODĒRETH DOSĒRE SYRE SUROE SAN-
KISTĒ DŌDEKAKISTĒ AKROUROBORE[119] KODĒRE RINŌTON KOUMETANA ROU-
BITHA NOUMILA PERPHEROU AROUŌRĒR / AROUĒR"[120] (say it seven times and add   685
the usual, whatever you wish).
*Tr.: E. N. O'Neil.

PGM VII. 686–702

*Bear charm: "Bear, Bear, you who rule the heaven, the stars, and the whole
world; you who make the axis turn and control the whole cosmic system by force
and compulsion;[121] / I appeal to you, imploring and supplicating that you may do   690
the NN thing, because I call upon you with your holy names at which your deity
rejoices, names which you are not able to ignore: BRIMŌ, earth-breaker, chief hunt-

---

116. Cf. on this title PGM VII. 405 and n.

117. These dactylic hexameters are also one version of the reconstructed Hymns 15–16, ll. 1–12; see
Preisendanz, vol. II, p. 249. This version is, however, quite different from that in PGM V. 400–421 and
XVIIb. 1–23. [E.N.O.]

118. At PGM V. 410, Preisendanz prints the word as a common noun, here as the proper noun.
[E.N.O.]

119. On this vox magica, see the Glossary, s.v. "YESSIMMIGADO/AKROUROBORE formula."

120. AROUĒR is Egyptian for Ḥr-wr, "Horus the great." [R.K.R.]

121. For this concept of the divine mover of the universe, see Bousset, Religionsgeschichtliche Studien
208–11.

ress,[122] BAUBŌ L[123] . . . I AUMŌR AMŌR AMŌR . . . IĒA [shooter] of deer[124] AMAM[A-
695   MAR] APHROU . . . MA, universal queen, queen of wishes, / AMAMA, well-bedded,[125]
Dardanian, all-seeing, night-running, man-attacker, man-subduer, man-summoner,
man-conqueror, LICHRISSA PHAESSA, O aerial one, O strong one,[126] O song and
700   dance, guard,[127] spy, delight, delicate, protector, adamant, adamantine, O / Dam-
nameneia, BREXERIKANDARA, most high, Taurian,[128] unutterable, fire-bodied,
light-giving, sharply armed. Do such-and-such things" (add the usual).
*Tr.: H. D. Betz. The purpose of the spell is not given, although directions to insert requests
come at the end. Cf. the Bear spells in *PGM* IV. 1275–1330, 1331–89; LXXII. 1–36.

PGM VII. 703–26

*Request for a dream oracle: Write [with myrrh] on clean papyrus:
705   "I call you, the one who shines on the whole inhabited / and uninhabited world,
whose name is composed of 30 letters, in which are the seven vowels, through
which you name [the] universe, gods, lords, RARAPAE ABRAIĒ IRARA PAUOUŌ
710   ARAŌACH (30 letters)[129] IEŌYŌĒ AIĒ IAŌĒ YŌEI: Reveal [to me], / lords, concerning the NN matter, dependably and through memory, PSICHOM[130] MORAIOUCH
PSICHOM ARASKELLITH ĒCHOMMORAKAUPS PSICHOMMO ARATOPOTH. Lords of
glory, reveal to me concerning the NN matter tonight, THŌOUTH PHEUBĒ CHAR-
715   PHRAUTHI / PHRĒ"[131] (add the usual, as you wish). Also write the name composed
of 30 letters in two wing formations,[132] thus: RARAPAEABRAIĒIRARAPAOUŌA-
BRAŌACHRARAPAEABRAIĒIRARAPAOUŌABRAŌACH: A

Ō

CHAŌARBAŌYOAPARARIĒIARBAEAPARAR
/ RAR A   A   R
Ō   Ō
IEŌYŌĒ[AIĒIAŌĒYŌEI]
R   E   E   R

Write also the ["heart"] as indicated [if] you want, and after placing the strip of
725   papyrus / under the lamp, go to sleep in a pure condition. Give answer to no one,
ENTYTHLCH.[133]
*Tr.: W. C. Grese.

122. The rendering of προκυνη is uncertain. See also *PGM* VII. 885–86; P. Reinach II, 88 which
has προκυνητε. For similar epithets, see LSJ, s.v. "κυναγέτις, προκυναγός, προκυνηγίς, προκύων."
The epithet "earthbreaker" has usually in *PGM* been transcribed RĒXICHTHŌN.
123. The following list of divine epithets comes from the cult of Artemis; it contains old material,
but not all is explainable and some renderings are quite tentative. Cf. for parallels *PGM* IV. 1301–8,
1345–79; also P. Reinach II, 88 (ed. P. Collart, *Les Papyrus Théodore Reinach*, BIFAO 39 [1940]:
29–32).
124. For this epithet, see Homeric Hymn 27. 2 and K. Wernicke, "Artemis," *PRE* 2 (1895):1384.
125. The rendering of εὐναία is uncertain. See Euripides, *Hippol.* 160, also Burkert, *Griechische Religion* 236.
126. Preisendanz translates, "O goddess of Erymna."
127. On this epithet of Artemis, see also *PGM* IV. 1298; *Orph. Frag.* 42.
128. The meaning of this epithet is uncertain; for similar expressions, see K. Wernicke, *PRE* 2
(1895):1399–1400.
129. The name is given below, ll. 716–18; cf. 708–9.
130. PSICHOM is Egyptian *p3 sḥm*, "the image/power." [R.K.R.]
131. THŌOUTH PHEUBĒ . . . PHRE corresponds to Egyptian "Thoth the ibis . . . Prē." [R.K.R.]
132. For the wing formation of magical words, see *PGM* I. 11 and n.
133. This is Demotic *mtw.f.ti ḥl.k* (?), "and he makes you fly" (?). [R.K.R.]

PGM VII. 727–39

*Charm for a direct vision of Apollo: In a ground-floor room without light, while you are crowned with a wreath of marjoram and while wearing wolf-skin sandals, recite this formula:

Formula: / "Helios, ruler of light, MER . . . EIPHIRA GARGERI PHTHA ER 730
. . . OIE . . . GERLYCHA MER . . . [OPHO] R ITHARA PHERXEI AR . . . EID . . .
PHŌRITHARZEI ERPHIBILCHIE ZEIRABELBĒ BICHA ARTHIA MĒLICHIA ERGA
GERPHI IŌ CHERPHEI KARGŌOARA EARMILICHA ATHERTHAPHTHŌ ATHTHERTHA-
PHI ARNACHERBBI." /

After you have said these things, the god Apollo will come having a cup for a 735
drink offering. Then you inquire concerning what you want. He gives from memory if you want, and if you ask, he will let you drink from his cup.

Dismissal: "ERKIKCHI BELTĒAMILICHA ARCHARZEIR PHIZŌR GEIRPHEI."
*Tr.: W. C. Grese.

PGM VII. 740–55

*[Request for a dream oracle: Write] on a strip of tinfoil, and after crowning the 740
strip of foil with myrtle, set up the censer. Then make a burnt offering of frankincense and carry the leaf of metal around the vapor while saying: "Lords, gods, reveal to me concerning the NN matter / tonight, in the coming hours. Emphatically 745
I beg, I supplicate, I your servant and enthroned [134] by you."

Then place the piece of foil under your pillow, and, without giving answer to anyone, go to sleep after having kept yourself pure for 3 days.

Formula to be written: / "MOU AMOU [135] AU IAŌ ABARBARASA AIŌ BAŌA CHPHĒ- 750
NOURIS AŌB AMO ADŌNAI ŌIG IIII OTHTHOUŌ AORCHA ARORCHA CHAXYNNĒRE
THIRARI OTHŌ CHOŌTH ERRE OCHŌ ANA ĒEPHRORE CHEIR ĒIN IĒIŌ ŌŌAA-
MADAA / OOO ŌŌŌ ŌŌA." Write [it] with a copper stylus. 755
*Tr.: W. C. Grese. This spell appears to be another version of a dream request; cf. *PGM* VII.
703–76. In this one, however, the title has been added by Preisendanz.

PGM VII. 756–94

*Prayer: "I call upon you who have all forms and many names, double-horned goddess, Mene, whose form no one knows except him who made the entire / world, IAŌ, the one who shaped [you] into the twenty-eight shapes of the world so 760
that you might complete every figure and distribute breath to every animal and plant, that it might flourish, you who wax from obscurity into light and wane from light into darkness" / (who begin to wane into a decrease). 765

"And the first companion of your name is silence, the second a popping sound, the third groaning, the fourth hissing, / the fifth a cry of joy, the sixth moaning, the 770
seventh barking, the eighth bellowing, the ninth neighing, / the tenth a musical 775
sound, the eleventh a sounding wind, the twelfth a wind-creating sound, the thirteenth a coercive sound, the fourteenth a coercive emanation from perfection. /

"Ox, vulture, bull, beetle, falcon, crab, dog, wolf, serpent, horse, she-goat, asp, 780
goat, he-goat, baboon, cat, lion, leopard, fieldmouse, deer, multiform, virgin, torch, / lightning, garland, a herald's wand, child, key.[136] 785

"I have said your signs and symbols of your name so that you might hear me, because I pray to you, mistress of the whole world. Hear me, you, the stable one,

134. On the ritual of the enthronement of the initiate, see A. D. Nock, "Notes on Beliefs and Myths," *JHS* 46 (1926):47–48; Nilsson, *GGR* II, 642, 680.
135. AMOU is Coptic for "come!" [R.K.R.]
136. See for the meaning of these symbols *PGM* LXX. 9–11 and nn.

the mighty one, / APHEIBOĒŌ MINTĒR OCHAŌ PIZEPHYDŌR CHANTHAR CHADĒ-   790
ROZO MOCHTHION EOTNEU PHĒRZON AINDĒS LACHABOŌ PITTŌ RIPHTHAMER
ZMOMOCHŌLEIE TIĒDRANTEIA OISOZOCHABĒDŌPHRA" (add the usual).
*Tr.: W. C. Grese.

PGM VII. 795–845

*Pythagoras' request for a dream oracle and Demokritos' dream divination: 795
The entering angel is subordinate to the sun, and as subordinate to the sun he enters—so he enters in the form of your friend whom you recognize, with a shining
star upon his head, and sometimes he enters / having a fiery star. Take, then, a   800
branch of laurel, and inscribe on each leaf a sign of the Zodiac with cinnabar, hav-   805
ing crowned yourself [with it]. (Also write its name in front of the sign of the
Zodiac.) / This rite is divine. Hence, keep in your breast the things revealed to you
by me even after the parting of my life, and if you perform them devoutly you will
be successful.

They are: [137]

1.	Aries	HAR MONTH [138] HAR THŌ CHE	810
2.	Taurus	NEOPHOBŌTHA THOPS	
3.	Gemini	ARISTANABA ZAŌ	
[4].	Cancer	PCHORBAZANACHAU	
[5].	Leo	ZALAMOIRLALITH	
[6].	Virgo	EILESILARMOU PHAI	815
[7].	Libra	TANTINOURACHTH	
[8].	Scorpio	CHORCHORNATHI	
9.	Sagittarius	PHANTHENPHYPHLIA	
[10].	Capricorn	AZAZAEISTHAILICH	
[11].	Aquarius	MENNY THYTH IAŌ	820
[12].	Pisces	SERYCHARRALMIŌ	

Take still another leaf of the royal laurel and write with cinnabar [ink] this name of
[the] living god: "CHALCHANA PHOE KOSKIANŌ (19) / ALĒMONTALL . . . ASEICH."   825
Having written it, do this for three days: wrap the leaves in a new handkerchief and
lay it under your head. Having come when it is evening, while burning frankincense, speak this *formula*:

"I call upon you, holy angel ZIZAUBIŌ, from the company of the Pleiades to
whom you are subordinate / and serve for all things, [for] whatever she might com-   830
mand you, you great, indestructible, fire-breathing one, who cast the rope of
heaven, through which rope all things turn upon earth. And I also call upon you
yourselves who are angels who have been stationed beneath his [ZIZAUBIŌ'S]
power. Hence I call upon you all that you may come quickly / in this night, and reveal   835
to me clearly and firmly, concerning those matters I desire. I conjure you, O lord,
who rise above the earth of the whole cosmic region, by the one ruling the whole
inhabited world and the benefactor of all. Hence, I call upon you in this night, / and   840
may you reveal all things to me through dreams with accuracy, O angel ZIZAUBIŌ."

Go to your house and having incensed the branch, put it on your head and sleep
pure. You must have [the place] where you perform absolutely pure, and the phylac-

137. In this list most of the numerical designations 1–12 can be recognized in the far right column
of the papyrus manuscript, numbering downward from Aries to Pisces. These numbers were erroneously
included in the magical symbols by Preisendanz.

138. Har-Month is Horus-Montu. Montu is the Egyptian god of war and therefore the proper counterpart of Ares, the ruler of the zodiacal sign Aries. Horus is also associated with this sign, for "Horus
the Red" was the name of Mars which governs Aries. [R.K.R.]

tery / where you have inscribed the name, put on your head and crown yourself   845
with the branch.
*Tr.: J. P. Hershbell.

PGM VII. 846–61

* **Shadow** [139] **on the sun**: After you have purified yourself, walk towards the sun in
the 5th hour, crowned with a tail of a cat, and say: "ERBETH BIO . . . PH . . . PH . . .
LL . . . III ANACH ABAREIR LATŌRŌCH ERBEBRITHA AMBRITHĒRA ŌRYKISTAR /
LAILAM AŌR XARXI THADARI ĒSYRPHA PHŌRPHI AGĒRŌCHĒ BEBATHA BARA   850
LIRYPŌ PHERCHĒ AMIARTH THERTHI GŌRĒ AMINACHARPHA IRGIRAMOU THAR-
PHI THEIRIŌRYS PHERIA PHORPHOROPHI."

When you have said these things, you will see a shadow in the sun. / Close your   855
eyes, look up, and you will see a shadow standing before you. Ask what you want,
"ERBAIGŌRYTHARPHTHEIR:"
Phylactery: The tail and the characters with the circle [on which] you will stand
after you have drawn it with chalk.
The characters are the following: 860
*Tr.: W. C. Grese.

PGM VII. 862–918

* **Lunar spell of Claudianus** [140] **and [ritual] of heaven and the north star** [141] **over
lunar offerings**: This papyrus itself, the personal property of the Twelve Gods, was
found [142] in Aphroditopolis [beside] the greatest goddess, / Aphrodite Urania, who   865
embraces the universe.

The preparation for Mistress Selene is made like this: Take clay from a potter's
wheel and mix a mixture [143] with sulfur, and add blood of a dappled goat and mold
an image of Mistress Selene the Egyptian, [144] as shown below, making her in / the   870
form of the Universe. And make a shrine of olive wood and do not let it face the
sun at all. [145] And after dedicating it with the ritual that works for everything, [put it
away,] and thus it will be dedicated in advance. And anoint it also with lunar ointment and wreathe it. And late / at night, at the 5th hour, put it away, facing Selene   875
in a [pure] room. And also offer the lunar offering and repeat the following in succession and you will send dreams, you will bind with spells. For the invocation to
Selene is very effective. And after anointing yourself in advance [with] the ointment, appeal to her.

And this is the lunar spell: / "I call upon you, Mistress of the entire world, ruler   880
of the entire cosmic system, greatly powerful goddess, gracious [daimon], lady of
night, who travel through the air, PHEROPHORĒ ANATHRA . . . OUTHRA. Heed

139. On the significance of the shadow, see Betz, "The Delphic Maxim," 163–64.

140. Preisendanz indicates the name Klaudianos may refer to a certain philosopher and alchemist
appearing in a list in Berthelot and Ruelle, *Collection des anciens alchimistes grecs* 26, l. 1.

141. The identity of the constellation of the Bear with Aphrodite-Selene is late. See Plutarch, *Amat.*
19, and F. Schwenn, "Selene," *PRE*, 2nd ser. 2 (1921): 1142; W. Fauth, "Arktos in den griechischen
Zauberpapyri," *ZPE* 57(1984): 93–99. [R.K.R.]

142. On this literary claim of having found books, see W. Speyer, *Bücherfunde in der Glaubenswerbung der Antike, Hypomnemata* 24 (Göttingen: Vandenhoeck and Ruprecht, 1970).

143. The pleonasm (μῖξον μίγματος, "mix a mixture,") is not uncommon in *PGM*; see *PGM* VII.
972. [E.N.O.]

144. The Egyptian Selene is the mistress of the night sky. See Bleeker, *Hathor and Thoth* 46.
[R.K.R.]

145. Preisendanz has incorrectly translated τὸ σύνολον with "das Ganze." Cf. l. 915 below, for the
sense of the instruction. [E.N.O.]

885 your sacred symbols and give a whirring sound,[146] [and] give a sacred angel or a holy assistant who serves / this very night, in this very hour, PROKYNĒ BAUBŌ PHOBEIOUS MĒE, and order the angel to go off to her, NN, to draw her by her hair, by her feet; may she, in fear, seeing phantoms, sleepless because of her passion for me and her love for me, NN, come to my bedroom."

890 So goes the song. But when / you see the goddess turning red, know that she is now attracting, and then say: "Mistress, send forth your angel from among those who assist you, one who is leader of night, because I adjure [you] by your great names, because of which no aerial or infernal daimon can ignore you, MESOUR-
895 PHABABOR BRAL IĒŌ ISI Ē. Come to me just as I have summoned you, / ORTHŌ BAUBŌ NOĒRE KODĒRE SOIRE SOIRE ERESCHIGAL SANKISTĒ DŌDEKAKISTĒ AKROUROBORE KODĒRE SAMPSEI; hear my words, and send forth your angel who is
900 appointed over the 1st hour: / MENEBAIN, and the one over the 2nd hour: NEBOUN, and the one over the 3rd hour: LĒMNEI, and the one over the 4th hour: MORMOTH, and the one over the 5th hour: NOUPHIĒR, and the one over the 6th hour: CHORBORBATH, and the one over the 7th hour: ORBEĒTH, and the one over
905 the 8th hour: PANMŌTH, and the one over the 9th hour: / THYMENPHRI, and the one over the 10th hour: SARNOCHOIBAL, and the one over the 11th hour: BATHIABĒL, and the one over the 12th hour: ARBRATHIABRI, so that you may do this for me; that you may attract, that you may tame on this very night, and so that she, NN
910 (or he, NN) be unable to have success until coming / to me, NN. [May she remain] fully satisfied, loving, desiring me, NN, and may she be unable to have intercourse with another man, except with me alone."

Now recite the spell many times, and it will attract and bind, and she will love you for all the time of her life. But when you attract her and she has had intercourse
915 with you, then pick up / the goddess and stow her away, giving her magical material, and do not show her to the sun and she will not stop coming, desiring you.

You will act in the same way for the spell to send dreams until you accomplish what you want. The power of the spell is strong. The figure is below.[147]
*Tr.: É. N. O'Neil.

PGM VII. 919–24

*Hermes' wondrous victory charm** which you are to keep in your sandals: Take a
920 tablet / gold like the sun[148] and inscribe on it with a bronze stylus and put it on whatever you want and see what it does on a boat, on a horse, and you will be amazed.

These are the characters: "⌐ ✕ Υ ϡ ϡ ~Η ✳ 𝓁∘⌐° σ Κ Ⴈ ϶Κ THŌOUTH, give victory, strength, influence to the wearer."
*Tr.: R. F. Hock.

PGM VII. 925–39

925 *Another[149] tablet charm** but **one to subject**: Take a lead tablet from a yoke for mules and inscribe [on it] with a bronze stylus the following names and characters,

---

146. ῥοῖζον, "whirring," most likely refers to the sistrum of Hathor, her constant emblem. The Egyptian name for the sistrum (*sšš.t*) is onomatopoetic for the rustling sound made by the shaking of its jingles. See on this point Bleeker, *Hathor and Thoth* 59–60. [J.B./R.K.R.]

147. See Preisendanz, apparatus ad loc. The figure is missing.

148. Literally, a "sun" or "solar" tablet, that is, a gold lamella.

149. Literally, "another one." However, the only connection with the preceding is the use of a metal tablet, hence the translation.

and put it under the sole of your left foot, after you have fumigated it carefully with incense.

/ **The names and characters are:**   930

```
 ∆ Ρ Ζ Χ
3  "NOLEANOUN
Γ  EBREBA
M  OLOTHIERON
○
Ζ  DENDENXOUN
↓  TOUBANTŌNI Restrain                         935
Ι  the wrath of him, NN, and the anger and
   tongues of everybody, in order that
   they might not be able to speak to him, NN."
 N Π ⊁ᚴ ω
```

*Tr.: R. R. Hock. As shown here the papyrus illustrates how the lead tablet is to be drawn. The language of the curse suggests the spell was designed for use in a courtroom scene.

PGM VII. 940–68

* **A charm to restrain anger** and **a charm to subject**: On clean papyrus write with   940
pure myrrh ink these names together with the "stele:"

IŌERBĒTH	IŌPAKERBĒTH
IŌERBĒ	ŌPAKERBĒTH
IŌERB	PAKERBĒTH
IŌER	AKERBĒTH 945
IŌE	KERBĒTH
IŌ	ERBĒTH
I	RBĒTH
	BĒTH
	ĒTH 950
	TH
IŌSESESRŌ	
ŌSESESRŌ	
SESESRŌ	IŌPĒMPS
ESESRŌ	ŌPĒMPS 955
SESRŌ	PĒMPS
ESRŌ	ĒMPS
SRŌ	MPS
RŌ	PS
Ō	960

"Come to me, you who are in the everlasting air,[150] you who are invisible, almighty, creator of the gods. Come to me, you who are the unconquerable daimon. Come to me, you who are never grieved for your own brother, Seth.[151] Come to me, / you fire-bright spirit. Come to me, you god who are not to be despised, you   965 daimon, and put to silence, subordinate, enslave him, NN, to him, NN, and cause him to come under my feet."
*Tr.: R. R. Hock.

150. For this expression see the parallel in *PGM* IV. 507–8.

151. This refers to Seth's murder of his brother Osiris. See H. te Velde, *Seth, God of Confusion* (Leiden: Brill, 1967) esp. 81–82. [R.K.R.]

PGM VII. 969–72

970 * **A good potion**: Take a piece of hieratic papyrus and / write on it: "IAŌ Ō ES-
TABISASĒ TOUREŌSAN ATHIACHIŌOUĒNOU ACHĒMACHOU. Let her, NN, whom
NN bore, love me, NN, when she has drunk the drink."[152]
*Tr.: E. N. O'Neil.

PGM VII. 973–80

* **A love spell of attraction through touch**: Take a scarab and boil it in a good
975 unguent,[153] / and take the beetle and grind it together with the plant vetch, and
place them in a glass cup and say the spell that follows twice: "THŌBARRABAU MI-
CHAĒL MICHAĒL OSIRIS PHOR PHORBA ABRIĒL SESEGGENBARPHARAGGĒS IAŌ
980 SABAŌTH ADŌNAIE LAILAM, compel / her, NN, whom NN bore, to follow me
should I touch her."
*Tr.: E. N. O'Neil.

PGM VII. 981–93

* [**Love spell of attraction**: Purify yourself from everything for . . .] days and say
[this] spell at sunrise: "Helios . . . but come here to me, [Mistress AKTIŌPHIS
985 ERESCHIGAL] PERSEPHONĒ; / attract [to me and bind her], NN, whom NN bore,
[to] the man who is [pining away] with [passion for her]; at this very moment,
inflame her that she fulfill the nightly desires of NN, whom NN bore. Aye, lord
990 NETHMOMAŌ [Helios, enter] into the [soul] of her, NN, whom NN bore, / and
[burn her heart], her guts, [her liver, her spirit, her bones. Perform] successfully for
me [this] charm,[154] immediately, immediately; [quickly, quickly]."
*Tr.: E. N. O'Neil.

PGM VII. 993–1009

* Look [to the] east [and say: "You are the one who thunders,] the one who rains
995 and / hurls lightning [at the] right time and dries [in the same way]; come to me,
reveal" (add the usual or [write] whatever [you want], and anoint your hand).

   Preparation of the ink: 3 dried figs, 3 stones of the Nicolaus date, 3 fragments of
1000 wormwood, and 3 lumps of myrrh; [mix together, / then] after pulverizing them,
[write] the following formula. Isis uttered [it and] wrote [it] when, after taking up
Osiris, she fit together his separated members. Asklepios[155] [saw] Osiris and admitted that he [could] not [put together] someone who was dead [even] with the help
of Hebe[156] or of [anyone else].

1005 [This is / ***the formula***: "Come to me, SESEGGENBARPHARAGGĒS SABAŌTH,] for
[I conjure] you, [daimon] of the dead, [by] bitter [Necessity]; open [your ears and]
hear [the] holy [words]." Also say [frequently] the [stele given] below.
*Tr.: W. C. Grese. This fragmentary spell has not preserved its title and so its exact purpose
cannot be known.

---

152. On the pleonasm πιοῦσα τὸν πότον, cf. *PGM* VII. 867. [E.N.O.]

153. μύρον is translated by Preisendanz as "Myrrhenöl." Both translations, however, may be too
specific for this unspecified aromatic concoction. [E.N.O.]

154. For this phrase, cf. *PGM* IV. 295, 2939; XX. 5.

155. Asklepios seems to have taken over the role of Anubis (thus Eitrem, in Preisendanz, apparatus
ad loc.).

156. The appearance of Hebe, daughter of Hera and Zeus, is surprising in this context. According to
Euripides, *Heraklid.* 847; Ovid, *Met.* 9. 400, she made Iolaos young again, a deed of proverbial fame.

PGM VII. 1009–16

*Divination by a dream: Say / to the . . . double . . . and rub your [head]; and   1010
[after descending], go to sleep without answering anyone.

"I call upon [you], Sabaoth, Michael, Raphael and you, [powerful archangel]
Gabriel, do not [simply] pass by me [as you bring visions], but let one of you enter / and reveal [to me] concerning the NN matter, AIAI ACHĒNĒ IAŌ." Write these   1015
things [on leaves . . .] of laurel and place them by your head.
*Tr.: W. C. Grese.

PGM VII. 1017–26

*"[Hail, Helios!] Hail, Helios! Hail, [Gabriel! Hail, Raphael! Hail,] Michael!
Hail, whole [universe! Give me] the [authority] and power of SABAŌTH, the /
[strength of IAŌ], and the success of ABLANATHANALBA, and [the might of] AK-   1020
RAMMACHAMAREI. Grant that I [gain] the victory, as I have summoned you" (then
write the 59-[letter] IAEŌ formula). "Grant [victory] because I know the names
of the Good Daimon, HARPON [CHNOUPHI] BRITATĒNŌPHRI BRISAROUAZAR
BASEN / KRIPHI NIPTOUMI CHMOUMAŌPHI (add the usual) and accomplish this   1025
for me." Speak to [no one].
*Tr.: R. F. Hock. Although untitled, this spell is a "favor and victory" charm. Cf. *PGM* XCII
for a similar request for the power and strength of various magical and mythological
personalities.

PGM VIII. 1–63

*Binding love spell of Astrapsoukos:[1]
Spell: "Come to me, lord Hermes, as fetuses do to the wombs[2] of women. Come to
me, lord Hermes, who collect the sustenance of gods and men; [come] to me, NN,
lord Hermes, and give me favor,[3] sustenance, / victory, prosperity, elegance, beauty   5
of face, strength of all men and women. Your names in heaven: LAMPHTHEN
OUŌTHI OUASTHEN OUŌTHI OAMENŌTH ENTHOMOUCH. These are the [names] in
the 4 quarters of heaven. I also know what your forms are:[4] in the east you have the
form / of an ibis, in the west you have the form of a dog-faced baboon, in the north   10
you have the form of a serpent, and in the south you have the form of a wolf. Your
plant is the grape which is the olive.[5] I also know your wood: ebony. I know you,
Hermes, who you are and where you come from and what your city is: Hermopolis. Come to me, lord Hermes, many-named one, who know / the things hid-   15
den beneath heaven and earth. Come [to me], NN, lord Hermes; serve well, benefactor of the world. Hear me and make me agreeable to all the forms throughout
the inhabited world. Open up for me the hands of everyone who [dispenses gifts][6]
and compel them to give me what they have in their / hands. I also know your for-   20
eign names: 'PHARNATHAR BARACHĒL CHTHA.' These are your foreign names.

"Whereas Isis, the greatest of all the gods, invoked you in every crisis, in every

1. According to Diogenes Laertius, *Prooem.* 2, Astrampsychos was the name of one or several Persian
magicians. See E. Reiss, "Astrampsychos," *PRE* 2 (1896):1796–97.
2. For parallels to this concept, see *PGM* III. 603 and n.
3. Here and throughout this section, χάρις is translated "favor," but the term comes close to meaning "grace." [E.N.O.]
4. The four animals represent the following deities: the ibis is Thoth, the dog-faced baboon is
Anubis, the serpent is Uto, the wolf is another form of Anubis. Their respective positions are partially
clear as well: Uto is often the north, Anubis the west (or the south), but why Thoth stands in the east
remains a puzzle. [J.B.]
5. The underscored words are Coptic written with Greek letters.
6. Accepting the emendation of Preisendanz.

district, against gods and men and daimons, creatures of water and earth and held
25   your favor, / victory against gods and men and [among] all the creatures beneath
the world, so also I, NN, invoke you.[7] Wherefore, give me favor, form, beauty.
Hear me, Hermes, benefactor, [inventor][8] of drugs; be easy to talk to and hear me,
just as you have done everything in the form of your Ethiopian dog-faced ba-
30   boon, / the lord of the chthonic daimons. Calm them all and give me strength,
form (add the usual), and let them give me gold and silver and every sustenance
which will never fail. Preserve me always, through all eternity, from drugs and de-
35   ceits, every slander and evil tongues, from / every daimonic possession,[9] from every
hatred of both gods and men. Let them give me favor and victory and business and
prosperity. For you are I, and I am you;[10] your name is mine, and mine is yours. For
I am your image.[11] If something should happen to me during this year or this
40   month or this day or this hour, it will happen to the great / god ACHCHEMEN ES-
TROPH, the one inscribed on the prow of the holy ship. Your true name has been
inscribed on the sacred stele in the shrine at Hermopolis where your birth is. Your
45   true name: OSERGARIACH NOMAPHI. This is your name with fifteen / letters,[12] a
number corresponding to the days of the rising moon; and the second name with
the number 7, corresponding to those who rule the world,[13] with the exact number
365,[14] corresponding to the days of the year. Truly: ABRASAX. I know you, Hermes,
50   and you know me. / I am you, and you are I. And so, do everything for me, and
may you turn to me[15] with Good Fortune and Good Daimon, immediately, immediately; quickly, quickly."

Take a piece of olive wood and make a small dog-faced baboon sitting down,
55   wearing the winged helmet of Hermes / and a box on its back, and inscribe the
name of Hermes on the papyrus and put it in the box. Write in myrrh ink, praying
for what you do or what you wish, and after putting a lid on, burn incense and
place it where you wish in the middle of the workshop.

60   ***And the name to be written is***: "PHTHORON PHTHIONĒ THŌYTH." / In addition, write also these great names: "IAŌ SABAŌTH ADŌNAIE ABLANATHANALBA
AKRAMMACHAMAREI, 365, give to the workshop business, favor, prosperity, elegance, both to NN himself and to his workshop, immediately, immediately;
quickly, quickly."

*Tr.: E. N. O'Neil. The title of the spell is misleading, for the spell has nothing to do with
love, sex, or attraction of a woman. This is a spell for some shopkeeper to ensure good business. There are traces of mysticism here. See Reitzenstein, *Poimandres* 19–20. [E.N.O.]

7. On Thoth as Isis' chief helper, see Bleeker, *Hathor and Thoth* 132–36. [R.K.R.]

8. The translation follows Preisendanz's emendation. Cf. below, l. 33 and *PGM* V. 247–48.

9. συνοχή occurs only here in *PGM*, and its meaning is uncertain. The verb συνέχω, however, occurs at *PGM* IV. 1408; V. 126, 131, where each time it seems to refer to daimonic possession. [E.N.O.]

10. For this formula of mutual identity, see *PGM* VIII. 49–50; XIII. 795. See Betz, "The Delphic
Maxim," 165–68.

11. The term εἴδωλον may show philosophical influence. See *PGM* XII. 235–36; LXI. 53–55. See
Betz, "The Delphic Maxim," 165–67; J. Bremmer, *The Early Greek Concept of the Soul* (Princeton:
Princeton University Press, 1983) 78–80, 83.

12. As the Greek text stands, the name has sixteen letters. The name should be separated OSER-
GARIACH NOMAPHI. The discrepancy must be in the first word because the second is correctly said to
have seven letters. The confusion may be due to underlying Egyptian words. [J.B.]

13. That is, the seven planets.

14. Cf. l. 61. The number has the numerical value of Abraxas. See Glossary, s.v. "Abraxas."

15. The term συρρέπω is rare. See Betz, "The Delphic Maxim," 164 n. 49.

PGM VIII. 64–110

*Request for a dream oracle of Besa: / On your left hand draw Besa in the way 65
shown to you below. Put around your hand a black cloth [16] of Isis and go to sleep
without giving answer to anyone. The remainder of the cloth wrap around your
neck.

This is the ink with which you draw: Blood of a crow, blood / of a white dove, 70
lumps of incense, myrrh, black writing ink, cinnabar, sap of mulberry tree, rainwater, juice of a single-stemmed wormwood and vetch. With this write.

Here is the text of the prayer [17] to the setting sun:

"Borne [18] on the breezes of the wand'ring winds, /
Golden-haired Helios who wield the flame's 75
Untiring light, who drive in lofty turns
Around the great pole; who create all things
Yourself which you again reduce to nothing.
For from you come the elements arranged
By your own laws which cause the whole world to
Rotate through its four yearly turning points. /
If you go to the depths of earth and reach 80
The region of the dead, send up the truthful
Prophet out of that innermost abode.

I beg you LAMPSOUĒR SOUMARTA BARIBAS DARDALAM PHORBĒX, lord, send forth
your holy daimon ANOUTH ANOUTH SALBANACHAMBRĒ BRĒITH, immediately, immediately; quickly, quickly; in this night, come." / If you wish to call him also for a 85
direct vision, [take] a strip [of linen], soak it in sesame oil you have mixed [with]
cinnabar, and place the linen as a wick in a lamp that is not colored red. The lamp
should be lighted with sesame oil. Place it opposite you, say the formula, and he
will come to you. Have near you / a small tablet so that you may write as much as 90
he says, [19] lest after going to sleep you forget.

"I call upon / you, the headless god, having your face beside your feet, [20] the one 95
who hurls lightning and thunders; you are the one whose mouth is continually full
of fire, the one placed over Necessity. I call upon you, the god placed over Necessity,
IAEŌ SABAŌTH ADŌNAI ZABARBATHIAŌ; you are the one lying on a coffin of myrrh,
having resin and asphalt as an elbow cushion, [21] [the one] whom they call ANOUTH
ANOUTH. Rise up, daimon. You are not a daimon, but the blood / of the two 100
falcons [22] who chatter and watch before the head of Osiris. You are the oracle-giving
god SALBANACHAMBRĒ ANOUTH ANOUTH SABAŌTH ADŌNAI IĒ IE IĒ IE" (add the
usual). Go to sleep on a rush mat, having an unbaked brick beside your head.

What you draw is / of this sort: A naked man, standing, having a diadem on his 105
head, and in his right hand a sword that by means of a bent [arm] rests on his neck,

---

16. See *PGM* VII. 227 and n.

17. The translation here is tentative because the reading of the papyrus is uncertain. See Preisendanz,
apparatus ad loc.

18. These dactylic hexameters are part of the reconstructed Hymn 4: vv. 1–6, 11 (7–8 [the identification of lines in Preisendanz, vol. II, p. 239, is incorrect: v. 13 is not included here]). For other versions
and sections of Hymn 4, see *PGM* I. 315–27; IV. 436–61; 1957–89. [E.N.O.]

19. Cf. the memory spells in *PGM* I. 233–47; II. 16–20, 40–42.

20. See on this point *PGM* VII. 234 and n.

21. See for a parallel *PGM* VII. 237.

22. See for the two falcons and their watch *PGM* VII. 239 and n.

and in the left hand a wand. If he reveals to you, wipe off your hand with rose
110   perfume. This is the figure / of the rite:

*Tr.: W. C. Grese (ll. 64–74; 81–110) and E. N. O'Neil (ll. 74–81). This particular charm
in its present form is actually two charms (a request for a dream oracle and a request for a
direct vision) directed to Bes, an originally non-Egyptian god who came to Egypt early and
was given many functions, one of which was to provide oracles. The request for a dream
oracle contains preparatory instructions and a hymn to the sun that also appears in *PGM* IV.
436–46 and 1957–68. The request for a direct vision has instructions and a formula of
invocation addressed to the "headless god." This invocation also appears in *PGM* VII.
233–48 and makes use of language that can also be found in a boast of the "headless god" in
PGM IV. 145–58.

PGM IX. 1–14

*"'I'll give you rest from wrath and soothe your raging.'[1] Come, lord BAIN-
CHŌŌŌCH, with your father ANIBAINCHŌŌŌCH, with your mother CHECHPHIŌ,
with your two bodyguards CHENGĒBIŌCHTHŌ MYSAGŌTH ECHE ŌŌ MYSAGŌTH
ACHPHIPHIŌ IAIA ŌCH SEBAU PHRĒ IŌ RĒXICHTHŌN YŌĒŌ AEAEĒIOYŌ CHYCH-
BACHYCH BAUACHYCH BAKAXICHYCH BAZABACHYCH MENEBACHYCH BADĒDO-
5   PHŌ BAINCHŌŌŌCH. Bring into subjection, put to silence, and enslave / every race
of people, both men and women, with their fits of wrath, and those who are under
the earth beneath the feet of him, NN, especially so-and-so (add the usual, as you
wish), for you have put beneath my feet, like my robe, the heart of SABAŌTH."

   On the back of the lamella: "EULAMŌ SISIRBBAIĒRSESI PHERMOU CHNOUŌR
ABRASAX. Bring into subjection, enslave, and put to silence the soul, the wrath [of
10   him, NN], because I adjure you by the / awful Necessity MASKELLI MASKELLŌ
PHMOUKENTABAŌTH OREOBAZAGRA RĒXICHTHŌN HIPPOCHTHŌN PYRIPĒGANYX
LEPETAN LEPETAN PHNOUNOBOĒ." On the front [write] the person's name.

   The introduction to the rite:
      "I'll[2] give you rest from wrath
         And soothe your raging.
      Come silently and bring
         Silence and keep it.
      Stop ev'ry wrath in souls
      And melt all anger
      Of those with temper,
because I call upon your authentic name, BAINCHŌŌŌCH." Say this name, [writ-
ten] at the top of the metal leaf: "IAŌMORMOROTOKONBAI."

1. The introduction to this spell cites only the first line of the "prologue" given in ll. 12–14.
2. These lines have been arranged in iambic trimeters and are the reconstructed Hymn 30. See Preisendanz, vol. II, p. 266. [E.N.O.]

[ON VERSO]:

*Tr.: R. F. Hock and E. N. O'Neil (verse sections, ll. 12–13). This spell to subject and silence gives instructions for engraving a so-called curse tablet, presumably made of lead.

PGM X. 1–23

*[While drinking] and eating take the first [morsels] and place them [into] a small dish [1] [of the temple while speaking] thus: "NN, may you have been sent [to me as a helper] to fulfill the commands / of the gods. My name is ŌI . . . IAŌ SABAŌTH ZABARBATHIAŌ [ADŌNAI . . .]; let her, [NN,] love me, NN, with a divine [and] indelible [love]." »»»»»»——

    Spell that is spoken: / "I adjure you and the spirit which is with you. To you speaks the great and powerful god, SATHIS [PEPHOOUTH MOU]RŌPH ANOUR [2] OUPH[IRIGCH]: let her, NN, be well [disposed toward me]; let her see me and, having seen me, let her fall in love with me, and no one [will be able] to speak in opposition, PHTHOROCHĒB ATHA / . . . N THARAMĒCHI EOPSĒRIPSOU ACHOR-SŌTHIA . . . THIE Ē NOUSOU PHTHAPA APOUOROTH . . . Ē CHOADOUSTRŌ PRŌ-THIAPSIŌR . . . S CHOMARCHŌCH CHANACHOUŌRRĒLOUKOUMPHA."

    [*The spell in another form*: "May she, NN,] fall in love when she sees [3] [me, and] may she [never] resist [me], / O great and powerful god, because of modesty." And when you see her, NN, take a long, deep breath three times while staring at her, and then she smiles at you. For [this is] a sign of [her love]. »»»»»»——
*Tr.: E. N. O'Neil. The text clearly preserves a love spell, but the beginning of the text is mutilated. The restoration by Preisendanz remains tentative, and so is the translation.

PGM X. 24–35

***Charm to restrain anger** which works in all cases, for it works against enemies, / accusers, brigands, phobias, and nightmares: Take a gold or silver lamella and engrave on it the characters and names, and when you have consecrated it, wear it in purity. *Now here it is*:

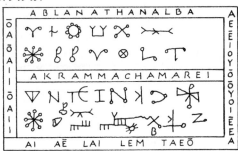

*Tr.: R. F. Hock.

1. παραψίδιον is taken here to be a misspelling of παροψίδιον, referring to a small food dish. [E.N.O.]
2. ANOUR is Egyptian *In-ḥr* (Greek Onouris), whose major role in mythology was to bring back the angry goddess Tefnut. Cf. Bonnet, *RÄRG* 545–47, s.v. "Onuris." [R.K.R.]
3. On the idea of love at first sight, a typically hellenistic idea, see, for example, Theocritus, *Idyll* 2.

PGM X. 36–50

*Another way: **Apollo's charm to subject**: Take a lamella [or metal leaf][4] from a yoke for mules and engrave on it the following names and put a frog's tongue in it.

40   **Spell**, when the metal leaf with the frog's tongue is put / into your right sandal: "Just as these sacred names are being trampled, so also let him, NN (add the usual), the trouble-maker, be trampled."

"ABRASAX

			IŌCHCH
AEĒIOYŌ	CHYCH	MICHAĒL	NYSEU
EĒIOYŌA	CHYBACHYCH	RAPHAĒL	NYCHIEU
ĒIOYŌAE	BACHACHYCH	GABRIĒL	AŌCHĒ
IOYŌAEĒ	BAKAXICHYCH	SOURIĒL	MECHEU
OYŌAEĒI	BAZABACHYCH	ZAZIĒL	IAŌ
YŌAEĒIO	BADĒTOPHŌTH	BADAKIĒL	SABAŌTH
ŌAEĒIOY.	BAINCHŌŌŌCH.	SYLIĒL.	ADŌNAI.

50   ✗ ABRASAX ✗ Subject him, NN, to me, / immediately; quickly, quickly."

✗   z   ✗

*Tr.: R. F. Hock.

PGM XI.a 1–40

*Apollonius of Tyana's old serving woman: Take Typhon's skull[1] and write the following characters on it with the blood of a black dog: "⌐ ⅔ ⊠ ⊙⌐ SABERRA." Then, going to a suitable place, by a river, the sea, or at the fork of a road, in the

5   middle of the night put the skull / on the ground, place it [under] your left foot, and speak as follows.

    The formula: "ERITHYIA[2] MEROPĒ GERGIRŌ CHĒTHIRA ANAPEROUCH . . . LYRŌPHIA GĒGETHIRA LOLYN GOUGŌGĒ AMBRACHA BI . . . AEBILĒ MARITHAIA MPROUCHE ABĒL ETHIRAŌ AP . . . ŌCHORIĒLA MŌRĒTHIRA PHECHIRŌ ŌSRI

10   PHOIRA AMERI . . . PHĒ. OUTHĒRA / GARGERGIŌ TITHEMYMĒ MĒRAPSĒCHIR AŌRIL. Come, appear, O goddess called Mistress of the House."[3]

    After you say this, you will behold sitting on an ass a woman of extraordinary loveliness, possessing a heavenly beauty, indescribably fair and youthful. As soon as you see her, make obeisance and say: "I thank [you], lady for appearing to me. /

15   Judge me worthy of you. May your Majesty be well disposed to me. And accomplish whatever task I impose on you."

---

82 (on a magical ritual), a line which Virgil, *Ecl.* 8. 41, and the author of the *Ciris* (l. 430) copied. See Gow's note to *Idyll* 2. 82, Theocritus, vol. II, 51–52. [E.N.O.]

   4. The translation follows the text of Preisendanz, which has the editor's insertion ⟨ἢ πέταλον⟩ to conform with the occurrence of the noun in l. 39. The emendation, however, may not be necessary.

   1. "Typhon's skull" is the semantic equivalent of the skull of an ass. See C. Colpe, "Geister (Dämonen)," *RAC* 9 (1978): 620–21; H. Kees, "Seth," *PRE*, 2nd ser. 4 (1923): 1896–1922; esp. 1899, 1920–21; W. Fauth, "Seth-Typhon, Onoel und der eselköpfige Sabaoth," *Oriens Christianus* 57 (1973): 79–120.

   2. This seems to be the reading of the papyrus, but it is not certain. Preisendanz treats the word as a proper name. One may also read ειλειθυια on the grounds that both it and μεροπε which follows immediately are names suitable for the goddess Nephthys. [J.B.]

   3. "Mistress of the house" is a direct translation of the Egyptian name Nephthys, sister of Isis, and (as is stressed in this spell) wife of Seth. Thus she is fittingly associated with an ass. See Bonnet, *RÄRG* 519–21, s.v. "Nephthys"; Griffiths, *Plutarch's De Iside et Osiride* 305, 447. [J.B./R.K.R.]

The goddess will reply to you, "What do you have in mind?"

You say, "I have need [of you] for domestic service."

At that, she will get off the ass, shed her beauty, and will be an old woman.[4] And the old woman will say to you, "I will serve and attend you."

After she tells you this, the goddess will again put on her own beauty, which she had just taken off, / and she will ask to be released.[5]   20

But you say to the goddess, "No, lady! I will use you until I get her."

As soon as the goddess hears this, she will go up to the old lady, and will take her molar tooth and a tooth from the ass and give both to you; and after that it will be impossible for the old woman to leave you, unless perhaps you want to release her. From that time forth, you will receive a bounty of great benefits, for everything that your soul desires will be accomplished by her. She will guard all your possessions[6] / and in particular will find out for you whatever anyone is thinking about   25 you.[7]

Indeed she will tell you everything and will never desert you: such is her store of good will toward you. But if ever you wish, there is a way to release her (but never do this!). Take her tooth and the ass's tooth, / make a bonfire, and throw them into   30 the fire, and with a shriek the old woman will flee without a trace. Do not be prone to release her, since it will be impossible for you to replace her.

But do release the goddess, when you are sure that the old woman will serve you, by speaking as follows: "MENERPHER PHIĒ PRACHĒRA LYLŌRI / MĒLICHARĒ   35 NĒCHIRA." When the old woman hears this, the goddess will mount the ass and depart.

The phylactery to be used throughout the rite: The skull of the ass. Fasten the ass's tooth with silver and the old lady's tooth with gold, and wear them always; for if you do this, it will be impossible for / the old woman to leave you. The rite has   40 been tested.

*Tr.: Hubert Martin, Jr. See on this spell, for general background and additional literature, E. L. Bowie, "Apollonius of Tyana: Tradition and Reality," *ANRW* II, 16, 2 (Berlin: De Gruyter, 1978) 1652–99, esp. 1686; J. Bergman, "Nephthys découverte dans un papyrus magique (*PGM* XIa.)," in *Mélanges Adolphe Gutbub* (Montpellier: Editions de l'université de Montpellier, 1984) 1–11.

PGM XIb. 1–5

*To make men who have drinking at a symposium appear to have donkey snouts[8] to outsiders, from afar**: In the dark [take] a wick from a lamp and dip it in donkey's blood; make a new lamp / with the new wick and touch the drinkers.   5 *Tr.: Roy Kotansky. For similar "gimmicks," see the translation and notes on *PGM* VII. 167–85. The translation adopts the restorations mentioned in the *apparatus criticus* of Preisendanz.

4. At this point, the old woman and the goddess assume separate identities. [H.M.]

5. On this point see *PGM* LXX. 11 and Betz, "Fragments," 291.

6. Reading with Eitrem πάντα δέ σοι, instead of Preisendanz's καὶ τάδε σοι. [H.M.]

7. Or "whatever anyone is plotting against you." [J.B.]

8. LSJ, s.v., cites this as a gloss (a plant name). But here and in Psellos, *Lect. Mirab.* (A. Westermann, *Paradoxographi Graeci* [Amsterdam: Hakkert, 1963; repr. of 1839 ed.] 147, 11; the *paignion* of Anaxilaos in Wellmann, *APAW.PH* 1928, p. 79, 7) the term can be rendered literally "donkey-faced" or "ass-snouted." The *paignion* of Anaxilaos reads: "If you wish your wife to appear 'ass-snouted' when she looks in the mirror, rub her mirror with donkey's tears." [R.D.K.]

PGM XIc. 1–19

*You write this on hieratic papyrus and [place . . . :]

"I adjure you, by the god
IABŌ: turn the heart of her,
NN, whom NN bore, to NN,
whom / NN bore, at the
command of IABŌ, MASKELLEI
MASKELLŌ PHAINOUKENTABAŌ;
cause me, NN, to obtain
intercourse,

God the [BAR]BARAI
let her, NN, [whom
NN bore, come
beneath my] / roof,
and let her love
[me, NN, whom NN
bore], for [all] the
time / [of her] life,
lusting [for me] with
[eternal] love, immediately,
[immediately; quickly,
quickly]."

ABLANATHANALBA
BLATHANABA
NATHANDA
ANATHANA
NABANAEI
ABTHŌŌTH
BARBACHA
ABRASAX
AŌ[IAMARI]
SERPHOUTHEI
E EI EI Ē I Ē I AAAAAAA IIIIIII

*Tr.: E. N. O'Neil.

PDM xii. 1–5

*". . . I am NA, come (?) . . . farmer (?), the millions of falcons, / this young
man. . . ."

*Tr.: Janet H. Johnson, following the edition and translation in OMRM 56 (1975): 32–33,
col. II*, ll. 1–5. The first line of this invocation of an uncertain purpose is missing. Section
titles are indicated in the Demotic texts only when they appear in red letters (see the Introduction to the Demotic magical papyri).

PDM xii. 6–20

*A ring to cause praise: You bring a ring of iron and you bring a white stone which
is in the shape of a grape [which] grows / as a fresh plant in the water, there being
[a] daimon with the face [of] a falcon . . . together with his snake tail,[1] there being
a nemes headdress (?) in (?) the . . . eye whose face goes to the. . . . Write / this
name on it . . . saying, "ABRAXAM PHILEN . . . CHNI . . . ," put a limb of a lion
under it together with a piece of gold; put them under it; and / make . . . it.

*Tr.: Janet H. Johnson, following the edition and translation in OMRM 56 (1975): 32–33,
col. II*, ll. 6–20.

PDM xii. 21–49

*"Open to me, O heaven! Open to me, O earth! Open to me, O underworld! Open
to me! I am Horus. Open to me! I went forth from the necropolis of Wen-nefer.

1. For a composite deity, cf. PGM XII. 121ff.; XIII. 50 with n.

May Iymhotep[2] the Great, the son of Ptah, born of Kherti-ankh, come to me tonight! May he tell me a prescription which is fitting to the illness / which has 25 [5] happened to me, together with the method of [using] it, there being no falsehood therein! Bear witness! Bear witness![3] O Iymhotep the Great, the son of Ptah, born of Kherti-ankh, and put this . . . of reed (?) on yourself while the bark of ʿ*rw*-wood is under you, while the . . . of . . . of Ptah is on you. Is it what is fitting? May he, Iymhotep the Great, the son of Ptah, / born of Kherti-ankh bear witness (?) to the 30 [10] fury against you in the presence of Nephthys saying, 'O Shu, live! O soul, live! Live, O Shu, live! Live, O Osiris! Live, O Ethiopian soul! Live, O Sokar who endures (?) who is [on] board . . . harbor . . . entire (?), he having ascended. Live O great (secret) image of Egypt who rests in the middle of Memphis, the place of Ptah' (another [manuscript] says: 'the House of the obelisk') 'without a prescription! If I am called / about it, . . . calls to me about a prescrip- 35 [15] tion, I shall tell him the prescription which is fitting to the illness in which he is.' Is it what is fitting? May Iymhotep the Great, the son of Ptah, born of Kherti-ankh bear witness (?). Come to me, O battler! Tell me the prescription which is fitting to the illness [which] has happened to me! Come to me, O great of face . . . O . . . the peak . . . soul! Come to me, O one whose face / is as the face of a falcon . . . hair of 40 [20] . . . ! O he who rests . . . necropolis of (?) Heliopolis (?). I (?) am the son . . . after swallowing. O son of the great Shu. Come to me . . . of man upon his egg (?) . . . of Thoth and his father! Come to me, O (?) . . . who is in the great ennead, not knowing his . . . , the . . . ! Are you steadfast against me, not to tell me the pre- scription which is fitting to the illness which has happened / in me? I will say much 45 [25] (?) . . . which is in . . . , the mysterious one (?), who is in . . . the heart of the . . . the . . . of . . . of . . . of the . . . soul" (*another [manuscript]* says: "Ruler of the western half"). "You will not live in the . . . without having come to me tonight to tell me a prescription which is fitting to the illness which has happened to me, to- gether with the method of using it, [there] being no falsehood therein."

*Tr.: Janet H. Johnson, following the edition and translation in *OMRM* 56 (1975): 35–37, col. I*, ll. 1–29. The purpose of this prayer is to secure a remedy for an unstated disease.

PGM XII. 1–13

*Rite: Unfold a funeral shroud at night and carry it;[4] also take a sword.
    Then say: "THERMOCH CHTHABOI ACHAPH MARMILYCHA BERTHIŌCH CHARĒL . . . BAIOCH . . . THACH DĒRPHO PHIRBSAT (?) SŌTHŌRAI PHAUXAI IŌA MEILICH IABAI EIA KARSE REUTHRA ENROUCH ZERPHRĒCH / PSERPHERCHŌ THNERBĒCH 5 CHARCHERBER YEICH PHCHYAR PA . . . CHA MILCHITHER CHLĒLŌR PHACHILER MAZ MACHAIRIŌCH."

After you say this, the Maiden will come carrying torches.[5] Say: "PHERTHELI- LŌCH PEIY . . . ," and her firebrands will be extinguished, and she will stand there in distress and complain.

You say, "Do such-and-such and I will light your torches." If she sends a dream, you are to light them and she will fly away. / If you send her to kill somebody, give 10

2. For Imhotep, the vizier and architect of the Step Pyramid of Djoser at Saqqara later divinized as the patron of scribes and physicians, see Dietrich Wildung, *Imhotep und Amenhotep* (München: Deut- scher Kunst Verlag, 1977); idem, "Imhotep," *LdÄ* 3, 145–48. [J.H.J.]
    3. The words "Bear witness!" were crossed out by the original scribe.
    4. It is not clear what the conjurer is to carry. Is it the funeral shroud? [H.M.]
    5. The reference is to Kore (Persephone). See the picture on the Niinnion Tablet in G. E. Mylonas, *Eleusis and the Eleusinian Mysteries* (Princeton: Princeton University Press, 1961), fig. 88, and the discus- sion, pp. 213–21.

her the sword and she will give you the torches and return with the sword covered
with blood. Tell her that the torches belong to her; they will catch fire, and she will
take flight.

While doing this, say: "MŌZĒRPHER TACHCHAPS." Attach a phylactery[6] to your
right and your left hand at night and wear it.
*Tr.: Hubert Martin, Jr.

PGM XII. 14–95

15   *Eros[7] as assistant. / A ritual of Eros: *consecration and preparation* (among his
operations, he sends dreams or causes sleeplessness; and he releases from an evil
spirit, if you use him in a proper and holy manner, for he can perform every operation). Take [wax] of Etruria[8] and mix with it [every] kind of aromatic plant. Then
make a statue of a torch-bearing Eros that is eight dactyls[9] high and has a large base
20   to support it. Put a bow / and arrow in [his left] hand, and fashion a Psyche[10] of
the same sort as Eros.

When you have completed all this, conduct a three-day consecration. You are to
present to Eros fresh fruits of every kind and 7 cakes, 7 pinecones, every kind of
sweetmeat, 7 lamps not colored red; also, [three] daggers, votive tablets, a bow and
arrow, dates, a bowl mixed with honey wine.

After you make the statues and the presentation as indicated, next place your
25   Eros on a table laden with the fruit / and holding both the 7 lamps, ablaze with
clear olive oil, and all else listed so as to win the favor of wondrous Eros.

On the first day, after you put him on the table and arrange things as prescribed—and I describe its form in full for you, that you may understand and lack
no detail—build a pure altar; that is, take two unbaked bricks and form them into 4
30   horn-shaped objects, on which you lay fruit-bearing branches. / Take also on the
first day 7 living creatures and strangle them: one cock, a partridge, a wren, a
pigeon, a turtledove, and any two nestlings you can get hold of. Do not make a
burnt offering[11] of any of these; instead, you are to take them in hand and choke
them, all the while holding them up to your Eros, until each of the creatures is
suffocated and their breath[12] enters him. After that, place the strangled creatures on
35   the altar together with aromatic plants / of every variety.

On the second day, strangle a male chick before your Eros and burn it as a whole
offering.

On the 3rd day, place another chick on the altar; while conducting this portion of
the ritual, consume the chick by yourself, allowing no one else to be present. I as-
sure you, if you perform the above actions in a holy and pure manner, you will have
complete success.

40   *First formula to be spoken* while making the burnt offering: / "I call upon you,
who are on the couch of beauty, who are in the mansion of desire: serve me and, no
matter where I send you, always bear the message I give you, likening yourself to
some god (or goddess) such as men and women there worship, announcing all that
is written out or imparted to you in speech, quickly!

6. It is not certain what the phylactery is, although it may be the shroud.
7. Cf. *PGM* VII. 479 for a parallel.
8. For this substance, see *PGM* IV. 3131.
9. That is, the measure of the finger's breadth, about 7/10 of an inch.
10. On Eros and Psyche, see *PGM* IV. 1741 and n.
11. This refers to the so-called holocaust, in which the sacrificial gifts are burnt completely (cf. *PGM*
IV. 2396, 3148–49). See Nilsson, *GGR* I, 132; J. Milgrom, *IDB.S* (1976): 769–70 on ʿŌlâ.
12. For this peculiar purpose of sacrifice, see *PGM* XIII. 377.

"Fire overtook the greatest phantoms, and heaven swallowed unawares the orb of the holy scarab / called 'PHŌREI.'[13] Scarab, the winged ruler in midheaven, was be- 45
headed, dismembered, and wasted his greatness and glory; they confined him and took another as master of heaven.[14] You take note, and serve as my minister to anyone I choose, man or woman.

"Come to me, O master of heaven, who shine upon the world of men; serve as my minister, whether to men or to women, whether to the small or to the great, and / compel them always to do everything written by me.   50

"Come to me, O master of forms, and arouse men and women for me; force them by your ever-strong and mighty authority to do everything written or spoken by me, EISAPHSANTA PHOUREI ARNAI SYSYN PHREŌ[15] RIŌBAIOSOI, you are ATEPHTHO AŌREL ADŌNAI; afflict them with fear, trembling, terror; trouble their thoughts / with fear of you. And do everything prescribed for [me], NN. If you 55
disobey me, the sun's orb will burn out and darkness will cover the whole world. The Scarab will come down until you do for me everything I write or say—in strict obedience to me; immediately, immediately; quickly, quickly."

Second [formula] to be spoken while making the burnt offering: "I conjure you by the one who controls the universe, laid the four foundations, and mixed the 4 / winds. You are the one who sends lightning, you are the one who thunders, you 60
are the one who shakes, you are the one who overturned all things and set them up again. Cause all men and all women to turn to love me, the man NN (or the woman NN), from the very hour when I make my petition with this binding charm,[16] on order from the most high god,[17] IAŌ ADŌNEAI ABLANATHANALBA. You are the one who embraces the Graces on the mountain top, LAMPSRĒ; you are the one who holds Necessity in your right hand, BELTEPIACH; you are the / one who loosens 65
and binds, SEMESIELAMP EKRIPH. Obey me from this day forth even unto all time."

Third formula for the same offering: "I call upon you, gods of heaven and gods of earth, gods aerial and gods terrestrial. And I conjure you by the one who controls the 4 foundations, to accomplish for me, the man NN (or the woman NN) such-and-such a matter and to give me favor, sweet speech, charm with all men / and all women under creation, that they may be submissive to my every wish, in- 70
asmuch as I am the slave of the most high god, the almighty who controls the universe, MARMARIŌTH LASIMIŌLĒTH ARAAS . . . S SĒBARBAŌTH NOŌ AŌI ŌIĒR (add the spice)[18] AAAAA ĒĒĒĒĒĒĒ ŌŌŌŌŌŌŌ. I give orders to Eros, who is charged with carrying out these my commandments, inasmuch as I am god of all gods, IAŌN SABAŌTH ADŌNAI [ABRASAX] IARABBAI / THŌURIŌ THANAKERMĒPH PAN- 75
CHONAPS."

The above formulas must be used and [spoken] during the 3 days if you are to endow the rite with full potency. But when you dispatch your Eros to accomplish

13. The relationship between the holy scarab and the name PHŌREI is not clear. Cf. the *voces magicae* below, l. 53 (PHOUREI) and the apparatus ad loc.

14. The reference to scarab mythology in ll. 45–47 is syncretistic and reminiscent of the dismemberment of Osiris. See S. Eitrem, "Sonnenkäfer und Falke in der synkretistischen Magie," in *Pisciculi. Festschrift für F. Dölger* (Münster: Aschendorff, 1939) 94–101.

15. PHREŌ is "Prē the great." It should be noted that the sun god is in conjunction with the scarab. [R.K.R.]

16. The papyrus reads παραψιμω (LSJ, s.v.: "charm acting by means of touch"); the translation follows Preisendanz's reading παραφιμω ("Zauberzwang"). See the apparatus ad loc.

17. For this epithet of IAŌ ADŌNAI, cf. *PGM* IV. 1068; XVI. 9. See G. Bertram, *TDNT* 8 (1972):618–19, s.v. "ὕψιστος."

18. The papyrus reads ἄρτημα, "ornament"; Preisendanz takes it to be ἄρτυμα, "spice."

your desires, utter only the formula below, removing him from the table together with the things presented to him; write instructions as to what you desire on a small piece of papyrus.

    Formula to be written on the piece of papyrus: "You are the babe, the living god, the creature of beauty[19] . . . SAMMŌTH / SABAŌTH TABAŌTH SORPHĒ SEOUR-PHOUTH MOUI SI SRŌ[20] SALAMA GŌUTH ETHEIMĒOUS OUSEIRI HESEIĒ E PHTHA NOUTH SATHAĒ ISIS[21] ACHTHI EPHANOUN BIBIOU BIBIOU SPHĒ SPHĒ ASĒĒAĒI. Go [to] every place and every dwelling to which I send you, to him, NN, [born of] her, NN (or to her, NN, [born of] her, NN), likening yourself to a god (or goddess) he [or she] worships. Force him to do such-and-such a matter (write as much as you wish on the piece of papyrus along with the formula). Awake, terrify him! I conjure you / by the [holy] and precious name to which all creation is subject: PAS-ICHTHŌN IBARBOU THARAKTITHEANŌ BABOUTHA KŌCHED, Amen.[22] Let such-and-such a matter come to pass immediately, immediately. . . .

    ". . . of the Red Sea, the one who drives the winds together from the 4 regions, the one who sits upon the lotus[23] and illumines the whole world; for you [sit on the] throne in the form of a crocodile, and in southerly regions you are a winged serpent. Such now in very / truth is your nature, IŌIŌ BARBAR ADŌNAI KOM-BALIŌPS THŌB IARMIŌOUTH. Come to me; heed this my request for service, this my request for action, O most great one, HARSAMŌSI MOUCHA LINOUCHA robber ADŌNEAI. I am he whom you met at the foot of the holy mount and to whom you gave the knowledge of your most great [name], which knowledge will I even keep in sanctity, imparting it to no one save the very initiates into your own holy myste-ries, IARBATHATRA MNĒPSIBAŌ / CHNĒMEŌPS. Come! Submit to this service and be my assistant."

    *Tr.: Hubert Martin, Jr.

PGM XII. 96–106

*Himerios'[24] recipes:

    Drawing made with Typhonian ink:[25] A fiery red poppy, juice from an ar-tichoke, seed of the Egyptian acacia, red Typhon's ocher, unslaked quicklime, wormwood with a single stem, gum, rainwater.

    To do well at the workshop: / On the egg of a male bird[26] write and then bury the egg near the threshold where you live. "CHPHYRIS,[27] egg, which is CHORBAI SANA-CHARSŌ AMOUN ⳨ SPHĒ SPHĒ GAKNEPHĒ SIETHŌ ⳨ NOUSI NOUSI, you are the sacred egg from birth, which is SELBIOUS BATHINI PHNIĒIAĒO AŌĒ AŌĒ AŌIAŌI A PHIAEA THŌUTH IAŌ SELETĒA THEŌĒPH OXYMBRĒ ĒĒĒ III."

19. The words "babe, living god, creature of beauty" translate Egyptian epithets: ḥwn, "youth," nṯr ꜥnḫ, "living god," and Wn-nfr, "Onnophris." See *PGM* IV. 1078. [R.K.R.]

20. For SERPOUTH MOUI SI SRO, "Lotus, lion, son (?) of Ram," cf. *PGM* III. 659 and n.

21. USIRI HESIE PHTHA NOUTH . . . ISI is Egyptian and means "Osiris, drowned one, Ptah, Nut . . . Isis." On Hesies, see Glossary, s.v. "Esies"; for Nut, the sky god, see Bonnet, *RÄRG* 536–38, s.v. "Nut." [R.K.R.]

22. The *amen* points to Jewish influence. Cf. *PGM* VII. 271; XXIIb. 21, 25.

23. For this epithet, see *PGM* II. 101 and n.; IV. 1684; LXI. 32.

24. The papyrus reads ημεριου, which Preisendanz assumes is a reference to the fourth-century phy-sician Himerios. See H. Goossen, "Himerios, 2," *PRE* 8 (1913):1635.

25. Cf. for this ink *PGM* VII. 653; XIa. 2.

26. Preisendanz translates "on the male egg of a bird." The idea is less of a problem when the egg is taken to be an image of the primordial egg, in which the first god comes to existence. See *PGM* III. 145 and n.

27. CHPHYRIS is the scarab. See *PGM* VII. 584 and n.

The prayer concerning the egg: "Great God, give favor, business to me and to this place where the egg lies, in the house I do my business, SELEPĒL THEŌĒPh and / Good Daimon, send to this place every business and good daily profit. You   105 are my work. You are the great Ammon,[28] who dwells in heaven. Come, help me."
*Tr.: R. F. Hock.

PGM XII. 107–21

*Charm of Agathokles[29] for sending dreams: Take a completely black cat that died a violent death, make a strip of papyrus and write with myrrh the following, together with the [dream] you want sent,[30] and place it into the mouth of the cat. /

"I am lying,[31] I am lying, I am the great one, the one lying in [the mouth], MOM-   110 MOU THŌTH NANOUMBRĒ CHARICHA KENYRŌ PAARMIATH, [to whom belongs] the holy name, IAOU IEĒ IEOU AĒŌI, the one above the heaven; arise, YMEU NEN-NANA SENNANA ABLANATHANALBA AKRAMMACHAMARI ABRASILOUA LAMPSŌREI EEI EIEI AŌĒĒŌ THĒOURIS[32] ŌA EPEIDEU EPERGA BRIŌN AMĒN. Reveal to him, NN, concerning this."

Compelling charm: "Come to me, NN, [you who] established the . . . by your own power, / you who rule the whole world, the fiery god.[33] Reveal to him,   115 NN, THARTHAR THAMAR ATHATHA MOMMOM THANABŌTH APRANOU BAMBALĒA CHRĒTH NABOUSOULĒTH ROMBROU THARAĒL ALBANA BRŌCHRĒX ABRANA ZOU-CHĒL. Hear me, because I am going to say the great name, AŌTH, before whom every god prostrates himself and every daimon shudders, for whom every angel completes those things which are assigned. Your divine name according to the seven[34] is AEĒIOYŌ IAYŌĒ EAŌOYEĒŌIA. I have spoken the / glorious name, the   120 name for all needs. Reveal to NN, lord god."

This is the name; this Apollobex[35] also used.
*Tr.: W. C. Grese.

PGM XII. 121–43

*Zminis[36] of Tentyra's spell for sending dreams:[37] Take a clean linen cloth, and (according to Ostanes) with myrrh ink draw a figure on it which is humanlike in

28. For the invocation of Amon and Thoth in conjunction with the cosmic egg, see Morenz, *Egyptian Religion* 178.

29. Nothing is known about this author.

30. Or "to whom you want to send this dream." [J.B.]

31. The papyrus has κειμι. It could be a reference to the Egyptian *kemi*, *kmj*, "the black one," an epithet of Osiris. See Schmidt, *Philologische Wochenschrift* 55 (1935): 1174, and the apparatus ad loc.

32. THĒOURIS is the Egyptian *T3-wr.t*, "Thoeris," the hippopotamus goddess who protected the bedside. See Bonnet, *RÄRG* 530–35, s.v. "Nilpferd." [R.K.R.] For the Greek name, see Plutarch, *De Is. et Os.* 19, 358C: Θούηρις; and Griffiths, Plutarch's *De Iside et Osiride* 347–48.

33. See on this epithet Bousset, *Religionsgeschichtliche Studien* 118–20, 164.

34. That is, the seven vowels.

35. Apuleius, *Apol.* 90 calls Apollobex a famous magician, and Pliny, *NH* 30. 9, makes him the fore-runner of Demokritos, who copied his works from him. But the name is also an epithet of Horus. See E. Riess, "Apollobex," *PRE* 1 (1894): 2847; Hopfner, *OZ* II, sec. 210; K. Preisendanz, "Apollobex," *PRE* 20 (1941): 1311–12.

36. The magician Zminis of Tentyra (Dendera on the Nile) is not otherwise known. See K. Preisendanz, "Zminis," Roscher 6 (1936): 762.

37. On dream sending, see I. E. S. Edwards, *Oracular Amuletic Decrees of the Late New Kingdom* (London: British Museum, 1960), vol. I, pp. xx, n. 11; 63. [R.K.R.]

appearance but has four wings,[38] having the left arm outstretched[39] along with the
125   two left wings, and having the other arm bent with the fist clenched. / Then upon
the head [draw] a royal headdress and a cloak over its arm, with two spirals on the
cloak. Atop the head [draw] bull horns and to the buttocks a bird's tail. Have his
right hand held near his stomach and clinched, and on either ankle have a sword
extended.

Also write on the strip the following names of the god and whatever you want
130   him, [NN], to see and how:[40] "CHALAMANDRIŌPH IDEARZŌ THREDAPHNIŌ /
ERTHIBELNIN RYTHADNIKŌ PSAMOMERICH,[41] to all of you I speak, also to you, ()
very powerful daimon: go into the house of this person and tell him such-and-such."

Next take a lamp neither colored red nor inscribed, and after you put a wick in it,
fill it with cedar oil, and light it. Invoke the following names of the god, three
[times]:[42] "CHALAMANDRIŌPH IDEARYŌTH THREDAPHNIŌ ERTHABEANIG RYTHA-
NIKŌ PSAMMORICH, O sacred names of the god, listen to me—you also, O Good
135   Daimon, whose might is very great / among the gods, listen to me: go to him, NN,
into his house, where he sleeps, into his bedroom, and stand beside him, causing
fear, trembling, by using the great and mighty names of the god. And tell him such-
and-such.

"I conjure you [by] your power, [by] the great god, SĒITH,[43] [by] the hour in
which you were begotten a great god,[44] [by] the god revealing[45] it now (?), [by] the
365 names of the great god, to go to him, NN, this very hour, this very night, and
140   to tell / him in a dream such-and-such.

"If you disobey me and don't go to him, NN, I will tell the great god, and after
he has speared you through, he will chop you up into pieces and feed your members
to the mangy dog who lies among the dungheaps.[46] For this reason, listen to me
immediately, immediately; quickly, quickly, so I won't have to tell you again."
*Tr.: Roy Kotansky.

PGM XII. 144–52

145   * **Request for a dream;** / **an exact method for everything**:[47] Using blood from a

38. The picture is of Bes-Pantheos known from Egyptian monuments and from gemstones. See Delatte and Derchain, *Les Intailles* 126–41; Bonner, *SMA* 25, also nos. 251–61, plates 24–25. On the
identification with El-Kronos, see A. Barb, *Gnomon* 41 (1969):304; P. Zazoff, ed., *Antike Gemmen in
Deutschen Sammlungen*, vol. IV (Wiesbaden: Steiner, 1975) 387 (no. 77). For a detailed picture and
description, see S. Sauneron, *Le Papyrus magique illustré de Brooklyn* (Brooklyn Museum 47.218.156)
(Oxford: Oxford University Press, 1970) 11–16.

39. Reading ἐκτεταμένον; see *apparatus criticus* in Preisendanz ad loc.

40. ὡς must be read here as a relative particle, with the meaning that the magician is to insert a
description of how the dream will appear to the sleeper. See LSJ, s.v. "ὡς," A.c.

41. The *voces magicae* here have been written to conform to the second occurrence of the list in ll.
133–34. The division of the words follows the edition of C. Leemans, *Papyri Graeci Musei Antiquarii
publici Lugduni-Batavi*, vol. II (Leiden: Brill, 1885), plate V, col. 4a. Preisendanz divides the names
differently in both series. [R.D.K.]

42. Or the "three names of the god."

43. That is, Seth.

44. Or "[by] the hour in which you were appointed a great god." This rendering follows Leemans's
edition.

45. The interpretation of the symbol, read by Preisendanz as χ(ρημ ατίσοντ)α, is open to question.
See the apparatus ad loc.

46. The god is threatened in the name of Seth with the same attack Seth committed against Osiris.
Cf. *PGM* VII. 940–68. [R.K.R.]

47. The translation follows the suggestion by W. B. that ἀκριβὴς εἰς πάντα is probably part of the
title.

quail, draw on a strip of linen the god Hermes, standing, ibis-faced.[48] Then with myrrh write also the name and say the *formula*:

"Come to me here quickly, you who have the power. I call upon you, the one appointed god of gods over the spirits, to show this[49] to me in dreams. I conjure [you] by your father, Osiris, and Isis,[50] your mother, to show me one of your forms, / and reveal concerning the things I want. Your name is ĒIIOUATHI PSRĒP-   150
NOUA NERTĒR DIOCHASBARA ZARACHŌ, whom they call BALCHAM. Reveal concerning this[51] concerning all things [about which] I inquire."
*Tr.: W. C. Grese.

PGM XII. 153–60

* **Spell for a divine revelation**: Invoke the great name in a time of great stress, in major and pressing crises. If not, you will blame yourself.[52] In addition say three times the "IAŌ," then the great name of god. /

"I call upon you, PHTHA RA PHTHA IĒ PHTHA OUN EMĒCHA ERŌCHTH BARŌCH   155
THO[RCH]THA THŌM CHAIEOUCH ARCHANDABAR ŌEAEŌ YNĒŌCH ĒRA ŌN ĒLŌPH
BOM PHTHA ATHABRASIA ABRIASŌTH BARBARBELŌCHA BARBAIAŌCH; let there be depth, breadth, length, brightness, ABLANATHANALBA ABRASIAOUA AKRAMMA-
CHAMAREI THŌTH HŌR ATHŌŌPŌ. Come in, lord, and reveal."

The serpent-faced god[53] will come in and answer you. When you dismiss [him], make an offering of / the skin of a serpent.   160
*Tr.: W. C. Grese.

PGM XII. 160–78

* [**Charm to release from bonds**:][54] If you want to do something spectacular and want to free yourself from danger, stand at the door and say the spell, and having said it, go out, adding: "Let the bonds of him, NN, be loosened, and let the doors be opened for him, and let no one see him."

You may even prove that it happens. Bind someone securely and shut him in a house. Stand outside and say the spell six or seven times thus: "I call upon you great gods, with a loud voice, / AISAR AIŌTH OUAIGNŌR MARSABŌOUTŌRTHE LABATH   165
ERMOU CHOŌRTHEN MANACHTHŌRPH PECHRĒPH TAŌPHPŌTHTHŌCHO THA-
RŌCH BALETHAN CHEBRŌOUTHAST ADŌNAI HARMIŌTH."

Whenever [you say] this spell, and he has been released, say this besides, in order that the doors might open: "OCHLOBARACHŌ LAILAM DARIDAM [DARDAM] DAR-
DARAMPTOU IARTHA IERBA DIERBA BARŌTHA THIARBA ARBITHŌ . . . Ō MAAR SE-
MESILAM MARMARACHNEU MANE THŌTH; holy one, enter and release him, NN, and give him a way / of escape, SESENGENBARPHARAGGĒS, you who loosen all   170

48. For an ibis-faced Hermes, see *PGM* VIII. 10.
49. Or "such and such." That is, the practitioner supplies here his request. See below, l. 151.
50. Osiris and Isis are the parents of Horus, not of Thoth/Hermes as one might infer from the preceding.
51. See n. 49 above.
52. Cf. the *lex sacra* from Halikarnassos, published by M. Çetin Şahin, "Five Inscriptions from Halicarnassus," *ZPE* 20 (1976): 22–23. [W.B.]
53. When depth, breadth, length, and brightness are summoned, this may indicate the reenactment of creation. In such a context, a serpent-faced deity (l. 159) would be appropriate, because the serpent form is the primordial form of the gods. See K. Sethe, *Amun und die Acht Urgötter von Hermopolis* (Berlin: Akademie-Verlag, 1929) 26–27. [R.K.R.]
54. This title for the spell does not appear in the papyrus manuscript and has been supplied by Preisendanz. It is, however, typical of other spells to begin with the phrase, "If you wish to do (this and this). . . ." Cf. e.g., *PGM* XII. 179–81; XIII. 239–64, and often. [R.D.K.]

bonds and you who loosen the iron fetter that has been placed around him, NN, because the great, unutterable, holy, righteous, awful, powerful, unspeakable, fearful and not-to-be-despised daimon of the great god commands you, SOROERMER [PHERGAR] BAX MAMPHRI OURIXG."

When the bonds break, say: "I thank you, lord, [because] the holy spirit, the unique one, the living one, has [released] me."

175   And say this spell again: / "Star-grouping god, you thunderbolt-with-great-clap-Zeus-confining-world-flashing-abundant-bolt-bestowing daimon, cracking-through-the-air, ray-producing, mind-piercing, you who [produce] cunning."

And use also the name of Helios for everything: "Fiery, ĒPHAIĒ, Hephaistos, who is shining with fire, brightly moving, ANANŌCHA AMARZA MARMARAMŌ."
*Tr.: R. F. Hock.

PGM XII. 179–81

180   *If you want someone to cease being angry with you, write with myrrh [on linen][55] this / name of anger: "CHNEŌM."[56] Hold it in your left [hand and say]: "I am restraining the anger of all, especially of him, NN, which is CHNEŌM."
*Tr.: R. F. Hock.

PGM XII. 182–89

*"Greetings, lord, you who are the means to obtain favor for the universe and for the inhabited [world]. Heaven has become a dancing place [for you], ARSENO-PHRĒ, O king of the heavenly [gods], ABLANATHANALBA, you who possess righ-
185   teousness, AKRAMMACHAMAREI, gracious [god,] SANKANTHARA, ruler / of nature, SATRAPERKMĒPH, origin of the heavenly [world], ATHTHANNOU ATHTHANNOU ASTRAPHAI IASTRAPHAI PAKEPTŌTH PA . . . ĒRINTASKLIOUTH ĒPHIŌ MARMA-RAŌTH.

"[Let] my outspokenness not leave me. [But] let every tongue and language listen to me, because I am PERTAŌ [MĒCH CHACH] MNĒCH SAKMĒPH[57] IAŌOYEĒ ŌĒŌ ŌĒŌ IEOYŌĒIĒIAĒA IĒŌYOEI, Give [me graciously] whatever you want."
*Tr.: R. F. Hock. Although untitled, the first line of this invocation shows it is a "favor charm."

PGM XII. 190–92

190   *Request for a dream oracle spoken to the Bear: Take olive oil [from] a clean[58] . . . onto the left hand and say the [names. Then] smear yourself and go to sleep having your head towards the east. "IĒSOUS[59] ANOUI. . . ."
*Tr.: W. C. Grese.

PGM XII. 193–201

*[To make] a tincture [viz., "reduction"] of gold:[60] Take thickened pungent vinegar and also have ready 8 drachmas of ordinary salt, 2 drachmas of rock alum that has clear cleavage, 4 drachmas of massicot, and triturate them [together] with the

55. Or byssus.
56. CHNEŌM here and in l. 181 is probably Egyptian Khnum. Cf. PGM I. 29. [R.K.R.]
57. MNĒCH SAKMĒPH corresponds to Egyptian "beneficient, son of Agathodaimon." For Kmeph, Knephis, cf. PGM I. 27; μνηχ is Egyptian mnḫ, an adjective of the preceding noun. Cf. PGM II. 77. [R.K.R.]
58. A noun seems to be missing here.
59. The name of Jesus appears at the beginning of an invocation; the rest is lost.
60. The term ἴωσις or ἐξίωσις (l. 198) probably refers to the process of reduction in alchemy. Since there is no gold included in the papyrus until l. 198, the process may actually be designed to produce

vinegar for 3 days, and strain off [and] / use. Then add one drachma blue vitriol   195
[cupric sulfate] to the vinegar, 1/2 obol in weight of chalcopyrite, 8 obols of rock
alum, 1/2 obol in weight of melanterite, a carat [viz., 1/1728 lb. = *siliqua*] of ordinary salt, 2 [carats] of Cappadocian [salt].

Make a leaf [of metal] of 2 fourths by weight, dip [it] 3 times into fire until the
leaf [breaks up] into fragments. Then take up the pieces [and] assume them as "reduced" to the metallic state of gold.

Treatment: Take [2] fourths by weight of gold, make a leaf and [purify it in]
fire, dip it in blue vitriol / triturated with water.   200

And another [treatment]: Pound dry cupric sulfate and dip [it] in the vinegar.

(Yet another [treatment]: with the compound): Pour off the verdigris and throw
it in.
*Tr.: John Scarborough.

PGM XII. 201–69

*Placing (a) ring.[61] **A little ring** [useful] for every [magical] operation and for
success. Kings and governors [try to get it]. Very effective. Taking an air-colored[62]
jasper, engrave on it a snake in a circle with its tail in its mouth, and also in the
middle of [the circle formed by] the snake [Selene][63] having two stars / on the two   205
horns, and above these, Helios, beside whom ABRASAX should be inscribed; and on
the opposite side of the stone from this inscription, the same name ABRASAX, and
around the border you will write the great and holy and omnicompetent [spell], the
name IAŌ SABAŌTH. And when you have consecrated the stone[64] wear it in a gold
ring, when you need it, [provided] you are pure [at that time], and you will succeed
in everything you may wish. You are to consecrate the ring together with the stone
in the rite used for all [such] objects. A similar engraving in gold, / too, is equally   210
effective.

The consecration [requires] the following equipment: Making a pit in a holy
place open to the sky, [or] if [you have none] in a clean, sanctified tomb looking
toward the east, and making over the pit an altar of wood from fruit trees, sacrifice
an unblemished goose, and 3 roosters and 3 pigeons. Make these whole burnt
offerings and burn, with the birds, all sorts of incense. Then, standing by the pit,
look / to the east and, pouring on a libation of wine, honey, milk, [and] saffron,   215
and holding over the smoke, while you pray, [the stone] in which are engraved the
inscriptions, say: see page 330

"I invoke and beseech the consecration, O gods of the heavens, O gods under the
earth, O gods circling in the middle region from one womb. O masters of all living
and dead, [O] heedful in many necessities of gods and / men. O concealers of   220
things now seen, O directors of the Nemeseis[65] who spend every hour with you,[66]

---

pseudo gold. This is in keeping with the fact that the section 193–201 is full of technical terminology
from alchemy. See M. P. Crosland, *Historical Studies in the Language of Chemistry* (London: Heinemann,
1962) 3–4, and esp. 54; A. J. Hopkins, "Transmutation by Colour: A Study of Earliest Alchemy," in
J. Ruska, ed., *Studien zur Geschichte der Chemie. Festgabe E. O. von Lippmann* (Berlin: Springer, 1927)
9–14. [J.S.]

61. The symbols printed in Preisendanz's text as magical characters are Demotic *wꜥ gswr*, "a ring." Cf.
PGM XII. 270. [R.K.R.]

62. According to LSJ, s.v., a "light-blue" or perhaps "grey, cloudy" color.

63. That is, a crescent moon.

64. On the consecration of amulets, see *PGM* IV. 2179 and n.

65. For the Nemeseis, cf. *PGM* VII. 503 and n.; Griffiths, *The Isis-Book* 311–12.

66. The papyrus here accidentally repeats the preceding clause about the Nemeseis.

O senders of Fate who travels around the whole world, O commanders of the rulers, O exalters of the abased, O revealers of the hidden, O guides of the winds,
225   O arousers of the waves, O bringers of / fire (at a certain time), O creators and benefactors of every race, O nourishers of every race, O lords and controllers of kings, come, benevolent, for that [purpose] for which I call you, as benevolent assistants in this rite for my benefit. I am a plant named Baïs (palm leaf); I am an outflow of blood from the tomb of the great One [between] the palm trees;[67] I am the faith[68] found in men, and am he who declares the holy names, who [is] always alike, who
230   came forth from the abyss.[69] I am / CHRATES[70] who came forth from the eye [of the sun].[71] I am the god whom no one sees or rashly names. I am the sacred bird, Phoinix.[72] I am Krates the holy, called MARMARAUŌTH. I am Helios who showed forth light. I am Aphrodite called TYPHI.[73] I am the holy sender of winds. I am Kronos who showed forth light. I am Mother of gods, called Heaven. I am Osiris,
235   called water. I am Isis, called dew.[74] / I am ĒSENEPHYS,[75] called spring. I am the image resembling the true images. I am SOUCHOS[76] [who appear as] a crocodile. Therefore, I beseech [you], come as my helpers, for I am about to call on the hidden and ineffable name, the forefather of gods, overseer and lord of all."

"Come to me, you from the four winds, god, ruler of all, who have breathed spirits into men for life, master of the good things in the world. Hear me, lord,
240   whose / hidden name is ineffable. The daimons, hearing it, are terrified—the name BARBAREICH ARSEMPHEMPHRŌTHOU—and of it the sun, of it the earth, hearing, rolls over; Hades, hearing, is shaken; rivers, sea, lakes, springs, hearing, are frozen; rocks, hearing it, are split. Heaven is your head; ether, body; earth, feet; and the water around you, ocean, [O] Agathos Daimon.[77] You are lord, the begetter and nourisher and increaser of all."

67. For the efflux of Osiris, see *Book of the Dead*, spells 63b sec. S 1; 119 sec. S 1; 147a sec. S 1; 147g sec. S 1; 149n sec. S 1; 149o. [R.K.R.]

68. Preisendanz treats the term as a hypostatized name (Pistis, "Faith"). See Reitzenstein, *Die hellenistischen Mysterienreligionen* 234–35; D. Lührmann, "Glaube," *RAC* 11 (1979): 84–86.

69. Preisendanz takes βύθος to be the name of a deity. Bythos is the name of the primordial deity in Valentinian gnosticism. For passages, see *PGL*, s.v. "Βύθος"; *The Nag Hammadi Library in English*, index s.v. "Bythos." See also Bousset, *Hauptprobleme*, passim; idem, *Religionsgeschichtliche Studien* 58.

70. Preisendanz, following Eitrem, takes this name to be Egyptian for *Chrat*, "child (Horus)." Actually, the papyrus reads σοκρατης; see C. Leemans, *Papyri Graeci Musei Antiquarii publici Lugduni-Batavi*, vol. 2 (Leiden: Brill, 1885) 26–27. Eitrem's emendation was taken up by J. Kroll, "Chrates," *PRE* 11 (1922): 1641–42; K. Preisendanz, "Pachrates," *PRE* 18 (1942): 2071–74, esp. 2072. The fact, however, remains that the papyrus reads Socrates in l. 230 and Crates in l. 231.

71. The papyrus reads ουαγιου; the translation follows Preisendanz's emendation ἐκ τοῦ οὐατίου. Cf. *PGM* V. 75.

72. On the Phoenix, see Tardieu, *Trois mythes gnostiques* 231–62. Cf. *PGM* II. 104.

73. Typhi, the epithet of Aphrodite, may correspond to Egyptian Triphis (*T3-rpy.t*), "the maiden." See Bonnet, *RÄRG* 838–39, s.v. "Triphis." [R.K.R.]

74. For Isis as dew, see Plutarch, *De Is. et Os.* 12, 355F–365A; 33, 364B, and Griffiths, *Plutarch's De Iside et Osiride* 303, 420, 424. [R.K.R.]

75. ĒSENEPHYS may correspond to Egyptian "Isis the beautiful." Preisendanz, however, understands it to refer to Isis-Neph[th]ys. [R.K.R.]

76. Souchos is Sobek, the Egyptian crocodile god. See Bonnet, *RÄRG* 755–59, s.v. "Suchos." [R.K.R.]

77. On the cosmic body of the deity, see *PGM* XIII. 767–72; XXI. 3–7. See J. Assmann, "Primat und Transzendenz: Struktur und Genese der ägyptischen Vorstellung eines höchsten Wesens," in *Aspekte der ägyptischen Religion*, ed. W. Westendorf, *Göttinger Orientforschungen*, 4th series 9 (Wiesbaden: Harrassowitz, 1979) 7–42.

"Who[78] molded the forms of the beasts [of the Zodiac]? Who / found [their]   245
routes? Who was the begetter of fruits? Who raises up the mountains? Who commanded the winds to hold to their annual tasks? What Aion nourishing an Aion
rules the Aions? One deathless god. You are the begetter of all and assign souls to all
and control all, king of the Aions and lord, [before] whom mountains and plains
together tremble, springs and streams of rivers, and valleys of earth, and spirits, and
[all things] that are. High shining heaven trembles before you, and every sea, / lord,   250
ruler of all, holy one, and master of all. By your power the elements exist and all
things come into being, the route of sun and moon, of night and dawn—all things
in air and earth and water and the breath of fire. Yours is the eternal processional
way [of heaven], in which your seven-lettered name is established for the harmony
of the seven sounds [of the planets] which utter [their] voices according to the 28
forms of the moon. Yours are the beneficent effluxes of the stars, daimons and for-
tunes / and fates. You give wealth, good old age, good children, strength, food.   255
You, lord of life, ruling the upper and the lower realm, whose justice is not thwarted,
whose glorious name the angels hymn, who have truth that never lies, hear me and
complete for me this operation so that I may wear this power in every place, in
every time, without being smitten or afflicted, / so as to be preserved intact from   260
every danger while I wear this power. Yea, lord, for to you, the god in heaven, all
things are subject, and none of the daimons or spirits will oppose me because I have
called on your great name for the consecration. And again I call upon you, according to Egyptians, PHNŌ EAI IABŌK; according to Jews, ADŌNAIE SABAŌTH; accord-
ing to Greeks, "the king of all, ruling alone"; / according to the high priests, "hid-   265
den, invisible, overseer of all"; according to Parthians, "OUERTŌ,[79] master of all."
Consecrate and empower this object for me, for the entire and glorious time of
my life."

The names inscribed on the back side of the stone are these: "IAŌ SABAŌTH
ABRASAX."

*Tr.: Morton Smith.

PGM XII. 270–350

*A Ring. A little ring for success and favor and victory. It makes men famous   270
and great and admired and rich as can be, or it makes possible friendships with
suchlike men. The circlet is always yours [to use] justly and successfully for all purposes. It contains a first-rate name.

Helios is to be engraved on a heliotrope stone[80] as follows: A thick-bodied
snake[81] in the shape of a wreath should be [shown] having its tail in its / mouth.   275
Inside [the circle formed by] the snake let there be a sacred scarab[82] [beetle surrounded by] rays. On the reverse side of the stone you are to inscribe the name in
hieroglyphics, as the prophets pronounce [it]. Then, having consecrated [the ring],
wear it when you are pure.

The world has had nothing greater than this. For when you have it with you you
will always get whatever you ask from anybody. Besides, it calms the angers of masters and kings. Wearing it, whatever you may say to anyone, you will be believed,

---

78. The dactylic hexameters (ll. 244–52) are also the reconstructed Hymn 1. See Preisendanz, vol.
II, p. 237. [E.N.O.]
   79. OUERTO corresponds to the Egyptian epithet "the great one of earth." [R.K.R.]
   80. A green chalcedony with small spots of red jasper. Cf. Pliny, NH 37. 165. [J.S.]
   81. That is, the Ouroboros serpent. See Glossary, s.v. "Ouroboros."
   82. On the scarab, see PGM IV. 943 and the Glossary, s.v. "Scarab."

and you will be pleasing to everybody. Anyone can open doors and break chains
280 and rocks if he / touches them with the stone, that is, the gem, and says the name
written below. It also works for demoniacs. Just give it [to one] to wear, and the
daimon will immediately flee. So at dawn stand facing the sun, holding the well-
planned, beneficent, divine, holy, useful, economical, merciful stone which provides your needs, the beautiful and becoming one, [say]:

285   "Greatest god, who exceed / all power, I call on you, IAŌ SABAŌTH ADŌNAI
EILŌEIN[83] SEBŌEIN TALLAM CHAUNAŌN SAGĒNAM ELEMMEDŌR CHAPSOUTHI
SETTŌRA SAPHTHA NOUCHITHA, Abraham, Isaac, Jacob,[84] CHATHATHICH ZEU-
PEIN NĒPHYGOR ASTAPHAIOS KATAKERKNĒPH KONTEOS KATOUT KĒRIDEU MAR-
290 MARIŌTH LIKYXANTA BESSOUM SYMEKONTEU, the opponent of Thoth, / MASKELLI
MASKELLŌTH PHNOU KENTABAŌTH OREOBAZAGRA HIPPOCHTHŌN RĒSICHTHŌN
PYRIPĒGANYX NYXIŌ ABRŌROKORE KODĒRE MOUISDRŌ, King, THATH PHATH
CHATH XEUZĒN ZEUZEI SOUSĒNĒ ELATHATH MELASIŌ KOUKŌR NEUSOŌ PACHIŌ
XIPHNŌ THEMEL NAUTH BIOKLĒTH SESSŌR CHAMEL CHASINEU XŌCHŌ IAL-
295 LINŌI / SEISENGPHARANGĒS MASICHIŌR IŌTABAAS CHENOUCHI CHAAM PHA-
CHIARATH NEEGŌTHARA IAM ZEŌCH AKRAMMACHAMAREI Cheroubei(m) BAIN-
CHŌŌCH EIOPHALEON ICHNAŌTH PŌE XEPHITHŌTH XOUTHOUTH THOŌTHIOU
XERIPHŌNAR EPHINARASŌR CHANIZARA ANAMEGAR IŌO XTOURORIAM IŌK NIŌR
300 CHETTAIOS ELOUMAIOS NŌIŌ DAMNAMENEU / AXIŌTHŌPH PSETHAIAKKLŌPS
SISAGETA NEORIPHRŌR HIPPOKELEPHOKLŌPS ZEINACHA IAPHETHANA A E Ē I O
Y Ō. I have called on you, greatest god, and through you on all things, that you may
give divine and supreme strength to this image and may make it effective and
powerful against all [opponents] and to be able to call back souls, move spirits,
subject legal opponents, strengthen friendships, produce all [sorts of] profits,
305 bring / dreams, give prophecies, cause psychological passions and bodily sufferings
and incapacitating illness, and perfect all erotic philters. Please, lord, bring to fulfillment a complete consecration."

When you perform this rite, say [the spell] three times each day, in the third,
sixth, and ninth hour, and this for fourteen days, beginning when the moon begins
its third quarter. And try to have the goddess [i.e., the moon] either [rising] in [the
Zodiacal sign of] the Bull or the Virgin or Scorpion or the Water Carrier or the
310 Fishes. Also when you are performing the consecration, each time / you recite
[the spell] pour as libation the [fluids] specified above and all kinds of perfumes
except frankincense. And when you have completed the consecration properly, have
a rooster with a double comb—either white or yellow; keep away from black—and
after the consecration cut the live rooster open and stick the [stone with its] image
well into the guts of the rooster, taking care that the entrails of the animal be not
315 broken. Leave [it there] for one day, / then in the ninth hour of the night take [it]
out and put [it] away in a holy place, and use as [seems] best.

Whenever you wish to command the god, give [your] command, saying the
greatest [name] OUPHŌR, and he will perform. You have [now] the consecration [to
secure] the supreme and divine action. This OUPHŌR is the [god] whom Urbicus
used, the holy, true OUPHŌR. Here is truly written out, with all brevity, [the rite]
320 by which all modeled images and engravings / and carved stones are made alive.
For this is the true [rite], and the others such as are widely circulated, are falsified
and made up of vain verbosity. So keep this in a secret place as a great mystery. Hide
it, hide it! It is—the beginning—

83. Almost certainly a misspelling of *elohîm*, a Hebrew word meaning "god."
84. The names are misspelled as Abraan, Isak, Iakkōbi.

"The gates of heaven were opened. The gates of earth were opened. / The route 325
of the sea was opened. The route of the rivers was opened. My spirit was heard by
all gods and daimons. My spirit was heard by the spirit of heaven. My spirit was
heard by the terrestrial spirit. My spirit was heard by the marine spirit. / My spirit 330
was heard by the riverine spirit. Therefore give spirit to the mystery[85] I have prepared, O gods whom I have named and have called on. Give breath to the mystery I
have prepared."

Hide, hide the true [spell to control?] OUPHŌR, / which contains the truth in 335
summary. *The invocation to* OUPHŌR:[86]

"ĒI IEOU MAREITH
ĒI IEOU MONTHEATHI MONGITH
ĒI IEOU CHAREŌTH MONKĒB
ĒI IEOU SŌCHOU SŌRSŌĒ
/ ĒI IEOU TIŌTIŌ OUIĒR   340
ĒI IEOU CHARŌCHSI CHARMIŌTH
ĒI IEOU SATHIMŌOYEĒOY
ĒI IEOU RAIRAI MOURIRAI
ĒI IEOU Amoun ĒEI Osiris
/ ĒI IEOŪ PHIRIMNOUN[87]   345
ĒI IEOU ANMORCHATHI OUĒR
ĒI IEOU ANCHEREPHRENEPSOUPHIRINGCH
ĒI IEOU ORCHIMORŌIPOUGTH
ĒI IEOU MACHPSACHATHANTH
/ ĒI IEOU MOROTH."   350
*Tr.: Morton Smith. The Demotic title (line 270) is written between the sections.

PGM XII. 351–64

*Demokritos' "sphere": prognostic of life and death.** Find out what day of the
month[88] the sick one took to bed. Add his name from birth[89] to the day of the
month and divide by thirty.[90] Look up on the "sphere" the quotient: if the number
is on the upper register, the person will live, but if it is on the lower register, he will
die.

85. That is, the magical ring.
86. These invocations begin with a formula corresponding to the Egyptian *i i3w,* "O, hail!" [R.K.R.]
87. PHIRIMNOUN corresponds to Egyptian "He who comes forth from Nun (the abyss)." Cf. *PGM*
XII. 229. [R.K.R.]
88. Literally, "know in relation to the moon." Beginning with the new moon, each day of the lunar
month can be given a number from one to thirty.
89. The *praenomen,* or first name, among the Romans. Each letter of the Greek alphabet has a numerical value.
90. Literally, "see how many times thirty there are." In other words, the sum of the numerical value
of the name and the value of the day on which the person took ill, is divided by thirty.

355

1	10	19
2	11	20
3	13	23
4	14	25
7	16	26
9	17	27
5	15	22
6	18	28
8	21	29
12	24	30

360

*Tr.: J. P. Hershbell. A similar "sphere" is attributed to Petosiris, the mythical Egyptian astrologer. The so-called sphere is only a circle or other plane figure, in this case a rectangle, but even when the circle is reduced to a rectangle, it is called a sphere. For full discussion of this kind of "astrological medicine," see A. Bouché-Leclercq, *L'astrologie grecque* (Paris 1899, repr. 1963) 537–42, esp. 538, and Thorndike, *A History of Magic I*, 682ff.; see also V. Alfieri, *Gli atomisti, frammenti e testimonianze* (Bari 1936) 305–6, n. 801 and Budge, *Egyptian Magic* 228–30.

PGM XII. 365–75

365 ***Charm for causing separation**: On a pot for smoked fish inscribe a spell with a bronze stylus and recite it afterwards and put it where they [i.e., your victims] are, where they usually return, repeating at the same time this spell: "I call upon you, god, you who are in the empty air, you who are terrible, invisible, and great, you who afflict the earth and shake the universe, you who love disturbances and hate

370 stability and scatter the clouds / from one another, IAIA IAKOUBIAI IŌ ERBĒTH, IŌ PAKERBĒTH IŌ BOLCHOSĒTH BASDOUMA PATATHNAX APOPSS OSESRŌ ATAPH THABRAOU ĒŌ THATHTHABRA BŌRARA AROBREITHA BOLCHOSĒTH KOKKOLOIPTOLĒ RAMBITHNIPS: give to him, NN, the son of her, NN, strife, war; and to him, NN, the son of her, NN, odiousness, enmity, just as Typhon and Osiris had"[91] (but if it is a husband and wife, "just as Typhon and Isis had"). "Strong Typhon, very / powerful one, perform your mighty acts."

*Tr.: R. F. Hock. This charm provides a means for effecting a breach between two men's friendship or love for each other, with a variant formula inserted to make the spell work against a husband and wife.

PGM XII. 376–96

***Charm to induce insomnia**: Take a living bat and on the right wing paint with myrrh the following figure, and on the left write the 7 names of the god as well as: "Let her, NN whom NN bore, lie awake until she consents." And so release the bat again.

Perform this spell at the waning of the moon[92] when the goddess is in her third

380 night, and the woman will die for lack of sleep, without lasting / 7 days.

This charm cannot at any time have an antidote. But if you at some time wish one, do not release the bat, but keep it in custody; and this does the same thing: when you want to release it, wash off with spring water [what] has been written on the wings and release the bird. But do not do this, save for a great intrigue.

91. On the enmity between Typhon/Seth and Osiris, see *PGM* VII. 964 and n.
92. That is, the moon goddess Selene.

This then is the figure:

/ ***The names to be written on the left wing are these***: "I call upon you, great god,   385
THATHABATHATH / PETENNABOUTHI PEPTOU BAST[93] EIĒSOUS OUAIR AMOUN   390
OUTHI ASCHELIDONĒTH / BATHARIBATH; let her, NN, lie awake through the whole   395
night and day, until she dies, immediately, immediately; quickly, quickly."
*Tr.: R. F. Hock.

PGM XII. 397–400

*To gain favor and friendship forever**: Take a pasithea or wormwood root and
write this name on it in a holy manner: ☩ ⋎ ⅄ ┘ ∫ – 3 ⋂ ⋂ L. Then carry it, and you
will be an object of favor, friendship, and admiration to people who see you. /

The formula: 1 dram of myrrh, 4 drams of truffle, 2 drams of blue vitriol, 2   400
drams of oak gall, 3 drams of gum arabic.
*Tr.: Hubert Martin, Jr.

PGM XII. 401–44

*Interpretations** which the temple scribes employed, from the holy writings, in
translation. Because of the curiosity of the masses they [i.e., the scribes] inscribed
the names of the herbs and other things which they employed on the statues of the
gods, so that they [i.e., the masses], since they do not take precaution, / might not   405
practice magic, [being prevented] by the consequence of their misunderstanding.[94]
But we have collected the explanations [of these names] from many copies [of the
sacred writings], all of them secret.

Here they are: [95]

A snake's head: a leech.

---

93. On Bastet, the Egyptian cat goddess, see *PGM* III. 1 and n.

94. Cf. V. F. Vanderlip, *The Four Greek Hymns of Isidorus and the Cult of Isis* (Toronto: Hakkert,
1972), Hymn IV. 37–39: "Reliably learning these facts from men who study history, I myself have set
them all up on inscribed pillars and translated (into Greek) for Greeks the power of a Prince who was a
god" (pp. 64–65). Isidorus himself cannot read the hieroglyphs.

95. For similar lists of names, cf. *De succedaneis* transmitted among the works of Galen, *Claudii
Galeni Opera Omnia*, ed. C. G. Kühn, vol. 19 (Lipsiae: Officina libraria Car. Cnoblochii, 1830) 721–

A snake's "ball of thread": this means soapstone. /
410   Blood of a snake: hematite.
A bone of an ibis: this is buckthorn.
Blood of a hyrax: [96] truly of a hyrax.
"Tears" [97] of a Hamadryas baboon: dill juice.
Crocodile dung: Ethiopian soil. /
415   Blood of a Hamadryas baboon: blood of a spotted gecko.
Lion semen: Human semen.
Blood of Hephaistos: wormwood.
Hairs of a Hamadryas baboon: dill seed.
Semen of Hermes: dill. /
420   Blood of Ares: purslane.
Blood of an eye: tamarisk gall. [98]
Blood from a shoulder: bear's breach [99]
From the loins: camomile.
A man's bile: turnip sap. [100] /
425   A pig's tail: leopard's bane. [101]
A physician's bone: sandstone.
Blood of Hestia: camomile.
An eagle: wild garlic (?). [102]
Blood of a goose: a mulberry tree's "milk." /
430   Kronos' spice: piglet's milk.
A lion's hairs: "tongue" of a turnip. [103]
Kronos' blood: . . . of cedar.
Semen of Helios: white hellebore.
Semen of Herakles: this is mustard-rocket. [104] /
435   [A Titan's] blood: wild lettuce. [105]
Blood from a head: lupine.
A bull's semen: egg of a blister beetle. [106]

47, as well as the adapted version of Galen's tract in Paul of Aegina, *Paulus Aegineta, Corpus Medicorum Graecorum IX/2*, ed. I. L. Heiberg, vol. II (Lipsiae: Teubner, 1924) 401–8; and Dioscorides' *Materia medica*, ed. M. Wellmann, 3 vols. (Berlin: Weidmann, 1907–14). [J.S.]

96. Probably the rock hyrax (*Procavia capensis*), also mentioned in the LXX Lv 11:6; Dt 14:7; Ps 103 (104): 18; Prv 24:61 (30:26). [J.S.]

97. Perhaps the "sleep sand" from the eyes of baboons. [J.S.]

98. Cf. Dioscorides 1. 75; also 1. 89. [J.S.]

99. Probably to be emended to ἄκανθος (*Acanthus mollis* L. or *Helleborus foetidus* L.). [J.S.]

100. Probably to be emended to βουνίας as in Dioscorides 2. 111, a kind of turnip (probably *Brassica napus* L.). [J.S.]

101. Literally, "scorpion-tail," probably a variety of "leopard's bane" in the genus *Boronicum*, or one of the heliotropes. Cf. Theophrastus, *Hist. plant.* 9. 13. 6; Nicander, *Alexiph.* 145; Dioscorides 4. 190. 1. See J. Scarborough, "Theophrastus on Herbals and Herbal Remedies," *Journal of the History of Biology* 11 (1978): 373–74, with n. 120; idem, "Nicander's Toxicology II: Spiders, Scorpions, Insects, and Myriapods," *Pharmacy in History* 21 (1979): 3–34, 73–92. [J.S.]

102. The papyrus reads οσελγεβει, which the editors read either as χελκβει, "wild garlic" (*Trigonella foenumgraecum*), following Griffith, ad loc.; *PGM* V. 70, or as ἑλλέβορος, "hellebore." [J.S.]

103. As emended in l. 425 (see above, n. 100), referring to the leaves of the taproot. [J.S.]

104. Probably *Eruca sativa* Mill. [J.S.]

105. See on this Dioscorides 2. 136. [J.S.]

106. The blister beetle played a role in the manufacture of the aphrodisiac known as Spanish fly. See J. Scarborough, "Some Beetles in Pliny's Natural History," *Coleopterists Bulletin* 31 (1977): 293–96; idem, "Nicander's Toxicology" (see above, n. 101). [J.S.]

A hawk's heart: heart of wormwood.
Semen of Hephaistos: this is fleabane. /
Semen of Ammon: houseleek.   440
Semen of Ares: clover.
Fat from a head: spurge.
From the belly: earth-apple.
From the foot: houseleek.[107]

*Tr.: H. D. Betz (ll. 401–7) and John Scarborough (ll. 408–45) who are also responsible for the respective notes. The "interpretations" refers to the secret list of plant names below; cf. the *Discourse on the Eighth and the Ninth* 61, 19ff., in *The Nag Hammadi Library in English*, 296–97; *2 Jeu*, chaps. 45–48; *Test Sol* 13.6; see Gudeman, "Lyseis," *PRE* 13 (1927):2511–29.

PDM xii. 50–61 [*PGM* XII. 445–48]

*A spell for separating one person from another: Dung of . . . and you put it [in] a   50 [1]
document, and you write on a document of papyrus these great names / together   55 [6]
with the name of the man, and you bury it under the doorsill of the house.

    Here are the names for (?) it and you recite them over it also, 7 times: "†IO-
ERBĒTH †IO-SĒTH[108] †IO-BŌLGHŌSĒTH[109] †IO-PAGERBĒTH †IO-PATATHNAGS †LĒE-   (445–48)
MENG.RĒ †IO-ŌSESRO[110] / †IO-GHLŌNTOĒPS, separate NN, born of NN, from NN,
born of NN!" It is . . . : "Separate Isis from . . ." (formula: 7 times).   60 [11]

*Tr.: Janet H. Johnson, following the edition and translation in *OMRM* 56 (1975):38–39, col. IV, ll. 1–12. The Old Coptic/Greek and Demotic *voces magicae* in ll. 57–60 [8–11] are transcribed as Greek in *PGM* XII. 445–48 (*Kol.* XIV) in Preisendanz. A variant of the same spell follows immediately in ll. 62–75, a spell in which a magical figure is supplied. Words preceded by † are written in the text in Demotic with Old Coptic glosses inserted above.

PDM xii. 62–75 [*PGM* XII. 449–52]

*Another: You bring a . . . and you write the names on it, and you bury [it] in the
road of. . . .

    Formula: †BRAG †GRAB †BRAGH †HŌSPERTHNAKS[111] / †BHRIENTHE(?)GH †BAS-   65 [16]
PHETHŌI †ATHRYPH †PATATHNAG †APŌPSI †IŌ-BĒTH †IŌ-BŌLGHŌSĒTH †IŌ-PAG-   (449–52)
ERBĒTH,[112] separate NN born of NN, from NN born of NN!" Two [times] . . . You
bring a sherd . . . of beer of . . . which is burnt, and you write [on] it a donkey / in   70 [21]
this manner:

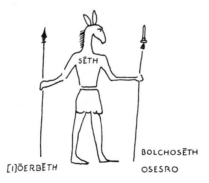

107. See on this plant Dioscorides 4. 88. [J.S.]
108. Ending includes Egyptian god Seth. [J.H.J.]
109. See n. 108 above.
110. Or, perhaps, IŌ ŌSEIRŌ, as in the label to the figure. [J.H.J.]
111. HŌSPER may be for ὥσπερ, "similarly." [R.K.R.]
112. See figure.

"Separate NN, born of NN, from NN, born of NN!" And you say this name to it again, 7 times, and you lift the sherd, and you . . . in the house in which they
75 [26]   are. / You do it. . . .

*Tr.: Janet H. Johnson, following the edition and translation in *OMRM* 56 (1975): 38–39, col. IV, ll. 13–26. The Demotic *voces magicae* in ll. 15–18 are transcribed as Greek in *PGM* XII. 449–52 (*Kol.* XIV). Words preceded by ˈ are written in the text in Demotic with Old Coptic glosses inserted above.

PDM xii. 76–107 [*PGM* XII. 453–65]

*Another: . . . of a black donkey,[113] and you put a . . . which is . . . , and you leave [it] in it for three days . . . it. You should cook it for one night . . . , and you should
80 [5]   bring a / strip of . . . , and you should write . . . the names on it with donkey blood, and you should gather outside . . . saying, "Separate NN, born of NN, from NN, born of NN!" And you should . . . and you should . . . the urine. . . .
85 [10]   Here is the *name* which you should write it: / . . . ˈTHALAMAXI, separate NN, born of NN, from NN, born of NN!"

. . . again on the day of separating (another [manuscript] says: "beating" [?]),
90 [15]   . . . of a donkey and a . . . / urine (?), and you put them in a new ladle (?) and you . . . until they come . . . , and you put . . . and you . . . the sherd . . . and you [write] these names . . . and you . . . in the above-mentioned house.
95 [20]   / Here are the names: "I call upon you, you who are in the [empty air], you who
(453–65) are terrible, you who are an invisible god, you who cause destruction and desolation, you who hate a stable household and you who do mischief.[114] I call upon your great name; cause him, NN, to be separated from him, NN, IŌ IŌ IŌBRACH KRA-BROUKRIOU BATRIOU APOMPS STROUTELIPS IAK[OUBIAI][115] IŌ PAKERBĒTH PAKERBĒTH, god of gods . . . at the gate of IAŌ. Separate him, NN, from him, NN, because I am the daimon XANTHIS[116] OUBATH . . . E . . . TEBERETERRI . . . EI . . . , separate him, [NN], from him, NN."

*Tr.: Janet H. Johnson (ll. 76–95), following the edition and translation in *OMRM* 56 (1975): 40–41, col. III, ll. 1–20; and R. F. Hock (ll. 96–107), following Preisendanz, *PGM* XII. 453–65.

PDM xii. 108–18 [*PGM* XII. 466–68]

*A spell [to] cause a woman to hate a man . . . : You bring dung, hair and hair . . .
110 [3]   which is dead, / and you mix them with fresh blooms, and you put it in a new papyrus after writing on the papyrus first with my ink, saying, "May NN, born of NN, hate NN, born of NN!" And you recite these true names over it 7 times, and you bind the papyrus, and you put it in the water of. . . .
115 [8]   Here are / the true names: ˈIAKYMBIAI IAŌ ˈIŌERBĒTH ˈIŌBOLGHOSĒTH ˈBA-
(466–68) SELE OM ˈGITATHNAGS ˈAPSOPS ˈŌ.EL.T, separate NN, born [of] NN, from NN, born of NN; hurry, hurry; be quick, be quick!"

*Tr.: Janet H. Johnson, following the edition and translation in *OMRM* 56 (1975): 42–43, col. II, ll. 1–18. The Demotic *voces magicae* in ll. 8–10 are transcribed by Preisendanz as Greek in *PGM* XII. 466–68. Words preceded by ˈ are written in the text in Demotic with Old Coptic glosses inserted above.

113. On the donkey as the image of Seth, see the Glossary, s.v. "Typhon-Seth."
114. So following the emendation in Preisendanz; cf. the apparatus ad loc.
115. Supplying in the lacuna Ἰακο[υβιαι], a name attested elsewhere.
116. The reading of this name is, however, textually uncertain.

PDM xii. 119–34 [*PGM* XII. 469–70; 471–73]

*A spell for it: Surround (?) . . . of . . . another [manuscript] says . . . : / You (?)   120 [13]
write [the] true names with ink . . . and you write at its bottom, . . . to me Anubis,
saying, "Surround (?) NN, born of NN!" . . . you should write on its bottom . . .
"vex NN, born of NN!" and you should . . . them to it again, and you should . . .
fire, flame (?), and you should [bind] . . . of the hair of the woman with . . . , / and   125 [18]
you should put a . . . a bitch which is dead.

   Its formula: "Rouse yourself and depart, at the undertaking ward off responses of   (469–70)
each penalty . . . woman." You write these words on a new papyrus with myrrh ink,
and you put it in . . . of a . . . / built (?), and you put it in a chest (?), and you give it   130 [23]
to an ibis.

   Here are the names: "†ALBANAGHAMBRE †AMESŌTSIE(?)R †ATHRŌER †ATHROI   (471–73)
†THYIN, surround NN, born of NN, . . . in her heart."

*Tr.: Janet H. Johnson (ll. 119–125, 128–31), following the edition in *OMRM* 56
(1975):42–43, col. II, ll. 12–27; and E. N. O'Neil (ll. 126–27), following the edition in
Preisendanz, *PGM* XII. 469–70. The Demotic *voces magicae* in ll. 132–33 are transcribed by
Preisendanz as Greek at *PGM* XII. 471–73. Words preceded by † are written in Demotic in
the text with Old Coptic glosses inserted above.

PDM xii. 135–46 [*PGM* XII. 474–79]

*. . . you bring a sealed . . . of copper . . . this lion, this mummy (?), and this   135 [1]
Anubis . . . while they seek . . . black scarab (?) . . . put . . . :

   / ". . . AIDIŌ ŌRICH THAMBITŌ, Abraham who at . . . PLANOIEGCHIBIŌTH   140 [6]
MOU ROU and the whole soul for her, NN [whom NN bore] . . . the female body   (474–79)
of her, NN [whom NN bore], I conjure by the . . . [and] to inflame her, NN whom
[NN bore]."

   [Write these] words together with this picture on a new papyrus:

*Tr.: Janet H. Johnson (ll. 135–39; 146), following the edition and translation in *OMRM*
56 (1975):44–45, col. I, ll. 1–5, 12; and E. N. O'Neil (ll. 140–45) following Preisendanz,
PGM XII. 474–79.

PDM xii. 147–64 [*PGM* XII. 480–95]

*Another: Cook it [in the (?)] bath: "ALLANTH BIREIBAMETIRA / EMETHIRE THA-   150 [16]
RABLATH PNOUTHE THOUCHARA ŌSOUCHARI SABACHAR . . . , / burn her, NN,   155 [21]
until she [comes] to me, NN, immediately, immediately; quickly, quickly. I conjure   (480–95)
you, daimons of the dead, [by] the dead and by the daimon of [Balsames], and
the / dog-faced god,[117] and the gods with him."   160 [26]

   117. The dog-faced god is Anubis.

Write these things . . . with the salt first . . . which is on it.

*Tr.: Janet H. Johnson (ll. 147, 163–64), following the edition and translation in *OMRM*
56 (1975): 44–45, col. I, ll. 13–14, 29–30; and E. N. O'Neil (ll. 148–62), following Preisendanz, *PGM* XII. 480–95.

PGM XIII. 1–343

*GOD/GODS.[1] **A sacred book called "Unique"[2] or "Eighth Book of Moses,"**
concerning the holy Name. Its content goes as follows: Remain / pure 41 days, hav-
5 ing calculated in advance so that your completion of them will coincide with the
dark of the moon which occurs in Aries.[3] Have a house on ground level, in which
no one has died during the past year. The door should face west. Now set up in the
middle of the house an earthen altar and have ready cypress wood, ten pinecones
10 full of seed,[4] two white roosters / uninjured and without blemish, and two lamps
each holding an eighth of a pint, filled with good oil. And don't pour in any more,
for when the god comes in they will burn more fiercely. Have the table prepared
with these following kinds of incense, which are cognate to the god (from this /
15 book Hermes plagiarized when he named the 7 kinds of incense[5] [in] his sacred
book called *Wing*).[6]

The proper incense of Kronos is styrax, for it is heavy and fragrant; of Zeus, malabathron;[7] of Ares, kostos; of Helios, frankincense; of Aphrodite, Indian nard; of
20 Hermes, cassia; / of Selene, myrrh. These are the secret incenses (the direction in
the *Key of Moses*,[8] "Prepare sun vetch on every occasion," refers with these [words]

---

1. ϑεοί ("gods") commonly stands at the beginning of sacral inscriptions from Athens and sites in
the Athenian sphere of influence; elsewhere it is rare (see the uses in F. Sokolowski, *Lois sacrées des cités
grecques*, Paris: E. de Boccard, 1969). The use here indicates literary and philosophical pretensions.
"GOD" is put above "GODS" both to suggest that the magician has access to a higher power, and to
conform to the fashion which, by the time this text was copied (under Constantine's successors), favored
monotheism.

2. "Unique" translates the Greek μόνας, "by oneself, solitary"; in philosophy, primarily Pythagorean, then Platonic, "monad." Hence also in *C.H.* 4. 10, on which see Festugière's n. 28. Philosophic use
for the primal deity made the word vague and prestigious, which accounts for its appearance here. The
attribution to Moses was due partly to the texts' content (see below, n. 16), partly to Moses' fame as a
magician. Pliny, *NH* 30. 11, credited him with starting his own school of magic. Both Jews and gentiles
helped the tradition grow by repeating stories about him and circulating magical texts under his name.
See J. Gager, *Moses in Greco-Roman Paganism* (Nashville, Abingdon Press, 1972), chap. 4, pp. 134–61.
The compiler of *PGM* XIII was both a composer and a collector of "Mosaic" texts. He had himself
written one called "The Key of Moses" (l. 229), which he often recommends; he had a variorum edition
of VIII Moses, giving three texts, and in his additions to it he cites "The Archangelic (Teaching?) of
Moses," Moses' "secret moon prayer," and "The Tenth Hidden (Book?) of Moses." The choice of
"eighth" as the number of the book is surprising, since we hear nothing of the sixth and seventh; it may
be due to the increasing prestige of the ogdoad (see below, nn. 29 and 112). The choice of "Tenth" for
the next numbered book (nothing is heard of a ninth) is also explicable from numerology, ten being the
Pythagorean perfect number.

3. The Greek σύνοδος here is ambiguous. It was also used loosely to refer to the new moon, and was
so understood by Preisendanz, but see l. 349.

4. So Preisendanz, translating δέξιος; alternatively, "with spirals (formed by the edges of the scales)
running to the right."

5. The promised list of incenses "cognate to the (one) god" can hardly be the following list of incenses proper for seven different gods. The author probably inserted a standard list taken from the book
of "Hermes" whom he therefore accused of plagiarism.

6. To this "Hermetic" book there is no other reference. Evidently it was the work of a rival author.
This comment by the compiler clearly interrupts the earlier text. That "Hermes" is attacked makes the
restoration of "Hermetic spell" (in l. 138) dubious.

7. Leaves of *Cinnamomum tamala* or *albiflorum*. "Kostos," which follows, is *Sassurea lappa*.

8. The two following statements by the compiler again interrupt the text. The *Key of Moses* was his
own book (l. 229), evidently a sort of magician's handbook with astrological information, etc. There is

to the Egyptian bean). Moreover, Manetho gave these directions in his own book.

Then take the 7 flowers of the 7 stars (which are marjoram, white lily, lotus, erephyllinon,[9] / narcissus, gillyflower, rose); take these flowers twenty-one days before   25
the initiation, and grind them fine in a white mortar[10] and dry them in the shade
and have them ready for that day.

First, however, present yourself, on / whatever auspicious new moon occurs,[11] to   30
the gods of the hours of the day, whose names you have in the *Key*. You will be
made their initiate[12] as follows: Make 3 figures from fine flour, one bull-faced, one
goat-faced, one ram-faced, each of them standing on the celestial pole and holding
an Egyptian flail.[13] And when you have / censed them, eat them, saying the spell for   35
the gods of the hours (which is in the *Key*) and the compulsive formula for them
and the names of the gods set over the weeks. Then you will have been made their
initiate.

Next, for the all-important meeting, have a square of natron[14] on which you will
write the great name with the seven vowels. Instead / of the popping noise and the   40
hissing [sound in the name] draw on the first part of the natron a falcon-faced crocodile[15] and the nine-formed god standing on him, for this falcon-faced crocodile at
the 4 turning points [of the year] greets the god with the popping noise. For, coming up to breathe from the deep, he goes "Pop, pop, pop," / and he of the 9 forms   45
replies to him antiphonally. Therefore, instead of the popping noise, draw the
falcon-faced crocodile, for the popping noise is the first element of the name. The
second is a hissing. Instead of the hissing [draw] a snake biting its / tail. So the two   50
elements, popping and hissing, are represented by a falcon-faced crocodile and the
nine-formed god standing on it, and around these a snake and the seven vowels.

Now [the great name] is [composed of] 9 names, before which you say [those of]
the gods of the hours, with [the prayer on] the stele, and [those of] the gods of the
days and of those / set over the weeks, and the compulsive formula for these; for   55
without these the god will not listen but will refuse to receive you as uninitiated,
unless you emphatically say in advance the [names of] the lord of the day and of the
hour, which information you will find at the end [of this tractate]; for without
these / you will not accomplish even one of the things you find in the *Key*:   60

---

no good reason to think it had anything to do with *C.H.* 10, which was also called *Key* but dealt with
totally different subjects. Manetho was an Egyptian priest who wrote a history of Egypt for Ptolemy II,
ca. 275 B.C. The success of this work made him famous; hence many other texts, especially of astrology,
but also of magic, were fathered onto him. Which this writer had in mind, is unknown. Cf. *PGM* III.
440 and n. The content of the *Key* is described in eight passages in *PGM* XIII, viz. ll. 21–22, 30–31,
35–36, 59–60, 228–29, 282–83, 431–32, and 735–43. From these it appears that the *Key* contained
directions for performance of rites, names of the gods of the days, hours, etc., spells to control these, and
the great name of 6 letters, Ogdoas. Some of the directions were allegorical or allegorized (see ll. 21–22
and 228–29).

9. Unknown.

10. Alternatively, "into white incense."

11. Literally, "a new moon favored by a god," meaning one which the god, by giving good auspices,
declares favorable for your purposes.

12. Literally, "initiated."

13. Alternatively, "Egyptian flails."

14. Sodium carbonate, a soapy substance. This was not a gourmet rite.

15. The falcon-faced crocodile appears on many Egyptian inscriptions. He was a fusion of the crocodile god Sobek and the hawk god Horus. The "nine-formed" was the "Ennead," an Egyptian complex of
nine gods who in the late period were thought to be the members of the body of a single god. See
H. Bonnet, *RÄRG*, 521–25, s.v. "Neunheit." The "four turning points of the year" are the equinoxes
and solstices. That crocodiles pop off at these periods is an example of the unnatural history surprisingly
common in ancient authors from Aristotle on.

Now the [text of the] sacred stele to be written in the natron is:

"I[16] call on you, who are greater than all, the creator of all, you, the self-begotten,
who see all and are not seen. For you gave Helios the glory and all the / power,
Selene [the privilege] to wax and wane and have fixed courses, yet you took nothing
from the earlier-born darkness, but apportioned things so that they should be
equal. For when you appeared, both order[17] arose and light appeared.[18] All things
are subject to you, whose true form none of the gods can / see; who change into all
forms. You are invisible, Aion of Aion.

"I call on you, lord, to appear to me in a good form, for under your order I serve
your angel, BIATHIARBAR BERBIR SCHILATOUR BOUPHROUMTRŌM, and your fear,
DANOUPH CHRATOR BELBALI BALBITH IAŌ. / Through you arose the celestial pole
and the earth.

"I call on you, lord, as do the gods who appeared under your [order?] that they
may have power; ECHEBYKRŌM of Helios, whose is the glory,[19] AAA ĒĒĒ ŌŌŌ III
AAA ŌŌŌ SABAŌTH ARBATHIAŌ / ZAGOURĒ, the god ARATHY ADŌNAIE.

"I call on you, lord, in 'birdglyphic'[20]: ARAI; in hieroglyphic: LAILAM; in He-
braic:[21] ANOCH BIATHIARBATH BERBIR ECHILATOUR BOUPHROUMTROM; in
Egyptian: ALDABAEIM; in 'baboonic': ABRASAX; / in 'falconic':[22] CHI CHI CHI CHI
CHI CHI CHI TIPH TIPH TIPH; in hieratic: MENEPHŌIPHŌTH CHA CHA CHA CHA
CHA CHA CHA." Then clap 3 times, go "pop, pop, pop" for a long time; hiss at
some length.

"Come [to me], lord, faultless and unflawed, who pollute / no place, for I have
been initiated into your name."

Have a tablet in which you will write what he says to you and a two-edged knife,
all of iron, so that, clean from all [impurities],[23] you may kill the sacrifices, and a
libation (a jug of wine and a flask full of honey /) that you may pour. Have all these
ready nearby you. And you be in clean linens, crowned with an olive wreath. Prepare the canopy[24] thus: Taking a clean sheet, write on the border [the names of] the

16. This invocation and that following (138–53) are essentially identical, both being variations of an
old Egyptian hymn in which the rising sun is greeted by the sacred animals, each kind making its appropriate noises. In both invocations (and their close parallels in the B version—443–61, 570–99; in C
only the first lines are cited) the sun god has been made the creator and sustainer of the world, and the
songs of the animals are preceded by and partly fused with the songs of the angels, many of whom are
Jewish. In both, the same angels and the same languages appear in the same orders. The roles given the
god and the angels, and the personnel, help explain the attribution to Moses, the more so because these
two invocations are the most important elements in the text—the active agents which make the deity
appear (this is particularly clear in B, which, since it put the first invocation after the rite as an appendix,
ll. 570–99, followed it by a second epiphany, 608–717).

17. Here "order" translates the Greek κόσμος, which means also "the cosmos."

18. I.e., light and darkness?

19. Or "the doxology" without following comma, the doxology being the following formula. Here
the choice is difficult because "glory" fits Helios, but "doxology" gives the magical words a function in
the text, as those in the preceding paragraph functioned as names of the angel and the fear. Δόξα meaning "spoken/sung praise" is found already in LXX; see G. Kittel and G. von Rad, *TDNT* 2 (1964):
233–55.

20. Greek ὀρνεογλυφιστί, formed by analogy from ἱερογλυφιστί, which follows.

21. In spite of the claim that this is Hebrew, the first word is a transliteration of the Egyptian word
for "I (am)," *anoch.* A similar Hebrew word, *ʾanoki,* has the same meaning. The author seems to have
known Hebrew and Egyptian badly enough to mix them up. See Glossary, s.v.

22. *Chi chi* is the cry appropriate for the morning sun; *tiph tiph,* for the evening sun. [J.B.]

23. This supposes a purity code in which iron neither received nor transmitted pollution.

24. That is, under which you will receive the god. Perhaps from some mystery rite. (Originally the
bridal tent?) Here an unexplained residuum.

365 gods,[25] and make it a tent / under which you go to be initiated. Also have a   100
cinnamon at your neck, for the deity is pleased by it and gave it power. And have
also the Apollo who will help you, carved from a root of laurel, with tripod standing beside him and / Pythian serpent. Carve around the Apollo the great name, in   105
Egyptian form; on his chest: BAINCHŌŌŌCHŌŌŌCHNIAB, written [the same]
forwards and backwards; and on the back of the figure this name: ILILLOU IL-
ILLOU / ILILLOU; and around the Pythian serpent and the tripod; ITHOR MAR-   110
MARAUGĒ PHŌCHŌ PHŌBŌCH. Have this too around your neck after you perform
the initiation; it is helpful in everything, along with the cinnamon.

Accordingly, as I said before, when you have purified yourself in advance [through
the last] / seven days while the moon is waning, at the dark of the moon[26] begin   115
sleeping on the ground on a pallet of rushes. Rising at dawn, greet Helios through
seven days, each day saying first the [names of the] gods of the hours, then those set
over the weeks. Also [each day], / learning who is the ruler of that day, keep after   120
him, saying, "Lord, on such-and-such a day I am calling the god to the sacred sacrifices"—doing so until the eighth day.

Then, when you come to this day, in the middle of the night at about eleven
o'clock / when there is quiet, light the altar fire and have at hand the two roosters   125
and the two lamps, lighted (the lamps should hold an eighth of a pint each, and you
must not put more oil into them). Begin to recite the stele and the mystery of the
god, which is [called?] "Scarab." Have standing by a mixing bowl containing milk
of a black cow / and wine not mixed with seawater, for this is beginning and end.[27]   130
Then, having written [the text of] the stele on the two faces of the natron plaque,
lick off the one side and, pouring [wine?] on the other, wash it off into the mixing
bowl. The natron should be written on [with ink made] both from the incense materials and from the flowers.

Then, before you drink off the milk and wine, say over it / this petition;[28] and   135
having said it, lie down on the mat, holding both the tablet and the stylus, and
say—*Hermetic* (?) [*spell*]:[29]

"I call on you who surround all things, I call in every language and in every dialect, as he first / hymned you who was by you appointed and entrusted with all   140
authorities, Helios ACHEBYKRŌM[30] (which signifies the flame and radiance of the
disk)[31] whose is the glory, AAA ĒĒĒ ŌŌŌ, because he was glorified by you—[you][32]

25. The gods of the days of the year.

26. Greek σύνοδον, the twenty-four-hour day in which the moon will come into line with the earth
and the sun.

27. I.e., essential, all important, cf. Rv 21:6; 22:13. [M.S.] Seawater was prohibited because the sea
was a symbol of Seth, the enemy of Osiris and of fertility. [R.K.R.]

28. The identity of "this petition" is not clear. The prayer on the stele has already been recited
(l. 127), the main invocation is to follow; perhaps something has fallen out. A similar problem is posed
by C, 684–95. B prescribes a prayer to the gods of the hours.

29. The Greek here is corrupt and the restoration uncertain. See above, n. 6. In B 443ff. this spell has
no such designation. The following "You who surround all things" found in all three versions refers to
the outermost celestial sphere conceived as a god, i.e., the Ogdoad. See below, n. 112.

30. *Ache* in Egyptian means "brightness." Cf. l. 34 above. [J.B.]

31. An obvious gloss. This hymn is full of such. They have been set off by parentheses and henceforth will not usually be pointed out. Many seem to be early, since they appear in both A and B.

32. As the text stands, Helios set the stars in their places and created the world in which, thereafter,
"you"—the highest god—set all things in order. This is not totally impossible, but not at all likely. Most
likely the writer attributed creation to the highest god (whom he was invoking) and did so either by
anacoluthon or by a σύ ("you," reduced to σ') before ἀέρας ("winds"), which fell out with the word it
preceded.

who set [in their places the winds] [33] and then, likewise, the stars of glittering
145   forms, and who, in divine light / create the cosmos, III AAA ŌŌŌ, in which you
have set in order all things. SABAŌTH ARBATHIAŌ ZAGOURĒ (these are the angels
who first appeared) [34] ARATH ADŌNAIE BASĒMM IAŌ. The first angel cries in 'birdglyphic' ARAI—which is ["Woe to my enemy"—and you have set him] in charge of
the punishments. Helios hymns you in hieroglyphic, LAILAM, and in Hebrew by his
own [35] name, ANOK [36] BIATHIARBAR BERBIR SCHILATOUR BOUPHROUMTRŌM
150   / (36 letters); [37] he says, 'I precede you, lord, I who rise on the boat of the sun, the
disk (?), [38] thanks to you.' Your magical [39] name in Egyptian is ALDABIAEIM" (9
letters, see below). Now he who appears on the boat rising together with you is a
155   clever / baboon; he greets you in his own language, saying 'You are the number of
[the days of] the year, ABRASAX.' [40] The falcon on the other end [of the boat] greets
you in his own language and cries out to receive food: CHI CHI CHI CHI CHI CHI
160   CHI TIP TIP TIP TIP TIP TIP TIP. He of the nine forms greets you in / hieratic, saying: MENEPHŌIPHŌTH. (He means, 'I go before you, lord'). . . ." [41]

So saying, he clapped 3 times, and the god [42] laughed 7 times [43]: "CHA CHA CHA
CHA CHA CHA CHA." When the god laughed, 7 gods were born [44] (who encompass
the cosmos—see above—for these are those who appeared before [the world was
formed]).

33. The text is corrupt; I follow Preisendanz's conjecture, ad loc.

34. This gloss interrupts a list of the first seven angels, probably thought to be the first creatures
within the cosmos, certainly the foremost subjects of the cosmocrator, Helios. We should next have a list
of their utterances, but it is broken off after the first and replaced by those of the Egyptian gods who
accompany the sun god's boat at sunrise, and among whom Helios (here the sun disk) is a minor deity
by relation to the god on the boat.

35. Reading αὑτοῦ for Preisendanz's αὐτοῦ.

36. See above, n. 21.

37. Numerical glosses of this sort, of which there are many, reflect a special interest of the compiler;
see ll. 737–57, his postscript after VIII Moses. Besides their convenience for numerological speculation, they helped copyists check their transcriptions of magical names. Not that copyists always took
advantage of the convenience. Here Preisendanz proposes to get the number of letters down to thirty-six
by omitting the final *r* of BERBIR. More interesting is the fact that the compiler evidently did not count
ANOK as part of the name, but gave it its Egyptian meaning, "I (am)."

38. "The disk" is an uncertain expansion of an abbreviation otherwise unknown.

39. φυσικόν, meaning "with power to produce physical effects."

40. The sum of the numerical values of the Greek letters *a b r a s a x* is 365. See Glossary, s.v.
"Abrasax."

41. Here the sudden change in content and style indicates that something has fallen out of the text.
What follows is a fragment from some theogonic and cosmogonic myth, an insertion which runs to
l. 206, where the invocation, here interrupted, is resumed. The insertion was found in all three versions
(C refers to it as "the account of the making of the world," but does not quote it, l. 697).

42. "The god" seems to be someone other than the preceding "he"—we have come into the middle
of some mythological scene.

43. Seven is common in cosmological contexts. Besides, Gn 1, Prof. Bergman reports that it appears,
for instance, in the temple of Esna, where, as here, seven utterances of one god become other gods. See
S. Sauneron, *Les Fêtes religieuses d'Esna* (Cairo: Imprimerie de l'Institut français d'archéologie orientale,
1962) 268–69. 2 Enoch 25–30 combined an Egyptian sequence of seven utterances that produce gods,
with the Hebrew sequence of seven commands that produce cosmic changes, and thus produced a
muddle.

44. What were born, according to the following text, were not seven but eight *pairs* of gods, not
angels, who do not encompass the cosmos but are involved in it as psychological and physical elements
(see n. 45). Therefore the words here set in parentheses look like two glosses, especially because the
wording of the second phrase echoes that of the clear gloss in l. 165 (see n. 45). However, the structure
of seven laughs—seven emanations seem basic to this cosmology. That the last pair of gods does not
come from a laugh but from a comment and an echo, makes it suspect; the list of eight looks like an

When he laughed first, / Phōs-Auge (Light-Radiance)[45] appeared and irradiated   165
everything and became god over the cosmos and fire, BESSYN BERITHEN BERIO.

Then he laughed a second time. All was water. Earth, hearing the sound, cried
out and heaved, and the water came to be divided into three parts. A god appeared;
he was given charge of the abyss [of primal waters], for without / him moisture   170
neither increases nor diminishes. And his name is ESCHAKLEŌ (for[46] you are ŌĒAI,
you are ŌN BETHELLE).

When he wanted to laugh the third time, Nous or Phrenes[47] [Mind or Wits]
appeared holding a heart,[48] because of the sharpness of the god. He was called
Hermes; he was called SEMESILAM. /

The god laughed the fourth time, and Genna [Generative Power] appeared, con-   175
trolling Spora [Procreation]. [This pair] was called BADĒTOPHŌTH ZŌTHAXATHŌZ.

He laughed the fifth time and was gloomy as he laughed, and Moira [Fate] appeared, holding scales indicating that justice was in her province. But Hermes[49]
contested / with her saying, "Justice is my province" (see above). While they were   180
fighting the god said, "What seems to be just will depend on both, but all things in
the world will be subject to you, [Moira]." And she was the first to receive the
scepter of the world—[Moira] of whom the name written first forward, then backwards, is great and holy and glorious, and it is this: THORIOBRITITAMMAŌR-
RANGADŌ Ī ŌDANGARRŌAMMATITIRBOIROTH[50] / (49 letters).   185

He laughed the sixth time and was much gladdened, and Kairos [Time] appeared
holding a scepter, indicating kingship, and he gave over the scepter to the first-
created god, [Phōs, who] receiving it, said, "You, wrapping yourself in the glory of

adaptation to the Ogdoad (see below, l. 743 and n. 112)—perhaps misunderstood as eight, rather than
four, pairs. The fact that this text was augmented by an appendix glorifying the Ogdoad (ll. 743–61), to
make up for its absence from the original form, increases our suspicion. Hence the statement that seven
gods were born is probably original. The fundamental problem presented by the text cannot be further
investigated within the limits of these notes.

45. Thus the papyrus in both passages—here (with αὐτή for αὐγή) and l. 476. This is generation in
syzygies, as in many ancient Egyptian and gnostic systems (see below, n. 111). Here the original structure may have been Phōs-Augē, Earth-Water, Nous-Phrenes, Genna-Spora, Moira-Hermes, Kairos-Basi-
lissa (i.e., Sun-Moon), Psyche-Serpent, Phobos-Iaō. In the document used by the sources of *PGM* XIII
this structure had been forgotten. Phōs and Augē had been identified, so had Nous and Phrenes. Nous
had also been identified with Hermes. Spora had been reduced to a process controlled by Genna. In at
least one version, Basilissa had been omitted. However, the original form is indicated by the needless
occurrence of a *pair* of names at each level, and the frequent pairing of magical names: BERITHEN-
BERIO, ESCHAKLEŌ-BETHELLE, HERMES-SEMESILAM, BADĒTHOPHŌTH-ZŌTHZXATHŌZ. Another piece
of evidence is the recurrence, in the Moira-Hermes and Phobos-Iaō pairs, of the story of original hos-
tility/rivalry followed by fusion of function and name. Another element true to form is that, in the Phōs-
Augē syzygy, Augē, being feminine and derivative from Phōs, is that aspect of the pair which is involved
in lower being. It is she who appears to the earth (480), and she is probably the δόξα (glory) of Phōs in
which sun and moon are clothed (189, 514–20, read αὐγήν for αυραν). So Christ is the ἀπαύγασμα
(radiance) of the Father's glory (Heb 1:3).

46. "For you are" introduces another gloss.

47. "Or Phrenes" is taken as a gloss by Preisendanz but may have come from the phrase "and Phrenes" and from an original syzygy (see above, n. 45). In privately written texts καί ("and") was often
abbreviated to *K'*, easily confused with *H* ("or").

48. From the Greek side, the heart was the seat of the intelligence in classical times; φρένες, "wits,"
literally "midriffs," had earlier been thought the seat of the intelligence, and the word continued in literary use with that sense. For the Egyptian side, cf. Bonnet, *RÄRG* 296–97, s.v. "Herz."

49. Among the things of which Hermes was patron was public speaking, especially argument in the
law courts. (The text here is extremely corrupt. I follow Preisendanz's conjecture.)

50. Double *g* in Greek is pronounced *ng*, so in the English transliteration of this palindrome the
letters *n* and *g* change places, but in Greek there is no change.

190   Phōs [Light] / will be after me. . . . .⁵¹ ANOCH BIATHIARBAR BERBIR SILATOUR
       BOUPHROUMTRŌM" (36 letters).

       When the god laughed a seventh time Psyche [Soul] came into being, and he
wept while laughing. On seeing Psyche, he hissed, and the earth heaved and gave
birth to the Pythian serpent who foreknew all things, so the god called him IL-
195 ILLOU / ILILLOU ILILLOU ILILLOU ITHŌR MARMARAUGĒ PHŌCHŌ PHŌBŌCH.
Seeing the serpent, the god was frightened and said, "Pop, pop, pop." When the
god said, "Pop, pop, pop," an armed man appeared who is called DANOUP
CHRATOR BERBALI BARBITH. Seeing him the god was again terrified, as seeing
200 someone stronger [than himself, fearing] / lest the earth had thrown up a god.
Looking down at the earth he said, "IAŌ." From the echo a god was born who is
lord of all. The preceding man contended with him, saying, "I am stronger than this
fellow." The [first] god said to the strong man, "You come from the popping noise,
and this [god] comes from an echo. Both of you will have charge of every need."
205 [The pair] was then called DANOUP / CHRATOR BERBALI BALBITH IAŌ.⁵²

       "Lord, I imitate [you by saying] the 7 vowels;⁵³ enter and hear me, A EE ĒĒĒ IIII
OOOOO YYYYYY ŌŌŌŌŌŌŌ ABRŌCH BRAŌCH CHRAMMAŌTH PROARBATHŌ IAŌ
OYAEĒIOYŌ."

210   / When the god comes in, look down and write the things he says and the Name
which he gives you for himself. And do not go out from under your canopy until he
tells you accurately, too, the things that concern you.

       The technique of determining which god is ruler of the celestial pole [at a given
time] goes as follows: Find out, child, to which god the day is subject in the Greek
215 reckoning [counting from the top down], and then coming to / *The Seven-Zoned*⁵⁴
count [the same number] from the bottom up, and you will find the answer. For if
the day be subject to Helios in the Greek reckoning, Selene rules the pole, and thus
the rest, as follows:

The Greek	The Seven-Zoned
Helios	Kronos
Selene	Zeus
220	Ares	Ares
Hermes	Helios
Zeus	Aphrodite
Aphrodite	Hermes
Kronos	Selene

225   / Of these things, child, I have declared to you the easy and godly solution which
not even kings were able to grasp.

       You are to write on the natron with the ink from the flowers of the 7 [stars] and
kinds of incense. Similarly, you are to make "the bean,"⁵⁵ which I described alle-
gorically in my *Key*, from the flowers and the kinds of incense.

       51. For the Kairos-Phōs relation, see ll. 509–19 and nn. Here the text has omitted "the Queen" (the
moon) who is the consort of Kairos in this syzygy. The following *Anoch* is again "I (am)" in Coptic.
       52. Here the cosmogonic insertion is broken off and the invocation it interrupted (above, l. 161) is
resumed.
       53. The supplement comes from the parallel, version C, l. 701. God's creative power issues in per-
petual harmony of which the seven vowels are the expression—"the music of the spheres."
       54. *The Seven-Zoned* was thought by Festugière, *La Révélation* I 343, n. 3, to be a planetary sphere,
but Festugière's opinion was based on other evidence; this author seems to have thought the thing a
table or treatise; see below, ll. 722–30.
       55. "The bean" was a bean-shaped ball of incense.

The initiation called *The Monad* has been fully declared to you, child. / Now I   230
shall add for you, child, also the practical uses of this sacred book, the things which
all the experts accomplished with this sacred and blessed book. As I made you
swear, child, in the temple of Jerusalem,[56] when you have been filled with the divine
wisdom, dispose of the book so that it will not be found.

The first, then, [of these uses] is the marvelous / *[spell for] invisibility*: Taking   235
the egg of a falcon, gild half of it and smear the other half with cinnabar. Wearing
this you will be invisible when you say the Name.[57]

To fetch a lover: Say the Name 3 times to the sun. It fetches woman to man and
man to woman in a way that will amaze you.

If you want someone to be repulsive / —either a woman to a man or a man to a   240
woman: Take a dog's excrement and put it in the post-hole of their door, saying
the Name 3 times and saying "I sever NN from NN."

If you say the Name to a demoniac while putting sulfur and asphalt to his nose,
the daimon will speak at once and will go away.[58]

If you say it over a man who has erysipelas,[59] / having rubbed him with crocodile   245
dung, he will be rid [of it] at once.

If you say the Name over a sprain or fracture 3 times, having rubbed it down
with earth and vinegar, you will make it go away.

If you say it over any bird, into its ear, it will die.

If you see an asp and want to fix it in its place, say / "Stay!" while turning your-   250
self around. When the names[60] are said it will stay.

To restrain anger: Enter the presence of a king or magnate, and while you have
your hands inside your garment say the name of the sun disk[61] while tying a knot in
your pallium or shawl.[62] You will marvel at the results.

If [you want] to break spells:[63] Having written the Name on a page of hieratic
papyrus, wear it.

To make Helios appear:[64] Say toward the east, "I am he / on the two cherubim,   255
between the two natures, heaven and earth, sun and moon, light and darkness,
night and day, rivers and sea. Appear to me, O archangel of those subject to the
cosmos, ruler Helios, set in authority under the One and Only Himself. The Eternal
and Only orders you." Say the Name. And if he appears glowering / say "Give[65] me   260

56. Pretentious hokum.

57. Presumably the Name revealed by the god in the climax of the ritual, l. 211.

58. Or, perhaps, "(the man) will speak and (the demon) will go away." For the technique, cf. Josephus, *Ant.* 8. 47.

59. Or, perhaps, "[the ἐρυσιπέλας] will go away." Cf. Mk 4:31; diseases were evil beings.

60. The plural here indicates that this list of applications drew on sources not originally connected with the preceding rite to learn the (one) Name. This probably explains the absence of the list from the other versions. "Say the Name" in many of these spells looks like an addition.

61. This, again, did not originally belong to the preceding rite. The god invoked there was not the sun god, but the creator and ruler of the sun; see 138–61. A number of similarly incompatible spells will be noticed in what follows.

62. The pallium was a cloak affected by persons claiming to be philosophers. The rare word translated "shawl" means "crosswise garment." If this magician were a Jew, it may have been the *talith*.

63. Or "as an antidote for poisons" or, most likely, both.

64. A spell of unmistakably Jewish background in which, however, the magician identifies himself with Yahweh ("he that sitteth upon the cherubim," 1 Sm 4:4; 2 Sm 6:2; etc.) and identifies Helios as an archangel. Compare the use of a Greek prayer, transliterated into Hebrew, for the same purpose, in *Sepher Ha-Razim*, ed. M. Margalioth (Jerusalem, 1966), pp. 12, 99. The prayer in our text is clearly an interpolation in the list of short (two- or three-line) prescriptions which it interrupts.

65. In these requests it is not clear whether "give" means "specify" (a time suitable for some magical operation) or "add" (to the time of my life).

a day; give an hour; give a month; give a year, lord of life." Say the Name.

If you want to kill a snake: Say, "Stay, for you are Aphyphis." And taking a green palm branch and holding its heart,[66] split it into two, saying the Name over it
265   7 times. At once the snake will be split / or will break open.

Prescience: This comes in the rite described above, that with the natron. And [you know] that the god will talk with you as with a fellow god, for I have often performed the rite when you were present.

Invisibility: Also thus: "Come to me, Darkness which appeared in the beginning, and hide me, NN, by the order of him who is self-begotten in heaven." Say the Name.

270   / *Another way*: "I call on you alone, the only one in the cosmos who gives orders to gods and men, who changes himself into holy forms and brings existence out of the nonexistent and nonexistence from existent things, holy Thayth,[67] the true sight of whose face none of the gods can endure to see; make me seem to be, to the eyes
275   of all creatures—a wolf, dog, lion, / fire, tree, vulture, wall, water, or whatever you want—for you are able." Say the Name.

Resurrection of a dead body: "I conjure you, spirit coming in air, enter, inspire,
280   empower, resurrect by the power / of the eternal god, this body; and let it walk about in this place, for I am he who acts with the power of Thayth, the holy god." Say the Name.

If you want to cross [the Nile] on a crocodile: Sit down and say, "Hear me, you who live your life in the water. I am one who is at leisure in heaven and goes about
285   in water and in fire and in air / and earth. Return the favor done you on the day when I created you and you made your request to me. You will take me [to] the other side, for I am so-and-so." Say the Name.

For release from bonds: [[Say, "Hear me, O Christ, in torments; help, in neces-
290   sities, / O merciful in violent hours, able to do much in the world, who created compulsion and punishment and torture." Say it 12 times by day,[68] hissing thrice eight times.]] Say the whole name of Helios beginning from ACHEBYKRŌM.[69]

"Let every bond be loosed, every force fail, let all iron be broken, every rope or
295   every strap, let every / knot, every chain be opened, and let no one compel me, for I am"—say the Name.

To quench fire: "Hear, fire, a work of the works of god's invention, glory of the honored luminary, be quenched, become snow, for the speaker himself is Aion who
300   puts on fire as if it were / asbestos. Let every flame be scattered from me, every physical power, by command of Him who exists forever. You shall not touch me, fire; you shall not harm my flesh, for I am"—say the Name.

66. The center of the triangular end of the branch.

67. Thoth, here and below, l. 283.

68. Not "twelve days" (Preisendanz). All these charms are for quick results, and in this case they were particularly wanted. The words in double brackets are a Christian interpolation as can be seen by the fact that it creates a doublet—a double recipe for a single purpose—and also by comparing form and content of this spell with those of the others in this series, which consistently contain just the elements left in this when the bracketed words are deleted. The interpolation is interesting as evidence that these pagan magical texts continued to be used by the newly Christian criminal class. It also makes conspicuous the absence of Christian elements from the rest of the text. Since the text with the Christian interpolation dates from the first half of the fourth century A.D., the pagan text that was interpolated was probably third century at the latest.

69. This refers to the full name given in ll. 590–92, ACHEBYKRŌN . . . IAŌ. See also ll. 78–79, and cf. ll. 141–47 and 446–53, where the elements of the name are separated by exegetic comments. The magician was to know this name by heart.

For fire to continue: "I conjure you, fire, daimon of holy love, the invisible and manifold, / the one and everywhere, to remain in this lamp at this time, shining and not dying out, by the command of NN." Say the Name.

To send dreams: Make a hippopotamus[70] of red wax, / hollow, and put into the belly of this hippopotamus both gold and silver and the so-called ballatha[71] of the Jews and array him in white linen and put him in a pure window and, taking a sheet of hieratic papyrus write on it with myrrh ink and baboon's blood / whatever you wish to send. Then, having rolled it into a wick and using it to light a new, pure lamp, put on the lamp the foot of the hippopotamus and say the Name, and he sends [the specified dream].

A philter to be drunk: Take the lion-wasps (?) in a spider's web / and, when you have ground them [to a powder, sprinkle the powder] on a drink and give it [to the appropriate person] to drink.[72]

If you want your wife[73] *not to be had by another man*: Take earth and make a crocodile, and add to it ink and myrrh, and put it into a lead coffin and write on this the great Name and that of your wife and, "Let NN not cohabit with any other man except me, NN." The name / to be written on the feet of the image is: BIBIOU OUÉR APSABARA KASONNAKA NESEBACH SPHĒ SPHĒ CHPHOURIS.

To open doors by use of the Name: "Open, open, 4 quarters of the cosmos, for the lord of the inhabited world comes forth. Archangels, decans, angels rejoice. For Aion of Aion himself, the only and / transcendant, invisible, goes through this place. Open, door! Hear, bar! Fall into two parts, lock! By the name AIA AINRY-CHATII, cast up, Earth, for the lord, all things you contain, for he is the storm-sender and controller of the abyss, master of fire. Open, for ACHEBYKRŌM commands you!" [Say ACHEBYKRŌM] 8 times; [it is] the name of Helios.

Another way. The spell for Helios: "I am he on the two cherubim, at the middle of the cosmos, between heaven and earth, light and darkness, night and day, rivers and sea. Appear to me, archangel of god, set in authority under the One and Only Himself." With this spell perform the acts of thanksgiving to Helios, rites to fetch lovers, send dreams, / ask for dreams, make Helios appear, attain goals, win victories, and in short, everything.

You have now received, child, the sacred and blessed book, *Unique*, which no one [hitherto] was able to translate[74] or put into practice. Keep well, child.[75]

*Tr.: Morton Smith. For a more extensive discussion of the composition, see Morton Smith, "The Eighth Book of Moses and How It Grew (PLeid. J 395)," in *Atti del XVII Congresso internazionale di papirologia* (Napoli: Centro Internazionale per lo studio di papiri ercolanesi, 1984) 683–93. PGM XIII (copied about A.D. 350) consists of two parts, first *The Eighth Book of Moses* (henceforth *VIII Moses*), ll. 1–733; second, a collection of miscellaneous spells, divine names, etc., ll. 734–1077.

VIII Moses consists of three parts—three different versions of a rite to get a visit from the supreme god; let us call them A (ll. 1–343), B (ll. 343–645) and C (ll. 646–734). These versions differ considerably by peripheral additions and omissions, but their essential parts are often closely parallel, though not always arranged in the same order. Because of the parallelism, questions raised by two or three have been dealt with only when they first appeared.

70. The word for "hippopotamus" here is uncertain, but written in Greek letters. See also M. J. Raven, "Wax in Egyptian Magic and Symbolism," *OMRM* 64 (1983): 7–47, esp. 17–18.

71. Unknown.

72. The expected result is not indicated. Perhaps death, but perhaps love—the wasps had been ensnared and held fast.

73. Reading γυναῖκά σου instead of Preisendanz's γυναῖκας οὐ.

74. More hokum.

75. A standard epistolary cliché. The use of epistolary beginnings and ending for treatises was a common ancient practice.

Hence readers of B and C who encounter difficulties should look for explanations in the notes on the parallel passages in A. Not all parallels are equally close, but those fairly clear are as follows:

Lines:

343–50 = 3–6	410–32 = 42–61	567–608 = 61–90
352–56 = 17–27	432–34 = 227–28	580–81 = 273–74
358 = 100–102	435–40 = 130–35	646–66 = 91–110
361–63 = 128–31	443–550 = 138–209	666–99 = 110–39
378–82 = 54–59	451ff. = 78ff.	692 = 227–28
384–88 = 35–43	562–70 = 138–209	700–701 = 206
		704–13 = 210–13
		718–30 = 213–24.

PGM XIII. 343–646

345 *The sacred, hidden book of Moses called "eighth" or "holy." [76] / This is the ritual using the name that encompasses all things. It also has directions for a meeting with the god in which you will succeed if you leave out nothing [of what is prescribed].

Keep yourself pure 41 days, having calculated the day and the hour in which the
350 last appearance of / the old moon will occur in Aries. And when the moon enters Aries sleep on the floor during the previous night, and when you have sacrificed burn also the seven approved kinds of incense [77] in which the god delights, for the seven censings of the seven stars. The incenses are these: malabathron, styrax, nard, kostos, cassia, frankincense, myrrh. [Take these] and the seven flowers of the seven
355 / stars, which are rose, lotus, narcissus, white lily, erephyllinon, gillyflower, marjoram. Having ground them all to a powder, with wine not mixed with seawater, burn all as incense. And [also] wear cinnamon, for the god has given it magical power. Burn the incenses after the twenty-first day, so as to complete [the prepara-
360 tion?]. As / food take milk of a black cow and wine without seawater and Greek natron ([the author] indicates that is beginning and end).

When the day is at hand, put aside for the sacrifice cypress wood or balsam
365 wood—so that even / without the incenses the sacrifice may give a pleasant odor— and five pinecones full of seed. And light two lamps, each holding about half a pint of oil, on this and that side of the altar. The altar, moreover, is to be made of earth. When you have prepared and filled the lamps, do not later pour any more oil into
370 them. Sacrifice an unblemished [78] white rooster, / and leave another alive, and similarly [sacrifice one] pigeon [and leave another] so that the god, when he comes in, may take the spirit from whichever he prefers. Also lay out a knife, and lay beside it the seven incenses and the seven flowers prepared [as] written [above] so that if, on
375 coming in, the god should wish to sacrifice again / he may find all in readiness. And leave the sacrifice lying on the altar.

The tasting of the victims is done [in] this way: When you are ready to taste them, sacrifice the rooster, so that [the god] may receive lots of spirit, and at the point of tasting, call on the god of the hour and him of the day, so that you may
380 have sponsorship from them. For if you do not invoke them, / they will not hear you, as being uninitiated. Now you will find [the names of] the gods of the hours and those of the days, and the compulsive formula for each of them in the *Key of Moses*, for he set them out one by one. [79]

76. The beginning of the second version; see the prefatory note above.
77. Translation dubious. Ἐπίθυμα, usually "incense," might mean "censing," which here seems required by the syntax.
78. Or one "without any fleck of color."
79. Or "brought them out [of secrecy]"? The verb means "pulled away/apart"; this use is unparalleled.

As for the name [of the great god], write all of it on the Greek natron. Instead of / the "pop, pop, pop" sound [in the name] draw on the Greek natron a falcon-   385 formed crocodile,[80] for he greets the god four times a year at the gods' true entries of new periods[81]—at the cosmos' first turning, called increase, then in his own elevation which they call "the birth / of Horus," [[then at the rising of the Dog   390 Star,]][82] then at the ascension of Sothis. At each increase of the sun and diminution he gives forth his popping noise. The nine-formed [the Ennead] gives him the power to make the noise at that time, so that the sun may ascend from the sound of water,[83] / for he himself appears together with him [the sun]. Therefore he [the   395 falcon-faced crocodile] received the forms and the power of the nine gods that rise with the sun. For at the downward turning [the autumnal equinox] he sends out the sound weaker and less / powerful, [[for this is the birth of cosmos and sun]].[84]   400 Then at the "increase" when the lights [of the heavens] begin to rise, he too sends out the noise more powerfully. And at the rise of the Dog Star, turning to the west, he sends out the noise most powerfully,[85] inasmuch as he does not have the / related   405 water near by, and because this solstice adds more [to his power], while the effects of the last equinox take away what he gained in the preceding solstice. For [the autumn equinox] is [the time of] the Nile flood's[86] departure and the sun's abasement.

Accordingly, draw the two, i.e., the falcon-faced crocodile / and the nine-formed   410 god standing on him, both with myrrhed ink. For the falcon-faced crocodile at the four turnings [of the year] greets the god with his popping noise. For coming up to breathe from the deep he goes "pop, pop, pop," / and he of the nine forms replies   415 to him antiphonally. Therefore, instead of the "pop, pop, pop" [in the god's name], draw the falcon-faced crocodile, for the "pop, pop, pop" is the first element of the name. The second is a hissing, and instead of the hissing [draw] a snake biting / its   420 tail. Thus the two elements, popping and hissing, are[87] [represented by] a falcon-

80. I.e., falcon-faced/headed. See above, l. 4 and n. 15.

81. The reference is to the four solar seasons. The "gods" are the sun and the planets, thought to accompany him. That the beginnings of the seasons are called "new moons" shows how this latter term has been generalized. The "increase" is the sun's return toward the north after the winter solstice. The falcon-faced crocodile was in part Horus (see above, n. 15); hence his elevation becomes "the birth of Horus," probably the spring equinox. (Preisendanz's reference to the winter solstice seems ruled out by the preceding "increase.") "The birth of Horus" was also a festival celebrated on the twenty-eighth of Pharmuthi (Brugsch, *Thesaurus Inscr. Aegypt.* 609. 71–72; cf. 370. 14) and in the ideal year, which began with the rising of Sirius/Sothis in July, just after the summer solstice, the twenty-eighth of Pharmuthi would have fallen near March 21, the spring equinox. Such a year actually occurred in Egypt in A.D. 139. Does this date the spell?

82. Omitting, "then (at) the rising of the Dog Star," a marginal gloss which Preisendanz put in his text. The fourth occasion of greeting, the autumn equinox, is not here specified.

83. The deity is here identified with water, and specifically with the Nile flood. Thus he sends out the popping noise (the sound of water, l. 394) most powerfully at the rise of Sirius/Sothis which begins the inundation in Egypt. At this time the god is said not to have "his kindred water" near him (ll. 404–5), because he has just begun to summon it with his popping. [R.K.R.]

84. This seems an explanatory gloss irreconcilable with the preceding location of "the birth of Horus" (the sun) at the spring equinox. The festival would not have coincided with the autumnal equinox until the end of the sixth century A.D., much too late for this fourth-century papyrus. (Its last previous coincidence was about the end of the eighth century B.C.) Plutarch, *De Is. et Os.* 52, 372B, reports a festival at "the birthday of the staff of the sun, after the fall equinox, indicating its need . . . of strengthening." This festival may explain the gloss.

85. Taking δυναμικώτερον as *litotes* for a superlative (as comparatives, in Greek, often are).

86. The Nile's flood, beginning after the summer solstice, declines before the autumn equinox.

87. Omitting καί ("and").

faced crocodile and the nine-formed god standing on it, and around these a snake and the seven vowels.

Now [the god's name] is [composed of] nine names,[88] in advance of which you
425   should say, with the [prayer on the] stele, [those of] the gods of the hours / and of the days [and] those set over the weeks, and the compulsive formula for these. For without these the god will not listen, but, thinking you uninitiated, will refuse to receive [you], unless you emphatically say to him the names of the lord of the
430   day and of the hour, / which information you will find at the end [of this tractate]. For without these you can accomplish nothing of the things you find written in the *Key*.

Then throw [the powder] of the seven flowers, which you have prepared, into the ink, and with this write on the natron. Write the same things on the two sides of the
435   plaque and lick off / the one side and wash off the other into the wine and the milk,

see page 330

first—before you wash it off—having sacrificed the rooster and made everything
440   read.[89] / Then call on the gods of the hours, as aforesaid, and then drink off [the wine and milk].[90]

"I call on you, you who surround all things, in every language, and in every di-
445   alect, I hymn you, / as he first hymned you who was by you appointed and entrusted with all authorities, Helios ACHEBYKRŌM" (which signifies the flame and radiance of the disk) "whose is the glory AAA ĒĒĒ ŌŌŌ, because he was glorified by you" (or, as other [texts read], "was given a glorious form")—"[you] who set [in
450   their places] the stars / and who, in divine light, create the cosmos, in which you have set in order all things III AAA ŌŌŌ. SABAŌTH ARBATHIAŌ ZAGOURĒ." (These are the angels who first appeared.) "ARAGA ARATH ADŌNAI BASĒMM IAŌ. The first
455   angel cries to you in birdglyphic, / 'ARAI' (which is, 'Woe to my enemy,') and you have set him in charge of the punishments. Helios hymns you thus in hieroglyphic, LAILAM, and in Hebrew by his very name, ANAG[91] BIATHIARBAR BERBI SCHI-
460   LATOUR BOUPHROUMTRŌM, / saying, 'I precede you, lord, I who rise on the boat of the sun, the disk (?), thanks to you. Your magical name in Egyptian is AL-DABAEIM." (This means the boat, on which he comes up, rising on the world.) "He
465   who appears on the boat rising together with you is a clever / baboon; he greets you in his own language, saying, 'You are the number of [the days of] the year, ABRASAX.' The falcon on the other end [of the boat] greets you in his own language and cries out, to receive food, CHI CHI CHI CHI CHI CHI CHI TI TI TI TI TI TI TI.
470   He of the nine forms greets / you in hieratic, 'MENEPHŌIPHŌTH,'" (meaning "I go before you, lord"). . . .[92]

88. The translation is conjectural, but conjecture seems required by the fact that none of the groups of names specified adds up to nine.

89. This contradicts the directions given above, ll. 369–75, and also requires more roosters than provided. Such internal inconcinnities prove version B composite. Most conspicuous is the doubling of the epiphany at the end.

90. Contrast l. 134, where the following petition precedes the drinking. For other discrepancies of detail between B and the other versions, cf. ll. 136, 440–41 (no reference to reclining), 695, and 702–3; and see above, nn. 16 and 28.

91. See above, n. 21, on l. 82. Here we have ANAG, a variant spelling of ANOCH, but equally Egyptian, not Hebrew. Several other variant spellings will occur below and be transcribed without further comment.

92. See above, l. 161. The same hiatus occurs here as in version A. Therefore both B and A were copied from a single source; but they differ considerably, therefore at least one was not copied directly from the source in which the hiatus first occurred. That source must therefore have been at least three literary generations prior to our fourth-century manuscript, and prior to it (by how many generations?) will have been the first copy of the correct text from a descendant of which (presumably) it was taken.

So saying he clapped three times and the god laughed seven times, CHA CHA CHA CHA CHA CHA CHA. When he laughed seven gods were born, who encompass all things. (For these are / those who appeared before [the world was formed].)   475

When he laughed first Phōs-Auge [Light-Radiance] appeared and divided all things, and became god over the cosmos and fire, BESEN BEREITHEN BERIO.

Then he laughed a second time—all was water, and the earth, hearing the / sound and seeing Auge, was amazed and heaved, and the water came to be divided   480 into three parts. And a god appeared and was given charge of the abyss, and therefore without him moisture neither increases nor diminishes. And his name is PROMSACHA ALEEIŌ. (For you / are ŌĒAI BETHE[LLE].)   485

When he wanted to laugh the third time Nous and Phrenes [Mind and Wits] appeared holding a heart, because of the sharpness of the god, and was called Hermes, [since it is he] by whom all things have been interpreted.[93] He is also in charge of the power of understanding by which everything is managed. / And he is   490 [called] SEMESILAMPS.

The god laughed the fourth time and Genna [Creative Force][94] appeared, controlling Spora [Procreation] of all things, by whom all things were sown, and [this pair] was called BADĒTOPHŌTH ZŌTHAXATHŌZO.

He laughed the fifth time and was gloomy as he laughed, and Moira [Fate] / appeared, holding scales, indicating that justice was in her province. But Hermes   495 contested with her, saying, "Justice is in my province." While they were fighting the god said to them, "What seems to be just / will depend on both, but all things in   500 the world will be subject to you [Moira]." And she was the first to receive the scepter of the world and was called by a holy name, fearsome and frightful, written first forwards, then backwards, and it is this: THORIOBRITI, etc. [[of whom the name written first forwards, then backwards is great / and holy and glorious, and   505 this is of great value, a powerful name: THORIOBRITITAMMAŌRRAGGADŌ I ŌDAG-GARRŌAMMATITIRBOIROTH—49 letters]].

He laughed the sixth time[95] and was much gladdened, and Kairos[96] appeared, holding a scepter, indicating kingship, and he gave over the scepter to / the first-   510 created god, [Phōs, who] receiving it said, "You, wrapping yourself in the glory of Phos [Light] will be after me, because you first gave me a scepter. All things will be subject to you, those that were before and those yet to be. All power will be in you." When he [Kairos] wrapped himself in the glory of Phos, / the character of the light   515 produced a certain effluence.[97] The god, [Phōs, then] said to the Queen,[98] "You, wrapping yourself in the effluence of Phōs, will be after him [Kairos—the sun] compassing all things. You will wax with the light you receive from him, and again you will wane because of him. With you all things will increase and / diminish." So   520

93. "Interpreted" in Greek seems to come from the same root as "Hermes."

94. The bracketed words seem a variant and expansion of the preceding text, probably with contamination from version A; cf. ll. 183–86.

95. καιρός ("time") is here not only time, but the sun god qua measure of time.

96. Here the relation of Kairos as world ruler, to Phōs, the first created god, who subjects all things to him and clothes him with his own glory (cf. Phil 2 : 9–11), is remarkably like that of Jesus as Messiah (who is to reign until he puts all enemies under his feet, 1 Cor 15 : 23–28) to the first god, the Father. The Christians have transposed the relation a step higher. Jesus himself is Phōs ("Light," Jn 1 : 7–9) and "first born of all creation" (Col 1 : 15), and the Father is the creator. However, it seems clear that the same sort of theogonic theorizing underlies both theological structures.

97. Reading ὁ δὲ τρόπος τοῦ φωτός with C. Leemans, *Papyri graeci Musei antiquarii publici Lugduni-Batavi*, vol. II (Leiden: Brill, 1885) ad loc.

98. The moon, probably Artemis-Selene-Isis.

the great and marvellous name is, ANAG BIATHIAR BARBERBI SCHILATOUR BOU-PHROUNTŌRM (36 letters).

He laughed the seventh time, breathing hard, and Psyche [Soul] came into being and all things were moved. So the god said, "You will move all things, and all shall
525 be made glad / so long as Hermes guides you." When the god said this all things were moved and filled with spirit unrestrainably. The god, seeing this, said, "Pop, pop, pop," and all things were terrified, and on account of the popping noise Pho-
530 bos [Fear] appeared, armed. So he is called DANOUP CHRATŌR / BERBALI BAL-BITHI (26 letters).

Then, looking down at the earth, the god gave a loud hiss and the earth was opened, receiving the echo. It gave birth to a creature of its own, the Pythian ser-pent, who foreknew all things through the utterance of the god. Its name is great
535 and / holy, ILILLOUI ILILLOUI ILILLOUI ITHŌR MARMARAUGĒ PHŌCHŌ PHŌ-BŌCH. When he appeared the earth heaved and was raised much higher, but the celestial pole stayed unmoved, so when they were about to collide the god said
540 "IAŌ," and everything was fixed in place / and a great, supreme god appeared who established the things that were before in the cosmos and the things yet to be, so that none of the aerial bodies was thenceforth out of place.

Phobos, seeing someone stronger than himself, opposed him, saying, "I am prior
545 to you." He, however, said, "But I fixed all things [in their places]." So the / [first] god said [to the serpent], "You come from an echo, but this god from an utterance. Now an utterance is better than an echo. However, [he said to Iao],[99] "the power of you, who appeared last, will derive from both, so that all things may be fixed in their places." And he was thenceforth called by the great and marvelous name
550 DANOUP CHRATŌR / BERBALI BALBITH IAŌ. And wishing to give honor also to the one who had assisted him, as having appeared together with him, the first god gave him precedence of the nine gods and possession of power and glory equal to theirs.
555 / And he was called [by a name derived] from the nine gods, as having taken away, along with their power, also the initials of their names, BOSBEADII,[100] and from the seven planets AEĒIOYŌ EĒIOYŌ ĒIOYŌ IOYŌ OYŌ YŌ Ō ŌYOIĒEA YOIĒEA OIĒEA IĒEA
560 ĒEA EA A— / when written forwards and backwards this is great and marvelous. But his greatest name, which is this following, is great and holy (of 27 letters) ABRŌCH BRAŌCH CHRAMMAŌTH PRŌARBATHŌ IAŌ. Another version: ABRŌCH BRAŌCH CHRAMMAŌTH PRŌARBATHŌ IAŌ OY AEĒIOYŌ.

565 When, then, the god comes in, / look down and write the things said and what-ever name he may give you for himself. And do not let him go out from under your canopy until he also tells you the things that concern you.

Now the text of the sacred stele to be written in the natron is as follows—and the invocation runs thus, as here given altogether accurately:
570 / "I call on you, the creator of all, who are greater than all, you, the self-begotten god, who see all and hear all and are not seen. For you gave Helios all the glory and
575 the power, / Selene the privilege to wax and wane and have fixed courses, yet you took nothing from the earlier-born darkness, but assigned them equality [with it?]. For when you appeared, both order arose and light appeared, and all things were

---

99. Since in this version only the serpent was born of an echo, and since the last half of the god's speech must be addressed to Iaō, the change of interlocutor, indicated by the translation, just be conjec-tured. Presumably the text is corrupt. Cf. the A version, ll. 191–206, which, however, may have been produced by excision of the difficulties. That the more difficult text is apt to be the original is a well-known rule.

100. In spite of this clue the names remain uncertain.

arranged by you. Therefore all things are also / subject to you, whose true form 580
none of the gods can see, who take different forms in [different] visions, Aion of
Aion.

"I call on you, lord, that you may show me your true form. For under your order
I serve / your angel, ANOG BIATHIABAR BERBI SCHILATOUR BOUPHROUNTŌRM, 585
and your fear DANOUP CHRANTŌR BELBALI BALBITH IAŌ. Through you arose the
[celestial] pole and the earth.

"I call on you, lord, as do those gods who appeared through you that they /
may have power, ACHEBYKRŌM, whose is the glory, AAA ĒĒĒ ŌŌŌ III AAA ŌŌŌ 590
SABAOTH ARBATHIAŌ ZAGOURĒ, the god ARATH ADŌNAI BASYMM IAŌ.

"I call on you, lord, in birdglyphic, ARAI; hieroglyphic, LAILAM; Hebraic, ANAG,
/ BIATHIARBAR BERBI SCHILATOUR BOURPHOUNTŌRM; Egyptian, ALDABAEIM; 595
baboonic, ABRASAX; falconic, CHI CHI CHI CHI CHI CHI [CHI] ti ti ti ti ti ti ti;
hieratic, MENEPHŌIPHŌTH / CHA CHA CHA CHA CHA CHA CHA." 600

Then clap three times, TAK TAK TAK, go "pop, pop, pop" for a long time; hiss a
great hiss, that is, one of some length.

"Come to me, lord, faultless, who pollute no place, joyful, unflawed, for I call on
/ you, King of kings, Tyrant of tyrants, most glorious of the glorious, daimon of 605
daimons, most warlike of the warlike, most holy of the holy. Come to me, willing,
joyful, unflawed."

An angel will come in, and you say to the angel, "Greetings, lord. Both initiate
me by these rites [101] I am performing / and present me [to the god], and let the fate 610
determined by my birth be revealed to me." And if he says anything bad, say, "Wash
off from me the evils of fate. Do not hold back, but reveal / to me everything, by 615
night and day and in every hour of the month, to me, NN, son of NN. Let your
auspicious form be revealed to me, for under your [order] I serve [your] angel,
ANAG BIATHI." (Repeat the formula.)

"I call on you, lord, holy, much hymned, greatly honored, ruler of the cosmos, /
[[Sarapis]];[102] consider my birth and turn me not away, me, NN whom NN [bore], 620
who know your true name and valid name, ŌAŌĒŌ ŌEOĒ IAŌ IIIAAŌ THOUTHĒ
THĒ AATHŌ ATHĒROUŌR AMIATHAR MIGARNA CHPHOURI IYEYĒOŌAEĒ A EE ĒĒĒ
/ IIII OOOOO YYYYYY ŌŌŌŌŌŌŌ SEMESILAMMPS AEĒIOYŌ ĒŌOYE LINOUCHA 625
NOUCHA HARSAMOSI [103] ISNORSAM OTHAMARMIM ACHYCH CHAMMŌ. I call on
you, lord; I hymn your holy power in a musical hymn, AEĒIOYŌŌ." [104] / Burn in- 630
cense, saying, "ĒIOYŌ IOYŌ OYŌ YŌ Ō A EE ĒĒĒ IIII OOOOO YYYYYY ŌŌŌŌŌŌŌ
ŌĒŌAŌAŌ OOOYO IIIIIAO IIYYYOAĒA YO. Protect me from all my own astrological
destiny; destroy my / foul fate; apportion good things for me in my horoscope; 635
increase my life even in the midst of many goods, for I am your slave and peti-
tioner and have hymned your valid and holy name, lord, glorious one, ruler of

101. Literally, "Initiate me in/by these my matters."

102. Sarapis (like Christ above, in ll. 289–92) is elsewhere of no importance in this text. Therefore
his name here and in l. 640 below is probably interpolated. However, this does not prove that the whole
section in which the name occurs is an interpolation. The section has the ideas and vocabulary of the rest
of the text, and understandably follows the visit of the angel as a spell to introduce the magician to the
supreme god himself. That no epiphany follows may be due either to the loss of the end of the text that
the compiler was using or to his desire to subordinate this to the C version, which now begins immediately, is much abbreviated, and so leads quickly to the final meeting with the god.

103. HARSAMOSI is "Horus the Elder." [R.K.R.] Other divine names are also embedded in the spell:
IAŌ, THOUTHE (probably from Thoth), SEMESILAM.

104. The seven Greek vowels, represented by the first seven letters of this group, were equated with
the notes of the musical scale, and so represented the basic harmony.

640 the cosmos, of ten thousand names (?),[105] greatest, nourisher, apportioner, /
[[Sarapis]]."

Having drawn in spirit with all your senses, say the first[106] name in one breath to
the east, the second to the south, the third to the north, the fourth to the west, and
having knelt to the left [on] your right knee once, say to the earth once and to the
645 moon once, to water once and to sky once, "ŌAOĒ ŌŌ EOĒIAŌ / III AAŌ THĒ THOU
THĒ AATHŌ ATHĒROYŌ" (36 letters).
*Tr.: Morton Smith.

PGM XIII. 646–734

*Have[107] a tablet on which you will write what he says to you, and a knife so that,
clean from all [impurities], you may kill the sacrifices, and a libation, that you may
650 pour one. Have all these / ready nearby you. And you be in clean linens, crowned
with an olive wreath. Prepare the canopy thus: taking a clean sheet write on the
655 border [the names of] the 365 gods. Make it like a tent / under which you go to be
initiated. Also have cinnamon at your neck, for the deity is pleased by it and gave it
power. And have also the Apollo who will help you, carved from a root of laurel,
660 / with tripod standing beside him and Pythian serpent. Carve around the Apollo
the great name in Egyptian form: on his chest this,[108] BAINCHŌŌŌCHŌŌŌCHNIAB,
665 written [the same] forwards and backwards; / on the back of [the] figure this name:
ILILLOU ILILLOU ILILLOU; and around the Pythian serpent and the tripod: ITHŌR
MARMARAUGĒ PHŌCHŌ PHŌBŌCH. Have this, too, around your neck when you
670 perform the initiation; / it is helpful in everything, along with the cinnamon.

Accordingly, as I said before, when you have purified yourself in advance [through
the last] seven days while the moon is waning, at the dark of the moon begin sleeping on the ground. Rising at dawn, greet the sun [Helios] through seven days, each
675 day saying first the [names of the] / gods of the hours, then those set over the
weeks. Also [each day], learning who is the ruler of that day, keep after him, saying,
"Lord, on such-and-such a day I am calling the god to the sacred sacrifices"—doing
so until the eighth day.

680 Then, / coming to this day, in the middle of the night, when there is quiet, light
the altar fire and have at hand the two roosters and the two lamps, lighted, into
685 which you must not put any more oil. Now begin to recite the stele and the / mystery of the god. Have standing by a mixing bowl containing milk of a black cow and
wine not mixed with seawater, for this is beginning and end. Then having written
on one side of the natron [plaque, the text of] the stele which begins "I call on you,
690 who are greater than all," / etc., as given above, lick it off, and pouring [wine?] on
the other side, on which is the figure drawing,[109] wash it off into the mixing bowl.
The natron should be written [with ink made] both from the incense materials and
695 from the flowers. Then, before you drink off the milk and the wine, / say over it this
petition and having said it lie down on the mat, holding the tablet and the stylus,
and recite the account of creation which begins, "I call on you who surround all

105. Reading μυριώνυμε for the papyrus's μυρικωτατες, and Preisendanz's μυριώτατε (otherwise
unknown?).
106. "First" of those in this section; above, ll. 622–27.
107. Here version C of the main ritual begins, paralleling version A, ll. 91–110, where the notes on
features common to both texts will be found.
108. Preisendanz's supplement, ὄνομα, is needless.
109. Of the nine-formed god standing on a falcon-faced crocodile inside an ouroboros, above,
ll. 39–45 and parallel. Contrast versions A and B in which the prayer is to be written on both sides of
the tablet, ll. 131 and 434.

things, I call in every language and in every dialect," etc. And when / you come to 700
the vowels, say, "Lord, I imitate you by [saying] the seven vowels; enter and hear
me." Then repeat the name [composed] of the 27 letters. You should be lying on a
rush mat spread under you on the ground.

Now when the god comes in do not stare / at his face, but look at his feet while 705
beseeching him, as written above, and giving thanks that he did not treat you con-
temptuously, but you were thought worthy of the things about to be said to you for
correction of your life. You, then, ask, "Master, what is fated for me?" And he will
tell you even / about your star, and what kind of daimon you have, and your horo- 710
scope and where you may live and where you will die. And if you hear something
bad, do not cry out or weep, but ask that he may wash it off or circumvent it, for
this god can do everything. Therefore, when you begin questioning, / thank him 715
for having heard you and not overlooked you. Always sacrifice to this [god] in this
way and offer your pious devotions, for thus he will hear you.

*The technique of determining which god is ruler of the celestial pole [at a given
time,] goes as follows*: Find out, child, to which god the day is subject in the Greek
reckoning, / and then, coming to the "Seven-Zoned," count from the bottom up, 720
and you will find the answer. For if the day be subject to Helios in the Greek reckoning, Selene rules the pole, and thus the rest, as follows:

Greek		The Seven-Zoned
Helios	The Monad of	Kronos
Selene	Moses,	Zeus
Ares	which is also a table	Ares
Hermes	called "The Seven-	Helios
Zeus	Zoned."	Aphrodite
Aphrodite		Hermes
Kronos		Selene

The Eighth, Hidden Book of Moses.[110] In another [manuscript] I found was written,
The Hidden Book of Moses concerning the Great Name, or,[111] *For Everything, in which
is the Name of Him Who Governs All.*
*Tr.: Morton Smith.

PGM XIII. 734–1077
*You should also take, child, for this personal / vision, [a list of] the gods of the 735
days and the hours and the weeks, those given in the book, and the twelve rulers of
the months, and the seven-letter name which is in the first book, and which you
also have written in the *Key*, which [name] is great and marvelous, as it is what
brings alive all your books. / I have also set out for you the oath that precedes each 740
book, since, when you have learned the power of the book, you are to keep it secret,
child, for in it there is the name of the lord, which is Ogdoas,[112] the god who com-

110. As often in ancient manuscripts, the title follows the text. Perhaps it did so in l. 344 and was
there fused with the beginning title of version B.

111. Reading "or" for Preisendanz's "which" (ἤ for ἡ). Evidently the copyist knew at least three
manuscripts.

112. An "ogdoad" is something composed of eight members or elements. Capitalized, the term is
used especially for a set of eight Egyptian gods, considered as a unit. They consisted of four pairs, representing the masculine and feminine aspects of the primeval world (Bonnet, *RÄRG* 5–6, s.v. "Achtheit";
cf. the similar "Ennead" discussed in n. 15 above). [R.K.R. adds that they were celebrated in the creation
myth of Hermopolis—in Egyptian, "Eight-Town"—as those who brought forth the universe. He refers

745   mands and directs all things, since to him angels, archangels, he-daimons, / she-daimons, and all things under the creation have been subjected.

There are also prefaced four other names, that of nine letters and that of fourteen letters and that of twenty-six letters and that of Zeus. You may use these on boy-
750   mediums who do not see the gods, so / that one will see unavoidably, and for all spells and needs: inquiries, prophecies by Helios, prophecies by visions in mirrors. And for the compulsive spell you should use the great name which is Ogdoas, the god who directs all things throughout the creation. [For] without him simply
755   nothing / will be accomplished. Learn and conceal, child, the name [composed] of the nine letters, AEĒ EĒI OYŌ, and that of the fourteen letters, YSAU SIAUE IAŌUS, and that of the twenty-six letters, ARABBAOUARABA (to be written forwards and backwards),[113] the name of Zeus, CHONAI IEMOI CHO ENI KA ABIA SKIBA PHO-ROUOM EPIERTHAT.

760   / *Here is the instruction [for recitation] of the heptagram,*[114] *and the spell to which the god gives attention: (The spell)* :

"Come to me, you from the four winds, ruler of all, who breathed spirit into men for life, whose is the hidden and unspeakable name—it cannot be uttered by hu-
765   man mouth / —at whose name even the daimons, when hearing, are terrified, whose is the sun, ARNEBOUAT BOLLOCH BARBARICH B BAALSAMĒN PTIDAIOY AR-NEBOUAT, and [the] moon, ARSENPENPRŌOUTH BARBARAIŌNE OSRAR MEMPSE-
770   CHEI—they are unwearied eyes / shining in the pupils of men's eyes—of whom heaven is head, ether body, earth feet, and the environment water, the Agathos Daimon. You are the ocean, begetter of good things and feeder of the civilized
775   world. Yours is the eternal processional way[115] / in which your seven-lettered name is established for the harmony of the seven sounds [of the planets which] utter their voices according to the twenty-eight forms of the moon, SAR APHARA APHARA I
780   ABRAARM ARAPHA ABRAACH PERTAŌMĒCH / AKMĒCH IAŌ OYE Ē IAŌ OYE EIOY AEŌ EĒOY IAŌ. Yours are[116] the beneficent effluxes of the stars, daimons and For-tunes and Fates, by whom is given wealth, good old age, good children, good luck,
785   a good burial.[117] And you, lord of life, King of the heavens and the / earth and all things living in them, you whose justice is not turned aside, you whose glorious name the Muses sing, you whom the eight guards attend, Ē Ō CHŌ CHOUCH NOUN
790   NAUNI AMOUN AMAUNI;[118] you who have / truth that never lies. Your name and

---

to Morenz, *Egyptian Religion* 175–77.] As gods who produced the cosmos, like those of Hesiod's *The-ogony*, they interested Greeks who speculated about cosmology. Since the precosmic world was that of divine perfection, they came to be thought both a heaven above the seven planetary heavens, and a deity above the cosmic gods. Greek speculation about a divine sphere beyond those of the planets was happy to find in them an ancient, arcane, and prestigious prototype. Hence their name became a popular term in second-century A.D. and later theosophy; it figures in Hermetic, Neoplatonic, and Christian writings, both "orthodox" and "gnostic," and reflections are found even in rabbinic literature. Such popularity accounts for this postscript, adding the fashionable Egyptian name to the preceding collection, which had lacked it. Perhaps the collection was made before the name became truly popular.

113. In the Greek text this direction is abbreviated to α′ (for ἀναγραμματίζε), of which Preisen-danz did not see the meaning.

114. I.e., the seven vowels. More pretentious terminology.

115. Of the sky, in which the luminaries revolve.

116. Reading σοῦ for οὑ, in accordance with Preisendanz's emendation in the parallel text, XII. 254.

117. This list of divine gifts (while admittedly at home in most cultures) is quite Egyptian in its emphasis on "good old age" and "good burial." Cf. the standard prayer, "that he be buried in the ne-cropolis of the desert in good old age," K. Sethe, *Urkunden des alten Reiches* (Leipzig: Hinrichs, 1933), vol. I, p. 120, and many parallels. [R.K.R.]

118. These are the names of the members of the Hermopolitan Ogdoad (see above, n. 112, and

your spirit rest upon the good. Come into my mind and my understanding for all the time of my life and accomplish for me all the desires of my soul. /

For you are I, and I, you. Whatever I say must happen, for I have your name as a unique phylactery in my heart, and no flesh, although moved, will overpower me; no spirit will stand against me—neither daimon nor visitation nor any other of the evil beings of Hades, / because of your name, which I have in my soul and invoke. Also [be] with me always for good, a good [god dwelling] on a good [man], yourself immune to magic, giving me health no magic can harm, well-being, prosperity, glory, victory, power, sex appeal. Restrain the evil eyes / of each and all of my legal opponents, whether men or women, but give me charm in everything I do. ANOCH AIEPHE SAKTIETĒ BIBIOU BIBIOU SPHĒ SPHĒ NOUSI NOUSI SEĒE SEĒE SIETHŌ SI-ETHŌ OUN CHOUNTIAI SEMBI IMENOUAI BAINPHNOUN PHNOUTH TOUCHAR SOUCHAR SABACHAR ANA[119] of [the] god IEOU ION EON THŌTHŌ / OUTHRO THRŌRESE ERIŌPŌ IYĒ AĒ IAŌAI AEĒIOYŌ AEĒIOYŌ ĒOCH MANEBI CHYCHIŌ AL-ARAŌ KOL KOL KAATŌN KOLKANTHŌ BALALACH ABLALACH OTHERCHENTHE BOULŌCH / BOULŌCH OSERCHNTHE MENTHEI,[120] for I have received the power of Abraham, Isaac, and Jacob, and of the great god, daimon IAŌ ABLANATHANALBA SIABRATHILAŌ LAMPSTĒR IĒI ŌŌ, god. Do [it], lord PERTAŌMECH / CHACHMĒCH IAŌ OYĒE IAŌ OYĒE IEOU AĒŌ EĒOY IAŌ."

The instruction: Speaking to the rising sun, stretching out your right hand to the left and your left hand / likewise to the left, say "A." To the north, putting forward only your right fist, say "E." Then to the west, extending both hands in front [of you], say "Ē." To the south, / [holding] both on your stomach, say, "I." To the earth, bending over, touching the ends of your toes, say "O." Looking into the air, having your hand on your heart, say "Y." Looking into the sky, having both hands on your head, say "Ō:"

795

800

805

810

815

820

825

830

		sky		835
A	Ō Ō Ō Ō Ō Ō		IIII	
east	Ō Ō Ō Ō Ō Ō O		south	
air	Y Y Y Y Y Y			
north	E E O O O O O Ē Ē Ē		west	840
		earth		

"I call on you, eternal and unbegotten, who are one, who alone hold together the whole creation of all things, whom none understands, whom the gods worship, / whose name not even the gods can utter. Inspire from your exhalation (?),[121] ruler

845

K. Sethe, *Amun und die Acht Urgötter von Hermopolis* [Berlin: de Gruyter, 1929], p. 65 and pl. I). The pairs are *Ḥḥ* and *Ḥḥ.t* ("Expansiveness" and "Female Expansiveness"), *Kk* and *Kk.t* ("Darkness" and "Female Darkness," cf. CHŌŌŌCH, "darkness," in BAINCHŌŌŌCH with the CHOUCH here), *Nwn* and *Nwn.t* ("Abyss" and "Female Abyss" *sc.* of water), and *Imn* and *Imn.t* ("the Hidden" and "the Female Hidden"). Cf. *PGM* XIII. 743 and XXI. 20. [R.K.R.] It should be noticed, too, that here the Ogdoad are merely assistants—the "eight guards" who "attend" the highest god—whereas in the preceding two paragraphs, which we saw reason to think interpolated (above, n. 112), the Ogdoad was itself and as a unit the supreme god. Detailed textual analysis is impossible here, but it seems clear that different sources have been used, and likely, that different writers used them.

119. Possibly "I [am]" in Aramaic, transliterated into Greek.

120. Besides the initial ANOCH "I am," this list has many Egyptian words: BAINPHOUN, "spirit of Nun" (the abyss); PHNOUTH, "the god"; THŌTHŌ, "Thoth the great"; OSERCHENTHE MENTHEI, "Osiris the foremost of the westerners," the standard epithet of Osiris. [R.K.R.]

121. Dubious restoration, in Preisendanz's text, of a word here plausible, but otherwise unknown.

of the pole, him who is under you; accomplish for me the NN thing.

"I call on you as by the voice of the male gods, IĒŌ OYE ŌĒI YE AŌ EI ŌY AOĒ OYĒ
850 / EŌA YĒI ŌEA OĒŌ IEOU AŌ. I call on you, as by the voice of the female gods, IAĒ
EŌO IOY EĒI ŌA EĒ IĒ AI YO ĒIAY EŌO OYĒE IAŌ ŌAI EOYĒ YŌĒI IŌA. I call on you,
855 as the winds / call you. I call on you, as the dawn." (Looking toward dawn [say], "A
EE ĒĒĒ IIII OOOOO YYYYY ŌŌŌŌŌŌŌ.") "I call on you as the south." (Looking
860 to the south say, "I OO YYY ŌŌŌŌ AAAAA EEEEE ĒĒĒĒĒĒĒ.") / "I call on you as the
west." (Standing [facing] the west, say, "E II OOO YYYY ŌŌŌŌŌ AAAAAA EEEEEEE.")
"I call on you as the north." (Standing looking toward the north say, "Ō AA EEE
865 ĒĒĒĒ IIIII OOOOOO YYYYYYY.") "I call on you / as the earth." (Looking toward the
earth say, "E ĒĒ III OOOO YYYYY ŌŌŌŌŌŌ AAAAAAA.") "I call on you as the sky."
(Looking into the sky say, "Y ŌŌ AAA EEEE ĒĒĒĒĒ IIIII OOOOOOO.") "I call on you
870 as the cosmos, "O YY ŌŌŌ AAAA / EEEEE ĒĒĒĒĒ IIIIIII. Accomplish for me NN
thing, quickly. I call on your name, the greatest among gods. If I say it complete,
there will be an earthquake, the sun will stop and the moon will be afraid and the
875 rocks and the mountains and the sea and the rivers / and every liquid will be petri-
fied; the whole cosmos will be thrown into confusion. I call on you, IYEYO ŌAEĒ
IAŌ AEĒ AI EĒ AĒ IOYŌ EYĒ IEOU AĒŌ ĒI ŌĒI IAĒ IŌOYĒ AYĒ YĒA IŌ IŌAI IŌAI ŌĒ
880 / EE OY IŌ IAŌ, the great name. Become for me lynx, eagle, snake, phoenix, life,
power, necessity, images of god, AIŌ IŌY IAŌ ĒIŌ AA OYI AAAA E IY IŌ ŌĒ IAŌ AI
885 AŌĒ OYEŌ AIEĒ IOYE YEIA EIŌ ĒII YY EE ĒĒ ŌAOĒ / CHECHAMPSIMM CHANGALAS
EĒIOY IĒEA ŌOĒOE (seven of the auspicious [names?]) ZŌIŌIĒR ŌMYRYROMRO-
MOS." [Say it?] thus, extending the second AIŌ: "Ē II YY ĒĒ OAOĒ."

This initiation is performed to the suns[122] of the thirteenth day of the month,
890 when the gold lamella is licked / off and one says over it: "IAIA IY OĒ IEYOŌ ĒŌI EO
Ē ŌY EĒ YŌĒ ŌŌO ŌŌI ŌAŌ EŌ OĒ YŌ." Then more completely, "AŌEYĒ OAI IO
895 ĒYEŌA OYŌ ŌO EI OY ĒO OIYY ŌYY ŌI A / EE ĒĒĒ IIII OOOOO YYYYY ŌŌŌŌŌŌŌ
AŌ EOĒ EŌĒ IAA ĒŌI ĒIŌ. In [the] initiation these things are said six times with all
[the rest?], and the seven vowels are written on the gold lamella to be licked off, and
900 on the silver lamella the seven vowels for the phylactery / OĒŌ AŌ OOO YOIĒ OY YĒI
SORRA THŌŌM CHRALAMPĒAPS ATOYĒGI. The following series of vowels [are written as] "wings";[123] and on the gold lamella write this: AŌEYĒOI; on the silver:
IOĒYEŌA, . . .[124]

905
AEĒIOYŌ	AEĒIOYŌŌ	AEĒIOYŌOYŌ
EĒIOYŌA	EĒIOYŌŌA	EĒIOYŌOYŌA
ĒIOYŌAE	ĒIOYŌŌAE	ĒIOYŌOYŌAE
IOYŌAEĒ	IOYŌŌAEĒ	IOYŌOYŌAEĒ
OYŌAEĒI	OYŌŌAEĒI	OYŌOYŌAEĒI
YŌAEĒIO	YŌŌAEĒIO	YŌOYŌAEĒIO
ŌAEĒIOY	ŌŌAEĒIOY	ŌOYŌAEĒIOY

910

and[125] the great heaven, eternal, incorruptible, OĒŌ AŌ THOOU OIĒ OY YĒI OR-
915 CHRA THŌŌMCHRA SEMESILAMPS / ATOYĒTI DROUSOUAR DROUĒSRŌ GNIDA

122. Of dawn, midday, and sunset (Preisendanz).
123. I.e., in triangles, produced by writing the words in successive lines, but in each line dropping
one letter from the same end (usually the front) until only one is left. A "wing" is the technical term in
magical jargon for the resultant form.
124. Something, probably directions from another rite, seems to have fallen out of the text. It resumes near the end of another spell.
125. This has no clear connection to the preceding vowels, so Preisendanz conjectures a lacuna.
However, this may be the continuation of the lost spell in which the vowels stood.

BATAIANA ANGASTA AMASOUROUR OUANA APAISTOU OUANDA ŌTI SATRAPERK-
MĒPH ALA Dionysus, blessed EYIE YOY YYY THENŌR conducting YYY EYEYEY YE
OYŌ XERTHENATHIA THAPHTHŌ / OIKROU ŌR ARAX GŌ Ō AAA ERARĒRAYIIĒR   920
THOUTH ASĒSENACHTHŌ LARNIBAI AIOŌ KOUPHIŌ ISŌTHŌNI PATHENI IEEEN-
THĒR PANCHOCHITAS OYE TIASOUTH PACHTHEESTH HYSEMMIGADŌN / ORTHŌ   925
BAUBŌ NOĒRADĒR SOIRE SOIRE SANKANTHARA ERESCHIGAL APARA KEŌPH IAŌ
SABAŌTH ABRATIAŌTH ADŌNAI ZAGOURĒ HARSAMOSI RANAKERNŌTH LAMP-
SOUŌR.[126] Therefore, I am brought together with you by the great commander-
in-chief Michael, lord, the great archangel of IEOY AĒ AIŌ EYAI / I Ē IĒ IŌA IĒIĒ AIŌ   930
EĒ AIŌ. Therefore, I am conjoined [127] [with you], O great one, and I have you in my
heart AŌ EĒ EŌĒI AIAĒ ŌĒ IŌAŌ EOĒE ŌĒI AAĒ ŌĒIŌ.

As the revelator Orpheus[128] *handed down in his private note*: "OISPAĒ IAŌ /
OYEA SEMESILAM AĒOI, son, CHOLOUE ARAARACHARARA ĒPHTHISIKĒRE ŌĒEYAIĒ   935
OIAI EAĒ EAĒ ŌEA BORKA BORKA PHRIX RIX ŌRZA ZICH MARTHAI OYTHIN LI-
LILILAM LILILILŌOU AAAAAAA ŌŌŌŌŌŌŌ / MOUAMECH, fluid boundary, AĒŌ ŌEA   940
ĒŌA." (Breathe out, in. Fill up); "EI AI OAI" (pushing more, bellow-howling.)
"Come to me, god of gods, AĒŌĒI ĒI IAŌ AE OIŌTK" (Pull in, fill up, / shutting your   945
eyes. Bellow as much as you can, then, sighing, give out [what air remains] in a hiss.)

Erotylos, in his "Orphica": [129] "YOĒEŌAI ŌAI YOĒEAI YOĒEŌ EREPE EYA / NAR-   950
BARNE ZAGEGŌĒ ĒCHRAĒM KAPHNAMIAS PSIIPHRI PSAIARORKIPHKA BRAKIŌ
BOLBALOCH SIAILASI MAROMALA MARMISAI BIRAITHATHI ŌO."

And Hieros[130] *writes thus*: "MARCHŌTH SAĒRMACHŌTH ZALTHAGAZATHA /
BABATHBATHAATHAB A III AAA OOO[131] ŌŌŌ ĒĒĒ ŌNTHĒR." Then, "Depth   955
AUMŌLACH."

And as it stands in the "Holy Name" pronounced by Thphes, the sacred scribe to
King Ochos: [132] "NETHMOMAŌ / MARCHACHTHA CHTHAMAR ZAXTHTHARN MA-   960
CHACH ZAROKOTHARA ŌSS IAŌ OUĒ SIALŌR TITĒ EAĒ IAŌ ĒS ZEATHE AAA ĒEEOY
THŌBARRABAU."

And in the Memoranda / of Euenos[133] he says the name is pronounced by the   965
Egyptians [and] the Syrians "CHTHETHŌNI."

As Zoroaster[134] *the Persian in* . . . "RNISSAR PSYCHISSAR."

And as is said in the works of / Pyrrhus: [135] "ZZA AAA EEE BBMŌEA ANBIŌŌŌ."   970

And as Moses says in the Archangelic [Teaching?] : [136] "ALDAZAŌ BATHAM MA-

126. Besides the Hebrew, Aramaic, and Egyptian divine names now familiar, this list has Baubo,
a comic figure from Eleusinian legend, and Ereschigal, the ancient Mesopotamian queen of the
underworld.

127. The verb is συνίστημι, usually "introduce, present," but the context here seems to require
some closer connection. Cf. above, ll. 795–804.

128. Orpheus, the legendary Thracian singer, had by this time become famous as a revelator. Many
bogus works were attributed to him; nothing is known of this one.

129. Or "as quoted in the *Orphica*." The translation given in the text follows Berthelot and Ruelle,
Collection des anciens alchimistes grecs I, 17. An Erotylus was once cited by the alchemist Zosimus as an
authority on "the All" (*ibidem*, III, 144). He is otherwise unknown.

130. Unknown?

131. Reading OOO for ŌOO, since the adjacent groups are all triplets of a single letter.

132. Ochos was Artaxerxes III, 358–338 B.C. Thphēs is unknown, and the conversation was probably fictitious.

133. Several authors named Euenos are known, but nothing connects any of them with this statement.

134. Zoroaster, like Orpheus, was a favorite victim of forgers, one of whom produced this.

135. We know of many men named Pyrrhus, but of none likely to have written this.

136. *The Archangelic Teaching* (?) of "Moses" is again cited in the Nag Hammadi documents (II. 5.
102) and may be reflected by a medieval manuscript which quotes an "archangelic hymn" given to

CHŌR," or "BA ADAM MACHŌR RIZXAĒ ŌKEŌN PNED MEŌYPS PSYCH PHRŌCH
PHER PHRŌ IAOTHCHŌ."

975   */ And as it is explained in Hebrew in "The Law"*:[137] "Abraham, Isaac, Jacob,
AĒŌ ĒOA ŌAĒ IEOY IEĒ IEO IAŌ IA ĒI AO EĒ OE EŌ."

   And as in the fifth book of the Ptolemaica,[138] the most excellent book entitled
980   */ One and the Whole.* (It contains [an account of] the birth of the spirit of fire and
of darkness:) "Lord of [the] Aion, who created all things, only god, unutterable,
985 THOROKOMPHOUTH PSONNAN / NEBOUĒTI TATTAKINTHAKOL SOONSOLOUKE
SOLBOSEPHĒTH BORKA BORKA PHRINX RIXŌ ZADICH AMARCHTHA IOU CHORIN
LI LI LAM LAM AAAAAAA IIIIIII ŌŌŌŌŌŌŌ EMACH ĒĒĒ NACH LILILI LAM CHENĒ
990 / LILILI ŌOY AĒŌ ŌAĒ IŌA ŌŌŌ ĒĒĒ, fluid boundary, MOTHRAĒ EIA OYŌ AOYE THOP-
TOCH A ŌŌ YYY OOOO IIII ĒĒĒĒĒĒĒ EEEEEE AMOUN IAAAAŌ ĒI ĒI ANOCH AI IŌ ŌI
995 ĒI ORTONGOUR ŌĒAI EIAI / ŌĒAI ŌĒOI AA ĒI OYŌ ĒI IOY ĒŌ ĒEAE THATH IER
THAINON ABOU, the great, great[139] Aion, god, lord (?), Aion."

   And the great name, that in Jerusalem, by which they bring out water when
1000 there is none in a cistern (?): "ACHMĒ IEŌĒ IEĒŌ IARABBAO / YCHRABAŌA, do the
NN thing, unutterable name of great god."

Taking a golden or silver lamella, engrave with an adamant[140] stone the unutterable characters given below. He who engraves them should be pure from all /
1005 impurity, his wrists wreathed with wreaths of flowers in season, and should also offer frankincense. The spell to annul this spell should be written on the reverse of the
1010 lamella. Then, taking it, inscribed, put it into a clean box / and put this on a clean
tripod covered with a linen cloth, and prepare an accompanying offering of pure
pinecones, a small basket[141] of bread, sweetmeats, flowers in season, Egyptian wine
1015 not mixed with seawater. Then / putting milk, wine, water in a new vessel, pour a
libation while burning frankincense. Also let a clean lamp be at hand, full of rose oil.
1020 And say, "I call on you the greatest god in the heaven, / strong lord, mighty IAŌ OYŌ
IŌ AIŌ OYŌ, who exist.[142] Perfect for me, lord, the great, lord, unutterable magical
1025 sign, so that I may have it and remain free of danger and unconquered and / undefeated, I, NN."

Moses for use as a phylactery. Unfortunately, neither "hymn" nor "phylactery" matches the gender of
"archangelic" as given in our text, and the quotations differ widely. See Reitzenstein, *Poimandres* 292–
93 and Gager, *Moses in Greco-Roman Paganism* 150. One of the works used by the author of *PGM* XIII
may have had a Hebrew source. The beginning of the second quotation is readable as Hebrew: "In
Adam was the source of secrets" (taking ριζξαη as a corruption of *razzaya*—Greek has no *y*).

137. The source of this may have been a targum in which the phrase, "the God of Abraham, the God
of Isaac, and the God of Jacob" (Ex 3:6, 15; 4:5, etc.) was followed by a magical gloss, like those
sometimes inserted in manuscripts of Homer; cf. *P. Oxy.* 412.

138. Claudius Ptolemaeus, ca. A.D. 100–178, the famous astronomer and astrologer, was another
favorite victim of false attributions; see Gundel, *Astrologoumena* 211. This adds one more.

139. Doubling is a common form of superlative, especially in Hebrew and Egyptian, but also in
Greek. See F. Blass and A. Debrunner, *A Greek Grammar of the New Testament* (Chicago: University of
Chicago Press, 1961), sec. 493.1.

140. Probably the legendary adamant, which nothing could break. The observable stone most often
called *adamas* was hematite, a relatively soft iron oxide not suitable for engraving. See A. A. Barb, "Lapis
Adamas," in *Hommages à Marcel Rénard*, vol. I, *Latomus* 101 (1969):67–86; R. K. Ritner, "A Uterine
Amulet in the Oriental Institute Collection," *JNES* 43 (1984):209–21.

141. Literally, one containing about a *kab*—roughly one-sixth of a bushel. However, the word thus
literally translated appears in Greek only in Preisendanz's text, where it is a conjectural correction of a
corruption.

142. Literally, "the being" (person or thing, masc.)—the famous Greek hypostatized principle which
LXX used in translating the obscure Hebrew gloss in Ex 3:14.

Try to prepare this when [the moon] is in the east and in conjunction with a beneficent planet, either Zeus or Aphrodite, and when / no maleficent one, Kronos 1030 or Ares, is in aspect. You may do it best when one of the three beneficent planets is in its own house, while the moon is taking / the position of conjunction or aspect or 1035 diametrical opposition and when the planet, too, is in the east, for then the rite will be effectual for you. Accordingly, do not / idly talk about the way to annul it, if you 1040 don't want to help damage yourself; but keep it to yourself.

Its uses are the following:

When you want to put down fear or anger: Taking a leaf of laurel, write on it the / sign, as it is, and having shown it to the sun, say, "I call on you, the great god in 1045 heaven, [strong] lord, mighty IAŌ OYŌ IŌ AIŌ OYŌ, who exist; protect me from all fear, from all danger that threatens / me in the present day, in the present hour." 1050 Having said these words thrice, lick off the leaf, and have the lamella with you. And if [things come to] hand-to-hand [fighting, wear it] on your hand.

    ✗ ⁴⁄∀⁊   **The spell to annul**, which   1055
    ✗+✝ ✝   is written on the reverse:
    ✗ ⁞⁞∧°+∣°   "PAITH PHTHA PHOŌZA."¹⁴³

A secret prayer of Moses to Selene: "OINEL of life, CHNOUB OUĒR AKROM-BOUS / OURAOI OYĒR AI HAPH HŌR OKI. ANOCH BŌRINTH MAMIKOURPH AEI AEI 1060 Ē AEI EIE EIĒ TETH OUR OUR OUĒR ME CHROUR CHOU TAIS ECHRĒZĒ ECHRINX MAMIA OURPH, goddess in woman's form, mistress Selene, do the NN thing."

For opening [doors]: Taking / the navel of a male crocodile (he means pond- 1065 weed)¹⁴⁴ and the egg of a scarab and a heart of a baboon (he means myrrh, perfume of lilies),¹⁴⁵ put these into a blue-green faïence vessel. And when you wish to open a door, bring the navel to the door, saying, "By / THAIM THOLACH THECHEMBAOR 1070 THEAGON PENTATHESCHI BŌTI, [I call on you] who have power in the deep, for myself, that there may now be a way open for me, for I say to you, SAUAMBOCH / MERA CHEOZAPH ŌSSALA BYMBĒL POUO TOUTHŌ OIRĒREI ARNOCH." 1075

If [you wish] to call phantoms: . . .

*The tenth (?) Hidden [Book of] Moses.*¹⁴⁶

*Tr.: Morton Smith.

PDM xiv. 1–92

*[**A vessel divination** which a physician ?] in the nome of Oxyrhynchus [gave to me]:¹ *Formula*: "[O god, NN,] . . . the edge of whose strap rests in Pelusium while his face is like a spark . . . of an obscene cat whose testicles² are like a rearing uraeus . . . quickly. Put the light and breadth in my vessel. . . . / Open to me, O earth! 5 Open to me, O underworld! Open to me, O primeval waters! . . . large . . . of cop- [col. I, 5]

143. PHTHA PHOŌZA is "Ptah, health." In the following prayer, CHNOUB OUĒR is "Khnum the great," OURAOI OUĒR is "great ureai," HAPH HOR is "Apis, Horus." [R.K.R.]

144. This is an example of the secret magical vocabulary by which everyday things were given pretentious names, partly to make magical rituals impractible for chance readers, partly to impress the ignorant.

145. Or possibly, "myrrh mixed with (oil of white) lilies."

146. In the manuscript "book" is lacking and "tenth" uncertain. Against Gager's argument for a repetition of "eighth" (*Moses*, p. 148, [above, n. 136]) stand the conspicuous differences of the material preceding this title from that of the better attested "eighth" books in ll. 1–730.

1. Restored by comparison with *PDM* xiv. 528.

2. Read, perhaps, *sn.ty*; see A. H. Gardiner, *Hieratic Papyri in the British Museum*, 3d ser., vol. 1 (London: British Museum, 1935), 115, n. 2; and cf. Griffith and Thompson, glossary #133 and 20, n. to l. I. 3.

per of Alkhah.[3] O gods who are in heaven, who are exalted, come! . . . [Put (the)] light and breadth in my vessel and my . . . [the] boy whose face is bent over this vessel.[4] May . . . prosper, for this vessel divination is the vessel divination of Isis

10 when she was searching / . . . . Come in to me, †O †my †compeller, for everything
[I, 10] . . . , and make †this youth[5] open his eyes to them all . . . , for I †am the Pharaoh Lion-Ram. Ram-Lion-Lotus[6] is my name; . . . to you here today, for I †am SIT-TAKO.[7] 'Hearing' is my name; 'hearing' [is my true name. I am GANTHA, GINTEY,

15 GIRITEY][8] HRENYTE (also called ARENOYTE)[9] †LAPPTTOTHA †LAKSANTHA SA/[RISA
[I, 15] . . . †BOLBYE]L[10] BYEL BYEL †LYTERI †KLOGASANTRA †IAHO [is my name; IAHO is my true name. BALKHAM the][11] powerful one of heaven, †ABLANATHANALBA, the griffin[12] [of the shrine of the god who stands today]."[13]

[You should] say, whispering, "O good oxherd,[14] my compeller, . . . in order to ask you about it here today, and †you †should †make †this [youth] open[15] his eyes . . . every . . . and you should protect †this youth whose face is bent [down over

20 this / vessel][16] . . . of god, †lord †of †earth, †the †survivor of the earth, †lord †of
[I, 20] †earth . . . I †am Hor-Amoun[17] who sits at this vessel divination here today . . . †[at][18] †this vessel divination here today. †MARIGHARI, you should . . . so that they say my inquiry for me."

Say to them twice, "O pure gods of the primeval waters, [I am] . . . of earth by

25 name, under the soles [of whose feet] the gods of Egypt are placed / . . . †THAR, for
[I, 25]

3. For Alkhah (Eg., ʿrq-ḥḥ), see *PGM* IV. 124 and n. One should, probably, use a standard transliteration of the name throughout; see Griffith and Thompson, *The Leyden Papyrus* 21, n. to l. I. 6.

4. Or oil; parallels allow either; see Griffith and Thompson, *The Leyden Papyrus* 21, n. to l. I. 8.

5. Restored by comparison with *PDM* xiv. 43, 72, etc.; see discussion in Johnson, *Verbal System* 274–75.

6. For this combination, see Griffith and Thompson, *The Leyden Papyrus* 22, n. to l. I. 12; also *PGM* III. 659 and n.

7. For a discussion of the possible meaning of this name, see Griffith and Thompson, *The Leyden Papyrus* 23, n. to l. I. 13.

8. Restored by comparison with *PDM* xiv. 1171–72. The spelling of magical names given here is based on the Demotic spelling supplemented by the Old Coptic spelling. If there is a disagreement between the two, the Demotic is accepted. See Johnson, "Dialect," 110–25 for a discussion of the correlations among Greek, Old Coptic, and Demotic found in this text. Transcriptions try to maintain a one-to-one correspondence between ancient script and modern.

9. "Also called' is inserted above the line, in front of the Old Coptic gloss ARENOYTE. Note that *PDM* xiv. 1174 writes this name ḥry ntr "lord god."

10. The missing magical names could be restored by comparison with *PDM* xiv. 1175–76.

11. Restored by comparison with *PDM* xiv. 1178.

12. The griffin is described by the author of the Demotic tale called "The Myth of the Sun's Eye" in the following terms (15. 1–4): His beak is (that of) an eagle; his eyes are (those of) a man; his limbs are (those of) a lion; his scaly ears are (those of) an ꜣbꜣḫ fish of the sea; his tail is (that of) a snake—the five [creatures] which breathe which are upon (the earth). The griffin is described as the "avenger upon whom no avenger can wreak vengeance" and the "herdsman of everything which is upon earth." The most recent discussion of this passage, and its translation into Greek, is by J. W. Tait, "A Duplicate Version of the Demotic *Kufi* Text," *Acta Orientalia* 36 (1974):23–27, and "The Fable of Sight and Hearing in the Demotic *Kufi* Text," *Acta Orientalia* 37 (1976):27–44.

13. Restored by comparison with *PDM* xiv. 1179.

14. Epithet of Anubis; cf. *PDM* xiv. 35, 400, and 422; see *PGM* I. 26 and n.

15. See n. 5 above.

16. See n. 4 above.

17. The formation of compound dieties occurs very early in Egyptian religion and remains a common feature.

18. Restoration based on Old Coptic gloss "a" = preposition r.

I am ⁺TA ⁺PISH⁺TEHEI¹⁹ of earth by name. . . . preserve you, O Pharaoh, PASHA-
MEI,²⁰ who rests opposite . . . these forearms of real gold. Truth is in my mouth,
honey [is on my lips]²¹ . . . MA . . . THA, for I ⁺am ⁺STEL ⁺IAHO, ⁺he ⁺who ⁺opens
⁺the ⁺land.”

You should say to the boy, “Open your eyes!” If he opens his eyes and sees the
light, you should make him cry out, / saying “Be great, be great, O light! Come   30
forth, come forth, O light! Rise up, rise up, O light! Be high, be high, O light! He   [II, 2]
who is outside, come in!”

If he opens his eyes and does not see the light, you should make him close his
eyes while you recite to him again.

Formula: “O darkness, remove yourself ⁺from ⁺before him! O light, bring the
light in to me! Pshai²² who is in the primeval waters, bring the light in to me! O
Osiris who is in the divine bark, bring the light in to me! O these four winds which
are outside, bring the light in to me! O he in whose hand is the ⁺moment, the one
who belongs to these hours,²³ / bring the light in to me! O Anubis, the good ox-   35
herd, bring the light in to me in order that you give me ⁺protection here today, for I   [II, 7]
am Horus, the son of Isis, the good son of Osiris! You should bring the gods of the
place of judgment, and you should cause them to take care of my affair so that they
make ⁺my business proceed. ⁺O ⁺those ⁺belonging ⁺to ⁺the ⁺avengers,²⁴ you should
cause them to do it, for [I am] . . . ⁺TYRAMNEI²⁵ ⁺AMNEI²⁶ ⁺A ⁺A ⁺MES MES
⁺ORNYORF ORNYORF ⁺ORNYORF ORNYORF ⁺PAHOROF²⁷ . . . ⁺PAHROF²⁸ ⁺IO ⁺little
king, ⁺mountain ⁺of ⁺Horus. May this youth whose face is bent down to this / oil   40
be saved [and may you] send Sobek to me until he comes forth. ‘Hearing’ is my   [II, 12]
name; ‘Hearing’ is my correct name, for I am L[OT ⁺MYLO]T²⁹ ⁺TYLOT. ⁺TAT
⁺PINTAT is my correct name. O great god whose name is great, appear to this youth
⁺without ⁺alarming or ⁺deceiving, ⁺truthfully.”³⁰ You should recite these *writings
seven times*.

If you make him open his eyes and the light is good and he says “Anubis is coming in,” you should recite before him,³¹

Formula: “O RIDJ MYRIDJ, O earth, great one of the earth, O this beautiful male
whom ⁺HERIEY, the daughter of the ⁺Neme³² bore, / come to me, for you are this   45

19. The final group is the Demotic word ⁽.*wy*, “house”; the first element of the first word may be a
phonetic rendering of *ta*, “she of.”

20. See n. 19 above.

21. Or “the truth of my mouth is the honey of my lips.” Restored by comparison with *PDM* xiv.
252.

22. On *š*(⁽)*y* “Fate” and *p3 š⁽y ⁽3* as the ἀγαθοδαίμων, see J. Quaegebeur, *Le dieu égyptien Shaï dans
la religion et l’onomastique* (Louvain: Leuven University Press, 1975). See also *PGM* III. 144–45.

23. I.e., the god who is “on duty” at this moment; see below, *PDM* xiv. 58–60.

24. On avengers, see *Mythus* 4/20. “The Avenger” is identified by the Coptic monk Shenute as Chronos. See also *PDM* xiv. 242.

25. The ending is written with Demotic *n3y*, “there” or “to me.”

26. See n. 25 above.

27. The ending is written *r.f*, “his mouth.”

28. See n. 27 above.

29. Restored by comparison with *PDM* xiv. 534.

30. “Without alarming or deceiving, truthfully” are Greek words written phonetically in Demotic, as
Griffith and Thompson, 28, n. to l. II. 14. The spelling of Greek επαληθια as *ep⁽letsy⁽* reflects the standard transcription of Greek τ/ϑ + ι as *tsy*; see Johnson, “Dialect,” 123–25. Greek π/φ + ι are written
ps/šy; Greek κ/χ + ι as *ksy*.

31. I.e., Anubis.

32. A goddess of destruction, as suggested by Griffith and Thompson, *The Leyden Papyrus* 28–29, n.
to l. II. 16.

[II, 17] lotus flower which came forth from †the †lotus bud †of †PNYSTOR which makes light for the entire land! Hail, Anubis! Come to me! †O †high †one, O mighty one, O master of secrets for those in the Underworld, O Pharaoh of those in Amenti,[33] O Chief Physician, O good [son] of Osiris, he whose face is strong among the gods, you should appear in the Underworld before the hand of Osiris. You should serve the souls of Abydos in order that they all live through you, these souls, the ones of the sacred Underworld. Come to the earth! Reveal yourself to me here to-day! You are Thoth. You are the one who went forth from the heart of the great
50   Agathodaimon,[34] the father of the fathers of all the gods. Come to the mouths / of
[II, 22] my vessel today and tell me an answer in truth concerning everything about which I am inquiring, without falsehood therein, for I am Isis the Wise, the sayings of whose mouth come to pass" *(formula: seven times).*

You should say to the youth, "Speak to Anubis, saying, 'Go forth; bring the gods in!'"

When he goes after them and brings them in, you should question the youth, saying, "Have the gods already come in?" If he says, "They have already come," and if you [*sic*] see them, you should recite before them.

Formula: "Awaken to me, awaken to me! PSHAI![35] Awaken, †MERA, †the †Great †One †of †Five,[36] †TSITSIY †TENNDJIY! Do justice to me! Thoth, may creation fill
55   the earth with light; O ibis[37] in / his noble countenance, noble one who entered
[II, 27] the heart,[38] create truth, O great god whose name is great!" *(Say seven times).*

You should say to the youth,[39] "Speak to Anubis, saying, 'Bring in a table for the gods! Let them sit.'"

When they are seated, you[40] should say, "Bring in a wine jar; open it for the gods! Bring in some bread! Let them eat, let them drink, (let them eat, let them drink),[41] let them make merry."

When they have finished, you[42] should say to Anubis, "Will you make inquiry for me?"

If he says, "Immediately," you[43] should say to him,[44] "The god who will make my inquiry today, let him stand up." When he[45] says, "He has stood up," you[46] should say to him, "Say to Anubis, 'Carry off the things from the midst!'"[47]
60   You[48] should recite / before him instantly, saying, "Agathodaimon of today, lord
[III, 3] of today, the one to whom these moments belong."[49]

33. Literally, the west; i.e., the necropolis and, by extension, the realm of the dead.
34. See n. 22 above.
35. See n. 22 above.
36. Probably an epithet of Thoth; originally the title of the high priest of Thoth in Hermopolis, as Griffith and Thompson, *The Leyden Papyrus* 30, n. to l. II. 26.
37. I.e., Thoth.
38. I.e., who pleases.
39. A similar passage, but without the youth, is found in *PDM* xiv. 550–54.
40. I.e., the youth.
41. Dittography in going from column II to column III.
42. I.e., the youth.
43. See n. 42 above.
44. I.e., Anubis.
45. I.e., the god who will make the inquiry.
46. I.e., the youth.
47. I.e., of the gods seated at the table, as noted by Griffith and Thompson, *The Leyden Papyrus* 32, n. to l. III. 2.
48. I.e., the youth.
49. I.e., Anubis.

You should cause him to say to Anubis, "The god who will inquire for me today, let him tell me his name." When he stands up and tells his name, you should ask him concerning everything which you wish.

Its preparation: [50] You bring seven new bricks which have not yet been moved in order to turn them (over) to the other face. You should lift them, you being pure, without touching them against anything on earth, and you should set them back in the[ir] manner in which they were set. You should set three bricks under the oil. The other four bricks; you should arrange them around the youth without / his   65 body touching the ground. Or seven palm staffs—you should treat them in this   [III, 8] fashion also. You should bring seven clean loaves [of bread] and arrange them around the oil, together with seven lumps of salt. You should bring a new bowl and fill it with clean oasis oil. You should put [it in]to the dish gradually without producing cloudiness so that it becomes exceedingly clear. You should bring a pure youth who has not yet gone with a woman; you should speak down into his head beforehand, he standing up, (to learn) whether he would be useful in going to the vessel. If he will be useful, you should make him lie down on his belly / and cover   70 him with a clean linen cloth (you should recite down into his head),[51] there being a   [III, 13] strap on the upper part of the cloth. You should recite this invocation which is above down into his head, he gazing downwards looking into the oil, up to *seven times*, his eyes being closed. When you have finished, you should make him open his eyes, and you should ask him about what you desire. You do it until the time of the seventh hour of the day.

The invocation which you should recite (them [*sic*]) down into his head beforehand to test him in his ears to learn whether he would be useful in going to the vessel. *Formula*: "Noble ibis, falcon, / hawk, noble and very mighty, let me be pu-   75 rified in the manner of the noble ibis, falcon, hawk, noble and very mighty." You   [III, 18] should recite this down into his head up to *seven* times.

When you announce this, his ears speak. If his two ears speak, he is very good; if it is his right ear, he is good; if it is the left (ear), he is bad.

Prescription for enchanting the vessel quickly so that the gods come in and tell you an answer truthfully: [52] You should put the shell of a crocodile's egg, or that which is inside it, on the flame. It enchants instantly.

Prescription to make them speak: You put a frog's head on the brazier. They speak.

Prescription for bringing the gods in by force: You should put bile / of a croco-   80 dile and ground myrrh on the brazier.   [III, 23]

If you wish to make them come in quickly, again: You should put stalks of anise on the brazier together with the eggshell, above. It enchants at once.

If you wish to bring in a living man: You should put sulphate of copper on the brazier. He comes in.

If you wish to bring in a spirit: You should put *s3-wr* stone[53] and glass(?) stone[54] on the brazier. The spirit comes in. You should put the heart of a hyena or a hare; (it is) very good.

If you wish to bring in a drowned man: You should put sea-*garab* (stone?) on the brazier.

---

50. Literally, "gathering of things." [R.K.R.]
51. Repeated, out of place, from *PDM* xiv. 68.
52. See n. 30 above.
53. Perhaps σῶρυ; see Harris, *Minerals* 179–80.
54. Ibid., 99–100.

If you wish to bring in a dead man: You should put ass's dung[55] and an amulet of Nephthys on the brazier. He comes in.

85   *If you / wish* to send them all away: You should put ape's dung on the brazier.
[III, 28] They all go away to their place. And you should recite their spell for dismissing them also.[56]

If you wish to bring in a thief: You should put crocus powder and alum on the brazier.

The spells which you should recite when you dismiss them to their place: "Go well, go in joy!"

If you wish to make the gods come in to you and (to make) the vessel enchant quickly: You should bring a scarab and drown it in the milk of a black cow and put it on the brazier. It enchants in the moment named and the light comes into being.

90   / An amulet to be bound to the body of the one who is carrying the vessel, to
[III, 34] cause it to enchant quickly: You should bring a band of linen of sixteen threads, four of white, four of [green], four of blue, four of red, and make them into one band and stain them with the blood of a hoopoe. You should bind it to a scarab in its attitude of the sun god,[57] drowned,[58] being wrapped in byssus. You should bind it to the body of the youth who is carrying the vessel. It enchants quickly, there [being nothing in the world better ?] than it (?).

*Tr.: Janet H. Johnson, following the edition and translation of Griffith and Thompson, *Demotic Magical Papyrus*, recto, cols. I/1–III/35. All words preceded by ˈ are written in the text in Demotic with Old Coptic glosses inserted above. Section titles are indicated in *PDM* xiv as they are marked in the papyrus (see the Introduction to the Demotic Magical Papyri).

PDM xiv. 93–114 [*PGM* XIVa. 1–11]

*A casting for inspection[59] which the great god Iymhotep makes: *Its preparation*:[60] You bring a ˈstool of olive wood having four legs,[61] upon which no man on

95   earth has ever sat, and you put it near you, it being clean. When you wish / to make
[col. IV, a "god's arrival"[62] with it truthfully without falsehood, *here is* its manner. You
3] should put the stool in a clean niche in the midst of the place, it being near your head; you should cover it with a cloth from its top to its bottom;[63] you should put four bricks under the table before it, one above another, there being a censer of clay before it [sc. the table]; you should put charcoal of olive wood on it;[64] you should add ˈwild ˈgoose fat pounded with myrrh and *qs-ʿnḥ*-stone;[65] you should make

55. The donkey was associated with the god Seth in the later periods. Seth, of course, had murdered his brother Osiris. For association of ass's dung with Seth, see *PGM* IV. 155–285 and n. The amulet is that of Nephthys, since she is the consort of Seth.

56. I.e., *PDM* xiv. 86–87.

57. The scarab beetle was identified with the sun god; cf. *PGM* I. 223; IV. 751 and 943; see R.K.R.'s notes there and Griffith and Thompson, *The Leyden Papyrus* 39, n. to l. III. 34.

58. See R.K.R.'s note to *PGM* I. 5 and Griffith and Thompson, *The Leyden Papyrus* 38–39, n. to l. III. 31.

59. Taking this noun as a compound from the two verbs *šš* "to spread" and *mšt* "to inspect," as Griffith and Thompson, *The Leyden Papyrus*, glossary #786. The translation "casting" was suggested by R.K.R. since what follows is a horoscope; see n. 66 below.

60. See *PDM* xiv. 1–92 with n. 50.

61. Literally, "feet."

62. For a discussion of the reading and meaning of this term, used to describe spells in which a god is seen in a vision, usually a dream, see J. H. Johnson, "Louvre E3229: A Demotic Magical Text," *Enchoria* 7 (1977): 90–91.

63. Literally, from its head to its feet. See also *PGM* IV. 88.

64. I.e., the censer.

65. Probably hematite; see Harris, *Minerals* 233–34.

them into balls; you should put one on the brazier; you should leave the remainder
near you; you should recite this spell in Greek[66] to it *(formula)*;[67] you should lie
down without speaking / to anyone on earth; and you should go to sleep. You see   100
the god, he being in the likeness of a priest wearing clothes of byssus on his back   [IV, 8]
and wearing sandals[68] on his feet.

"I call upon you [sing.] who are seated in impenetrable darkness and are in the   [XIVa.1]
midst of the great gods, you who set; take with you the solar rays, and send up the
light-bringing goddess NEBOUTOSOUALĒTH; [you are the] great god, BARZAN
BOUBARZAN NARZAZOUZAN BARZABOUZATH, / Sun. Send up to me this night   105
your archangel, ZEBOURTHAUNĒN. Respond with truth, truly, not falsely, unam-   [IV, 13]
biguously concerning such-and-such a matter, because I conjure you by him who is   [*PGM*
seated in the fiery cloak on the serpentine head of the Agathos Daimon, the al-   XIVa. 5]
mighty, four-faced, highest daimon, dark / and conjuring, PHŌX. Do not ignore   110
me, but send up quickly tonight [in accordance with the] command of the god."   [IV, 18]
Say this three times.   [*PGM*
He speaks with you truthfully with his mouth opposite your mouth concerning   XIVa. 10]
anything which you wish. When he has finished, he will go away again. You place a
tablet for reading the hours upon the bricks, and you place the stars upon it, and
you write your business on a new roll of papyrus, and you place it on the tablet. It
sends your stars to you whether they are favorable for your business.

*Tr.: Janet H. Johnson, following the edition and translation of Griffith and Thompson, *De-
motic Magical Papyrus*, recto. col. IV/1–22, and W. C. Grese (Greek sections). All words preceded by ˙ are written in the text in Demotic with Old Coptic glosses inserted above.

PDM xiv. 115

*[A] tested [spell] for the security of shadows: Hawk's egg and myrrh; rub, put   115
[some] of it on your eye(s). You secure shadows.   [col. IV,
                                                                                         23]
*Tr.: Janet H. Johnson, following the edition and translation of Griffith and Thompson, *De-
motic Magical Papyrus*, recto. col. IV/23. Or could this be a spell to protect against loss of
vision? The following spell makes such an interpretation less likely. Griffith and Thompson,
43, n. to l. IV/23, suggest that the shadow is that of the god of the lamp. If so, this and the
next should be considered part of the last spell; cf. *PGM* II. 612–13 and n.

PDM xiv. 116

*Another, again: Head and blood of a hoopoe; cook them and make them into a   [col. IV,
dry medicine. Paint your eye(s) with it. You see them again.   24]

*Tr.: Janet H. Johnson, following the edition and translation of Griffith and Thompson, *De-
motic Magical Papyrus*, recto, col. IV/24. See note to the preceding spell.

PDM xiv. 117–49

*A tested "god's arrival":[69] You should set up your . . . ; you should stamp on the   115
ground with your foot seven times. You should recite these spells to the Foreleg,[70] [col. V,
you having turned to the North, seven times; you should turn down;[71] (you should   1f]

---

66. I.e., the procedure for reading a horoscope.
67. I.e., *PDM* xiv. 101–11.
68. The word written *še*, "nose," is a scribal error for *tb.ty*, "sandals." See R. K. Ritner, "Gleanings
from Magical Texts," *Enchoria* (forthcoming).
69. See n. 62 above.
70. I.e., Ursa Major.
71. I.e., away from the constellation.

go to a dark room).[72] You should go to a dark, clean room whose face opens to the
120   south; you should purify it with / natron water; you should bring a new white
[V, 4]   lamp to which no red lead[73] or gum water has been applied; you should put a clean
wick in it; you should fill it with real oil after first writing this name and these figures[74] on the wick with ink of myrrh; you should put it on a new brick in front of
yourself, its underside being spread with sand; and you should recite these spells[75]
at the lamp again another seven times. If you put frankincense up in front of the
lamp and you look at the lamp, you see the god near the lamp; you sleep on a reed
mat without having spoken to anyone on earth, and he tells you the answer in a
dream. ***Here is its invocation.***

(124a–   ***Formula***: / (Here are the writings which you should write on the wick of the
126a)   lamp: "BAXYXSIXYX[76] 𓂝𓏏𓆑𓊪 𓋴𓏏𓏏.")[77]
125   / "Hail, I[78] am MYRAI MYRIBI[79] †BABEL †BAOTH BAMYI,[80] the great Agathodai-
[V, 9]   mon,[81] MYRATHO, the . . . form of soul which rests above in the heaven of heavens,
†TATOT TATOT †BYLAI BYLAI †MYIHTAHI MYIHTAHI †LAHI LAHI †BOLBYEL[82] †II
†AA †TAT TAT[83] †BYEL BYEL †IOHEL IOHEL, the first servant of the great god, he who
gives light exceedingly, the companion of the flame, he is whose mouth is the flame
which is never extinguished, the great god who is seated in the flame, he who is in
the midst of the flame which is in the lake of heaven,[84] in whose hand is the great-
130   ness and the power of the god: reveal yourself to me / here today in the †manner of
[V, 14]   the †form of revealing yourself to Moses which you made upon the mountain, before which you had already created darkness and light."
(Insert above):[85] "I beseech you. You should reveal yourself to me here tonight
and speak with me and tell me [an] answer, in truth, concerning the given matter
about which I am asking you. (I beseech you. You should reveal yourself to me here
tonight and speak with me and tell me [an] answer in truth)[86] without falsehood,
for I shall glorify you in Abydos; I shall praise you in heaven before Phre;[87] I shall
praise you before the Moon; I shall praise you before him who is upon the throne,

---

72. An overlap with what is in the next line, showing where to insert these two lines.
73. See R.K.R.'s note in Glossary, *s.v.* "Lamps, not painted red."
74. Written in the left margin opposite *PDM* xiv. 124–26; here called *PDM* xiv. 124a–126a.
75. See *PDM* xiv. 124–249 below.
76. This is Egyptian and can be translated "Soul (*Ba*) of darkness, son of darkness." [R.K.R.]
77. These figures all resemble Egyptian hieroglyphs but cannot be translated by me.
78. The independent pronoun, which gives the translation "I am . . . ," was a later addition, above
the line. Thus all the following magical names and descriptions may originally have been vocatives addressed to the god who is asked to appear and give the answer. This analysis is reinforced by the parallel
in *PDM* xiv. 194–204, which has all as vocatives.
79. Ending written as *by*, "Soul."
80. Ending written as *m3y*, "lion."
81. See n. 22 above.
82. An almost identical version of this section appears in *PDM* xiv. 194–204, 489–99, and
516–26.
83. Written with the hieroglyph of the *dd*-column.
84. Astrological term for noon, in contrast to the "lake of the underworld," which is midnight.
85. Added at the bottom of the column when the scribe realized he had left out part of one of the
clauses in *PDM* xiv. 131. He began making the addition above the line in 131, but there was not space
for all of it. Thus, as with the addition to *PDM* xiv. 119, he repeated much of the line in order to show
the exact spot where the correction and additions override the original.
86. The overlap with *PDM* xiv. 148–49; see n. 85 above.
87. The sun god.

who is never destroyed. O he of great praise, †PETERI PETERI †PATER[88] †ENPHE †ENPHE, the god who is in the upper part of heaven, in whose hand is the beautiful staff, who created deity, deity not having created him; come to me / down into the midst of this flame which is here before you, †O †he †of †BYEL †BYEL, and let me see the business about which I am praying tonight, truly, without falsehood! Let [me] see it, let [me] hear it. O great god †SISIHOYT[89] SISIHOUT (also called ARMI-OOUTH),[90] come in before me and tell me [an] answer to that about which I am asking, truly, without falsehood. O great god who is on the mountain of ATYGI[91] †CHABAHO,[92] come in to me, let me learn[93] tonight about the given thing about which I am asking, truly, without falsehood . . . voice (?)[94] †of †the †LEASPHYT NEBLOT NEB LILAS" ([say it] seven times and go to sleep / without speaking).

135
[V, 19]

140
[V, 24]

The ointment which you should put on your eye(s) when you are going to question the lamp in any lamp divination: You bring some flowers of the Greek bean plant.[95] You find them in the place of the garland seller (also called the lupine seller). You should bring them while they are fresh; you should put them in a glass bowl; you should seal its mouth with clay very well for twenty days in a hidden, dark place. After twenty days, if you bring it up and open it, you find some testicles in it together with a phallus. If you leave it for forty days and bring it up and open it, you find that it has already become bloody. In a place which is hidden at all times, you put it in a glass object, and you put the glass object into a pottery object. / If you desire to make a "god's arrival"[96] of the lamp with it at any time, you should fill your eye(s) with this aforementioned blood while you are going in to recite the spell to the lamp. You see a secret figure of a god standing outside the lamp, and he speaks with you concerning the question which you wish; or you should lie down and he comes to you. If he does not come to you, you should awaken and recite his summons. You lie down on [a mat of] green reeds only while you are pure from a woman, the back of your head being turned to the south, your face being turned to the north, and the face of the lamp being turned to the north likewise.

145
[V, 29]

*Tr.: Janet H. Johnson, following the edition and translation of Griffith and Thompson, *Demotic Magical Papyrus*, recto, col. V/1–33. All words preceded by † are written in the text in Demotic with Old Coptic glosses inserted above.

88. This magical name is determined with the "man"-determinative rather than the "divine"-determinative normally found with the magical names. It is probably Greek πατήρ, "father." The preceding may consist of this Greek word plus the Egyptian first-person singular suffix pronoun .*y*, "my." The following word, written alphabetically, corresponds to the Coptic for "in/of heaven" (*n p.t*). Thus these glosses may well mean "my father, my father, father in (the) heaven of the heaven(s)." (For the analysis of the repeat of the last word, cf. *PDM* xiv. 126, as noted by R.K.R.)

89. The last word of this name is probably the Egyptian word "male." The first word, which is repeated, might be the word "son" or the verb "to be satisfied." In *PDM* xiv. 202 it is written as the verb "to be satisfied."

90. "Also called" is inserted above the end of the line and the Old Coptic gloss ARMIOUUTH is added in the left margin.

91. The Old Coptic gloss gives "of KABAON"; in *PDM* xiv. 204 the scribe changed Demotic ꝫ*twgy* into *g̣ꝫbꝫwn*.

92. The Old Coptic gloss adds TAKRTAT after XABA[H]O.

93. Literally, "let my eyes open out"; the idiom *ti-wn ir.t*, "to cause that (the) eye(s) open" means "to instruct." See Ritner above, n. 68.

94. Or is this sign the determinative (used with foreign words) of the preceding word, which ends in *ṭ*?

95. Literally, "eye-of-raven" plant.

96. See n. 62 above.

PDM xiv. 150–231

150   ***An inquiry of the** lamp: You go to a clean, dark room without light; you dig a
[col. VI, new niche in an eastern wall; you bring a white lamp on which no red lead[97] or
1] gum water has been put and whose wick is clean; you fill it with clean, genuine
oasis oil; you recite the spells of praising Ra at dawn when he rises; you bring the
lamp, it being lit, opposite the sun; you recite the spells which are below[98] to it *four*
times; you take it into the room, you being pure, together with the youth; you
recite the spells to the youth[99] while he is not looking at the lamp, his eye(s) being
closed, *seven* times. You should put pure frankincense on the brazier while you are
155   putting your finger on the youth's head, his eye(s) being closed. / When you have
[VI, 6] finished, you make him open his eye(s) toward the lamp: he sees the shadow of the
god near the lamp, and he inquires for you concerning that which you desire. At
midday in a place without light you do it.

     If you are inquiring for a demonic spirit, a wick of sailcloth is what you should
give to the lamp, and you should fill it with clean butter.

     If it is another matter, a clean wick and pure genuine oil are what you should give
to the lamp.

     If you will do it to bring a woman to a man, oil of roses[100] is what you should put
in the lamp.

     It is on a new brick that you put the lamp, and it is upon another brick that the
youth seats himself while his eye(s) are closed, while you recite[101] down into his
head four times.

160   / *The spells* which you should recite to the wick[102] beforehand before you have
[VI, 16] recited to the youth: *Formula*:

     "Are you the unique, great wick of the linen of Thoth? Are you the byssus robe of
Osiris, the divine Drowned,[103] woven by the hand of Isis, spun by the hand of
Nephthys? Are you the original bandage which was made for Osiris Khenty-
amenti?[104] Are you the great bandage with which Anubis lifted his hand to the
body of Osiris the mighty god?[105] It is in order to cause the youth to look into you
so that you may make reply concerning everything about which I am asking here
today, that I am bringing you today, O wick. (If not doing it is what you will do, O
wick, it is in the hand of the black cow that I am putting you, and it is in the hand
165   / of the black cow that I am burning you. Blood of the Drowned One is what I am
[VI, 16] giving to you for oil. The hand of Anubis is that which is laid against you. The
spells of the great Sorcerer are those which I am reciting to you.) And so that[106] you
bring me the god in whose hand the command[107] is today, so that he tell me [an]
answer to everything about which I am inquiring here today, truly, without false-

97. See n. 73 above.
98. *PDM* xiv. 160–69.
99. *PDM* xiv. 194–231.
100. *Skn/sgn* is a cheaper oil than *nḥḥ*-oil (probably sesame oil); here it has been scented with rose
scent. See J. J. Janssen, *Commodity Prices from the Ramessid Period* (Leyden: E. J. Brill, 1975) 336–37.
101. See n. 99 above.
102. Corrected above, n. 99.
103. See references collected by R.K.R., n. to *PGM* I. 5.
104. "Foremost of the west," i.e., ruler of the world.
105. Anubis mummifying Osiris, using the fine bandages described in *PDM* xiv. 160–62.
106. Continuing from *PDM* xiv. 163.
107. For the god of the hour, i.e., the god who is "on duty," see n. 23 above. See also, as Griffith and
Thompson, *The Leyden Papyrus* 53, n. to l. VI. 17, the reference to 365 gods in *PDM* xiv. 1224.

hood. O Nut, mother of water, O Opet,[108] mother of fire, come to me, Nut, mother of water; come, Opet, mother of fire; come to me IAHO." You should say it whispering exceedingly. You should also say: "ᵗESEKS ᵗPOE EF CHTN" (also called "CHT ON"), seven times.

If it is a "god's arrival"[109] these alone are what you should recite / to the lamp, and you should go to sleep without speaking. If obstinacy occurs, you should wake up and recite his summons, which is his compulsion: *Formula*:

"I am the Ram's face; Youth is my name. Under the venerable persea[110] tree in Abydos was I born. I am the soul of the great chief[111] who is in Abydos; I am the guardian of the great corpse[112] which is in Wu-poke.[113] I am he whose eye(s) are the eye(s) of a falcon watching over Osiris by night; I am 'He who is upon his mountain'[114] upon the necropolis of Abydos; I am he that watches over the great corpse which is in Busiris;[115] I am he who watches for R-Khepri-Atum[116] / whose name is hidden in my heart. 'Soul of souls' is his name" (*formula*: seven times).

[*In margin*]: The writings which you should write on the lamp: "BAXYXSIXYX ⸗𝔅𝔛𝔛𝔞." [117]

If it is a "god's arrival,"[118] these things alone are what you should recite.

If an inquiry by the youth is what you will do, you should recite these aforesaid to the lamp before you have recited[119] down into the head of the youth. You should turn around,[120] and you should recite this other invocation to the lamp also. *Formula*: "O Osiris, O lamp, it will cause [me] to see those above;[121] it will cause [me] to see those below, and vice versa. O lamp, O lamp, Amoun is moored in you. O lamp, O lamp, I call to you while you are going up upon the great sea, the sea of Syria, the sea of Osiris.[122] Am I speaking / to you? Are you coming that I may send you? O lamp, ᵗbearᵗ witness! When you have found Osiris upon his boat of papyrus and faïence, Isis being at his head, Nephthys at his feet, and the male and female divinities about him, ᵗsay [to] Isis, 'Let them speak to Osiris concerning the things about which I am asking, to send the god in whose hand the command is,[123] so that he say to me an answer to everything about which I am inquiring here today.'"

"When Isis said, 'Let a god who is serious[124] concerning the business which he

170
[VI, 21]

175
[VI, 26]

(174a–
176a)

180
[VI, 31]

108. On the identification of Opet with Nut, see Griffith and Thompson, *The Leyden Papyrus* 53–54, n. to l. VI. 18.

109. See n. 62 above.

110. For the persea tree, cf. Bonnet, *RÄRG* 82–87 and *LdÄ* III 182–83, and n. to *PGM* I. 34–36.

111. Osiris.

112. Osiris.

113. Precinct of Osiris at Abydos.

114. Anubis.

115. See n. 113 above.

116. The three forms of the sun god. For the reading of this trigram, see M-L. Ryhiner, "A Propos de Trigrammes Panthéistes," *Revue d'Égyptologie* 29 (1977): 125–37, and R.K.R. notes to *PGM* II. 104ff, III. 659, and IV. 1649ff.

117. See nn. 74 and 76 above. These three lines are written in the left margin and should be set apart, as ll. 174a–176a, presumably at the break in the middle of l. 175.

118. See n. 62 above.

119. See n. 99 above.

120. Or "withdraw."

121. Corrected by the scribe from "those of the day," the words for "day" and "above" being pronounced almost identically.

122. Cf. the Osiris legend as preserved in Plutarch.

123. See n. 107 above.

124. For the meaning "sober, serious," see the discussion by Johnson, *Verbal System* 127, n. 248.

will undertake be summoned for me so that I may send him and so that he may complete them,' they went and brought [one] to her. You are the lamp, ⁺the [thing] which was brought to her. The fury of Sakhmet, your mother, and of Hike,¹²⁵ your

185 father, is / cast at you. You shall not burn for Osiris and Isis; you shall not burn for

[VI, 36] Anubis until you have told me an answer to everything about which I am asking here today truly, without telling me falsehood. If not doing it is what you will do, I will not give you oil, (I will not give you oil);¹²⁶ I will not give you fat, O lamp. It is in the belly of the [female] cow that ⁺I ⁺shall put you,¹²⁷ and I shall put blood of the [male] bull after you,¹²⁸ and I shall put your hand to the testicles of the enemy of Horus."¹²⁹

"Open to me, O you¹³⁰ of the underworld, O box of myrrh that is in my hand! Receive me before you, O souls, excellent ones¹³¹ belonging to Bi-wekem,¹³² O box

190 of myrrh which has four corners. O dog who / is called Anubis by name, who rests

[VII, 4] on the box of myrrh, whose feet are set on the box of myrrh,¹³³ send to me the ointment for the youth of the lamp so that he may tell me [an] answer to everything about which I am asking here today, truly, there being no falsehood therein. ⁺IO ⁺TABAO ⁺SYGAMAMY ⁺AKHAKHA-NBY ⁺SANAYANI ⁺ETSIE¹³⁴ ⁺GOMTO¹³⁵ ⁺GETHOS ⁺BASA-ETHORI ⁺THMILA ⁺AKHKHY, make for me [an] answer to everything about which I am asking here today" *(seven times)*.

The spells for the youth:¹³⁶ "⁺BOEL ⁺BOEL BOEL ⁺I ⁺I ⁺I ⁺A ⁺A A ⁺TAT ⁺TAT

195 ⁺TAT,¹³⁷ he that gives light very exceedingly, the companion of the flame, / he in

[VII, 9] whose mouth is the flame which is never extinguished, the great god who sits in the flame, he who is in the midst of the flame, he who is in the lake of heaven,¹³⁸ in whose hand are the greatness and strength of the god, reveal yourself to ⁺this youth who is carrying my vessel today so that he may tell me [an] answer truly, without falsehood. I shall glorify you in Abydos; I shall praise you in heaven before Pre; I shall praise you before the moon; I shall praise you on earth; I shall praise you before him who is upon the throne, who is never destroyed. O he of great praise, ⁺PETERI ⁺PETERI ⁺PATER ⁺ENPHE ⁺ENPHE,¹³⁹ the god who is in the upper part of

200 heaven, in whose hand is the beautiful staff, / who created deity, deity not having

[VII, 14] created him, come into the midst of this flame which is here before you, O he of ⁺BYEL.¹⁴⁰

125. The god of magic. For the association of Hike with Sakhmet, see Griffith and Thompson, *The Leyden Papyrus* 56–57, n. to l. VI. 35.

126. Dittography going from column VI to column VII.

127. Or, perhaps better, "that I shall give to you," since *n.k* should be the dative, not the oblique object.

128. The term to be "after" someone is also used in legal texts with the meaning "to have a legal claim against" someone.

129. I.e., Seth, whose testicles were cut off by Horus.

130. Plural.

131. Or, possibly, "of Aker," the earth god.

132. The eastern desert.

133. Note common depiction of Anubis, as jackal, on top of a chest.

134. See n. 30 above.

135. Perhaps "earthquake," as Crum, *Coptic Dictionary* 396a; if *gm* is for *qm*, this could be "creator of the earth."

136. An almost identical version of this section appears in *PDM* xiv. 128–38, 489–99, and 516–26.

137. See n. 83 above.

138. See n. 84 above.

139. See n. 88 above.

140. Old Coptic gloss above end of line adds ANIEL.

cause me to see the business about which I am inquiring here today! Let [me] see it; let [me] hear it.[141]

give strength to the eyes of the youth who is carrying my vessel, to cause him to see it and [give strength] to his ears to cause him to hear [it].[142]

O great god ⁺SISIHYT,[143] come in to the midst of this flame! before me today and instruct me[144] concerning everything concerning which I am praying here today!

O great god who is upon the mountain of GABAYN,[145] ⁺CHABAHO."[146]

You should recite this / until the light appears. When the light appears, you should turn around[147] and recite this other document again also. *Here is* the copy of the summons itself which you should recite: "O, speak to me, speak to me, ⁺THES ⁺TENOR, the father of eternity and everlastingness, the god who is over the entire land, ⁺SALGMO ⁺BALKMO ⁺BRAK ⁺NEPHRO-BANPRE[148] ⁺BRIAS ⁺SARINTER[149] ⁺MELIKHRIPHS ⁺LARNKNANES ⁺HEREPHES ⁺MEPHRO-BRIAS ⁺PHRGA ⁺PHEKSE ⁺NTSIYPSHIA[150] ⁺MARMAREKE ⁺LAORE-GREPSHIE! Let me see the answer to the inquiry on account of which I am here. Let an answer be made to me / concerning everything about which I am asking here today, truly, without falsehood. ⁺O ⁺ATAEL ⁺APTHE ⁺GHO-GHO-MOLE ⁺HESEN-MINGA-NTON-ROTHO-BAYBO[151] ⁺NOERE ⁺SERE-SERE ⁺SAN[152] ⁺GATHARA ⁺ERESGSHINGAL[153] ⁺SAKGISTE ⁺NTOTE-GAGISTE[154] ⁺AKRYRO-BORE[155] ⁺GONTERE."[156]

You should make him open his eye(s) so that he can look at the lamp, and you should ask him about what you wish. If obstinacy occurs, he not having seen the god, you should turn around[157] and recite his compulsion.

Formula: " ⁺SEMEA-GANTEY[158] ⁺GENTEY ⁺GONTEY ⁺GERINTEY[159] ⁺NTARENGO[160] ⁺LEKAYKS, / come to me! ⁺GANAB ⁺ARI ⁺KATEI[161] ⁺BARI KATEI,[162] sun disk, moon of the gods, sun disk, hear my voice! Let me be told an answer to everything about which I am asking here today. O perfume of ⁺SALABAHO ⁺NASIRA ⁺HAKE, arise! O

205
[VII, 19]

210
[VII, 24]

215
[VII, 29]

141. *PDM* xiv. 202 and 204 are for use when a youth is consulting the lamp; xiv. 201 and 203 are to be used when the magician is not using a youth as intermediary.

142. See n. 141 above.

143. See n. 89 above. Here the scribe has added the Old Coptic gloss AXREMTO above the beginning of the next line (i.e., over the Demotic "come!").

144. Literally, "cause that my eyes open out"; see n. 93 above.

145. Modified by the Demotic scribe from ATYGI; see Griffith and Thompson, *The Leyden Papyrus*, n. to column VII of the autograph volume.

146. Old Coptic gloss adds TAKARTAT after CHBAHO; cf. *PDM* xiv. 138 and n. 92 there.

147. See n. 122 above.

148. The end is written in Demotic as "of Pre," perhaps "soul of Pre."

149. NTER is the Old Coptic gloss; the Demotic writes *ntr.w*, "gods."

150. See n. 30 above (*nts* for *d* before *i*).

151. The last section shows a metathesis in the Demotic (apparently for graphic reasons) of the common ORTHO found in the gloss. See also n. 8 above (*nt.* for *d.*).

152. Written in Demotic as *sn*, "brother."

153. and 154. See n.8 above.

155. AKRYROBORE is Greek ἀκρουροβόρε (LSJ, s.v.: "swallowing the tip of her tail"). See also *PGM* I. 146 and the Glossary s.v. "YESSIMMIGADON formula." [H.D.B.]

156. See n. 8 above.

157. See n. 120 above.

158. SEMEA is Greek for "image," σεμέα/σημεία. [R.K.R.]

159. All four names end with Egyptian *t3w*, "breath, wind."

160. See n. 8 above.

161. The ending is written ⸗3 "linen."

162. See n. 161 above.

Lion-ram,[163] let me see the light today, together with the gods, so that they may tell me an answer to everything about which I am asking here today, truly. †NA †NA †NA †NA is your name; †NA †NA is your true name."

You should utter a loud whisper, calling out, saying, "Come to me †IAHO[164] †IAEY †IAHO †AYHO †IAHO, husband,[165] †bull, †high day,[166] †NASHBOT †ARPI-HPE ABLA-

220   †'eye of raven,' / 'face of falcon,' †NI-ABIT THATLAT †MIRIBAL."

[VIII, 1]   (If [the gods] delay so as not to come in, you should cry out: †"MIRIBAL)[167] †QMLA †KIKH, †the †father †of †the †fathers of the gods, enchant, 'One eye weeps; the other laughs, †Moon, moon, moon, moon, †HA †HA †HE †ST †ST †ST †ST †IHA †IAHO, seek! Send to me the god in whose hand the command[168] is today so that he may tell me an answer to everything about which I am asking here today."

You should speak [to] that god with your mouth each time, and you should cry out, "I am throwing fury at you, [fury] of him who cuts you, of him who devours

225   you. / Let the darkness separate from the light before me. O god, †HYHOS[169] sealed

[VIII, 5]   portion (?), be sated, be sated, †AHO[170] †AH;[171] I do not †appear †without portion, awe, soul of souls †IAHO †ARIAHA[172] ARIAHA; act for her; they will turn the face of [the] rebel; GS GS GS GS †IANIAN; 'we do' EIBS[173] KS KS KS KS, send to me the god in whose hand the command is[174] so that he may tell me an answer to everything about which I am asking here today. Come in, †PIATOY †CHITRE! O SHOP SHOPE SHOP[175] †ABRAHME,[176] the pupil of the sound eye,[177] †QMR QMR QMR QMR KMRO,[178] who created †creation, great flourishing creation. †SH[]KNYSH is your real name.

230   Let an answer be told to me / about everything concerning which I am asking here

[VIII, 10] today. Come to me BAKAKSIKHEKH![179] Tell me an answer to everything about which I am asking here today, truly, without telling me falsehood" (*formula*: seven times).

*Tr.: Janet H. Johnson, following the edition and translation of Griffith and Thompson, *Demotic Magical Papyrus*, recto, col. VI/1–VIII/11. All words preceded by † are written in the text in Demotic with Old Coptic glosses inserted above.

163. See n. 6 above.
164. Written with the Egyptian verb *iw*, "to come."
165. Although with animal determinative rather than phallus.
166. Or, if we do not believe the determinative on *q3*, "day of (the) bull."
167. Overlap with the end of the preceding column. Note that, as Griffith and Thompson remark, *The Leyden Papyrus* 62, n. to l. VIII. 1, this heading is simply a reminder of the subject matter and is not a new heading; it is put in the middle of the column, not flush with the right margin.
168. See n. 107 above.
169. Ending written as *hs*, "praise."
170. The Demotic uses the verb *iw*, "to come."
171. See n. 170 above.
172. Perhaps "lifetime maker." [R.K.R.]
173. R.K.R. suggests translating "I shall induct (?)."
174. See n. 107 above.
175. Written with the Egyptian verb *hpr* "to be, become," Coptic *šōpe*; the middle example has an added final *e*.
176. With seated man determinative; the Old Coptic gloss reads ABRAHAM.
177. The *wd3.t*-eye of Horus.
178. "Creator (or creation) of the mouth."
179. "Soul of darkness, son of darkness." See n. 76 above.

PDM xiv. 232–38

*A "god's arrival"[180] at the request of Paysakh, the priest of Cusae,[181] who says that it has been tested nine times: "I am †RAMSHY[182] †SHY RAMSHY son †of PSHY of his mother †she †of PSHY. If such-and-such a thing is going to happen, do not come to me in your face of Pekhe.[183] You should come to me in your form of a priest, / in your figure of a man of the temple. If it will not happen, you should come to me in your form of a soldier, for I am RAMSHY SHY RAMSHY, the son †of PSHY, of his mother †she †of PSHY."

235
[col. VIII,
15]

[Say it] opposite Ursa Major on the third day of the lunar month, there being a clove of three-lobed white garlic with three iron needles piercing it; recite this to it seven times, and put it before you. He sees you and speaks with you.

*Tr.: Janet H. Johnson, following the edition and translation of Griffith and Thompson, *Demotic Magical Papyrus*, recto, col. VIII/12–18. Words preceded by † are written in the text in Demotic with Old Coptic glosses inserted above.

PDM xiv. 239–95

*The vessel inquiry of Khonsu: "[Hail][184] to you, Khonsu in Thebes Nefer-hotep, the noble child who came forth from the lotus,[185] Horus, lord of time,[186] †he †is †one. . . . / O silver,[187] lord of silver, o circuit of the underworld, lord of the circuit of the underworld,[188] lord of the disk, the great god, the †vigorous bull, the Son of the Ethiopian,[189] come to me. O noble child, the great god who is in the disk, who pleases[190] . . . , †POMO[191] who is called the bull, the great bull, the great god who is in the sound-eye,[192] who came forth from the four . . .[193] of eternity, the avenger of flesh, whose name cannot be known, whose form cannot be known, whose manner cannot be known.

240
[col. IX,
2]

180. See n. 62 above.

181. A town in Middle Egypt; see Gardiner, *Onomastica* II, 77*, #374. As Griffith and Thompson, *The Leyden Papyrus* 64, n. to l. VIII. 12, there is no determinative to show that Paysakh is a personal name, but it is hard to suggest an alternative interpretation.

182. Although SHY is written phonetically in the Demotic, this may well be the Egyptian god Shu, the god of the air. The first element of the name is written with the Egyptian word *r*, "mouth," and the whole name could possibly mean "mouth of Shu." If this is the god Shu, the P of PSHOU is the definite article, which is also found with *rᵉ* "the sun (god)" in the late form Pre.

183. A lion-headed goddess worshiped especially in Middle Egypt; see Griffith and Thompson, *The Leyden Papyrus* 65, n. to l. VIII. 14.

184. Restoring *ind*.

185. *Nfr-ḥtp* means "beautiful of setting" (of the sun and moon). Khonsu (son of Amoun and Mut and preeminently a Theban god) is a moon god, here identified with Horus (also a moon god) in the form of the "noble child who came forth from the lotus," i.e., *Nrf-tm*; see R.K.R.'s note to *PGM* IV. 1110.

186. The moon regulating the days of the month, as Griffith and Thompson, *The Leyden Papyrus* 66, n. to l. IX. 2.

187. The color of the moon, as noted by Griffith and Thompson, *The Leyden Papyrus* 66, n. to l. IX. 2.

188. As suggested by Griffith and Thompson, ibid.

189. Amoun, who in the late period was considered the god of Meroe; cf. l. 1097 and see Griffith and Thompson, ibid.

190. Or does this involve the verb *ḥn* "to command," "to entrust"? Then the rendering would be "to whom is commanded" (*ḥn.w n.f*). [R.K.R.]

191. Perhaps "the great one of/among the great one(s)." [R.K.R.]

192. The *wḏꜣ.t*-eye, the sound-eye of Horus. See Bonnet, *RÄRG* 854–56, s.v. "Uzatauge."

193. The identical epithets occur below, *PDM* xiv. 250–58. The word *ḥn* which is to be restored here means literally "vessel." The plural means "things" and the Coptic derivative means not only "vessel" or "pot" but any material "thing." Griffith and Thompson translate "boundaries" in 241 and 250 and "cycle" in 246. R.K.R. suggests that the idea of "four eternal things" is an Egyptian rendering of the Greek concept of the four elements.

"I know your name, I know your form, I [know] your manner. ⁺'Great' is your name; ⁺'Heir' is your name; ⁺'Beneficial' is your name; 'Hidden' is your name; 'Great one of the gods' is your name; 'He whose name is hidden from all the gods'¹⁹⁴ is your name; ⁺OM, Great One, ⁺Am is your name; 'All the gods' is your name; 'Lotus Lion Ram'¹⁹⁵ is your name; ⁺'LOY is coming, Lord of the ⁺lands' 'Lord of the lands' is your name; ⁺'AMAKHR of heaven' is your name; 'Lotus flower of stars

245   (?) / is coming EI IO NE EI O' is your name.

[IX, 7]   'Your [secret] form is [that of] a scarab with the face of a ram whose tail is a falcon and which is wearing two panther skins.¹⁹⁶ Your [serpent is a serpent] of eternity;¹⁹⁷ your . . .¹⁹⁸ is a lunar month; your wood is vine wood and persea; your herb is the herb of Amoun; your bird of heaven is a heron; your fish of [the sea] is a black *lebis*.¹⁹⁹ They are established on earth. 'Sickness' is your name in your body in the sea; your [secret] form of stone in which you came forth is a [. . .], Heaven is your shrine, the Earth is your forecourt. My desire was to seize you here today, for I am one who appears [shining] and who ⁺endures. My . . .²⁰⁰ ⁺grows ⁺old when I have not done it through delay, when I have not discovered your name, O great god whose name is great, the lord of the ⁺threshing-floor of heaven. Bearing [hunger]

250   / for bread and thirst for water I did it. You should save me and make me well and

[IX, 12] give me praise, love, and respect before every man. For I am the [great] bull, the great god who is in the sound-eye, who came forth from the four . . . ⁺²⁰¹ of eternity.

"I am youth, the great name who is in heaven, who is called ⁺AMPHOY²⁰² AMPHOY truly, truly; ⁺He ⁺who ⁺was ⁺praised at Abydos;²⁰³ Ra. 'Horus the youth'²⁰⁴ is my name; 'Chief of the gods' is my correct name. Save me! Let me be healthy. Let my vessel become [successful?].

"Open to me Alkhah²⁰⁵ before every god and all men who came forth from the stone of Ptah,²⁰⁶ for I am the serpent who came forth from Nun,²⁰⁷ I am the youthful Ethiopian,²⁰⁸ the rearing uraeus of real gold! In ⁺my ⁺lips is honey. That which I shall say comes to pass at once. Hail . . . / mighty one! I am Anubis, the

255   youthful creation. I am Isis; I shall bind²⁰⁹ him. I am Osiris; I shall bind him. I am

[IX, 17] Anubis; [I shall bind] him. You should save me from every [misery?] and all confusion. ⁺LASMATNYT ⁺LESMATOT, save me! Heal me! Give me praise, love and respect in²¹⁰ my vessel, and (?) my bandage here today! Come to me, Isis, mistress of

---

194. An epithet of Amoun-Ra, as Griffith and Thompson, *The Leyden Papyrus* 67, n. to l. XI. 5.

195. See n. 6 above.

196. A figure found on late period coffins, as noted by Griffith and Thompson, *The Leyden Papyrus* 68, n. to l. IX. 7.

197. For the various possible meanings of this image, see the discussion in F. Ll. Griffith, *Stories of the High Priests of Memphis* (Oxford: Clarendon Press, 1900) 22, n. to l. III/20.

198. See n. 192 above.

199. Probably Labeo Niloticus; see Griffith and Thompson, *The Leyden Papyrus* 68, n. to l. IX. 9.

200. With flesh determinative; it should be a part of the body.

201. See n. 192 above.

202. Could this be a phonetic rendering of the "great one in (the) heavens," ʿ3 m p.w(t)?

203. Osiris.

204. See n. 185 above.

205. See n. 2 above.

206. For Ptah as creator god, see H. Bonnet, *RÄRG* 614–19, s.v. "Ptah."

207. The primeval waters.

208. See n. 189 above.

209. The binding of the body as part of mummification.

210. I.e., through.

magic, the great sorceress of all the gods. Horus is before me; Isis is behind me; Nephthys is as my diadem. A snake, being the son of Atoum,[211] is that which †lies[212] in the uraeus diadem at my head in order that he who will strike me will strike the king. Mont is here today . . . Mighty Mihos[213] will send out a lion of the sons of Mihos, he being forced to bring to me quickly[214] †the divine †souls, the human souls, / the souls of the Underworld, the souls of the horizon, the spirits, the dead,[215] so that they tell me the truth today concerning that about which I am inquiring, for I am Horus, son of Isis, who is going across to Alkhah[216] to cast embalming wrappings before the amulets and to put linen on the Drowned one, the good Drowned one of the drowned ones.[217] They should[218] awaken and flourish at the mouths of my vessel, my bandage, my word-gathering. Awaken for me the spirits, the dead; awaken their souls and their forms at the mouths of my vessel! Awaken them for me together with the dead! Awaken [them] for me! Awaken them for me! Awaken their souls and their forms. O fury of Pessiwont[219] the daughter of ARB . . . , / awaken for me, awaken for me the Wontes from their misfortune! Let them speak with their mouths; let them talk with their lips; let them say that which I have said [concerning that which] I am asking here today. Let them speak before me; let truth happen to me. Do not substitute a face for a face, a name for a true name, truly [without] falsehood in it! [O] scarab of true lapis lazuli that sits at the pool of Pharaoh Osiris Unnefer,[220] fill your mouth with the water of [the pool?]! Pour it out on my head together with that which is at my hand! Heal me; heal him, and vice versa until what I said [happens]! Let that which I said come to pass, for if that which I said does not come to pass, I will cause the flame to circulate around this †bandage (?)[221] until that which I said does come to pass, for [they came] / to the earth, they listened to me . . . , and they said to me, Who are you? Who are you? I am Atum in the sun boat of Pre; I am †ARIATATY, †the †chest[222] of. . . . I looked out before [me] to see Osiris the Ethiopian while he was coming in at me, there being two sons of Anubis in front of him, [two] sons of Wepwawet[223] behind him, two sons of Rere[224] mooring him. They said to me Who are you? Who are you? . . . I am one of those two falcons who watch over Isis and Osiris, the diadem, the . . . with its greatness. . . . Bring to me, bring to me the divine souls, the human souls, the souls of the Underworld, the souls of the horizon, the spirits, the dead![225] Let them tell me the truth today concerning that about which I am asking,

260
[IX, 22]

265
[IX, 27]

270
[IX, 32]

---

211. For the connection between Atoum and serpents, see Karol Myśliwiec, *Studien zum Gott Atum*, vol. 1 (Hildesheim: Gerstenberg Verlag, 1978) 95–124.

212. Reading by W. Spiegelberg, "Demotische Miszellen, 5. Eine unerklärte Glosse im magischen Papyrus," *ZÄS* 53 (1917):123.

213. A lion god.

214. Actually written *sp sn*, "twice."

215. To the Egyptian, the range of forceful beings in the world.

216. See n. 3 above.

217. The drowned one is Osiris, who is here being cared for by his dutiful son Horus; see n. 58 above.

218. Corrected in Coptic from "you should" in Demotic.

219. To be translated "her son Wonte"; Wonte is a designation of Apophis, the enemy of Ra. See Erman and Grapow, *Wörterbuch* I. 325, #14. On Wonte and Apophis, see also *PGM* IV. 993–95 and n.

220. Unnefer is Onnophris. See *PGM* IV. 1078.

221. See F. Ll. Griffith, "The Glosses in the Magical Papyrus of London and Leiden," *ZÄS* 46 (1909–10):128, and Crum, *Coptic Dictionary* 368b.

222. Perhaps "sarcophagus."

223. Jackal-headed god.

224. Usually the "sow" but here determined with the snake and perhaps indicating a snake goddess.

225. See n. 214 above.

275
[X, 2]

for I am ˈARTEMI²²⁶ . . . womb when he rises in the east. / Come in to me, Anubis, in your beautiful face! It is in order to worship you that I come. Woe (?), woe (?), fire, fire, [south, north,] west, east, every breeze of Amenti,²²⁷ let them come into being in very good condition, established, correct, enchanted, like the fury [of the one great] of reverence, for I am ˈIAE ˈIAO ˈIAEA ˈIAO ˈSABAOTH ˈATONE,²²⁸ I am casting [fury] at you, ˈTSIE²²⁹ ˈGLATE ˈARKHE²³⁰ ˈIAO ˈPHALEKMI ˈIAO ˈMAKHA-HAI ˈIEE KHO . . . ˈN ˈKHOKHREKHI ˈE-EOTH ˈSARBIAQY ˈIGRA ˈPSHIBIEG²³¹

280
[X, 7]

ˈMOMY ˈMYNEKH ˈSTSITHO²³² ˈSOTHON ˈNAON ˈKHARMAI. / O fury of all these gods, whose names I have uttered here today, awaken for me, awaken for me the drowned, the [dead]! Let your souls and your [secret] forms live for me at the mouths of my lamp, my bandage, my word-gathering. Let it answer me concerning every word [about] which I am asking here today in truth, truly, without falsehood therein. Hasten, hasten, quickly, quickly!"

Its preparation:²³³ You go to a dark storeroom whose [face] opens to the south or east in a clean place. You should spread it with clean sand brought from the great river.²³⁴ You should bring a clean copper beaker or a new vessel [made] of pottery; you should put a *lok*-measure of water that has settled or of pure water into the

285
[X, 12]

beaker together with a *lok*-measure of pure real oil, / or oil alone without putting water into it; you should put a *qs-ˁnḥ* stone²³⁵ in the vessel with the oil; you should put a "heart-of-the-good-house" plant²³⁶ in the bottom of the vessel; you should put three new bricks around the vessel; you should place seven clean loaves [of bread] on the bricks which are around the vessel; and you should bring a pure youth who has been tested in his ears beforehand (that is, he will be profitable in going with the vessel). You should make him sit on a new [brick]; you yourself should sit on another brick, you being before him (another [manuscript] says, be-hind him); you should put your hand up to [his] eye(s), [his eye(s) being] closed

290
[X, 17]

while you recite down / into the middle of his head seven times. When you have finished, you should lift your hand from before his eye(s), you should [make him bend over] the vessel and you should put your hands to his ears. You should take hold of them with your own hands while you ask the child saying, "Did you [see the great god]?"

If he says, "I see a darkness," you should say to him "Speak, saying, 'I see your beautiful face, . . . you . . . O great god Anubis!'"

If you wish to do it by vessel [you being] alone,²³⁷ you should fill your eye(s) with this ointment,²³⁸ and you should sit [near the vessel?] in accordance with what is above, your eyes being closed. You should recite the above invocation seven times, open your eye(s), and question him concerning everything [that you wish]. . . . You

226. Artemis?
227. The west and, therefore, the necropolis.
228. Adonai?
229. See n. 30 above.
230. Greek ἀρχή, "beginning, first cause."
231. See n. 30 above.
232. See n. 30 above.
233. See n. 50 above.
234. The Nile.
235. See n. 65 above.
236. "The good house" is the place of embalming.
237. I.e., without using the youth.
238. Cf. *PDM* xiv. 140. [R.K.R.]

do it from the / fourth day of the lunar month until the fifteenth day, which is the   295
half-month when the moon fills the sound-eye.[239]   [X, 22]

*Tr.: Janet H. Johnson, following the edition and translation of Griffith and Thompson, *Demotic Magical Papyrus*, recto, col. IX/1–X/22. Words preceded by * are written in the text in Demotic with Old Coptic glosses inserted above.

PDM xiv. 295–308

*[A] vessel [inquiry, the magician being] alone[240] in order to see the bark of Pre.[241] *Formula*: "Open to me, O heaven, mother of the gods! Let [me see the bark] of Pre [descending and ascending] in it, for I am Geb, heir of the gods. Praying is what am doing before Pre, my father, [on account of] the things[242] which have gone forth from me. O great Heknet,[243] mistress of the shrine, the Rishtret (?),[244] open to me, mistress of spirits! [Open] to me, O primal heaven! Let me worship the messengers, [for] I am Geb, heir of the gods! O you seven Kings; O you [seven Montus],[245] bull who engenders, lord of awe / who illuminates the earth,   300
soul of the primeval waters. Hail, lion like a lion of the primeval waters, bull of   [col. X,
darkness! Hail, foremost one of the people of the east, Nun,[246] great one, lofty one!   27]
Hail, soul of the ram, soul of the people of the west! Hail, [soul of souls, bull] of darkness, bull (?) of bulls, son of Nut,[247] open to me! I am the Opener of earth, who came forth from Geb. Hail! [I am †I †I] †I †E †E †E [HE HE HE] †HO †HO †HO; I am †ANEPO[248] †MIRI †PO †RE MAAT IB THIBIO ARYI[249] †YAY [IAHO]."

  Formula: blood of a Nile goose, blood of a hoopoe, blood of a [nightjar], "live-on-them" plant, [mustard], / "Great-of-Amoun" plant,[250] *qs-ʿnḫ* stone,[251] genuine   305
lapis-lazuli, myrrh, "footprint-of-Isis" plant.[252] Pound [them]; make [them] into a   [X, 32]
ball [and paint] your [eye(s)] with it! Put a goat's-[tear] in (?) a "pleasure-wood"[253] of juniper or ebony wood [and bind it] around you [with a] strip of male palm fiber in [an] elevated place opposite the sun after putting [the ointment as above on] your eye(s) . . . according to what is written concerning it.

*Tr.: Janet H. Johnson, following the edition and translation of Griffith and Thompson, *Demotic Magical Papyrus*, recto, col. X/22–35. Words preceded by † are written in the text in Demotic with Old Coptic glosses inserted above.

PDM xiv. 309–34

*A spell for causing favor: "Come to me O . . . your beautiful name [of] Thoth! Hurry, hurry! Come to me. / Let me see your beautiful face here today . . . I being   310

239. I.e., full moon; on the sound-eye, see above, n. 192.
240. I.e., without using a youth.
241. This spell is repeated in *PDM* xiv. 805–16.
242. Literally, "words."
243. "Joyful" or "acclaimed one."
244. An epithet of Heknet?
245. For discussion of seven as a magical number in ancient Egypt, see Griffith and Thompson, *The Leyden Papyrus* 78–79, n. to l. X. 26. Note that *ḥknw* is the name of one of the seven oils found in offering lists.
246. Primeval waters.
247. Goddess of the sky.
248. Great Anubis.
249. Perhaps, "May the greatness of Ra, just (?) of heart, and the great lamb act." [R.K.R.]
250. Suggested by Griffith and Thompson, *The Leyden Papyrus*, glossary [3], to be flax.
251. See n. 65 above.
252. See Griffith and Thompson, *The Leyden Papyrus* 80, n. to l. X. 32, for the suggested identification of this plant as πίτταξις.
253. Suggested by Griffith and Thompson, ibid., n. to l. X. 33, to be a kohl stick.

[col. XI, 2] in the form of a baboon; may you rejoice over (?)[254] [me (?)] in praise and honor with your tongue of. . . . May you hear my voice today and may you save me from all evil things and all evil spells. Hail, he whose form is of . . . his great and mysterious form, from whose begetting a god came forth, who rests in the midst of Thebes! I am . . . of the great Lady, under whom Hapy[255] comes forth. I am the face of great awe . . . soul in his protection; I am the noble child / who is in the House of Re.[256] I am the noble dwarf who is in the cavern . . . the ibis as a true protection, who rests in Heliopolis. I am the master of the great foe,[257] the lord who obstructs semen, the very strong one . . . is my [name]. I am the ram, son of the ram; Lotus Lion Ram[258] (and vice versa) is my name. Ra-Khepri-Atum[259] is my true name, truly. Give me praise and love [before NN, son of] NN today, so that he give me all good things, so that he give me food and nourishment, and so that he do everything which I [shall desire. And do not let him] injure me so as to do me any harm, so that he say to me a thing which [I] hate, today, tonight, this month, this year, [this] hour. . . . [But as for my enemies (?)] the sun shall impede their hearts and blind / their eyes, and create darkness in their faces, for I am †BIRAI . . . †RAI; be far off †from †me![260] I am the son of Sakhmet; I am †BIGT, the bull of †LAT. I am GAT, son of GAT, whose . . . the underworld, who rests in the depths of the great temple[261] in Heliopolis. I am a greatly praised one, the mistress of protection, who binds with leather thongs . . . in whose protection are great and powerful divine powers, who rests in Bubastis. I am the divine shrew-mouse[262] who [rests in] Letopolis. Lord of Letopolis, unique lord . . . is my name; Ra-Khepri-Atum[263] is my true name, truly. O all you gods [whose names I have spoken] here today, come to me in order that you might hear what I said today / and in order that you might rescue [me] from all weakness, every defect, everything, every evil today! Give me praise, love [and respect before] NN,[264] the king and his people, the mountain and its animals so that he does everything which I shall say to him together with [every man who will see] me [or] to whom I shall speak [or] who will speak to me from among all men, all women, all youths, all old people, all people [or animals or things in the] whole land, [who] shall see me in these hours today so that they create my praise in their hearts in everything which I will [do] daily, together with those who will come to me in order to overthrow every enemy! Hurry, hurry! Quickly, quickly, before I have said them and repeated saying them!"

[330] [To be said] over an ape of wax and a fish; put it / in first-quality lotus oil (another [manuscript] says *tšps* oil)[265] or moringa oil which is . . . ; add styrax to it together with first quality myrrh and seeds of "great-of-love" plant in a faïence vessel; bring a wreath of . . . , anoint it with this oil as above, recite these [spells] to it seven times before the sun at dawn, before you have spoken to any man at all; pu-

[column markers: 315, [XI, 7], 320, [XI, 12], 325, [XI, 17], 330, [XI, 22]]

---

254. Suggested by R.K.R.

255. The Nile, especially the inundation.

256. I.e., Heliopolis.

257. Perhaps *ḫr.wy* "foe" is a mistake for *ḫr.wy* "testicles," as suggested by Griffith and Thompson, *The Leyden Papyrus* 82, n. to l. XI. 8.

258. See n. 6 above.

259. See n. 116 above.

260. See Griffith and Thompson, *The Leyden Papyrus* 83, n. to l. XI. 12.

261. Of the sun god, (P)re.

262. See Griffith and Thompson, *The Leyden Papyrus* 84, n. to l. XI. 15.

263. See n. 116 above.

264. Feminine.

265. For a possible identification, see Griffith and Thompson, *The Leyden Papyrus* 85, n. to l. XI. 22.

rify it; anoint your face with it; place the wreath in your hand; go to any place; [and be] among any people. It creates for you very great praise among them indeed. This scribe's feat is that of King [Darius].[266] There is none better than it.

*Tr.: Janet H. Johnson, following the edition and translation of Griffith and Thompson, *Demotic Magical Papyrus*, recto, col. XI/1–26. Words preceded by † are written in the text in Demotic with Old Coptic glosses inserted above.

PDM xiv. 335–55

*[A spell for making] a woman love a man: †Juice †of †balsam †tree, **one stater**; †malabathrum, **one stater**. qwšt, **one stater**; . . . scented . . . , **one stater**; mrwe, **one stater**; genuine oil, two *lok*-measures.[267] You should grind these [ingredients]. You should put them into a clean [vessel]; you should put the oil on top of them one day before the beginning of the lunar month. When the lunar month occurs, you should bring a black Nile fish[268] measuring nine fingers (another [manuscript] says seven), its eye(s) being variegated(?) in color . . . [which you] find in [a] water(?) . . . ; you should put it into this above-mentioned oil for two days; you should recite this formula to it at dawn . . . / before you have come [out of your] house and before you have spoken to any man on earth. When the two days have passed [you should] arise at dawn. You should [go] to a garden. You should bring a vine shoot which has not yet formed grapes. You should lift it in your left [hand]; you should put it in your right hand. It should amount to seven fingers [in length]. You should take it [to your] house; you should bring the [fish] up out of the oil; you should tie it by its tail with a strip of flax; you should hang it up [by the head on] the vine; and [you should place] the thing containing oil under it for another three days until it[269] pours out by drops downwards that which is in it, while / the vessel which is under [it] is on a new brick. When the three days have passed, you should [bring it] down. You should embalm [it] with myrrh, natron, and byssus. You should put it in a hidden place or in [your house]. You should spend two more days, reciting to the oil again, making seven days. You should keep it. When you [wish] to make it do its work, you should anoint your phallus and your face and you should lie with the woman to whom you will do it.

The spells which you should recite to the oil: "I am Shu[270] †GLABANO. I am Ra; I am the †creation[271] of †Ra; I am the son of Ra. I am / SISHT[272] the son of Shu, a water reed of Heliopolis, this griffin which is in Abydos. You[273] are the first one, the great one, great of magic, the living,[274] uraeus. You[275] are the sun boat, the lake of Wu-poke.[276] Give me praise, love, and respect before every womb, every woman. Love is my true name."

[Another] spell pertaining to it,[277] again: "I am Shu KLAKINOK; I am IARN, I am

335
[col. XII,
1]

340
[XII, 6]

345
[XII, 11]

350
[XII, 16]

266. For the restoration, see ibid., 86, n. to l. XI. 26.
267. A *lok*-measure is about one pint.
268. For a discussion of the type of fish, see Griffith and Thompson, *The Leyden Papyrus* 87–88, n. to l. XII. 4.
269. The fish.
270. God of air.
271. Or the "reed" of Ra.
272. "The image of." [R.K.R.]
273. Feminine singular.
274. Or "rearing": cf. *PDM* xiv. 3.
275. Feminine singular.
276. See n. 113 above.
277. The fish.

GAMREN. I am SE . . . PAER(?) IPAF INPEN NTINHS GAMRY,[278] water of Heliopolis. I am Shu SHABY SHA . . . , SHABAHO LAHEI[279]LAHS LAHEI,[280] the great god who is in the east, / LABRATHAA. I am the griffin which is in Abydos."

355

[XII, 21] *Tr.: Janet H. Johnson following the edition and translation of Griffith and Thompson, *Demotic Magical Papyrus*, recto, col. XII/1–21. Words preceded by ᐟ are written in the text in Demotic with Old Coptic glosses inserted above.

PDM xiv. 355–65

*[Another] manner of them[281] to give favor to a man before a woman and vice versa before . . . : "You[282] are the great one,[283] the great of magic, the Ethiopian [cat], daughter of Ra,[284] the mistress of the uraeus.[285] You are Sakhmet[286] the great, the mistress of Ast,[287] who has destroyed every enemy . . . [eye (?)] of the sun in the sound-eye,[288] born of the moon at midmonth at night.[289] You are the great creation of the primeval waters. You[290] are creation . . . the great one who is in the House of the obelisk[291] in Heliopolis. You[292] are the golden mirror: [you are] the morning bark [of the sun], the sun bark of Ra, . . . LANDJA, the youth, the son of the Greek

360   woman, the Libyan woman of the . . . / of dom palm fruit, these secrets (?) . . . of

[col. XII,   Bi-weken.[293] The favor and the love which Pre, your father, has given to you, send

26]   [them] down to me into this oil before every heart and eye of every woman before whom I am going in."

[Invocation,] to a black Nile fish[294] nine fingers [long]: [You should put it] in oil of roses;[295] you should drown it in it; you should bring it [up]; you should hang [it] up by [the] head [for . . . days]. When you have finished you should put it in a glass vessel; you should [add] a little water of sisymbrium[296] and a small "amulet plant(?)-of-Isis" which is . . . and pounded; and you should recite this to it seven times for

365   seven days opposite the rising of the sun. You should anoint your face with it / at

[XII, 31]   the time when you lie with the woman; [you should] embalm the fish in myrrh and natron. You should bury it in your house or in a hidden place.

*Tr.: Janet H. Johnson, following the edition and translation of Griffith and Thompson, *Demotic Magical Papyrus*, recto, col. XII/21–31.

278. The end is written *r.w*, "mouths."
279. The end is written *iy*, "to come."
280. The end is written *ʿe.t*, "limb."
281. Written "me" rather than "them."
282. Feminine singular.
283. *t3.wr.t*, identified by Griffith and Thompson as Thoueris, a goddess usually presented in the form of a hippopotamus.
284. In the story of the Myth of the Sun's Eye (see n. 19 to xiv. 1–92), Tefnut, the daughter of Ra, fled to Ethiopia.
285. For all these epithets, cf. *PDM* xiv. 350–51.
286. Cat goddess, goddess of war.
287. See Griffith and Thompson, *The Leyden Papyrus* 90, n. to l. XII. 22.
288. See n. 192 above and *PDM* xiv. 295.
289. The sun and moon were thought of as the eyes of heaven, as Griffith and Thompson, *The Leyden Papyrus* 90, n. to l. XII. 23.
290. Feminine singular.
291. Within the great temple of the sun god, Ra.
292. Feminine singular.
293. The eastern desert.
294. See n. 268 above.
295. See n. 100 above.
296. See Griffith and Thompson, *The Leyden Papyrus* 92, n. to l. XII. 29.

PDM xiv. 366–75

***The method** of separating a man from a woman and a woman from her husband: "Woe; woe, flame; flame; Geb made his form into (that of) a bull, he had intercourse [with][297] his mother, Tefnet, †again . . . as the heart of his father cursed his face, the fury of him whose soul is as a flame, while his body is as a pillar, so that he . . . fill the earth with flame and so that the mountains shoot with tongues. The fury of every god and every goddess, the great living one,[298] †LALAT / †BARESHAK eye of Ethiopia[299] be cast upon NN, the son of NN, [and] NN, the daughter of NN. Put the fire behind his heart and the flame in his place of sleeping, the . . . fire of hatred never [ceasing to enter] into his heart at any time, until he casts NN, the daughter of NN, out of his house(s), she carrying (?) hatred to his heart, she carrying quarrelling to his face. Give him nagging and squabbling, fighting and quarreling between them at all times, until they are separated from each other, without having been at peace forever and ever." Gum, . . . / myrrh. You should add wine to them; you should make them into a figure[300] of Geb, there being a *w3s*-scepter[301] in his hand.

370
[col. XIII, 5]

375
[XIII, 10]

*Tr.: Janet H. Johnson, following the edition and translation of Griffith and Thompson, *Demotic Magical Papyrus*, recto, col. XIII/1–10. Words preceded by † are written in the text in Demotic with Old Coptic glosses inserted above.

PDM xiv. 376–94

*[The recipes] into which the shrew-mouse goes: If you bring a shrew-mouse, you drown it in some water, and you make the man drink it; [then] he is blinded in both eyes. If you grind its body(?) with any piece of food and you make the man eat it, [then] he makes a blistering death(?),[302] he swells up, and he dies.

If you do it to fetch a woman, you should bring a shrew-mouse; you should place it on a Syrian potsherd; you should put it on the backbone of a donkey; you should put its tail on a Syrian potsherd or [piece of] a glass; also, you should let it loose alive in / the door of a bathroom of the woman; you should gild it. You should embalm its tail; you should add pounded myrrh to it; you should put it in a gold[303] ring(?); you should put it on your finger after reciting these[304] spells to it; and you should go with it to any place. Every woman whom you shall seize, she [wants?] you. You do it when the moon is full.

380
[col. XIII, 15]

If you do it to make a woman mad after a man,[305] you should take its body when it is dry; you should pound [it; you should] take a little of it together with a little blood from your second finger and the little finger[306] of your left hand; you should mix it with it; you should put it in a cup of wine; you should give it to the woman so that she drinks it. [Then] she rages after you.

If you put its gall into a [measure of] wine / and the man drinks it, he dies at

385

297. See J. G. Griffiths, "A Note on P. Demot. Mag. Lond. et Leid. XIII, 2," *ZÄS* 84 (1959): 156–57.
298. Perhaps the uraeus serpent; cf. *PDM* xiv. 3 and 351.
299. Tefnut; see n. 284 above.
300. The star-determinative suggested to Griffith and Thompson, *The Leyden Papyrus* 94, n. to l. XIII. 10, that this is a reference to the planet Κρόνος/Geb, otherwise called Horus the Bull and depicted as a bull-headed man holding a *w3s* scepter.
301. Symbol of dominion.
302. See Griffith and Thompson, *The Leyden Papyrus* 95, n. to l. XIII. 13.
303. Cf. *PDM* xiv. 392, as suggested by Griffith and Thompson, *The Leyden Papyrus* 95, n. to l. XIII. 15.
304. *PDM* xiv. 392–94.
305. A similar spell occurs in *PDM* xiv. 1206–18.
306. Crum, *Coptic Dictionary* 331b.

[XIII, 20] once; or [if you] put it into any piece [of food]. If you put its heart into a [seal] ring of gold, you put it on your hand, and you go anywhere, [then] it creates for you [favor, love and] respect.

If you drown a hawk in a [measure of] wine, and you make the man drink it, [then] he dies. If you put the gall of an Alexandrian [weasel] into any piece of food, [then] he dies. If you put a two-tailed lizard into [the] oil, [cook] it, and anoint the man with it, [then he dies?].

If you wish to produce a skin disease on a man so that it does not heal: A *hantous*
390   lizard [and?] a *haflela* lizard; you should cook them with [oil?], / and you should
[XIII, 25] wash the man with them.

If you wish to make it . . . :[307] you should put . . . ; [then] it. . . . If you put beer . . . to the man's eye(s), he is blinded.

The spells which you recite to the ring[308] at the time when you seize the woman: "[O] . . . IAHO ABRASAKS, may NN, whom NN bore, love me! May she burn for me in (?) the road!" . . . you . . .[309] she follows after you. You write [it] also on the strip with which you embalm the [shrew-mouse?].

*Tr.: Janet H. Johnson, following the edition and translation of Griffith and Thompson, *Demotic Magical Papyrus*, recto, col. XIII/11–29.

PDM xiv. 395–427

[col. XIV, *[**A vessel divination:**] "Open my eyes! Open your eyes!" and vice versa, up to
1]   three times. (That which another man said to me, "Open, O my eyes! Open, O my eyes!" up to *four* times.) "Open, ⸢Tat! Open Nap! Open Tat! Open, Nap! Open, Tat! Open, Nap! Open [to me]! Open [to me]! for I am ⸢ARTAMO, whom the great craftsman[310] bore, the great serpent of the east, who rises with your father at dawn! Hail, hail, Heh![311] Open to me, flame!"[312] You say whispering, ⸢"ARTAMO, open to me, flame. If you do not open to me, flame, I will make you open to me, flame. O ibis, ibis, sprinkle, ⸢so ⸢that ⸢I may see the great god Anubis, the powerful one,
400   / who is before me, the great strength of the sound-eye![313] O powerful Anubis, the
[XIV, 6] good oxherd, open every[thing] to me! Reveal yourself to me, for I am ⸢NESTHOM ⸢NESDJOT ⸢NESHOTB ⸢BORILAMMAI BORILAMMAI ⸢MASTSINKS[314] Anubis, ⸢great ⸢one, Arian[315] the one who is great, Arian, this bringer of safety, Arian, the one who is outside! Hail, ⸢PHRIKS ⸢IKS lord ⸢IBROKS ⸢AMBROKS ⸢EBORKS ⸢KSON[316] ⸢NBROKHRIA, the great child, Anubis, for I am this soldier.

405   "O those of the Atef crown,[317] those of PEPHNUN[318] MASPHONEGE; / hail! Let
[XIV, 11] all that I have said come to pass here today, for hail! You are ⸢THAM ⸢THAMTHOM

307. Written in cipher; reading and meaning uncertain. Griffith and Thompson read ṮOYR and translated "to be troublesome." It might read ḌOYR, in which case could it mean "to be strong" (*ḏr*) or "to scatter, disperse" (*ḏrꜥ*)? Depending on the meaning of this verb, the preceding subject might be "he" (the man) rather than "it" (the animal).

308. See *PDM* xiv. 381.

309. The verb *ḏrp*, which is what appears to have been written, means "to stumble" or, transitively, "to trip (someone), to hinder, to impede."

310. A reference to Ptah, the craftsman god of Memphis.

311. Personification of high numbers and everlastingness.

312. Or a phonetic spelling of the name Heh, written in hieratic.

313. See n. 177 above.

314. With flesh determinative; cf., perhaps, μάστιξ, "whip."

315. Arianus, written with seated man determinative.

316. The Old Coptic gloss adds another KSON.

317. A crown worn by the king and Osiris.

318. Perhaps "he of the primeval waters (Nun)."

⌐THAMATHOM ⌐THAMATHOMTHAM ⌐THAMATHYTSI [319] Amoun. Amoun is your correct name, who is called ⌐THOM ANKTHOM.[320] You are ⌐ITTH; ⌐Thoth[321] is your name. ⌐Son ⌐of ⌐THOM ⌐ANITHOM ⌐OP[322] ⌐SAO ⌐SHATNSRO black,[323] open to me the mouths of my vessel here today! Come to me at the mouths of my vessel, my bandage! Let my cup make the reflection (?) of heaven. May the hounds of the Phulot[324] give me that which is just in the primeval waters. May they tell me / that about which I am asking here today, in truth, truly, there being no falsehood therein AEĒIOYŌ[325] ⌐spirit ⌐of ⌐strife!"[326]

Formula: You bring a copper cup; you engrave a figure of Anubis in it; you fill it with settled water guarded which the sun cannot find; you fill the top[327] [of the water] with true oil; you place it on [three] new bricks, whose undersides are spread with sand; you put another four bricks under the youth; you make the youth lie down on his stomach; you make him put his chin on the bricks of the vessel; you make him look into the oil, while a cloth is stretched over him, / and while a lighted lamp is in his right hand and a burning censer in his left hand; you put a lobe of Anubis plant on the lamp; you put this incense up [on the censer]; and you recite these writings which are above[328] to the vessel *seven* times.

The incense which you should put up [on the censer]: frankincense (?), oil, ammoniac, incense,[329] dates. Pound them with wine, make them into a ball and offer up this scent.

When you have finished, you should make the youth open his eyes and you should ask him, "Is the god coming in?" If he says, "The god has already come in," you should recite before him. *Formula*: "Your bull(?), ⌐MAO, O Anubis, this [soldier?],[330] this ⌐bull[331] / this blackness[332]. . . . This . . . ⌐this ⌐ITSI[333] this SRITSI[334] ⌐SRITSI SRITSI ⌐ABRITSI[335] is your name, being your correct name."

And you should ask him concerning that which you [desire]; when you have finished your inquiry about which you are asking, you should recite to him seven times and you should dismiss [the god] to his home.

His dismissal: *Formula*: "Farewell, farewell, [Anubis] the good oxherd, Anubis, Anubis, the son of a wolf and a dog, the . . ." (another papyrus says: "the child of

410
[XIV, 16]

415
[XIV, 21]

420
[XIV, 26]

319. See n. 30 above.
320. I.e., I am THOM.
321. See n. 30 above.
322. Written as the verb *ip* "to count, reckon."
323. Perhaps, as Griffith and Thompson, *The Leyden Papyrus* 100, n. to ll. XIV. 13–14, "[sacrifice (lit., cutting) of (a) black ram."
324. A geographical name; see H. Gauthier, *Dictionnaire des noms géographiques* . . . , vol. 4 (Cairo: Institut Français d'Archéologie Orientale: 1925–31), 4, for a discussion of the suggested identifications.
325. The vowels of the Greek alphabet, in order.
326. Written in Demotic with a foreign word determinative; a compound from μάχομαι, "to fight" and πνεῦμα, "spirit."
327. Literally, "its (the water's) face."
328. *PDM* xiv. 395–410.
329. See Griffith and Thompson, *The Leyden Papyrus* 102, n. to l. XIV. 23.
330. Assuming the partially preserved word is the *mty*, "soldier" (Coptic *matoi*), from "Mede."
331. If this is identical with Coptic *qam* (Černý, *Coptic Etymological Dictionary* 330).
332. This, like the preceding, would have been pronounced KAM, as that is glossed.
333. See n. 30 above.
334. See n. 30 above.
335. See n. 30 above.

her of [?] Isis and a dog, ⸢NABRISHOTHT, the Cherub[336] of Amenti,[337] king of those
of . . .”). Say *seven* times.

425

[XIV, 31]

You should take the lamp from the child, you should take the vessel containing
water, you should take the cloth off him. You can also do it / alone[338] by vessel inquiry. [It is] very good, tried, tested nine times.

The Anubis *plant*:[339] It grows in millions of places. Its leaf is like the leaf of Syrian [plant] which grows white; its flower is like the flower of conyza[340] . . . you . . .
eye . . . before you have . . . the vessel.

*Tr.: Janet H. Johnson, following the edition and translation of Griffith and Thompson, *De-
motic Magical Papyrus*, recto, col. XIV/1–34. Words preceded by ⸢ are written in the text in
Demotic with Old Coptic glosses inserted above. Note the change in line arrangement.

PDM xiv. 428–50

430

[col. XV,
3]

435

[XV, 8]

440

[XV, 13]

*A potion: You should bring a small shaving from the head of a man who was
murdered together with seven grains of barley buried in a grave of a dead man; you
should grind them with ten *oipe* / (another [manuscript] says, nine) of apple seeds;
you should add blood of a tick[341] of a black dog to them together with a little blood
of your second finger and the little finger[342] of your left hand and your semen;[343]
you should press them together; you should put them in a cup of wine; you should
add three ladles to it of the first fruits of the wine, before you have tasted it and
before an offering has been poured out from it; you should recite this spell[344] to it
seven times; you should make the woman drink it; you should tie the skin of the
tick aforesaid with a band of byssus; / and you should tie it to your left arm.

Its invocation. Formula: “I am he of ⸢Abydos, in truth, in the completion of
birth in her name of Isis, the bringer of flame, ⸢she ⸢of the seat of mercy of the
Agathodaimon.[345] I am this figure of the sun, ⸢the son ⸢of ⸢TAMESRO[346] is my name.
I am this figure of the strong general, this sword, this great overthrower. The great
flame is my name. I am this figure of Horus, this fortress, this sword; this great
overthrower is my name. I am this figure of the Drowned one,[347] who testifies in
writing, who rests on board here under / the great offering table of Abydos, to
whose name of Isis the blood of Osiris bore witness when it was put in this cup.
This wine, give it, the blood of Osiris [which] he gave to Isis, to make her feel love
in her heart for him at night, at noon, at any time, there not being time of change.
⸢Give it, the blood of NN, whom NN bore, to give it to NN, whom NN bore, in

336. For this interpretation, see Griffith and Thompson, *The Leyden Papyrus* 102, n. to l. XIV. 29.

337. The west, the necropolis, and thus the realm of the dead, over which Anubis presided.

338. I.e., without a youth.

339. *PDM* xiv. 415–16.

340. Thus Griffith and Thompson, *The Leyden Papyrus*; see pp. 103–4, n. to XIV. 32. The identification has been questioned by D. Devauchelle and M. Pezin, “Un papyrus médical démotique,” *CEg* 53
(1978):59. H. von Deines and H. Grapow (*Wörterbuch der Ägyptischen Drogennamen*, *Grundriss der
Medizin der Alten Ägypter*, vol. 6 [Berlin: Akademie-Verlag, 1959], 39–41) identified this plant as “men-
tha aquatica.”

341. The identification of *ḥꜣlꜥmꜥtꜥ* of *PDM* xiv. 430 with *syb* of *PDM* xiv. 434 indicates the meaning
“tick,” as Crum, *Coptic Dictionary*, 318b–319a.

342. See n. 306 above.

343. Or “urine.”

344. *PDM* civ. 435–48.

345. See n. 22 above.

346. Or “the daughter of Ra.” [R.K.R.]

347. Osiris.

this cup, this bowl of wine today, to cause her to feel a love for him in her heart. The love which Isis felt for Osiris, when she was seeking after him everywhere, let NN, the daughter of NN, feel it, / while seeking after NN, the son of NN, every- where. The love which Isis felt for Horus the Behedite,[348] let NN feel it for NN, she loving him, she being mad after him, she being inflamed by him, she seeking him everywhere, there being a flame of fire in her heart in her moment of not seeing him."

   Another method [of doing it] again: The fragment[349] of the tip of your fingernail and apple seed together with blood from your aforesaid finger also. You should pound the apple, you should add blood to it, you should put it in the cup of wine; / you should recite[350] it *seven* times, and you should make the woman drink it at the above-mentioned time.

445

[XV, 18]

450

[XV, 23]

*Tr.: Janet H. Johnson, following the edition and translation of Griffith and Thompson, *Demotic Magical Papyrus*, recto, col. XV/1–23. Words preceded by † are written in the text in Demotic with Old Coptic glosses inserted above.

PDM xiv. 451–58 [*PGM* XIVb. 12–15]

*[A spell] for going before a superior if he fights with you and he will not speak with you:

   "Do not pursue me, you, so-and-so, I am PAPIPETOU METOUBANES. I am carry- ing the mummy of Osiris, and I go to take it to Abydos, to take it to Tastai, and to bury it at Alkhah.[351] If he, NN, causes me trouble, / I will throw the mummy at him."

   Its invocation in Egyptian[352] again is this which is below:

   "Do not run after me, NN.[353] I am PAPIPETY METYBANES, carrying the mummy of Osiris, going to take it to Abydos to let it rest in Alkhah. If NN fights with me today, I shall cast it out." (Say seven times!)

455

[col. XV, 28] (15)

*Tr.: Janet H. Johnson, following the edition and translation of Griffith and Thompson, *Demotic Magical Papyrus*, recto, col. XV/24–31, and R. F. Hock (Greek section).

PDM xiv. 459–75

*The words of the lamp: / "†BOTH †THEY †IE †YE †O †OE †IA †YA (another manu- script [says], †THEY †IE †OE †ON †IA †YA) PTHAKH ELOE (another manuscript [says] ELON; very good) †IATH †EON †PERIPHAE †IEY †IA †IO †IA †IYE, come down to the light of this lamp, appear to this youth, and ask for me about that which I am asking here today, †IAO †IAOLO †THERENTHO †PSIKSHIMEA KHE-LO[354] †BLAK- HANSPLA †IAE †YEBAI[355] †BARBARETHY †IEY †ARPON-GNYPH / †BRINTATENOPHRI †HEA †GARHRE †BALMENTHRE †MENEBARIAKHEGH †IA †KHEKH[356] †BRIN-SKALMA †ARYNSARBA[357] †MESEGHRIPH †NIPTYMIKH †MAORKHARAM. †O, †LAANKHEKH †OMPH †BRIMBAINYIOTH †SENGENBAI †GHOYGHE †LAIKHAM †ARMIOYTH."

460

[col. XVI, 1, 2]

465

[XIV, 7]

348. I.e., of Edfu.
349. Literally, "measure." See R. H. Pierce, "*Dnf*, A Problem in Demotic Lexicography," *Journal of the American Research Center in Egypt* 4 (1965): 74.
350. *PDM* xiv. 435–48.
351. See n. 3 above.
352. Note the bilingual abilities of the scribe. The text is Egyptian in theme (the burial of Osiris) and the Greek text even includes one sentence in Egyptian. This indicates the Egyptian origin of the whole, despite the placement of the Greek version before the Egyptian one. [R.K.R.]
353. Feminine or, possibly, plural.
354. See n. 30 above.
355. Ending written *by*, "soul."
356. Glossed xyx, Egyptian *kky* "darkness": see n. 76 above.
357. See n. 8 above.

You should speak, you[358] being pure, in this manner: "O god who lives, O lamp
470   which is lit, †TAGRTAT, he of eternity, bring in / †BOEL! Bring BOEL in! Bring BOEL
[XVI, 12]   in! †ARBETH-BAI †YTSIO,[359] O doubly †great god, bring †BOEL in! †TAT TAT, bring
†BOEL in! Bring BOEL in! Bring BOEL in! TAGRTAT, he of Eternity, bring BOEL in!
Bring BOEL in! Bring BOEL in! BEYTSI[360] O great god, bring †BOEL in! Bring BOEL
in! Bring BOEL in!

    The invocation which you should recite before Pre early in the morning before
you have recited to the youth, in order that that which you will do will come about:
"O great god, †TABAO †BASYKHAM †AMO †AKHA-GHAR-KHAN-GRABYNSA-NYNI
475   / †TSIKOMETO[361] †GATHYBASATHYRITHMILAALO" ([say] *seven times*).
[XVI, 17]   *Tr.: Janet H. Johnson, following the edition and translation of Griffith and Thompson, *Demotic Magical Papyrus*, recto, col. XVI/1–17. Words preceded by † are written in the text in
Demotic with Old Coptic glosses inserted above.

PDM xiv. 475–88

*Another manner of [doing] it also: You should rise at dawn from your bed, early
in the day on which you will do it, or any day, in order that everything which you
will do will be exact through your agency,[362] you being pure from all evil. You should
recite this spell before Pre three times or seven times: "†IO †TA-BAO †SOKHAM-MYA
†OKHOKH-KHAN-BYNSANAY[363] †AN-IESI †EGOMPTO[364] †GETHO †SETHYRI †THMILA
480   †ALYAPOKHRI, let everything / that I shall undertake here today, let it happen."
[col. XVI,   *Its manner*: You bring a new lamp in which no red lead[365] has been put; you
22]   [put] a clean wick in it; you fill it with pure genuine oil; you put it in a hidden place
cleansed with natron water; you lay it on a new brick; you bring a youth; you seat
him on another new brick, his face being turned to the lamp; you close his eyes;
and you recite these [words] above,[366] down into the youth's head, seven times. You
should make him open his eyes while you say to him, "Do you see the light?" If he
says to you, "I see the light in the flame of the lamp," you should cry out at that
485   moment saying / "†HEYE" nine times. You should ask him about everything you
[XVI, 27]   wish after reciting the invocation which you did previously before Pre early in the
morning.[367] You do it in a place whose door opens to the east; you leave the face of
the lamp turned . . . ; and you leave the youth's faced turned . . .[368] facing the lamp,
you being on his left. You should recite down into his head, while you touch his
head with your second finger of the . . . of your right hand.

    *Tr.: Janet H. Johnson, following the edition and translation of Griffith and Thompson, *De-
motic Magical Papyrus*, recto, col. XVI/18–30. Words preceded by † are written in the text in
Demotic with Old Coptic glosses inserted above.

358. Actually written "it."
359. See n. 30 above.
360. See n. 30 above.
361. Ending written *qme t3*, "creator of the earth": for the correspondence of Egyptian and Greek
letters, see n. 30 above.
362. Literally, "through your hand."
363. Ending written *nw*, "time"; for correspondences between Greek and Egyptian letters, see n. 8
above.
364. Old Coptic gloss aspirated; Demotic writes *m p3 t3*, "in the earth."
365. See R.K.R.'s note to *PGM* I. 277.
366. *PDM* xiv. 478–79.
367. xiv. 476.
368. Left blank in the manuscript.

PDM xiv. 489–515

*__Another__ manner of [doing] it also; [it is] very good for the lamp. You should [say]:[369] "⸗BOEL BOEL BOEL ⸗I ⸗I ⸗I ⸗A ⸗A ⸗A ⸗TAT ⸗TAT ⸗TAT, the first servant of the great god, he who gives light exceedingly / the companion of the flame, in whose mouth is the flame, he of the flame which is never extinguished, the god who lives, who never dies, the great god, he who sits in the flame, who is in the midst of the flame, who is in the lake of heaven,[370] in whose hand is the greatness and might of the god, come into the midst of this flame. Reveal yourself to this youth here today, have him inquire for me concerning everything about which I shall ask him here today, for I shall praise you in heaven before Pre; I shall praise you before the moon; I shall praise you on earth; I shall praise you before the one who is on the throne, who is never destroyed! O he of great praise, in whose hand is the greatness and might of the god, he of great praise, ⸗PETERI PETERI PATER ⸗EMPHE EMPHE,[371] O ⸗doubly ⸗great god, who is in the upper part of heaven, in whose hand is the beautiful staff, who created deity, deity not having / created him, come in to me with ⸗BOEL ⸗ANIEL; give strength to the eyes of this youth who is carrying my vessel today, in order to let him see you, in order to let his ears hear you while you are speaking; and ask for him about everything and all things about which I shall ask him here today! O great god, ⸗SI-SAOTH ⸗AKHREMPTO,[372] come into the midst of this flame! O he who sits on the mountain ⸗of ⸗Gabaon, ⸗TAGRTAT, he of eternity, he who does not die, who lives forever, bring[373] ⸗BOEL in ⸗BOEL BOEL, ⸗ARBETH-BAI-NOUTSI[374] ⸗O ⸗great ⸗one, great god, great god, bring[375] ⸗BOEL in! ⸗TAT TAT bring[376] BOEL in!" You should / say these [things] __seven times__ down into the youth's head. You should make him open his eyes; you should ask him, "Has the light already appeared?" If the light has not come forth, you should have the youth himself speak with his mouth to the lamp.

   __Formula__: "Be great, O light! Come forth, O light! Rise up, O light! Be high, O light! Come forth, O light of the god! Reveal yourself to me, O servant of the god, in whose hand is command today, who will ask for me."[377]

   He reveals himself to the youth in the moment named. You recite these things down into the head of the boy, while he is looking / at the lamp. Do not let him look at another place except only the lamp. If he does not look at it, he is afraid. You should do all these [things]. When you finish your inquiry, you should turn around, you should have him close his eyes, and you should say down into his head this __other__ invocation, below, that is, if the gods go away[378] and the youth ceases to see them: "⸗Beginning ⸗KHEM-PHE, ⸗Zeus, ⸗Sun[379] ⸗SATRA-PERMET, watch over this youth! Do not let him be frightened, terrified, or afraid, and make him return to his original path! Open, O ⸗Underworld! Open, ⸗here."[380] I say [it] that this vessel inquiry of the lamp is better / than the first.

490 [col. XVII, 2]

495 [XVII, 7]

500 [XVII, 11]

505 [XVII, 16]

510

369. A very similar invocation appears in PDM xiv. 127–40, 194–204, and 516–26.
370. See n. 84 above.
371. On this group, see n. 88 above.
372. Ending written *m pȝ tȝ*, "in the earth."
373. *R-iny* written above *r-wy*, both imperatives meaning "Bring!"
374. Could the end of this mean "Bas (souls) of the gods"? For the correspondence between Egyptian and Greek letters, see n. 30 above.
375. *R-iny* written above *r-wy*, both imperatives meaning "Bring!"
376. See n. 375 above.
377. See n. 23 above.
378. Or "in order that the gods go away."
379. The gloss consists of the Greek symbol for the sun.
380. A pun between "here" (*ty*) and "underworld" (*tei*).

[XVII,   This is the form again. ***Its manner***: you bring a new lamp in which no red lead[381]
21]   has been put; you put a clean cloth wick in it; you fill it with genuine clean oil; you
place it on a new brick; you seat the boy on another brick opposite the lamp; you
make him shut his eyes; and you recite down into his head according to the other
form also.

    Another invocation which you recite opposite Pre at dawn three times, or seven
times: ***Formula***: †IO-TABEO †SOKHOMMYA †OKHO-KH-KHAN †BYNSANAY[382] †AN-
515   IESI †EGOM(PH)THO †GETHO †SETHORI / †THMILA-ALYAPO-KHRI, may everything
[XVII,   which I shall do today come about." And they succeed.[383] If you do not purify it, it
26]   does not come about. Purity is its chief factor.

    *Tr.: Janet H. Johnson following the edition and translation of Griffith and Thompson, *De-
motic Magical Papyrus*, recto, col. XVII/1–26. Words preceded by † are written in the text in
Demotic with Old Coptic glosses inserted above.

PDM xiv. 516–27

    *****Another*** invocation according to what is above, again:[384] ***Formula***: " †BOEL BOEL
BOEL †I †I †I †A †I †I †I †A †TAT TAT TAT he who gives the light exceedingly, the
companion of the flame, he of the flame which is never extinguished, the god who
lives, who never dies, he who sits in the flame, who is in the midst of the flame, who
is in the lake of heaven,[385] in whose hand is the greatness and might of the god,
reveal yourself to this youth, HEY HOY HOY †HE-O so that he may inquire for me;
make him look so that he sees and hears[386] everything about which I shall ask him,
for I shall praise you in heaven, I shall praise you on earth, I shall praise you be-
520   fore the one who is on the throne, who is never destroyed. / O he of greatness,
[col.   †PETERI PETERI †EMPHE EMPHE,[387] O †great god[388] who is in the upper part of
XVII, 31] heaven, in whose hand is the beautiful staff, who created deity, deity not having
created him, come into the midst of this flame with BOEL †ANIEL. Give strength to
the eyes of †HEY †HEY, [†HEY †HEY],[389] the son of †HEY †HEY, in order that he see
you with his eyes; make his ears hear; speak with him of anything about which he
will ask you; tell me an answer truly! You are the great god †SABAOTH. Come down
525   with †BOEL TAT TAT! Bring BOEL in! Come into the midst of this flame / and ques-
[XVIII, 4] tion for me concerning that which is good! †TAGRTAT, he of eternity, bring †BOEL
in! Bring BOEL in! Bring BOEL in! ARBTH BAINYTSIO,[390] O †great god,[391] bring
BOEL in! Bring BOEL in! Bring BOEL in!" You should say these [things] down into
the youth's head; you should have him open his eyes and you should ask him about
everything according to the manner which is outside,[392] also.

    *Tr.: Janet H. Johnson, following the edition and translation of Griffith and Thompson, *De-*

    381. See n. 73 above.
    382. Ending written *nw*, "time"; for the correspondences between Egyptian and Greek letters, see
n. 8 above.
    383. Continuing from the instructions in *PDM* xiv. 512–13.
    384. A very similar invocation appears in *PDM* xiv. 127–40, 194–204, and 489–99.
    385. See n. 84 above.
    386. Or "obey."
    387. On this group, see n. 88 above.
    388. Glossed "doubly great."
    389. Intentional dittography in going from column XVII to column XVIII. Note that HEY here and
in the next line is written in Demotic with the silver determinative, as if it were the word "money, silver."
    390. See n. 374 above; here the adjective ꜥꜣ, "great," has been added to the end of the invocation
name. ARBETHBAINOYTHIŌ is "Horus-Falcon, spirit of the great god"; see *PDM* xiv. 500.
    391. Glossed "doubly great."
    392. On the verso, but see Griffith and Thompson, *The Leyden Papyrus* 118, n. to l. XVIII. 6.

motic Magical Papyrus, recto, col. XVII/26–XVIII/6. Words preceded by † are written in the text in Demotic or in Greek letters with Old Coptic glosses inserted above.

PDM xiv. 528–53

*[Another?] vessel inquiry which a physician in the Oxyrhynchite nome gave me. You can also do it as a vessel inquiry by yourself: [393] "SABANEM [394] NN BIRIBAT Hail! Hail, O god, †SISIAHO who is on the mountain of Qabaho, / in whose hand is the begetting of Fate,[395] go[396] to this boy! Let him enchant the light, for I am 'beautiful of face'[397] (another manuscript says "I am the face of Nun") at dawn, HALAHO[398] at midday; I am 'joyful of face' in the evening. I am Pre, the noble youth who is called GARTA by name. I am he who came forth on the arm of Triphis[399] in the east. I am †great; 'Great' is my name; 'Great' is my real name. I am †OY; †OY is my name; †AY is my real name. I †am †LOT †MULOT, the one who prevailed, he whose / strength is in the flame, he of that golden wreath which is on his head, THEIT THEIT[400] TO TO[401] HATRA HATRA, dog-face, dog-face. Hail, Anubis, Pharaoh of the underworld! Let the darkness depart. Bring the light to me in my vessel inquiry, for I am Horus, son of Osiris, whom Isis bore, the noble youth whom Isis loves, who seeks after his father Osiris Unnefer. Hail Anubis, Pharaoh of the underworld! Let the darkness depart. Bring the light to me in my vessel inquiry / my bandage here today! Let me flourish; let the one whose face is bent down to this vessel here today flourish until the gods come in and tell me [an] answer in truth concerning my question about which I am inquiring here today, truly, without falsehood, immediately. Hail, Anubis, creature and youth![402] Go forth at once! Bring to me the gods of this city and the god who gives answer today[403] so that he tell me my question about which I am asking today." Nine times.

/ When you open your eyes, or the youth [opens his eyes] and you see the light, you should recite to the light, "Hail, O light! Come forth, come forth, O light! Rise up, rise up, O light! Be great, be great, O light! O that which is outside, come in!" You should say it nine times until the light is great and Anubis comes in.

When Anubis has come in and established himself, you should say to Anubis, "Arise! Go out and bring in to me the gods of this city or town." He goes out at that moment and brings the gods in. When you know / that the gods have come in, you should say to Anubis, "Bring in a table for the gods so that they may sit down!" When they are seated, you say to Anubis,[404] "Bring in a wine jar and some bread! Let them eat; let them drink." When he has had them eat and drink, you should say to Anubis, "Are they going to inquire for me today?" If he says they [are] again, you

(marginal line references)
530
[col.
XVIII, 9]

535
[XVIII, 14]

540
[XVIII, 19]

545
[XVIII, 24]

550
[XVIII, 29]

---

393. I.e., without using a youth as intermediary.

394. Ending written *nm*, "dwarf."

395. See n. 22 above.

396. This verb also appears in *P. BM* 10507, 6/9, where it is translated "to approach" by M. Smith (not yet published).

397. Or, perhaps, "baboon-face," as Griffith and Thompson, *The Leyden Papyrus* 120, n. to l. XVIII. 10.

398. Ending written *ḥr*, "face."

399. A goddess whose name meant "the noble lady"; Griffith and Thompson suggest, *The Leyden Papyrus*, 120, n. to l. XVIII. 12, that this might be a reference to the constellation Virgo.

400. The middle of this name is written with the word ꜥ.*wy*, "house."

401. Written *t3*, "land."

402. Perhaps seen as half-canine, half-human. [R.K.R.]

403. See n. 23 above.

404. A very similar passage, but spoken by the youth, occurs in *PDM* xiv. 56–62.

should say to him, "The god who will question for me,[405] let him raise his hand for me and let him tell me his name." When he tells you his name, you should ask him concerning that which you desire. When you are finished asking about what you desire, you should send them away.

*Tr.: Janet H. Johnson, following the edition and translation of Griffith and Thompson, *Demotic Magical Papyrus*, recto, col. XVIII/7–33. Words preceded by ˙ are written in the text in Demotic with Old Coptic glosses inserted above.

PDM xiv. 554–62

555
[col. XIX, 2]

*[Spell] to be said to the bite of the dog: / "My mouth being full of blood of a black dog, I spitting out the redness[406] of a dog, I come forth from Alkhah.[407] O this dog who is among the ten dogs which belong to Anubis, the son of his body, extract your venom, remove your saliva from me also! If you do not extract your venom and remove your saliva, I shall take you up to the forecourt of [the temple

560
[XIX, 7]

of] Osiris, my watchtower (?). I will do for ˙you[408] . . . / according to the voice of Isis, the magician, the lady of magic, who bewitches everything, who is never bewitched in her name of Isis, the magician."

You [should] pound garlic with gum (?), put it on the wound of the dog bite, and speak to it daily until it is well.

*Tr.: Janet H. Johnson, following the edition and translation of Griffith and Thompson, *Demotic Magical Papyrus*, recto, col. XIX/1–9. The word preceded by ˙ is written in the text in Demotic with an Old Coptic gloss inserted above.

PDM xiv. 563–74

565
[col. XIX, 12]

570
[XIX, 17]

*[Spell] to be said in order to extract the venom from the heart of a man who has already been made to drink a potion or poison[409] (?): "Hail, hail, IABLY, O golden cup of Osiris! / From you have drunk Isis, Osiris, and the great Agathodaimon.[410] The three gods drank and after them I myself drank in order that you will not let me get drunk, you will not let me list, you will not make me fall, you will not make me be thrown down, you will not make me be troubled of heart, you will not make my mouth curse. May I be healed of all poison, pus, [and] venom. They shall be removed (?) from my heart. When I drink you, may I vomit[411] them up in her name of ˙SARBITHA, the daughter / of the Agathodaimon,[412] for I am SABRA BRIATHA BRISARA. HER is my name. I am Horus SHARON[413] coming from receiving greetings. IAHO, ˙the ˙child, is my name, being my real name" [to be said] to a cup of wine. Add fresh rue; add it to it; speak to it seven times, and make the man drink it at dawn before he has eaten.

*Tr.: Janet H. Johnson, following the editions and translation of Griffith and Thompson, *Demotic Magical Papyrus*, recto, col. XIX/10–21. Words preceded by ˙ are written in the text in Demotic with Old Coptic glosses inserted above.

405. See n. 23 above.
406. I.e., blood.
407. See n. 3 above.
408. Or, "act for you as . . . ": see the discussion of his passage in Johnson, *Verbal System* 11, n. 1. Or, "I shall do to you that which this other bird (?) did," seeing a reference to Isis as a kite. [R.K.R.]
409. Or "hang over" (?). [R.K.R.]
410. See n. 22 above.
411. Literally, "cause them to be thrown up."
412. See n. 22 above.
413. Written *ẖˁ r.n*, "to our mouths."

PDM xiv. 574–85

*[Spell] to be said to the man, when a bone is stuck / in his throat: "You are SHLATE LATE BALATE the white crocodile, which is under the foam of the sea of flame whose belly is full of bones of every drowned man. Hail, you should spit out this bone for me today, it acting as a harpoon head, it making a point, it acting as a sack piercer,[414] it doing[415] everything, without change, for I am[416] a lion's forepart, I am[417] a ram's horn,[418] I am[419] a panther's tooth. / Griffin[420] is my real name, for Osiris is he who is in my hand. The man named is the opener[421] of my neck"[422] (seven times).

575
[col. XIX, 22]

580
[XIX, 27]

You should speak to a little oil, you should put the man's face up; you should put it down in his mouth; you should move[423] your finger and your thumb[424] [to the] two sinews[425] of his throat; you should make him swallow the oil; you should make him rise up suddenly; and you should eject the oil which is in his throat immediately. / The bone comes up with the oil.

585
[XIX, 32]

*Tr.: Janet H. Johnson, following the edition and translation of Griffith and Thompson, *Demotic Magical Papyrus*, recto, col. XIX/21–32.

PDM xiv. 585–93

* Spell to be said to the bite of the dog: the fury of Amoun and Triphis:[426] "I am this strong Arab SHLAMALA MALET secret one, mighty one SHETEI[427] GRSHEI[428] GRSHEI[429] NEBRNT TAHNE BAHNE this dog, this black one,[430] the dog which has bewitched this dog, he of these four bitch-pups, the wolf[431] son of Wepwawet.[432] O son of Anubis, seize by your teeth! Put down your secretion, your face being that / of Seth against Osiris, your face being that of Apophis against the sun! Horus, the son of Osiris, whom Isis bore [is the one] with whom you filled your mouth,[433] NN whom NN bore [is the one] with whom you filled your mouth. Hear this speech of Horus, who stopped heat, who went to the primeval water, who established the earth; listen, O IAHO SABAHO ABIAHO by name!" You should cleanse the wound and grind salt with Nubian hematite.[434] Apply [it] to it.

590
[col. XIX, 37]

414. Meaning suggested by George R. Hughes; for harpoon head and point, see Griffith and Thompson, *The Leyden Papyrus* 126, n. to l. XIX. 25.

415. Or "acting as."

416. Or "to me belongs," as suggested by Griffith and Thompson, *The Leyden Papyrus* 126, n. to l. XIX. 26.

417. See n. 416 above.

418. See n. 416 above.

419. See n. 416 above.

420. See n. 12 above.

421. Reading *wn*.

422. Reading *nḥbe.t*.

423. Reading *ḥn*, "to approach," "move toward."

424. So William F. Edgerton, comparing it to Coptic *mout*, "thumb": Crum, *Coptic Dictionary* 81a.

425. Coptic *eine* means "sinew, nerve" or "neck"; Crum, *Coptic Dictionary* 189a.

426. See n. 399 above.

427. Ending written ʿ*e.t*, "limb."

428. See n. 427 above.

429. See n. 427 above.

430. Cf. *PDM* xiv. 555.

431. Or jackal, given the association with Wepwawet.

432. See n. 223 above.

433. I.e., whom you bit.

434. For this identification, see J. R. Harris, *Minerals* 156–57.

Another: You should grind rue with honey. Apply to it and say it also to a cup of water and make him drink it.

*Tr.: Janet H. Johnson, following the edition and translation of Griffith and Thompson, *Demotic Magical Papyrus*, recto, col. XIX/32–40.

PDM xiv. 594–620

595
[col. XX, 2]
*[Spell] to be said to the sting.[435] / "I am the King's son, greatest and first, Anubis. My mother Sekhmet-Isis comes[436] after me all the way to the land of Syria, to the hill of the land of Heh,[437] to the nome of these cannibals, saying, 'Hurry, hurry! Quickly, quickly, my child, King's son, greatest and first, Anubis,' saying, 'Arise and come to Egypt, for your father Osiris is King of Egypt; he is ruler over the whole land; all the gods of Egypt are assembled to receive the crown from his hand.'

600
[XX, 7]
/ "At the moment of saying these [things] she jumped[438] at me. My strength fell from me. She coiled[439] and she came to me with a sting; I sat down and I wept. Isis, my mother, sat near me, saying to me, 'Do not weep, do not weep, my child, King's son, greatest and first, Anubis! Lick from your tongue to your heart, and vice versa, as far as the edges of the wound! Lick from the edges of the wound up to the limits

605
[XX, 12]
of your / strength!' What you will lick up, you should swallow it. Do not spit it out on the ground, for your tongue is the tongue of the Agathodaimon,[440] your tongue is that of Atum!"

You should lick it with your tongue while it is bleeding. Immediately afterwards, you should speak to a little oil and you should speak[441] to it seven times while putting it on the sting daily. You should dye a strip of linen and put it on it.

610
[XX, 17]
/ [The spell] which you should say to the oil to put it on the sting daily: "Isis sat speaking to the oil, ABARTAT, and lamenting to the true oil, saying, 'You are praised. I am going to praise you, O oil; I am going to praise you. By the Agathodaimon you are praised. By me myself you are honored. I am going to praise you forever, O oil, O vegetable oil'" (another [manuscript] says "true oil"), "'O sweat of the

615
[XX, 22]
Agathodaimon, amulet of Geb. Isis is the one who / is speaking to the oil. O true oil, O drop of rain, O water-drawing of the planet Jupiter[442] which comes down from the sun bark at dawn, you should do the good [deeds] of the dew of dawn which heaven cast to the ground upon every tree. You should heal the limb which is paralyzed and you should act as remedy for him who lives, for I shall employ you for the sting of the King's son, greatest and first, Anubis, my child, in order that you fill it and make it well. For I shall employ you for [the] sting of NN, whom NN

620
[XX, 27]
bore, / in order that you fill it and make it well'" (seven times).

*Tr.: Janet H. Johnson, following the editions and translation of Griffith and Thompson, *Demotic Magical Papyrus*, recto, col. XX/1–27.

435. Probably of a scorpion, as Griffith and Thompson, *The Leyden Papyrus* 128, n. to l. XX. 1. This interpretation is reinforced by the suggested new translation of *PDM* xiv. 601; see n. 439 below.
436. For this interpretation, see J. Johnson, *Verbal Systems* 102, n. 167.
437. Literally, "millions."
438. See n. 456 below.
439. Literally, "gather"; this meaning was suggested by George R. Hughes.
440. See n. 22 above.
441. *PDM* xiv. 610–20.
442. Literally, "Horus the red" or "Horus the mysterious."

PDM xiv. 620–26

* Spell to be said to bring a bone out of a throat: "I am he whose head reaches the sky while his feet reach the primeval waters,[443] who awakened this crocodile . . . in Pidjeme[444] in Thebes, for I am ˈSA ˈSIME. TAMAHO is my correct name, ˈANYG ANYG, for a hawk's egg is what is in my mouth, an ibis egg is what is in my belly, saying, ˈbone of god, bone of man, bone of bird, bone of fish, bone of animal, bone of everything, there being nothing besides, for let that which is in your belly come to your heart; let that which is in your heart / come to your mouth; let that which is in your mouth come to my hand here today, for I am he who is in the seven heavens, who is established in the seven shrines; for I am the son of the living god!" [Say it] to a cup of water seven times and make the woman drink it.

625
[col. XX,
32]

* Tr.: Janet H. Johnson, following the edition and translation of Griffith and Thompson, *Demotic Magical Papyrus*, recto, col. XX/27–33. Words preceded by ˈ are written in the text in Demotic with Old Coptic glosses inserted above.

PDM xiv. 627–35

*The vessel inquiry of Osiris:[445] "Hail, Osiris, King of the Underworld, lord of burial, whose head is in Thinis[446] while his feet are in Thebes,[447] the one who gives answer in Abydos, while his protection[448] (?) is [in?] Pshilom,[449] he who is under the *nubs* tree in Meroë, who is on the mountain of Poranous,[450] who is on my house forever, / the house of the avengers[451] forever; he whose face[452] resembles the face of a hawk of byssus, mighty one whose tail is as the tail of a serpent while his back is as the back of a ˈdragon,ˈ[453] while his hand is [that of] a man, who is girded (?) with this girdle of bandage, ˈinˈ whose hand is this palm staff of command. Hail, IAHO SABAHO ATONAI[454] MISTEMY IAYIY! Hail, MIKHAEL[455] SABAEL! Hail, Anubis in the nome of the dog-faces, he to whom this earth belongs, who leaps[456] on only one foot! Hide the darkness in the deep! Bring in the light for me! Come in to me; tell me the answer to that about which I am inquiring here today!" [Say] nine times, / until the god comes and the light appears.

630
[col. XXI,
4]

You do it according to the forms of the remainder above, again while the youth's face is to the east and your own face is to the west, you reciting down into his head.

635
[XXI, 9]

* Tr.: Janet H. Johnson, following the edition and translation of Griffith and Thompson, *Demotic Magical Papyrus*, recto, col. XXI/1–9. Words preceded by ˈ are written in the text in Demotic with Old Coptic glosses inserted above.

443. Reaching from sky to abyss; see also *PGM* IV n. 160.

444. Western Thebes.

445. A partial parallel in Old Coptic is found in *PGM* IV. 10–25.

446. A town in the nome of Abydos; see A. H. Gardner, *Onomastica*, vol. II, p. 38*.

447. See Griffith and Thompson, *The Leyden Papyrus* 134, n. to l. XXI. 2.

448. The Old Coptic parallel (see n. 445 above) has "whose glory is in Pashalom."

449. For possible identifications, see Griffith and Thompson, *The Leyden Papyrus* 134, n. to l. XXI. 3.

450. Perhaps the Egyptian definite article *p* + οὐρανός, "firmament" of heaven, and Griffith and Thompson, ibid., 135, n. to l. XXI. 4.

451. On avengers, see also n. 24 above.

452. See the description of a griffin taken from the Myth of the Sun's Eye quoted in n. 12 above.

453. Literally, perhaps, "crocodile" or "guardian (dragon)"; see Griffith and Thompson, *The Leyden Papyrus* 135, n. to l. XXI. 5.

454. Adonai? The Old Coptic parallel (see n. 445 above) has *althōnai*.

455. The Old Coptic text (see n. 445 above) also invokes Michael.

456. Coptic *fi foqs*, "to leap, hop," Crum, *Coptic Dictionary* 627b, as suggested by George R. Hughes.

PDM xiv. 636–69

*[The method] of the scarab in the cup of wine in order to make a woman love a man: You should bring a scarab of Mars[457] (which is this small scarab which has no horn), it having three shields on the front of its head—you find its face shrunken—or also the one which has two horns.[458] You should bring it at the rising of the sun; you should bind yourself with a cloth on the upper part of your back; you should bind yourself at your face with a strip of palm fiber while the scarab is on the palm[459] of your hand; and you should speak[460] to it before the sun when it is about to rise, seven times. When you have finished, you should drown it in milk of a black cow. You should put a [unit of?] 10[461] (pieces) of olive wood to its head. You

640 should leave it until evening in the milk. When evening comes, you should / bring
[col. XXI, it up, you should spread under it with sand, and you should put a band of cloth
14] under it upon the sand, for four days. You should put myrrh on a flame before it.

When the four days have passed, and it is dry, you should bring it before you, a cloth being spread under it. You should divide it in its middle with a copper knife. You should take its right half and nail parings of your right hand and foot, and you should cook them on a new potsherd with vine wood. You should pound them with nine apple seeds and your urine or your sweat free from bath oil; you should make it into a ball; you should put it in the wine; you should speak[462] over it seven times; you should make the woman drink it; you should take its other half, the left one, together with the nail parings of your left hand and foot also; you should bind them in a strip of byssus with myrrh and saffron; you should bind them to your left arm; and you should lie with the woman while they are bound to you.

645 / If you wish to do it also without drowning it, you do it also on the third of the
[XXI, 19] lunar month, you doing this manner above for it also. You should recite its invocation to it before the sun at dawn; you should cook [it]; you should divide it; you should do it according to that which is above also in everything.

[The invocation] which you should recite to it before the sun at dawn: "You are the scarab of real lapis-lazuli. Bring yourself out of the door of my temple! You should lift (?) a copper vessel (?) to your nose, [O he] who knew how to eat the herbage, who tramples the field plants (?), who damages the great cult images of those of Egypt, I sending you against NN whom NN bore, to strike her from her heart to her belly, from her belly to her intestines, from her intestines to her womb, for she is the one who urinated before the sun at dawn, saying to the sun, 'Do not come forth!'; to the moon, 'Do not rise!'; to the water, 'Do not come to those of Egypt!'; to the field, 'Do not bloom!'; and to the great trees of those of Egypt, 'Do

650 not grow green!' / I sending you to NN, whom NN bore, in order to beat her from
[XXI, 24] her heart to her belly, from her belly to her intestines, from her intestines to her womb, so that she put herself on the road following after NN, whom NN bore, at all times."

[The spell] which you should recite to it while it is in the milk: "Woe, doubly great one; woe, my doubly great one; woe, his (?) Nun,[463] woe, his love, O scarab,

457. See Ritner, "Gleanings" (above, n. 68).
458. For the possible identification as the "stag beetle," see ibid., n. to l. XXI. 11.
459. Lit., "body": translation suggested by George R. Hughes.
460. *PDM* xiv. 646–50.
461. For the use of ten as a "round number," see K. Sethe, *Von Zahlen und Zahlworten bei den alten Ägypter* (Strassburg: Trübner, 1916) 39.
462. *PDM* xiv. 658–69.
463. Primeval waters.
464. See n. 306 above.

O scarab; you are the eye of Pre, the little finger[464] of Osiris, the fingers of Shu.[465] You should go in this form[466] in which Osiris your father went, on account of NN, whom NN bore, until fire is put after her heart, the flame after her flesh, until she goes to NN, whom NN bore, at every place in which he is."

[The spell] which you should recite to it while you are cooking it: "Hail, my beautiful child, the youth of oil-eating (?), who cast semen and who casts semen among all the gods, this one whom the small one and the great one found among the two great enneads on the east of Egypt, / while he was coming forth as a black scarab on a stem of papyrus reed! I know your name; I know your craft[467] (?). 'The work of two stars' is your name. I am casting fury against you today; NPHALAM BALLABALKHA IOPHPHE, in order that every burning, every heat, every fire in which you are today, you will make them in the heart, the lungs, the liver, the spleen, the womb, the large intestine, the small intestine, the ribs, the flesh, the bones, in every limb, in the skin of NN, whom NN bore, until she goes to NN, whom NN bore, at every place in which he is."

 655
 [XXI, 29]

[The spell] which you should recite to it in the wine:

"O scarab, O scarab, you are the scarab of real lapis-lazuli; you are the eye of Pre; you are the eye of Atum, the finger of Shu, the little finger of Osiris. You are the black bull, the foremost one, who came forth from Nun, / the beauty of Isis being with you. You are RAKS RAPARAKS, the blood of this wild boar which they brought from the land of Syria to Egypt."

 660
 [XXI, 34]

From outside to the wine: "I shall send you. Will you go on my business? Will you do it? May you say, 'Send me to the thirsty so that his thirst may be quenched, to the canal that it may be dried up, to the sand of the . . . that it may be scattered without wind, to the papyrus of Buto that the copper [blade] may be applied to it, while Horus is saved for Isis from the great destructions for those of Egypt, so that not a man or woman is left in their midst,' while I send you. Do the like of these while I am sending you down to the heart of NN, whom NN bore; make a flame in her body, flame in her intestines. Put madness after her heart, fever after her flesh. Let her make the travels of the Shoulder constellation[468] after the 'Hippopotamus' constellation.[469] Let her make / the movements of the sunshine after the shadow while she is searching after NN, whom NN bore, at every place in which he is, she loving him, she being mad about him, she not knowing a place of the earth in which she is. Take away her sleep by night! Give her grief and anxiety by day! Do not let her eat! Do not let her drink! Do not let her lie down! Do not let her sit in the shadow of her house until she goes to him at every place in which he is, her heart forgetting, her eye flying, her glances turned upside down, she not knowing a place of the earth in which she is, until she sees him, her eye after his eye, her heart after his heart, her hand after his hand, she giving to him every. . . . Let [her] put the tip of her feet after his heels in the street at all times, without a time changed. Quickly, quickly! Hurry, hurry!"

 665
 [XXI, 39]

*Tr.: Janet H. Johnson, following the edition and translation of Griffith and Thompson, *Demotic Magical Papyrus*, recto, col. XXI/10–43.

465. The god of air, whose hands/fingers supported the sky.
466. I.e., drowned, as Osiris.
467. As suggested by Griffith and Thompson, *The Leyden Papyrus* 141, n. to l. XXI. 29.
468. I.e., the Big Dipper.
469. See the references in Griffith and Thompson, *The Leyden Papyrus* 142, n. to l. XXI. 38.

PDM xiv. 670–74

670
[col.
XXII, 1]

*Here is [the spell ?] of the name of the Great One of Five [470] which should be recited to every spirit, there being nothing which is stronger than it in the books: if you recite these spells to any vessel, the gods never go away without your having questioned them about everything so that they say to you the answer about heaven, earth, the underworld, a distant inquiry, water, and fields. [It is] a writing which is in the power [471] of a man to recite. [472]

*Tr.: Janet H. Johnson, following the edition and translation of Griffith and Thompson, *Demotic Magical Papyrus*, recto, col. XXII/1–5.

PDM xiv. 675–94 [PGM XIVc. 16–27]

675
[col.
XXIII, 1]

680
[XXIII, 6]

*A spell to cause "evil sleep" [473] to fall. *Formula*: You bring a donkey's head; you place it between your feet opposite the sun at dawn when it is about to rise, opposite it again in the evening when it is going to set; you anoint your right foot with yellow ocher [474] of Syria, your left foot with clay, the soles of your feet also; you place your right hand in front and your left hand behind, the head being between them; you anoint one of your two hands with donkey's blood, / and the two corners (?) of your mouth; and you recite these writings before the sun at dawn and in the evening for four days. He sleeps.

If you wish to make him die, you should do it for seven days. If you do its magic, you should bind a thread of palm fiber to your hand, a piece of male palm fiber to your phallus and your head. It is very good.

This spell which you should recite before the sun:

(15)

685
[XXIII,
11]
(*PGM*
XIVc. 17)
(20)
690
[XXIII,
16]
(*PGM*
XIVc. 23)
(25)

/ "I call upon you who are in the empty air, you who are terrible, invisible, almighty, a god of gods, you who cause destruction and desolation, you who hate a stable / household, you who were driven out of Egypt and have roamed foreign lands, you who shatter everything and are not defeated. / I call upon you, Typhon Seth; I command your prophetic powers because I call upon your authoritative name to which you cannot refuse to listen, IŌ ERBĒTH IŌ PAKERBĒTH IŌ BOLCHŌSĒTH IŌ PATATHNAX / IŌ SŌRŌ IŌ NEBOUTOSOUALĒTH AKTIŌPHI ERESCHIGAL NEBOUTOSOALĒTH ABERAMENTHŌOULERTHEXANAXETHRELUŌTHENEMAREBA AEMINA / (the whole formula). Come to me and go and strike down him, NN (or her, NN) with chills and fever. That very person has wronged me and he (or she) has spilled the blood of Typhon in his own (or her own) house. For this reason I am doing this" (add the usual).

*Tr.: Janet H. Johnson, following the edition and translation of Griffith and Thompson, *Demotic Magical Papyrus*, recto, col. XXIII/1–20; and R. F. Hock, following the edition of Preisendanz.

PDM xiv. 695–700

695
[col.
XXIII, 21]

*To inquire opposite the moon: you should do it as a vessel inquiry alone or [with] a youth. If you are the one who is going to inquire, you should equip your eye with green eyepaint and black eyepaint. You should stand on a high place on the top of

---

470. See n. 36 above.
471. Literally, "hand."
472. As Griffith and Thompson note, *The Leyden Papyrus* 144, n. to l. XXII. 5, the remainder of the column, where the spell would have been written, was left blank.
473. Reading *nktk bin*. [R.K.R.] Griffith and Thompson, ibid., n. to l. XXIII. 1, suggest "catalepsy."
474. See Harris, *Minerals* 151.

your house. You should speak to the moon when it fills[475] the sound-eye[476] on the 15th day, you being pure for three days. You should recite this spell opposite the moon seven or nine times until he appears to you and speaks to you: "Hail, †SAKS †Amoun †SAKS †ABRASAKS, for you are the moon, the great one of the stars, he who formed them! Listen to these things which I said! Walk in accordance with the [words] of my mouth! Reveal yourself to me, †THAN / †THANA †THANATHA" (another [manuscript] says "THEI"); "this is my correct name." Nine [times] of saying it until she[477] reveals herself to you.

700
[XXIII, 26]

*Tr.: Janet H. Johnson, following the edition and translation of Griffith and Thompson, *Demotic Magical Papyrus*, recto, col. XXIII/21–26. Words preceded by † are written in Demotic in the text with Old Coptic glosses inserted above.

PDM xiv. 701–5

*Another form of it again, to be recited opposite the moon: You should paint your eye with this paint, you [going] up before the moon. When it fills the sound-eye,[478] you see the figure of the god in sound-eye speaking to you:

"I am flame, high, AMRO[479] MAAMT, true is my name, for I am . . . soul so †AGANAGYP Mars[480] spirit, spirit, joy-Mars[481] is my real, true name . . . eternity. I am KHELBAI[482] SETET; HEN EM-NEFER[483] is my name; SRO OSHENBET[484] is my correct name." Say [it] nine times, while you are standing opposite the moon, your eye equipped with this ointment: green and black eyepaint. Grind with Syrian honey; put the gall of a / full-grown chick to it; put it on a glass object; and leave it for yourself in a hidden place until the time in which you will need it. You do it also according to what is above.

705
[col. XXIII, 31]

*Tr.: Janet H. Johnson, following the edition and translation of Griffith and Thompson, *Demotic Magical Papyrus*, recto, col. XIII/27–31. The word preceded by † is written in the text in Demotic with an Old Coptic gloss inserted above.

PDM xiv. 706–10

*Against "evil sleep"[485]—another: flour of wild dates which has been beaten with milk[486] . . . ; / you should make them together into a ball. Put in the wine!

710
[col. XXIV, 5a]

*Tr.: Janet H. Johnson, following the edition and translation of Griffith and Thompson, *Demotic Magical Papyrus*, recto, col. XXIV/1a–5a.

PDM xiv. 711–15

*A tested **prescription** if you wish to "evil sleep"[487] a man: scammony root, 1 dram; opium, 1 dram; pound with milk; make it into a ball, and put it in some food (?) / which is cooked so that he eats it. He is upset.

715
[col. XXIV, 5]

*Tr.: Janet H. Johnson, following the edition and translation of Griffith and Thompson, *Demotic Magical Papyrus*, recto, col. XXIV/1–5.

475. See *PDM* xiv. 295 and n. 239 therewith.

476. See n. 192 above.

477. The moon, which is feminine in Greek although masculine in Egyptian.

478. See n. 192 above.

479. Written ʿm, "to swallow" or "to know" plus r, "mouth."

480. The planet; see W. Erichsen, *Demotisches Glossar* (Kopenhagen: Munksgaard, 1954) 170.

481. See n. 480 above.

482. Written ḫl, "young" (?), plus by, "soul."

483. Written ḫn, "to approach," plus preposition m, "in," plus nfr, "good."

484. Or, perhaps, "prince, great of throat." [R.K.R.]

485. See n. 473 above.

486. Griffith and Thompson, *The Leyden Papyrus*, vol. III, p. 109, suggest that this might be ʿgyr, "rush/reed."

487. See n. 473 above.

PDM xiv. 716–24

720
[col.
XXIV, 10]

Another, if you wish to make a man sleep for *two* days: mandrake root, 1 ounce; water and honey,[488] 1 ounce; henbane,[489] 1 ounce / ivy, 1 ounce. You should grind them with[490] a *lok*-measure of wine. If you wish to do it cleverly, you should put four portions to each one of them with a glass of wine; you should moisten them from morning to evening; you should clarify them; and you should make them drink it. [It is] very good.

*Tr.: Janet H. Johnson, following the edition and translation of Griffith and Thompson, *Demotic Magical Papyrus*, recto, col. XXIV/6–14.

PDM xiv. 724–26

725
[col.
XXIV]

Another, the third: apple / seeds, 1 stater, 1 kite; pound with flour; make it into a cake, and make the man whom you wish eat it.

*Tr.: Janet H. Johnson, following the edition and translation of Griffith and Thompson, *Demotic Magical Papyrus*, recto, col. XXIV/14–16.

PDM xiv. 727–36

730
[col.
XXIV, 20]
735
[XXIV,
25]

A prescription to cause a man to sleep; [it is] very good: apple seeds, 1 stater, 1 dram; mandrake root, 4 drams; ivy, 4 drams; pound together; add fifteen / measures of wine to it; put it in a glass vessel and guard it! When you wish to give it, you should put a little in a cup of wine, and you should give it to the man. The ivy—it grows in gardens; its leaf is like the leaf of a shekam plant, being divided into three lobes like a grape leaf. It is one palm in measurement; its blossom / is like silver (another [manuscript] says gold).

Another: Gall of an Alexandrian weasel; you should add [it] to any food.

Another: A two-tailed lizard.

*Tr.: Janet H. Johnson, following the edition and translation of Griffith and Thompson, *Demotic Magical Papyrus*, recto, col. XXIV/17–26.

PDM xiv. 737–38

A prescription for "evil sleep":[491] gall of horned viper, seeds of western apples, poisonous herb; pound them together; make into a ball and put [it] into the food!

*Tr.: Janet H. Johnson, following the edition and translation of Griffith and Thompson, *Demotic Magical Papyrus*, recto, col. XXIV/27–28.

PDM xiv. 739–40

·740
[col. XXV,
30]

Another: If you put camel's blood and the blood of a dead man / into the wine and you make the man drink it, he dies.

*Tr.: Janet H. Johnson, following the edition and translation of Griffith and Thompson, *Demotic Magical Papyrus*, recto, col. XXIV/29–30.

PDM xiv. 741

Another: If you put a nightjar's blood to his eye, he is blinded.

*Tr.: Janet H. Johnson, following the edition and translation of Griffith and Thompson, *Demotic Magical Papyrus*, recto, col. XXIV/3.

488. See Griffith and Thompson, *The Leyden Papyrus* 149–50, n. to l. XXIV. 8.
489. Ibid., 150, n. to l. XXIV. 9.
490. Literally, *r-ḫ.t*, "according to."
491. See n. 473 above; there is a parallel in *PDM* xiv. 917–19.

PDM xiv. 742

*Another: If you put bat's blood, it is [in] this manner again.

*Tr.: Janet H. Johnson, following the edition and translation of Griffith and Thompson, *Demotic Magical Papyrus*.

PDM xiv. 743–49

*Another: If you drown a hawk in wine and you make the man drink it, it does its work. A shrew-mouse in this manner again; it does / its work also. Its gall also, if you put it in the wine, it does its work very well. If you put the gall of an Alexandrian weasel on any food, it does its work. If you put a two-tailed lizard in the oil and cook it with it and anoint the man with it, it does its work.

745
[col.
XXIV, 35]

*Tr.: Janet H. Johnson, following the text and edition of Griffith and Thompson, *Demotic Magical Papyrus*, recto, col. XXIV/33–39.

PDM xiv. 750–71

*The words of the lamp to question the youth: *Formula*: "†TE †TE †IG †TATAK THETHE SATI †SAN-TASKL †KROMAKAT †PATAKSYRAI †KALEY-PANKT †A-A-TSIEYI[492] MAKT-SITAKAT HATI[493] HAT †RO-I[494]O-I †HAY[495] (?) †I; may they say to me an answer to everything about which I am asking here today, for I am Harpokrates[496] in Mendes, for I am Isis the wise; the sayings of my mouth come to pass" *(say seven times)*.

750
[col. XXV,
1]
755
[XXV, 6]

You bring a new lamp; you put a clean cloth wick into it brought from a temple; you set it on a new clean brick brought from the brick mold on which / no man has mounted; you set it upright; you place the lamp on it; you put genuine oil in it, or oasis oil; you set two new bricks under yourself; you place the youth between your feet; you recite the aforementioned spells down into the youth' head, your hand being over his eyes; and you offer up myrrh and willow leaf / before the lamp. You do it in a dark place whose door opens to the east or the south and under which there is no cellar. You let no light come in to the aforementioned place; you purify the said place beforehand; you put the youth's back to the opening of the room. When you finish reciting the spell, you should take your hand from his eyes—a youth who has not yet gone with a woman, / [is he] whom you should send before it[497]—and you should question him, saying, "What do you see?" He speaks with you of everything about which you will ask him.

760
[XXV, 6]
765
[XXV, 16]
770
[XXV, 21]

*Tr.: Janet H. Johnson, following the edition and translation of Griffith and Thompson, *Demotic Magical Papyrus*, recto, col. XXV/1–22. Words preceded by † are written in the text in Demotic with Old Coptic glosses inserted above.

PDM xiv. 772–804

*A method to put the heart of a woman after a man: Done in one moment (?) and it comes to pass instantly. You bring a live swallow and a live hoopoe.

Ointment made for them: Blood of a male donkey, blood of the tick of a black cow. You should anoint / *their* heads with lotus ointment and cry out before the sun in his moment of rising. You should cut off the heads of the two; you should

775
[col. XXV,

492. See n. 30 above.
493. Written *ḥȝt.y*, "my heart."
494. Written *ḥȝt r.y*, "heart of my mouth."
495. Demotic apparently written *ʿb.w*, but see Griffith and Thompson, *The Leyden Papyrus* 153, n. to l. XXV. 6.
496. Horus the Child, son of Isis and Osiris.
497. See Griffith and Thompson, *The Leyden Papyrus* 155, n. to l. XXV. 21.

26] bring their hearts out from their right ribs [of the two] and anoint them with the
donkey's blood and the blood of the tick of a black cow, above. You should put them
into donkey's skin and leave them in the sun until they dry up in four days. When
780 the four days have passed, you should pound them, put them into a / box, and leave
[XXV, 31] it in your house.

When you wish to make a woman love a man, you should take the piece[498] of
"pleasure wood,"[499] recite these[500] true names before them, put it in a cup of wine
or beer, and give it to the woman so that she drinks it: "I am †BIRA-AQHL †LA-AQH
785 †SASMRIALO †PLS-PLYN. I am †IOANE[501] †SABAATHL †SASYPY / †NITHI. Put the
[XXV, 36] heart of NN, whom NN bore, after NN, whom NN bore, in these hours today!"
([Say] seven times). You do it on the fourteenth of the lunar month. [it is] very
good.

790 / Another spell again for this cup of wine: "†BIRAGETHT †SAMARA †PILPIYN
[XXVI, 1] †IAHYT †SABAYTH †SAIPYNITHAS."

Another spell belonging to it again, on another papyrus: "I am †BIRAGATHT
795 †LATHT †SASMIRA †PLIPRN / †IAHY[502] †SABAQHT SASYPYNITHA. Put the heart of
[XXVI, 4] NN after SASYPYNITHAS."

*Tr.: Janet H. Johnson, following the edition and translation of Griffith and Thompson, *De-
motic Magical Papyrus*, col. XXV/23–XXVI/18. Words preceded by † are written in Demotic
with Old Coptic glosses inserted above.

PDM xiv. 805–40

805 * **Another** vessel inquiry,[503] [the magician being] alone[504] in order to see the bark of
[col. Pre: *The spell which you should recite*: "Open to me, O heaven, mother of the gods!
XXVII, 1] Let me see the bark of Pre, he going up and going down in it, for I am Geb, heir of
the gods; praying is what I am doing before Pre, my father, on account of the thing
which went forth from me. O great Heknet,[505] lady of the shrine, the Rishtret[506]
(?), open to me, mistress of spirits! Open to me, O primal heaven! Let me worship
the messengers, for I am Geb, heir of the gods! O, you seven[507] kings; O, you seven
Montus, bull who engenders, lord of awe, who illuminates the earth; soul of the
primeval waters; hail, lion like a lion of the primeval waters, bull of the darkness!
810 / Hail, foremost one of the people of the east, Nun,[508] great one, lofty one! Hail,
[XXVII, soul of the ram, sould of the people of the west! Hail, soul of souls, bull of darkness,
6] bull of [two] bulls, son of Nut! Open to me; I am the opener of earth, who came
forth from Geb. Hail! I am †I-I-I †E-E-E †HE-HE-HE †HO-HO-HO. I am ANEPO[509]
MIRI-PO-RE MAAT IB great THIBAI, †ARYI[510] †YOY †IAHO."

The preparation:[511] Blood of a Nile goose, blood of a hoopoe, blood of a night-

498. Literally, "measure."
499. See n. 253 above.
500. *PDM* xiv. 783–86.
501. Written ꜥ3, "donkey"; ꜥn, "again"; n3, "these."
502. Beginning written ꜥ3, "donkey."
503. This same vessel inquiry occurs in *PDM* xiv. 295–308.
504. I.e., without using a youth.
505. See n. 243 above.
506. See n. 244 above.
507. See n. 245 above.
508. Primeval waters.
509. Great Anubis.
510. See n. 249 above.
511. See n. 50 above.

jar, "live-on-them" plant, mustard,[512] "Great-of-Amoun" plant, *qs-ʿnḥ* stone,[513]
genuine lapis-lazuli, myrrh, "footprint-of-Isis" plant. Pound, make into a ball, and
paint / your eyes with it. Put a goat's tear in a "pleasure-wood"[514] of juniper or   815
ebony, and tie around you a strip of male palm fiber.   [XXVII,
    The way of making the vessel inquiry of the lamp: You should bring a clean,   11]
white lamp without putting red lead[515] or gum water in it, its wick being of byssus;
you should fill it with genuine oil or oil of dew; you should tie it with four linen
threads which have not been burned;[516] you should hang in on an eastern wall [on]
a peg of laurel wood; you should make the youth stand before it, he being pure, he
not having gone with a woman; you should cover his eyes with your hand; / you   820
should light the lamp; you should recite down into his head,[517] *seven* times; you   [XXVII,
should make him open his eyes; and you should ask him, saying, "What are the   16]
things which you have seen?" If he says, "I have [already] seen the gods near the
lamp," they tell him an answer concerning that which they will be asked.
    If you wish to do it by yourself alone, you should fill your eyes with the afore-
mentioned ointment. You should stand up opposite the lamp while it is lit and recite to it *seven* times while your eyes are shut. When you have finished, you should
open your eyes. You see the gods behind you and you speak with them concerning
that which you desire, you regularly doing it in a dark place.
    The spell which you should recite: *Formula*: "I am MANEBAI[518] †GHTHE-
THONI KHA-BA-KHEL; let me worship you, the child of ARPHITNA / PIRA PILE-ASA   825
†GNYRIPH-ARISA †TENI-IRISSA †PSI[519] †PSI †IRIS-SA †GIMITHYRY-PHYS-SA OQMAT   [XXVII,
SISA OREOBAZAGRA PERTAOMEKH PERAGOMEKH SAKMEPH.[520] Come in to me and   21]
inquire for me about the question about which I am inquiring, truthfully, without
falsehood."
    Its preparation:[521] The ointment[522] which you should put on your eyes when
you are going to make any "god's arrival"[523] with the lamp. You bring some flowers
of the Greek bean plant.[524] You find them in the place of the lupine sellers. You
should bring them while they are tender / and put them into a glass vessel. You   830
should seal its mouth very carefully for *twenty* days in a dark, hidden place. After   [XXVII,
twenty days, if you take it up and open it, you find testicles and a phallus in it. If   26]
you leave it for *forty* days and bring it up and open it, you find it having [already]
become bloody. In something of glass, you put it and you put the glass object in a
pottery object in a place hidden at all times.
    When you wish to make a "god's arrival" of the lamp with it, you should fill your
eyes with this blood aforesaid, while you are going to sleep. Or you should stand

    512. Literally, "bread-of-heaven" plant; Griffith and Thompson, *The Leyden Papyrus* 158, n. to l.
XXVII. 10, suggest an identification with σίναπι, "mustard."
    513. See n. 65 above.
    514. See n. 253 above.
    515. See n. 73 above.
    516. Or see Griffith and Thompson, *The Leyden Papyrus* 158, n. to l. XXVII. 14.
    517. *PDM* xiv. 823–28.
    518. Ending written *by*, "soul."
    519. PSI for "Agathodaimon"? Cf. *PGM* IV. 1644.
    520. SAKMEPH is "son of Kneph (Agathodaimon)"; see *PGM* I. 27.
    521. See n. 50 above.
    522. See the parallel in *PDM* xiv. 140–46.
    523. See n. 62 above.
    524. See n. 95 above.

opposite the lamp, reciting this spell aforesaid. You see the god beyond you while
835   you are standing or sleeping. [It is] very good, proven. / You write this name on the
[XXVII, strip of the wick of the lamp in myrrh ink: "BAKHYKH-SIKHYKH"[525] (what another
31]   papyrus said: "KIMITHORO PHOSSE"). This method which is written above is the
        method of the "god's arrival" of MANEBAI.[526] If you wish to do it by questioning the
        lamp, it is this form again. It is also profitable for a "god's arrival" of MYRIBAI.[527] If
        you will do it by vessel inquiry of the lamp, you should fill the lamp aforesaid on a
        new brick; you should make the youth stand up before the lamp while his face is
        covered; and you should recite to his head this spell in Greek while you are standing
840   over him. When you have finished, you should uncover / his face. He answers you
[XXVII, truthfully.
26]   *Tr.: Janet H. Johnson, following the text and translation of Griffith and Thompson, *De-
        motic Magical Papyrus*, recto, col. XXVII/13–36. Words preceded by † are written in the text
        in Demotic with Old Coptic glosses inserted above.

PDM xiv. 841–50

Another method of vessel inquiry [the magician being] alone: **Formula**: "I am
†the †lord †of †Spirits, †ORITSIMBAI[528] SONATSIR EPISGHES[529] EMMIME; THO-GOM-
PHRYR PHIRIM-PHYNI is your name; MIMI soul of souls soul of souls GTHETHO-NI, I
am Bastet PTHO[530] BALKHAM whom BINYI SPHE PHAS bore. I am BAPTHO;[531] GAM-
MI-SATRA is your name, MI-MEO, IANYME."

         Its preparation:[532] you go to a clean place; you bring a copper vessel; you wash it
845   with natron water; you put a *lok*-measure / of oil in it; you place it on the ground;
        you light a copper lamp; you put it on the ground near the copper vessel; you cover
        yourself with a clean robe, you and the vessel; and you recite into the vessel, your
[col.   eyes being shut, **seven** times. / You should open your eyes and ask it concerning
XXVIII] what you wish. If you wish to make the gods of the vessel speak with you with their
        mouths opposite your mouth, **you should recite**: "IAHO IPH †EOE †GINNTETHYR
        †NEPHAR †APHOE." They give you an answer concerning everything about which
        you will ask also.
        If they do not tell you an answer, you should **recite** this other name "†NGO-
        NGETHIGS †MANTYNOBOE †GOKSHIR-HRONTOR[533] †NTONTROMA †LEPHOGER
850   / †GEPHAER-SORE." If you recite these, they inquire for you truthfully.
[XXVIII, *Tr.: Janet H. Johnson, following the edition and translation of Griffith and Thompson, *De-
10]   motic Magical Papyrus*, recto, col. XXVIII/1–10. Words preceded by † are written in Demotic
        in the text with Old Coptic glosses inserted above.

PDM xiv. 851–55

Another vessel inquiry to which you add vegetable oil, you doing it according to
what is above: **Formula**: "Speak to me, speak to me, HAMST, god of the gods of
darkness, every spirit, every shadow which is in the west and the east! Do it, O he

525. See n. 76 above.
526. I.e., the formula beginning with MANEBAI in *PDM* xiv. 824.
527. I.e., the formula beginning with MYRAI MYRIBI in *PDM* xiv. 125.
528. Ending written *by*, "soul": see also n. 30 above.
529. For a possible translation of this name, see Griffith and Thompson, *The Leyden Papyrus* 163, n.
   to l. XXVIII. 1.
530. Ptah? [R.K.R.]
531. Spirit of Ptah? [R.K.R.]
532. See n. 50 above.
533. See nn. 8 and 30 above.

who has died! Awaken to me, awaken to me, O soul of life, O soul of breath! Let my vessel, my bandage go forth here today, because of the vessel of great Isis seeking her husband, searching for her brother; MNASH MNASH MNANF MNANF." Say, "MNASH MNASH MNANF MNANF PHONI PHONI" a multitude of times, and say to the youth, "Say, / 'Go away, O darkness! Come to me, O light!' and open your eyes at once." The gods come in and tell you an answer to everything.

*Tr.: Janet H. Johnson, following the edition and translation of Griffith and Thompson, *Demotic Magical Papyrus*, recto, col. XXVIII/11–15.

855
[col.
XXVII,
15]

PDM xiv. 856–75

***Here is** a form of inquiry of the sun of which it is said that it is well tested: *Its preparation*:[534] you bring a pure youth; you do the spirit formula which is written for it; you bring him before the sun; you make him stand on a new brick at the moment in which the sun is going to rise, so that he comes up entirely in the disk; you draw a new linen curtain[535] (?) around him; you make him shut his eyes; you stand up over him, reciting down into his head and striking down on / his head with your sun-finger[536] of your right hand, after filling his eyes with the paint which you made before: "†NASIRA †OAPKIS †SHFE †SHFE soul of †souls; soul of souls is your true name, truly. †O †Lotus, open to me heaven in its breadth and height! Bring me the light which is pure! Let the god in whose hand command[537] is come to me and tell me an answer to everything about which I am asking here today, in truth without falsehood therein. †Chief †god,[538] †ETALE †TAL †NASIRA †IARMEKH †NASERA †AMPTHY †CHO †AMAMARKAR †TEL IAAO / †NASIRA †HAKIA lotus †CHDJISIPHTH †AHO †ATONE[539] †I †I †E †O †BALBEL, let the pure light come to me. Let the youth *enchant*; let him tell me an answer. Let the god in whose hand command is come to me and tell me an answer to everything about which I shall *ask*, in truth, without falsehood therein."

   Afterwards you should recite his compulsion *another seven times*, his eyes being shut. *Formula*: "†SI †SI †PI †TSIRIPI[540] †SA-AO-NKHAB †HRABAOT †PHAKTHIOP †ANASAN †KRAANA †KRATRIS TMA-/PTARA-†PHNE †ARAPHNY, come to the youth! Let the god in whose hand command is come to him and tell me an answer to everything about which I am asking here today."

   If the light is slow to come within, you should say, "†KE †KE †SALSOATHA †IPPEL †SIRBA" *seven times*. You should put frankincense on the brazier; you should utter this great name after all these; you should utter it from beginning to end and vice versa, *four times*: "†AYEBOTH-IABATHABAITHOBEYA." You should say, "Let the youth see the light; let the god in whose hand command is come in and tell me an answer to everything about which I am asking / here today, in truth, without falsehood therein."

*Tr.: Janet H. Johnson, following the edition and translation of Griffith and Thompson, *Demotic Magical Papyrus*, recto, col. XXIX/1–20. Words preceded by † are written in Demotic with Old Coptic glosses inserted above.

860
[col.
XXIX, 5]

865
[XXIX,
10]

870
[XXIX,
20]

875
[XXIX,
15]

   534. See n. 50 above.
   535. Suggested by Sir Herbert Thompson.
   536. For a possible explanation of this term, see Griffith and Thompson, *The Leyden Papyrus* 166, n. to l. XXIX. 5.
   537. See n. 107 above.
   538. A phonetic rendering of the combination of Greek ἀρχός, "chief," and Egyptian *nṯr* (Coptic *noute*), "god."
   539. Adonai?
   540. See n. 30 above. TSIRIPI is Thriphis; cf. *PGM* XI. 232.

PDM xiv. 875–85

*Here is another form of it again: You should take the youth to a high, upper place. You should make him stand up in a place which has a large window in its presence, whose door opens to the east, and inside which the sun shines; you should paint the youth's eyes with the paint which is prescribed for it; you should recite to him 8 times (another [manuscript] says seven times) while you are standing over him; and you should make him look at the sun when it fills the sound-eye,[541] he standing up on a new brick, there being a new linen robe over him, and his eyes being closed. You should recite down into his head while striking his head with your finger which is written above[542] also. You should offer up frankincense before him. When you have finished, you should make him open his eyes. / He sees the gods beyond him, speaking with him.

880
[col.
XXIX, 25]

[*The ointment*] which you put in the youth's eyes when he goes to any vessel inquiry of the sun: you bring two *buri* fish[543] of the river, both being alive; you burn one of them with vinewood before the sun; you add the blood of the other to it; you make it smooth with it and myrrh; and you make them into balls which measure one finger [in length]. You should spread (?) [it] in his eyes. You should bring a vessel of vine wood (?) and a "pleasure-wood"[544] of vine wood (?) also; you should grind this drug with a little yellow ocher[545] of Nubia and juice of Egyptian grapes; and you should fill your eyes with it. If you fill your eyes with this drug and look at the sun when it fills the sound-eye, your eyes being open toward it, he reveals himself to you and tells you an answer / to everything. Its chief factor is purity. It is more profitable than the youth; it is profitable for you yourself as a person [acting] alone.

885
[XXIX,
30]

*Tr.: Janet H. Johnson, following the edition and translation of Griffith and Thompson, *Demotic Magical Papyrus*, recto, col. XXIX/20–30.

890
[v. col. i,
5]
895
[v. i, 10]

PDM xiv. 886–96

*Eyebrow of the sun.[546] Eyebrow of the moon.[547] (These are herbs.) Heliogonon.[548] / Selenogonon.[549] (These are herbs.) Spurge,[550] which is this small herb which is in the gardens and which exudes milk. / If you put its milk on a man's skin, it eats.[551]

*Tr.: Janet H. Johnson, following the edition and translation of Griffith and Thompson, *Demotic Magical Papyrus*, verso, col. i/1–11.

541. See n. 192 above. The summer solstice.

542. *PDM* xiv. 860 and n. 536 above.

543. Assuming cipher *iiḏ* is for ꜥ*ḏ*.

544. See n. 253 above; Griffith and Thompson, *The Leyden Papyrus* 169, translate "kohl-pot" and "kohl-stick" (?).

545. See *PDM* xiv. 677 and n. 474 above.

546. Written in both Demotic and Greek.

547. Written in both Demotic and Greek.

548. Griffith and Thompson, *The Leyden Papyrus* 170, n. to V. l. I. 4, suggest this is a synonym for *qouč*, "safflower, cardamom," Crum, *Coptic Dictionary* 840b.

549. Peonies, according to Griffith and Thompson, *The Leyden Papyrus* 170, n. to V. l. I. 5.

550. Written in both Demotic and Greek.

551. Suggested by W. F. Edgerton; Coptic *bolbl* means "burrow, dig," Crum, *Coptic Dictionary* 37a–b.

PDM xiv. 897–910

*Camomile: "Clean straw" is its name.

"White flower": ". . .-horse"[552] is its name.

Martagon lily:[553] "There is none better than I" is its name.

/ Chrysanthemum: "Beautiful of face" is its name (another [manuscript] says, "the golden flower" of the wreath seller). Its leaf is strong; its stem is cold; its flower is of gold; its leaf is like martagon lily.

Magnesium:[554] / A stone of stone which is black like galena. You should grind it while it is black.

Magnetite;[555] it is brought. You should scrape it while it is black.

Human magnesium:[556] It is brought / from the land of India. If you scrape it, it sends out blood.

900
[v. col. ii, 4]

905
[v. ii, 7]

910
[v. ii, 14]

*Tr.: Janet H. Johnson, following the edition and translation of Griffith and Thompson, *Demotic Magical Papyrus*, verso, col. ii/1–15.

PDM xiv. 911–16

*To "evil sleep"[557] your enemy: A beetle: you should burn it with styrax (?), you should pound it together with one drachma of apples / and a . . . ; you should . . . ; and you should put a. . . .

915
[v. col. ii, 20]

*Tr.: Janet H. Johnson, following the edition and translation of Griffith and Thompson, *Demotic Magical Papyrus*, verso, col. ii/16–20.

PDM xiv. 917–19

***Prescription** for "evil sleep":[558] Gall of horned viper, seeds of western apples, and poisonous herbs. Grind them together, make into a ball, and put [it] in wine!

*Tr.: Janet H. Johnson, following the edition and translation of Griffith and Thompson, *Demotic Magical Papyrus*, verso, col. iii/1–3.

PDM xiv. 920–29

***Lees of wine**: It is a white stone like galbanum. There is another one which is made into lime. (This is) the way to know about it, whether it is genuine. If you grind a little / with water and apply it to the skin of a man for a short time, it cuts the skin. Its name in Greek [is] "foam of the moon."[559] It is a white stone.

920
[v. col. iii, 4]

925
[v. iii, 9]

*Tr.: Janet H. Johnson, following the edition and translation of Griffith and Thompson, *Demotic Magical Papyrus*, verso, col. iii/4–13.

PDM xiv. 930–32

***A prescription**[560] to cause a woman to love a man: Fruit of acacia; grind with honey; anoint his[561] phallus with it; and lie with the woman!

930
[v. col. iii, 14]

*Tr.: Janet H. Johnson, following the edition and translation of Griffith and Thompson, *Demotic Magical Papyrus*, verso, col. iii/14–16.

552. The Egyptian word may be from the root *šq*, "to dig."

553. See Griffith and Thompson, *The Leyden Papyrus* 171, n. to V. l. II. 3.

554. Written in Egyptian and Greek.

555. Glossed twice in Greek. Demotic says lit., "living iron"; see J. R. Harris, *Minerals* 170, who suggests that it is being confused with hematite.

556. See Griffith and Thompson, *The Leyden Papyrus* 173, n. to V. l. II. 13, and n. 555 above.

557. See *PDM* xiv. 675 and n. 473 thereto.

558. See *PDM* xiv. 675 and n.; there is a parallel in *PDM* xiv. 737–38.

559. Written in both Greek and Egyptian.

560. There is a parallel in *PDM* xiv. 1046–47.

561. *Sic*, for "your."

PDM xiv. 933–34

*"Foam of the moon": It is a white stone like glass, which is rubbed into tiny fragments like orpiment.

*Tr.: Janet H. Johnson, following the edition and translation of Griffith and Thompson, *Demotic Magical Papyrus*, verso, col. iii/17–18.

PDM xiv. 935–39

935

[v. col. iv,

1]

*Prescription for an ear which is watery: Salt; heat with good wine and apply to it after first cleaning it. You [should] rub copper salt,[562] heat with wine, and apply to it for four days.

*Tr.: Janet H. Johnson, following the edition and translation of Griffith and Thompson, *Demotic Magical Papyrus*, verso, col. iv/1–5.

PDM xiv. 940–52

940

[v. col. iv,

6]

945

[v. iv, 11]

950

[v. iv, 17]

*Salamander, a small lizard which is blue-green[563] in color and which has no feet. "Ram's-horn"[564] is its name, / an herb which is like a wild fennel bush. Its leaf and its stem are incised like the "love-man" plant. You should pound it when it is dry, sift[565] it, make it into a dry powder, and apply it to any wound. It stops.

Styrax; it grows like . . . / with regard to its leaf. Its seeds are twisted like a "ram's-horn" plant which has a small thorn at its end.

*Tr.: Janet H. Johnson, following the edition and translation of Griffith and Thompson, *Demotic Magical Papyrus*, verso, col. iv/6–19.

PDM xiv. 953–55

955

[v. col. v,

3]

*A *prescription* to stop blood: Juice of "Great-Nile" plant together with beer; you should make the woman drink it at dawn / before she has eaten. It stops.

*Tr.: Janet H. Johnson, following the edition and translation of Griffith and Thompson, *Demotic Magical Papyrus*, verso, col. v/1–3.

PDM xiv. 956–60

960

[v. col. v,

8]

*The *way* to know it of a woman whether she will be pregnant: You should make the woman urinate on this plant, above, again, at night. When morning comes, if you find the plant scorched, she will not conceive. If you find it / green, she will conceive.

*Tr.: Janet H. Johnson, following the edition and translation of Griffith and Thompson, *Demotic Magical Papyrus*, verso, col. v/4–8.

PDM xiv. 961–65

965

[v. col. v,

13]

*A *prescription* to stop blood: Leaf of [†]. . . , leaf of fresh "copper-fly" plant. Pound, put [it] on yourself while you lie with the woman. *Another*: Myrrh, garlic, gall of a gazelle; pound with / old scented wine; put [it] on yourself while you lie with her.

*Tr.: Janet H. Johnson, following the edition and translation of Griffith and Thompson, *Demotic Magical Papyrus*, verso. col. v/9–13. The word preceded by [†] is written in Demotic with Old Coptic gloss inserted above.

562. Reading ḥmꜣ ḥmt, as Griffith and Thompson, *The Leyden Papyrus* 175, n. to V. l. IV. 7. Copper-based medicines were common in Pharaonic medicine, presumably since the copper helped kill bacteria.

563. See *PGM* IV. 1090.

564. Written in Egyptian and Greek.

565. Coptic šolšl, "sift," Crum, *Coptic Dictionary* 561b.

PDM xiv. 966–69

*Asphodel, also called wild onion.[566]
  Garlic, also called wild garlic.

*Tr.: Janet H. Johnson, following the edition and translation of Griffith and Thompson, *Demotic Magical Papyrus*, verso, col. v/14–17.

PDM xiv. 970–77

***A prescription** to stop liquid in a woman: The first prescription: salt and oil; pound; . . .[567] two days, after the two days.

The second ***prescription***: White lead; you should pound it with a little salt paste[568] of an oil dealer very carefully; you should put true oil of fine quality to it, together with an egg; you should pound them; you should bring a strip of fine-woven linen; you should dye it in this medicine (she should wash in the bath and wash in good wine); you should put the medicated strip up in her; you should push it in and / out in her womb for a short time, in the manner of a man's phallus, until the medication permeates; you should remove it; and you should leave her until evening. When evening comes, you should dye a bandage in genuine honey and put it up in her until dawn, for ***three*** (another [manuscript] says, four) days.

*Tr.: Janet H. Johnson, following the edition and translation of Griffith and Thompson, *Demotic Magical Papyrus*, verso, col. vi/1–8.

970
[v. col. vi, 2]

975
[v. vi, 6]

PDM xiv. 978–80

***Another**, after it: Juice of a cucumber which has been rubbed, one measure; water of the ear of a . . . animal, one measure, in accordance with the measure of a wine cup; you should add a measure of good wine to them and she should drink it at midday without having / eaten anything at all after bathing in the bath, which she did beforehand. When evening comes, you should put the rag with honey up in her as above for seven days.

*Tr.: Janet H. Johnson, following the edition and translation of Griffith and Thompson, *Demotic Magical Papyrus*, verso, col. vii/1–4.

980
[v. col. vii, 3]

PDM xiv. 981–84

***Another**, after it: You should bring a new dish; you should put ten measure of old sweet wine in it; and you should put a drachma of fresh rue in it from dawn until midday. She should wash in the bath, come out, and drink it. When evening comes, you should put honey up in her as above again for seven days.

*Tr.: Janet H. Johnson, following the edition and translation of Griffith and Thompson, *Demotic Magical Papyrus*, verso, col. vii/4–7.

PDM xiv. 985–92

*Gout: You should make the man sit down, place clay under the man's feet, and place . . . after it[569] while his feet are on it. You should ask the man, "Has it [already] heard?"[570] for three days. Afterwards you should bring an ant; you should cook it in henna oil; and you should anoint his foot / with it. When you have finished, you should bring Alexandrian figs, dried grapes, and † potentilla.[571] You

985
[v. col. viii, 1]

990
[v. viii, 6]

566. See Griffith and Thompson, *The Leyden Papyrus* 177, n. to verso col. V, l. 15.
567. See ibid., 178, n. to V. VI. 1, for a discussion of the passage omitted.
568. Crum, *Coptic Dictionary* 781a.
569. Or "him."
570. Or "whether he has (already) heard."
571. See Griffith and Thompson, *The Leyden Papyrus* 180, n. to V. l. VIII. 7.

should pound them with wine and anoint him. In addition to this, you should breathe at him with your mouth.

*Tr.: Janet H. Johnson, following the edition and translation of Griffith and Thompson, *Demotic Magical Papyrus*, verso, col. viii/1–8. The word preceded by † is written in Demotic with an Old Coptic gloss inserted above.

PDM xiv. 993–1002

995
[v. col. ix, 3]
1000
[v. ix, 8]

*Another: 1 dram of spurge; / 1 drachma of pepper; 1 stater of pyrethrum; 1 stater of adarces;[572] 1 stater of native sulfur; 6 staters of [any] wine; / 8 [measures] of genuine oil. You should pound them and make them into a poultice. Apply to the place which pains the man.

*Tr.: Janet H. Johnson, following the edition and translation of Griffith and Thompson, *Demotic Magical Papyrus*, verso, col. ix/1–10.

PDM xiv. 1003–14

1005
[v. col. x, 3]
1010
[v. x, 8]

*Another amulet for the foot of the gouty man: You should write these names on a strip / of silver or tin. You should put it on a deerskin[573] and bind it to the foot of the man named, on his two feet: "THEMBARATHEM OUREMBRENOUTIPE / AIOX-THOU SEMMARATHEMMOU NAIOOU, let NN, whom NN bore, recover from every pain which is in his knees and two feet." You do it when the moon is [in the constellation] Leo.

*Tr.: Janet H. Johnson, following the edition and translation of Griffith and Thompson, *Demotic Magical Papyrus*, verso, col. x/1–12.

PDM xiv. 1015–20

1015
[v. col. xi, 1]
1020
[v. xi, 6]

*Prescription for a . . . : Garlic, frankincense, old . . . , genuine oil. Pound them; anoint him with it. When it is dry, you should wash it / with cold water. It stops.

*Tr.: Janet H. Johnson, following the edition and translation of Griffith and Thompson, *Demotic Magical Papyrus*, verso, col. xi/1–6.

PDM xiv. 1021–23

*Prescription for a foot which is very stiff: [It is] very good. You should wash his foot with cucumber juice and rub it on his foot very well.

*Tr.: Janet H. Johnson, following the edition and translation of Griffith and Thompson, *Demotic Magical Papyrus*, verso, col. xi/7–9.

PDM xiv. 1024–25

1025
[v. col. xi, 11]

*Another: Sycamore figs of . . . ; fruit of acacia, / persea fruit. Pound [them]; apply [it] to him.

*Tr.: Janet H. Johnson, following the edition and translation of Griffith and Thompson, *Demotic Magical Papyrus*, verso, col. xi/10–11.

PDM xiv. 1026–45

*"I am this great one, SHAEI"[574] (another [manuscript] says, "the great one, SHE-ray"), "who makes magic against the great Triphis,[575] the lady of Koou, †LL †MYLL The water of Mut[576] is what is in my mouth; the fat[577] of Hathor, worthy of love, is

---

572. See ibid., 181, n. to V. l. IX. 5.
573. Written in Egyptian and Greek.
574. Ending written ꜥ3, "linen."
575. See n. 399 above.
576. Thus R.K.R.
577. See Griffith and Thompson, *The Leyden Papyrus* 184, n. to V. l. XII. 3.

what is in my heart. My heart yearns, my heart loves with (?) a longing which a she-
cat / feels for a tomcat, a longing which a she-wolf feels for a wolf, a longing which   1030
a bitch feels for a dog, the longing the god, the son of Sirius, felt for Moses while   [v. col.
he was going to the hill of NINARETOS to offer water to his god, his lord, his †IAHO   xii, 5]
†sabaho, his GLEMYRA MYSE PLERYBE S MI ABRASAKS SENKLAI. Let NN, whom
NN bore, feel it for NN, whom NN bore. Let her feel a yearning, a love, a great
madness . . . , she seeking after him everywhere. O fury / of IAHO SABAHY HORION   1035
(?) all-mighty ANTOGRATOR[578] ARBANTHALA THALO THALAKS, 'I cast fury against   [v. xii, 10]
you[579] of the great gods of Egypt. Fill your hands with flames and fire! Use it! Cast
it on the heart of NN, whom NN bore! Wither her, O spirit! Take her sleep, O man
of the west![580] Let the house of her father and her mother, the places where she is.
. . . Call out while the flame of fire / is against her, while she speaks, saying,   1040
"mercy," she standing outside murmuring "mercy," for I am an agent (?) of Geb,   [v. xiii, 4]
Horus RON. Pre is my name. Tear her name out of Egypt for 40 days, 33 months,
175 days, the complement of six months, O GIRE †THEE PISITY EKOIMI ATAM!'"[581]
([Say] seven times.)
    Crocodile dung, a little donkey placenta, and sisymbrium, 7 *oipe* of antelope
dung, gall of a male goat, and first fruits of oil. You should heat them with flax
stalks; you should recite to it seven times for seven days; you should anoint your
phallus / with it; and you should lie with the woman; and you should anoint the   1045
woman's heart,[582] also.   [v. xiii, 9]

*Tr.: Janet H. Johnson, following the edition and translation of Griffith and Thompson, *De-
motic Magical Papyrus*, verso, col. xii/1–xiii/9. Words preceded by † are written in the text in
Demotic with Old Coptic glosses inserted above.

PDM xiv. 1046–47

*[A prescription] to cause a woman to love her husband:[583] Acacia, fruit. Pound
with honey, anoint your phallus with it, and lie with the woman.

*Tr.: Janet H. Johnson, following the edition and translation of Griffith and Thompson, *De-
motic Magical Papyrus*, verso, col. xiii/11–12.

PDM xiv. 1047–48

*To make a woman love copulating with her: Foam of a stallion's mouth. Anoint
your phallus with it and lie with the woman.

*Tr.: Janet H. Johnson, following the edition and translation of Griffith and Thompson, *De-
motic Magical Papyrus*, verso, col. xiii/11–12.

PDM xiv. 1049–55

*To make [a woman love copulating with her (?)]: / Alum, 1 dram; pepper, 1   1050
dram: dry *mhnknwt* plant, 4 drams; orchid, 4 drams. Pound into a dry medication!   [v. col.
Do [your] business with / it in accordance with what you know with any woman.   xiv, 2]

*Tr.: Janet H. Johnson, following the edition and translation of Griffith and Thompson, *De-*   1055
motic Magical Papyrus, verso, col. xiv/1–7.   [v. xiv, 7]

578. Is this the preceding with the initial *p* interpreted as the Egyptian masculine singular definite
article and omitted?
579. Plural.
580. See n. 33 above.
581. Perhaps "O divine faithful lord, I cast out Adam," as Griffith and Thompson, *The Leyden Papyrus* 186–87, n. to V. l. XIII. 6.
582. Or "breast" (?), as Griffith and Thompson, ibid., 187.
583. There is a parallel in *PDM* xiv. 930–32.

PDM xiv. 1056–62

*The names of the gods whom you seek when you are going to bring in a thief [by vase questioning?]:[584] "†MASKELLI †MASKELLO †PHNYGENTABAO †HREKSIGTHO †PERIGTHEON †PERIPEGANEKS †AREOBASAGRA" (also called †OBASAGRA).

1060
[v. col. xv, / This name, you say it before a ship which is about to founder on account of the names of Dioscorus,[585] which are within, so that it is safe.

5]
If you recite them to the beaker of Adonai,[586] which is inscribed outside, it will do a great work which will bring in a thief.

*Tr.: Janet H. Johnson, following the edition and translation of Griffith and Thompson, *Demotic Magical Papyrus*, verso, col. xv/1–7. Words preceded by † are written in Demotic with Old Coptic glosses inserted above.

PDM xiv. 1063–69

*"†ARMIOYT[587] †SITHANI †YTHANI †ARIAMYSI †SOBRTAT[588] †BIRBAT †MISIRITHAT

1065
[v. col. / †AMSIETHARMITHAT,[589] bring NN, whom NN bore, out of her abodes in which she is, to any house, any place in which NN, whom NN bore, is while she loves him

xvi, 3]
and craves him, she making the gift of his heart at every moment!"

You should write this in myrrh ink on a strip of clean byssus and put it in a clean new lamp, which is filled with genuine oil, in your house from evening until dawn. If you find the hair of the woman, put it in the wick! It is good.

*Tr.: Janet H. Johnson, following the edition and translation of Griffith and Thompson, *Demotic Magical Papyrus*, verso, col. xv/1–7. Words preceded by † are written in Demotic with Old Coptic glosses inserted above.

PDM xiv. 1070–77

1070
[v. col. *A spell to bring [a woman] to a man, to send dreams (another [manuscript] says, to dream dreams) again: [[A line of symbols of secret signs.]] You should write this

xvii, 1]
on a reed leaf and put [it] under your head while you sleep. It makes dreams and sends dreams. If you will do it to send dreams, you should put it on the mouth of a mummy. It brings a woman also. You should write this name on the reed leaf with

1075
the blood of a . . . or a hoopoe; you should put the hair of the woman in the leaf;

[v. xvii, 6] you should put it on the mouth of the mummy; and you should write this name on the ground, saying: "Bring NN, the daughter of NN, to the house, to the sleeping-place in which is NN, the son of NN!" Now it is also a fetching charm.

*Tr.: Janet H. Johnson, following the edition and translation of Griffith and Thompson, *Demotic Magical Papyrus*, verso, col. xvii/1–8.

PDM xiv. 1078–89

1080
[v. col. *"ERYBITHY EKTYLA / ERREPHEDI, reveal yourself to me, god NN, and speak to me concerning that about which I shall ask you, truthfully, without having told me

xviii, 3] falsehood."

1085
[v. xviii, Saffron, 2 [measures]; / black eye paint of Koptos, 2 [measures]; pound with blood of a lizard, make into a ball, and rub it with milk of a [woman who has born

8] a] male child! Put [it] in his right eye and recite to it before any lamp or the Big Dipper at night!

*Tr.: Janet H. Johnson, following the edition and translation of Griffith and Thompson, *Demotic Magical Papyrus*, verso, col. xviii/1–12.

584. See Griffith and Thompson, *The Leyden Papyrus* 188, n. to V. l. XV. 1.

585. The patron gods of sailors, as Griffith and Thompson, ibid., n. to V. l. XV. 6.

586. See ibid., 189, n. to V. l. XV. 6.

587. Preceding this line is a line showing three scarab beetles, three falcons, and three goats. In the right margin next to this line is the addition "also called ARMIOYTH."

588. Ending written with the hieratic *ḏd*-pillar.

589. Beginning written *r-ms*, "whom . . . bore."

PDM xiv. 1090–96

*A spell for bringing a woman out of her house: You bring a . . . of a wild cat; you dry it; you take a tendon (?) [of a . . . which has been] drowned; and you fashion a ring whose body is blended with gold [in the form of two] lions whose mouths are open, the face of each being turned to the other. You should put the thing . . . it face.

When you wish to bring a woman to you at any time, you should place the ring in the upper part of a lamp / which is lit and you should say to it, "Bring NN, the daughter of NN, to this place in which I am, quickly, in these moments of today!" She comes at once.

*Tr.: Janet H. Johnson, following the edition and translation of Griffith and Thompson, *Demotic Magical Papyrus*, verso, col. xix/1–7.

1090
[v. col. xix, 1]

1095
[v. xix, 6]

PDM xiv. 1097–1103

*To heal ophthalmia[590] in a man: "O Amoun,[591] this †lofty male, this male of Ethiopia, who came down from Meroe to Egypt and who found my son Horus hurrying on his feet.[592] He beat (?) him on his head with three spells in the Ethiopian language. When he finds NN, whom NN bore, he will hurry on / his feet, and he will beat (?) him on his head with three spells in the Ethiopian language: "GENTINI †tentina qyqybi [ak]khe akha."

[Say it] to a little oil; add salt and nasturtium seed to it, anoint the man who has opthhalmia with it, also write this on a new papyrus, and make it into a papyrus roll on his body: "You are the eye of heaven," in the writings. . . .[593]

*Tr.: Janet H. Johnson, following the edition and translation of Griffith and Thompson, *Demotic Magical Papyrus*, verso, col. xx/1–7. Words preceded by † are written in the text in Demotic with Old Coptic glosses inserted above.

1100
[v. col. xx,
4]

PDM xiv. 1104–9

*. . . / "live-on-them" plant: . . . Pound, make . . . of the river. . . . Paint your eye with it!

*Tr.: Janet H. Johnson, following the edition and translation of Griffith and Thompson, *Demotic Magical Papyrus*, verso, col. xxi/1–6.

1105
[v. col.
xxi, 3]

PDM xiv. 1110–29

*A tested . . . : . . . *Here is* [the ointment which you] put on your eyes when you go to the vessel of inquiry alone: Green eyepaint, black eyepaint, *qes-ꜥnḥ* stone,[594] amulet of . . . , flowers of black . . .[595] which are vetch, blood of hoopoe. / Pound, [make] into a ball, and paint your eye with it, together with juice of Egyptian grapes and yellow ocher[596] of Nubia. You see the shadow of every god and every goddess.

Its . . . : "I call to you, O great gods who appear with the sun, †TSEMYKS[597] †AMP

1110
[v. col.
xxii, 1]

1115
[v. xxii, 6]

590. Or "evil eye"; see Griffith and Thompson, *The Leyden Papyrus* 192, n. to V. l. XX. 1.

591. See n. 189 above.

592. Or, perhaps, "as fast as his feet (could go)," as Griffith and Thompson, *The Leyden Papyrus* 193, with n. to V. l. XX. 3.

593. What is left blank here is written in the papyrus as the hieroglyph of an eye with rays rising up from it.

594. See n. 65 above.

595. See Griffith and Thompson, *The Leyden Papyrus* 194–95, n. to V. l. XXII. 4.

596. See *PDM* xiv. 677 and n. 474.

597. Or OEMYKS. [R.K.R.]

1120
[v. xxii,
11]

...⁵⁹⁸ ⁺PIAM ⁺ENPAIA ⁺IBOTH ⁺IAE SABAOTH. / Open to me, open to me, O great gods who appear with the sun! Let my eyes open to the light, and let me see the god who inquires today.⁵⁹⁹ Hurry, hurry, for the protection . . . ⁺ABLANATHANLBA, the great god, ⁺MARARAANTONE⁶⁰⁰ ⁺ABIATH N . . . SENEN Agathodaimon NTOSA-TRAPERQEMAI⁶⁰¹ Osiris ⁺LILAM is his name. Open to me, Open to me, O great

1125
[v. xxii,
16]

gods! Let my eyes open to the light, / and let me see the god who inquires today. Open to me, open to me! I cast fury of the doubly great god . . . whose strength is great, who lives forever, against you. Give strength to the name . . . the name of the god. . . . Open to me, open to me, O great [gods] who appear with the sun! Let [my eyes] open [to the light, and let] me [see the god] who inquires today. Hurry, hurry" (. . . times).

*Tr.: Janet H. Johnson, following the edition and translation of Griffith and Thompson, *Demotic Magical Papyrus*, verso, col. xx/1–20. Words preceded by ⁺ are written in Demotic with Old Coptic glosses inserted above.

PDM xiv. 1130–40

1130
[v. col.
xxiii, 1]
1135
[v. xxiii,

*. . . grind . . . with. . . . Another: . . . NAKS . . . / juniper . . . seeds. . . . Another:. . . again. Dung . . . dried and burned, 2 [measures]; / pound [with oil of] henna and honey, anoint [your phallus] with it, and lie with her!

6]
1140
[v. xxiii,
11]

*Tr.: Janet H. Johnson, following the edition and translation of Griffith and Thompson, *Demotic Magical Papyrus*, verso, col. xxiii/1–12.

PDM xiv. 1141–54

*. . . to it, and you should . . . of byssus to it, these three names being written on

1045
[v. col.
xxiv, 4]

it; . . . / and myrrh; you should light it; you should place it . . . your head; and you should recite them to it again nine times . . . the lamp. You do it at the time of the third hour of night . . . alone.

1050
[v. xxiv,
9]

Formula: "⁺IOBASAYMPTHO [⁺GHROME (?) ⁺LY]GHAR, instruct⁶⁰² me / in truth concerning any given matter about which I am praying here [today, in] truth, without telling you⁶⁰³ falsehood. IOBASAYMPTHOKHROMELOYKHAR, instruct me in truth concerning any given matter about which I am praying here today."

*Tr.: Janet H. Johnson, following the edition and translation of Griffith and Thompson, *Demotic Magical Papyrus*, verso, col. xxiv/1–13. Words preceded by ⁺ are written in the text in Demotic with Old Coptic glosses inserted above.

PDM xiv. 1155–62

1155
[v. col.
xxv, 1]

*. . .⁶⁰⁴ hawk's dung; salt, reed, *bele* plant. Pound together. Anoint your phallus with it and lie with the woman. If it is dry, you should / pound a little of it with wine, anoint your phallus with it, and lie with the woman. [It is] very good.

*Tr.: Janet H. Johnson, following the edition and translation of Griffith and Thompson, *Demotic Magical Papyrus*, verso, col. xxv/1–8.

598. With water determinative, presumably *p₃ y‘m*, "the sea."
599. See n. 23 above.
600. For Adonai?
601. See n. 8 above.
602. Literally, "Let my eyes open out." Cf. n. 93 above. [R.K.R.]
603. *Sic.*
604. The first line is perhaps to be restored "in order to make a woman love copulation, again," as

PDM xiv. 1163–79

*If you [wish to make] the gods of the vessel speak with you,[605] when the gods come in, you should say this name [to them], nine times: / "†IAO †IPH †EOE †GINN-TATHYR[606] †NEPHAR †APHOE." He commands to you concerning that about which you will ask him.

1165
[v. col. xxvi, 3]

If delay occurs in order not to tell you an answer, you should say this other name to them, nine times until they inquire for you truthfully: "†NGONGETSIKS †MANTY †NOBOE †GOGHIR †HRONTOR[607] †NTONTROMA †LEPHOGER †GEPHAERSORE" (seven times). "IAYO EIPHE ON KINDATHOYR NEPHAR APHOE."

1170
[v. xxvi, 8]

According to what is above,[608] on the recto, "I am SIT-TA-KO.[609] 'Hearing' is my name; 'hearing' is my correct name. I am GANTHA GINTEY[610] GIRITEY, lord god, ARENOYTE[611] LABTATHA LAPTYTHA / LAKSANTHA SARISA MARKHARAHYTEY[612] †AR-SINGA-GHLA" (another manuscript [says], ARSI-NGALABEL) "*Bolboel* BOEL BOEL LOTERI †GLO-GASANTRA. IAHO is my name; IAHO is my correct name. BALKHAM, the powerful one of heaven, ABLANATHANALBA, the griffin[613] of the shrine of the god who stands today."

1175
[v. xxvii, 4]

*Tr.: Janet H. Johnson, following the edition and translation of Griffith and Thompson, *Demotic Magical Papyrus*, verso, col. xxvi/1–xxvii/8. Words preceded by † are written in the text in Demotic with Old Coptic glosses inserted above.

PDM xiv. 1180–81

*You are going to send a star . . . down while the moon is [in the constellation] Scorpio.

1180
[v. col. xxviii, 2]

*Tr.: Janet H. Johnson, following the edition and translation of Griffith and Thompson, *Demotic Magical Papyrus*, verso, col. xxviii/1–2.

PDM xiv. 1182–87

*[Spell to] make mad any man or any woman: You should take the hair of the man whom you wish together with the hair of a dead man; you should tie them to each other; / you should tie them to the body of the hawk; and you should release it alive. If you wish to do it for some days, you should put the hawk in a place, feeding it in your house.

1185
[v. col. xxix, 4]

*Tr.: Janet H. Johnson, following the edition and translation of Griffith and Thompson, *Demotic Magical Papyrus*, verso, col. xxix/1–6.

PDM xiv. 1188–89

*If you . . . dung of a Nile goose. Her body falls.[614]

*Tr.: Janet H. Johnson, following the edition and translation of Griffith and Thompson, *Demotic Magical Papyrus*, verso, col. xxx/1–2.

Griffith and Thompson, *The Leyden Papyrus*, in the hand copy.

605. There is a parallel in *PDM* xiv. 847–50.
606. See n. 23 above.
607. See n. 23 above.
608. *PDM* xiv. 13–16.
609. See n. 7 above.
610. Ending written ṱꜣw, "wind."
611. See n. 9 above.
612. Ending written ṱꜣw, "wind."
613. See n. 12 above.
614. Perhaps "abortion," as Griffith and Thompson, *The Leyden Papyrus* 201, n. to V. l. XXX. 1.

PDM xiv. 1190–93

1190
[v. col.
xxx, 3]

*Another: You should anoint your phallus with dung of weasel[615] and lie with [the] woman. She loves you. You should pound dung of . . . with honey and anoint your phallus with it according to what is above, again.

*Tr.: Janet H. Johnson, following the edition and translation of Griffith and Thompson, *Demotic Magical Papyrus*, verso, col. xxx/3–6.

PDM xiv. 1194–95

1195
[v. col.
xxx, 8]

*Another: Dung of hyena with oil of / roses[616] in accordance with what is above, again.

*Tr.: Janet H. Johnson, following the edition and translation of Griffith and Thompson, *Demotic Magical Papyrus*, verso, col. xxx/7–8.

PDM xiv. 1196–98

*Another: You should fumigate a woman with ichneumon's dung when the menstruation is on her. She stops. Ass's dung also—this method [of treatment].

*Tr.: Janet H. Johnson, following the edition and translation of Griffith and Thompson, *Demotic Magical Papyrus*, verso, col. xxx/9–11.

PDM xiv. 1199–1205

1200
[v. col.
xxxi, 2]
1205
[v. xxxi,
7]

*"SISIOOYT" / (another [manuscript] says, ARMIOYTH), "O living god, O burning lamp, come in before me and tell me an answer concerning that about which I am asking here / today."

*Tr.: Janet H. Johnson, following the edition and translation of Griffith and Thompson, *Demotic Magical Papyrus*, verso, col. xxxi/1–7.

PDM xiv. 1206–18

1210
[v. col.
xxxii, 5]

*To make [a woman] mad after a man:[617] You should bring a live shrew-mouse, remove its gall and put it in one place; and remove its heart and put it in another place. You should / take its whole body. You should pound it very much while it is dry; you should take a little of what is pounded with a little blood of your second finger and the little finger[618] of your left hand; you should put it in a cup of wine; and you should make the woman drink it. She is mad after you.

/ If you put its gall into a cup of wine, she dies instantly. Or put it in meat or some food.

1215
[v. xxxii,
10]

If you put its heart in ring of gold and put it on your hand, it gives you great praise, love, and awe.

*Tr.: Janet H. Johnson, following the edition and translation of Griffith and Thompson, *Demotic Magical Papyrus*, verso, col. xxxii/1–13.

PDM xiv. 1219–27

1220
[v. col.
xxxiii, 2]

*Horus . . . went up the mountain[619] at midday during the season of inundation, mounted on a white horse . . . on a black horse, / the papyrus rolls [of . . .] being on (?) him, those of the Great of Five in his breast. He found all the gods seated at the place of judgment eating [of the produce] of the Nile, my great one. Said they, "Horus, come and eat! Horus, come! Are you going to eat?"

615. Identification suggested by R.K.R., identifying Griffith and Thompson, cipher number 22 with cipher number 83.

616. See n. 100 above.

617. A similar spell occurs in *PDM* xiv. 382–86.

618. See n. 411 above.

619. For the mountain of Horus, see M. Smith's commentary to P. BM. 10507, l. 5 (not yet published).

He said, "Go away ' from ' me! I have no [way] to eat. My head hurts; my body hurts. A fever has taken hold of me; a south wind has seized me. Does Isis [stop] making magic? Does Nephthys stop curing? Are the sixteen [620] those of the avenger? Is my one a divine power of a god? Are [the 365] gods sitting down to eat the produce of the fields of the Nile (?), my great one, until they remove the fever / from the head of the son of Isis, from the head of NN, whom NN bore, being the fever of night, the fever of midday, headache, this burning, this heat of the fevers of those below the brow to his feet,[621] [until they] remove [it] from the head of NN, whom NN bore?"

1225
[v. xxxiii,
7]

[Say it] over genuine oil, seven times; anoint his hand, his body, his feet; and speak to him.

*Tr.: Janet H. Johnson, following the edition and translation of Griffith and Thompson, *Demotic Magical Papyrus*, verso, col. xxxiii/1–9. Words preceded by ' are written in the text in Demotic with Old Coptic glosses inserted above.

PGM XV. 1–21

*"I will bind you, Nilos, who is also [called] Agathos Daimon, whom Demetria bore, with great evils. Neither gods nor men will procure[1] a clean getaway[2] for you! On the contrary, you will love me, Capitolina whom Peperous bore, with a divine passion, and in every way you will be for me an escort, as long as I want, that you might do for me what I wish and nothing for anyone else, and that you might obey no one save only me, Capitolina, and that you might forget your parents, / children, and friends. I also conjure you, daimons, who are in this place, ALYĒAĒL . . . LIONŌ SOUAPH ALŌ LYBALOLYBĒL OIKALLISSAMAEŌ LYBALALŌNĒ LYLŌĒY LYOTHNOIS ODISSASON ALELADA. I, Capitolina, have the power, and, on meeting you, Nilos, you will return the favors. They are releasing all who have drowned, have died unmarried, and have been carried away by the wind. Let me insert this deposit, in order that you might accomplish for me what has been written on the strip of papyrus, on account of which I am conjuring / you, daimons, by the force and fate that constrains you. Accomplish everything for me and rush in and take away the mind of Nilos, to whom this magical material belongs, in order that he might love me, Capitolina, and that Nilos, whom Demetria bore, might be inseparable from me, every hour and every day. I conjure you daimons by your spiteful fates that hold you and by those carried by the wind, IŌ IŌĒ PHTHOUTH EIŌ PHRĒ, the greatest daimon, IAŌ SABAŌ / BARBARE THIŌTH[3] LAILAMPS OSORNŌPHRI EMPHERA, the only-begotten god in heaven, who shakes the deep, sending out waters and winds— discharge the spirits of the daimons where my deposit box is, in order that they, either male or female, small or great, might perform for me the things in the tablet, in order that they might come and accomplish the things in this tablet and might bind Nilos, who is also [called] / Agathos Daimon, whom Demetria bore, to me, Capitolina, whom Piperous bore, for his [whole] life. Nilos shall love me with an eternal affection; immediately, immediately; quickly, [quickly]."

5

10

15

20

*Tr.: R. F. Hock.

620. See Griffith and Thompson, *The Leyden Papyrus* 204, n. to V. l. XXXIII. 5.

621. I.e., from his head to his feet. [R.K.R.]

1. The papyrus has ευρωσι, which A. Henrichs emends to εὕρω σοι, "I will procure." The meaning is, however, unclear.

2. Lit., "a pure release."

3. THIŌTH was accidentally omitted in Preisendanz's text.

PGM XVI. 1–75

*"I adjure you, [daimon] of the dead, by the MĒTH . . . OU MACHEREMA PHA-
CHE[LEZETHI] ALŌIA BATHABLEOUCHACHI ABAŌS OMŌCHAL ARACHRAUCH . . .
OU AMERRA MACHERTHA PHACHELEZETHI; cause Sarapion to pine [and] melt
5   away for the passion of Dioskorous, whom [Tikoi bore]. [Inflame / his] heart,
cause it to melt, and [suck out his] blood because of love, passion, and pain for me,
until Sarapion, whom [Pasametra] bore, [comes] to Dioskorous, whom Tikoi bore.
[And] let him [do] all the things in my [mind] and let him [continue] loving me,
[until] he [arrives] in Hades."

"I adjure you, as a daimon of the dead, by ADŌNAIOS SABAŌTH AMARACHTHEI /
10   AXIAŌTHAZAR, god, ATHRŌA SOU . . . AMALAXA, god, . . . EN MARATA ACHŌ
CHIMMI NEMEGAIPH Y . . . ACHILTHTEE [MARADTHA] THARBI APSŌCH . . . ;
cause Sarapion, whom Pasametra[1] bore, to pine and melt away out of passion for
Dioskorous, whom Tikoi bore. Brand his heart, cause it to melt, and suck out his
15   blood because of love, passion, pain, / until Sarapion, whom Pasametra [bore],
comes to Dioskorous, whom Tikoui bore. And let him do all the things in my mind
and let him continue loving me until he arrives in Hades."

"I adjure you, [daimon] of the dead, by the heart of Kronos' son . . . ŌURŌNY
20   . . . LI . . . EULAMŌSI . . . MERATHA; cause Sarapiōn, whom Pasametra bore, / to
pine and melt away out of passion for [Dioskorous], whom Tikoi bore. And cause
his heart to melt, [and] suck out [his] blood because of love, passion, pain, [until]
Sarapion, whom Pasametra bore, comes to Dioskorous, whom Takoui bore. And
25   let him do all the things in my mind, and let him continue loving me, until / he
arrives in Hades."

"I adjure you, daimon of the dead, by the one under STĒĒAALEBMOU EYA . . .
NEKELA . . . TOSAN . . . AKETORIMISEPHONYMI STASACHĒ AMŌTILŌ NEBOU
[TOSOUALĒTH cause] Sarapion, whom [Pasametra bore], to pine and melt away out
of passion for Dioskorous, whom Tikoui bore. Cause [his heart] to melt [and] suck
30   out [his] blood / because of love, passion, pain, until Sarapion, whom Pasametra
bore, comes [out of passion for Dioskorous, whom Tikoi bore]. And [let him do all
the things in my mind], and let him continue loving me until [he arrives in Hades]."

"I adjure you, daimon of the dead, by the M . . . MASĒ LEAI . . . MEA . . . RMŌ
35   . . . SEGE B . . . DĒSAŌOUA / PHESPHTOU undefiled EI, names . . . XAI BAIMEBOTĒ-
SAI PHTHASIAU SAIEXEETHA CHTHETHŌ OU NEBIŌTHY LAIOUTH, cause Sarapion,
whom Pasametra bore, to pine and melt away out of passion [for Dioskorous],
40   whom Tikoui bore. And [cause] his [heart to melt and] suck out his blood / because of love, passion, pain, until Sarapion, whom Pasametra bore, comes [to] Dioskorous, [whom] Tikaui [bore]. And let him do [all the things in my] mind, [and let
him continue] loving me until [he arrives] in [Hades], and again I adjure you,
45   [daimon of the dead], by the PHTHOI KI . . . ŌSE . . . AUTHEIOKRA . . . EI / APO
EIRRATHEIBŌTHIMIA PROSĒMOPERNAI . . . ENE A . . . S . . . TASĒTHŌNNEBAI
LEISEI; cause Sarapion, [whom Pasametra] bore, [to pine and melt away] out of
passion for Dioskorous, whom [Tikoi] bore. And cause his heart to melt [and suck
50   out his blood] because of love, passion, pain, until Sarapion, whom / Pasametra
bore, comes to Dioskorous, [whom] Tikoui bore. [And let him] do all [the things]
in my mind, and let him continue loving [me], until he arrives [in Hades]."

"I adjure you, daimon of the dead, by SIIA the MEGON ABAŌTH OU . . . OUOG-
55   DOUKO . . . ĒRĒ . . . OMMA KELARO . . . ONTBEIA; [cause Sarapion], / whom Pasa-

1. Cf. D. R. Jordan, *Philologus* 120 (1976): 132, who reads πᾶσα μήτρα, "the whole womb," here
and throughout the text.

metra bore, [to pine] and melt away [out of] passion for Dioskorous, whom Ti-
kouou bore. And cause his [heart] to melt and suck out his blood because of [love],
passion, pain, unless Sarapion, whom Pasametra bore, comes to Dioskorous, whom
[Tikoi] bore. [And let him do] all the things in / my mind, [and let him continue   60
loving me until he arrives in Hades]."

"I adjure you, [daimon of the] dead, by [ADONAIOS] . . . DŌ . . . EXIAKĒN
NEIKAROPLĒX MIDEKLIBAIA AUKA . . . LEUEIMETH . . . EXENNE KOMMI BIOU;
cause Sarapion, whom Pasametra bore, to pine [and melt away] out of passion for
[Dioskorous], whom [Tikoi bore. Brand his heart] and [cause it to melt]; / [suck   65
out his] blood because of love, passion, pain, until Sarapion, whom Pasametra bore,
[comes out of passion for Dioskorous, whom Tikoi bore. And let him do] all [the]
things in my mind, [and let him continue loving me until he arrives in Hades]."

"[I adjure you, daimon of the dead, by] the greatest MY . . . PRŌTĒSKAINO-
NEONTI ERĒ[KISISPHĒ] ARARACHARARA ĒPHSISIKĒRE . . . / and inflame [his heart   70
until Sarapion, whom] Pasametra [bore, comes] to Dioskorous, whom [Tikoi] bore.
[Cause Sarapion, whom] Pasametra [bore, to pine and melt away] out of passion
for Dioskorous, [whom] Tikoi bore; [cause him to melt away and suck out his
blood] because of love, [passion, pain] for me, [O daimon of the dead]. Wherefore,
do [and complete] for me all the things [written on this] / [strip of papyrus].   75
*Tr.: E. N. O'Neil.

PGM XVIIa. 1–25

*"ᘐᶴᵃᴿᶴ⫸ DAMNIPPE PĒPĒ ŌŌ 𝑥𝖊𝖝𝖞𝖞=39	A	A
LYKYXUVHYCH NN CHYCH	BA	AK
XYKYL ⵍᶾ⵰ᵞ PSCH ⬚⵰ ŌŌ ĒPĒP ⸻	LBA	AKR
ĒPP[1] INMAD, Anubis, god on earth	ALBA	AKRA
and under earth and heavenly;	NALBA	AKRAM
dog, dog, dog, assume all your /	ANALBA	AKRAMM
authority and all your power	THANALBA	AKRAMMA	5
against Tigerous, whom Sophia	ATHANALBA	AKRAMMACH
bore. Make her cease from	NATHANALBA	AKRAMMACHA
her arrogance, calculation,	ANATHANALBA	AKRAMMACHAM
and her shamefulness, and attract	LANATHANALBA	AKRAMMACHAMA
her to me, beneath my feet,	BLANATHANALBA	AKRAMMACHAMAR
melting with passionate	ABLANATHANALBA	AKRAMMACHAMARI
desire / at every hour of the	BLANATHANALBA	AKRAMMACHAMAR	10
day and night, always	LANATHANALBA	AKRAMMACHAMA
remembering me while she is	ANATHANALBA	AKRAMMACHAM
eating, drinking, working,	NATHANALBA	AKRAMMACHA
conversing, sleeping / dreaming,	ATHANALBA	AKRAMMACH	15
having an orgasm in her dreams,	THANALBA	AKRAMMA
until she is scourged by you and	ANALBA	AKRAMM
comes desiring me, with her	NALBA	AKRAM
hands full, with a generous	ALBA	AKRA
soul and graciously giving me	LBA	AKR
both herself and her possessions	BA	AK
and fulfilling / what is	A	A	20

appropriate for women in regards to men: serving both my desire and her own

---

1. The *voces magicae* PĒPĒ, ĒPĒP, etc., may be related to the Hebrew tetragrammaton, the name for
god. See *PGM* IV. 595 and n.

unhesitatingly and unabashedly, joining thigh to thigh and belly to belly and
her black to my black, most pleasantly. Aye, lord, attract to me Titerous, whom
25 Sophia bore, to me, Hermeias, whom Hermione bore, / immediately, immediately;
quickly, quickly—driven by your scourge."
*Tr.: E. N. O'Neil.

PGM XVIIb. 1–23

*"[Hermes, lord of the world], who're in the heart,
[O orbit of Selene, spherical]
[And] square, the founder of the words [of speech]
[Pleader of justice's cause,] garbed in a mantle,
[With winged sandals,] who rule [expressive] speech
5   [Prophet to mortals] / . . .
For he inspires . . .
. . . within a short time . . .
[Whene'er] the fateful [day arrives] again[1]
10 . . . [who send] some [oracle] that's true, / you're said
To be [the Moirai's thread] and [Dream divine],
[The all-subduer, Unsub]dued, just as
. . . may you judge . . .
You offer good things to the good, [but grief]
[To those who're worthless.][2] Dawn comes up for you,
15 For you swift [night draws] near. / You lord it o'er
The elements: fire, air, [water, and earth][3]
When you became helmsman of [all the] world;
And you escort the souls of those you wish,
But some you rouse again. For you've become
The order of the world, for you [cure], too,
20 Man's [every] ailment, / [who send oracles]
By day and night; [send] me, I pray your [form],
For I'm a man, a pious suppliant,
And your [soldier];[4] and so, [while I'm asleep],
[Send to me your unerring] mantic skill."
*Tr.: E. N. O'Neil. This badly damaged papyrus contains a spell in dactylic hexameters
which is similar in part to *PGM* V. 400–421 and VII. 668–80. Heitsch (in Preisendanz, vol.
II, p. 249) has reconstructed the passages to form Hymns 15–16.

1. Cf. Homer, *Od.* 10. 175.
2. Cf. Homer, *Il.* 24. 530–33; Rom 13:3–4.
3. Cf. *PGM* XII. 250–51.
4. Cf. *PGM* IV. 185–94, esp. 193.

PGM XVIIc. 1–14

```
             *"ABLANATHANATHANABLA
         A    XXXXΠ↙     G
             BAEĒIOYŌ AAAAAAA     R
                                  A
             L EEEEEEE IIIIIII     M          5
         A                        A
             NAKRAKAMARPITAR       CH
             AKOMMŌTEU M P O       A
             THNIRA . . . IPHEL
             PETHION                          10
             AEU.LEIĒ . . . ꝝITAPE
             AṂ̃ÑNEBALESITŌT
             ATACHIT
             O. . . ."
```

*Tr.: Roy Kotansky. This slip of papyrus was evidently used as an amulet or protective charm.

PGM XVIIIa. 1–4

*"Lord Sabaoth, repel the pain from me, the headache pain, I pray, take [from me]. . . ."

*Tr.: John Scarborough.

PGM XVIIIb. 1–7

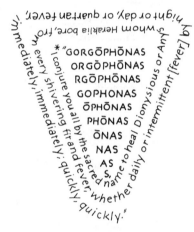

"GORGŌPHŌNAS	*"I conjure you all by the
ORGŌPHŌNAS	sacred name to heal Dionysius
RGŌPHŌNAS	or Anys, whom Heraklia bore,
GŌPHŌNAS	from every shivering fit and fever,
ŌPHŌNAS	whether daily or intermittent [fever]
PHŌNAS	by night or day, or quartan fever,
ŌNAS	immediately, immediately, quickly,
NAS	quickly."
AS	
S"	

*Tr.: John Scarborough. The name GORGŌPHŌNA, here apparently feminine accusative plural, may refer to the epithet of Athena, "Gorgo-slayer."

PGM XIXa. 1–54

* "ENTHI ENTHŌ BOSOU ĒRIS ĒRIS I . . . NOUŌ OUI DE BATHAR NĒITH NĒITH [1]
ĒIAŌTH OUOR KAŌTHIS SAMI SAMIS OPHOR ANOUIPHŌ XTHETHŌNI NOUĒRIŌTH
AŌTH OUŌR TENOCH TENOCH BIBIOU BIBIOU MOUAU MOUAU SMŌSOM THEU-
OUTH OKEBENEUSI ENSI EIPSĒI OUŌR OUŌR OSARAMŌKS THAT THAT ENTHOUŌ
KOMMOUOA PHIANOCH PHIANOCH SŌPH CHTHENTHEBENCH ENTHEBECH ĒCH-
THENTHEBETH YIIABŌY LAILAM HARMIOŌUTH SŌN APS IPHIŌS DIAR NEBES CHI-
NEI NOUTHI NOUTHI KOMŌA RAPHŌR HARSAMŌSI STEOBAOCH ANOCH PHRĒ
5   PHRI CHORBAI MAI ABAŌTH IAŌ IPHI ROMBAOTH / CHAOUCH CHŌOUCH RINGCH
SPHĒCH CHOOUCHORPHI MOUISRŌ [2] KAMPYCHRĒ GORGIŌRIE LAMPIPYRSI SEI-
ROE OMBRIME MATEORSI NAPHSISAŌTHA Ō OSOR MNEUEI Ō OSARAPI SARAPI [3] Ō
OSOR NOBĒCHIS OSOR MNEUEI Ō OSOR NŌPHRIS THŌ THŌ THŌ ITHI ITHI [ITHI]
MOU THOURI [4] CHAOUCH CHTHETHŌNI MAPSITHYRIMAPS TITI NYXBI AMOUN
BLAMOUNITH BIŌTH THŌDIARAX PHORBORBABŌR CHŌSOĒTH BOLCHOSĒTH
ERESCHIGAL HARSAMŌ HARSENOPHRĒ BIRBĒ KAPHIŌ IAŌ ĒIA IAĒ ĒI ĒAIA CHIM-
NOUTH HARBIŌTH KARACHARAX PHRAX AX NOUMŌR TO TACHAN TO PHRĒ TAUAN
CHOUCHE CHOUCHE CHŌX CHŌX CHOUCHOTHI MASKELLI MASKELLI PHNOU-
CHENTABAŌTH OREOBAZAGRA HYPOCHTHŌN IŌOUTH IAŌOUTH AI AI AI OU OU
10   OU BARBARAI BALĒMAĒTH KĒCHI ATHŌR / SENEZEZOUTH SORO ORMEA CHTH
. . . BARMAR PHRIOUREINGX MASKELLI MASKELLŌ PHNOUKENTABAŌTH OREO-
BAZAGRA RĒXICHTHŌN HIPPOCHTHŌN PYRIPEGANYX OREOPEGANYX LEPETAN
LEPETAN PHRIX PHRŌX BIA MASTIGX ANAGKĒ MANTOUENOBOĒL THOURA KRINI
ZOUCHE PIPPĒ BECHOCH TA NIKA AKŌY . . . ĒTO KOURA SANKANTHARA SAN-
KISTĒ DŌDEKAKISTĒ IE ĒI EĒ KINXTABAKINX TABAKINX IŌ MOLPĒ IO KABALTH
SAMAS SAIŌBOTHŌR . . . BAIŌOR BAIŌR ATHARBAIŌ ZASAR THARAIŌ, guardian [5] of
strong Destiny, who manages my affairs, the thoughts of my soul, which no one
can speak out against, not a god, not an angel, not a daimon: arouse yourself for
15   me, / daimon of the dead, and do not use force but fulfill what has been inscribed
and inserted into your mouth, immediately, immediately; quickly, quickly.

---

1. Neith is the Egyptian goddess of Sais. See Bonnet, *RÄRG* 512–17, s.v. "Neith."

2. MOUISRO is "Lion-Ram." See l. 36 below, and *PGM* III. 659 and n.; XXXVI. 351. [R.K.R.]

3. This invocation of Sarapis is peculiar because the god is named by his two names, the older Osar-apis and the common Sarapis. In addition, the three sacred bulls of Apis are named: Osor Nobechis (Buchis), Osor Mnevis, and Osor Nophris (Onuphis). Cf. *PGM* IV. 140; XL. For bull cults in Egypt, see E. Otto, *Beiträge zur Geschichte der Stierkulte in Ägypten* (Leipzig: Hinrichs, 1938). [R.K.R.]

4. THOURI is Egyptian Thoeris, the hippopotamus goddess. See *PGM* XII. 113 and n. [R.K.R.]

5. μελητής, "guardian," seems to occur only here. The common term is ἐπιμελητής. [E.N.O.]

```
ABRASAX            IAEŌBAPHRENEMOUNOTHILARIKRIPHIAEYEAIPHIRKIRALITHONUOMENERPHABŌEAI    BAINCHŌŌŌCH                                      16
ŌYOIĒEA            AEŌBAPHRENEMOUNOTHILARIKRIPHIAEYEAIPHIRKIRALITHONUOMENERPHABŌEA      AEĒIOYŌ        DAMNAMENEU
YOIĒEAŌ            EŌBAPHRENEMOUNOTHILARIKRIPHIAEYEAIPHIRKIRALITHONUOMENERPHABŌE        EĒIOYŌA        AMNAMENEU
OIĒEAŌY            ŌBAPHRENEMOUNOTHILARIKRIPHIAEYEAIPHIRKIRALITHONUOMENERPHABŌ          ĒIOYŌAE        MNAMENEU
IĒEAŌYO            BAPHRENEMOUNOTHILARIKRIPHIAEYEAIPHIRKIRALITHONUOMENERPHAB            IOYŌAEĒ        NAMENEU           20
ĒEAŌYOI IAŌ        APHRENEMOUNOTHILARIKRIPHIAEYEAIPHIRKIRALITHONUOMENERPHA             OYŌAEĒI     Ō  AMENEU
EAŌYOIĒ IAŌ        PHRENEMOUNOTHILARIKRIPHIAEYEAIPHIRKIRALITHONUOMENERPH               YŌAEĒIO     YŌ MENEU
AŌYOIĒE IŌIA       RENEMOUNOTHILARIKRIPHIAEYEAIPHIRKIRALITHONUOMENER      IAŌ AŌI ŌAEĒIOY         OYŌ    ENEU
AIŌIAŌIIIAAAŌ      ENEMOUNOTHILARIKRIPHIAEYEAIPHIRKIRALITHONUOMENE
ŌŌIIIOOOYYYŌŌŌ     NEMOUNOTHILARIKRIPHIAEYEAIPHIRKIRALITHONUOMEN        ŌIAAIŌIAŌ III AAA        IOYŌ    NEU          25
ŌIA AŌI AIŌ ŌIA ŌIA    EMOUNOTHILARIKRIPHIAEYEAIPHIRKIRALITHONUOME       EŌŌŌIIIOOOYYY ŌŌ
III AAA EEE ĒĒEIIIOOOO  MOUNOTHILARIKRIPHIAEYEAIPHIRKIRALITHONUOM         ŌIA IŌIAIŌ I AŌIAŌ     ĒIOYŌ   EU
O YYYYY ŌŌŌŌŌŌŌ    OUNOTHILARIKRIPHIAEYEAIPHIRKIRALITHONUO             IIIAAAEEEĒĒĒIII IOOOO  EĒIOYŌ   U
ABLANATHANALBA    UNOTHILARIKRIPHIAEYEAIPHIRKIRALITHONU               O YYYY ŌŌŌŌŌŌŌ          AEĒIOYŌ
BLANATHANALBA     NOTHILARIKRIPHIAEYEAIPHIRKIRALITHON         AKRAMMACHAMARI SYREMĒNĒ BAKERBĒTH PAKERBĒTH          30
LANATHANALBA      OTHILARIKRIPHIAEYEAIPHIRKIRALITHO           KRAMMACHAMARI ABRASAX ARSAMŌ ACHIŌNOUTH
ANATHANALBA       THILARIKRIPHIAEYEAIPHIRKIRALITH             RAMMACHAMARI ANOUPHI AŌTH ZŌI ZŌPH CHMOUIE
NATHANALBA        ILARIKRIPHIAEYEAIPHIRKIRALI         A       AMMACHAMARI ACHŌR ARCHITŌR IAĒTH ARNTHI-
ATHANALBA         LARIKRIPHIAEYEAIPHIRKIRAL         E   E     MMACHAMARI MORIAM BIŌCH BIŌCH APHROU PHILA
      Ō THANALBA      A   ARIKRIPHIAEYEAIPHIRKIRA       Ē  Ē  Ē    MACHAMARI BRAUPŌPA / . . . CHOUCH ĒEURĒNITHE-    35
     YŌ ANALBA       EA   RIKRIPHIAEYEAIPHIRKIR        I I I I    ACHAMARI PALASŌCH . . . IŌ MOUISRŌ RŌS
    OYŌ NALBA       ĒĒA   IKRIPHIAEYEAIPHIRKI        O O O O O   CHAMARI MOUISRŌ . . . BALBA . . . AIAŌ PAGOURĒ
   IOYŌ ALBA       IĒEA   KRIPHIAEYEAIPHIRK         Y Y Y Y Y Y   AMARI PAAGOURĒ MA . . . PSYLŌ PARNAB
  ĒIOYŌ LBA       OIĒEA   RIPHIAEYEAIPHIR       Ō Ō Ō Ō Ō Ō Ō   MARI LO . . . ARKABERRŌTH MARMARIILĒSA
 EĒIOYŌ BA       YOIĒEA   IPHIAEYEAIPHI       A A A A A A A   ARI RIANYRRĒSON CHORITGRĒE ANŌCH                    40
AEĒIOYŌ A      ŌYOIĒEA   PHIAEYEAIPH          E E E E E E   RI PRĒCHTHENITH ASŌCH NYCHEUNE-
OYOIBĒL OUAIBĒL OUAI IAIŌTHŌ BARRABAU   IAEYEAI      Ē Ē Ē Ē Ē   I CHAPEA PAICHŌRSARI ASISINĒITH
SEMESILAM ABRASAX ORCHRATH BIOURA ZAZER   AEYEA       I I I I   ANASŌCH RĒ . . . EUNI PHŌR PHŌR
MABE CHACHAR ZAS^ CHLABATAR AŌTH AROUĒR CHŌ   EYE       O O O   ABAŌTH DŌI DŌI KOLYPHMYŌTH
BLATHATH ALĒTH BĒIGAMA CHRAEIŌ MEEUAAŌĒŌTH   Y         Y Y   EPONCHŌTH SEUEISĒI SĒTH BOILŌTH TELES-              45
ĒIOYŌ EĒIOYŌ ĒIOYŌ IOYŌOYŌ OYŌŌAAEAEĒ                    Ō   PHEUCHA . . . ASŌRĒTERIŌNICH PHYGRIS SCHĒIK
AEĒI AEĒIO AEĒIOU AEĒIOUŌ . . . BARA OYAAMOU                 PANTA PAREREITHŌSD . . . PHARCHĒLAMA
CHMĒCHEEMEAY ARAREBAICHI PHIANOCHŌ                           DINACHARPAULI PODRYPHORIPH THŌRI ZŌRI ŌN
                                                            AŌ ABRASAX PHONOBOUBOĒL IAŌ
```

IAI IAŌ ĒII AII AŌEA IIII YYY, draw off, thrust away every member of this dead body and the spirit of this tent[7] and cause him to serve / against Karosa, whom Thelo bore. Aye, lord daimon, attract, inflame, destroy, burn, cause her to swoon[8] from love as she is being burnt, inflamed. Sting the tortured soul, the heart, of Karosa, whom Thelo bore, until she leaps forth[9] and comes to Apalos, whom Theonilla bore, out of passion and love, in this very hour, immediately, immediately; quickly, quickly. As long as the divine mystery remains within you,[10] do not allow Karosa herself, whom Thelo bore, to think of her [own] husband,[11] her child, drink, food, but let her come melting for passion and love and intercourse, especially[12] yearning for the intercourse of Apalos whom Theonilla bore, in this very hour, immediately, immediately; quickly, quickly."
*Tr.: E. N. O'Neil and R. Kotansky (ll. 16–47).

PGM XIXb. 1–3

*" . . . may he [bring] him, NN, to her, NN" (add the usual). Write with myrrh mixed with blood on leaves of flax.
*Tr.: E. N. O'Neil.

6. On the name Zas, see PGM II. 117 and n.

7. For similar anthropological terms for "body," see PGM I. 319; IV. 448, 1951, 1970, 2141.

8. σκότωσον (Preisendanz: "umfinstern") refers to the Hellenistic topos of women swooning with love. See, for example, Apollonius, Argon. 3. 960–72 of Medea, for even a witch may swoon with love. [E.N.O.]

9. That is, from her house. Cf. PGM XXXVI. 71, 359 for the same expression.

10. According to A. D. Nock, JEA 11 (1925): 158, μυστήριον is the magical act. So the meaning seems to be "as long as the magical spell which I have worked remains in effect on you." [E.N.O.]

11. ἀνδρί is strange and probably incorrect. The verb μνημονεύω requires either a genitive or an accusative, and the words in parallel construction here are genitive. [E.N.O.]

12. πλείστω[ς], which Preisendanz has retained despite the fact that this adverbial form occurs only in a quotation by Galen from Hippocrates where the manuscripts actually have the regular form πλεῖστα. Schubart (in Preisendanz's apparatus) suggests πλεῖστα. [E.N.O.]

PGM XIXb. 4–18

5   *Love spell of attraction over a dog:[1] Onto a cutting[2] / of hieratic papyrus write
with myrrh and dedicate it[3] to one who has died a violent death.[4] "[I adjure you]
by the SENAKŌTHO ARPOPSYG KAMOUO ORPS THŌ OUCH PETI ANOUP PETIO-
10   PARIN AUT KINOTHEN CHYCH AAA ROPS UICHTHEN / KREMME SECHAXTHNE
NEOUPHTHE AKĒCH CHAKE PŌPHOPI KACHE ANOCH[5] . . . ĒTHMĒ ARI MĒS
15   THOD . . . PE; you, who are able, / [raise] your body and go [to her, NN], until she
is [willing]. . . . "
*Tr.: E. N. O'Neil.

PGM XX. 1–4

*. . . [Spell for] head[ache]:
    ". . . for you to mortals are . . .
        . . .
    . . . fulfill my perfect charm."
*Tr.: E. N. O'Neil. Among the numerous studies of this papyrus, three are especially helpful:
P. Maas, JHS 62 (1942): 33–38; L. Koenen, CEg 37 (1962): 167–74; A. Henrichs, ZPE 6
(1970): 193–212. The text has been restored on the basis of Pap. Berol. 7504, Pap. Amherst
and Pap. Oxyr. ined. D. L. Page, Select Papyri, vol. III (L.C.L.): Literary Papyri Poetry,
no. 146 (pp. 604–5) has reprinted part of Wilamowitz's text of Pap. Berol. 7504. His interpretation of the situation and translation of the text is almost comic.

PGM XX. 4–12

5   *[The charm] of the Syrian woman of Gadara, / for any inflammation:
        "[The[1] most majestic goddess' child] was set
        Aflame as an initiate[2]—and on
        The highest mountain peak was set aflame—
        [And fire did greedily gulp] seven springs
        Of wolves, seven of bears, seven of lions,[3]
10   But seven dark-eyed maidens[4] / with dark urns

1. For a love spell over a dog, see PGM XXXVI. 370.
2. The term τομίον, found only once in PGM, is most likely a reference to a cutting of papyrus; cf.
the technical term ἱερατικόν. See Lewis, Papyrus in Classical Antiquity 181.
3. Preisendanz understands this as "deposit with."
4. Preisendanz assumes that this term refers to the dog (cf. PGM IV. 1882–85, 2578; XXXVI. 370),
but the spell is too fragmentary to be sure.
5. For the interpretation of these magical words see Preisendanz, apparatus ad loc. PETIANOUP is a
personal name and means "He whom Anubis has given"; cf. Ranke, Ägyptische Personennamen I, 122,
no. 11. CHAKE PŌPHOPI KACHE ANOCH, etc., is equivalent to "Darkness, Apophis, darkness I am. . . ."
[R.K.R./J.B.]
1. These lines offer some whole and partial dactylic hexameters. They have been rearranged and used
as the reconstructed Hymn 28; see Preisendanz, vol. II, p. 265. This reconstructed hymn has been translated here. [E.N.O.]
2. L. Koenen, "Der brennende Horusknabe. Zu einem Zauberspruch des Philinna-Papyrus," CEg
37 (1962): 167–74, identifies the παῖς μυστοδόκος as the Horus child. Cf. the story of Isis and the
child of the rulers of Byblos in Plutarch, De Is. et Os. 15–16, 357B–C, and Griffiths, Plutarch's De
Iside et Osiride 328. Cf. also the story of Demeter and Demophoon in Homeric Hymn to Demeter
231–55, with commentary by N. J. Richardson, The Homeric Hymn to Demeter (Oxford: Clarendon
Press, 1974) 231–34. Furthermore, see the note by J. G. Frazer, Apollodorus, vol. II, LCL (Cambridge,
Mass.: Harvard University Press, 1979) 311–17. [E.N.O.]
3. On these springs and animals, see Koenen, "Der brennende Horusknabe," 171–74. Cf. P. Maas,
"The Philinna Papyrus," JHS 62 (1942): 33–38, esp. 37: "I see no plausible connection of wells with
wild beasts." [E.N.O.]

Drew water and becalmed the restless fire."
*Tr.: E. N. O'Neil.

PGM XX. 13–19

**The charm⁵ of the Thessalian Philinna, [for] headache:*
/ "Flee, headache, [lion] flees beneath a rock, 15
Wolves flee; horses flee on uncloven hoof
[And speed] beneath blows [of my perfect charm]."
*Tr.: E. N. O'Neil.

PGM XXI. 1–29

*"[Hear me, lord, whose secret name is unspeakable,] at whose [name, when] the daimons [hear it, even they are terrified; you of whom the sun] BAAL BNICH BAALA [AMĒN PTIDAIOU ARNEBOUAT, and the moon], ASENPEMPH [THŌOUTH BARBA-RAIŌNĒ OSRARMEMPSECHEI], / are [tireless] eyes¹ [shining in the pupils] of men's 5
[eyes; you of whom heaven is the head,] air the body, [earth the feet, the water around you, ocean. You are the Good] Daimon, the lord, [the one who begets good things, nurtures and increases] the [whole] inhabited [earth and all the] / universe. 10
Yours is the eternal [processional way, in which is established] your name which is seven-lettered [in] harmony with the seven [vowel sounds, which are pronounced according to] the twenty-eight forms of the moon, [AEĒIOYŌ AE]ĒIOYŌ AE[Ē]IOYŌ AEĒ[I]OYŌ, / you whose good emanations from the [stars are daimons,] Fortunes 15
and Fates by whom [are given wealth, success,] a happy old age, a good burial.²

"[And] you, [lord of life, ruling] the upper and lower regions,³ [whose justice is not shut off,] whose glorious [name] the Muses praise, [you whom the eight] / guards (Ē, Ō, CHŌ, CHOUCH, [NOUN, NAUNI,] AMOUN and IO)⁴ [attend], you who 20
possess the inerrant [truth]; many moving bodies [will not overpower] me; no spirit, no visitation, [no daimon, no evil being will oppose me, for I will have your name as a single phylactery [in my heart] /, PHIRIMNOUN [A]NOCH⁵ SOLBAI SANA- 25
CHESRŌ . . . ARCHĒN SE KOPŌ⁶ K . . . OAI . . . NOUST [NOUSI SIETHŌ] SIETHŌ BENOUAI.⁷ . . ."
*Tr.: W. C. Grese. See also the parallels in XII. 239–44, 252–57; XII. 765–99.

4. On the identity and role of these maidens see Maas, "The Philinna Papyrus," 37–38; Koenen, "Der brennende Horusknabe," 169.

5. This charm seems to be a *historiola*. Cf. Maas, "The Philinna Papyrus," 37; Koenen, "Der brennende Horusknabe," 169, 173–74.

1. For sun and moon as cosmic eyes, cf. the cosmic body of the deity in *PGM* XII. 242–45.

2. For the divine gifts, see also *PGM* XIII. 782–83.

3. Or "Upper and Lower Egypt"; cf. *PGM* XII. 256.

4. This is the "Ogdoad" of Hermopolis; see S. Morenz, *Ägyptische Religion* 184; Nun-Naunet, Huh-Hauket, Kuk-Kauket, Amun-Amaunet. [J.B.] For these eight guards, see *PGM* XIII. 743–45, 788–89.

5. These words are equivalent to Egyptian and mean "I am he who came forth from Nun." Cf. *PGM* XII. 345; III. 549–58. [R.K.R.]

6. These three groups of letters may be Greek words: ". . . rule. I weary you. . . ." If so, their context cannot be determined, as they are set amid magical words. [M.S.]

7. BENOU is the Phoenix. Cf. *PGM* II. 104 and n. See Bonnet, *RÄRG* 594–96, s.v. "Phönix."

PGM XXIIa. 1

*"We would flee [from Trojan battle before death and ruin."]
*Tr.: John Scarborough. This verse, probably Homer, *Iliad* 17. 714, has not preserved its
title, though Preisendanz (on the basis of the following spell) believed it was a recipe for
hemorrhage. The verse begins *P. Berol.* 9873, a collection of Homeric verses to be used for
magico-medical purposes.

PGM XXIIa. 2–9

Another, for bloody flux:
> "the wrath of Apollo, far-darting lord."[1]

5   Spoken to blood, this [verse] cures bloody flux. / But if [the patient] recovers
and shows ingratitude, take a pan of coals, throw [it in the altar (?)], and place the
amulets over the smoke; add a root, and write this verse in addition:
> "the Far-shooter, having attained his aim, has, therefore, given pain and will
> give it further."[2]

*Tr.: John Scarborough.

PGM XXIIa. 9–10

Write [this] for pain in the breasts and uterus:
10   "[him] / daughter of Zeus suckled and the wheat-bearing earth bore."[3]
*Tr.: John Scarborough.

PGM XXIIa. 11–14

*Carried [with a magnetic] stone, or even spoken, [this verse] serves as a **contraceptive**:
> "Would that you be fated to be unborn and to die unmarried."[4]

Write this on a piece of new [papyrus] and tie it up with hairs of a mule.
*Tr.: John Scarborough.

PGM XXIIa. 15–17

15   *[For one who suffers from elephantiasis*, write this] verse and give it [to him] to
wear:
> "[As when a] woman stains ivory with Phoenician purple."[5]

*Tr.: John Scarborough.

PGM XXIIa. 18–27

*"Greetings, Helios; greetings, Helios; greetings, god over the heavens, with your
20   name [being that] of the all-powerful! From the / seventh heaven [give] me [steady]
favor before every race of men and all women, but especially before her, NN. Make
25   me as beautiful in her presence as IAŌ is, as rich as SABAŌTH, to be loved / like
LAILAM, as great as BARBARAS, as honored as MICHAĒL, as famous as GABRIĒL, and
[I shall be] highly favored."
*Tr.: John Scarborough.

1. Cf. Homer, *Il.* 1. 75.
2. Cf. Homer, *Il.* 1. 96.
3. Cf. Homer, *Il.* 2. 548; also 8. 486; *Od.* 7. 332. But metaphorically ἄρουρα can mean the receiving of seed by a woman and bearing fruit (see, e.g., Theognis 582).
4. Cf. Homer, *Il.* 3. 40.
5. Cf. Homer, *Il.* 4. 141.

PGM XXIIb. 1–26

***Prayer of Jacob**: "O Father of the patriarchs, Father of the All, [Father] of the [cosmic] powers, [Creator of all] . . . , Creator of angels and archangels, the Creator of the [saving] names. I summon you, Father of all powers, Father of the entire [cosmos] and of all / creation inhabited and uninhabited, to whom the [cherubim]   5
are subjected, [who] favored Abraam by [giving the] kingdom [to him] . . . : hear me, O God of the powers, O [God] of angels [and] archangels, [King]. . . .
LELEACH . . . ARŌACH TOU ACHABOL . . . Ō . . . YRAM TOU . . . BOACH KA . . . TH
. . . RA . . . CHACH MARIROK . . . YRAM . . . ITHTH SESOIK, / he who sits upon   10
[holy] Mount Sinai; . . . I . . . BO . . . ATHEM . . . he who sits upon the sea; . . . EA
. . . BL . . . D . . . K . . . E . . . THĒS . . . PARACHTHĒ . . . , he who sits upon the
serpentine gods; the [god who sits upon the] sun, IAŌ; he who sits [upon] . . . TA
. . . Ō . . . I . . . CH; he [who sits] upon the . . . the . . . MA . . . SI, ABRIĒL LOUĒL
. . . M . . . resting place of the [cherubim] . . . CHIRE . . . OZ . . . I . . . / to the ages   15
of ages, God ABAŌTH ABRATHIAŌTH [SABAŌTH] ADŌNAI star . . . and BRILEŌNAI
ADŌNAI CHA . . . AŌTH the Lord of the all.

"I call upon you who give power [over] the Abyss [to those] above, to those below, and to those under the earth; hear the one who has [this] prayer, O Lord God of the Hebrews, EPAGAĒL ALAMN, of whom is [the] eternal power, ELŌĒL SOUĒL. Maintain the one who possesses this prayer, who is from the stock of Israel and from those / who have been favored by you, O god of gods, you who have the   20
secret name, SABAŌTH . . . I . . . CH, O god of gods, amen, amen. You who produce the snow, over the stars, beyond the ages, [and] who constantly traverse [the cosmos], and who cause the fixed and movable stars to pursue all things by your creative activity, fill me with wisdom. Strengthen me, Master; fill my heart with good, Master, as a terrestrial angel, as one who has become / immortal, as one who has   25
received this gift from you, Amen, amen!"

Pronounce the *[Prayer of] Jacob* seven times facing north and east.
*Tr.: D. E. Aune.

PGM XXIIb. 27–31

***Request for a dream oracle, to a lamp**: Purify yourself before your everyday lamp, and speak [the following] to the lamplight, until it is extinguished: "Be well, O lamp, who light the way to Harsentephtha and to Harsentechtha, and to the great [father] Osiris-Michael. / [If] the petition I have made is appropriate, [show]   30
me water [and] a grove. If otherwise, show me water and a stone."
*Tr.: D. E. Aune.

PGM XXIIb. 32–35

*Another **request for a dream oracle**: Take your last morsel of food, and [show it to the] lamp, and while showing it, say [the invocation]. After saying [it] chew up [the morsel], drink wine on top of it, and go to sleep without speaking to anyone. If this is [performed, immediately] you will see someone speaking to you.

". . . OI . . . AL . . . OSMŌ . . . PRA, . . . / I am LAMPSYS, if this matter[1] has been   35
granted to me, show a courtesan; otherwise, a soldier."
*Tr.: D. E. Aune.

---

1. Or "such-and-such a matter."

PGM XXIII. 1–70

    *[But¹ when with vows] and prayers [I had appealed]
    [To them], the tribes of dead, I took [the] sheep
    And slit their throats [beside the trough, and down]
    The dark blood [flowed. From out of Ere]bos
5   Came gathering [the spirits] of the dead: /
(5)   [New brides, unmarried youths,] toil-worn old men,
    [And] tender [maidens] with fresh-mourning hearts,
    [And many] pierced by bronze-tipped spears, [men] slain
    In battle, still in armor stained with gore.
10   [These many] thronged from ev'ry side around
(10)   The trough / with [awful] cry. Pale fear seized me.
    [But]² having drawn the sharp sword at my thigh,
    [I sat,] allowing not the flitting heads
    Of the dead to draw nearer to [the blood],
15   And I in conversation spoke with them.
               (He has said what must be done:) /
(15)   "O³ rivers, earth, and you below, punish
    Men done with life, whoe'er has falsely sworn;
    Be witnesses, fulfill for us this charm.
20   I've come to ask how I may reach the land
    Of that Telemachus, my own son whom /
(20)   I left still in a nurse's arms." For in
    This fashion went the charm most excellent.
               (He tells what charms must be sung:)
25   "[Hear]⁴ me, gracious and guardian, well-born
    [An]ubis; [hear, sly] one, O secret mate,
    Osiris' savior; come, Hermes, come, robber,
(25)   Well-trussed, infernal Zeus; / †Grant [my desire]†,⁵
    Fulfill this charm. [Come hither, Hades,] Earth,
30   Unfailing Fire, O Titan Helios;
    [Come,] Iaweh, Phthas, Phre, guardian of laws,
    [And Neph]tho, much revered; Ablanatho,
    In blessings rich, with [fiery] serpents girded,
(30)   Earth-plowing, goddess with head high, [Abrax]as,
35   A daimon famous by your cosmic name,
    Who rule earth's [axis], starry dance, the Bears'
    Cold light. [And come] to me, surpassing all
    In self-control, O Phren. I'm calling [you],

1. Vv. 1–10 equal Homer, *Od.* 11. 34–43.
2. Vv. 11–13 equal Homer, *Od.* 11. 48–50.
3. Vv. 15–17 equal Homer, *Il.* 3. 278–80 except that in v. 15 the *Iliad* has καί in place of ὦ. In v. 16 the *Iliad* has τίννσθον and the second hemistich of v. 17 appears in the *Iliad* as φυλάσσετε δ'ὅρ-κια πίστα.
4. Because of the fragmentary condition of the following lines (25–43) the reconstructed text of Hymn 24 has been used.
5. "Grant my desire": [κῦρσ]αι δωσάμενοι. The translation is very tentative, for the Greek is uncer-tain. Preisendanz translates "schenkt Gewährung"; Vieillefond (p. 286) translates "ratifiez mes voeux" but in this commentary says: "Il faut comprendre: κῦρσαι δ—'ayant accordé de ratifier.'" Preisendanz reports that this line begins with a space for six letters, but Wünsch's κῦρσα]ι fills only five spaces. Per-haps we should read καὶ ἐπ]ὶ, i.e., καὶ ἐπιδωσάμενοι, "and having given freely."

O B[r]i[ar]eus and Ph[r]asios and you,
O Ixion and Birth and youth's decline,   40
Fair-burning Fire, / [and may you come,] Infernal   (35)
And Heav'nly One, and [you who govern] dreams,
And Sirius, who. . . ."⁶
Standing beside the trough, I cried [these words],
[For well] did I remember Circe's counsels,⁷   45
[Who] knew [all] poisons which the broad earth grows.⁸ /
[Then came] a lofty wave of Acheron   (40)
Which fights with lions, [Cocytus] and Lethe
And mighty Polyphlegethon.⁹ A host
[Of dead] stood round the trough, [and first] there came   50
The spirit of Elpenor, my comrade.¹⁰
          (And so on.)

So, since this is the situation, either the poet himself suppressed¹¹ the remainder   55
because it was an elaboration of the spell in order to preserve the decorum of the   (45)
work, or the Peisistratides,¹² as they were assembling the other verses, withheld
these because they considered them foreign to the passage here. ᵗThis is my opinion for many reasons. And soᵗ¹³ I have myself inserted the lines as a rather valuable   60
creation of epic poetry.¹⁴ / You will find this whole document on the shelves in the   (50)
archives of our former home town, the colony of Aelia Capitolina¹⁵ in Palestine,
and in Nysa in Caria and, up to the thirteenth verse,¹⁶ in Rome near the baths of   65
Alexander¹⁷ in the beautiful library in the Pantheon,¹⁸ whose collection of books I

6. Preisendanz's version ends here. The remaining lines are taken from Vieillefond.

7. Cf. Homer, *Il.* 15. 412.

8. V. 39 equals Homer, *Il.* 7. 741 where ἤδη instead of οἶδα is read.

9. Cf. Homer, *Od.* 10. 513–14. In v. 41 the noun Πολυφλεγέθων is a hapax legomenon (see O. Höfer, in Roscher 3/2 [1902–9] 2713). *Od.* 10. 513 has Πυριφλεγέθων.

10. Cf. Homer, *Od.* 11. 51. With this Homeric line the verse portion of the papyrus concludes. The remaining section contains Julius Africanus' own evaluation of the verses.

11. We seem to have another example here of Homeric criticism in antiquity. Interestingly enough, *Od.* 11. 38–43 were rejected by several ancient scholars, including Zenodotus, Aristophanes of Byzantium, and Aristarchus.

12. A reference to the tradition in late antiquity that Peisistratus was responsible for the earliest recension of the Homeric poems. For a discussion of the subject, see J. A. Davison, "The Transmission of the Text," in A. J. B. Wace and F. H. Stubbings, eds., *A Companion to Homer* (London: Macmillan, 1962) 215–33, esp. 219–20.

13. The translation is tentative. Vieillefond daggers these words, for they seem hopelessly corrupt.

14. Line 49 translates ἅτε κύημα πολυτελέστερον ἐπιεικῆς, but this a strange and otherwise unparalleled meaning of κύημα.

15. Aelia Capitolina is the name given by Hadrian (A.D. 131) to the rebuilt Jerusalem. The statement seems to confirm, at least partially, Jerome's claim (*De viris illustr.* 63) that Julian was born at Emmaus in Palestine. Others call him a Libyan by birth.

16. This is a strange remark, for the first thirteen verses are Homeric. Surely this collection of volumes included the *Iliad* and *Odyssey*.

17. The Thermae Alexandrinae were constructed by rebuilding and enlarging the Thermae Neronianae in the Campus Martinus just northeast of the Pantheon. These baths had their own water supply from the Alexandrian Aqueduct. See *Life of Severus Alexander* 20. 3–5 and 44. 4–6. Cf. *CAH* vol. 12 (1939), pp. 66 and 477.

18. Others, including Vieillefond, understood the words in ll. 53–54 to mean that Africanus built or served as the architect of the library. Yet we have no evidence that he was an architect but abundant testimony that he was a writer and intellect. It seems more probable, therefore, that Africanus here is saying that he "built the collection of books which constituted the library."

myself built for Augustus.[19] /

(55)   Kestos 18[20] of Julius Africanus
*Tr.: E. N. O'Neil. P. Oxy. 412 contains an excerpt from book 18 of the *Kestoi* of Sextus
Julius Africanus, a Christian writer of the third century A.D. The work dealt with numerous
subjects, including medicine, agriculture, natural history, military art, and, as this passage
shows, with Homeric criticism and magic. Since Preisendanz prints only a part of the pa-
pyrus, the translation uses the full text as provided by Jean-René Vieillefond, *Les "Cestes" de
Julius Africanus. Étude sur l'ensemble des fragments avec édition, traduction et commentaires*
(Firenze: Edizioni Sansoni Antiquariato; Paris: Librairie Marcel Didier, 1970) 277–91.

PGM XXIVa. 1–25
*"Great is the Lady Isis!" Copy of a holy book found in the archives of Hermes: /
5   The method is that concerning the 29 letters[1] through which letters Hermes and
10   Isis, who was seeking / Osiris,[2] her brother and husband, [found him].
          Call upon Helios and all the gods in the deep concerning those things for which
15   you want to receive an omen. Take / 29 leaves of a male date palm and write on each
20   of the leaves the names of the gods. Pray and then pick them up two / by two. Read
         the last remaining leaf and you will find your omen, how things are,[3] and you will
25   be answered / clearly.
*Tr.: W. C. Grese.

PGM XXIVb. 1–15
*On the right . . . on the left parts of [the neck . . .] upon the right shoulder . . .
5   on the nipple of the [right breast,] / on the left [shoulder] . . . shall receive . . . on
10   the nipple of the [left breast] . . . on the breast . . . for, the . . . receiving, great . . .
15   and the woman will (?) flee outside, men on . . . drugs . . .
*Tr.: Roy Kotansky. This very fragmentary text describes the engraving of a magic doll or
similar object. The fragment may contain portions of a love charm similar to that of *PGM* IV.
296ff.

PGM XXV. a–d.
a. *P.Oxy.* 959, 7.2 × 13 cm, contains a text of eight lines of magical characters and
letters dated to about the third century A.D. The text remains unpublished.
       b. *P. Freib. inedit.* (described by Preisendanz, P. Un. Bibl. Freiburg i. Br., O. Nr.
7.5 × 9 cm) is an unpublished, opisthographic text containing "characters" and a
magical figure. Sixth century A.D.
       c. *P. Cair.* 10434 measures 5.1 × 6.6 cm (no date provided) and contains the
following text: "[1]Holy Lord Zabaot" (var. of SABAŌTH).
       d. *PSI inedit.*, 6.5 × 5 cm, is described by Preisendanz as a tiny fragment con-
taining a figure with a long nose, the point of which ends in what appear to be
droplets. Behind it is a similar figure, and above both heads there is yet another

19. Augustus is Severus Alexander.
20. Notice that, although the title of the work is in the plural κεστοί, each individual book seems to
have the singular title κεστός.
1. According to W. Schubart, *Einführung in die Papyruskunde* (Berlin: Weidmann, 1918) 369, the
twenty-nine letters represent the Coptic alphabet.
2. On Isis seeking Osiris, see Plutarch, *De Is. et Os.* 18, 358 A–B; 52, 372 B–C, and Griffiths, *Plutarch's De Iside et Osiride* 339–40, 499; idem, *The Isis-Book* 219.
3. Grenfell and Hunt, *P. Oxy.* 6, pp. 200–201, translate: "and you will find wherein [Milligan, *Selec-
tions from the Greek Papyri* 110–11, ". . . in what things"] your omen consists." The translation follows
the punctuation of Preisendanz, who translates: "und du wirst dein Orakel finden darüber, worauf es dir
[Hopfner, *OZ* II, 299 adds ⟨σα⟩] ankommt." [W.C.G.]

head with a very long nose. On the reverse side appear three words of which only
"PHOIBIŌN" can be made out.

PGM XXVI. 1–21

The numerically arranged oracular text, *P.Oxy.* XII. 1477, is here omitted as it has
been shown to belong to the corpus known as the *Sortes Astrampsychi*, for which see
Gerald M. Browne, *The Papyri of the Sortes Astampsychi*, Beiträge zur klassischen
Philologie 58 (Meisenheim am Glan: Hain, 1974); see also idem, "The Date of the
Sortes Astrampsychi," *ICS* 1 (1976): 53–58; idem, "A New Papyrus Codex of the
Sortes Astrampsychi," in *Arktouros. Hellenic Studies presented to Bernard M. W. Knox
on the Occasion of his 65th birthday* (Berlin/New York: de Gruyter, 1979) 434–39;
see also *P.Oxy.* XLVII. 3330. The editor is also preparing an edition of the *Sortes* for
the Bibliotheca Teubneriana.

PGM XXVII. 1–5

Victory charm**, for Sarapammon, son of Apollonius: "[1] Give victory and
safety at the stadium and in the crowd to the above-mentioned Sarapammon. In the
name of SYLIKYS Ē SYS. . . ."
*Tr.: R. F. Hock.

PGM XXVIIIa. 1–7

*"OR OR[1] PHOR PHOR SABAŌTH ADŌNE SALAMA TARCHEI ABRASAX, I bind you,
scorpion of Artemisia, / three-hundred and fifteen times, on the fifteenth day of   5
Pachon. . . ."
*Tr.: Roy Kotansky.

PGM XXVIIIb. 1–9

*"ŌR ŌR[2] PHŌR PHŌR IAŌ ADŌNAEI / SABAŌTH SALAMAN TARCHCHEI, I bind   5
you, scorpion of Artemisos, on the 13th."
*Tr.: Roy Kotansky.

PGM XXVIIIc. 1–11

*[††††] ŌR ŌR[3] PHŌR PHŌR [ADŌNAI] / SALAMA RTHACHI, I bind you, Artemisian   5
scorpion, on the fourth day of Phamenoth, / PHŌR OR OR OSOA DDD RRR."
*Tr.: Roy Kotansky.

PGM XXIX. 1–10

  *"I used to command the Rhodian[1] winds
    And your regions of the sea
    Whenever I'd want to set sail.
    Whenever I'd want to stay there,
    I'd say to the regions of the sea: 5
    'Don't [smite] the seas with your blows;

1. According to Grenfell and Hunt, *P.Oxy.* 12 (1916) 237, magical symbols are given in the papyrus
at this point, but the editors did not provide them.
    1. The name should probably be articulated HŌR, i.e., Horus, who is often invoked in Egyptian
scorpion spells. See Borghouts, *Ancient Egyptian Magical Texts* 51–85. [R.K.R.]
    2. See n. 1 above.
    3. See n. 1 above.
    1. It seems preferable to retain the ʽΡοδίοις of the papyrus rather than to follow Preisendanz in
emending to ʽΡοϑίοις. See Preisendanz, apparatus ad loc.

Lay smooth the brine for seafarers.'
Then ev'ry fair wind[2] is raised;
They shut out the blasts, and so, lord,[3] grant
10   The impassable to be passable."
*Tr.: E. N. O'Neil. This rather charming and unpretentious poem is surely not a part of the regular *PGM* material. It is rather a poem—or a fragment of a poem—which is perhaps an ancient treatment of the theme that appears in Goethe's two poems, *Meeresstille* and *Glückliche Fahrt*. Because of the literary aspect, J. U. Powell included these lines among the *Lyrica Adespota* in his *Collectanea Alexandrina* (Oxford: Clarendon Press, 1925) 195, no. 33. Despite the obvious poetic quality, no one has satisfactorily explained the meter (cf. Powell, p. 196). Grenfell thought that the verses are accentual, while Schmidt believed that they are a blend of trochaic and Cretic. For the references, see Preisendanz, ad loc. Whatever the case, the present translation uses a blend of iambic and anapaestic feet in an attempt to give in English some of the general effect of the Greek. These verses have been emended and stand as the reconstructed Hymn 29; see Preisendanz, vol. II, pp. 265–66.

PGM XXXII. 1–19

*"I adjure you, Evangelos, by Anubis and Hermes and all the rest down below;
5   attract and bind / Sarapias whom Helen bore, to this Herais, whom Thermoutha-
10   rin bore,[1] now, now; quickly, quickly. By her soul and heart / attract Sarapias herself, whom [Helen] bore from her own womb,[2] MAEI OTE ELBŌSATOK ALAOUBĒTŌ
15   ŌEIO . . . AĒN. Attract and [bind / the soul and heart of Sarapias], whom [Helen bore, to this] Herais, [whom] Thermoutharin [bore] from her womb [now, now; quickly, quickly]."
*Tr.: E. N. O'Neil. This spell, without a title, is clearly a love spell in which one woman seeks to attract another woman. Thus it belongs to the small group of lesbian spells. In form, these lines contain one spell repeated, with slight variations, three times: 1–9, 10–14, 14–19.

PGM XXXIIa. 1–25

*"As[1] Typhon is the adversary of Helios, so inflame the heart and soul of that[2]
5   Amoneios whom / Helen bore, even from her own womb, ADŌNAI ABRASAX PI-
NOUTI[3] and SABAŌS; burn the soul and heart of that Amoneios whom Helen /
10   bore, for [love of] this Serapiakos whom Threpte bore, now, now; quickly, quickly."
      "In this same hour and on this same day, from this [moment] on, mingle /
15   together[4] the souls of both and cause that Amoneios whom Helen bore to be this
20   Serapiakos whom / Threpte bore, through every hour, every day and every night.
25   Wherefore, ADŌNAI, loftiest of gods, whose name is the true / one, carry out the matter, ADŌNAI."
*Tr.: E. N. O'Neil. This section contains two spells—or one spell repeated with variations.

2. For ὅλος of the papyrus perhaps οὖρος should be read: "fair wind" is what the author seems to mean.

3. Can ἄναξ be Helios as represented by the famous Colossus Rhodius? Powell dates this poem to the period ca. A.D. 250–80, and the huge statue of Helios was complete ca. A.D. 168 and destroyed ca. A.D. 224. Yet the memory of this "wonder" continued for centuries. In any case, Helios was an important god on the island of Rhodes, and a reference to him seems appropriate.

1. Herais has a Greek name, while her mother, Thermoutarin, has an Egyptian name. [R.K.R.] The spelling of the names follows Preisendanz; cf. the apparatus ad loc.

2. On this formula, see D. Jordan, *Philologus* 120 (1976): 131–32.

1. The opening statement is troublesome and has attracted some attention. See A. S. Hunt, "An Incantation in the Ashmolean Museum," *JEA* 15 (1929): 155–57; A. D. Nock, *JEA* 16 (1931): 124; K. Preisendanz, *Philologische Wochenschrift* 50 (1930): 748–49.

2. As the pronouns indicate, this spell is concerned with homosexual attraction.

3. This is Egyptian and means "O/The god." See Preisendanz, apparatus ad loc.

4. συγκαταμείγνυμι is a concept from friendship literature: true friends are two souls in one body, *amicus est alter ego*. The term is also erotic just as the simple μείγνυμι is regularly. [E.N.O.]

PGM XXXIII. 1–25

*"ABLANATHANABLANAMACHARAMARACHARAMARACH

BLANATHANABLANAMACHARAMARACHARAMARA

LANATHANABLANAMACHARAMARACHARAMAR

ANATHANABLANAMACHARAMARACHARAMA

NATHANABLANAMACHARAMARACHARAM   5

ATHANABLANAMACHARAMARACHARA

THANABLANAMACHARAMARACHAR

ANABLANAMACHARAMARACHA

NABLANAMACHARAMARACH

ABLANAMACHARAMARA   10

BLANAMACHARAMAR

LANAMACHARAMA

ANAMACHARAM

NAMACHARA

AMACHAR   15

MACHA

ACH

A

"O Tireless one, KOK KOUK KOUL, save / Tais whom [Taraus] bore from every shiv-   20
ering fit,[1] whether tertian[2] or quartan[3] or quotidian fever, or an every-other-day
fever,[4] or [one] by night, or [even] a mild fever,[5] because I am the ancestral, tireless
god, KOK KOUK[6] KOUL, / immediately, immediately; quickly, quickly."   25
*Tr.: John Scarborough.

PGM XXXIV. 1–24

*". . . [the sun] will stand still; and should I order the moon, it will come down;
and should I wish to delay the day, the night will remain for me; and should / we[1]   5
in turn ask for day, the light will not depart; and should I wish to sail the sea, I do
not need[2] a ship; and should I wish to go through the air, / I will be lifted up. It is   10
only[3] an erotic drug that I do not find, not one that can cause, not one that can stop
love. For the earth, in fear of the / god, does not produce one. But if anyone has it   15
and gives it, I beg, I beseech him: 'Give! I wish to drink, I wish to anoint myself.'"[4]

    "You[5] say that a handsome phantom keeps appearing to your daughter, / and   20
this seems unreasonable[6] to you? Yet how many others have fallen in love with 'un-

1. Cf. *PGM* XVIIIb. 5.
2. τριταῖος (πυρετός), as in the Hippocratic *Aphorisms* 3. 21 and *Nature of Man* 1. 5, is literally "every-third-day-fever."
3. In contrast to *PGM* XVIIIb. 6, the papyrus has the normal τεταρταῖος.
4. Pollux, *On.* 1. 65 cod. B suggests the reading παρημέρινος; it does not occur in the medical writers. [J.S.]
5. λεπτοπυρετοῦ is a textual emendation; however, the word is unattested in LSJ, s.v. Cf. LSJ, *Suppl.* s.v. "λεπτοπυρέτιον."
6. KOUK is Egyptian *kky*, "darkness"; cf. *PGM* XIII. 788–89.
1. The sudden appearance of the person plural is strange.
2. This use of the present tense occurs in the midst of a series of future tenses. [E.N.O.]
3. Although μόνον οὐ regularly means "almost," that sense does not seem to fit here. [E.N.O.]
4. The text here is uncertain. For the translation, the text of Preisendanz has been used.
5. For the following lines see, especially, the study of Dodds mentioned below.
6. The papyrus reads παράδοξον here and παρ' ἀλόγων (παραλόγων) in l. 22, and so both Dodds and Preisendanz print their versions; but in a conversation it is reasonable to expect the second person to repeat the word which the first speaker has used. The translation understands παραδόξων in l. 22. [E.N.O.]

reasonable' bodies[7] . . .?"[8]

*Tr.: E. N. O'Neil. This fragment belongs not to a magical spell but rather to some literary piece, perhaps a Greek romance. See C. Bonner, "A Papyrus Describing Magical Powers," *TAPA* 52 (1921): 111–18; E. R. Dodds, "A Fragment of a Greek Novel (P.Mich. inv. no. 5)" in *Studies in Honor of Gilbert Norwood, Phoenix Supp.* I (Toronto: University of Toronto Press, 1952) 133–37. Dodds's theory that this fragment is part of a lost Greek romance seems logical in light of the conversational tone throughout, but the tone of ll. 19–24 makes this theory almost certain.

PGM XXXV. 1–42

*"I call upon you, who sit over the Abyss, BYTHATH; I also call upon the one who sits in the first heaven, MARMAR; I call upon you, who sit in the 2nd heaven,
5   RAPHAËL; I call upon you, who sit in the 3rd heaven, SOURIËL;[1] / I call upon you, who sit in the 4th heaven, IPHIAPH;[2] I call upon you, who sit in the 5th heaven, PITIËL; I call upon you, who sit in the [6th] heaven, MOURIATHA.

"I call upon you, who sit over the snow, TELZË; I call upon you, EDANÔTH, who
10   sit over the sea; I call upon you, SAESECHEL, who sit over the serpents; / I call upon you, TABIYM, who sit over the rivers; I call upon you, BIMADAM; I call upon you, CHADRAOUN, who sit in the midst of CHADRALLOU, in between the two cherubim and seraphim, as they praise you, the lord of the whole host which is under heaven.

"I conjure you all by the god of Abraham, Isaac, and Jacob,[3] that / you obey my
15   authority completely, each one of you obeying perfectly, and that you stay beside me and give me favor, influence, victory, and strength, before all, small men and great, as well as gladiators, soldiers, civilians, women, girls, boys, and everybody,
20   quickly, quickly, because of the / power of IAÔ, the strength of SABAÔTH, the clothing of ELOË,[4] the might of ADÔNAI, and the crown of ADÔNAI. Grant also to me favor and victory before all, as you have given good gifts to ALBANATHANALBA
25   and AKRAMACHAMARI; and this is why, then, I am exhorting and conjuring / you that you give favor, victory, power, and spirit on behalf of me, the three-crown-bearing ruler, quickly, [quickly,] because I conjure you, IAÔ SABAÔTH AÔ SABAÔTH Ô SABAÔTH SABAÔTH A ABAÔTH BAÔTH AÔTH ÔTH TH."

30
"Look above the spir   PAULUS   "I conjure
its of the opponent to-   you by the
ward the spirits of dig-   god SARA-
nity [and] exaltation. I   JULIANUS   CHAEL [by]
35   call upon / and exhort   BILIAM,[5] and
and conjure you that   [by] the god
you obey unfailingly   who made
my every command, for   heaven and

7. σωμάτων is synonomous with εἴδωλον.

8. Dodds (see n. 4 above) 137 assumes the speaker is female, but the gender is not indicated in the text.

1. For the name SURIEL, see the discussion by Scholem, *Jewish Gnosticism* 46. A number of other parallels esp. with Judaism are noted in Preisendanz's apparatus.

2. For the name IPHIAPH, see Scholem, *Jewish Gnosticism* 12, n. 7.

3. The papyrus reads Abram, Isaka, Iachôb.

4. For the garment of ELOË, see Scholem, *Jewish Gnosticism* 64.

5. The prophet Bileam from Pethor is known from Nm 22:5–24, 25; 31:8, 16; Dt 23:4, etc. His

my sake, the three [crown-] bearing one, SABATH. . . ." earth and everything in it. . . ."

*Tr.: R. F. Hock. The spell has a number of parallels in a Christianized Jewish silver lamella from Beirut; see A. Heron de Villefosse, *Florilegium . . . dédiés à . . . de Vogüé* (Paris: Imprimerie nationale, 1909) 287–95.

PGM XXXVI. 1–34

*Charm to restrain. Works on everything: Taking a lead lamella, hammered out while cold, inscribe with a bronze stylus the creature below and the names, and deposit it nearby and in front [the person]: "Come Typhon, who sit on the under-[world] gate; / IŌ ERBĒTH, who killed his own brother,[1] IŌ PAKERBĒTH IŌ BOL- 5
CHOSĒTH IŌ APOMPS IŌ SESENRŌ IŌ BIMAT IAKOYMBIAI ABERRAMENTHŌOY LERTHEXANAX ETHRELYOŌTH MEMAREBA, of Seth, BOLKOL, fear your uninhibited son."

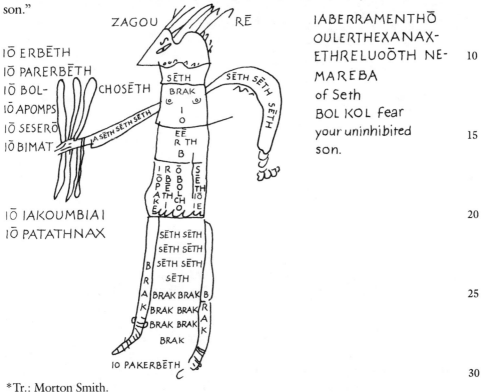

ZAGOU RĒ

IŌ ERBĒTH
IŌ PARERBĒTH
IŌ BOL- CHOSĒTH
IŌ APOMPS
IŌ SESERŌ
IŌ BIMAT

IŌ IAKOUMBIAI
IŌ PATATHNAX

IABERRAMENTHŌ
OULERTHEXANAX-
ETHRELUOŌTH NE- 10
MAREBA
of Seth
BOL KOL fear
your uninhibited 15
son.

20

25

30

*Tr.: Morton Smith.

PGM XXXVI. 35–68

*Charm to restrain anger and to secure favor and an excellent charm for gain- 35
ing victory in the courts (it works even against kings; no charm is greater): Take a silver lamella and inscribe with a bronze stylus the following seal of the figure and the names, / and wear it under your garment, and you will have a victory. 40

connection with magic was proverbial. See Ginzberg, *The Legends of the Jews* III, 354–82; H. Karp, "Bileam," *RAC* 2 (1954) : 262–73.

  1. Cf. the denial of this deed in *PGM* VII. 964.

The names to be written are these: "ΙΑῶ SABAῶTH ADῶNAI ELῶAI ABRASAX
ABLANATHANALBA AKRAMMACHAMARI PEPHTHA PHῶZA PHNEBENNOUNI,[2] supreme angels, give to me, / NN whom NN bore, victory, favor, reputation, advantage over all men and over all women, especially over NN, whom NN bore, for ever
and all time." Consecrate it.

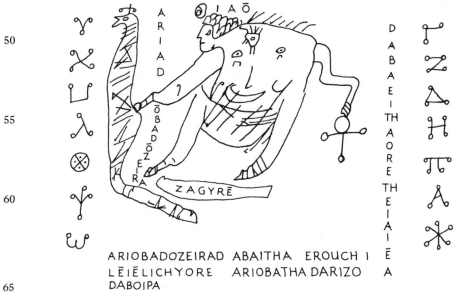

ARIOBADOZEIRAD ABAITHA EROUCH I Ē
LĒIĒLICHYORE ARIOBATHA DARIZO A
DABOIPA

*Tr.: R. F. Hock.

PGM XXXVI. 69–101

*Love spell of attraction, excellent inflamer, than which none is greater. It at-
tracts men to women and women to men / and makes virgins rush out of their
homes. Take a pure papyrus and with blood of an ass[3] write the following names
and figure, and put in the magical material from the woman you desire. Smear the
strip of papyrus with moistened vinegar gum[4] / and glue[5] it to the dry vaulted
vapor room of a bath,[6] and you will marvel. But watch yourself so that you are not
struck.

The writing is this: "Come, Typhon, who sit on top of the gate, Iῶ ERBĒTH IῶPAKERBĒTH IῶBALCHOSĒTH Iῶ APOMPS Iῶ SESENRῶ Iῶ BIMAT IAKOUMBIAI AB-
ERRAMENTHῶ OULER- / THEXANAX ETHRELUOῶTH MEMAREBA TOU SĒTH, as you
are in flames and on fire, so also the soul, the heart of her, NN, whom NN bore,
until she comes loving me, NN, and glues her female pudenda to my male one,
immediately, immediately; quickly, quickly."

2. PEPHTHA PHῶZA PHNEBENNOUNI is equivalent to Egyptian "He is Ptah the healthy, the lord of the Abyss." [R.K.R.]
3. This is to connect the spell with Typhon, invoked below. Cf. *PGM* IV. 2015, 2100, 2220.
4. ὀξοκόμι is from ὀξυκόμμι according to LSJ, s.v. It is also a hapax legomenon. The papyrus has ὀξωκόμῃ, which LSJ explains as dative of ὀξυκόμμι. See Schmidt, *GGA* 189 (1927):464–56, who refers to Pliny, *NH* 24. 3, 106; cf. also *NH* 13. 20, 66–67 for a discussion of Egyptian gums. [E.N.O.]
5. For the glue, cf. l. 83 below. As the operator does with the strip of papyrus, so may NN do with the operator. [E.N.O.]
6. Cf. *PGM* II. 51.

*Tr.: E. N. O'Neil.

PGM XXXVI. 102–33

*Another divination by fire: Take clean papyrus and write the following names and figure with myrrh ink and say the spell three times.

The names / and the figure to be written are these: 105

"Hear me, you who founded and destroyed and became the mighty god whom a white sow bore,[7] ALTHAKA EIATHALLATHA SALAIOTH, who appeared in Pelousion,[8] in Heliopolis possessing an iron staff[9] with which you opened up the sea and passed through after you had completely / dried up all the plants. Attract to me,   110 NN, her, NN, aflame, on fire, flying through the air, hungry, thirsty, not finding sleep, loving me, NN whom NN bore, until she come and glue[10] her female pudenda to my male one, immediately, immediately; quickly, quickly." /

---

7. The one born of the white sow is Min of Koptos, born of Isis. For discussion, see J. Bergman, "Isis auf der Sau," *Acta Universitatis Upsaliensis Boreas* 6 (1974): 81–109, esp. 91–92. [R.K.R.]

8. Pelusium was a city in Egypt, situated on the Nile. See Plutarch, *De Is. et Os.* 17, 375E, and Griffiths, *Plutarch's De Iside et Osiride* 334–35. Cf. *PGM* VII. 499 and n.

9. See for the iron staff Ex 7:17–24; 14:21–31. For Egyptian parallels, see W. K. Simpson, ed., *The Literature of Ancient Egypt* (New Haven: Yale University Press, 1973) 21. [R.K.R.]

10. Cf. above, l. 75 and n.

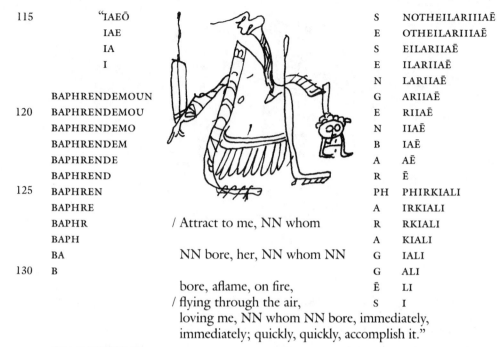

115	῾IAEŌ
	IAE
	IA
	I
	BAPHRENDEMOUN
120	BAPHRENDEMOU
	BAPHRENDEMO
	BAPHRENDEM
	BAPHRENDE
	BAPHREND
125	BAPHREN
	BAPHRE
	BAPHR
	BAPH
	BA
130	B

S	NOTHEILARIIIAĒ
E	OTHEILARIIIAĒ
S	EILARIIAĒ
E	ILARIIAĒ
N	LARIIAĒ
G	ARIIAĒ
E	RIIAĒ
N	IIAĒ
B	IAĒ
A	AĒ
R	Ē
PH	PHIRKIALI
A	IRKIALI
R	RKIALI
A	KIALI
G	IALI
G	ALI
Ē	LI
S	I

/ Attract to me, NN whom

NN bore, her, NN whom NN

bore, aflame, on fire,
/ flying through the air,
loving me, NN whom NN bore, immediately,
immediately; quickly, quickly, accomplish it."

*Tr.: E. N. O'Neil.

PGM XXXVI. 134–60

*Marvelous love spell of attraction**, than which none is greater: Take myrrh /
135 and male frankincense, put them in a drinking cup and add an *archē*[11] of vinegar,
and at the third hour of the night put it into the socket of your door and say the
spell 7 times.

The spell to be spoken is this: "Arise, daimons in the dark; leap up onto the bricks
and beat your breasts after you have smeared your faces with mud. For because
140 of / her, NN whom NN bore, unlawful eggs are being sacrificed: fire, fire, unlawfulness, unlawfulness.[12] For Isis raised up a loud cry, and the world was thrown
into confusion. She tosses and turns on her holy bed, and its bonds and those of the
daimon world are smashed to pieces[13] because of the enmity and impiety of her,
145 NN, whom NN bore. But you,[14] Isis / and Osiris and [daimons] of the chthonic
world, ABLAMGOUNCHŌTHŌ ABRASAX, and daimons who are beneath the earth,
arise, you who are from the depth, and cause her, NN, whom NN bore, to be sleepless, to fly through the air, hungry, thirsty, not finding sleep,[15] to love me, NN
150 whom NN bore, passionately with passion in her guts, until she comes / and glues
her female pudenda to my male one. But if she wishes to fall asleep, spread under
her knotted leather scourges and thorns upon her temples, so that she may nod

11. ἀρχή occurs only here as a unit of measure. See A. Erman, *ZÄS* 33 (1895): 46.
12. For an Egyptian parallel to this exclamation see the *historiola* in H. O. Lange, *Der magische Papyrus Harris, Det Kgl. Danske Videnskabernes Selskab, Historisk-filologiske Meddelelser* 14/2 (Copenhagen:
Høst, 1927) 75, 81: "Woe! Woe! Fire! Fire!" [R.K.R.]
13. Cf. Preisendanz's translation (accepting Hopfner's reconstruction in *Archiv Orientální* 3 [1931]:
122): "hin wandte sie sich zum heiligen Lager, gesprengt werden seine Bande und zugleich die der
Dämonenwelt . . ." (she turned to the holy bed [i.e., of Osiris], smashed to pieces are his bonds and
those of the daimons' world . . .).
14. Despite the appeal to several deities, the Greek has σύ, "you," sing. here.
15. The idea of sleeplessness is repeated. Cf. l. 112 above where there is no such repetition. [E.N.O.]

agreement to a courtesan's love, because I adjure you who have been stationed over
the fire, MASKELLI MASKELLŌ PHNOUKENTABAŌTH / OREOBAZAGRA RĒXICH- 155
THŌN HIPPICHTHŌN PYRIPĒGANAX."

"You, NN, have been bound by the fibers of the sacred palm tree, so that you may
love NN forever. And may no barking dog release you, no braying ass, no Gallus, no
priest who removed magic spells, no clash of cymbals, no whining of flute; indeed,
no protective charm from heaven that works for anything; / rather, let her be pos- 160
sessed by the spirit."
*Tr.: E. N. O'Neil.

PGM XXXVI. 161–77

*Charm to restrain anger and charm for success. (No charm is greater, and it is
to be performed by means of words alone:) Hold your thumbs and repeat the spell
7 times: "ERMALLŌTH ARCHIMALLŌTH stop the mouths / that speak against me, 165
because I glorify your sacred and honored names which are in heaven."

To augment the words: Take papyrus and write thus: "I am / CHPHYRIS.[16] I must 170
be successful. MICHAĒL RAPHAĒL ROUBĒL NARIĒL KATTIĒL ROUMBOUTHIĒL
AZARIĒL IOĒL IOUĒL EZRIĒL SOURIĒL NARIĒL METMOURIĒL AZAĒL AZIĒL SAOU-
MIĒL / ROUBOUTHIĒL RABIĒĒL RABIĒĒL RABCHLOU ENAEZRAĒL, angels, protect 175
me from every bad situation that comes upon me."
*Tr.: R. F. Hock.

PGM XXXVI. 178–87

*A charm to break spells: Take lead and draw on it a unique figure[17] holding a
torch in its right / hand, in its left—and at the left—a knife, and on its head three 180
falcons, and under its legs a scarab, and under the scarab[18] an ouroboros serpent.
The things to be written around / the figure are these: 185

*Tr.: Morton Smith.

16. CHPHYRIS is the god Khepri, the scarab. See *PGM* IV. 943 and n.; VII. 584 and n., and the
Glossary, s.v. "Scarab."
17. The figure drawn below on the papyrus does not correspond to the description.
18. On the scarab see n. 16 above.

PGM XXXVI. 187–210

*Love spell of attraction: On an unbaked piece of pottery write with a bronze stylus: "Hecate, you, Hecate, triple-formed, since every seal of every [19] [love spell of

190 attraction] has been completed, I adjure you / by the great name of ABLANATHANA and by the power of AGRAMARI,[20] because I adjure you, you who possess the fire,

195 ONYR,[21] and those in it, that she, NN, / be set afire,[22] that she come in pursuit of me, NN, because I am holding[23] in my right hand the two serpents and the victory of IAŌ SABAŌTH and the great name BILKATRI MOPHECHE, who brandishes fire,

200 . . . ,[24] that she love me / completely and be aflame and on fire for me; aye, and tortured too. I am SYNKOUTOUEL."

[Write] 8 characters like this: "Grant me, indeed the favor of all, ADŌNAI ✳⌐ ∫𝔇 𝕀𝔸Ō ⊹⸓⸞."

```
Λ Λ Λ Λ Λ Λ Λ
Ε Ε Ε Ε Ε Ε Ε
Ε Ε Ε Ε Ε Ε Ε
Ι Ι Ι Ι Ι Ι Ι
Ο Ο Ο Ο Ο Ο Ο
Υ Υ Υ Υ Υ Υ Υ
Ȯ Ȯ Ȯ Ȯ Ȯ Ȯ Ȯ
```

*Tr.: E. N. O'Neil. The text of this spell appears to be corrupt at a number of places, so that by necessity the translation remains tentative.

PGM XXXVI. 211–30

*Prayer to Helios: A charm to restrain anger and for victory and for securing favor (none is greater): Say to the sun (Helios) [the prayer] 7 times, and anoint your hand with oil and wipe it on your head and face.

215   *Now [the prayer] is*: "Rejoice with me, you who are set over the east wind / and the world, for whom all the gods serve as bodyguards at your good hour and on your good day, you who are the Good Daimon of the world, the crown of the inhabited world, you who rise from the abyss, you who each day rise a young man

220 and set an old man, HARPENKNOUPHI BRINTANTĒNŌPHRI BRISSKYLMAS / AROUR-ZORBOROBA MESINTRIPHI [25] NIPTOUMI CHMOUMMAŌPHI. I beg you, lord, do not allow me to be overthrown, to be plotted against, to receive dangerous drugs, to go into exile, to fall upon hard times. Rather, I ask to obtain and receive from you life,

225 health, reputation, wealth, influence, strength, success, charm, / favor with all men and all women, victory over all men and all women. Yes, lord, ABLANATHAN-ALBA AKRAMMACHAMARI PEPHNA PHŌZA PHNEBENNOUNI [26] NAACHTHIP . . .

230 OUNORBA, accomplish the matter which I want, / by means of your power."
*Tr.: R. F. Hock.

PGM XXXVI. 231–55

*Take a lead lamella and inscribe with a bronze stylus the following names and the figure, and after smearing it with blood from a bat, roll up the lamella in the usual

---

19. The isolated πάσης is vague. Preisendanz adds "Gestalt." [E.N.O.]

20. The *voces magicae* in ll. 190–91 are abbreviated forms of the ABLANATHANALBA and AKRAMMACHAMARI formulas. See the Glossary, s.v.

21. Preisendanz understands ONYR to be a form of Coptic NOYRE, "vulture, falcon." But more likely the god Onouris is meant. Cf. *PGM* X. 12 and n.

22. The text of these lines is very uncertain and probably corrupt. The translation is tentative. [E.N.O.]

23. Read perhaps κατέχομαι, since κατέχω μέ makes no sense. [E.N.O.]

24. The text contains here incomprehensible letters, probably because of corruption rather than their being *voces magicae*.

25. MESINTRIPHI is Egyptian and means "born of Triphis," an epithet of Isis. See *PGM* XII. 232 and n. [R.K.R.]

26. PEPHNA (read PEPHTHA), PHŌZA, PHNBENNOUNI is Egyptian and means "He is Ptah the healthy, the lord of the Abyss." Cf. above, ll. 43–44; *PGM* XIII. 1055. [R.K.R.]

fashion. / Cut open a frog and put it into its stomach. After stiching it up with   235
Anubian thread and a bronze needle, hang it up on a reed from your property by
means of hairs from the tip of the tail of a black ox, / at the east of the property near   240
the rising of the sun.

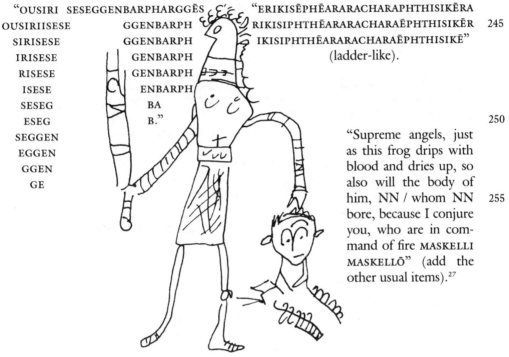

"OUSIRI SESEGGENBARPHARGGĒS   "ERIKISĒPHĒARARACHARAPHTHISIKĒRA
OUSIRIISESE   GGENBARPH   RIKISIPHTHĒARARACHARAĒPHTHISIKĒR   245
   SIRISESE   GGENBARPH   IKISIPHTHĒARARACHARAĒPHTHISIKĒ"
    IRISESE   GENBARPH   (ladder-like).
     RISESE   GENBARPH
      ISESE   ENBARPH
      SESEG   BA
       ESEG   B."   250
     SEGGEN   "Supreme angels, just
      EGGEN   as this frog drips with
       GGEN   blood and dries up, so
         GE   also will the body of
                                         him, NN / whom NN   255
                                         bore, because I conjure
                                         you, who are in com-
                                         mand of fire MASKELLI
                                         MASKELLŌ" (add the
                                         other usual items).[27]

*Tr.: R. F. Hock.

PGM XXXVI. 256–64

*Taking a three-cornered sherd from the fork of a road—pick it up with your left
hand—inscribe it with myrrhed ink and hide it. [Write:] ASSTRAELOS[28] CHRAELOS,
dissolve every enchantment against me, NN, for I conjure you / by the great   260
and terrible names which the winds fear and the rocks split when they hear it."
ϒ Χ Ц ⌐ ϡ ԑ Ꝃ
*Tr.: Morton Smith.

PGM XXXVI. 264–74

*Take blood from a nightowl and myrrh ink, and mix the two together, and draw   265
the figure[29] as appended, with a new reed pen on a clean strip of papyrus. At the
same time stare[30] at a clean wall and look toward the east. Fasten the figure to an
all-linen handkerchief with thorns / from a male date palm and hide it and stand   270
back from it six cubits. After hiding it, measure and step back fifty-nine paces three
times, standing on the mark of the six cubits.
*Tr.: R. F. Hock. The purpose of this ritual is not stated.

27. Or "(add the rest, and the usual items)."
28. On the name ASTRAĒLOS, see Scholem, *Jewish Gnosticism* 95.
29. The figure is not provided in the payrus. The preceding characters are marked off from this spell
by a dividing line.
30. Preisendanz suggests that the two phrases in ll. 268–69 may be variants.

PGM XXXVI. 275–83

275 *A great charm for gaining the favor of people in your presence and of crowds
280 (but it also works on those afflicted by daimons): / Offer a sacrifice, inscribe the
following characters on a silver tablet and put frankincense over them. Wear it as an
amulet. It will freely render service:

"⌇⌇⌇⌇⌇⌇⌇⌇⌇⌇⌇⌇⌇⌇⌇⌇⌇⌇⌇⌇⌇⌇⌇⌇⌇⌇⌇⌇⌇⌇⌇⌇⌇⌇⌇⌇⌇⌇

ERĒKISIPHTHĒARARCHARAĒPHTHISIKĒRE."
*Tr.: Hubert Martin, Jr.

PGM XXXVI. 283–94

*Pudenda key spell: Take an egg of a crow and the juice of the plant crow's-foot
285 and gall of a river electric eel,[31] and grind them with honey and say / the spell
whenever you grind and whenever you smear it on your genitals.

This is the spell that is to be spoken: "I say to you, womb of NN, open and receive
the seed of NN and the uncontrollable seed of the IARPHE ARPHE (write it).[32] Let
her, NN, love me for all her time as Isis loved Osiris[33] and let her remain chaste for
290 me as Penelope[34] did for Odysseus. / And do you, womb, remember me for all the
time of my life, because I am AKARNACHTHAS."

Say this while grinding and whenever you rub your genitals, and in this way have
intercourse with the woman you wish, and she will love you alone and by no one
else will she ever be laid, just by you alone.
*Tr.: E. N. O'Neil.

PGM XXXVI. 295–311

295 *Love spell of attraction, fire divination over unburnt sulfur, thus: Take seven
lumps of unburnt sulfur and make an altar fire from vine wood. Say this spell over
the lumps one by one and throw them into the fire.

This is the spell: "The heavens of heavens opened, and the angels of God
300 descended and overturned the five / cities of Sodom and Gomorrah, Admah,
Zeboiim, and Segor.[35] A woman who heard the voice became a pillar of salt.[36] You
are the sulfur which God rained down on the middle of Sodom and Gomorrah,
Admah and Zeboiim and Segor; you are the sulfur[37] which served God—so also
305 serve me, NN, in regards to her, NN, / and do not allow her to go to bed or to find
sleep until she comes and fulfills the mystery rite of Aphrodite."[38]

As you throw [the lumps] into the fire, say: "If I throw you into the fire, I adjure
you by the great PAP TAPHEIAŌ SABAŌTH ARBATHIAŌ ZAGOURĒ PAGOURĒ, and
310 by the great MICHAĒL / ZOURIĒL GABRIĒL SESENGENBARPHARANGĒS ISTRAĒL
ABRAAM, attract her, NN, to NN."
*Tr.: E. N. O'Neil.

31. Probably the Nile, in which this eel was found. [E.N.O.]

32. The papyrus has γραφ, which Preisendanz interprets as γράφε and understands to mean "write
the formula in the diminishing pattern IARPHE, ARPHE, RPHE, PHE, E." Although he may be correct,
the instruction to write in the midst of an oral spell is strange. [E.N.O.]

33. See on this point the discussion in Wortmann, "Neue magische Texte," 83–84.

34. The papyrus reads Pēlenopē.

35. The papyrus has the following names, all in need of correction in the light of Old Testament texts
(esp. Dt 29:23): Sodoma, Gomora, Adama, Sebouiē, Sēgōr. The last name should be Zoar. See
Ginzberg, *The Legends of the Jews* I, 252.

36. A reference to the story of Lot's wife, Gn 19:26.

37. A reference to Gn 19:24.

38. The mystery rite of Aphrodite is the sex act.

PGM XXXVI. 312–20

*Charm to open a door: Take from a firstborn ram an umbilical cord that has not fallen to the ground, and after mixing in myrrh, apply it to the door bolts when you want to open a door, and say this spell, and you will open it immediately.

Now this is the spell: / "Open up for me, open up for me, door bolt; be opened,   315
be opened, door bolt, because I am Horos the Great, ARCHEPHRENEPSOU PHI-
RIGX, son of Osiris and Isis. I want to flee the godless Typhon; [39] immediately, immediately; quickly, / quickly."   320
*Tr.: R. F. Hock.

PGM XXXVI. 320–32

*A contraceptive, the only one in the world: Take as many bittervetch seeds as you want for the number of years you wish to remain sterile. Steep them in the menses of a menstruating woman. Let her steep them in her own genitals. And take a frog [40] / that is alive and throw the bittervetch seeds into its mouth so that the frog   325
swallows them, and release the frog alive at the place where you captured him. And take a seed of henbane, steep it in mare's milk; and take the nasal mucus of an ox, with grains of barley, put these into a [piece of] leather skin made from a fawn and on the outside bind it up with mulehide skin, / and attach it as an amulet during   330
the waning of the moon [which is] in a female sign of the zodiac on a day of Kronos or Hermes, [41] Mix in also with the barley grains cerumen from the ear [42] of a mule.
*Tr.: John Scarborough.

PGM XXXVI. 333–60

*Love spell of attraction over myrrh: [43] Say the spell and [put it on the] flat stone of the bath.

The spell is this: / "Myrrh, Myrrh, who serve at the side of gods, who stir up   335
rivers and mountains, who burn up the marsh of Achalda, [44] who consume with fire the godless Typhon, who are ally of Horos, the protection of Anubis, the guide of Isis. Whenever I throw you, Myrrh, upon the *strobilos* [45] of the / flat stone of this   340
bath, as you burn, so also will you burn her, NN, because I adjure you by the strong and inexorable Destiny, MASKELLI MASKELLŌ PHNOUKENTABAŌTH OREOBAZA-
GRAS REXICHTHŌN HIPPOCHTHŌN PYRICHTHŌN PYRIPAGANYX LEPETAN / LEPE-   345
TAN MANTOUNOBOĒ, and by the Destiny of this, LAKI LAKIŌ LAKIŌYD LAKIŌYDA.
Attract, burn her, NN (add the usual, whatever you wish), because I adjure you by the strong and great names, THEILŌCHNOU ITHI PESKOUTHI TETOCHNOUPHI SPEUSOUTI IAŌ SABAŌTH / ADŌNAI PAGOURĒ ZAGOURĒ ABRASAX ABRATHIAŌ   350
TERĒPHAĒL MOUISRŌ [46] LEILAM SEMESILAM THOOOU IIE ĒŌ OSIR [47] ATHOM [48]

---

39. This passage contains a *historiola* of Horus escaping from Seth/Typhon. See for a parallel Lich-theim, *Ancient Egyptian Literature* II, 214–23. [R.K.R.]

40. The frog was associated with fertility, and therefore in Egypt with Heket, the goddess of birth. See Bonnet, *RÄRG* 198–99, s.v. "Frosch"; M. Weber, "Frosch," *RAC* 8 (1972): 524–38, esp. 524–29. [R.K.R.]

41. That is, the planets Saturn and Mercury.

42. Also possible is "dirt from the ear," but "ear wax" is more likely, given Aristophanes, *Lys.* 1198.

43. Cf. the parallel to the spell in *PGM* IV. 1495–1595.

44. This locality is not identified.

45. The meaning of the term is obscure; it may refer to some item having the shape of a pinecone. See LSJ, s.v. "στρόβιλος." Cf. *PGM* II. 25 and n.

46. See on this detail *PGM* III. 659 and n.

47. OSIR is Osiris. [R.K.R.]

48. ATHOM is Atum. [R.K.R.]

CHAMNEUS PHEPHAŌN PHEPHEŌPHAI PHEPHEŌPHTHA. Arouse yourself, Myrrh,
355 and go into every place[49] and seek out her, NN, and / open her right side and enter
like thunder, like lightning, like a burning flame, and make her thin, [pale,] weak,
limp, incapable of [action] in [any part of her body] until she leaps forth and comes
360 to me, [NN, son of] NN (add the usual, / whatever you wish), immediately, immediately; quickly, quickly."
*Tr.: E. N. O'Neil.

PGM XXXVI. 361–71

Fetching charm for an unmanageable woman, which works on the same day:
Take the skin of an ass[50] and write the following in the blood from the womb of a
silurus[51] after mixing in the juice of the plant Sarapis.

365   *The writing is this*: "SISISŌTH, attract to me / her, NN on this very day, in this
very hour, because I adjure you by the name CHYCHACHAMER MEROUTH[52] CHMĒ-
MINOUTH THIŌNTHOUTH PHIOPHAŌ[53] BELECHAS AAA EEE ĒĒĒ L' S' S' S' N' N'.
Attract her, NN, to NN" (add the usual).

370   And put the magical material inside / with vetch and place it in the mouth of a
dead dog, and it will attract her in the same hour.
*Tr.: E. N. O'Neil.

PGM XXXVII. 1–26

*. . . not one of the unclean men . . . I did not have intercourse with a woman . . .
[knowingly]. Whenever I swear, the [existing? . . .] relatives, that on my father's
5 side and / [mother?], friends and my father's relatives with . . . not, and this
one . . . into a container, thus taking . . . [into a] suburb, with the loud voice . . . of
10 the prophets and pro[phetesses]. / And whenever in . . . swear, lest . . . such as
heard. . . .
15   . . . / [of Theodoros?], that is, of Selenion(?), [it is not necessary] to subtract or
add a thing. If . . . these . . . cast from the . . . as mentioned before; and another
20 . . . from every rite / . . . your . . . is unlawful . . . should receive a letter . . . pi-
25 ously . . . receive extreme ill-luck, it is . . . lest you . . . taken . . . / the. . . .
*Tr.: Roy Kotansky. This fragmentary text was acquired in Egypt with the other magical
papyri, *PGM* XXXVI and XXXVIII, and is thus presumed to contain portions of a magical
spell; however, the recto (ll. 1–14) was written in a hand different from that of the verso (ll.
14–26) and seems to contain a text of a biblical or theological nature. The verso may contain
a text on some type of divination.

PGM XXXVIII. 1–26

*. . . at the proper time purify [yourself for seven days and][1] take myrrh ink and
[write] on [pure] papyrus . . . of baths: "Come here to me . . . who have the power

49. See on this point Wortmann, "Neue magische Texte," 71, 101.
50. The animal of Seth/Typhon.
51. The silurus is a large river fish which seems to have been a part of the common fare, either pickled
or salted. Cf. Pliny, *NH* 9. 17, 44; Aelian, *NA* 14. 25; Juvenal, *Sat.* 4. 33; 14. 132. The silurus also
occurs in *PGM* IV. 3097, but Preisendanz there altered the text to read αἴλουρος, "cat." Diehl, in Preisendanz's apparatus, proposes the same emendation here. [E.N.O.]
52. MEROUTH is Egyptian *mrw.t*, "love." [R.K.R.]
53. THOUTH PHIOPHAŌ is Egyptian and means "Thoth the great, the great." [R.K.R.]
1. Eitrem reads ἄγνευσον [ἕπτα ἡμέρας καὶ . . .], which D. Moke, *Eroticism in the Greek Magical
Papyri: Selected Studies* (Ann Arbor: University Microfilms, 1975) 72, translates with "Be purified for
seven days." The verb, however, is active and requires an object. Furthermore, the papyrus uses numerals, not words, so it is better to read ἄγνευσον [σὲ ζ' ἡμέρας καὶ . . .]. [E.N.O.]

.../... and go into the house ... after causing fright and [after] hiding ... of the 5
door. For by the contribution(?)² of her ... by your [power, attract] to me her, NN,
whose mother is NN, because .../... to find sleep and ... brain ... of sacred 10
phantoms ... of the sea ... / [who copulate in the ocean, PSOI PHNOUTHI 15
NINTHĒR,³ you are the one who are] daily visible [and who set in the northwest] of
heaven, [and rise in the southeast. In the 1st hour] you have [the form of a cat; your
name is PHARAKOUNĒTH. In the 2nd hour you have the form] of a dog; your name is
/ [SOUPHI. In the 3rd hour you have the form of a snake; your name is] ABERAN 20
NEMANE [THŌUTH. In the 4th hour you have the form of a scarab]: [your] name is
[SESENIPS. In the 5th hour you have the form] of an ass; [your] name is [EN-
PHANCHOUPH. In the 6th hour you have the form of a lion]; your name is
[BAISOLBAI ... who control] time. / [In the 7th hour you have the form of a goat; 25
your name is] OUMESTHŌTH. In the 8th hour you have the form of a bull; your name
is [DIATI-PHĒ, who becomes invisible]. ... .⁴

*Tr.: E. N. O'Neil. This papyrus is so fragmentary that the text owes more to Eitrem's inge-
nuity than to the copyist. Ll. 15–26 seem to be a doublet and, in part, an abridged version
of IV. 1642–79. The edition of Preisendanz provides no translation; Moke offers one only
of ll. 1–12.

PGM XXXIX. 1–21

*"THATTHARATHAUTHŌLTHARA	THATTHARATHAUTHŌLTHARA
ATTHARATHAUTHŌLTHARA	ATTHARATHAUTHŌLTHARA
TTHARATHAUTHŌLTHARA	TTHARATHAUTHŌLTHARA
THARATHAUTHŌLTHARA	THARATHAUTHŌLTHARA
ARATHAUTHŌLTHARA	ARATHAUTHŌLTHARA 5
RATHAUTHŌLTHARA	RATHAUTHŌLTHARA
ATHAUTHŌLTHARA	ATHAUTHŌLTHARA
THAUTHŌLTHARA	THAUTHŌLTHARA
AUTHŌLTHARA	AUTHŌLTHARA
UTHŌLTHARA	UTHŌLTHARA 10
THŌLTHARA	THŌLTHARA
ŌLTHARA	ŌLTHARA
LTHARA	LTHARA
THARA	THARA
ARA	ARA 15
RA	RA
A	A

I adjure you by the twelve elements of heaven and the twenty-four elements / of 20
the world, that you attract Herakles whom Taaipis bore, to me, to Allous, whom
Alexandria bore, immediately, immediately; quickly, quickly."

*Tr.: E. N. O'Neil. The figure on the left is that of the dwarf god Bes. In the Greco-Roman
period the erotic associates of Bes became so pronounced that he seems to have become a
patron of brothels. See J. E. Quibell, *Excavations at Saqqara (1905–1906)* (Cairo: Imprimerie
de l'Institute français d'archéologie orientale, 1907) 12–14. [R.K.R.]

2. The papyrus has προσδόσι, for which Eitrem suggests προσδόσει, hence "by the contribution,"
but the papyrus is so mutilated that any translation must be tentative. [E.N.O.]

3. PSOI PHNOUTHI NINTHĒR corresponds to Egyptian "Fate, the god (of) the gods." Cf. PGM III.
144–45. [R.K.R.]

4. The list of forms continues at PGM IV. 1679. This papyrus is clearly a fragment as well as fragmentary. [E.N.O.]

PGM XL. 1–18

*"O master Oserapis and the gods who sit with Oserapis, I [pray] to you, I
Artemisie, daughter of Amasis, against my daughter's father, [who] robbed [her] of
the funeral gifts and tomb. So if he has not acted justly toward me and his own
children—as indeed he has acted unjustly toward me and his own children—let

5   Oserapis and the gods / grant that he not approach the grave of his children, nor
that he bury his own parents. As long as my cry for help is deposited here, he and
what belongs to him should be utterly destroyed badly, both on earth and on sea,
by Oserapis and the gods who sit together with Oserapis, nor should he attain propitiation from Oserapis nor from the gods who sit with Oserapis.

10   Artemisie has deposited this supplication, supplicating / Oserapis and the gods
who sit with Oserapis to punish justly. As long as my supplication [is deposited]
here, the father of this girl should not by any means attain propitiation from the
gods. [Who]ever [seizes] this document [and] does an injustice to Artemisie, the
god will inflict a penalty on him . . . to no one . . . except . . . Artemisie commands

15   that . . . as . . . / not suffice . . . observed me in need of . . . and to me who lives
. . . observed . . . in need of. . . ."

*Tr.: R. F. Hock. For similar curses against desecrating a tomb, see G. Björck, *Der Fluch des
Christen Sabinus. Papyrus Upsaliensis 8* (Uppsala: Almqvist and Wiksell, 1938) esp. 131–38;
B. Boyaval, "Une malédiction pour viol de sépulture," *ZPE* 14 (1974): 71–73.

PGM XLI. 1–9

5   *"CHRIA . . . BĒEI[NŌR; SOUSI[NEPHI] . . . trembles / ENTOKE KENTA[BAŌTH]
. . . thence, [trembles] . . . NITHIORA BAINCHŌŌŌŌCH. . . ."
*Tr.: Roy Kotansky. This fragmentary spell contains only a few recognizable words, mostly
magical.

PGM XLII. 1–10

*"A A A A A A
E E E E E E
Ē Ē Ē Ē Ē Ē
I I I I I I O O O O
5   Y Y Y Y Y
Ō Ō Ō Ō Ō
["magical characters"]
. . . ARAĒL SAB[AŌTH
O]URIEL ASABA . . .
10   . . . OSĒPRAK."

*Tr.: Roy Kotansky. The magical characters mentioned in the text are unavailable for tran-
scription. The slip of papyrus probably served as an amulet.

PGM XLIII. 1–27

```
*"[ABLANA]THANALBA   EMANOUĒL
  [BLA]NATHANALBA     ASOUĒL
     LANATHANALBA     MARMARĒL
      ANATHANALBA     MELCHIĒL
        NATHANALBA    OURIĒL                                          5
          ATHANALBA   THOURIĒL
            THANALBA  MARMARIŌTH
              ANALBA  ATHANAĒL
                ALBA  AŌĒ . . .                                       10
                 LBA  SABAŌTH
                  BA  ADŌNAI
                   A  ELŌAI
```

ABŌ . . . / SESENGEN SPHRANGĒS MICHAĒL SABAŌTH LAPAPA / . . . GABRIĒL   15/20
SOURIĒL RAPHAĒL, protect Sophia / whom Theoneilla bore from every shivering   25
fit and fever, immediately, quickly."
*Tr.: John Scarborough.

PGM XLIV. 1–18

*"THŌPHŌPHA. MOS . . . AMOU K . . .

A A A A A A A	. . . OUABEIO . . . S BAMERM . . . L . . .	
E E E E E E E	earache EY . . . MATI unwritten SYRID	
Ē Ē Ē Ē Ē Ē Ē	partaking (?), might ascend (?) driving away . . .	
I I I I I I I	fever (?), just (?) PAĒ . . . X	5
O O O O O O O	TAI, burning these things until N	
Y Y Y Y Y Y Y	ATHIAL PYRON MOLOS I	10
Ō Ō Ō Ō Ō Ō Ō	R	
Y MICHAĒL	ŌZ Y	
Ō ICHAĒL	YZ O	
CHAĒL	OZ	
E E E E E E E AĒL	IZ	
P ĒL		
L		
MICHAĒL	. . . Z	15
[ICHAĒL]	EZ	
[CHAĒL]		
CH S AĒL	. . . Z."	
```

```

*Tr.: Roy Kotansky. This fragmentary text may have served as a phylactery for earache and
possibly fever. On the right side of the papyrus there is a figure holding a staff and with the
letters "A" and "Ō" on either side; the representation of the figure, however, was never
published.

PGM XLV. 1–8

*". . . R . . . RPHEĒ ABRAXAS IRMOUN ⁺ACHOA BRĒPHAUTH IOU ATHĒTHAL
KATHŌLŌ . . . NITASPHIN BAROUCH BAROUCH DAULA ADŌNAIA CHAITA SIAMOUR
5   ERBELMŌN ELŌE ADŌNAIA MELĒ . . . A SESEMIE . . . LAMEBDO / ELŌE ACHRAI
ĒNNANAI AZAĒL CHERMAIŌ B . . . ROBBAN J(erusa)lem . . . N⁺"
*Tr.: Roy Kotansky.

PGM XLVI. 1–4

*. . . *[If] you wish the god to speak*: . . . These names . . . "SON LALEIKACHRI . . .
KAIE. . . ."
*Tr.: R. F. Hock. This fragmentary papyrus, which contains portions of only two spells,
contains here a request for a revelation. In the series of words to be spoken or written some
Greek can be read.

PGM XLVI. 4–8

5   *Spell to silence and [subject]: . . . on an unbaked potsherd . . . : / "IŌ SĒTH IŌ
ERBĒTH IŌ . . . IŌ SĒTH IŌ PATATHNAX . . . IŌ [OSIRIS]."
*Tr.: R. F. Hock.

PGM XLVII. 1–17

5   *"ĒL ĒL¹ STRAGĒL STRAKOUĒL, the god, / the SATOUCHEOS, the PSATOUCHEOS,²
10   protect, shelter [the wearer against fever] whether [it is] every other day, / or daily,
15   or equinoctial, or perpetual; purify us, EIAOTH / SABAOTH . . . [[two lines of
characters]].
*Tr.: Morton Smith.

PGM XLVIII. 1–21

*"KLE¹ [[characters]] AAAAAAA KLE ANNNGL . . . O SESEGGESBARPHARAGGES,
5   help us, Atikhis; bring aid (?) / with all your powers. They must move like the one
whom the Cherubim have led,² the Father Pantokrator, who is in heaven . . . the
Cherubim. You must fly like the birds of heaven. He³ must move like a piercing
10   wind, . . . good, through / the power of these names and their saving acts and the
phylacteries and the power of the honored (?) Place.⁴ Yes, yes! Quickly, quickly!
[[2 lines of characters]]. And a blessing upon the name SESSEGGES, together
15   with / . . . AI SACHLAS EL and MEFEJRAHIEU . . . names, aid . . . the place SA . . .
20   aid (?) . . . [the] whole house . . . INETENEI great (?) . . . IĒL EŌN / . . . the birds
of great (?)⁵ [[characters]] . . . OU."
*Tr.: Marvin W. Meyer.

1. *El* is the common Hebrew word for "god" but was also the name of a particular god worshiped
mostly along the Palestine-Syrian coast.
2. Perhaps the definite articles before this and the two following terms should be omitted, and they
should be taken as names of gods or demons. These magical texts rarely use the definite article before
the names of deities invoked, and SATOUCHEOS looks like an epithet ("loaded, burdened"?) and
PSATOUCHEOS like a byform of it.
1. Or, in Greek, "etc."
2. Or "they must lead forth," "who move like," or "who lead forth."
3. Or "you."
4. In later Jewish writings, God is frequently designated as "the Place."
5. Or "which we come" or "your fathers."

PGM XLIX
*

AIONO Y

*Tr.: Roy Kotansky. An amulet with a series of characters and the name "Aion."

PGM L. 1–18
*. . . out of . . . the . . . and if their principal (lots ?) should [fall] on the side of [the
lots] of "Tyche" or "Daimon" [it is good ?] for a spell (?) concerning sorcery / —the   5
same principal (tosses?) of the lot producing the same result, with a "Tyche" or
"Daimon" being an excellent toss. And the one who tosses concerning sorcery . . .
executes the same given results for the given toss. These things mentioned before
will be . . . / . . . of "Daimon." If ever . . . it happens in your own place or even . . .   10
by malevolent ones (?), / as it testifies of an exile, it signifies either . . . or dis-   15
graceful ones; if then a benevolent one occurs, a malevolent one by the benevolent
ones is changed (?). . . .
*Tr.: Roy Kotansky. Very little sense can be made from this scrappy fragment. The text seems
to deal with responses to a type of knucklebone or dice oracle.

PGM LI. 1–27
*"I exhort you, daimon of the dead [and] the necessity of death which has hap-
pened in your case, image of the gods, to hear / my request and to avenge me,   5
Neilammon, whom Tereus bore, because Etes has brought a charge against me, / or   10
against my daughter Aynchis or her children or those who might ever be [with]
me. And I exhort you not to listen to those who have brought charges against us,
either / [from] Hermes, whom . . . bore, [or] EU . . . s, who is known as [Apelles],   15
or from Harpochrates, whom Tereus bore, [who is] a wicked man and / ungodly   20
toward me, his father. I ask you, daimon of the dead, not to listen to them [but to]
listen [only] to me, Neilammon, [since I am] / pious [toward the] gods, [and to   25
cause them to be] ill for their [whole] life."
*Tr.: R. F. Hock. This necromantic request is directed against Neilammon's legal opponents,
one of whom appears to be his own son. The text follows the format of an Egyptian letter to
the dead. Cf. Alan Gardiner and Kurt Sethe, *Egyptian Letters to the Dead Mainly from the Old
and Middle Kingdoms* (London: Egypt Exploration Society, 1928). [R.K.R.]

PGM LII. 1–9
* . . . *the formula*:
   ". . . stout of heart, silver-eddying,
    And with the Graces CHŌOS EU . . .
    Both Hera and Selene, thus
    / The wits, which come upon to . . .   5
    . . . nothing, about the bed-chamber,
    . . . s . . . ES . . . ES . . . however much
    . . . ."
*Tr.: Roy Kotansky. This very fragmentary papyrus contains portions of two or three spells

probably dealing with love magic. The first of these, translated here, preserves a poetic incantation whose first few lines scan as dactylic hexameters.

PGM LII. 9–19

10 *Take an ichneumon / from the countryside and throw in some vinegar myrrh and boil for 3 days . . . but. . . .

15 ". . . and . . . / Peitho . . . will see a . . . with mighty . . . or might grant me favor . . . or love me in . . . from a mighty (?). . . ."
*Tr.: Roy Kotansky.

PGM LII. 20–26

20 ***Spell to induce insomnia**: Take some . . . grasp, speak the formula . . . speak . . . : ". . . ēōs mother's, summoning Eros."

25 Speak *the formula*: ". . . through night and day, from (?) / . . . set a flame in the heart. . . ."
*Tr.: Roy Kotansky.

PGM LIII–LVI

PGM LIII and LIV correspond to the unpublished texts of the papyrus rolls cataloged together as *P. Strassb.* I. 39 (P. gr. 1769 and 1770 in F. Preisigke, *Griechische Papyrus der kaiserlichen Universitäts—und Landesbibliothek zu Strassburg*, I. Leipzig: J. C. Hinrichs, 1912, 134–35). *PGM* LIII (no. 1769) measures 32 × 22 cm and contains fifteen lines; *PGM* LIV (no. 1770) measures 22 × 16 cm and contains ten lines. Both date from the Arabic period.

PGM LV and LVI correspond to the two unpublished texts, *P. Strassb.* I. 39A (P. gr. 762 and 788; Preisigke 136). They are written by the same hand and stem also from the Arabic period. *PGM* LV measures 28 × 22 cm and contains twelve lines; *PGM* LVI (17 × 11 cm) contains eight lines primarily made up of letter permutations, with sy sz and sch predominating.

PGM LVII. 1–37

*. . . ADŌNAI . . . *These are the words*: "[Accomplish] for him, NN, all that I have written on [this] for you, and I will[1] leave [the east] and the west[2] [where] he was established [formerly], and [I will preserve] the flesh of Osiris[3] [always] and I

5 will not break / [the] bonds with which you bound Typhon,[4] and I will not call those who have died a violent death but will leave them alone, and I will not pour out the oil of Syrian cedar [but] will leave it alone, and I will save Ammon and not kill him, and I will [not] scatter the limbs of Osiris, and I will hide you [from the]

10 giants;[5] EI EI EI EI [EI EI] EI EI CHOIN / [APHOUTH] CHENNONEU APHOUTH ANOU AŌTH EI EI EI PEOOE [IAKŌB] MANNOZ ARANNOUTH CHAL . . . APH KOULIX

---

1. For these implied threats see *PGM* II. 54, and Papyrus Ebers, col. 30, ll. 12–16: "If the stroke dispells itself . . . I shall not speak (the threat), I shall not repeat the statement." [R.K.R.]

2. For this notion of the collapse of the east and west, see *PGM* V. 284.

3. For mythical details regarding the death of Osiris, see Plutarch, *De Is. et Os.* 18, 358A–B; 35, 364F; 42, 368A; and Griffiths, *Plutarch's De Iside et Osiride* 340–42, 434–35, 460; Diodorus Siculus 1. 11, with the commentary by Burton, *Diodorus Siculus* 60–61, 89, 95.

4. For the binding of Typhon, see Plutarch, *De Is. et Os.* 19, 358D, and the commentary by Griffiths, *Plutarch's De Iside et Osiride* 349–50.

5. For the role of the giants, see Plutarch, *De Is. et Os.* 25, 360E, and Griffiths, *Plutarch's De Iside et Osiride* 385–86; W. Speyer, "Gigant," *RAC* 10 (1978): 1247–76, esp. 1263.

NOĒ N . . . K BORNATH LOUBEINE AOUĒR OUEIRE ITIN LOTOL. Recite the secrets of the many-named goddess, Isis."[6]

[The] compulsive spell in order to show you whether the matter has been carried out: / Burn cypress with the strip of papyrus and say: "[Isis,] holy maiden, give   15 me a sign of the things that are going to happen, reveal your holy veil, shake your black [Tyche] and move the constellation of the bear, holy [IŌTHĒ] PNOUN GMOĒRMENDOUMBA[7] great-named [IAKŌ] / PHTHOĒRI, THERMOĒR, PHTHAŌ,[8]   20 great-named IOTHĒ [PHNOU]THOUĒR BŌB HELIX, great-named IAKŌ."

When you have said this and at the same time have opened your hands, the goddess will remove the [edge] of your hand from your breast. For you will see [a star being led] of necessity [to you], at which you are to look / [intently], as it flashes [a   25 picture] while rushing [toward you], so that you become stricken of God. [Wear the] above picture [for protection]. [For], in the name of [the goddess], it is a [picture] of Kronos who encourages you. After you have received this sign, rejoice / at your [fortune] and say once: "CHAITHRAI." For when you have said this,   30 she will cooperate with you [in whatever] you pray for. And immediately say these words, [lest] there occur a removal of the stars and your lucky day: "THA . . . OUSIR[9] PHNOUCH MELLANCHIŌ KERDŌ MELIBEU . . . KASP . . . NEBENTHTRIX GARN . . . Ō THRAŌ SAU TRAIS TRAIS / BASYM; immediately, immediately, accom-   35 plish this, within this moment. Very glorious Pronoia,[10] make the one who yesterday was [unlovable] beautiful [in the sight of all], make . . . [former]. . . ."
*Tr.: R. F. Hock.

PGM LVIII. 1–14

*. . . [**Spell to bind** . . . (?)]:[1] / Take a lamella [made of lead] . . . : "I say to you,   5 you who died prematurely and who were [called and taken] away by the wicked [Typhon. Commanding you] is / the great god who has [dominion above and rules   10 over the lower [gods]. Take into custody this wicked [and impious] man,[2] because this [is the one who burned the papyrus boat of Osiris][3] and who [ate[4] the sacred fish].[5] Take into custody [him, NN, whom NN bore . . .]."[6]
*Tr.: R. F. Hock. The exact purpose of this spell is not known, though it is clearly a type of curse.

6. On Isis with a myriad of names see *PGM* LIX. 13; Apuleius, *Met.* 11. 22, p. 284, l. 9: *deae multinominis*; Plutarch, *De Is. et Os.* 53, 372E: μυριώνυμος. See Griffiths, *Plutarch's De Iside et Osiride* 502–3.

7. PNOUN GMOĒR is equivalent to Egyptian, "Nun (the Abyss), great power." [R.K.R.]

8. The sequence of PHTHOĒRI . . . PHTHAŌ is equivalent to Egyptian *Ptḥ wr* and *Ptḥ ʿȝ*, "Ptah the great." [R.K.R.]

9. This is Osiris.

10. On the identification of Isis and Providence (Pronoia), see Apuleius, *Met.* 11. 15, p. 277, l. 4; and on this see Griffiths, *The Isis-Book* 241–44, 323.

1. The full title is not preserved. The opening line may have read κατά[δεσμος]. Cf. Preisendanz, apparatus ad loc.

2. Or "such-and-such a wicked and impious man." [R.D.K.]

3. The restoration is based on the parallel in Audollent, *Defixionum Tabellae*, no. 188, reprinted in Preisendanz, vol. II, p. 187. See on this point Plutarch, *De Is. et Os.* 18, 358A, where the burning of the boat is not mentioned, however. See for further references Griffiths, *Plutarch's De Iside et Osiride* 339–40.

4. The filling of the lacuna is based on the parallel in Audollent, *Defixionum Tabellae*, no. 188.

5. For sacred fish, see *PGM* V. 270–80, and J. F. Borghouts, "The Magical Texts of Papyrus Leiden I. 348," *OMRM* 51 (1971):26 (a similar sacrilege), and *Excursus III* 210–17. See Bonnet, *RÄRG* 191–94, s.v. "Fische, heilige." [R.K.R.]

6. Assuming the restoration in Preisendanz as correct. However, it seems more likely to restore the parallel phrase from above, "take into custody [this wicked and impious . . . man]. [R.D.K.]

PGM LVIII. 15–39

15/20 *. . . when the [moon] is full . . . , make an offering of incense . . . / . . . lick clean,
SITOULAS EK . . . KŌS, . . . *[under] the middle of the chest*:

"IŌ ERBĒTH
IAKOUMBIA
IŌ PAKERBĒTH
25 / IŌ BOLCHOSĒTH
BASAOUM
KOCHLŌTA
TETOMĒ
[[Remains of a magical figure]] BASSAOUM
30 / PATATHNAX
OSESRŌ
IŌ IŌ PAKERBĒTH
KEACH, come
[I]O ABRASAX
35 / (add the usual).

"[ABER]AMENTHŌOULERTHEXANAXETHRELYŌTHNEMAREBA."
*Tr.: R. F. Hock. The translation differs from Preisendanz in ll. 20, 34, 35.

PGM LIX. 1–15

*". . . Saioneis, whom [Sentaesis] bore. You, slave of the [glorious] god ABLANA-
THANALBA, you servant of the [good] god AKRAMMACHAMAREI, you, slave of
5 [IAEŌ] SABAŌ ABRASAX ADŌNAI, / you, servant of the [four] good [and] glorious
gods, ABERAMENTHOOYLERTHEXANAXETHRELYOŌTHNEMAREBA AEMEINAEBA-
RŌTHERRETHŌRABEANIEMEA ERĒKISITHPHĒARARACHARARAĒPHTHISIKĒRE IA-
EŌBAPHRENEMOUNOTHILARIKRIPHIAEYEAIPHIRKIRALITHONYOMENERPHA-
10 BŌEAI, / you, the good and glorious gods, protect the mummy and the body and
all the grave of the younger Phtheious, who is also [called] Saioneis, whom Sen-
15 taesis bore . . . the everlasting [punishments given by] the Lady [Isis], / goddess of
many names."[1]
*Tr.: Morton Smith.

PGM LX. 1–5

*"OBPHŌCHONMPOUO
AIEROĒNIONO
IBOPHA
IKON"
*Reading: Morton Smith.

PDM lxi. 1–30

5 *. . . to Truth . . . before you / incense (?) . . . to the . . . your head . . . land
[col. I, 5] . . . / look . . . above / these . . . Lady of the Flood (?) [. . . I]A IA OO . . . in truth
10 . . . and we come into . . . above after the . . . Teach me.[1] Show . . . Anubis of . . .
[I, 10] [Spirit of] Darkness . . . / Anubis . . . Anubis of the . . . Do not. . . . Do not let
15 . . . know (?) . . . true manner [without a matter (?)] of falsehood . . . saying: "I am

1. For this epithet of Isis, see *PGM* LVII. 13 and n.

1. Restored *[tun] eiat*ꞏ as a parallel to *tamo*. Both mean "to instruct." See Crum, *Coptic Dictionary*
73b. For the restorations by R.K.R. here and in the notes below, see his forthcoming article, "Gleanings
from Magical Texts," *Enchoria* 1985.

[OR]THOBAUBO . . . my name . . . OOO is my name. My name in [truth (?) . . .]   [I, 15]
. . . May you be exalted. Work . . . Anubis of the horizon. Anubis . . . / Anubis of   20
the son. Do not . . . twice. The great ruler. . . . It is this god who . . . face of a   [II, 5]
donkey. This . . . come . . . to me from them (?) which are before you . . . which   25
you. . . .   [II, 10]

*Tr.: Robert K. Ritner, following the edition and translation in Bell, Nock, and Thompson, *Magical Texts*, recto, col. I/1–16 (original translation from plate; not previously read by the editors), and col. II/1–13. Sections titles in the Demotic texts are indicated only if they are written in red letters (see the Introduction to the Demotic Magical Papyri).

PDM lxi. 30–41

*. . . which . . . / seven . . . dead . . . rue seven, bone of . . . wax (?) . . . seven   31
. . . / . . . seven, mix them all. Recite all the spells of the vessel over them at dawn,   [col. III,
midday [and] night at the beginning of the month and eat (?) seven of them each   2]
and every month. / You find his heart.[2]   36

*Tr.: Janet H. Johnson, following the edition and translation of Sir Hubert Thompson in   [III, 7]
Bell, Nock, and Thompson, *Magical Texts*, recto, col. III.   41
  [III, 12]

PDM lxi. 42

*" . . . *you and those who are*. . . .

*Tr.: Janet H. Johnson, following the edition and translation of Thompson, in Bell, Nock, and Thompson, *Magical Texts*, recto, col. IV/1. This fragmentary line may be part of the rubric of col. III (see Bell et al. p. 14, ad loc.). The fact that these words are written in red ink (in the original manuscript) suggests this is the title (or subtitle) of a new spell.

PDM lxi. 43–48 [*PGM* LXI. i–v (not in Preisendanz)]

*. . . *remedy* for [an] ulcer (?)[3] of the head . . . : one mina (?); this is what is [to be
spoken?] . . . of frankincense and [celandine? . . .] / of a male ass [together with   46
. . .], excellently, and add . . . a little, and smear it on the. . . .   (4)

*Tr.: Janet H. Johnson, following the edition and translation of Thompson in Bell, Nock, and Thompson, *Magical Texts*, recto, col. IV/2; and Roy Kotansky (Greek section), following the edition of Bell, Nock, and Thompson, ibid., ll. 3–7.

PDM lxi. 49–57

*. . . *head*: . . . . [papyrus ?], it being broken (?) in the place / . . . oil; you should   51
utter the name of . . . while they are not dry; you should utter the spell (?) twice . . .   [col. IV,
one grain to the name of the . . . name of palm, persea, [and] cypress[4] / mulberry,   10]
laurel, black poplar, pine. . . .   56

*Tr.: Janet H. Johnson, following the edition and translation of Thompson in Bell, Nock,   [IV, 15]
and Thompson, *Magical Texts*, recto, col. IV/8–16. The spell presumably describes another remedy for the head.

PDM lxi. 58–62 [*PGM* LXI. vi.x (not in Preisendanz)]

**For an erection*: Woad plant [or corn flag?] grows in the oasis in abundance; it's both female and [male]. Boil these in a pot and grind them up [in wine with] pep-

2. Or "wish."
3. As suggested by R.K.R.
4. Written in Demotic and Greek.

61
[col. IV,
19]

per; / smear it on [your] genitals. [If you wish it] to relax again, [provide] with the
decoction. . . .

*Tr.: Roy Kotansky, following the edition of Bell, Nock, and Thompson, *Magical Texts*, recto
A (p. 22). For a similar spell, compare *PGM* VII. 184–85.

PDM lxi. 63–78

*. . . **Har-Thoth**: You write on the [front of a] laurel leaf [and you light] a lamp on
a table and you speak to the laurel opposite the lamp. Do not look at the lamp! You

65
[col. V, 4]

should come; you should lie down; you should place the laurel / under your head;
and you should pray to Har-Thoth. He answers you in a dream. The front of the
laurel leaf, write these [words] on it; you write it in ink of myrrh and wine:

    The first: "THOYTHKH"
    The second: "LABINOYTHKH."
    The third: "PHRĒKH."
    The fourth: "SALBANAKHA."
    The fifth: "falcon."
    The sixth: "ape."
    The seventh: "ibis."

70
[V, 9]

And say these words: "Come to me, Thoth, Eldest one, Eldest one . . . of Re,
who went forth from Atum, who was born / in the form . . . from the limb of
Atum! Come to me, Thoth, heart of Re, tongue[5] of Tatenen,[6] throat[7] of the one
whose name is hidden![8] Come to me, HEFKAE HEPKA HEBIKE NEKHE-P-KAI!

75
[V, 14]

Come to me, Lord of Truth, who loves Truth, / who reckons [lifetime?],[9] who
judges Truth, who does Truth![10] Come to me in your beautiful face in this good
night and make answer to me concerning everything about which I am entreating
here today, truly without falsehood therein! Come to me in your form of excellent
one, in your [secret] image . . . ! Come to me and [tell me] an answer to everything, [truly,] without falsehood therein." [It is] very good.

*Tr.: Janet H. Johnson, following the edition and translation of Thompson in Bell, Nock,
and Thompson, *Magical Texts*, col. V, 1–5a/6.

PDM lxi. 79–94

80
[col. VI,
2]

*A way of finding a thief . . . : You bring a head of a drowned man; / you carry it
to the fields; you bury it; you put flax seed over it until you gather the flax; you
gather [it] upon it when it is high and alone; you [bring] the flax to the village;
you[11] wash the head by itself in milk; you cover it; and you take it to the place
which you wish.

    When you want to discover a thief, you should bring a small amount[12] of flax;
you should utter a spell to it; you should say the name of the man twice, one by one

85
[VI, 7]

(?) / you should make a knot and draw it together. If he is the one who stole it,[13] he
speaks while you tie the knot.

5. As read by R.K.R.
6. A holy place in Memphis. See Bonnet, *RÄRG* 769–70.
7. As read by R.K.R.
8. A pun on Amoun/hidden.
9. As read by R.K.R.
10. For these epithets, see P. Boylan, *Thoth the Hermes of Egypt* (Chicago: Ares, 1979 [reprint]),
appendix B. [R.K.R.]
11. Actually written "they."
12. Translation by R.K.R.
13. Literally, "carried/lifted it."

The spells which you should recite: *Formula*: "To me belongs the word of Khu;[14] to me belongs the word of Geb; to me belongs the word of . . . of Isis; to me belongs the word of this ibis, son of Thoth; Lo, all hail! Lo, all hail! I shall gather here today my sister SAMAL[A], saying, 'I shall give them. the words / of Geb which he gave to Isis when Shu (?) concealed them in the papyrus (swamp) of Buto, she bringing the small amount of flax in her hand, she forming it into a knot, she tying these forelegs (?)[15] until he was revealed to Horus in the papyrus (swamp). I will bring this small amount of flax in my own hand, I making it into a knot until NN is revealed . . . the sound-eye.' After (?) answering, he will lift (?)." [It is] very good. 90 [VI, 12]

*Tr.: Janet H. Johnson, following the edition and translation of Thompson in Bell, Nock, and Thompson, *Magical Texts*, col. VI/1–16.

PDM lxi. 95–99

* **Spell of giving praise** [and] love in Nubian: "SYMYTH KESYTH HRBABA BRASAKHS LAT, son of (?) NAPH, son of (?) BAKHA." Say these; put gum on your hand; and kiss your shoulder twice,[16] and go before the man whom you desire. 95 [col. VII, 1]

*Tr.: Janet H. Johnson, following the edition and translation of Thompson in Bell, Nock, and Thompson, *Magical Texts*, col. VII/1–5.

PDM lxi. 100–105

* **The red cloth of Nephthys**: "Pre arose; he sent forth the *Seket* boat[17] of heaven; the water under the bark of Pre has dried up. The gods and the two crowns (of the south and the north) complain until NN is brought to NN. If not doing it is what will be done, the gods whose names I said will bend down so that they fall into the fire. . . . I am the one who said it; she will repeat it 'Be destroyed, impious one!' She is the one who said it; / she is the one who heard it [and] repeated it." [It is] very good when he says it. 100 [col. VII, 6] 105 [VII, 11]

*Tr.: Janet H. Johnson, following the edition and translation of Thompson in Bell, Nock, and Thompson, *Magical Texts*, col. VI/6–11.

PDM lxi. 106–11

* **Prescription** for a donkey not moving: Rue, dung of falcon, dung of crocodile; you should apply it and you should anoint the ears or its nose or the nostril of its nose.

Formula: "He of the heart. . . . Horus [is] behind you; Geb is pursuing you, Isis being with them (?) . . . many hours. / The arrow of Horus[18] will go into you in order to. . . ." 111 [col. VII, 16]

*Tr.: Janet H. Johnson, following the edition and translation of Thompson in Bell, Nock, and Thompson, *Magical Texts*, col. VII/12–16.

14. Name of the twenty-second decan. [R.K.R.]
15. That is the foreleg of Seth (as bull) when killed. [R.K.R.]
16. Translation by R.K.R.
17. The morning bark of the sun.
18. Translation by R.K.R.

PDM lxi. 112–27

*A prescription** for making a [woman] love you: An image of Osiris [made] of wax—you should . . . , you bringing hair (?) and [wool] of a donkey together with

116   a bone of a lizard. / You should [bury them under the] doorsill of her house.[19] If stubbornness occurs, you should bring it . . . the image of Osiris with (?) ram's

[col. VIII,   wool; you should put the lizard bone . . . ; / you should bury it again under the

5]   doorsill of her house; and you should recite . . . before Isis in the evening when the moon has risen. Listen before you bury. . . .

"O secret image of Osiris [made] of wax, O powerful one, O protection of . . . , O lord of praise, love, and respect, may you go to every house which so-and-so is [in and send so-and-so] to every house which so-and-so is in; the tips of her feet

121   follow after his heels . . . / while her eyes are crying, while her heart longs (?)

[VIII, 10]   her . . . which she will do. O image of Osiris [made] of wax, if you will be stubborn [and not send so-and-so] after so-and-so, I shall go to the chest which . . . and I shall come . . . black, I shall gather it with a tooth . . . black, and I shall cause [Isis]

126   to receive . . . after Osiris her husband and [brother . . .]. / Hail to you, O lord of

[VIII, 15]   time, the one whom I caused [. . .] who is in the House of the Obelisk.[20] Come [to me . . .]."

*Tr.: Janet H. Johnson, following the edition and translation of Thompson in Bell, Nock, and Thompson, *Magical Texts*, col. VIII/1–16.

PDM lxi. 128–47

*. . . You should cause a man to drink (?) . . . [tick] of a black dog in the right ear

132   . . . [wool?][21] of the offspring of a black ram / . . . the face (?) of your foot on the

[v. col. i,   day of immersing without blood; you should kill the tick. . . . When you finish you

4]   should sleep with the woman; [you should anoint] your phallus with it; you should

137   wash it . . . ; you should cause her to drink; you should send the wool / . . . of

[v. i, 9]   olive; you should bind it to [your] right arm . . . ; [you] should cause the woman

142   to drink . . .of the tongue of a bull . . . name . . . them in your matter / . . . your

[v. i, 14]   blood; you should . . . PHAMOYROYTH THTO . . . T . . . ; wash it in [sweet?] wine

147   . . . to it / . . . to it. . . .

[v. i, 19]   *Tr.: Janet H. Johnson, following the edition and translation of Thompson in Bell, Nock, and Thompson, *Magical Texts*, verso, col. i/1–20.

PDM lxi. 148–58

151   *Here are their names: [22] "ORNAI SORNIN . . . OZO RANAY SARZANA IAO / XOINAI

[v. col. ii,   OOO NAIO MELOI NAI ERIANA E . . . ASNAI ENAMPHE, let her, NN, love me."

4]   Their (?) green ink: you should dye / . . . myrrh . . . ; you should burn them;

156   and you should pound them . . . of a child for drinking (?) burnt date[wine?].

[v. ii, 9]   *Tr.: Janet H. Johnson, following the edition and translation of Thompson in Bell, Nock, and Thompson, *Magical Texts*, verso, col. ii/1–12.

PDM lxi. 159–96
PGM LXI. 1–38

*Commendable love charm**: . . . take pure olive oil and a beet plant and olive branches; and take seven leaves and grind them all together and pour them into the

19. Cf. *PDM* xii. 55.
20. Cf. *PDM* xii. 34.
21. As suggested by R.K.R.
22. End of the line as read by R.K.R.

olive oil until they become like olive oil. / And put it into a jar, and go up onto a   5
housetop (or on the ground) facing the moon, and say the spell 7 times: [A, 1,
                                                                                        148]

"You are the olive oil; you are not the olive oil [23] but the sweat of Good Daimon,
the mucus of Isis, the utterance of Helios, the power of Osiris, the favor of the
gods. / I release you against her, NN, the one NN bore. Aye,[24] serve me against her,   10
NN, before I bring the gods of compulsion against you, if you do not send her. For   [A, 1,
otherwise I will break down iron doors [25] myself. No longer will I send you for these 153]
things,[26] nor is there need of them, but I will send you for her, NN, whom NN
bore, so that, if she dismisses you, / you can seize her head.[27] Cause her to swoon.   15
Let her not know where she is. Become fire beneath her until she comes to me, so   [A, 1,
that she may love me for all time; and may she not be able either to drink or eat,   158]
until she comes to me, so that she may love me for all time. I adjure you by the great
god / who is over the vault of heaven, ARBAIĒTH MOUTH NOUTH PHTHŌTHŌ   20
PHRĒ THŌOUTH BREISON THŌTH. Hear me, greatest god, on this very day (on this   [A, 2,
night), so that you may inflame her heart, and let her love me because I have in my   165]
possession the power of the great god, whose name it is impossible / for anyone to   25
speak, except me alone because I possess his power . . . EURIŌ MOI AEETHI EŌ Ē   [A, 2,
PHĒOUAB PHTHA ACHE ANOU // ĒSI ENES . . . E THOUL PHIMOIOU. Hear me be-   170]
cause of Necessity, for I have spoken your name because of her, NN, whom NN
bore, so that she may love me and do whatever I wish [and] so that she may forget
her father and mother, brothers, husband, / friend, so that, except for me alone, she   30
may forget them all."

And whenever you perform this spell, have an iron ring with yourself, // on   [A, 2,
which has been engraved Harpokrates sitting on a lotus,[28] and his name is ABRASAX.   175]

If, however, you should wish her to stop,[29] take a sun scarab and place it in the
middle of her / head and say to it: "Gulp down my love charm, image of Helios; he   35
himself orders you to do so." And pick up the scarab // and release it alive. Then   [A, 2,
take the ring and give it to her to wear, and immediately she will depart.   180]
*Tr.: E. N. O'Neil.

PDM lxi. 197–216
PGM LXI. 39–71

*Love spell of attraction: It attracts a woman who has been wronged by her hus-
band. / Take from the place where bodies are mummified a spotted lizard [30] which   40
lives around those places, and throw the same lizard into an iron vessel, and // take [B, 185]
coals from the forge whenever they light the fire and put them into the vessel with
the lizard; burn it up on the coals and while doing it say:

---

23. For this formula, see *PGM* VII. 644–46.

24. For this affirmation (ἠ), see *PGM* IV. 2288, 2331.

25. That is, the iron doors of Hades. See Betz, *Lukian* 82.

26. Or οὐκέτι ἐπὶ ταῦτα σὲ πέμψω may mean "no longer will I send you on these missions."
[E.N.O.]

27. See Antoninus Liberalis 6. 3 for a similar use of πιάζω in a similar action. [E.N.O.]

28. For Harpokrates sitting on the lotus flower, see *PGM* II. 101 and n.; XII. 87.

29. The language of παῦσαι and ἀπαλλαγήσεται (l. 38) contains two meanings: the vulgar and
the dismissal from the spell. See H. J. Bell, A. D. Nock, H. Thompson, "Magical Texts from a Bilingual
Papyrus in the British Museum," *Proceedings of the British Academy* 17 (1931):235–88, pp. 271–72.
[E.N.O.]

30. On the role of the lizard in magic, see *PGM* VII. 628 and n.

45   "Lizard, lizard, / as Helios and all the gods have hated you,[31] so let her, NN, hate
[B, 190] her husband for all time and // her husband hate her."
            Now when it has been completely cooked, keep the lizard ready for use and not
          touching the vessel.[32] Pick up the vessel in which it was burned and approach the
50   gateway itself / saying: "Lizard, lizard, let Helios and all men hate you because she,
[B, 195] NN, says that the mummy of the god // OSERONNŌPHRIOS PHAPRŌ OUSIRIS has
          been removed and devoured by you. Image of BIANDATHRĒ . . . image of TYPHON
55   SAKTIETĒ SOGGĒTH, image of ABRASAX ANAX[IBOA], / image of [IAŌ; do not let]
          her, NN, come through the gateway from whatever hour Helios brightens the
          earth for the whole time, as long as it also increases the River out of the River,[33]
[B, 200] as // long as the wild fig tree grows" ([state the usual and whatever you] wish, and
          depart).
60   / *[Spell written] on papyrus* . . . with [blood] of Typhon,[34] which is . . . : "Come,
65   father, whom the plow . . . IAKEMBRAŌTH . . . PHLOUDOUNTAS . . . / , [separate]
          him, NN, from her, NN, . . . turbulence . . . OENAI SORNIN . . . ŌXŌ RANAU
70   SARXANA IAŌ LOINAI ŌŌŌ NAIŌ MELŌI NAI ERIANA / E SASTIAI ENAMPHE, let her,
          NN, love me."
          *Tr.: E. N. O'Neil.

PGM LXII. 1–24

*[Now let] this [lamp], not colored red, be hung. Light the lamp[1] with good oil
[and] cedar oil.
          "You are the fire that is unquenchable, that lies beside the great god, OSORNŌPHRI
5   OSOR[NŌPHRI];[2] in service to him when he was smitten with love for his own / sis-
          ter Senephthys,[3] you not only ran as much as sixty-six *schoeni*[4] but you encircled as
          many as sixty-six mountains. In this way, too, serve me, NN, against her, NN. If
10   you do not, I will say the eight letters of Selene / which have been established in the
          heart of Helios. But if I am on the point of saying them and you have not set out on
          your way, I will go inside the seven gates around Dardaniel,[5] and I will shake the
15   foundation of earth,[6] and the 4 elements of the world will come together[7] / so that
          nothing will be created from them. Dissolve into your own nature and mingle with
          the air, and go to her, NN, whom NN bore (add the usual) and attract her down to

31. Cf. Antoninus Liberalis 24. 3. [E.N.O.]
32. The sense is obscure because the text is uncertain. Hence the translation is tentative. [E.N.O.]
33. A reference to the Nile and its periodic overflow. [E.N.O.]
34. For the blood of Seth/Typhon, see *PGM* IV. 2100 and n.
1. λυχνίζω occurs only here; ἐνλυχνιάζω is the regular verb. Cf. *PGM* I. 293; III. 585; IV. 1089; etc. [E.N.O.]
2. The repetition here, which is an Egyptian form of emphasis, has troubled Preisendanz. He omits one word and adds "(du bist es)." [E.N.O.]
3. Preisendanz takes this to be Isis-Nephthys, with reference to *PGM* XII. 235. [R.K.R.]
4. A measure of length which has no fixed value. Strabo (17. 1, 24) says that it varied from 30 to 120 stades (i.e., about 1,820–7,280 feet). [E.N.O.]
5. The name Dardaniel occurs only here. The city remains unidentified. The epithet ἑπτάπυλος (with seven gates) is usually associated with Thebes in Boiotia (see LSJ, s.v.), a city that plays a role in the sagas about the Trojan War. According to some traditions, Dardanos was the founder of Dardania (Troy); see Homer, *Il.* 20. 215–16. Whether there is a connection between these names is unclear. Cf. also *PGM* IV. 1716 and n.; IV. 2612; VII. 695.
6. On the threat to disrupt the cosmos, see *PGM* V. 284 and n.
7. The doctrine is similar to the creation myth in *C. H.* I. 17–19. See for further references Bousset, *Religionsgeschichtliche Studien* 117–18. In the lines of the papyrus only three elements are named; water is omitted.

me with fire of the thunderbolt. I adjure you by the great god / lying in the   20
pure earth, beside whom the unquenchable fire forever lies, ATHOUIN ATHOUIN
ATHOUIN IATHAOUIN SIBELTHIOUTH IATĒT ATATĒT ADŌNE" (add the usual).

Protective spell: Wrap three peonies around your left arm and wear them.
*Tr.: E. N. O'Neil.

PGM LXII. 24–46

*"Come to me, god of the gods, the only one who appears from fire and wind,[8] / you   .25
who have truth on your head, who disperse the darkness, you the lord of the winds[9]
LŌTH MOULŌTH[10] PNOUT EI[11] ESIŌTH, hail, lord LAMPSOURĒ IAAŌ IA . . . D."

Say these things many times. If, while you are reciting, the apparition delays:
"Open up, open up, Olympos; open up, Hades; open up, Abyss. Let / the darkness   30
be dispelled by command of the highest god and let the holy light come forth from
the infinite into the abyss." Whenever it still delays, cry out in this way and again
close the eyes of the boy: "Hail, holy light! Hail, eye of the world! Hail, brightness
of the dawn of the world,[12] ABRA Á Ó[13] NA BABROUTHI BIE BARACHE, god. Come
in, lord, / and reveal to me about the things I request of you." Then ask what you   35
wish. . . .

Dismissal: "I give thanks to you because you came in accordance with the command of god. I request that you keep me healthy, free from terror and free from
demonic attacks, ATHATHE ATHATHACHTHE ADŌNAI. Return to your holy places."

[Recite these things] over a saucer, in which you will pour 1 measure of good
olive oil, and will place it on a brick, / and will carve these characters on a magnet   40
that is [still] "breathing."

These are the characters to be made: ➤ ⊂⊃ ↵ ✳ ↙⊗ Ⴤ

Fasten the stone to the left side of the saucer, on the outside, and having em-
braced it with two hands, recite as shown to you. Cast (sink) in the saucer (a good
dish) / the afterbirth of a dog called "white" which is born of a white dog. On the   45
boy's chest write with myrrh: "KARBAŌTH."
*Tr.: W. C. Grese (ll. 24–38) and J. Hershbell (ll. 39–46).

PGM LXII. 47–51

A means to learn from a die whether a man is alive or has died, for example:
Make the inquirer throw this die in the [above] bowl. Let him fill this with water.
Add to the [cast of the] die 612, which is [the numerical value of][14] the name
of / god, i.e., "Zeus," and subtract from the sum 353, which is [the numerical value   50
of] "Hermes." If then the number [remaining] be found divisible by two, he lives;
if not, death has [him].
*Tr.: Morton Smith.

PGM LXII. 52–75

*(Year) 2 (of) Antoninus . . . 6th of Mecheir to the 7th; 7th hour of the night. / Sat-   55

---

8. Or "from fire and spirit."
9. Or "lord of the spirits."
10. Cf. *PDM* xiv. 534: "I am Lot Mulot."
11. PNOUTEI is Egyptian *p3 ntr*, "the god." [R.K.R.]
12. "Hail, holy light . . . dawn on the world" is written in the margin of the papyrus in seven parts
next to ll. 34–39. See Preisendanz, apparatus ad loc.
13. The text has ABRA A/ O/ NA. . . . It may indicate abbreviations for ABRASAX, ADŌNAI.
14. Greek letters also served as numbers, so each word had a numerical value, the sum of the numbers
signified by the letters composing it. [M.S.]

urn, horoscope in Scorpio; Jupiter, (sun) in Aquarius; Mars in Aries; Venus, (moon), Mercury in Capricorn.

60 (Year) 2 of the same (ruler): / Mexeir, 17th to 18th, 11th hour of the night:
65 Saturn in Scorpio, Jupiter, (sun), [Mercury] in Aquarius; Mars in Aries; / Venus horoscope, Mercury in Capricorn; moon in Gemini.

70 [Didymos.] Saturn in Libra; Jupiter, (moon), in Capricorn; Venus in Aries; / (sun) in Taurus; Mercury, Mars in Gemini; horoscope in Leo.

Dionysia. (Year?) I (of) Philip; 8th of Epeiph; 2nd hour of the day; Saturn,
75 Mars [in Virgo]; Jupiter, Venus in Taurus; / Mercury [in Gemini, horoscope?], (sun?) in Cancer, [moon in Libra].

*Tr.: Roy Kotansky. This horoscope appears on the verso, col. i of the Warren Magical Papyrus (*PGM* LXII) but is not included in Preisendanz's edition.

PGM LXII. 76–106

*"AR . . .

PHNOON PHEIOOUŌ ERMĒ THŌAR . . . IBARAREOUBEO . . . EA ALAŌ

ARIOUATHŌRMENERTIOUMAISI

RIOUATHŌRMENERTIOUMIAISI

80   I

                        EN"

(in this manner, shaped like a heart).

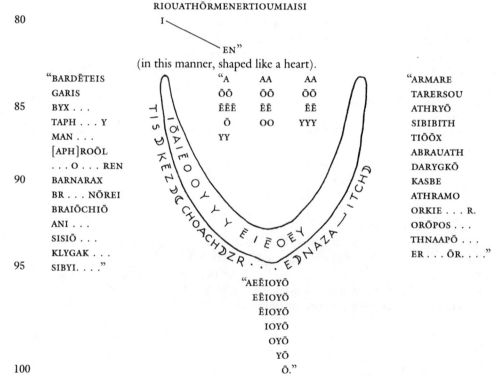

"BARDĒTEIS   "A   AA   AA   "ARMARE
GARIS   ŌŌ   ŌŌ   ŌŌ   TARERSOU
85 BYX . . .   ĒĒĒ   ĒĒ   ĒĒ   ATHRYŌ
TAPH . . . Y   Ō   OO   YYY   SIBIBITH
MAN . . .   YY   TIŌŌX
[APH]ROŌL   ABRAUATH
. . . O . . . REN   DARYGKŌ
90 BARNARAX   KASBE
BR . . . NŌREI   ATHRAMO
BRAIŌCHIŌ   ORKIE . . . R.
ANI . . .   ORŌPOS . . .
SISIŌ . . .   THNAAPŌ . . .
KLYGAK . . .   ER . . . ŌR. . . ."
95 SIBYI. . . ."

                    "AEĒIOYŌ
                     EĒIOYŌ
                     ĒIOYŌ
                     IOYŌ
                     OYŌ
                     YŌ
100   Ō."

"Let the genitals and the womb of her, NN, be open, and let her become bloody
105 by night and day." And [these things must be written] in sheep's blood, and recite before nightfall, the offerings / (?) . . . first she harmed . . . , and bury it near sumac, or near . . . on a slip of papyrus.

*Tr.: John Scarborough.

PGM LXIII. 1–7

*. . . pour two quarts of salt and honey wine, thus making a drink. / And say the   5

seven letters of magicians.[1]

The seven letters are: [A E Ē I O Y Ō].

*Tr.: E. N. O'Neil. This papyrus is severely damaged, and little remains. Of necessity, the translation is tentative in several places.

PGM LXIII. 7–12

*[For a sleeping woman] to confess the name of the man she loves: Place a bird's / [tongue] under her lip or on her heart and put your question, and she calls   10 the name three times.

*Tr.: E. N. O'Neil.

PGM LXIII. 13–20

*[Put in a new basket] a peppercorn and depart, leaving / the basket behind. Many   15 a flask . . . SARA . . . TĒ TE . . . a [useful tablet] . . . R . . . R . . . SM . . . ELA . . . YO . . . ĒS. ISN / . . . ĒN MEL . . . ERĒSA.   20

*Tr.: E. N. O'Neil. The text is too mutilated to yield any sense in this short spell.

PGM LXIII. 21–24

*Find a [spotted lizard],[2] pick it up with a new[3] piece of papyrus, [write] the characters on it, and then place it under the table: Ɔ λ ⌐ ⊕ ✳

*Tr.: E. N. O'Neil. A recipe of uncertain purpose.

PGM LXIII. 24–25

*A contraceptive: Pick up a bean[4] / that has a small bug in it, and attach it as an   25 amulet.

*Tr.: John Scarborough.

PGM LXIII. 26–28

*A contraceptive: Take a pierced bean and attach it as an amulet after tying it up in a piece of mule hide.

*Tr.: John Scarborough.

PGM LXIV. 1–12

*"Strike ill, attract, send [a dream]. I call upon you by your / sacred names, PSINA PSINA KRA-   5 DIDA PSIŌMOIPS. . . . [Make her] writhe at my / feet[1] for a short time [?]."[2]   10

*Tr.: R. F. Hock.

1. μάγων is Hopfner's logical emendation for the ματων of the papyrus. The seven vowels occur often enough to make them the logical "seven letters of the magicians." [E.N.O.]

2. On the role of the lizard in magic see *PGM* VII. 628 and n.

3. Preisendanz restores the mutilated word here as καινοῦ (cf. also *PGM* XXIIa. 14), but καθαροῦ is also possible because of the parallels (see *PGM* VII. 193, 703; XXXVI. 72, 102).

4. Cf. *PGM* IV. 769, 941.

1. Reading προκυλίνδομαι. See Preisendanz, apparatus ad loc.

2. Reading ἀ[καριαίῳ]. See Preisendanz, apparatus ad loc.

PGM LXV. 1–4

***To [prevent pregnancy]**: ". . . OCHTHIA, protect from the archetypal daimon[1] ꙮ [of pregnancy]."

*Tr.: John Scarborough. The recto of this papyrus contains fragmentary portions of household recipes. The verso, given here and in the spell to follow, gives portions of two magico-medical recipes.

PGM LXV. 4–7

5   ***For migraine headache**:[2] ✳ ✗ ✳ / . . . I . . . NA . . . TA. . . ."
*Tr.: John Scarborough.

PGM LXVI. 1–11

*"CHAŌR   ("CHOAR"[1] to the bottom)   "I conjure you
CHTHŌR   by the great
CHARARBA   names: throw
CHOLBAS   Philoxenos the
5   CHTHRYTHYR   harpist into
CHORBATH   strife with his
CHTHAMNŌ   friend Genna-
CHTHODYCHRA   dios. Throw Pe-
10   CHYCHCHYCH   lagios the elder
                                                                           into strife with
                                                                           Philoxenos the
                                                                           harpist."

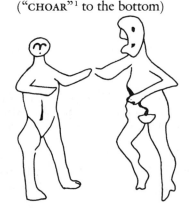

*Tr.: R. F. Hock.

PGM LXVII. 1–24

*. . . The speaker of [the] spell for those dead and those alive [must write]: "AGE . . . AOUMA . . . EB . . . THNOBAMA . . . BABOUA . . . EU DALANALAD . . . ALKOUMI
5   . . . OUTIZTAI AAAA IIIII EOYA BOUBITHA . . . CHANACH SANMACHANA / and KECHNOU BOUZA SANMACHANA . . . SAMMACHARA SPHAMBĒS EPOKR . . . ACHTH KAT ETA BAI KARKOPTŌ KOPTŌ KARBAR . . . AĒA PTOKOPTO KARABARBAROUTA THATH . . . CHRENPSENTHAĒS BERBAL IŌ PARP . . . RPAR, I adjure you by [the
10   holy name of the] daimon of ĒIOY [SOU] / ŌOUS BARBARATHAM of [ADONAIŌS, the god] SABAŌTH [ABRASAX] . . . PSE . . . TA [PHONOBOUBOĒL] [of chthonic Hermes-Thouoth, arch-subduer, PHŌKENSEPSEU AREEKTATHOU MIS[ONKTAI . . . ĒI IAŌ] ĒŌĒŌ KA . . . ĒŌIŌ ŌIŌĒ [SESENGENBARPHARAGGĒS ERĒKISITHPHE]
15   ARARACHARARA   [ĒPHTHISIKĒRE / IABEZEBYTH]   IAŌ . . . SAM . . . [ERĒKISI-PHTHĒ] ARARACHARARA ĒPHTHISIKĒRE . . . ĒI IAŌ [ĒŌĒ]Ō KA. By this oath I
20   adjure [you, who . . . and] the one who has been sworn . . . remaining / [. . . of those who have died] in an [untimely] death . . . [. . . her, NN, whom] NN [bore], . . . [him, NN, whom] NN bore . . . has spoken. . . ."
*Tr.: E. N. O'Neil. This papyrus is made up of five separate pieces. Preisendanz has printed basically the text of L. Koenen published in *ZPE* 8 (1971):199ff. and has omitted a translation.

---

1. So the rendering in LSJ, s.v. "αὐτοδαίμων," with reference to Plotinus, *Enn.* 3. 5. 6.
2. Cf. *PGM* VII. 199–201.
1. Either the *voces magicae* are to be read first or CHOAR is to be read before each word in col. 2.

PGM LXVIII. 1–20

*"As Typhon is the [adversary] of [Helios, so] also inflame [the soul] of Eutyches whom Zosime[1] / [bore], for her, [Eriea] whom [Ercheelio] bore; ABRASAX, in-   5
flame the soul and heart of him, Eutyches for him / Eutyches whom Zosime bore,   10
now, quickly, quickly, in this same hour and on this same day. ADŌNAI, inflame the
soul / and heart of Eutyches, for her Eriea [whom Ercheelio bore], now, quickly,   15
quickly, in this same hour / and on this same day."   20
*Tr.: E. N. O'Neil.

PGM LXIX. 1–3

*"PHNOUNEBEĒ (2 times), give me your strength, IŌ ABRASAX, give me your strength, for I am ABRASAX." Say it 7 times while holding your two thumbs.[1]
*Tr.: D. E. Aune.

PGM LXX. 1–4

*[This] name [is] a *favor charm*, *a charm to dissolve a spell*, *a phylactery*, and *a victory charm*: "AA EMPTŌKOM BASYM,[1] protect me."
*Tr.: H. D. Betz. On this charm and others of this papyrus, see the note on *PGM LXX. 4–25*, below. Ll. 1–3 may contain the end of a spell now lost, or they may represent a complete spell.

PGM LXX. 4–25

*Charm of Hekate Ereschigal against fear[2] of punishment: / If he comes forth,[3]   5
say to him: "I am Ereschigal, the one holding her thumbs,[4] and not even one evil
can befall her."

   If, however, he comes close to you, take hold of your right heel[5] and recite the
following:[6] "Ereschigal, virgin, bitch, / serpent, wreath, key, herald's wand, golden   10
sandal of the Lady of Tartaros." And you will avert him.

   "ASKEI KATASKEI ERŌN OREŌN IŌR MEGA SAMNYĒR BAUI[7] (3 times) PHOBANTIA
SEMNĒ,[8] I have been initiated, and I went down into the [underground] chamber of
the Dactyls, and I saw / the other things down below, virgin, bitch, and all the   15
rest." Say it at the crossroad,[9] and turn around and flee, because it is at those places
that she appears. Saying it late at night, about what you wish, it will reveal it in your
sleep; and if you are led away to death, say it while scattering seeds of sesame, and it
will save you.

   / "PHORBA PHORBA BRIMŌ AZZIEBYA." Take bran of first quality and sandal-   20
wood and vinegar of the sharpest sort and mold a cake. And write the name of so-
and-so upon it, and inscribe it in such a way that you speak over it into the light the

   1. The names seem confused here and should be corrected in accordance with ll. 16–17.
   1. On this magical gesture, see *PGM LXX*. 6 and n.
   1. For an explanation of this name, see *PGM IV*. 1377 and n.
   2. The fear refers to punishment in the underworld.
   3. This refers to a threatening approach by a punishment daimon.
   4. For this magical gesture, see *PGM IV*. 2329; XXXVI. 163; LXIX. 3. See Betz, "Fragments," 290, n. 14.
   5. Another magical gesture, for which see *PGM IV*. 1054 and Betz, "Fragments," 291, n. 18.
   6. For this peculiar list of signs, see *PGM IV*. 2334–38; VII. 780–85; and Betz, "Fragments," 291, nn. 20 and 21.
   7. The Greek has BAUI, perhaps referring to the dog's bark. Cf. *PGM IV*. 1911; XXXVI. 156. [W.B.]
   8. This formula is usually called *Ephesia grammata*, or in *PGM VII*. 451 "the Orphic formula." See Betz, "Fragments," 291–92 with notes.
   9. These instructions refer again to underworld experiences. See Betz, "Fragments," 293–94.

name of Hekate, and this: "Take away his sleep from such-and-such a person,"
25   and / he will be sleepless and worried.
*Tr.: H. D. Betz. Important in this spell are what appear to be liturgical remnants from the
mystery cult of the Idaean Dactyls. For a more detailed commentary, see H. D. Betz, "Fragments from a Catabasis Ritual in a Greek Magical Papyrus," *HR* 19 (1980): 287–95.

PGM LXX. 26–51

*Against fear and to dissolve spells: Speak through [two] knives [sounding
loudly] this formula; but [against] evil animals it does not work [compellingly], for
30   . . . you . . . over the . . . [speak] . . . : ". . . E . . . PHATE . . . CHNON A . . . / GE
35   . . . OIPS . . . SĒ . . . PSO . . . SIL . . . / MO . . . and . . . CHIL . . . PER . . . PAN
40/45   . . . / CHIO . . . CHO . . . AB. . . . POI . . . TOS . . . / IEO . . . DOI . . . ĒNE, so that
50   (?) CHY . . . / ERE . . . TOU. . . ."
*Tr.: H. D. Betz. See note to *PGM* LXX. 4–25. In this spell, the sense of ll. 30ff. cannot be
recovered, though the text probably contained the invocation.

PGM LXXI. 1–8

*A phylactery: "Great [god] in heaven revolving the world, the true god, IAŌ!
5   Lord, ruler of all, ABLANATHANALBA, grant, grant me this favor, / let me have the
name of the great god in this phylactery, and protect, from every evil thing, me
whom NN bore, [NN] begot."
*Tr.: Morton Smith.

PGM LXXII. 1–36

*[Rite concerning the Bear: Prepare] an earthen [censer, and] during the 6th
hour of the night [offer to the Bear] moss of a savin [in it. Do it before] three
5   days / [after you called on] the Bear nine times after going up to a roof top. Write [on
a piece of papyrus] with a mixture of ink and myrrh [concerning everything] which
10   you want, [add] the name, NEB/[OUTOSOUALĒTH"] and [show] both the strip of
papyrus [and] what is written on [it to the goddess . . .] within [one hour. Speak
15   with your hands] folded / on your head, [praying in a loud voice to the Bear:
"Hail,] O queen of mortals [and of gods. Hail,] heavenly ruler, [queen] of men.
20   Depart[1] . . . / I beseech you. . . ."
*Tr.: W. C. Grese. This spell, a cryptogram from the same source as *PGM* LVII, is edited
and commented upon by S. Eitrem, *Mélanges Maspero* 2, 113–17; see also Eitrem and
L. Amundsen, *Papyri Osloenses*, vol. III (Oslo: Dybwad, 1936) 38–40, no. 75.

PGM LXXVII. 1–24

*If you wish to receive a revelation concerning whatever you wish, say this formula
5   to yourself, saying nothing aloud: / "I call upon you, who are seated in the middle
of a field,[1] you who with power direct the universe, at whom the daimons tremble,
10   whom the mountains dread, / whom angels fall down to worship, whom the
sun and moon fall down to worship, you who have heaven for your throne, ether
15   as a place for your dancing place, and earth as your footstool, IOU IOU / APHARA
. . . THOMARA ARABRŌ . . . IOU IOU. Holy, [holy,] boundless, boundless, star-
20   organizer, [fire-breathing, SANTHĒNŌR, gold]-/sandaled [god], reveal." And without causing fear or trembling he will, clearly and soberly, reveal concerning the NN
thing. Do this while you are pure, and burn frankincense at the place.
*Tr.: W. C. Grese.

1. Text and translation are uncertain at this point. Preisendanz translates differently.
1. See on this point the parallels in *PGM* IV. 3023; XIV. 8.

PGM LXXVIII. 1–14

*[For any place], either home or workshop. [It attracts a woman] to a man. The same one [makes them steadfast] and faithful: Take a leaf [of lead] and with a nail write the figure[1] while saying [the name / that follows and]: "I shall burn up the   5 house and the [soul of him, NN, to] cause desire for her, NN, whom NN bore, whom NN bore,[2] as Typhon did [not] allow Osiris to find sleep. For I am [master of] MASKELLI MASKELLŌ PHNOUN[KENTABAŌTH / OREOBA]ZAGRA RĒSICHTHŌN   10 HIPPOCHTHŌN [PYRIPĒ]GANYX. Fulfill this for me, all-brightener, august light-bringer [of gods and daimons]."

Name of the all-[powerful] god: IAŌ IAŌ IAŌ.

*Tr.: E. N. O'Neil. For notes on the text, see also F. Maltomini, "Osservazioni al testo di alcuni papiri magici greci, II," *Civiltà classica e cristiana* 1 (1980): 371–74.

PGM LXXIX. 1–7

*<u>**Charm to restrain anger**</u>, which is to be spoken three times: "I am the soul of darkness, ABRASAX, the eternal one, MICHAĒL, but my true name <u>is THŌOUTH, THŌOUTH</u>.[1] Restrain the anger and / wrath [of him, NN] toward me, NN, [with]   5 the authority of the great god NEOUPHNEIŌTH."
*Tr.: R. F. Hock. The text is the same as in *PGM* LXXX., but by another scribe and in better condition.

PGM LXXX. 1–5

*<u>**Charm to restrain anger**</u>, [which is to be spoken] three times: "I am the soul of darkness, ABRASAX, the eternal one, MICHAĒL, but my true name <u>is THŌOUTH</u>, <u>THŌOUTH</u>. Restrain the anger and wrath of him, NN, toward me, NN, with the <u>authority</u> of the great / god NEOUPHNEIŌTH."   5
*Tr.: R. F. Hock. The text is the same as *PGM* LXXIX. 1–7.

PGM LXXXI. 1–10

*"Hail, Helios! Hail SAPEIPHNĒP! Hail, savior! Hail, ABRASAKX! / Hail, PETKĒI-   5 ERCHENEIN KAMTĒROU. Hail, ĒLOUAI. Hail, ELOUEIN. Hail, PETAIPINAKSNEUEI . . . XA . . . PETENTAETKĒPKEIEICHIN DONAIROUBI OPIANOS OPIANOS BASI[L]I-SKOS / TIARKAMIKEINTEU." Pronouncement of the name.   10
*Tr.: W. C. Grese. According to Preisendanz (ad loc.), this list of greetings was supposed to give protection, perhaps protection for a house—an interpretation he derives from his read-ing of the other side of the papyrus, "defense for a house."

---

1. The figure is given below, following the spell. See Preisendanz, vol. II, plate IV, figure 2. For a collection of images of Artemis *multimammaea*, see R. Fleischer, *Artemis von Ephesus und verwandte Kultstatuen aus Anatolien und Syrien*, EPRO 35 (Leiden: Brill, 1973).

2. The apparent duplication is in the papyrus.

1. The *voces magicae* are Coptic, written in Greek letters.

PGM LXXXII. 1–12

*. . . divide[1] . . . glue it together[2] . . . [the lamellae,] that is, much . . . having de-
5   termined, to water . . . / weave the roots[3] [from all the trees] . . . having separated,
10 with the rain waters . . . having determined . . . from one another, / having mea-
sured out the evergreen [plants] . . . fire from the . . . and anoint the cups. . . .

*Tr.: Roy Kotansky, following the edition of G. Manteuffel, *Papyri Varsovienses* (Warsaw: University of Warsaw, 1935) no. 4: Fragmentum libri magici, 6–7. All that can be said of this fragmentary text is that it seems to have preserved a section of a magical textbook dealing with the making of a certain ingredient.

PGM LXXXIII. 1–20

*For [fever with shivering fits]:[1] "GŌBA . . . S . . . MŌ . . . NOUSĒA . . . EIEGE
. . . OSARK . . . AUSE fever with shivering fits, / I conjure you, MICHAĒL, archangel
5   of the earth; [whether] it is daily or nightly / or quartan fever; I conjure you, the
Almighty SABAŌTH, that it no longer touch the soul of the one who carries [this],
nor [touch] his whole body; also the dead, deliver, . . . the distress IDOT . . .
YGRSBŌNŌE. . . . / "

10 "He who dwells in the help of the Most High shall abide in the shadow of the
God of heaven. He will say of God, 'thou art my refuge and my help; I will put my
trust in him.'"[2]

15 "Our Father who art in heaven, hallowed be thy will; / our daily bread."[3]

"Holy, holy is the Lord SABAŌTH, heaven is full of justice, holy is the one of
glory."[4]

"ANIAADA . . . IA, MIGAĒL[5] of lords, Abraham Isaac Jacob ELŌEI ELŌE Solo-
20 mon(?) / SABAŌTH ŌĒL. . . ."

*Tr.: Roy Kotansky, following the edition of E. H. Kase, Jr., *Papyri in the Princeton University Collections, II* (Princeton: Princeton University Press, 1936) no. 107: Gnostic Fever Amulet, 102–3. This fever amulet is of special interest because it cites several biblical verses. Despite the writer's use of these citations, the character of the spell shows it is syncretistic rather than distinctively Christian. In fact, the incoherent manner by which the verses are quoted suggests that the writer was ignorant of their context and meaning.

PGM LXXXIV. 1–21

*". . . KOACHAMIPHŌNCHŌŌTHPSACHE
KOACHAMIPHŌNCHŌŌTHPSACH
OACHAMIPHŌNCHŌŌTHPSA
ACHAMIPHŌNCHŌŌTHPS
5   CHAMIPHŌNCHŌŌTH
AMIPHŌNCHŌŌ
MIRPHŌNCHŌ
IPHŌNCH
PHŌN
10 Ō."

[magical symbols, about ten in number]

1. In accordance with our standard translation of the aorist participle λάβων, these participles are rendered as imperatives.
2. Or συνπεριπήγνυμι may mean "make to congeal around together." The word is apparently attested nowhere else in Greek literature.
3. For the use of roots in magic, cf. *PGM* XXIIa. 6; XII. 103, 397, 659, etc.
1. As the editor points out, the reading of the text at this point is far from certain.
2. This is a quotation of LXX Ps 90:1–2, with some peculiar variations.
3. This is a somewhat confused quotation of the Lord's Prayer, Mt 6:9–11. The papyrus may read "your father."
4. Apparently this is an allusion to LXX Is 6:3.
5. Read "Michael."

"Fetch Ptolemais whom Helen bore, for Ptolemaios whom Didyme bore. / In-   15
flame her liver and spirit and heart and soul until she leaps up and comes, that is,
Ptolemais whom / Helena bore, to Ptolemaios whom Didyme bore; immediately,   20
quickly."
*Tr.: Roy Kotansky, following the edition of Edmund Harris Kase, Jr., *Papyri in Princeton
University Collections, II* (Princeton: Princeton University Press, 1936) no. 76: Erotic Incantation, 73–74.

PGM LXXXV. 1–6

*". . . let him marvel, all THAE . . . drive away, make the daimons (?).[1] . . ."
Let the one who has written [this] be glad, and the haunts [of spirits][2] . . . he
knows not, but beautifully a picture (?).[3] . . . /
  Another: 5
  [Another]: . . . .
*Tr.: Roy Kotansky, following the edition of J. Enoch Powell, *The Rendel Harris Papyri*
(Cambridge: Cambridge University Press, 1936) no. 56: Magical Spells, p. 38. This text is
taken from three tiny fragments which date to the first or second century A.D. Although the
text is quite fragmentary, its early date makes it important. Furthermore, the recurring expression "another [spell]," shows that we are dealing with a collection from a magical
handbook.

PGM LXXXVI. 1–2

*"Protect him, NN, whom [she, NN bore]." Attach [this] as an amulet around
the neck.[1]
*Tr.: Roy Kotansky, following the edition of P. Collart, *Les Papyrus Théodore Reinach*, II
(Cairo: L'Institut français d'archéologie orientale, 1940) no. 89: Formulaire magique,
32–33. This tiny fragment preserves portions of two spells; the first contains instructions
for making a simple amulet. The second preserves the beginning of a magical procedure of
an uncertain nature.

PGM LXXXVI. 3–7

*At sunrise,[2] on the 10th day of the month of Didymon . . . the next day, during
the ninth hour, write . . . / of a female goat . . . XEONTA . . . DONO . . . ZOU. . . .   5
*Tr.: Roy Kotansky; see the note on *PGM* LXXXVI. 1–2, above.

PGM LXXXVII. 1–11

*"SAMOUSOUM SOUMA SOUMĒ SOUMĒIA MEISOUAT . . . SROUAT, my lord, ROUAT
. . . [deliver ?] John from the shivering fit and fever that has (him); [cleanse?] the
daily fever from this (?) shivering (?) . . . / [all] the headache, daily fevers, nightly,   5
quartan, semitertian, immediately, immediately; quickly, quickly. . . . TA. ĒMŌNO
. . . ARA the angel; . . . [deliver?] John from every shivering fit and fever, from this
very day, from the present [hour throughout] / his entire lifetime; [grant him heal-   10
ing?], immediately, immediately; quickly, quickly."
*Tr.: Roy Kotansky, following the new reading of F. Maltomini, "Osservazioni al testo di
alcuni papiri magici greci. (III.)," *Studi classici e orientali* 32 (1982) : 235–40 (tav. XXVI),

1. Reading δαιμόνια instead of δαιμονιε.
2. Reading τὰ ἤϑε[α . . . πν]ευμά[των
3. Reading γράμμα, "picture," "character," in the sequence γραμμασ[. . .
1. For similar instructions, cf. *PGM* VII. 198, 208; XIII. 669.
2. The editor restores the first letters of this word. Performing a magical ritual on a specified day is
common in the *PGM*; see, e.g., *PGM* VII. 155–67; XIII. 15, 349, 1037.

esp. 235–38. Cf. the original edition of W. Schubert, *Die Papyri der Universitätsbibliothek Erlangen* (Leipzig: Harrassowitz, 1942), *P. Erl.* 37: *Zaubertext*. For commentary and the suggested readings in the lacunae, consult the notes of Maltomini in the work cited here.

PGM LXXXVIII. 1–19

*"ZAGOURĒ PAGOURĒ
AGOURĒ PAGOUR
GOURĒ PAGOU
OURĒ PAGO
5 URĒ PAG
RĒ PA
Ē P
E."

10/15   "O excellent / ruling angels, give [him, NN] whom Sophia bore, rest from / the fever that restrains him; this very day, this very hour; immediately, immediately; quickly, quickly."
*Tr.: Roy Kotansky, following the edition of A. C. Johnson and S. P. Goodrich, *Papyri in the Princeton University Collections, III* (Princeton University Studies in Papyrology 4; Princeton: Princeton University Press, 1942), no. 159: Fever Amulet, 78–79. The text has also been published by Bruce M. Metzger, "A Magical Amulet for Curing Fevers," in Boyd L. Daniels and M. Jack Suggs, eds., *Studies in the History and Text of the New Testament in Honor of Kenneth Willis Clark* (Studies and Documents 20; Salt Lake City: University of Utah, 1967) 89–94; reprinted in Metzger, *Historical and Literary Studies: Pagan, Jewish, and Christian* (Leiden: Brill, 1968) 104–10.

PGM LXXXIX. 1–27

*"I, Abrasax, shall deliver. Abrasax am I! ABRASAX ABRASICHŌOU, help little /
5   Sophia-Priskilla. Get hold of and do away with what comes to little Sophia-
10 / Priskilla, whether it is a shivering fit—get hold of it! Whether a phantom—get
15 hold of it! Whether a daimon—get hold of it! / I, Abrasax, shall deliver. Abrasax
20 am I! ABRASAX ABRASICHŌOU. Get hold of, get hold of / and do away with . . .
25 what comes to little Sophia-Priskilla on this very day, / whether it is a shivering
fit—do away with it! Whether a daimon—do away with it!"
*Tr.: Roy Kotansky, following the edition of Erik J. Knudtzon, "Aus der Papyrussammlung der Universitätsbibliothek in Lund, IV," *Kungl. Humanistiska Vetenskapssamfundet i Lund, Årsberättelse*, 1945–1946 (Lund: Gleerup, 1946) no. 12: *Zauberspruch*, 74–75 (taf. 6).

PGM XC. 1–13

*". . . [calling] the lord, him [healthy(?)], and PANNANOM, in addition, MICHAĒL
5   MICHAĒL MICHAĒL GABRIĒL / RAPHAĒL OURIĒL EMANOUĒL SACHAPHAPABA SAB-
AŌTH [BAŌTH] IĒ PHA BRIĒL god, god IAŌ SOEOSTYOU . . . ŌNAAMIN BIĒCHENO
10 . . . MAS / ĒMRAĒL ANAĒL KEMOUĒL BIAMLISONTOMIPANIAŌ BAŌBBBB (add the
usual). ⳨⳦ ✳⳨⊛⳧⳺⳨ " (add the usual).
*Tr.: H. D. Betz, following the text given by Augusto Traversa, "Frammento di papiro magico," *Aegyptus* 33 (1953): 57–62. The text is mutilated; it contains some Coptic letters.

PGM XC. 14–18

15 *A salve [for] fever: Write: "▽ ▽⳽⳼ ABRAAM ĒHĒ (add the usual) TIT AA M
ŌŌ . . . ICHAU . . . TĒR . . . CHOUAS . . . EKIRA . . . OSTA . . . MAR . . . LOHĒ . . .
SĒTĒ . . . TAS."
*Tr.: H. D. Betz. For the reference to the edition of this papyrus, see the note on *PGM XC*. 1–13. The charm apparently served as a fever amulet.

PGM XCI. 1–14

＊ ˝ABLANATHANALBA

BLANATHANALB

[LA]NATHANAL

ANATHANA

NATHAN   5

ATHA

TH.

"Melt (?) . . . [NN], whom NN bore . . . / who has . . . the daily . . . reaching   10
out this very day, this very hour; immediately, immediately; quickly, quickly."
*Tr.: Roy Kotansky, following the edition of D. S. Crawford, *Papyri Michaelidae* (Aberdeen:
The Egypt Exploration Society, 1955) no. 27: Magical Charm, 49–50. The editor suggests
that this fragment is a curse or a love charm; however, the mention of "daily" in l. 11, as well
as "who has" in l. 10 (a typical description in the *PGM* for an affliction) suggests it is a fever
amulet.

PGM XCII. 1–16

*＊*Your great name, for*[1] favor*: "Everyone fears your great might. Grant me the
good things:[2] the strength of AKRYSKYLOS,[3] / the speech of EUŌNOS, the eyes of   5
Solomon,[4] the voice of ABRASAX, the grace of ADŌNIOS, the god.[5] Come to me,
Kypris, / every day.[6] The hidden name bestowed to you(?) [is this]: THOATHO-   10
ĒTHʹATHOOYTHAETHŌUSTHOAITHITHĒTHOINTHŌ; grant me victory, / repute,   15
beauty toward all men and all women."
*Tr.: Roy Kotansky, following the edition of B. R. Rees, H. I. Bell, and J. W. B. Barns, eds.,
A Descriptive Catalogue of the Greek Papyri in the Collection of Wilfred Merton, F.S.A., II (Dub-
lin: Hodges Figgis, 1959), no. 58: Magical Charm, 22–24 (pl. VII).

PGM XCIII. 1–6

*. . . [sacrifice and] . . . bury[1] . . . the same all [around?] . . . ; pour blood into a   5
vessel . . . / and on the outside besprinkle[2] . . . to Hekate. . . .   [i, 5]
*Tr.: Roy Kotansky, following the edition of J. W. B. Barnes and H. Zilliacus, eds., *The Anti-
noopolis Papyri*, vol. II (London: Egypt Exploration Society, 1960) no. 65: Magical Prescriptions (?), 45–47 (pl. III, i). The ascription of this fragment of a parchment leaf to a Greco-

1. The editors suggest the first three letters are a magical name, EIE. L. 1, they admit, makes little
sense regardless of what is read; however, the photograph of the papyrus shows that one might read the
preposition εἰς, "for, unto." The sentence thus seems clearer, although the reading and translation remain tentative.

2. The language and temper of this charm show that this spell is one used to acquire favor and victory. Cf. for example *PGM* XII. 397–400 etc.

3. The following list of names whose powers the client is requesting suggests that each person named
is recognized for his special attribute. Thus, Akryskylos is recognized for his strength, Euōnos for his
speech, and so on. Neither Akryskylos nor Euōnos (*sic* for Euō[nym]os? [so the editors]) can be identified; however, each of the following personalities is recognizable. Cf. *PGM* VII. 1017–26.

4. Or, possibly, "the glances of Solomon," according to the editors. Although Solomon was a popular magical figure, the mention of his "eyes" is not common. Consult the note in the original cited above,
p. 23, n. 6. On the other hand, cf. the αὐγή that illumines Solomon's mind in the *Test. Sol.*, Rec. C,
Prologus, 2 (McCown, *Testament* 76).

5. Adonis is here rendered by the variant spelling Adōnios. Adonis is often associated with Kypris, a
popular name for Aphrodite.

6. Or, if accusative of duration, "for the whole day," that is, presumably for the duration of each day
which the person wears the charm.

1. The command to bury something occurs in *PGM* IV. 2215; XII. 100, where an inscribed tablet
and an egg are referred to. The context here, however, gives no hint of what is to be buried.

2. On sprinkling dove's blood to dismiss a deity, see *PGM* II. 177.

Egyptian magical handbook is fairly certain. Although the two sides contain no *voces magicae*, and thus we may have a simple manual of sacrificial procedures, the presence of the name Hekate in l. 6 (side 1) suggests a magical text. Also, in the margin of l. 7 the number 43 occurs, which the editor describes as a numbering of the magical procedures.

PGM XCIII. 7–21

10   *43 . . . and whatever you wish[3] . . . blind, on . . . / stomach (?) . . . a cock [which
[i, 10]   is alive] . . . ; bring it and set it on the . . . the piglet[4] and the / . . . carrying, out-
15   side of many (?) . . . the house; . . . and offer this . . . nine women . . . in front of
[ii, 15]   the doors . . . / [it is] believed (?). . . .
20
[ii, 20]

*Tr.: Roy Kotansky, following the edition of J. W. B. Barnes and H. Zilliacus (see introductory note on previous spell), 46, side i, ll. 7–10; side ii, ll. 11–21. The procedure described here is of an uncertain purpose. The spell after l. 10 (side ii) may be independent of the preceding lines.

PGM XCIV. 1–6

*". . . YNYEL . . . STOOU . . . M . . . SEGEIR . . . Y . . . Y ERBĒTH . . . E . . . OUCHI."[1]
5   ***Drying powder made with saffron [for] sharp eyesight***: / KA . . . AL . . . 2 drams.
Use a dram of boar skin which has been dried in the sun.
*Tr.: Roy Kotansky, following the edition of J. W. B. Barns and H. Zilliacus, eds., *The Antinoopolis Papyri*, II (London: Egypt Exploration Society, 1960) no. 66: Magico-Medical Prescriptions, 47–49. The papyrus begins with the fragments of an invocation of unknown purpose. The prescriptions are separated by paragraph marks.

PGM XCIV. 7–9

For excellent health:[2] Write on an amulet: "ABRAŌ . . . ARŌN BARA BAR . . . A . . . Ō."
*Tr.: Roy Kotansky. See above, on *PGM* XCIV. 1–6.

PGM XCIV. 10–16

10   **A phylactery for [fever]**: . . . RARA . . . leather . . . seven days . . . [and] wear
15   / . . ." ⊗⋈ Z S . . . S . . . ⊗⋈ . . . Z ✕ . . . "
*Tr.: Roy Kotansky. See above, on *PGM* XCIV. 1–6.

PGM XCIV. 17–21

For those possessed by daimons: ". . . T . . . Y . . . depart . . . YT. . . ." The things
20   prescribed below . . . / "ATR . . . Y SOLŌMŌN . . . is washed. . . ."
*Tr.: Roy Kotansky. See above, on *PGM* XCIV. 1–6.

PGM XCIV. 22–26

For the eyes: Make a gothic (?) [figure][3] and carve [on it the] following: one who

---

3. References to stating one's wish are regularly found throughout the *PGM*. For very similar wording, cf. *PGM* IV. 1907.

4. As the editor points out, the cock and the pig probably serve as sacrificial animals. For the use of a cock in magical sacrifices, see *PGM* IV. 2370; XII. 312; XIII. 377, 437–38, and so on. Pigs are found less often as sacrificial animals in the *PGM*.

1. As the editors suggest, these lines may have consisted entirely of magical words. In the sequence ERBĒTH can be read.

2. Or "easy healing." The word is a hapax legomenon, as the editors point out.

3. Following the interpretation of the editors.

[holds (?) with the left] / hand, in the middle . . . : "CHACH. . . ."   25
*Tr.: Roy Kotansky. See above, on *PGM* XCIV. 1–6. The instructions seem to describe the manufacturing of a *figura magica*.

PGM XCIV. 27–35
[For] tumors [and] . . . . [the] following . . . / [write] on a grapeleaf [the] follow-   30
ing things and boil . . . the leaf . . . "⊗⊗ BB⚡⚡ . . . Z⌇⌇, flesh (?). . . ."
*Tr.: Roy Kotansky. See above, on *PGM* XCIV. 1–6.

PGM XCIV. 36–38
[For . . .] and strangury: [write on a] tin lamella [the following]: "MARŌTHA . . .
M. . . ."
*Tr.: Roy Kotansky. See above, on *PGM* XCIV. 1–6.

PGM XCIV. 39–60
Another, for migraine headache:

/ ". . . IYIŌ
. . . YAŌŌ
. . . ŌYOŌ
. . . OY."

40

It delivers (?). *And this is the formula of (over) water:*
/ "OURBEDERAEIS OUROURBEDERAEIS OUROUROUBEDERAEIS EISTHES ABRASA   45
ELECH BELLENOURE OUNOURE BAPHAMMĒCH, to you I speak, pounding headache: don't throb, don't rage, / don't shake the teeth, don't produce mucus, don't   50
produce a 'black-out', don't stir up convulsions. For if there is throbbing, raging,
shaking of teeth, producings of mucus, producings of a 'black-out,' / or stirrings of   55
a convulsion . . . BŌ . . . G . . . A . . . ✕ . . . CH . . . / . . . A. . . ."   60
*Tr.: Roy Kotansky.

PGM XCV. 1–6
*. . . on the left sole of one foot,[1] near (?) . . . having subjected . . . [upon?] . . .
and there will a be reward for the. . . . Take the skin of a mouse . . . / and have in   5
the workshop, beneath. . . .   [col. i, 5]
*Tr.: Roy Kotansky, following the edition of J. W. B. Barns and H. Zilliacus, *The Antinoopolis Papyri*, III (London: Egypt Exploration Society, 1967) no. 140: Magico-Medical Prescriptions, 71, Fr. (a). This portion of the formulary describes the engraving of parts of a figure, perhaps a magical doll for the purpose of subjugating someone. The description of the mouse skin either begins a new spell or introduces part of a procedure belonging to the previous charm.

PGM XCV. 7–13
Concerning the mole[-rat]:[2] one (?) mole-rat that is alive . . . a remedy (?) for (?)

---

1. The prescription is describing what to engrave on a waxen or clay figure such as we find in *PGM* IV. 296–335, 2373–2440; and VII. 927. These references describe the function of the left sole of the foot (along with other parts of the body) in a specified magical procedure. *PGM* VII. 927 (a charm to subject someone) commands one to place a tablet under the left sole of the foot. The mention of subjection in the spell above suggests that we have here a "charm to subject" (*hypotaktikon*).

2. The editors point out that the blind-rat or mole-rat (*Spalax typhlus*) may possibly be used as the remedy for the epilepsy.

10   epilepsy (?)³ . . . / on the first of the month . . . [altar?]. . . .
[col. ii, 4]

> *Tr.: Roy Kotansky, following the edition of J. W. B. Barns and H. Zilliacus (see note on previous spell) 71, col. ii. The editors identify this spell as a prescription for the "sacred disease." The spell, we should note, comes under a heading apparently arranged according to the magical virtues of the animal. Such arrangements are typical for a number of magico-medical prescriptions, in which case this section would enumerate the medicinal or magical values of the blind-rat (*Spalax typhlus*).

PGM XCV. 14–18

15   *. . . *This will be a remedy for you for all cases* of . . . : / . . . ATHOU, given thrice,
[(b), 2]   in the month it delivers, in the same manner both those afflicted by epileptic sei-
            zures and by . . . thus by our returning thanks . . . *those affected by lung dis-
            ease*. . . .

> *Tr.: Roy Kotansky, following the edition of J. W. B. Barns and H. Zilliacus (see note on previous papyrus) 71, fr. (b). The formulary at this point seems to provide a remedy for epilepsy. The beginning of a new remedy seems to be given at the end.

PGM XCVI. 1–8

5   *". . . AS (7 times) MELI XARO ŌRO AAAAAAA BAINCHŌŌŌCH MAI ĒEI / LĒNA-
            GKOLI, protect him who carries [this amulet]."

> *Tr.: Roy Kotansky, following the revised text of R. W. Daniel, "Some PHYLAKTĒRIA," *ZPE* 25 (1977):150–53 (text two). The text was originally published by J. O'Callaghan in *Chronique d'Egypte* 43 (1968):111–13, and subsequently commented upon by M. Vandoni in *Istituto Lombardo, Rendiconti* 102 (1968):532–34 and again by J. O'Callaghan in *Studia Papyrologica* 8 (1969):115–18. It is recognized that the text is a version of ll. 7–8 of *P. Oslo* I.5 (= *PGM* 3); however, whereas *PGM* 3 is Christian, this one is not. This text, moreover, is virtually complete, save for the slightly cut-away edges which suggest the papyrus was inserted in a case to be worn as an amulet.

PGM XCVII. 1–6

            *. . . [wrap it up in purple] cloth. . . .

5   [*Another*:] Cut out the right [eye] of a lizard and / [enclose it] in [goat skin];
            attach it to [your] left [eye].

> *Tr.: H. D. Betz, following the edition and commentary by D. Wortmann, "Neue magische Texte," *Bonner Jahrbücher* 168 (1968):109–11. Extant are only a few remnants of two columns, the first of which is too fragmentary to translate here. The individual spells in this collection of recipes are divided by *paragraphi*. Wortmann thinks the spell is against eye disease because the lizard is often used to that effect in magic. See A. D. Nock, "The Lizard in Magic and Religion," *Essays I*, 271–76. The purpose of the first recipe cannot be recovered.

PGM XCVII. 7–9

            Another: Grind up the heart¹ of a nightowl² [with . . .], and [anoint yourself].³
            *Tr.: H. D. Betz.

PGM XCVII. 10–13

10   / *Another*: KR . . . ĒS, and TŌ . . . OS at the same time [attach as an amulet] . . . of
            a bull⁴ . . . with one thong of a male goat. . . .
            *Tr.: H. D. Betz.

> 3. Remedies for epilepsy are not found often in *PGM*. For literature and discussion of epilepsy in antiquity, see in particular E. Lesky and J. H. Waszink, "Epilepsie," *RAC* 5 (1965):819–31.
> 1. Cf. *PGM* III. 427.
> 2. For the nightowl, see *PGM* I. 223; XXXVI. 264.
> 3. Cf. *PGM* II. 19; VIII. 185, 192; XXXVI. 291–92
> 4. Cf. the reading by F. Maltomini, "Osservazioni al testo di alcuni papiri magici greci, I," *Miscellanea Papyrologica, Papyrologica Florentina* 7 (Firenze: Gonnelli, 1980) 176.

PGM XCVII. 15–17

/ *For every [*disease*: Take] a scarab . . . K . . . IO . . . THEN. . . .   15
*Tr.: H. D. Betz.

PGM XCVIII. 1–7

*"A	Victorious[2] in everything is
EE	the nourisher[3] of
ĒĒĒ	the whole inhabited
IIII	world, lord Sarapis;
OOOOO	deliver[4] 5
YYYYYY	Artemidora."
ŌŌŌŌŌŌŌ[1]	

*Tr.: H. D. Betz, following the edition and commentary by D. Wortmann, "Neue magische Texte," *Bonner Jahrbücher* 168 (1969): 107–8.

PGM XCIX. 1–3

*"God is one who heals every sickness."
*Tr.: H. D. Betz, following the edition and commentary by D. Wortmann, "Neue magische Texte," *Bonner Jahrbücher* 168 (1968): 105.

PGM C. 1–7

*"A /// EE ĒĒĒ IIII OOOOO YYYYYY ŌŌŌŌŌŌŌ[1] ABLANATHAMALA[2] . . . EŌ AKRAM-
MACHAMARI KAI CHA K AI; lord god of gods,[3] heal everything with Thaēs . . . E . . .
ECHAIMA / ĒLO . . . OYEA dissolve.[4] The name of the father of Christ[5] BB [BBBB][6]   5
✗✗✗✷✶✗✂🏵 Heal Thaes, immediately, immediately; quickly, quickly."
*Tr.: H. D. Betz, following the edition and commentary by D. Wortmann, "Neue magische Texte," *Bonner Jahrbücher* 168 (1968): 102–04.

PGM CI. 1–53

*"I bind you[1] with the indissoluble fetters of the underworld Fates and mighty Necessity, for I conjure you, daimons, who lie here[2] and who move about here and who keep busy here, and the boys here who have died prematurely.[3]

"I conjure you by the invincible god, IAŌ BARBATHIAŌ BRIMIAŌ CHERMARI, to rise up, O daimons who are lying / here, and to search for Euphemia, whom   5
Dorothea bore, [for] Theon, whom Proechia bore. During the whole night let her not find sleep, but fetch her until she comes before his feet and loves him with mad love and affection and intercourse. For I have bound her brain and her hands and her intestines and her genitals, and her heart to love me, Theon.

1. For this formation of the vowels in form of a grape, cf. *PGM* I. 13 and n.; C and n. 1.
2. For this important epithet of Sarapis, see Wortmann's commentary, 107.
3. This epithet of Sarapis also occurs in *PGM* XIII. 638–39; XII. 244; XIII. 772–73; XXI. 7–10.
4. Probably from daimons; cf. *PGM* IV. 86–87; V. 125–26.
1. This series of vowels is called κλίμα. See *PGM* I. 13 and n.; XIXa. 33, etc. On the whole, see C. Lenz, "Carmina figurata," *RAC* 2 (1954): 910–12.
2. Misspelled for the common palindrome ABLANATHANALBA.
3. So the restoration by Wortmann on the basis of *PGM* II. 53; IV. 180.
4. Probably referring to the disease.
5. This Christian influence shows the syncretism of the spell.
6. The BBBB have been lined out in the manuscript.
1. The second-person singular, apparently referring to Euphemia; the daimons are addressed in the second person plural.
2. Cemeteries are the preferred dwelling places of the daimons.
3. The spirits of infants of premature death are preferred mediums of the magicians.

10   "But if you disobey and do not quickly / carry out what I tell you, the sun will not set under the earth, and neither Hades nor the world [will] exist.[4] But if you fetch for me Euphemia, whom Dorothea bore, for me, Theon whom Proechia bore, I shall give you Osiris Nophrioth, the brother of Isis, and he [will] bring you fresh water and he shall give rest, too, for your souls.[5] But if you do not carry out

15 for me what I tell you, / the EŌNEBYŌTH[6] shall burn you.

    "I conjure you, daimons, who are lying here, IEŌ IIIIAIA ĒIA IAŌ IAĒ IAŌ ALILAMPS. I deposit [this spell] for you in this land of the dogs.[7] Bind Euphemia to love me, Theon. O daimons, I adjure you by the stele of the gods, I adjure you by the ones in the innermost shrines, I adjure you by the names of the all-seeing god,

20 IA IA / IA IŌ IŌ IŌ IE IE IE OYŌA ADŌNAI. With pleasure I conjure the one in the temple,[8] and the blood[9] which the great god IŌTHATH[10] has received. I conjure you by the one who sits upon the four pinnacles of [the] winds.[11]

    "Do not disobey me, but do [it] quickly, because ordering you is[12] AKRAM-MACHAMARI BOULOMENTOREB GENIOMOUTHIG DĒMOGENĒD ENKYKLIE ZĒNO-

25 BIŌTHIZ / ĒSKŌTHŌRĒ THŌTHOUTHŌTH IAEOUŌI KORKOOUNOŌK LOULOENĒL, MOROTHOĒPNAM NERXIARXIN XONOPHOĒNAX ORNEOPHAO PYROBARYP REROU-TOĒR SESENMENOURES TAUROPOLIT YPEPHENOURY PHIMEMAMEPH CHENNEO-PHEOCH PSYCHOMPOIAPS ŌRIŌN, the true one. May I not be compelled to say the

30 same things again, IŌĒ IŌĒ. Fetch Euphemia, whom / Dorothea bore, for Theon, whom his mother Proechia bore, to love me with love and longing and affection and intercourse, with mad love. Burn her members, her liver, her female parts, until she comes to me, longing for me and not disobeying me. For I conjure you by the mighty Necessity, MASKELLI MASKELLŌ[13] PHENOUKENTABAŌTH OREOBAZAGRA

35 RĒXICHTHŌN / HIPPOCHTHŌN PYRICHTHŌN PYRIPĒGANYX LEPETAN LEPETAN MANTOUNOBOĒL, in order that you bind for me Euphemia, for me, Theon, in affec-tion and in love and in longing for a period of ten months[14] from today, which is the 25th of Hathyr of the second year of the indiction.

    "And again I conjure you by the one who rules over you, in order that you do not disobey me. And again I conjure you by the one who is in charge of the air.

40 And / again I conjure you by the seven thrones, ACHLAL LALAPHENOURPHEN

---

4. The operator threatens the gods with upsetting the cosmic order; see *PGM* IV. 185–86; XXXIV, and Wortmann, "Neue magische Texte," 92–93.

5. The dead in the netherworld suffer from thirst, while Osiris brings them the drink of life. See Wortmann, "Neue magische Texte," 94–95.

6. This name is otherwise not known. See Wortmann, "Neue magische Texte," 95.

7. Apparently referring to the desert cemetery where hyenas roam about. Thus Wortmann, "Neue magische Texte," 96.

8. Following Wortmann's interpretation of ōap as "temple" (97). (I should prefer to take ōap as abaton, "innermost shrine" [see l. 18] and the god as Osiris. Note that Osiris is called "he who rests in the abaton," whereby "rest" in Egyptian is ḥtp, which corresponds to Greek εὐδοκεῖν. [J.B.])

9. The blood is that of the enemies of the gods, especially that of Seth. See D. Wortmann, "Das Blut des Seth," *ZPE* 2 (1968):227–30, who refers to Plutarch, *De Is. et Os.* 6, 353 B, and Rv 16:4 as parallels.

10. That is, Hermes-Thoth.

11. For the four winds, see *PGM* III. 496; XII. 84, 238; XIII. 761, and Wortmann, "Neue magische Texte," 97–98.

12. The list of names contains the twenty-four names of the Greek alphabet; each name, except the first and the last, also ends with the letter of the alphabet. See Dornseiff, *Das Alphabet* 146–51; Wortmann, "Neue magische Texte," 98, who calls attention to the unique character of this list.

13. For the MASKELLI MASKELLŌ formula, see Glossary, s.v.

14. Ten lunar months was considered the normal period of pregnancy. See J. Bergman, "Decem illis diebus," *Ex Orbe Religionum. Studia Geo Widengren oblata* (Leiden: Brill, 1972) I, 332–46.

BALEŌ BOLBEŌ BOLBEŌCH BOLBESRŌ YYPHTHŌ,[15] and by the relentless god, CHMOUŌR ABRASAX IPSENTHANCHOUCHAINCHOUCHEŌCH. Seize Euphemia and fetch her for me, Theon, to love me with mad love, and bind her with indissoluble, strong, adamantine fetters / to love me, Theon; and do not let her eat, or drink, or   45 find sleep, or have fun, or laugh; but make her run away from every place and from every house, and leave father, mother, brothers, sisters,[16] until she comes to me, Theon, being fond of me, loving me, Theon, in unending love and mad affection. But if she has another one at her / bosom, move her to push him away and forget   50 him and hate him, but me she shall be fond of and love with affection and grant[17] me her favors, and she shall do nothing against my will. You, these holy names and these powers, confirm and carry out this perfect enchantment; immediately, immediately; quickly, quickly."

*Tr.: H. D. Betz, following the edition and commentary by D. Wortmann, "Neue magische Texte," *Bonner Jahrbücher* 168 (1968): 85–102. The papyrus was found folded up in a clay vessel and deposited in a cemetery. Inside the folded papyrus were found two wax figurines in erotic embrace (cf. *PGM* IV. 296ff.).

PGM CII. 1–17 [frag. E, D, C]

*. . . over [the lamp] . . . your hand, and [when you are almost awake] the god   [fr. E][1]
[will come and speak to you, and . . .] / [. . . and smear the picture with the black   [fr. D][2]
(?) of Isis . . .] But [the strip of cloth . . .]. Take rainwater[3] . . . Speak this [*formula* over the] lamp:

["I call upon you,] / the headless god,[4] the one who [has his head and] his face   5
[upon his feet;[5]] you who are hurling lightning [and who are thundering]; you are the one whose mouth [constantly pours forth] fire;[6] [you are the one who is over] Necessity. I call upon you, [the headless] god . . . [the one who has his head and his face upon his feet,] / strong[7] BĒSAS, [the dim-sighted one. You are the one lying on   10 a coffin] and having at the side of the head . . . an elbow cushion . . . and of bitumen[8] . . . , the one whom they call, ANOUTH ANOUTH, lord. . . . You are not a daimon, but the blood of . . . , / and of the 30 and of the 104 falcons[9] who are also   15 chattering and watching before the head of Osiris.[10] . . ."

/ . . . and from impurity . . . over the lamp . . . wholely black. . . .   [fr. C][11]

*Tr.: H. D. Betz, according to the edition by R. A. Coles et al., *The Oxyrhynchus Papyri*, vol. 36 (London: The Egypt Exploration Society, 1970), no. 2753: Magical Spells, 27–28. The papyrus, a request for a dream oracle, was cut into several pieces, all severely damaged. It is not clear whether there were one or two spells. Some of the lines can be restored on the basis of remarkably close parallels elsewhere in *PGM*.

15. The names of the seven thrones are attested here for the first time completely. See Wortmann, "Neue magische Texte," 101.

16. For parallels see *PGM* IV. 2756–59; XV. 4–5; and Wortmann, "Neue magische Texte," 101.

17. See Wortmann, "Neue magische Texte," 102, who refers to *PGM* IV. 2740–41, 2759–61.

1. Almost all is restored on the basis of *PGM* VII. 226–30.

2. As restored from *PGM* VII. 231–41.

3. For the association of the headless god with rainwater, see *PGM* VII. 224, 319–20; V. 152; LXI. 7.

4. For the headless god, see *PGM* II. 11; V. 98, 125, 145–46; VII. 233, 243, 442; VIII. 91; *Test. Sol.* 9. 1, and the discussion in Bonner, *SMA* 58, 110–11, 164–66.

5. Cf. *PGM* VII. 234; VIII. 91. See Bonner, *SMA* 110.

6. The fire has been omitted in *PGM* VII. 234.

7. Cf. on this epithet *PGM* V. 129.

8. Cf. *PGM* VII. 237; VIII. 98.

9. The number of falcons varies: cf. *PGM* VII. 239–40 (with Preisendanz's note); *PGM* VIII. 100.

10. Cf. *PGM* VII. 240; VIII. 100.

11. Cf. *PGM* I. 55–60; VII. 539.

PGM CIII. 1–18

5   *"... TAR thus P ... ŌTHOI and ... from every place ... place and every. ... / If
she lies down ... let ... [not] eat, if she drinks ... B ... SON NN and ... and the
10   ... most loved / ... immediately, immediately ... [NN, whom NN] bore ... to
15   every place ... but not ... fire, and throwing / ... RI of gain THI ... CHIŌCH
... upon. ..."
*Tr.: Roy Kotansky, following the edition of Georgios A. Petropulos, *Papyri Societatis Ar-
chaeologicae Atheniensis (P. S. A. Athen.)* (Milan: Cisalpino-Goliardica, 1972; repr. of 1939
edition), no. 70, pp. 430–31. The ostensible purpose of this second-century magical text is
the acquisition of a lover. For similar love charms that seek to disrupt the victim's eating,
sleeping, and so on, compare *PGM* IV. 1510ff.; CVIII, etc. For further commentary, see
F. Maltomini, "Osservazioni al testo di alcuni papiri magici greci, I," *Miscellanea Papyrologica*,
Papyrologica Florentina 7 (Firenze: Gonnelli, 1980) 169–72.

PGM CIV. 1–8

*"AEŌ[1] ... AEEŌ[2] ... THYRINERE[3] ... ARMARINNE ... ARI ... OCH ... SOZO-
CHABAI ... ACHABOZO ... OUEDDOUCHAI,[4] get rid of all Althea's (?) daily
5   fever with shivering fits. Give [Althea (?)] / rest from the daily fever with shivering fits. ..."
*Tr.: Roy Kotansky, following the edition of M. Amelotti and L. Z. Migliardi, *Papiri
dell'Università di Genova (PUG)*, vol. I (Milan: Giuffrè, 1974) no. 6: Amuleto contro la
febbre, 17–18 (tav. V).

PGM CV. 1–15

*"The one having appeared [before][1] the universe in [accordance with your] eter-
nal nature, the untiring one, the one who ... the one from the south ... guard;
5   I call upon you, lord [Almighty], / the unknown one, the pure soul, I, the one ...
having been sanctified. Be merciful to me, O Zeus-Iao-Zen-Helios, IOUS ...
SANBALCHANBAL THANŌAMA ... CHŌCH, so that I may speak ... of the gods
10   ... / AŌT[2] ABAŌT BASYM[3] ISAAC [ABRAHAM] JACŌB, hearken to me, the one ...
ŌROU ŌROU ŌROU AE IAI A ... SOUŌ I IYAOĒ IAŌ, [always,] the god who com-
15   mands, the god ... / the inhabited world. ..."
*Tr.: Roy Kotansky, following the edition of W. Brashear, "Vier Berliner Zaubertexte," *ZPE*
17 (1975) : 25–27. On the basis of the Zeus/Helios identification in l. 7, Brashear labels this
spell *Anrufung an Sarapis*, "an invocation to Sarapis." See also F. Maltomini, "Osservazioni
al testo di alcuni papiri magici greci, II," *Civiltà classica e cristiana* 1 (1980) : 375.

PGM CVI. 1–10

*"ADŌNAI ELO[AI SA]BAŌTH ABLANATHANAB[LA AKR]AMMACHAMARI ... SES-
ENGERBARPHARANGĒS AEĒIOYŌ IAŌ PHRĒ ... ĒAŌ IAŌ EAŌ ...

   1. There is space for a single letter here, perhaps *Ē*; see n. 2, below.
   2. After the *Ō*, there is one letter to make out. It is probably an omicron. The first nine letters, then,
probably contain a series of vowels, viz., AEŌĒ AEEŌŌ.
   3. The editor suggests that these letters may contain the Greek for "portal of Erebos" (reading ϑύριν
ἐρέβου). Erebos was the mythological place of nether darkness which formed a passage from Earth to
Hades.
   4. Supplying here an alpha before the final iota.
   1. Following the likely restoration of A. Henrichs.
   2. On this Aoth-*logos*, Brashear points the reader to *PGM* IV. 1376; Delatte and Derchain 416, 487;
Audollent, *Defixionum Tabellae*, no. 242. 9.
   3. BASYM, in Greek letters, corresponds to Aramaic *besum*, "in the name of": see Glossary, s.v. Thus
the text perhaps reads, "in the name of Isaac, [Abraham,] Jacob." In the lacuna, Brashear restores instead
"... Isaac [Sabaōth, Īaō], Jacob"; however, "Abraham" is another possible reading, as the three names
form a natural, formulaic grouping in magical literature. See M. Rist, "The God of Abraham, Isaac, and
Jacob: A Liturgical and Magical Formula," *JBL* 57 (1938) : 289–303.

AEĒIOYŌ   5
OURIĒL
MICHAĒL
GABRIĒL
SOURIĒL
RAPHAĒL

SEME-SILAM / AEĒIOY / Ō

SALAMABA ZZZ BAM IACHA

ABLANATHANABLA
ACHRAMMACHAMARI
SESENGHBPHARAGĒS
IAŌ / SABAŌTH
ŌRIPHER LOU.

Protect Touthous, whom
Sara bore, from every
shivering fit and fever:
tertian, quartian, quoti-
dian, daily, or every
other day [it occurs]
. . . ADŌNIAS, / ADŌNAEI,   10
protect in. . . ."

*Tr.: Roy Kotansky, following the edition of W. Brashear, *ZPE* 17 (1975): 27–30 (see note on previous papyrus).

PGM CVII. 1–19

*" 𐤉IOCHO – SIM ∕PHNOUĒ[1] PHTHONTHŌN 2B2–L–И˃Υ L'2 PERKMĒM[2] BIOU
BIOU BIBIOU[3]

˃ΥLΥL И–h⊥/h–Ȯ⊥Ɔ–CL–ᴧ7–cL–4–η–ηˊˊˌ∕B2–2h [4]   5
OCHERO⊬ NOURI[5] EPNEBAI[6] SERPŌT' MOUISRO[7] RINT'[8] MĒI MĒI[9] ĒI OU OUSIRI[10]
SERPHOUTH MOUISRO MĒI / MĒI. Quickly fetch here Tapias whom Demetria   10
bore, for Achillas whom Helene bore, by means of the soul of the one who died
prematurely, / BAKAXICHYCH,[11] by the one whom all things are entrusted to, EU-   15
LAMŌ;[12] fetch Tapias for Achillas, immediately, immediately; quickly, quickly."
*Tr.: Roy Kotansky, following the edition of Robert Daniel, "Two Love-Charms," *ZPE* 19
(1975): 255–64 (text two). Daniel provides copious notes and parallels to the *PGM*. Only
his most essential comments are noted below.

PGM CVIII. 1–12

*"THŌBARABAU TEUTHRAIAIAIAŌ BAKAŌPHLEN NOPH EPHOPHTHE AMOU AMIM
BAIN BAARA AALŌ B . . . NAARA AAAAAAA EEEEEEE ĒĒĒĒĒĒĒ / IIIIIII OOOOOOO   5
YYYYYYY ŌŌŌŌŌŌŌ, make fly through the air[1] the soul and the heart of Leontia
whom Ailia[2] bore in her womb, and don't allow her to eat or drink or to fall

1. PHNOU may be equated with the Coptic word *pnoun*, "the abyss." Otherwise it is the magical name for a god in *PGM* XII. 290 and is found in frequent combinations throughout the *PGM*.

2. PERKMEN, perhaps Coptic for "the Lord of darkness" or "house of darkness."

3. BIOU BIOU BIBIOU: BIOU is frequent in the *PGM* and is identical to the name of a decan. Cf. W. Gundel, "Dekane und Dekansternbilder," *Studien der Bibliothek Warburg* 19 (1936): 233–34.

4. In these lines there are thirty-six characters which correspond to the number of decans and their deities.

5. NOURI is Coptic for "vulture."

6. EPNEBAI may reflect the words *p nb by*, "the lord of souls," in *DMP* XXVIII, 1 (cf. Copt. *neb bai*).

7. For this Egyptian formula: lotus (*serphouth*)—lion (*moui*)—ram (*sro*), cf. *PGM* III. 659.

8. RINT' is Sahidic for "my name." Cf. *PGM* IV. 83–84.

9. MĒI MĒI (also in ll. 9–10) is Fayumic and Bohairic for "truth."

10. The god Osiris.

11. This name is to be equated with BAINCHŌŌŌCH: both names mean "spirit of darkness." See Glossary, s.v.

12. This popular name can be equated with "eternal" and has become the subject of some etymological speculation (see Daniel, "Two Love-Charms," 264, n. 17, for literature).

1. This verb, ἀεροπετέω, is used only in magical texts, as Daniel points out, pp. 249–50.

2. Reading Ailia instead of Elia.

10 asleep / until she comes to me, Dioskouros whom Thekla bore, immediately, immediately; quickly, quickly." |⎯⊦⎯

*Tr.: Roy Kotansky, following the edition of Robert Daniel, "Two Love-Charms," *ZPE* 19 (1975): 249–55 (text one).

PGM CIX. 1–8

*"As Hermes turns in his marrow[1] and this strip of papyrus becomes reality,[2] so

5   turn the brain[3] and the / heart[4] and search out[5] all the mind of her who is called Kalemera, immediately, immediately; quickly, quickly."

*Tr.: H. D. Betz, following the edition by Eric G. Turner, "The Marrow of Hermes," in *Images of Man in Ancient and Medieval Thought. Studia Gerardo Verbeke . . . dicata* (Louvain: Louvain University Press, 1976) 169–73. The love spell from Oxyrhynchus (ca. A.D. 300) presents very difficult problems, so that the translation by necessity remains tentative. See also the different readings and interpretations by J. Gwyn Griffiths, "Hermes and the Marrow in a Love-charm," *ZPE* 26 (1977): 287–88; Giuseppe Giangrande, "The Marrow of Hermes: A Papyrus Love-Spell," *Ancient Society* 9 (1978): 101–16; and P. Gorissen, "Once More the Love-Spell, Hermes and the Marrow," *ZPE* 37 (1980): 199–200.

PGM CX. 1–12

*. . . a voice comes to you in conversation. Lay out the stars on the board in their natural order,[1] with the exception of the sun[2] and the moon.[3] Make the sun[4]

5   gold, / the moon[5] silver, Kronos[6] of obsidian, Ares[7] of yellow-green onyx, Aphro-

10 dite[8] of lapis-lazuli streaked with gold, Hermes[9] / of turquoise; make Zeus[10] of a [dark blue] stone, but underneath of crystal. But the horoscope. . . .

*Tr.: Roy Kotansky, following the edition of Z. M. Packman, "Three Magical Texts from the Washington University Collection," *BASP* 13 (1976), no. 1: Astrological Text, 175–77 (plate). The text, constructed from two separate fragments, seems to contain instructions for a special type of astrological divination. The incomplete text at the beginning of the horoscope shows that the client participates in an auditory revelation of a god. This probably contains the end of the procedure section of the magical spell.

1. The phrase is unknown. Perhaps it is Hermes himself who "is turned around by the marrow," the marrow referring to a magical substance used in the ritual operation. In this case the verb is construed as passive, with "marrow" as the genitive of agent. This avoids the need to emend the word to the accusative case (so P. Gorissen), or to take the genitive as "locative" (so Turner), since this normally requires the dative case. [R.D.K.]

2. Perhaps the words are an interjected "commercial": "and this sheet really 'works.'" The πιττάκιον is the sheet or piece of papyrus on which the spell itself is written; see Turner, 172; Giangrande, 107, for parallels. [R.D.K.]

3. Cf. on this notion *PGM* IV. 1544–45.

4. Cf. the parallel in *PGM* XIc. 3. For another interpretation, see Giangrande, 109.

5. Thus Turner's translation. Gorissen takes ζητουν, "search out," to be a personal name.

1. Packman translates this more literally: "Let the stars be set upon the board where (they belong) by nature. . . ." The sense may suggest that the planets and stars are to be arranged in their acknowledged order in their sphere of orbit.

2. The term for "sun" is represented in the papyrus by the symbol ☼.

3. The term for "moon" is represented by the symbol ☾.

4. That is, Helios.

5. That is, Selene.

6. That is, the planet Saturn.

7. That is, the planet Mars.

8. That is, the planet Venus.

9. That is, the planet Mercury.

10. That is, the planet Jupiter.

PGM CXI. 1–15

*. . . in Egyptian, [Kneph;]¹ . . . in Greek; and the great sculptor . . . and after
forming two cows alike . . . and their sexes male and . . . / and after shaping an- 5
other . . . [make] its body that of a serpent which has [no tail], but from either end
[three-headed: on the right] human heads, [and on the left] geese heads, [and in
the middle heads of] / golden gazelles with solar disks matching the shapes of their 10
horns. [And after forming another] with its body, on the one hand . . . on the
other hand, its appearance that of a sea falcon . . . , in Egyptian . . . / slight inter- 15
pretations. . . .
*Tr.: Roy Kotansky, following the edition of Z. M. Packman, "Three Magical Texts from the
Washington University Collection," *BASP* 13 (1976) no. 2: Description of Magical Figures,
177–79 (plate).

PGM CXII. 1–5

* "SABAPSYRA	IOEL	
SEBAŌN	SBAŌTH."	
NAPSERNOUSOR	*[For] scorpion [sting]*.	
ANAX		
/ IRĒ		5

*Tr.: Roy Kotansky, following the edition of Z. M. Packman, "Three Magical Texts from the
Washington University Collection," *BASP* 13 (1976), no. 3: Amulet, 179–80 (plate). The
text is presumably a charm for scorpion sting.

PGM CXIII. 1–4

*". . . PENCHIRAASARA . . . DA, drive out¹ . . . and scorpion . . .   XAXAP. . . ."

*Tr.: Roy Kotansky, following the edition of P. J. Sijpesteijn, "Amulett gegen Skorpions-
stich," *ZPE* 22 (1976) : 108 (Taf. IIIb). This spell is similar to other amulets against scorpion
sting in the *PGM* (cf., e.g. *PGM* XXVIII a–c).

PGM CXIV. 1–14

*"[Protect] her, NN, O lord, [from all] evil acts [and from every] demonic visita-
tion [and] . . . of Hekate and from . . . / attack and [from every onslaught (?)] in 5
sleep . . . [from] mute daimons [and from every] epileptic fit [and from all] epilepsy / and . . . and. . . . 10
*Tr.: Roy Kotansky, following the revised edition of R. W. Daniel, "Some ΦΥΛΑΚΤΗΡΙΑ,"
ZPE 25 (1977) : 145–49 (text one). Daniel greatly improved the reading of the original edition in P. Proulx and J. O'Callaghan, *Studia Papyrologica* 13 (1974) : 83–88. Daniel also offers a tentative reconstruction of the lacunae in the text. The translation above reflects
Daniel's improved text, but not all of his tentative reconstructions. For further commentary
see F. Maltomini, "Osservazioni al testo di alcuni papiri magici greci, I," *Miscellanea Papyrologica, Papyrologica Florentina* 7 (Firenze: Gonnelli, 1980) 173–75.

1. Following the restoration suggested by R. Merkelbach.
    1. The imperative is in the plural, thus suggesting that the preceding text contained a list of magical
names.

PGM CXV. 1–7

*"PHĒG GĒ . . . BALOCHRA THAMRA ZARACHTHŌ, I conjure you all by the bitter compulsion: MASKELI MASKELŌ PHNOUKENTABAŌTH OREOBAZAGAR RHĒZICHTHŌN HIPPOCHTHŌN / PYRIPĒGANYX. Deliver Ammon from the fever and shivering fit that restrains him, immediately, immediately; quickly, quickly; today!"

*Tr.: Roy Kotansky, following the text of R. W. Daniel, "Some ΦΥΛΑΚΤΗΡΙΑ," *ZPE* 25 (1977): 153–54. The papyrus was first published with photographs and commentary by Z. Ritoók in *Antik Tanulmányok* 22 (1975): 30–43. Daniel's text offers some changes.

PGM CXVI. 1–17

*"IAIŌ ERBĒTH	IŌBRAK	IŌBRAK	IŌBRAK
IŌKABRA	ŌBRAK	ŌBRAK	ŌBRAK
ŌKABRA	BRAK	RAK	BRAK
ARBA	RAK	AB	RAK
ABA	AK	B	AK
BA	K		K."

"IAŌ IAKOUNBATT IŌ ERBĒTH IŌ BOLCHOSĒTH IŌ PAKERBĒTH IŌ PATATHNAX IŌ ERAPOMPS IŌ TANONO IŌ ERBĒTH IŌ ABRASAX IŌ PSAAPOPSI / IŌ PHTHEAPOPS IŌ ISIŌR IŌ PAKERBĒTH IŌ PAKERBIŌTH AMOUNAUEIEOUN PEITŌRE AU EN KTENOUATEI . . . KOX . . . OUS PSĒTAĒSEEBOLNOURTOU METHERENOUBTANOUN / TEB IMETHE . . . LENE EUINASMA, immediately, immediately; quickly, quickly."

*Tr.: H. D. Betz, following the edition and commentary of Rosario Pintaudi, "Invocazione a Seth-Typhon," *ZPE* 26 (1977): 245–48. Ll. 1–6 contain four "wing formations"; the rest seems to be an invocation using typical Seth-Typhon acclamations.

PGM CXVII

**Fr. 1* . . . [the elder?] . . . *Fr. 2* . . . the house [she?] leaves, [her] husband [forgetting] . . . to sleep most sweetly by me, [her waist] . . . until earth and heaven . . . *Fr. 4* . . . a cow . . . *Fr. 5* . . . with black, join together . . . into a new cup . . . *Fr. 6* . . . come to me . . . *Fr. 7* . . . and . . . in the middle of the night, the streets . . . OSIRIS ESIĒS, to meet . . . to pour out my fruits . . . *Fr. 8* . . . fulfill . . . *Fr. 9* . . . [what is prescribed below]: . . . ANOUBIS, ANOUBIS, I love her [NN] . . . *Fr. 10* . . . pluck two strands of her hair and [throw them] into a [new drinking vessel] . . . *Fr. 11* . . . her, possessed by your . . . *Fr. 12* . . . from . . . a white [thorn-apple tree] . . . speak the spell . . . *Fr. 13* . . . the Dioskouroi . . . the destroyer . . . *Fr. 14* . . . I conjure the gods in Hades . . . all, fetch her, [NN] . . . *Fr. 18* . . . of much knowledge . . . demand starry heaven . . . and the Eternal Mistress . . . *Fr. 19* . . . dreadful, everlasting [Hekate?], with grievous suffering, with . . . pains . . . *Fr. 21* . . . carry out [for me this perfect] spell . . . *Fr. 22* . . . AKRA . . . SO O . . . and . . . black . . . bring insomnia to her, NN . . . *Fr. 23* . . . [offer] to him as a drink . . . take it, for it is . . .

*Tr.: Roy Kotansky, following the edition of P. Fabrini and F. Maltomini, in A. Carlini et al., *Papiri Letterari Greci* (Pisa: Giardini, 1978) no. 34: P. Mon. Gr. Inv. 216: Formulario magico, 237–66. Although this text is comprised of twenty-three tiny fragments of which little sense can be made, its importance should not be underestimated, for it is one of a few magical papyri which antedates the Christian period. This, along with the so-called Philinna Papyrus (*PGM* XX), dates to the first century. Fragmentary as it is, one can detect that the papyrus contains portions of a love spell. Of special importance are the occasional Egyptian deities mentioned along with the Greek, thus showing that a syncretistic influence was already at work in the magic of this early period.

PGM CXVIII

P. Palau Rib. inv. 200 another "magical scroll" similar to those published by G. M. Parássoglou in *Studia Papyrologica* 13 (1974) (= *PGM* CIII a–c.). A description and photograph of the scroll, with no transcription of the text, was published by José O'Callaghan, "Rollo mágico (PPalau Rib. inv. 200)," *Studia Papyrologica* 17 (1978) : 85–87.

PGM CXIXa. 1–3

*"... fortune, I conjure. ..."

Love spell through touch: Take milk . . . 9 *echthei*, 12 *ealē*. . . .
*Tr.: Roy Kotansky, following the edition of R. Pintaudi, *Dai Papiri della Biblioteca Medicea Laurenziana* (PLaur. III), *Papyrologica Florentina* 5 (Firenze: Gonnelli, 1979) no. 57: "Frammenti di Manuale Magico (PL II/52)," 34–36. This papyrus contains fragments of approximately eight short spells. The opening line preserves the end of a conjuration of uncertain purpose; portions of a love spell follow.

PGM CXIXa. 4–6

Fetching charm: On an ostracon . . . : / "BOLSAK SAR . . . , the thoughts. . . ."   5
*Tr.: Roy Kotansky. On this magical papyrus, see the introductory note above. Since this tiny, fragmentary spell has preserved its title, it can be assumed the invocation is to be engraved on a potsherd with the aim of binding the thoughts (i.e. "brains") of a desired woman, as well as other parts of the human constitution.

PGM CXIXa. 7–11

Charm to subject: ". . . subject [to me] . . . CHR." Write . . . / an aphrodisiac (?).   10
*Tr.: Roy Kotansky. See the introductory note to *PGM* CXIXa. 1–3 for the bibliographical reference to this text. The fragmentary word translated "aphrodisiac" may introduce a new spell or may simply show that the spell to subject can work as an aphrodisiac as well.

PGM CXIXb. 1–5

*". . . A . . . EDĒS wounds . . . vain babbling, and also mingle. . . ."

[**For fever with shivering fits**:] Take an olive leaf and engrave: ". . . ." / [For   5
daily] and nightly fever. KELLIOTON. Take. . . .
*Tr.: Roy Kotansky. See the introductory note to *PGM* CXIXa. 1–3. This portion of the magical manual deals in part with a spell for fever. The invocation preceding it serves an unknown purpose. Furthermore, it is not clear whether another formula follows the charm for fever. The editor of the papyrus suggests that κάλλιστον (sc. φίλτρον), "an excellent philtre" could be read in the letters KELLIOTON.

PGM CXX. 1–13

*"cutting the uvula
utting the uvula
tting the uvula
ting the uvula
ing the uvula
ng the uvula
g the uvula
the uvula
he uvula
e uvula
uvula
vula
ula
la
a"

*Tr.: Roy Kotansky, following the edition of R. Pintaudi, *Dai Papiri della Biblioteca Medicea Laurenziana (PLaur. III)* (Firenze: Gonnelli, 1979) no. 58: Ὄνομα πτερυγοειδῶς (PL III/1442) 37–38 (Tav. LIII). This "winged" formation is made up of an adjective, στα-φυλότομος, attested in only one other place. According to the *Thesaurus Graecae Linguae,* cited by Pintaudi, the adjective means *uvam incidens,* "cutting the uvula." This term contains a play on words, as words with the same root can also refer to a bunch of grapes. It is no coincidence, then, that in magical literature winged formations such as that shown above were also referred to as grape-shapes (cf. *PGM* III. 70). The manner in which the formation is written allows one to read "cutting the uvula" down the left margin. Conceivably, this spell served as an amulet to heal its wearer from inflammation of the uvula. For a parallel, see the gemstone published by A. Sambon, *Le Musée* 6 (1909): 111.

PGM CXXI. 1–14

*. . . [cessation]:

column 1:	column 2:
death	rudeness
darkness	evil
mental illness	the evil eye
grief	debauchery
fear	slavery
illness	indecency
poverty	lamentation
disturbance	troublesomeness
	emptiness
	malignancy
	bitterness
	arrogance

*Tr.: Roy Kotansky, following the edition of Giovanni Geraci, "Un'*actio* magica contro af-flizioni fisiche e morali," *Aegyptus* 59 (1979): 63–72. This magical text has no real parallel in the corpus of magical literature. It appears to be an elaborate phylactery, listing a number of ailments both physical and psychological. The initial lines of the spell probably contained a plea that the vices listed in the two columns should cease or come to an end. The entire spell is enclosed in an ouroboros figure which has not been well preserved on the papyrus.

PGM CXXII. 1–55

*An excerpt of enchantments[1] from the holy book called Hermes,[2] found in He-liopolis in the innermost shrine of the temple,[3] written in Egyptian letters and translated into Greek. /

5   *Enchantment [spoken] three times over apples:*[4] "I shall throw apples, . . . and
[col. I, 5] thereby I shall provide this timely love spell for both mortal people and immortal
10   gods. I . . . , I threw the apple and I hit [her] with the apple. / Setting everything
[I, 10]   aside, may she fall madly in love with me; whether she takes it in her hand and
                eats . . . or holds it in her bosom, may she not stop loving me. O goddess born on
15   Cyprus,[5] / carry out this perfect charm. . . .

1. So according to Brashear's interpretation, p. 265.
2. That is, Hermes Trismegistos. Cf. *PGM* IV. 885–87.
3. This refers to the temple library.
4. Although reportedly coming from an Egyptian holy book, this love spell contains Greek magic. The importance of apples in declarations of love and in oracles is well known. See A. R. Littlewood, "The Symbolism of the Apple in Greek and Roman Literature," *HSCP* 72 (1967): 154–55, 157.
5. That is, Aphrodite; for commentary, see Brashear, 268–69.

"I have taken your . . . eye.[6] I, NN, have taken your soul.[7] I, NN, have drunk   [I, 15]
from your blood. I, NN, have used . . . I, NN, have devoured your liver.[8] I, NN,
have / [put on] your [skin]. I, NN, have done it.   20
                                                                                     [I, 20]

"The goddess[9] in heaven looked down upon him, and it happened to him according to every wish of his soul . . . NN says: From the day [and] from the hour I,
NN, [do this act] to you; you will love me, be fond of me, and value me . . . I
die. / O Lady, goddess, [Isis] . . . , carry out for me this perfect charm."   25
                                                                                     [I, 25]

Having[10] raised your hands toward the stars, let down . . . NN, and . . . and
black night; and standing [awake] and sleeplessness and . . . you shall use [these?]
before you see the sun. Take myrrh and chant and anoint your face:
"You are the myrrh with which Isis[11] was anointed / when she went to the   30
bosom of Osiris, her . . . brother, and gave him her favor on that day. Give me. . . ." [II, 5]
"Wake up him, NN, or her, NN, Mistress Isis, and carry out this perfect charm.
Hail,[12] Helios; hail you who rise; hail also to you, the gods who rise together with
him . . . / let rejoice . . . nor concerning a silver coin, but concerning him, NN, . . .   35
remain . . . I am running, but he is escaping me . . . to you . . . and having done the   [II, 10]
sacred [acts?] . . . at sunrise . . . neither . . . nor drink nor / lie down . . . nor . . . ,   40
but have me in . . . and anguished, until she [comes] to me, until . . . everlasting   [II, 15]
god . . . if she leaves [me] . . . I will bewitch you until she comes back to me and
goes . . . / [that] you bring him, NN, O Helios . . . the ever . . . day, him NN, . . .   45
a coin . . . ; / O goddess born on Cyprus,[13] carry out this perfect charm."   [II, 20]
                                                                                     50
                                                                                     [II, 25]

For headache:[14] "Osiris has a headache; Ammon has a headache at the temples of
his head; Esenephthys[15] has a headache all over her head. May Osiris' headache not
stop, may Ammon's headache at the temples of his head not stop, until / first he,   55
NN, stops everything. . . ."   [II, 30]
*Tr.: H. D. Betz, following the edition and commentary by W. Brashear, "Ein Berliner
Zauberpapyrus," *ZPE* 33 (1979): 261–78. The love spell is one of the oldest Greek magical
papyri; it was found in Abusir el Melek, Egypt (first c. A.D.). For further notes see F. Maltomini, "Osservazioni al testo di alcuni papiri magici greci, II," *Civiltà classica e cristiana* 1
(1980): 375–76.

6. Apparently, the lines refer to some sort of cannibalistic ceremony done for the purpose of erotic
magic. See Brashear, 269–71, who refers to *PGM* IV. 296–335, and A. Henrichs, *Die Phoinikika des
Lollianos, Fragmente eines neuen griechischen Romans, Papyrologische Texte und Abhandlungen* 14 (Bonn:
Habelt, 1972) 70, n. 77.
7. The term may be a euphemism for the sexual organs (see Glossary, s.v. "Soul"). See Brashear, 272.
8. The liver plays a special role in erotic magic. See Brashear, 272.
9. A reference to some mythical detail.
10. Apparently some kind of nocturnal ceremony is described. See Brashear, 273.
11. The second column contains Egyptian magic. The mythical love of Isis is imitated here; cf. *PGM*
XXXVI. 288–89 and Brashear, 274–75.
12. Apparently the beginning of a hymnic passage, addressed to Helios.
13. See n. 5 above.
14. A charm against headache, using a threat against the gods that they will not stop suffering head-
aches until they have healed the operator. See Brashear, 276, for parallels.
15. That is, Isis-Nephthys; cf. *PGM* XII. 234.

PGM CXXIII a–f

a.

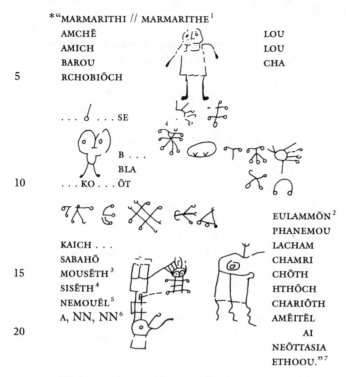

```
*"MARMARITHI // MARMARITHE¹
    AMCHĒ                                        LOU
    AMICH                                        LOU
    BAROU                                        CHA
5   RCHOBIŌCH

    . . . ƌ . . . SE

                B . . .
                BLA
10  . . . KO . . . ŌT



                                        EULAMMŌN²
                                        PHANEMOU
    KAICH . . .                         LACHAM
    SABAHŌ                              CHAMRI
15  MOUSĒTH³                            CHŌTH
    SISĒTH⁴                             HTHŌCH
    NEMOUĒL⁵                            CHARIŌTH
    A, NN, NN⁶                          AMĒITĒL
20                                          AI
                                        NEŌTTASIA
                                        ETHOOU."⁷
```

25   Write on tin:⁸ onion, rue, frankincense. ***Erōtylos***:⁹ / "Born of blood,¹⁰ shedding

1. A variation of the common magical name MARMARIŌTH, on which see K. Preisendanz, *PRE* 14 (1930):1881; Kropp, *Koptische Zaubertexte* IV sec. 3206; Hopfner, *OZ* I, sec. 746.

2. A form of the magical word EULAMŌ. For literature and additional occurrences of the term outside the *PGM*, consult Maltomini, 71–72, n. 11.

3. This name may be a conflation of the names "Moses" and "Seth." Alternatively, the name may be explained from Coptic and Demotic as "lion-Seth." See Maltomini, 72–73, n. 15.

4. Possibly Coptic for "Offspring of Seth"; see Maltomini, 73–74, n. 16.

5. An angelic name meaning "God has spoken." See Schwab, *Vocabulaire de l'Angélologie* 299. Cf. Nm 26:12.

6. In the papyrus we have ⇡ ⇡, the usual symbols for "so-and-so" (NN).

7. Perhaps Coptic *ethoou*, "evil," thus Maltomini, 75, n. 22.

8. The reference is probably to writing the words on a tin plate. Cf. *PGM* VII. 459, 462; *PGM* XCIV. 37.

9. This word also occurs in *PGM* XIII. 946; VII. 478. According to *LSJ*, this Doric term can mean the following: (1) "a darling, sweetheart"; (2) as an adjective, it refers to singing love songs; (3) a name of a small star; and (4) the name of a gem. In the *PGM*, both the context and the etymology suggest the term means "a love charm."

10. Reading αἱμοφυη, an apparent neologism in the *PGM*. Such formations of new words—usually epithets—abound in the magical papyri. Many of the new formations in the list that follows represent appropriate designations for Hekate and other chthonic deities. For parallels in each case, consult Maltomini, ad loc.

blood,[11] putting out roots,[12] androgynous,[13] manly,[14] / born with blood,[15] saffron- 30
dyed,[16] with golden arrows,[17] golden-haired,[18] like a white onion,[19] / MENOU- 35
LATH, CHARBATHA, STHŌMBAULĒ, ZANXMNA, CHŌNOUTHA, / MENOUBA, BELER- 40
THI, ZACHTHAĒR, CHALIOUBĒ

OUAMIRATH ... ⊗ ↲ ZAZEAS

BRIMŌ CHA-
URA ⊥ ⊕   45
ITPHIKASY
IOU."

For childbearing: "Come out of your tomb, Christ is calling you."[20] / [Place] a 50
potsherd on the right thigh. ***For sleep***: on a bay leaf [write]: "⸓THARA
THARŌ." ***For strangury***: "MŌGIB⸓THTHYS⸓" / ***For a shiver-*** 55
ing fit: on a piece of papyrus: "[A]BLANATHANAPAMBALANATHANATH ...
NATHANAMATHANATHANATHA ⸓ . ⸓ Raphaēl, EI ...
ŌI ☓ THNĒ," / Take a marble statuette, scratch with the right hand the right side of 60
a penis. Pound it on a table with wax. Take the wood from the heart of a plum tree,
the stock of a cabbage plant, chickpea; boil some garlic and give it as / a before- 65
dinner drink. Pellitory, pepper, grain, 23 parts kohl . . . bay leaf. Pound two pepper
grains and mix it with gum of "Hercules' woundwort."
For a victory: / [Wear] a tooth of a hyena, from the right side of the jaw . . . one of 70
the upper ones. . . .

11. Reading αἰμωχυη. Apparently a new formation from αἷμα, "blood" and χέω, "to pour out, shed." Related epithets having to do with blood and applying to Hekate are listed by Maltomini, 77, n. 26.

12. Reading perhaps ῥιζοποιε for ῥιζοπνε. The expression is problematic and the restoration very tentative; nevertheless the association of roots with both Selene and Hekate is attested. Consult the references in Maltomini, 78, n. 27.

13. Reading ἀνδρογύνη for ἀνδρωγενη (cf. the variant spelling of the Greek in *PGM* CXXIIIf., fr. A., 5). In *PGM* IV. 2610, Hekate is coupled with Hermes as an androgynous being.

14. The meaning of this unattested word ἀνδρως is at best very speculative; however, there is no question that the word originally formed a meaningful Greek epithet having to do with ἀνήρ, "man." For similar, anomalous formations, consult the occurrences in *PGM* as cited by Maltomini, 78, n. 29. In addition to his philological parallels, compare the term ἀνήνωρ, "unmanly."

15. The word αἰμογενής is now attested on a second-century inscription from Egypt, *SEG* 8. 374. Although LSJ, Supplement, s.v., p. 5, translates this "related by blood," Maltomini is correct in suggesting here "born of/with blood."

16. Reading κροκοβαφή for κροκοβανιη? [R.D.K.] Maltomini suggests perhaps κροκοφανη (unattested). Saffron is associated with Hekate in Orphic Hymn 1. 2; 71. 1, and elsewhere with Demeter and Persephone.

17. The word is attested in Tzetzes, *Alleg. Il.* XX. 226, p. 132, Matranga. A similar epithet is used of Hekate in Lydus, *De mens.* 3. 10.

18. An appropriate epithet of Hekate (-Selene), thus Maltomini, 79, n. 33.

19. Reading κρονν⟨ον⟩ λευκον.

20. Parallels adduced by Maltomini, 82–83, show that in Christian magic a *historiola* was used, according to which Elizabeth says to John the Baptist in her womb: "Come out, child, Christ is calling you. . . ." In our papyrus this *historiola* appears to have been confused with the account of Lazarus in the tomb, thus attesting the analogy of womb and tomb.

(pap. 2) *b.*

"KAICHABŌ, SABAHŌ, MOUSĒTH, SISĒTH, NEMOUĒL."

(Pap. 3) *c.*

5   *Fr. A:* "KAICHABO, SABAHŌ, MOUSĒTH, SISĒTH, NEMOUĒL, A, NN, NN . . ." *Fr. B*
". . . CHAR . . . AMĒI . . . NEŌT . . . ETHOO. . . ."

d. ". . . ATH . . . PHAĒL EL. . . ."

e.

"Born of blood, shedding blood, putting out roots, androgynous, manly, [born
with blood, saffron-dyed, with golden arrows]. . . . E . . . THCHARBATH, STHŌM-

5   BAULĒ,   ZANXMNA // CHŌNOUTHA // MENOUBA // BELERTHI // ZACHTHAĒR [//
CHALIOUBĒ]

f.

5   *Fr. A:* ". . . YBĒ . . . A . . . ROS. Born of blood, shedding blood, / putting out roots,
androgynous, ANTHROROCH,[21] born with blood, saffron-dyed, with gold arrows,
golden-haired, dog-faced baboon. . . ."

Fr. B.

────────────────────────────────

*Tr.: Roy Kotansky, following the edition and notes of Franco Maltomini, "I Papiri greci," in
G. Arrighetti et al., "Nuovi papiri magici in copto, greco e aramaico," *Studi Classici e Orientali* 29 (1979), section II, pp. 55–124. The six papyrus fragments translated here correspond to those numbered 1–6 consecutively by Maltomini. They have been grouped here
under the same Roman numeral because they represent duplications (with some variations)
of the same magical text. The text, which contains a series of peculiar and difficult epithets,
perserves portions of a magico-medical handbook. Unless otherwise stated, the notes that
follow are summarized from those of the editor. For a full discussion of each of the terms and
of the *voces magicae*, one should consult the edition of Maltomini.

21. Cf. n. 14. Something peculiar has occurred in the transmission of this epithet.

PGM CXXIV. 1–43

*ʹ·ΛᲒ𝔚𝖸𝟊⁎ʕʯ〉𝗭ΛⲞ CHAR ... OBBA being written, and the one throw into a public latrine, / the other bury in the house β⸗ʕʮᾗγʹⱵ THATHĒ THATHŌ.   5
Charm to inflict illness:[1] [Take] the blood of a weasel and write on a triangular potsherd and bury it in the house: ³𝘛⸓𝘒ℋ𝔛ʕΝ

THRAX TRAX BRAX. /

27 / and fill it with water, up
to the [shoulder] of the

33 [manikin]   only. / Crush
rhododendron plants with
some vinegar and sprinkle
the entrances to the tomb. /

35 Take a garland made from
the plant, and while pro-
nouncing the formula, at-
tach it to the tomb: "Principal angel of those below
the earth, BAROUCH, and
you, angel of many forms,
OLAMPTĒR; in this hour /

40 do not disobey me, but
send to me . . . without
fear, without harm, doing
my every. . . ."

Take unsmoked[2] beeswax   10
and make a little manikin.
Write the characters / on a   15
tiny piece of papyrus and
place it inside the beeswax.
Also write the three "ō's"
and the letters that follow,
on the head of the manikin,
and the bones of the victim
(?).[3] . . . / Prick the left   20
one[4] into the left eye of the
manikin and the right one[5]
into the right. Hold the
figure upside-down on its
head[6] / and put it into a   25
new pot. Leave the pot in
the dark

*Tr.: Roy Kotansky, following the edition of Franco Maltomini, in *Studi Classici e Orientali* 29 (1979), sec. II, pp. 94–112 (Pap. 7) (see previous papyrus, *PGM* CXXIII. a–f). The instructions call for the manufacturing of a waxen doll; for this phenomenon in magic, consult the literature cited by Maltomini; cf. *PGM* IV. 296ff.

PGM CXXV a–f

Papyri nos. 8–15 in Maltomini's edition in *Studi Classici e Orientali* 29 (1979): 113–20 (see *PGM* CXXIII a–f for full reference) contain texts too fragmentary to translate.

a. Papyrus no. 8 (Tav. XI) 113–16, dates to the fifth or sixth century and is made up of three fragments: Fragment A contains several legible *voces magicae*, viz.,

1. Reading κατακλιτικόν for κατακλητικόν. Cf. *PGM* VII. 430 for the same expression and *PGM* IV. 2076, 2442, 2450, 2497, 2624; LXIV. 1 for the use of the verb in this sense.

2. That is, presumably wax taken without smoking the bees. Cf. *PGM* IV. 2378, 2945 for a similar practice in reference to honey.

3. The text is hopelessly corrupt at this point and thus defies explanation. The text seems to contain a reference to the bones of a victim, thus we read σφάκτης (thus Maltomini) in the series of letters immediately following "bones."

4. The reference to "left one" and "right one" is not clear. Maltomini assumes the references are to "the left *part*" and "the right *part*" of the mannikin, respectively. That is, the magician is to prick the left part of the mannikin *up to* the left eye, and the same on the right. However, it is more likely on the basis of spells like *PGM* IV. 296–335 that "the left (one)" and "the right (one)" refer to left and right "needles" pricked into the matching eyes. The "left one" means a needle held in the left hand, the "right one" a needle held in the right. Cf. *PGM* IV. 2943–50 for a similar rite in which the eye of a magic doll is pricked.

5. See n. 4 above.

6. The text is unclear at this point. Literally, the text seems to direct the performer to hold the head of the mannikin "to the south." Judging from the description that follows, the mannikin is placed head-first into the pot, which is then filled up with water to cover its head.

SALAKALOU, KERKĒBI, and KAULYOUKAU. Fragment B contains only a handful of letters, whereas fragment C preserves an elaborate magical figure.

b. Papyrus no. 9 (Tav. XII) 116–17, contains nine lines of which only a few words can be positively identified: ALLELOUIA, SABAŌTH, and ADONAI. The other side of the papyrus preserves portions of an Aramaic magical text published by Marrassini in the same journal, p. 128.

c. Papyrus 10 (Tav. VIII) 117–18 dates to the fifth century and is made up of two tiny fragments which cannot be read. Fragment B contains portions of a Coptic formula.

d. Papyrus 11 (Tav. XII) 118, is made up of two fragments that are too small even to assign a date.

e. Papyrus 12 (Tav. XII) 119, is paleographically akin to Papyrus 6 (*PGM* CXXIII f.). Only the names ADONAI and SABAŌTH can be recognized.

f. Papyrus 13 (Tav. XI) 119–20, assigned to the end of the fifth century, also contains an Aramaic text on the other side (see Marrassini, pap. no. 3, p. 129). The text preserves portions of a formula which reads, "I conjure you by your holy name . . . BAROCH SĒMO. . . ."

PGM CXXVIa. 1–21

5   *". . . ATĒS . . . [sweet wine?] . . . / ATA . . . ASSA . . . NN [add the usual] . . . K
    . . . B . . . BRIAPS . . . [IŌ ERBĒTH IŌ] PAKERBĒTH IŌ BOLCH[OSĒTH BASDOUMA] /
10 OSESRŌ APOMPS P[ATATHNAX KOKKO]LOPTOLIN CH . . . K . . . [. . . IŌ THATHTHA]
    BRABO, without violence . . . [spell of Typhon] Seth [carrying] out the whole
    magic [procedure and] separate her, NN, from him, NN. ABERAMENTHŌ /
15 OUTHLERTHEXANAX [ETHRELTHYOŌTHNEMA]REBA, and say, 'Mustard, [you are
20 not Mustard,] but the eye . . . the inner parts of the bull of Apis'" / (add the usual)
    . . . "from Osiris . . . and separate. . . ."
    *Tr.: H. D. Betz, following the edition by Franco Maltomini, "Frammento di formulario magico (PL III/472)," in R. Pintaudi, ed., *Dai Papiri della Biblioteca Medicea Laurenziana (P. Laur. IV)*, *Papyrologica Florentina* vol. 12 (Firenze: Gonnelli, 1983) 46–53. Cf. the earlier edition by Rosario Pintaudi, "PL III/472: Frammento magico," *ZPE* 38 (1980): 261–64, and the new readings by F. Maltomini, "Osservazioni al testo di alcuni papiri magici greci, (III.)," *Studi classici e orientali* 32 (1982): 239–40. The poorly preserved text appears to be a spell for separation. L. 20 may begin another such spell, as it is separated by a paragraph mark. For parallel texts and commentary, see Maltomini's notes.

PGM CXXVIb. 1–17

5   *". . . O . . . [add the usual] . . . but the sight . . . the damage of ADŌNAI . . . / of
    the great god . . . [Mustard], in order to separate . . . enmity until [death] . . . [in
10 order that] you might enter into the . . . them as the . . . / having heard about . . .
15 of Osiris ANE . . . and frightful and . . . having burnt . . . / and you, Mustard
    . . . / [the] house of her, NN . . . passageway. . . .
    *Tr.: H. D. Betz, following the edition by Franco Maltomini (see note on the previous papyrus). This piece also appears to be from a spell for separation.

PGM CXXVII. 1–12

To make one bend down and not get up: Anoint the loins with the brain of an electric eel.

To get a certain [lover] at the baths: Rub a tick from a dead dog on the loins. /
5   To "play" with a woman: Anoint the phallus with the juice of the deadly carrot.

To cause a fight [1] **at a banquet**: Throw a dog-bitten stone into the middle.
To make wine sour: Throw burning / pebbles into it.   10

In order "to screw" many times: Drink beforehand seed of celery and of rocket.
*Tr.: Roy Kotansky, following the edition of G. M. Parássoglou, "Greek Papyri from Roman Egypt," *Hellenica* 27 (1974) : 251–53, no. 9: "Magico-Medical Prescriptions." Note also F. Maltomini, "Osservazioni al testo di alcuni papiri magici greci, II," *Civiltà classica e christiana* 1 (1980) : 374.

PGM CXXVIII. 1–11
A phylactery for fever:

"SARICH	"Of Jesus Christ, son of IAŌ (?),
AORKACH	quickly, quickly,
/ ROUGACH	heal!
CHIOSNĒCH	John,
KOCH."	/ Son,
	Life."

*Tr.: Roy Kotansky, following the edition of F. Maltomini, "Due papiri magici inediti," *Studi classici e orientali* 31 (1981) : 111–14: *P. Heid. G. 1386*.

PGM CXXIX. 1–7
*". . . [concerning] the certain matter . . . [a tin?] lamella from a certain . . . and tie it up in a cloth . . . / of a black wolf from . . . and . . . it in a little case . . . again   5
and again it will be of service to you.
*Tr.: Roy Kotansky, following the edition of F. Maltomini, "Due papiri magici inediti," *Studi classici e orientali* 31 (1981) : 115–17: *P. Berol. 21260*.

PGM CXXX
*[IA]RBATH AGRAMMĒ PHIBLŌ CHŌĒMEŌ
[A E]E ĒĒĒ IIII OOOOO YYYYYY ŌŌŌŌŌŌ[Ō]
Lord gods, heal Helene, whom [NN] bore, from every
illness and every fit of shivering [fever].
/ daily, daylong, tertian, quartan.   5
IARBATH AGRAMMĒ PHIBLŌ CHNĒMEŌ

	AEĒIOYŌŌYOIĒEA	
	EĒIOYŌŌYOIĒE	
	ĒIOYŌŌYOIĒ	✳️𝔻
YYY	IOYŌŌYOI	10
	OYŌŌYO	
	YŌŌY	YYYYY
	ŌŌ	
	[traces]	

*Tr.: H. D. Betz, following the edition and commentary by R. W. Daniel, "P. Mich. inv. 6666: Magic," *ZPE* 50 (1983) : 147–54. For a parallel to this spell, see *PGM* XVIII b; for the stellar and lunar symbols, see the parallels in Delatte and Derchain, *Les Intailles*, nos. 296, 301.

PDM Suppl. 1–6
[Another spell for] sending a dream: [. . . I] am the youth without . . . scarab of
. . . soul of the four faces (?) and I . . . you . . . complete. . . .
/ *Formula*: On a leaf . . . , and you put a . . . it, and you write . . . embalming   5
house.

---

1. Reading, with Maltomini (see introductory note above), μά[χ]ην for μά[ν]ην.

*Tr.: Janet H. Johnson, following the edition and translation in *Enchoria* 7 (1977):66, col.
1/1–6. Section titles are indicated in the Demotic text only when they are written in red
letters (see the Introduction to the Demotic Magical Papyri).

PDM Suppl. 7–18

*[*Another spell* for] sending a dream: ". . . Come to me in your [form] . . . you

10   . . . before I have gone to the . . . which is therein / . . . without a skin of . . . they
took it . . . your town . . . and I know . . . [in] your secret form . . . power (?) . . .
while it . . . is bearing witness what I did . . . noble mummy . . . face of a lion

15   which . . . is your name, I having done / . . . you . . . so-and-so guard his hand."
      Formula: . . . [body] of a white donkey . . . cow's fat . . . again; "great-of-love"
plant, tear apart . . . gather . . . skin of a donkey. . . . It is very good.

*Tr.: Janet H. Johnson, following the edition and translation in *Enchoria* 7 (1977):66, col.
1/7–18.

PDM Suppl. 19–27

20   *[*Another*] spell for sending a dream: ". . . anger / . . . great . . . of the sea . . .
Nun[1] at night . . . anger of the one who is in the water . . . the mountains. . . . Let
the . . . speak to me . . . under me . . . in them. If not doing it . . . enemy of the
praised one . . . me in the water at [night], in the day at [any time] . . . him."

25   *Formula*: / . . . reed leaf and you write an image of . . . the ear . . . drowned,
and you should recite these writings . . . *four* times . . . [wreath] to it and you say
the thing [in the ear (?). . . . It is] very good.

*Tr.: Janet H. Johnson, following the edition and translation in *Enchoria* 7 (1977):66, col.
1/19–27.

PDM Suppl. 28–40

*[*Another spell* for] sending a dream: *Formula*: You bring . . . and you do it . . . in

30[1]   an oil of lotus[2] and [you] . . . wick / . . . and you protect it and you . . . [write?]
these names in . . . falcon (?) with (?) its claw (?) and you write . . . of the . . . wick
on (?) a new lamp of . . . of . . . which is above and you bring a new brick . . . the

35 [5]   [lamp] . . . leave the lizard before the lamp . . . , / these again which you should
write on the strip of the wick [of] the [lamp . . .].
      Formula: ". . . BAH[E (?)] P[A]IRE PSIR PAH[. . .]BPS [. . .] A BAT LA BATL-
[A]ATE,[3] come [to] me tonight and tell [me] an answer to [everything] about
[which] I am praying (another [manuscript] says: . . . it goes in the place under the
head of . . .) [stand?][4] before him in the form of his god who is great in his heart

40 [10]   and make him dream a dream [about such-and-such] / a thing which I shall tell him
today."
      Formula: *7 times.*

*Tr.: Janet H. Johnson, following the edition and translation in *Enchoria* 7 (1977):67,
col. 1/28–30; col. 2/1–10.

PDM Suppl. 40–60

40 [10]   *Another spell* for sending a dream: *Formula*: "Listen to my voice, O noble
mummy-spirit of a man of the necropolis who assumes [all his] forms; come to me
and do for me such-and-such a thing today because I am calling you in your (?)

1. Primeval waters.
2. Scented with lotus.
3. Written *ʿte*, "limb."
4. See *PDM Suppl.* 120.

name . . . in Abydos who rests in the house of the official[5] whose name is 'this [one] who rests in truth' (another [manuscript] says, 'who . . . in truth'). Nun[6] . . . oath (?), 'great image of Nun' is your true name; / SHLBI NYH[R] is your true name, truly; Nun, NEO soul of Ha[. . .] 'very great one of Nun' is your true [name]. Soul of souls (another papyrus says, 'soul of a bull [?]') . . . of Nun is your true name. Soul of souls SHLBI NYHR is your true name. NEO soul of H[A . . .] Nun NEO great one of Nun [is your] true [name]. May you listen to the voice . . . in all his forms [of a spirit, noble mummy] of a man of the necropolis because [I] am [calling to you] / in your name of S . . . ISIRA SIRATHMA, saying, 'I am . . . land.' O SYAL[. . . †NEBOY]TOSYALTH SIRATHMA saying, 'I am . . . S.' O SY[. . . †NEBOYTOS]YALTH, let the [soul of the] noble spirit awaken to me; let him go [to the place] in which such-and-such is; let him greet (?) . . . have him do for me such-and-such a [thing] about [which I am] asking. . . . "

45 [15]

50 [20]

Its preparation:[7] . . . / these names with blood of . . . reed leaf; you put it . . . of a dead man; you leave . . . of clay under the head . . . on (?) it; and you recite them to him again. You do . . . lunar month and it is left in a place. . . . If stubbornness occurs, you should [put] the hoof . . . of a male donkey and myrrh . . . on it and you should beat on the ground until it stops. . . . If you [will act against a man / you should . . .] of a male. If you will act against a woman, you should [. . . of a] woman.

55 [25]

60 [1]

*Tr.: Janet H. Johnson, following the edition and translation in *Enchoria* 7 (1977):67–68, col. 2/10–29; col. 3/1. Words preceded by † are written in the text in Demotic with Old Coptic glosses inserted above.

PDM Suppl. 60–101

**Another spell* for sending a dream: *Formula*: "[O] noble divine spirit [whose soul is in heaven] whose body is in the underworld, whose mummy [is among the living,] O good messenger of Osiris, O great follower of 'he who is in his bed,' the god . . . him (?). O guardian of the one who is in Alkhah,[8] I am the soul of . . . the one who is in his [two sound] eyes, who protected his limbs in the soundness daily . . . / I am the offspring of khepri[9] [whose] name is the divine [son?] of Amoun . . . scarab . . . body of the noble mummy in the sarcophagus which rests in the underworld . . . true, of the house of embalming. . . . I am the bull of the . . . ; I am the lion; I am the lion; I am . . . ; I am the soul of Pre, the breast of Shu; I am the egg of the snake; [I am] the dung ball of the beetle.[10] I am the lord of the Amhet-underworld;[11] I am the divine fluid / of the living . . . ; I am the noble head which is in Abydos.[12] Come to me at night, quickly, quickly; hurry [hurry, O] soul

65 [6]

70 [11]

5. Perhaps one of the liked-named chapels listed in H. Gauthier, *Dictionnaire des noms géographiques contenus dans les textes hiéroglyphiques*, vol. IV (Le Caire: Imprimerie de l'Institut français d'archéologie orientale, 1927), 127–28.

6. Nun here and throughout this spell is the primeval waters.

7. Literally, "gathering of things"; the same term is used in *PDM* xii as a label for the directions.

8. See *PGM* IV. 124 and n.; cf. Griffith and Thompson, *The Leyden Papyrus* 21, n. to I. 3.

9. A sun god in the shape of the scarab beetle, whose dung ball represents the sun rolled across the sky. See *PGM* IV. 943 and n.

10. See n. 9 above.

11. I.e., the "upper" part of the underworld in contrast to *tph.t*, the "lower" part. See E. Chassinat, *Le mystère d'Osiris au mois de Khoiak*, vol. II (Le Caire: Imprimerie de l'Institut français d'archéologie orientale, 1968), par. 33, especially p. 622.

12. Osiris; see *PDM* xii. 628. On the dismemberment and burial of Osiris, see J. G. Griffiths, *The Origins of Osiris and His Cult, Studies in the History of Religions* (*Supplement to Numen*) 40 (Leiden: Brill, 1980), 24–25, 27, 51–52.

without the body, dead one without the noble mummy, the noble mummy without the netherworld, [the] netherworld without the funerary bed, without the sarcophagus without . . . shrine (?) . . . born of Horus . . . Seth acts . . . against Apophis, the slaughter (?) against the evil one [13] again. The brazier is in your hand . . .[14]

75 [16] morning bark / [at?] dawn, the evening bark greets heaven and earth with (?) a great fire. Woe, woe . . . until you send to him, NN, whom she, NN, bore, and you send his heart after NN . . . thing . . . at night, in the daytime, at any time, every day, quickly, quickly, hurry, hurry . . . I [will?] say them and I [will? . . .] specification (?) of saying them." *Formula: 7 times.*

80 [21] ***Its preparation:***[15] . . . kill it. You should bring it at the lunar month; / [you should] wash it in cow's [milk] . . . ; you [should] anoint it with oil of lotus[16] . . . of the leaf . . . reed; you should put [them?] at the seven(?) openings of the head and and bind them [with] linen . . . made by the hand of . . . bind them to its head; you should put its head . . . before the sun at dawn in the lunar month . . . to yourself barley and grain; you should leave them . . . you should put water of the divine lake

85 [26] . . . after them for 7 days until they grow; / [you should] bring them up; you should dry them until the 15th of the month; you [should] pound them with myrrh, green eyepaint, [black] eyepaint (?), *qs-ꜥnḫ* stone,[17] "live-thereby" plant, mustard . . . 7 reed leaves which are above.

[col. 4] Afterwards, [you should put] a scarab into [fat?] of a bull; you should put [it?] in a vessel of copper which is full of cow's [milk]. . . . until it . . . ; you should bring it up; you should put the . . . to the head of the . . . ; you should put blood of your

90 [4] left thigh and your [right] thigh / on them; you should . . . the time; you should [shape them] into a mummy of the foremost of the westerners[18] which amounts to 7 fingers [in length]; you should embalm it with myrrh, with ointment [and a covering of] byssus. Afterwards you should [sprinkle] pure sand; you should make a layer of sand under it in your . . . ; you should set the image on the layer of sand; you should leave the scarab on the body of the . . . after the embalming (it) which you did first with myrrh, with ointment and a covering of byssus itself (?); you should write the things which you desire on a new papyrus with carob tree (?) /

95 [9] water; you should leave it before the image; you should cause the head which is on it to bend down; you should put a bandage of 4 [colors] on it, blue, red, white, black, on the head; you should leave it in a hidden place; you should put frankincense (?), [†]barley, a great recipe to the brazier before it; you should offer to it bread, beer, and milk, in its midst; you should have blood fall from you on the brazier; you

100 [14] should put a piece of a red lizard / before it; you should recite these writings to it up to 7 times at night while you are in a [hidden] place which is clean; and you should make . . . settle (?)[19] before it. It is very good.

*Tr.: Janet H. Johnson, following the edition and translation in *Enchoria* 7 (1977): 68–70, col. 3/1–27; col. 4/1–15. The word preceded by [†] is written in the text in Demotic with Old Coptic inserted above.

13. Identical with *nk* of Erman and Grapow, *Wörterbuch* II, 205, 14–15, as suggested by Mr. Mark Smith.

14. The section left untranslated is glossed *KN* in old Coptic.

15. See n. 7 above.

16. Scented with lotus.

17. See *PDM* xiv. 98 and n.

18. An epithet of Osiris.

19. Literally, "lie down."

PDM Suppl. 101–16

Another spell for sending a dream: *Formula*: "O Anubis, the high one of heaven,   101 [15]
go to the underworld! Let the head of Osiris stop being far from him.[20] Give praise,
love, and respect to NN before NN. Let him do everything which he will write for
him, entirely. Move him! Give your iron staff / which is in your hand to the spirit!   105[19]
. . . Let him go to NN, whom NN bore. Let him stand before the image of the god
who is great in his heart until he brings him to the road which NN is in, he seeking
after him. And may you send a breathing spirit to NN so that he may stand before
[him] in the image of the god who is great in his heart, and may you say, 'Give every
good . . . thing to NN. . . .'"

Hear everything which he will say to you, entirely, while the crocodile of Isis, the
great goddess, / is therein. [Let?] it be commanded before the gods to happen or   110 [24]
you will delay because of it: "Is steadfastness [of] heart against me what you will
do, so that you scorn (?) the blood of Osiris the moon, Thoth,[21] at night at midmonth?"

Its preparation:[22] On a new papyrus: you should draw an image of Anubis with
blood of a black dog on it; you should write these writings under it; you should put
it to the mouth of black dog of the embalming house; you should make great offerings before it; you should put frankincense on the brazier before him; / you should   115 [29]
do it as a libation of milk of a black cow or a spirit whose face . . . ; and you should
put its recitation in its mouth. [It is] very good.

*Tr.: Janet H. Johnson, following the edition and translation in *Enchoria* 7 (1977): 70–71;
col. 4/15–30.

PDM Suppl. 117–30

Another form for sending a dream: *Formula*: "O praised one, call to heaven!
Speak to the underworld; Let Osiris stop sleeping while his head is far from him[23]
until a forceful spirit which does not sleep at night is sent / so that he stand above   120 [4]
NN in the form of the god who is great in his heart, so that he say to him, 'Arise
and do such-and-such a command of NN! Do all that which he will desire!' Come
to me, [O] divine spirit whom Anubis sent to NN, saying, 'Do the every command
which NN will desire!' Is not doing it what you will do, O noble spirit? Your soul
will not be allowed to rise up to heaven on day 25 of the fourth month of Inundation to dawn of day 26, while the excellent spirits are awake."

Formula: / On a jackal of clean clay which is lying down, its body moistened   125 [9]
with milk and fluid of a jackal of the embalming house with a . . .[24] on its foot. You
should write your words on a new papyrus; you should put it in the jackal's mouth;
and you should leave the jackal on a copper lamp which a brazier is heating. You
should recite these writings to it at night; you should stamp / on the ground with   130 [14]
your foot.

*Tr.: Janet H. Johnson, following the edition and translation in *Enchoria* 7 (1977): 71, col.
5/1–14.

20. See n. 12 above.

21. For the association Osiris-moon-Thoth, see J. G. Griffiths, "Osiris and the Moon in Iconogra-
phy," *JEA* 62 (1976): 153–59, although this Demotic evidence shows that the ibis in the hieroglyphic
examples is not just a determinative, as he thought (noted by Dr. Mark Smith).

22. See n. 7 above.

23. See n. 12 above.

24. Perhaps "sound-eye" of Horus.

PDM Suppl. 130–38

130 [14] *A "god's arrival"[25] of Osiris: "O Isis, O Nephthys, O noble soul of Osiris Wennefer, come to me! I am your beloved son, Horus. O gods who are in heaven, O gods who are in the earth, O gods who are in the primeval waters, O gods who are in the south, O gods who are in the north, O gods who are in the west, O gods who are in the east, come to me tonight! Teach me about such and such a thing /
135 [19] about which I am asking; quickly, quickly; hurry, hurry."

Formula: On a phoenix written with myrrh water and juniper water. Put a pellet (?) of gum on your right hand; recite these writings to it in the evening while your hand is stretched out to the moon, while you are going to sleep; and leave your hand before you. (It is) very good. 4 times.

*Tr.: Janet H. Johnson, following the edition and translation in *Enchoria* 7 (1977): 71–72, col. 5/15–22.

PDM Suppl. 138–49

*A spell for ———.[26] *Formula*: "The copper is bent down. The *neshmet* bark[27] will
140 [24] not stop sinking. The great / river draws blood. Isis is ill. [Neph]thys. . . . The copper will not stop bending. The *neshmet* bark will not stop sinking. The great river will not stop drawing blood. Isis will not stop being sick. Nephthys will not stop. . . . The copper is bent toward the one who is (?) in the sun bark. Re[28] is bent toward him while Amun is bent after him until sleep is taken from NN, whom NN bore, at night and care is given by day . . . until they [make] him do the thing which NN desires from him."

145 [2] *Formula*: A / vessel of copper [in] which an image [of] Osiris is drawn with human blood; you should bend [it] down before a lamp with an [image] of Anubis drawn on the wick with blood of a black dog; you should put cedar oil in it out of a new vessel, it being established on a brick standing on its (?) . . . ; you should recite these writings to it up to 4 times. (It is) very good. There is not its like . . . in her (?) hand. . . .

*Tr.: Janet H. Johnson, following the edition and translation in *Enchoria* 7 (1977): 72, col. 5/22–28; col. 6/1–6.

PDM Suppl. 149–62

150 [7] *A "god's arrival"[29] of Thoth according to what is outside,[30] also, *saying / Formula*: "I call to you, O Thoth, the hearing-ear,[31] who listens to everything. I call to you in your names which are great, which are divine: ʿALIPS THABLIPS STSILIPS ⸵GAGARPAOTHAR THANASIMA QHAH ⸵ORTHŌMENKH-ROŌN ⸵BALSA ʿALABAKHABEL.' Awaken to me, O lord of truth! Tell me an answer in
155 [12] truth to the "god's arrival" / concerning such-and-such a thing, in truth, without falsehood therein, so that I may awaken and find it (out)."

Its preparations:[32] A new lamp whose wick is of byssus cloth which is very clean; you should fill it with genuine oil; you should burn (it); you should write your command on a new papyrus; you should put it under the lamp; you should put a

25. See *PDM* xiv. 93–114.
26. Erased.
27. Sacred bark of Osiris.
28. The sun god, more commonly written Prē.
29. See n. 25 above.
30. On the other side of the papyrus?
31. I.e., who listens to the petitions of the average man.
32. See n. 7 above.

lobe of "great-of-love" plant under the lamp's mouth; and you should recite these
names above to it 8 times. / It comes to you.   160 [17]

Here is the ink with which you should write your command on the bookroll:
"Great-of-love" plant, a leaf of olive tree; you should cook them, make them into
myrrh ink and write with it.

*Tr.: Janet H. Johnson, following the edition and translation in *Enchoria* 7 (1977): 72–73,
col. 6/1–19. Words preceded by ˙ are written in the text in Demotic with Old Coptic glosses
inserted above.

PDM Suppl. 162–68

Another spell for finding your house of life. Formula: "Open to me! I am the
noble ibis; I am the ape of Edfu;[33] I am the great male, the scarab; I am the guardian of the great body; I am the snake of the 4 gods / who were with Isis while she   165 [22]
was searching for the good [one].[34] SHAPL is [my] name as Sothis.[35] The Ethiopian
is [my] name. Osiris the bull of magic is [my] name. The divine Ra-Shu is my
name, I going to all the gods in order to cause that I find my house in which I shall
live."

Formula: On an ibis written with black ink on the left hand of a man when he
sees that house of life.

*Tr.: Janet H. Johnson, following the edition and translation in *Enchoria* 7 (1977): 73, col.
6/19–25.

PDM Suppl. 168–84

* A spell for reciting a document which is. . . . It is a "god's arrival"[36] of Iymhotep
to whom the tenth belong also.

Formula: "Awaken! / Awaken in the underworld, Osiris Wennefer, l p h,[37]   170 [27]
Iymhotep the great, son of Ptah! . . . I am [. . . is] my name; I gather a box [. . . the
sound-] eye is [my] name (?) . . . ; the moon, Thoth . . . [Iymhotep the great], the
son of [Ptah . . .], excellent mother, fashioner of the underworld, go forth. . . .
They will not stand in / their box . . . [moisten ?] their box. You should awaken   175 [5]
before Iymhotep the great, son of [Ptah . . .] son, daughter, that I might live, and
you should tell [me] an answer [to] the thing which is on . . . bookroll . . . every
voice. Come to me, Thoth the great, the lord of Hermopolis . . . him. Give watch
to the head for [the] day."

Formula: write . . . on (?) it [with] your hand with / myrrh ink; likewise under   180 [10]
. . . lick it; you should open your mouth to the ground in a cry, saying, ". . . the
sound-eye; the sound-eye is what I ate." You should open your mouth to it in order
to lick it. Awaken at dawn; you should say: "Horus is my name; I am Horus, the
triumphant." . . .

. . . *day* on which *you will do the "god's arrival"* while the moon is in Leo, Sagittarius, Aquarius, or Virgo.

*Tr.: Janet H. Johnson, following the edition and translation in *Enchoria* 7 (1977): 73–74,
col. 6/25–27; col. 7/1–14.

PDM Suppl. 185–208

*"Face . . . which is at rest . . . except you also; my magical speech. I will take the   185 [1]

33. Presumably Thoth.
34. Osiris.
35. The star Sirius, by whose helical rising the beginning of the year is marked.
36. See n. 25 above.
37. "Life, prosperity, health."

. . . Ō MITHRA A . . . BARSA . . . THŌMI, the great one who is pure, the one who [grows . . .] I putting them in your hand, NN, whom NN bore. [I cast] anger against you in the head (?), NĒ[. . . stand]ing (?) without listening to your mes-
190 [6] sengers, saying . . . them in [the] hand saying . . . concerning these things, / standing [without] listening to my prayer, my magical speech (?) . . . it."

Its preparations:[38] . . . draw . . . of a crocodile . . . of a snake . . . make your hand stand (?) on . . . which belongs to you (?). . . .

Formula: TERETA TABE KR . . . N [ĒN?]Ē . . . (another [manuscript] says N[?] ELATS . . . BATSY . . .) ˈYO YAO SABATK M . . . hand."

195 [11] Formula: ". . . O NĒNĒBR . . . / ——————————————————

dog. The one who is in bandages removes bandages; the one who is above . . . saying, 'I am Anubis, the . . . of the underworld . . . , Isis, the great goddess, Osiris, the one who is in your hand, the lord of the gods . . . against me in the . . . the dog . . . the . . . dog, the red dog, the red dog . . . every. . . . You should . . . at night. Here is the . . . of your tongue in the. . . . I am Anubis, the master of secrets.
200 [16] . . . You should . . . / to me at night, during the day. [I] will give you the greetings of my mouth . . . I am Anubis the master of secrets. . . . Formula: 4 times . . . worm (?) saying "I am Isis . . . ," saying, "I am Osiris . . . saying, "I am . . . I am the lord who came before the ruler . . . wick. . . . I . . . you will stand, you will . . . , while he will go (?) [to? Horus?] the son of Isis, the [son of Osiris] . . . of this
205 [21] . . . will do it to a young bird . . . will do it to a young bird . . . / saying . . . of the harem, son of the harem, ... 7 times . . . heart. Be deaf, head! Come . . . ! Come . . . head of. . . . Open (your) mouth to me for I am Isis . . . , I am Osiris, I am Harsiese. . . ." 2 palm trees. . . .

*Tr.: Janet H. Johnson, following the edition and translation in *Enchoria* 7 (1977): 74–75, verso, ll. 1–24. Words preceded by ˈ are written in the text in Demotic with Old Coptic glosses inserted above.

38. See n. 7 above.

Errata

p. 161 at PGM XII.217 read:
"I invoke and beseech the consecration, O gods of the heavens, O gods under the earth, O gods circling in the middle region, three suns, Anoch, Mane, Barchych, who daily come forth in part from one womb."

p. 184 at PGM XIII.439 read:
"ready.[89] After killing the rooster, throw in one by one also the two others and the dove, getting things ready."

Glossary

The glossary provides explanations for some of the more difficult technical terms and names occurring in the *PGM*. Bibliographical data have been added for further study. More common terminology and names have not been explained since they can be found in easily available dictionaries.

ABERAMEN **formula**: The abbreviated formula stands for the long palindrome ABERA-MENTHŌOUTHLERTHEXANAXETHRELTHUOŌTHENEMAREBA, a magical name occurring several times in the *PGM* (see I. 294; II. 125–26; III. 67–68, 116–17; IV. 181; V. 180; XIV. 25; CXXVIa. 13–15, etc.). In it the name of the god Thoth can be read, although no meaningful decipherment of the word has been put forward. See K. Preisendanz, "Miszellen zu den Zauberpapyri, 3," *WSt* 41 (1919): 11–12; M. Tardieu, "Aberamenthō," in *Studies in Gnosticism and Hellenistic Religions, Presented to G. Quispel on the Occasion of His 65th Birthday*, ed. R. van den Broek and M. J. Vermaseren, *EPRO* 91 (Leiden: Brill, 1981) 412–18.

ABLANATHANALBA: This palindrome, perhaps the most common in magic literature, often occurs in company with SESENGENBARPHARANGĒS. Usually invoked for beneficent results, this magical name has not been adequately explained although it has been suggested that the name contains Hebrew.

ABRASAX: This popular deity in magic (also spelled ABRAXAS) is identified with a variety of other names of gods and was explained by *gematria* (assigning the numerical value to the letters of the name) as the magic number 365 (see *PGM* IV. 331–32; VIII. 49, 611; XIII. 156, 466, etc.). Accordingly the deity is recognized as a solar god and is pictured on amulets as a snake-footed creature (the so-called *anguipede*), armored, and with the head of a cock. See Bonner, *SMA* 162–63; Delatte and Derchain, *Les intailles* 24–42; Barb, "Abrasax-Studien," *Hommages à W. Deonna, Collection Latomus* 28 (1957): 67–86; C. Colpe, "Geister (Dämonen)," *RAC* 9 (1974): 618–19; Marcel Le Glay, "Abrasax," *Lexicon Iconographicum Mythologiae Classicae*, vol. I/2 (Zürich and Munich: Artemis, 1981) 2–7, pls. 1–63.

ADŌNAI: An important angelic figure in gnosticism and in magic. The name originally came from the Old Testament designation "my Lord," although this meaning had been long lost to the practitioners of the Roman Empire. See J. Michl, "Engelnamen," *RAC* 5 (1965): 202. For the variant angel forms Adonael, Adonail, Adoniel, Adonaiel, see E. Peterson, "Engel- und Dämonennamen. Nomina Barbara," *RhM* 75 (1926): 394.

ADONAIOS: Adonaios (an alternative reading of Adonai; note the Greek termination) is regarded in *PGM* as a name of the deity rather than as an epithet meaning "Lord" (cf. *PGM* I. 305). The Jewish origin, however, is still recognized (see *PGM* XII. 264). See J. Michl, *RAC* 5 (1965): 203.

Agathos Daimon: "The good genius" was originally an epithet of a god invoked at Greek banquets. In the *PGM* the name has become a designation for a god—one, however, who can be identified with a number of different deities. See Hopfner, *OZ* II, sec. 264, 294–95; R. Ganschinietz, "Agathodaimon," *PRE.S* 3 (1918): 37–59; Nilsson, *GGR* II, 213ff.; Colpe, *RAC* 9 (1974): 619–20; W. Fauth, "Agathos Daimon," *KP* 1 (1979): 121–22.

Aion: The god Aion, whose name signifies "long period of time," "eon," "eternity," plays an important role in the *PGM*. For the complicated history of the god, see A. J. Festugière, *La révélation d'Hermès Trismégiste*, vol. 4 (Paris: Les belles lettres, [3]1954) 182–99; W. Bousset,

"Der Gott Aion," in *Religionsgeschichtliche Studien* 192–230; Fauth, *KP* 1 (1979) : 185–88; A. I. Baumgarten, *The Phoenician History of Philo of Byblos*, *EPRO* 89 (Leiden: Brill, 1981) : 146–48; Marcel Le Glay, "Aion," *Lexicon Iconographicum Mythologiae Classicae* vol. I/2 (Zürich and Munich: Artemis, 1981) 405.

AKRAMMACHAMAREI: This magical name, with variant spellings, occurs frequently in beneficent magical incantations in company with ABLANATHANALBA and SESENGENBARPHARANGĒS. For a possible explanation of the name from Hebrew, see G. Scholem, *Jewish Gnosticism, Merkabah Mysticism, and Talmudic Tradition* (New York: The Jewish Theological Seminary of America, [2]1965) 94–100.

Aktiophi(s): Hopfner has suggested that this name is an epithet of Selene, goddess of the moon, a name which occurs elsewhere in *PGM* (see IV. 2473, 2484, 2601, 2664, 2749, 2913; VII. 317, 984; XVI. 23).

Ammon/Parammon: Hermes Parammon was honored as an Olympian god alongside Zeus Ammon and Hera Ammonia. The epithet Parammon probably means "he next to Ammon."

Amon (Amoun): The Egyptian god Amon. See Bonnet, *RÄRG* 31–37, s.v. "Amun"; E. Otto, "Amun," *LdÄ* 1 (1975) : 237–48.

Anoch (Anog, anok): These letters, occurring often at the beginning of an invocation, correspond to the Egyptian *ink* (Coptic *anok*), "I am." See S. Sauneron, "Le Monde du Magicien Egyptien," *Le Monde du Sorcier* (Paris 1966) 36–39.

Anouth: Name of Osiris (see VII. 238, 243, 247; VIII. 83, 98–99, 102).

Anubis: Anubis is the jackal god of mummification, the son of Osiris and Nephthys. On Anubis as key holder and guard (*PGM* IV. 1465), see S. Morenz, "Anubis mit dem Schlüssel," *Religion und Geschichte des alten Ägypten* (Köln: Bohlau, 1975) 510–20; J.-C. Grenier, *Anubis alexandrin et romain*, *EPRO* 57 (Leiden: Brill, 1977); Jean Leclant, "Anubis," *Lexicon Iconographicum Mythologiae Classicae*, vol. I/2 (Zürich and Munich: Artemis, 1981) 862–73 and plates.

Aphrodite Ourania: "Heavenly Aphrodite," whose city is Aphroditopolis (Dendera), refers to Hathor; see Bleeker, *Hathor and Thoth* 46; Bonnet, *RÄRG* 277–82, s.v. "Hathor."

Apollonius of Tyana: This famous first-century philosopher/magician is the subject of an extant biography by Philostratus. The attribution of a spell to him at *PGM* XIa. 1 is unique in ancient magical literature. For a survey of the problems and bibliography, consult E. L. Bowie, "Apollonius of Tyana: Tradition and Reality," *ANRW* II. 16. 2 (1978) 1652–99, esp. 1686.

Apophis (Aphyphis): The "unseen serpent" (see *PGM* IV. 190–91; cf. *PGM* III. 87) is Apophis, who is slain daily by Seth/Typhon in the barge of Ra. See E. Hornung and A. Badawy, "Apophis, " *LdÄ* 1 (1975) : 350–52; Bonnet, *RÄRG* 51–53, s.v. "Apophis."

Archenthechtha (Harchentechtha): This is the Egyptian god Har-Khenty-Khet; cf. *PGM* III. 170. See Bonnet, *RÄRG* 131–33, s.v. "Chentechtai"; U. Rössler-Köhler, "Horus-Chentechtai," *LdÄ* 3 (1980) : 27–33. [R.K.R.]

Arsenophre: The Egyptian god Arsenouphis (note also *PGM* II. 117; IV. 1629; XII. 183; XIXa. 7). See Bonnet, *RÄRG* 54–55, s.v. "Arsnuphis"; E. Winter, "Arsenuphis," *LdÄ* 1 (1975) : 424–25. [R.K.R.]

Arsentechtha (Harsentechtha): Perhaps the Egyptian name can be read Harsennechtha, "Horus, child of the strong one." [J.B.]

Arsentephtha: The name is probably Egyptian, "Horus, child of Ptah." [J.B.]

Artemis: In the *PGM* the goddess Artemis is identical with Selene, Hekate, and Persephone (see also IV. 2523, 2720–21, 2816ff.; LXXVIII. 11–12, with a drawing of Artemis Multimammaea). The invocations to Artemis, however, do contain archaic elements of her original cult. See T. Hopfner, "Hekate-Selene-Artemis und Verwandte in den griechischen Zauberpapyri und auf den Fluchtafeln," *Pisciculi, Festschrift F. J. Dölger* (Münster: Aschendorff, 1939) 125–45.

Assistant Daimon (paredros): Hellenistic magic knows of a special type of daimon called *paredros* ("assistant" or "attendant spirit"). The name refers to a deity who has been summoned as a servant to carry out any number of specified magical tasks. Cf. also *PGM* IV.

1348, 1841, 1851 (with *parastatēs*), 2083, 2109, 2145 (note); VII. 884; XII. 14ff. and surrounding contexts. See M. Eliade, *Shamanism: Archaic Techniques of Ecstasy*, Bollingen Series 76 (Princeton: Princeton University Press, 1964) 88–95; Hopfner, *OZ* I, secs. 1ff.; C. Colpe, "Geister (*Dämonen*)," *RAC* 10 (1974): 621ff.; C. Zintzen, "Paredros (*paredros*)," *KP* 4 (1972): 510–11.

Astrapsouchos: According to Diogenes Laertius, *Prooem.* 2, Astrampsychos was the name of one or several magicians; see E. Riess, "Astrampsychos," *PRE* 2 (1896): 179–80.

athor: See **Hathor**.

BAINCHŌŌŌCH: This formula, which invokes the god whose name corresponds to "spirit (soul) of darkness" (*b3 n kky*), occurs regularly in magical papyri and on curse tablets. [R.K.R.] See Bonner, *SMA* 26, 146; Bousset, *Religionsgeschichtliche Studien* 224 and n. 23.

Balsames: This angelic name served originally as the name of a Phoenician sun god, but in *PGM* IV. 1019 the god plays the role of a light divinity from heaven. Cf. XII. 494. See A. I. Baumgarten, *The Phoenician History of Philo of Byblos*, *EPRO* 89 (Leiden: Brill, 1981) 149–51, 185–86.

Basym: This magical name may have originally come from the Aramaic words meaning, "In the name of. . . ." For the magician, however, the word serves as a magical name. See G. Alon, *Jews, Judaism, and the Classical World* (Jerusalem: Magnes Press, 1977) 235–51.

Baubo: Baubo may have originally come as an independent deity from Asia Minor, where Hekate also came from; she then entered into the circle of Demeter and the mysteries of Eleusis. See W. Fauth, *KP* 1, s.v. "Baubo."

Bear constellation: The identification of the constellation of the Bear with Artemis occurs at *PGM* VII. 687. The Great Bear was believed to be Callisto, Artemis' fellow huntress, who was transformed into a constellation. Callisto was a manifestation of Artemis herself, who played an important role as a she-bear, especially at Brauronia. See also *PGM* IV. 1302; VII. 862; XII. 190; XIIb. 26; LXXII. See W. Sale, "The Temple Legends of the Arkteia," *RhM* 118 (1975): 265–84; L. Kahl, "L'Artemis de Brauron. Rites et mystères," *Antike Kunst* (1977): 86–98: W. Fauth, "Arktos in den griechischen Zauberpapyri, *ZPE* 57 (1984): 93–99.

Bes (Besa, Besas): Ancient Egyptian religion knew of an entire class of so-called Bes-demons (in Greek, Besas), distinguished by their dwarf-sized ugliness, who served as protectors of sleep and childbirth. In Hellenistic Egypt, Bes became a pantheistic deity, and in this form he appears in *PGM* VII. 222–49 and VIII. 64–110 (see also LXXXVIII: his plant, IV. 807). His role as an oracle giver was popular at Abydos (Ammianus Marcellinus 19. 12). In *PGM* the god was identified also with the Headless One (see n. on *PGM* II. 11). On Bes, see Bonnet, *RÄRG* 101–9; H. Altenmüller, *LdÄ* 1 (1975): 720–24, with bibliography.

Biaiothanatos Daimon: The *biaiothanatoi*, those who died violent deaths, were unable to enter the underworld because their time on earth had not been completed. After death, they lingered as evil spirits and were subject to magical compulsion. See J. H. Waszink, "Biothanati," *RAC* 2 (1954): 391–92.

Breathing stone: The magnet. Magnetism fascinated ancient philosophers and scientists, who explained the phenomenon in a variety of ways. Already Thales explained it in magical terms when he stated that "life" (*psychē*) is in a magnet. Magnetic stones, not surprisingly, played a great role in the magic of all periods. See A. Barb, "Lapis Adamas," *Hommages à Marcel Rénard*, I (Bruxelles: Latomus, 1969) 67ff.

Brimo: For this epithet of Artemis of Pherai in Thessaly, see *PGM* IV. 2270, 2291, 2611, 2964; VII. 692; LXX. 20, where the epithet is attributed to Hekate, Selene, Persephone. Etymologically, she is the "snorting" and "angry" and therefore "terrible" goddess of the netherworld; cf. the command in *PGM* IV. 2247; Lucian, *Necyom.* 20. See O. Kern, "Brimo," *PRE* 3 (1887): 853–54.

Chnouph (Chnoubis): The lion-headed serpent was popular in magic and is often found pictured on amulets. The daimon is a syncretistic combination of the Egyptian creator god Chnoum, the serpent Kneph, and the star *Knm*. In the *PGM* the name occurs mostly in *voces magicae*, especially in the Harpon-Knouphi formula (see, e.g., *PGM* III. 435–36, 560–63;

IV. 2433; VII. 1023–25; XXXVI. 219–20; *DMP* 16, 6–9). For the amulets, see Bonner, *SMA* 54–60; Delatte and Derchain, *Les intailles* 54–73; for references, see Bonnet, *RÄRG* 135–40, s.v. "Chnum"; E. Otto, "Chnum," *LdÄ* 1 (1975): 950–54; Colpe, *RAC* 9 (1974): 619.

Daimon, pl. daimons: In the *PGM*, as often in Greek literature, this term is used of deities and lesser spirits whose influential control is sought. In the New Testament, the word is used of an evil spirit, "demon," a sense not generally used in the *PGM*.

Decans: The Decans are the thirty-six deities each of whom presides over ten degrees of the zodiac. See in general, Gundel, *Dekane und Dekansternbilder*; cf. also G. J. Turner, "Mathematics and Astronomy," in J. R. Harris, ed., *The Legacy of Egypt* (Oxford: Oxford University Press, ²1971) 46–53; O. Neugebauer and R. A. Parker, *Egyptian Astronomical Texts*, I (Providence and London: Brown University Press, 1960) 95–121. [R.K.R.]

Demokritos: Strangely, the philosopher of Abdera (fifth century B.C.) was thought in antiquity to have been involved in magic. See E. Wellmann, "Demokritos (6)," *PRE* 5 (1903): 135–40; I. Hammer-Jensen, *PRE.S* 4 (1924): 219–23; H. Steckle, *PRE.S* 12 (1970): 191–223, esp. 193–94, 199–200. See also **Ostanes**.

EI LANCHYCH formula: For this magical formula, see *PGM* III. 131ff.; IV. 1625, 1630 (with corrupt or variant spellings). **EI** is perhaps Coptic for "house." [R.K.R.]

Eloaios: Eloaios occurs in *PGM* in various forms (*Eloe, Elouein, Elouai*) as a name for the Jewish god (see *PGM* I. 311; IV. 1577; VII. 564; XXXVI. 42). In Gnosticism he is one of the light-aeons and is described as having a donkey's face. See J. Michl, *RAC* 5 (1965) 212, no. 73: Eloaios.

ERBETH formula: The formula "IŌ ERBĒTH, IŌ PAKERBĒTH, IŌ BOLCHOSĒTH, IŌ APOMPS" occurs quite often in magical texts, especially in malicious invocations. See Hopfner, *OZ* II, secs. 142–43.

Erebos: An old Greek expression for the dark underworld, the place of the dead. Sometimes in literature it describes a place for the impious only, other times for the good before they are admitted to the Elysian fields. See O. Waser, "Erebos," *PRE* 6 (1907): 403–4.

Ereschigal: This name of the Babylonian underworld goddess is regularly associated with the Greek Hekate. The deity already occurs in the lead curse tablets of the fourth century B.C.

Erotylos: A writer of Orphica (see *PGM* XIII. 945) by this name is not otherwise known but may be the person mentioned by Zosimus in Bertholet and Ruelle, *Collection des anciens alchimistes grecques* II (1888) 144, 7. See Kern, *Orph. Fr.* p. 71, no. 235; idem, "Erotylos," *PRE.S* 4 (1924): 386. For the possible Greek meaning of the word, consult LSJ s.v.; cf. also *PGM* VII. 478; CXXIIIa. 24 and comments by F. Maltomini, *Studi classici e orientali* 29 (1979): 76–77.

Esies: Esies (Egyptian *ḥsy*, "praised") is an epithet of the sacred dead often applied to Osiris who was drowned and restored to life. See S. Eitrem, "Tertullian *de Bapt. 5*. Sanctified by Drowning," *ClR* 38 (1924): 69; A. Hermann, "Ertrinken/Ertränken," *RAC* 6 (1966): 370–409; C. Strauss, *LdÄ* 2 (1977): 17–19.

Eulamo: For literature and a possible interpretation of this magical name, see H. C. Youtie and C. Bonner, "Two Curse Tablets from Beisan," *TAPA* 68 (1937): 62; cf. *PGM* III. 57; VII. 401; IX. 8; XVI. 18.

Faïence: Faïence is a blue-green earthenware material popularly used in ancient Egypt for jewelry and other objects.

Good Daimon. See **Agathos Daimon**.

Hapi and Mnevis: The Apis (Hapi) and Mnevis bulls were incarnations of Ptah, Osiris, and Ra, respectively. See Bonnet, *RÄRG* 46–51, s.v. "Apis"; 468–470, s.v. "Mnevis."

Harpocrates: Harpokrates ("Horus the child") typically is portrayed with a finger of his right hand to his mouth, and he also may hold a crook and flail in his left hand. Harpokrates is the son of Isis and Osiris and is identified with the rising sun. See Bonnet, *RÄRG* 273–75, s.v. "Harpokrates"; D. Meek, "Harpokrates," *LdÄ* 2 (1977): 1003–11.

Harpon-Knouphi formula: This is Horus Knephis. On "Knephis" (*Km-3t.f*) as the

Agathos Daimon, see *LdÄ* I, 94; II. 1011–12. For this as Horus Khnum (and on the formula in general), see P. Pedrizet, "BRINTATĒNŌPHRIS: 1' un des noms magiques du dieu Chnoum," *Mélanges Maspero, II: Orient grec, romain et byzantin* 137–44; G. M. El-Khachab, "Some Gem Amulets Depicting Harpocrates," *JEA* 57 (1971): 132–33; D. Meeks, "Harponknuphi," *LdÄ* 2 (1977): 1011–12. [R.K.R.]

Harsamosi: According to W. W. Schmidt, *GGA* 193 (1931): 452, the name is Egyptian *Hrsmsw*, "Horus the Firstborn." See also *PGM* II. 155; XI. 91–92; XIII. 626; cf. I. 240–41. See D. Jankuhn, "Horsemsu," *LdÄ* 3 (1980): 13.

Hathor: The Egyptian goddess of love; see Bleeker, *Hathor and Thoth* 22–105; F. Daumas, "Hathor," *LdÄ* 2 (1977): 1024–33.

Headless One (Greek *Akephalos*): The Headless God is one of the most peculiar deities of the *PGM*. His origin seems to be in the older Egyptian religion, but he became very popular in Hellenistic Egypt, where he could be identified with Osiris (as in *PGM* II. 98–117) and Besas (as in *PGM* VII. 222–49; VIII. 64–110). Headless deities are also known outside Egypt. Plutarch tells about the headless Molos in Crete (*Def. orac.* 417E), Pausanias of the headless Triton in the temple of Dionysos at Tanagra (9. 20. 5); see A. Delatte, "Etudes sur la magie grecque V," *BCH* 38 (1914): 189–249; K. Preisendanz, "Akephalos," *RAC* 1 (1950): 211–16; K. Abel, "Akephalos," *PRE.S* 12 (1970): 9–14, with bibliography. For depictions of the god, see Preisendanz, *PGM* vol. I, plate I, 2; Bonner, *SMA* 58, 110, 164–66, 178, 243; Delatte and Derchain, *Les intailles* 42–54.

Helios: The Greek word for the sun (Helios) can stand for the celestial body or for the deity representative of that body. In the *PGM*, Helios is usually transcribed from Greek instead of translated as "sun," unless that term seems completely devoid of the sense of a deity.

Helios-Osiris: Although this link is possible through the fusion with Sarapis, for the older link of Osiris and Re, see A. Piankoff, *The Litany of Re* (New York: Bollingen, 1964) 19–21.

Hephaistos: The important connection of Hephaistos, the Greek god of the hearth and of fire, with magic is reflected a few times in *PGM* (see VII. 379; XII. 177, 417, 439). Since Herodotus, Hephaistos was the Greek interpretation of Ptah. See M. Delcourt, *Hephaistos ou la légende du magicien* (Paris: Les belles lettres, 1957).

Hermopolis: Hermopolis is "the city of Hermes," the cult center of Thoth in upper Egypt, the modern Ashmunein; cf. *PGM* III. 664; 670. See Bonnet, *RÄRG* 293–95, s.v. "Hermopolis."

Hesies: See Esies.

Horus: The great Egyptian god, son of Osiris and Isis. See Bonnet, *RÄRG* 307–15, s.v. "Horus"; W. Schenkel, "Horus," *LdÄ* 3 (1980): 14–25.

Iabas (**Iabo, Iabai, Iapos**): This is apparently the Samaritan enunciation of the tetragrammaton YHWH (Yahweh), elsewhere rendered *Iabe* or *Iabai*; cf. *PGM* V. 102; XIc. 1; XII. 4 and S. Lowy, *The Principles of Samaritan Bible Exegesis* (Leiden: Brill, 1977) 273–74 and passim. See also IAŌ.

IAEŌBAPHRENEMOUN formula: This magical formula (often abbreviated) is intended to read as the long palindrome IAEŌBAPHRENEMOUNOTHILARIKRIPHIAEYEAIPIRKIRALITHONUOMENERPHABŌEAI; see *PGM* I. 140, 195; III. 60–61 (var.), 77, 268, etc.

IAŌ: Iaō, originally derived from the name of the Hebrew god YHWH, became an important deity in magical literature. See J. Michl, *RAC* 5 (1965): 215, no. 102; R. Ganschinietz, "IAŌ," *PRE* 9 (1914): 698–721. In addition to being attested in the Nag Hammadi Library (see Robinson, *The Nag Hammadi Library in English*, index), Iaō is also found at Qumran, 4Q Lev[b] LXX; cf. H. Stegemann, "Religionsgeschichtliche Erwägungen zu den Gottesbezeichnungen in den Qumrantexten," in M. Delcor, ed., *Qumrân, sa piété, sa théologie et son milieu* (Gembloux: Duculot, 1978) 195–217.

IARBATHA formula: A common magical name, which, when spelled out fully and with allowance for variant spellings, reads IARBATHACHRAMNĒPHIBAŌCHNĒMEŌ (see *PGM* I. 142, 195; III. 472, 535; XII. 94–95). PHIBAŌCHNĒMEŌ may be equivalent to the Egyptian *p3 ḥib ꜥ3 Ḥnm ꜥ3*, "the great lamb, Khnum the great." [R.K.R.]

Ieu (**Jeu**): The scribe Jeu is mentioned only in *PGM* V. 97 (cf. also l. 141) in *PGM*, but the name is known in Gnostic literature. Elsewhere in *PGM* the name occurs rather frequently as a god or magical name. See C. Schmidt, ed., and V. MacDermot, trans., *The Books of Jeu and the Untitled Text in the Bruce Codex*, *NHSt* 9 (Leiden: Brill, 1978).

Isis band: Cloth or material taken from the dresses of statues of the gods, especially of Isis, was considered magically potent. Isis is a widow of Osiris and thus identified with the color black. See *PGM* I. 59; VII. 227, 231; VIII. 67; see Griffiths, Plutarch's *De Iside et Osiride* 90, 451; Hopfner, *OZ* I, sec. 678. [R.K.R.]

Jacob: The patriarch Jacob named at *PGM* XXIb. 1, together with Abraham and Isaac in XIII. 817, XXV. 14, occurs frequently in the context of magic. See Ginzberg, *The Legends of the Jews* I, 349–58; M. Rist, "The God of Abraham, Isaac, and Jacob: A Liturgical and Magical Formula," *JBL* 57 (1938): 289–303.

Khnum (Chnum): The Egyptian ram god; see *PGM* I. 27–28; IV. 327. See Bonnet, *RÄRG* 135–40, s.v. "Chnum"; E. Otto, "Chnum," *LdÄ* 1 (1975): 950–54.

Kmeph: The Egyptian serpent god Kmeph or Kneph occurs in *PGM* IV. 1705; III. 142; IV. 2094; VIII col. 17 with picture. See Bonnet, *RÄRG* 378–79, s.v. "Kneph."

Kommes: The name Kommes is still unexplained (see also II. 122; cf. "Kommi" in XVI. 63; Kom-Re in *DMP* xii, xv). See Gundel, *Dekane und Dekansternbilder* 233–34.

Lamella, pl. lamellae: From the Latin for a thin, metal plate. The word is used to translate a number of Greek terms for tablets of thin gold, silver, iron, or lead. The lamellae are usually engraved and worn as amulets or talismans (phylacteries). If lead is described, the tablets usually intend malicious or harmful magic.

Lamps, not painted red: In the *PGM* we find frequent references to the use of lamps with no red coloring (see I. 277, 293; II. 57; IV. 2372, 3191; VII. 542, 594; VIII. 87; XII. 27, 131; LXII. 1). Dipping the clay into red ocher (*miltos*) or painting it on before the firing, as customarily done, would give the lamp a reddish color. In lamp divination, however, the red color had to be avoided because of its association with Seth-Typhon. See W. Kroll, "Minium," *PRE* 15 (1932): 1848–54; R. Ganszyniec, "*Lychnomanteia*," *PRE* 13 (1927): 2115–19. Cf. also *DMP* col. V, 4, pp. 44–45 (with note), where the lamp is said to be white, without the application of red lead (*prš*). On the significance of red, cf. G. Posener, "Les signes noirs dans les rubriques," *JEA* 35 (1949): 77–81. [R.K.R.]

MASKELLI-MASKELLŌ formula: This well-known formula, written fully as MASKELLI MASKELLŌ PHNOUKENTABAŌ OREOBAZAGRA RHĒXICHTHŌN HIPPOCHTHŌN PYRIPĒGANYX, occurs often in magical literature (note *PGM* VII. 302; IX. 10; XXXVI. 342–46; *DMP* xv. 2; *Pistis Sophia* IV, chap. 140 [McDermot 365]). On the meaning see Hopfner, *OZ* I, sec. 747; Preisendanz, "Maskelli Maskellō," *PRE* 14 (1930): 2120. Within this formula, among other things, occur four words which may be old Greek epithets: *Oreobazagra*, perhaps an epithet of Hekate or of the moon goddess (thus *LSJ*, but of uncertain meaning); *Rhēzichthōn*, a word which may be translated "bursting forth from the earth" (thus *LSJ*; see Cook, *Zeus*, *III* 4–5 for parallels and discussion. See also Bonner, *SMA* 170; *Orph. H.* 52. 9); *Hippochthōn* (meaning unexplained, thus *LSJ*: Audollent, *Tab. Def.* 38129; cf. Hermann, "Erdbeben," *RAC* 5 [1965]: 1082ff.); *Pyripēganyx*, perhaps "lord of the fount of fire" (*LSJ* s.v.; Audollent, *Defixionum Tabellae* 38. 29).

Material, magical: "Material" (*ousia*; see *PGM* I. 99, IV. 2336, etc.) is the magical substance such as hair, thread from clothing, etc., which is often necessary to make sympathetic magic effective. See K. Preisendanz, "Miszellen zu den Zauberpapyri, I," *WSt* 40 (1918): 1–8; Hopfner, *OZ* I, secs. 667–77.

Meliouchos: The meaning of this epithet is still unexplained. In the magical texts it can be attributed to various deities. See *PGM* III. 45–46, 99; V. 4; VI. 33; Audollent, *Defixionum Tabellae* 22. 32; 38. 12; see P. E. Göbel, "Meliuchos," *PRE* 15 (1931): 554–55.

Mene: This is an epithet of the moon goddess, Selene; see *Hymn. Hom.* 32. 1; *Hymn. Orph.* 9. 3, 4; *PGM* IV. 2264, 2546, 2815; VII. 758.

Mithras: The Persian god is mentioned only a few times in *PGM* (note III. 100, 462; IV. 482) and each time as being identical with Helios or with Zeus-Helios-Sarapis (see *PGM* V. 4). See Nilsson, *GGR* II, 668–72; Dieterich, *Mithrasliturgie* 67ff.; M. J. Vermaseren, "Mithras in der Römerzeit," in M. J. Vermaseren, ed., *Die orientalischen Religionen in Römerreich*, *EPRO* 93 (Leiden: Brill, 1981) 96–120, with bibliography.

Moses: In Greco-Roman antiquity, Moses was widely recognized as a great magician. See Gager, *Moses in Greco-Roman Paganism* 134–61.

Myrrh(ed) ink: This ingredient used for writing on papyrus occurs throughout the *PGM*. Cf. the note on the Demotic equivalent *r′ w ḥl* in *DMP* v. 5.

Nature (Greek *Physis*): *Physis* appears from early times as a deified conception of nature's powers of creation and creativity. As such, Physis has an important role in most philosophical schools, especially where the concept of *kata physin* ("in accordance with nature") seems at times to rise almost to the level of a religious credo (so in Seneca, *De Prov.* IV. 15 and often). Physis appears often elsewhere as a goddess: cf., for example, *Hymn. Orph.* 10 which is addressed to Physis. Much of its language closely resembles that in the *PGM* hymns to the moon (to whom *Hymn. Orph.* 9 is addressed). In *PGM* Physis the goddess appears elsewhere at IV. 2883, 2917; see also IV. 939 and n. The surprising thing is that she does not appear more often in *PGM*. See K. Kerényi, "Die Göttin Natur," *Eranos-Jahrbuch* 14 (1947): 39–86.

NEBOUTOSOUALĒTH: The name occurs frequently in magical literature and is often connected with Aktiophis and Ereschigal. In *PGM* the triad is often attributed to deities of the underworld, especially Hekate. The name Nebutosoualēth may be derived from the Babylonian god Nebo, but the origin is not clear. See K. Preisendanz, "Nebutosualeth," *PRE* 16 (1935): 2158–60; Bonner, *SMA* 30, 197–98.

Nephotes: The name appears to be a hellenized form of the Egyptian Nefer-hotep (*Nfr-ḥtp*), but it is uncertain to whom it refers. Originally, it was the name of an Egyptian deity. See A. Rusch, "Nephotes" *PRE* 16 (1935): 2493–94; cf. Bonnet, *RÄRG* 518–19, s.v. "Nephotes." [R.K.R.]

(On)nophris: An epithet of Osiris, "The Beautiful Being." For the common proper name Onnophris, see Preisigke, *Namenbuch* 242. Cf. *PGM* IV. 1078; IV. 128. [R.K.R.]

Oserapis: The occurrence of the old name Oserapis (cf. *PGM* XL. 1) for Serapis on the fourth century B.C. curse found in the Serapeum of Memphis is important for the origins of this cult. See on this issue Nilsson, *GGR* II, 156. Cf. also the note on *PGM* XIXa. 6.

Osoronnophris: This is equivalent to the Egyptian *Wsir Wn-nfr*, "Osiris the Beautiful Being"; cf. *PGM* V. 101 and IV. 1078. [R.K.R.]

Ostanes (Osthanes): The historical Ostanes was a theologian at the court of Xerxes, with whom he went to Greece. He is said to have taught Demokritos the philosopher (who is also mentioned in *PGM* IV. 2006; VII. 167, 795; XII. 122, 351) and to have introduced magic to Greece (Pliny *NH* 30. 8). Later, many different writings were transmitted under the name of Ostanes. See J. Bidez and F. Cumont, *Les mages hellénisés. Zoroastre, Ostanès, et Hystaspe d'après la tradition grecque* (Paris: "Les belles lettres," 1938), vol. II, 267–356; K. Preisendanz, "Ostanes," *PRE* 18 (1942): 1610–42.

Ouroboros: The serpent who swallows its own tail is a widely used figure in magic. See W. Deonna, "Ouroboros," *Artibus Asiae* 15 (1952): 163–70; K. Preisendanz, "Aus der Geschichte des Uroboros," in *Brauch und Sinnbild. Eugen Fehrle zum 60. Geburstag gewidmet von seinen Schülern und Freunden* (Karlsruhe: Kommissionsverlag Südwestdeutsche Druck- und Verlagsgesellschaft, 1940) 194–209. For examples of the figure on Egyptian monuments, see A. Piankoff, *The Shrines of Tut-Ankh-Amon* (Princeton: Pantheon Books, 1955) pl. 48; idem, *Mythological Papyri* (Princeton: Pantheon Books, 1957) 22, fig. 3; 174, fig. 74; papyri 20, 27. [R.K.R.] See *PGM* I. 145–46; XII. 203–4, 274–75; VII. 58–59; XXXVI. 184.

Ouserrannouphthi: This is Egyptian *Wsir-rn-nfr*, "Osiris of the good name." [R.K.R.]

Palindrome: Palindrome (lit. "running back again") refers to magical words, usually of no recognizable sense, which can be read and pronounced the same forward as backwards.

Persian: The epithet "Persia," used of Artemis-Hekate (cf. *PGM* IV. 2271, 2715, 2781) shows evidence of the identification of the goddess with the Persian goddess Anahita. See Diod. V. 77 and Nilsson, *GGR* II, 672ff.

Phre: See Ra.

Phtha: See Ptah.

Phylactery: A phylactery (Greek *phylaktērion*) in the *PGM* refers to any stone, material, papyrus amulet, or lamella, engraved with a spell or otherwise, which is worn about the person for protection. The term should not be confused with the Jewish technical term referring to the *tefillin* cases with Scripture verses.

Pitys: W. Bousset, *Hauptprobleme der Gnosis* ([Göttingen: Vandenhoeck and Ruprecht, 1907] 192, n. 1; cf. *Religionsgeschichtliche Studien* 59, 105, 157, 210) has suggested that the Thessalian Pitys named in *PGM* IV. 1928, 2006, 2140 is in fact identical with the Egyptian priest and prophet Bitys (Iamblichus, *De myst.* 8. 5; 10. 7), the Bitos named in Zosimos' *On the Letter Omega*, and Bithus of Dyrrhachium mentioned in Pliny, *NH* 28. 82. See Festugière, *La Révélation* I, 268; Nilsson, *GGR* II, 610; K. Preisendanz, "Pitys (3)," *PRE* 20 1950): 1882–83.

Pnouthis: Pnouthis, or Pnythios, is an Egyptian name and means "He of God." See K. Preisedanz, "Pnuthis," *PRE* 41 (1951): 1104.

Priestly papyrus: Or "hieratic papyrus" refers to the best quality of paper for the writing of magical spells (cf. for example, *PGM* I. 233; IV. 2363, 2512–13; VII. 412). For this technical distinction on the quality of papyrus, see Lewis, *Papyrus in Classical Antiquity* 43–45. [R.K.R.]

Processional way (Greek *kōmastērion*): Ordinarily refers to the meeting place of the revelers of Dionysos, but in *PGM* it is used several times as a metaphor describing heaven as a place of procession of the stars (see also *PGM* IV. 1608–9; XII. 184, 252; XIII. 774; XXI. 10; LXXVII. 13).

Psammetichos: The name is the hellenized form of the Egyptian name *Psmtk*. A legendary figure, Psammetichos I (663–609 B.C.) was the first king of the twenty-sixth Dynasty, but other figures also bore this name. See W. Helck, "Psammetichos," *PRE* 23 (1959): 1305–8.

Psychē: See **Soul**.

Punishments, the (*Greek hai Timōrias*): These are the Greek deities responsible for retributive punishment and hence appropriately cited in spells dealing with malicious magic. See *PGM* VII. 303; XIII. 149, 291, 457; and K. Ziegler, "Timoros," *PRE* 2nd ser. 6 (1937): 1308–9.

Ptah: This is the Egyptian creator god, for which see Bonnet, *RÄRG* 614–19, s.v. "Ptah."

Pythagoras: Because of his interest in the mysticism of numbers, this philosopher's name became attached to late texts associated with mantic and magic. see W. Burkert, *Lore and Science in Ancient Pythagoreanism* (Cambridge, Mass.: Harvard University Press, 1972) 109ff.; idem, *Griechische Religon* 445–47.

Ra (Re, Phre): The Egyptian god of the sun (P)rē, without the definite article. Re means simply "sun," while Prē, the form of the god's name from the New Kingdom onward, means "the Sun." See Bonnet, *RÄRG* 626–30, s.v. "Re."

Sarapis (Serapis): The god Sarapis, closely associated with Osiris in *PGM* IV. 226, appears mostly in the *PGM* as identical with Zeus and Helios (see, e.g., IV. 1715; V. 4–5; LXXIV. 4–5, 14, and Nilsson, *GGR* II, 513), but not with Dionysos, with whom the Greeks identified Osiris (Herod. 2. 42; Plut. *Is. et Os.* 356C). See G. Roeder, "Sarapis," *PRE*, 2nd ser. 2 (1920) 2394–2496; John E. Stambaugh, *Sarapis under the Early Ptolemies*, *EPRO* 25 (Leiden: Brill, 1972); G. Mussies, "The *Interpretatio Judaica* of Sarapis," in M. J. Vermaseren, ed., *Studies in Hellenistic Religions*, *EPRO* 78 (Leiden: Brill, 1979) 188–214; L. Vidman, "Isis und Sarapis," in M. J. Vermaseren, ed., *Die orientalischen Religionen im Römerreich*, *EPRO* 93 (Leiden: Brill, 1981) 121–56. See *PGM* XIXa 6 and n.

Sachmou: This is the Egyptian goddess of war and plague (*PGM* VII. 300), Sakhmer; see Bonnet, *RÄRG* 643–46, s.v. "Sachmet." [R.K.R.]

Scarab: The beetle (*Ateuchus sacer*) regarded as holy by the Egyptians and associated with various deities. See Bonnet, *RÄRG* 720–22, s.v. "Skarabäus"; J. Assmann, "Chepre, *LdÄ* 1 (1975): 934–40; J. German, "Ancient Egyptian Theogony in a Greek Magical Papyrus (*PGM* VII, 11. 516–521)," in *Studies in Egyptian Religion Dedicated to Professor Jan Zandee* (Leiden: Brill, 1982) 28–37.

Selene: The Greek word for the moon (*selēnē*) can stand for the celestial body or for the deity representative of that body. In the *PGM*, Selene is usually transcribed from Greek instead of translated as "moon" unless that term seems completely devoid of the sense of deity.

SESENGENBARPHARANGĒS: A magical name very common in the *PGM*. It is often found together with ABLANATHANALBA. For possible derivations of the name and further references, see W. Fauth, "SSM PDRŠŠA," *Zeitschrift der Deutschen Morgenländischen Gesellschaft* 120 (1970): 229–56, esp. 254–55.

Seth: See **Typhon/Seth**.

Soul: The word *psychē* occurs frequently in *PGM* where it usually means "soul," "mind," etc., and "spirits of the dead." But in several passages (VI. 277, 2488; VII. 414, 472; XVIIa. 18) *psychē* means female pudendum, i.e., a synonym of *physis*, another regular term for the pudendum both in *PGM* and elsewhere. In addition, there are other places (i.e., IV. 1040, 1526, 1752, etc.) where *psychē* is translated "soul," but the erotic context also suggests the added meaning of pudendum. Indeed, it is entirely possible that such a double entendre was the origin of the extended meaning (see esp. IV. 1752, 2924; XXXII. 9, 15; XXXIIa. 15). This meaning of *psychē* occurs also outside of *PGM*. See, e.g., Juvenal, *Sat.* 6. 193–99, esp. 195; Martial, *Epigr.* 68. 5–12, esp. 5–7; and also Sophocles, *El.* 775. [E.N.O.]

Systasis: "Divine encounter," *vel sim.* is a technical term for a rite (*PGM* IV. 778–79; VII. 505ff.) or prayer (*PGM* III. 197–98, 494ff.; IV. 260ff.) to establish an association between a god and a person. Sometimes the association is really only a meeting between the god and the human in order for the human to receive a revelation (*PGM* III. 197ff.; see ll. 192–96; cf. also II. 43, 73; III. 698–99) or a blessing (see ll. 576ff. in *PGM* III. 494ff., and in IV. 260ff., ll. 272 and 284–85). At other times, the association is to be more long-lasting, and the god is to ally himself with the human (*PGM* I. 57, 79–80, 177–81) even to the point of some real sort of union (*PGM* IV. 209, 219–21; cf. ll. 215–17; XIII. 927–31). There is no single English word to encompass this variety of meanings, and therefore *systasis* and cognate words are translated in a variety of ways throughout this volume. For a different interpretation of *systasis*, see K. Preisendanz, "Miszellen zu den Zauberpapyri," *WSt* 40 (1913): 2–5.

THERNOPSI **formula**: This formula in *PGM* III. 186, IV. 828–29, VII. 316 (with corruptions or variant readings) refers to the magical incantation "PSINŌTHER NŌPSITHER THERNŌPSI." For possible Egyptian meaning, see Hopfner, *OZ* I, sec. 750. Note, however, that the three words form rearranged groupings of the syllables PSI, NŌ, and THER. [R.D.K.]

Thoth (**Thouth, Thoouth, Thayth, Theouth, Thooth**): The Egyptian god of wisdom and magic, whom the Greeks identified with Hermes. See Bonnet, *RÄRG* 805–12, s.v. "Thot"; P. Boylan, *Thoth, the Hermes of Egypt* (Chicago: Ares, ²1979), esp. 124ff.; G. Mussies, "The *Interpretatio Judaica* of Thot-Hermes," in *Studies in Egyptian Religion, Dedicated to Professor Jan Zandee* (Leiden: Brill, 1982) 89–120.

Typhon/Seth: The identification of the Egyptian god Seth with the Greek Typhoios or Typhos was already made by the Greeks of the Classical period (Hesiod, *Theog.* 820ff.) and was common in the Greco-Roman Period (see Plut. *De Is. et Os.* 2, 351F and often), a fact reflected also in the *PGM* (see, e.g., VII. 964; XII. 138; XIV. 20). For references, see Colpe, *RAC* 9 (1974): 556–57, 620–21. Because the figure of Seth was believed to be donkey-headed, Typhon in *PGM* IV. 3260 and elsewhere (cf. XIa. 1–2; IV. 2220) probably means "ass." See H. te Velde, *Seth, God of Confusion* (Leiden: Brill, 1967).

YESSIMMIGADON/AKROUROBORE **formula**: For this formula (with variants) see *PGM* II. 32; IV. 2771ff. (cf. IV. 337); V. 424ff.; VII. 680ff.; 895ff.; XIII. 923ff.; XIXa. 12; *DMP* vii. 25–26. In this formula, AKROUROBORE is believed to mean in Greek "eater of the tip of your tail" (thus *LSJ*), a reference to the ouroboros (see Glossary, s.v.). On the formula, see Drexler in Roscher, I, 2. 2771; J. M. R. Cormack, "A *Tabella Defixionis* in the Museum of the University of Reading, England," *HTR* 44 (1951): 25–34, esp. 31–32.

Appendix: Supplemental Bibliography

In the following readers are alerted to new literature on the PGM and the present volume of translations. The bibliography is organized as follows:

I. Important reviews of the GMPT
II. General literature
III. Literature on specific passages of the PGM

I. Important reviews of the GMPT

Biblical Archaeology Review 13:3 (1987) 6–9.
Culianu, Ioan P. *Journal for the Study of Judaism* 18 (1987), 81–83.
Danker, Frederick. *Journal of Biblical Literature* 108 (1988), 348–51.
Duling, Dennis. *The Second Century* 7 (1989–90), 180–82.
Faraone, Christopher A. *The Classical World* 80 (1987), 325–26.
Gager, John. *The Journal of Religion* 67 (1987), 80–86.
Klimkeit, Hans-Joachim. *Zeitschrift für Religions- und Geistesgeschichte* 39 (1987), 286.
Parsons, Peter. *Times Literary Supplement,* Nov. 21, 1986, p. 1316.
Stroumsa, Gedaliahu G. *History of Religions* 28.2 (1988), 182–83.

II. General Literature

Alexander, P. S. "Incantations and Books of Magic," in Emil Schürer, ed., *The History of the Jewish People in the Age of Jesus Christ III/1* (Edinburgh: T.& T. Clark, 1986), 342–79.
Arnold, Clinton E. *Ephesians: Power and Magic. The Concept of Power in Ephesians in Light of its Historical Setting.* Society for New Testament Studies Monograph Series 63 (Cambridge: Cambridge University Press, 1989).
Assmann, Jan. *Ägypten: Theologie und Frömmigkeit einer frühen Hochkultur.* Urban-Taschenbücher 366 (Stuttgart: Kohlhammer, 1984).
Aune, David E. "Jesus II (im Zauber)," *RAC* 17 (1995), 821–37.
———. "Jeu," *RAC* 17 (1995), 906–12.
Bernand, André. *Sorciers grecs* (Paris: Fayard, 1991).
Betz, Hans Dieter. *Hellenismus und Urchristentum. Gesammelte Aufsätze I* (Tübingen: J. C. B. Mohr [Paul Siebeck], 1990).
———. "Magic and Mystery in the Greek Magical Papyri," in Christopher A. Faraone and Dirk Obbink, *Magika Hiera: Ancient Greek Magic and Religion* (New York: Oxford University Press, 1991), 244–59. Reprinted in Hans Dieter Betz, *Hellenismus und Urchristentum,* 209–29.
———. "Secrecy in the Greek Magical Papyri," in Hans G. Kippenberg and Guy G. Stroumsa, eds., *Secrecy and Concealment: Studies in the History of Mediterranean and Near Eastern Religions.* Studies in the History of Religions, *Numen* Book Series 64 (Leiden: Brill, 1995), 153–75.
———. "The Changing Self of the Magician according to the Greek Magical Papyri." Paper read at the International Conference on Magic and Magic in Judaism, Jerusalem and Tel Aviv, October 28–November 2, 1995 (forthcoming).
Brashear, William M. "Trifles," *ZPE* 56 (1984), 61–68.

———. "Zauberformular," *Archiv für Papyrusforschung und verwandte Gebiete* 36 (1990), 49–74.

———. *Magica Varia*. Papyrologica Bruxellensia 25 (Bruxelles: Fondation Égyptologique Reine Élisabeth, 1991).

———. "Magical Papyri: Magic in Bookform," in Peter Ganz, ed., *Das Buch als magisches und als Repräsentationsobjekt* (Wiesbaden: Harrassowitz, 1992), 25–57.

———. *A Mithraic Catechism from Egypt: <P. Berol. 21196>*. Tyche: Supplementband, v. 1 (Wien: Verlag Adolf Holzhausens, 1992).

———. "Nachtrag zum Zauberformular P. Berol. 11734," *Archiv für Papyrusforschung und verwandte Gebiete* 38 (1992), 27–32.

———. "À propos des tablettes magiques," in Elisabeth Lalou, ed., *Les tablettes à écrire de l'antiquité à l'époque moderne* (Turnhout: Brepols, 1992), 149–58.

———. "Ein mithräischer Katechismus aus Ägypten in Berlin," *Antike Welt* 24 (1993), 2–19.

———. "Horos," *RAC* 16 (1994), 574–97.

———. "New Greek Magical and Divinatory Texts in Berlin," in Marvin Meyer and Paul Mirecki, eds., *Ancient Magic and Ritual Power*. Religions in the Graeco-Roman World 129 (Leiden: Brill, 1995), 209–42.

———. "The Greek Magical Papyri: an Introduction and Survey; Annotated Bibliography (1928–1994)," *ANRW* II, 18.5 (1995), 3380–3684.

Bremmer, Jan N. *Greek Religion*. Greece and Rome: New Surveys in the Classics 24 (Oxford: Oxford University Press, 1994).

Calvo Martínez, José Luis, and Maria Dolores Sánchez Romero. *Textos de magia en papiros griegos*. Bibl. clás. Gredos CV (Madrid: Gredos, 1987).

Ciraolo, Leda Jean. "Supernatural Assistants in the Greek Magical Papyri," in Marvin Meyer and Paul Mirecki, eds., *Ancient Magic and Ritual Power*. Religions in the Graeco-Roman World 129 (Leiden: Brill, 1995), 279–95.

Colpe, Carsten. "Heilige Schriften," *RAC* 14 (1988), 184–223.

———. "Jenseitsfahrt II (Unterwelts- oder Höllenfahrt)," *RAC* 17 (1994), 466–89.

Colpe, Carsten, Ernst Dassmann, Josef Engemann, and Peter Habermehl. "Jenseitsfahrt I (Himmelfahrt)," *RAC* 17 (1994), 407–66.

Compagni, V. Perrone, ed. *Cornelius Agrippa. De occulta philosophia libri tres*. Studies in the History of Christian Thought 48 (Leiden: Brill, 1992).

Daniel, Robert W. "3834. Magical Formulas," *The Oxyrynchus Papyri* 56 (1989), 54–57.

Daniel, Robert W., and Franco Maltomini. *Supplementum Magicum*. 2 vols. Abhandlungen der Rheinisch-Westfälischen Akademie der Wissenschaften. Sonderreihe Papyrologica Coloniensia 16.1–2 (Opladen: Westdeutscher Verlag, 1990–92).

Eitrem, Samson. "Dreams and Divination in Magical Ritual," in Christopher A. Faraone and Dirk Obbink, *Magika Hiera: Ancient Greek Magic and Religion* (New York: Oxford University Press, 1991), 175–87.

Elior, Rachel. "Mysticism, Magic, and Angelology—The Perception of Angels in Hekhalot Literature," *Jewish Studies Quarterly* 1 (1993–94), 3–53.

Eschweiler, Peter. *Bildzauber im alten Ägypten: die Verwendung von Bildern und Gegenständen in magischen Handlungen nach den Texten des Mittleren und Neuen Reiches* (Freiburg: Universitätsverlag; Göttingen: Vandenhoeck & Ruprecht, 1994).

Faraone, Christopher A. "Hephaestus the Magician and Near Eastern Parallels for Alcinous' Watchdogs," *Greek, Roman, and Byzantine Studies* 28 (1987), 257–80.

———. "The Agonistic Context of Early Greek Binding Spells," in Christopher A. Faraone and Dirk Obbink, eds., *Magika Hiera: Ancient Greek Magic and Religion* (New York: Oxford University Press, 1991), 3–32.

———. "Binding and Burying the Forces of Evil: The Defensive Use of 'Voodoo Dolls' in Ancient Greece," *Classical Antiquity* 10 (1991), 165–205.

———. "Sex and Power: Male-Targetting Aphrodisiacs in the Greek Magical Tradition," *Helios* 19 (1992), 92–103.

———. *Talismans and Trojan Horses: Guardian Statues in Ancient Greek Myth and Ritual* (New York: Oxford University Press, 1992).

———. "Molten Wax, Spilt Wine and Mutilated Animals: Sympathetic Magic in Near Eastern and Early Greek Oath Ceremonies," *JHS* 113 (1993), 60–80.

———. "The Wheel, the Whip and other Implements of Torture: Erotic Magic in Pindar *Pythian* 4.213–19," *Classical Journal* 89 (1993), 1–19.

———. "The 'Performative Future' in Three Hellenistic Incantations and Theocritus' Second *Idyll*," *Classical Philology* 90 (1995), 1–15.

———. "Magic," in Jan N. Bremmer, ed., *Encyclopedia of Ancient Religions* (forthcoming).

Faraone, Christopher A., and Dirk Obbink, eds. *Magika Hiera: Ancient Greek Magic and Religion* (New York: Oxford University Press, 1991).

Faraone, Christopher A., and Roy Kotansky. "An Inscribed Gold Phylactery in Stamford, Connecticut," *ZPE* 75 (1988), 257–66.

Fauth, Wolfgang. "Arbath Jao. Zur mystischen Vierheit in griechischen und koptischen Zaubertexten und in gnostischen oder apokryphen Schriften des christlichen Orients," *Oriens Christianus* 67 (1983), 65–103.

———. "Arktos in den griechischen Zauberpapyri," *ZPE* 57 (1984), 93–99.

———. "Ṭaṭrosjah-Ṭoṭrosjah und Meṭaṭron in der jüdischen Merkabah-Mystik," *Journal for the Study of Judaism in the Persian, Hellenistic, and Roman Periods* 22 (1991), 40–87.

———. *Helios megistos. Zur synkretistischen Theologie der Spätantike.* Religions in the Graeco-Roman World 125 (Leiden: Brill, 1995).

Feldman, Louis H., "Proselytes and 'Sympathizers' in the Light of the New Inscriptions from Aphrodisias," *Revue des études juives* 148 (1989), 265–305.

Fodor, S. "Traces of the Isis Cult in an Arabic Love Spell from Egypt," in Ulrich Luft, ed., *The Intellectual Heritage of Egypt. Studies Presented to László Kákosy by Friends and Colleagues on the Occasion of His 60th Birthday.* Studia Aegyptiaca 14 (Budapest, 1992), 171–86.

Fossum, Jarl, and Brian Glazer. "Seth in the Magical Texts," *ZPE* 100 (1994), 86–92.

Fowden, Garth. *The Egyptian Hermes: A Historical Approach to the Late Pagan Mind* (Princeton: Princeton University Press, 1986).

Frankfurter, David. "The Magic of Writing and the Writing of Magic: The Power of the Word in Egyptian and Greek Traditions," *Helios* 21 (1994), 189–221.

———. "Narrating Power. The Theory and Practice of the Magical *Historiola* in Ritual Spells," in Marvin Meyer and Paul Mirecki, eds., *Ancient Magic and Ritual Power.* Religions in the Graeco-Roman World 129 (Leiden: Brill, 1995), 457–76.

Gager, John G., ed. *Curse Tablets and Binding Spells from the Ancient World* (New York: Oxford University Press, 1992).

Gager, John G. "Moses the Magician: Hero of an Ancient Counter-Culture?" *Helios* 21 (1994), 179–88.

Ganz, Peter, ed. *Das Buch als magisches und als Repräsentationsobjekt.* Wolfenbütteler Mittelalter-Studien 5 (Wiesbaden: Harrassowitz, 1992).

Graf, Fritz. "Prayer in Magic and Ritual," in Christopher A. Faraone and Dirk Obbink, *Magika Hiera: Ancient Greek Magic and Religion* (New York: Oxford University Press, 1991), 188–97.

———. "The Magician's Initiation," *Helios* 21 (1994), 161–77.

———. *La magie dans l'antiquité gréco-romaine: Idéologie et pratique* (Paris: Les Belles Lettres, 1994).

———. "Excluding the Charming: The Development of the Greek Concept of Magic," in Marvin Meyer and Paul Mirecki, eds., *Ancient Magic and Ritual Power.* Religions in the Graeco-Roman World 129 (Leiden: Brill, 1995), 29–42.

———. *Schadenzauber und Gottesnähe. Die Magie in der griechisch-römischen Antike* (Munich: Beck, 1996).

Grözinger, Karl Erich, "Singen und ekstatische Sprache in der frühen jüdischen Mystik," *Journal for the Study of Judaism* 11 (1980), 66–77.

———. "The Names of God and the Celestial Powers: Their Function and Meaning in the Hekhalot Literature," *Jerusalem Studies in Jewish Thought* 6: 1–2 (1987), 53–64.

Gruenwald, I. *Apocalyptic and Merkabah Mysticism.* Arbeiten zur Geschichte des antiken Judentums 14 (Leiden: Brill, 1980).

————. *From Apocalypticism to Gnosticism. Studies in Apocalypticism, Merkavah Mysticism and Gnosticism.* Beiträge zur Erforschung des Alten Testaments und des antiken Judentums 14 (Frankfurt a.M., Bern, New York, Paris: Lang, 1988).

Gundel, Hans Georg, and Alois Kehl. "Horoskop," *RAC* 16 (1994), 597–662.

Gutekunst, Wilfried. "Zauber(er)(-Mittel, -Praktiken, -Spruch)," *LdÄ* 6 (1986), 1320–55.

Hanig, Roman. "Christus als 'wahrer Salomo' in der frühen Kirche." *Zeitschrift für die Neutestamentliche Wissenschaft und die Kunde der älteren Kirche* 84 (1993), 111–34.

Harrauer, Christine. *Meliouchos. Studien zur Entwicklung religiöser Vorstellungen in griechischen synkretistischen Zaubertexten.* Wiener Studien, Beiheft XI, Arbeiten zur antiken Religionsgeschichte I (Wien: Verlag der Österreichischen Akademie der Wissenschaften, 1987).

Himmelfarb, Martha. "The Practice of Ascent in the Ancient Mediterranean World," in John J. Collins and Michael Fishbane, eds., *Death, Ecstasy, and Other Worldly Journeys* (Albany, New York: State University of New York Press, 1995), 123–37.

Hoheisel, Karl. "Jesus III (außerchristlich)," *RAC* 17 (1995), 837–78.

Hornung, Erik. "Hieroglyphen: Die Welt im Spiegel der Zeichen," *Eranos-Jahrbuch* 55 (1986), 403–38.

Horsley, G. H. R., ed. *New Documents Illustrating Early Christianity.* 7 vols. (North Ryde, N.S.W., Australia: Macquarie University, 1981–94).

Jameson, Michael H., David R. Jordan, and Roy D. Kotansky. *A Lex Sacra from Selinous.* Greek, Roman, and Byzantine Studies, Monograph Series 11 (Durham, North Carolina: Duke University, 1994).

Johnston, Sarah Iles. *Hekate Soteira: A Study of Hekate's Roles in the Chaldean Oracles and Related Literature.* American Classical Studies 21 (Atlanta: Scholars Press, 1990).

————. "Defining the Dreadful: Remarks on the Greek Child-Killing Demon," in Marvin Meyer and Paul Mirecki, eds., *Ancient Magic and Ritual Power.* Religions in the Graeco-Roman World 129 (Leiden: Brill, 1995), 361–87.

Jordan, David R. "A Survey of Greek Defixiones Not Included in the Special Corpora," *Greek, Roman and Byzantine Studies* 26 (1985), 151–97.

————. "Defixiones from a Well near the Southwest Corner of the Athenian Agora," *Hesperia* 54 (1985), 205–55.

————. "A New Reading of a Phylactery from Beirut," *ZPE* 88 (1991), 61–69.

————. "Late Feasts for Ghosts," in Robin Hägg, ed., *Ancient Greek Cult Practice from the Epigraphic Evidence: Proceedings of the Second International Seminar on Ancient Greek Cult* (Stockholm: Svenska institutet i Athen, P. Åströms Förlag, 1994), 131–43.

————. "Magica Graeca Parvula," *ZPE* 100 (1994), 321–35.

Jüttner, Guido. "Heilmittel," *RAC* 14 (1988), 249–74.

Kákosy, László. *Zauberei im alten Ägypten* (Leipzig: Köhler & Amelang, 1989).

————. "Probleme der Religion im römerzeitlichen Ägypten," *ANRW* II, 18.5 (1995), 2894–3049.

Kehl, Alois. "Hekate," *RAC* 14 (1988), 310–38.

Kingsley, Peter. *Ancient Philosophy, Mystery, and Magic: Empedocles and Pythagorean Tradition* (Oxford: Clarendon Press; New York: Oxford University Press, 1995).

Kippenberg, Hans G., and Guy G. Stroumsa, eds. *Secrecy and Concealment: Studies in the History of Mediterranean and Near Eastern Religions.* Studies in the History of Religions, *Numen* Book Series 65 (Leiden: Brill, 1995).

Klauck, Hans-Josef. *Die religiöse Umwelt des Urchristentums.* 2 vols. (Stuttgart: Kohlhammer, 1995–1996).

Koenig, Yvan. *Magie et Magiciens dans l'Egypte ancienne* (Paris: Pygmalion/Gérard Watelet, 1994).

Kornfeld, W. et al. "Satan (et démons)," *Supplément au Dictionnaire de la Bible,* tome XII (Paris: Letouzey & Ané, 1992), 1–21.

Kotansky, Roy. *Texts and Studies in the Graeco-Egyptian Magic Lamellae.* Ph. D. Dissertation (University of Chicago, 1988).

————. "A Magic Gem Inscribed in Greek and Artificial Phoenician," *ZPE* 85 (1991), 237–38, and plate I: b, c.

———. "Magic in the Court of the Governor of Arabia," *ZPE* 88 (1991), 41–60, and plate I.

———. "Incantations and Prayers for Salvation on Inscribed Greek Amulets," in Christopher A. Faraone and Dirk Obbink, *Magika Hiera: Ancient Greek Magic and Religion* (New York: Oxford University Press, 1991), 107–37.

———. "Two Inscribed Jewish Aramaic Amulets from Syria," *Israel Exploration Journal* 41 (1991), 267–81.

———. *Greek Magical Amulets: The Inscribed Gold, Silver, Copper, and Bronze "Lamellae": Text and Commentary. Part I: Published Texts of Known Provenance.* Abhandlungen der Nordrhein-Westfälischen Akademie der Wissenschaften. Sonderreihe Papyrologica Coloniensia 22.1 (Opladen: Westdeutscher Verlag, 1994).

———. "θωβαρραβαυ = 'The Deposit is Good,'" *Harvard Theological Review* 87 (1994), 367–69.

———. "Greek Exorcistic Amulets," in Marvin Meyer and Paul Mirecki, eds., *Ancient Magic and Ritual Power.* Religions in the Graeco-Roman World 129 (Leiden; New York; Köln: Brill, 1995), 243–77.

———. "Remnants of a Liturgical Exorcism on a Gem," *Le Muséon* 108 (1995), 143–56.

Kotansky, Roy D., and Jeffrey Spier. "The 'Horned Hunter' on a Lost Gnostic Gem," *Harvard Theological Review* 88 (1995), 315–37.

Kotansky, Roy D., Joseph Naveh, and Shaul Shaked. "A Greek-Aramaic Silver Amulet from Egypt in the Ashmolean Museum," *Le Muséon* 105 (1992), 5–24.

Köves-Zulauf, Thomas. *Reden und Schweigen. Römische Religion bei Plinius Maior.* Studia et Testimonia Antiqua, 12 (Munich: Fink, 1972).

Larsen, Tage, and Adam Bülow-Jacobsen. *Papyri Graecae Haunienses. Fasciculus tertius (P. Haun. III, 45–69).* Papyrologische Texte und Abhandlungen 36 (Bonn: Habelt, 1985), 30–37.

Luck, Georg. *Arcana mundi. Magic and the Occult in the Greek and Roman Worlds* (Baltimore: Johns Hopkins University Press, 1985).

———. *Magie und andere Geheimlehren in der Antike* (Stuttgart: Kröner, 1990).

Maguire, Henry, ed. *Byzantine Magic* (Washington, D.C.: Dumbarton Oaks Research Library and Collection, 1995).

Maltomini, Franco. "Due Papiri Magici della Bibliothèque Publique et Universitaire di Ginevra," *Studi classici e orientali* 36 (1986), 293–305.

———. "3835. Magic," *The Oxyrynchus Papyri* 56 (1989), 57–61.

Marcovich, Miroslav P. *Studies in Graeco-Roman Religions and Gnosticism* (Leiden: Brill, 1988).

Martinez, David G. "T. Köln inv. 2.25 and Erotic δαμάζειν," *ZPE* 83 (1990), 235–36.

———. *P. Michigan XVI. A Greek Love Charm from Egypt (P. Mich. 757).* American Studies in Papyrology 30 (Atlanta: Scholars Press, 1991).

———. "'May she neither eat nor drink': Love Magic and Vows of Abstinence," in Marvin Meyer and Paul Mirecki, eds., *Ancient Magic and Ritual Power.* Religions in the Graeco-Roman World 129 (Leiden: Brill, 1995), 335–59.

Merkelbach, Reinhold, and Maria Totti. *Abrasax: Ausgewählte Papyri religiösen und magischen Inhalts. Band 1: Gebete.* Papyrologica Coloniensia 17.1 (Opladen: Westdeutscher Verlag, 1990).

———. *Abrasax: Ausgewählte Papyri religiösen und magischen Inhalts. Band 2: Gebete (Fortsetzung).* Papyrologica Coloniensia 17.2 (Opladen: Westdeutscher Verlag, 1991).

Merkelbach, Reinhold. *Abrasax: Ausgewählte Papyri religiösen und magischen Inhalts. Band 3: Zwei griechisch-ägyptische Weihezeremonien (die Leidener Weltschöpfung; die Pschai-Aion-Liturgie).* Papyrologica Coloniensia 17.3 (Opladen: Westdeutscher Verlag, 1992).

———. "Die Götter Hosios und Dikaios in Mäonien und Phrygien," *ZPE* 97 (1993), 291–96.

———. *Isis regina-Zeus Sarapis. Die griechisch-ägyptische Religion nach den Quellen dargestellt* (Stuttgart und Leipzig: Teubner, 1995).

Meyer, Marvin, Richard Smith, and Neal Kelsey, eds. *Ancient Christian Magic: Coptic Texts of Ritual Power* (San Francisco: Harper, 1994).

Meyer, Marvin, and Paul Mirecki, eds. *Ancient Magic and Ritual Power*. Religions in the Graeco-Roman World 129 (Leiden: Brill, 1995).

Miller, Patricia C. "In Praise of Nonsense," in A. H. Armstrong, ed., *Classical Mediterranean Spirituality: Egyptian, Greek, Roman*, World Spirituality 15 (London: Routledge & Kegan Paul, 1986), 481–505.

Miller, Patricia C. *Dreams in Late Antiquity. Studies in the Imagination of a Culture* (Princeton: Princeton University Press, 1994).

Montevecchi, Orsolina. *La Papirologia. Ristampa riveduta e corretta con adenda*, 2d ed. (Milano: Vita e Pensiero, 1988).

Morray-Jones, C. R. A. "Transformational Mysticism in the Apocalyptic-Merkabah Tradition," *Journal of Jewish Studies* 43 (1992), 1–31.

Nasemann, Beate. *Theurgie und Philosophie in Jamblichs De mysteriis*. Beiträge zur Altertumskunde 11 (Stuttgart: Teubner, 1991).

Naveh, Joseph, and Shaul Shaked. *Amulets and Magic Bowls. Aramaic Incantations of Late Antiquity* (Jerusalem: Magnes Press; Leiden: Brill, 1985).

———. *Magic Spells and Formulae: Aramaic Incantations of Late Antiquity* (Jerusalem: Magnes Press, 1993).

Niggemeyer, Jens-Heinrich. *Beschwörungsformeln aus dem "Buch der Geheimmisse" (Sefär harazim). Zur Topologie der magischen Rede*. Judaistische Texte und Studien 3 (Hildesheim: Olms, 1975).

Oberhelman, Steven M. "Dreams in Graeco-Roman Medicine," *ANRW* II, 37.1 (1993), 121–56.

Onnerfors, Alf. "Zaubersprüche in Texten der römischen und frühmittelalterlichen Medizin," in Sabbah Guy, ed., *Etudes de medicine romaine*. Mémoire de Centre Jean-Palerne VIII (Saint-Etienne: Publ. de l'Univ., 1988), 113–56.

———. "Magische Formeln im Dienste römischer Medizin," *ANRW* II 37.1 (1993), 157–224.

Parry, Hugh. *Thelxis: Magic and Imagination in Greek Myth and Poetry* (Lanham, Md.: University Press of America, 1992).

Patai, Raphael. *The Jewish Alchemists: A History and Source Book* (Princeton: Princeton University Press, 1994).

Pestman, P. W. *The New Papyrological Primer*, 5th ed. (Leiden: Brill, 1990).

Philipp, Hanna. *Mira et magica: Gemmen im Ägyptischen Museum der Staatlichen Museen Preussischer Kulturbesitz, Berlin-Charlottenburg* (Mainz: von Zabern, 1986).

Phillips, C. Robert. "In Search of the Occult. An Annotated Anthology," *Helios* 15 (1988), 151–70.

Quack, Joachim F. "Dekane und Gliedervergottung. Altägyptische Traditionen im Apokryphon Johannis," *Jahrbuch für Antike und Christentum* 38 (1995), 97–122.

Rea, J. R. with Tim Bateson. "3931. Magic," in J. R. Rea, ed., *The Oxyrhynchus Papyri* 58 (1991), 44–47.

Ritner, Robert K. "Gleanings from Magical Texts," *Enchoria* 14 (1986) 95–106.

———. *The Mechanics of Ancient Egyptian Magical Practice*, 2 vols. Ph. D. Dissertation (University of Chicago, 1987).

———. "Horus on the Crocodiles: A Juncture of Religion and Magic," in William Kelly Simpson, ed., *Religion and Philosophy in Ancient Egypt*. Yale Egyptological Studies 3 (New Haven: Yale Egyptological Seminar, Dept. of Near Eastern Languages and Civilizations, Yale University, 1989), 103–16.

———. "Religion vs. Magic. The Evidence of the Magical Statue Bases," in Ulrich Luft, ed., *The Intellectual Heritage of Egypt. Studies Presented to László Kákosy by Friends and Colleagues on the Occasion of His 60th Birthday*. Studia Aegyptiaca 14 (Budapest, 1992), 495–501.

———. "Egyptian Magic: Questions of Legitimacy, Religious Orthodoxy, and Social Deviance," in Alan B. Lloyd, ed., *Religion and Society in Ancient Egypt* (Swansea, Wales: University of Swansea, 1993), 189–200.

———. *The Mechanics of Ancient Egyptian Magical Practice*. Studies in Ancient Oriental Civilization 54 (Chicago: Oriental Institute of the University of Chicago, 1993).

———. "Egyptian Magical Practice under the Roman Empire: The Demotic Spells and their Religious Context," *ANRW* II, 18.5 (1995), 3333–79.

———. "The Religious, Social, and Legal Parameters of Traditional Egyptian Magic," in Marvin Meyer and Paul Mirecki, eds., *Ancient Magic and Ritual Power*. Religions in the Graeco-Roman World 129 (New York: Brill, 1995), 43–60.

Ritoók, Zsigmond. "Horkos und Exorkismos," in Ulrich Luft, ed., *The Intellectual Heritage of Egypt. Studies Presented to Lásló Kákosy by Friends and Colleagues on the Occasion of His 60th Birthday*. Studia Aegyptiaca 14 (Budapest, 1992), 503–8.

Roccati, Alessandro, and Alberto Siliotti, eds. *La magia in Egitto ai Tempi dei Faraoni*. Atti Convegno Internazionale di Studi, Milano 29–31 Ottobre 1985 (Verona: Rassegna internazionale di cinematografia archeologica, 1987).

Römer, Cornelia, and Heinz J. Thissen. "Eine magische Anrufung in koptischer Sprache," *ZPE* 84 (1990), 175–81.

Rosenberger, Veit. "Der Ring des Polykrates im Lichte der Zauberpapyri," *ZPE* 108 (1995), 69–71.

Scarborough, John. "Classical Antiquity, Medicine and Allied Sciences," in *Trends in History I* (New York: The Institute for Research in History, 1979), 1.2, pp. 3–14.

———. "Early Byzantine Pharmacology," *Dumbarton Oaks Papers* 38 (1984), 213–32.

———. *Folklore and Folk Medicines* (Madison, Wisconsin: American Institute of the History of Pharmacy, 1987).

———. *Some Rituals for Gathering Herbs in Greco-Roman Egypt* (Summary in *Abstracts of the American Philological Association* [1987], 70).

———. "The Pharmacology of Sacred Plants, Herbs, and Roots," in Christopher A. Faraone and Dirk Obbink, *Magika Hiera: Ancient Greek Magic and Religion* (New York: Oxford University Press, 1991), 138–74.

———. "Roman Medicine to Galen," *ANRW* II, 37.1 (1993), 3–48.

Schäfer, Peter, ed. *Übersetzung der Hekhalot-Literatur II (§§ 81–334)*. Texte und Studien zum antiken Judentum 17 (Tübingen: J. C. B. Mohr [Paul Siebeck], 1987).

———. *Hekhalot-Studien*. Texte und Studien zum antiken Judentum 19 (Tübingen: J. C. B. Mohr [Paul Siebeck], 1988).

———. *Übersetzung der Hekhalot-Literatur III*. Texte und Studien zum antiken Judentum 22 (Tübingen: J. C. B. Mohr [Paul Siebeck], 1989).

———. "Jewish Magic Literature in Late Antiquity and Early Middle Ages," *Journal of Jewish Studies* 41 (1990), 75–91.

Schäfer, Peter, and Shaul Shaked, eds. *Magische Texte aus der Kairoer Geniza. vol. I*. Texte und Studien zum antiken Judentum 42 (Tübingen: J. C. B. Mohr [Paul Siebeck], 1994).

Schäfer, Peter, and Klaus Herrmann, eds. *Übersetzung der Hekhalot-Literatur I (§§ 1–80)*. Texte und Studien zum antiken Judentum 46 (Tübingen: J. C. B. Mohr [Paul Siebeck], 1995).

Scholem, Gershom G. *Jewish Gnosticism, Merkabah Mysticism, and Talmudic Tradition*, 2d ed. (New York: Jewish Theological Seminary of America, 1965).

Segal, Alan F. *The Other Judaisms of Late Antiquity*. Brown Judaic Studies 127 (Atlanta: Scholars Press, 1987).

Shaked, Shaul. *Dualism in Transformation: Varieties of Religion in Sasanian Iran*. Jordan Lectures in Comparative Literature 16 (London: School of Oriental and African Studies, University of London, 1994).

Sheppard, Harry, Alois Kehl, and Robert McL. Wilson, "Hermetik," *RAC* 14 (1988), 780–808.

Shimoff, Sandra R. "Hellenization among the Rabbis: Some Evidence from Early Aggadot concerning David and Solomon," *Journal for the Study of Judaism* 18 (1987), 168–87.

Siker, Jeffrey S. "Abraham in Graeco-Roman Paganism," *Journal for the Study of Judaism* 18 (1987), 188–208.

Singer, Thomas C. "Hieroglyphs, Real Characters and the Idea of Natural Language in English Seventeenth-Century Thought," *Journal of the History of Ideas* 50 (1989), 49–70.

Smith, Jonathan Z. "Trading Places," in Marvin Meyer and Paul Mirecki, eds., *Ancient*

Magic and Ritual Power. Religions in the Graeco-Roman World 129 (Leiden: Brill, 1995), 13–27.

Smith, Morton. "Salvation in the Gospels, Paul, and the Magical Papyri," *Helios* 13 (1986), 63–74.

———. *Studies in the Cult of Yahweh. Volume 2: New Testament, Early Christianity, and Magic.* Edited by Shaye J. D. Cohen. Religions in the Graeco-Roman World 130/2 (Leiden: Brill, 1996).

Sørensen, Jørgen Podemann. "The Argument in Ancient Egyptian Magical Formulae," *Acta Orientalia* 45 (1984), 5–19.

Sperber, Daniel. "Some Rabbinic Themes in Magical Papyri," *Journal for the Study of Judaism* 16 (1985), 93–103.

———. *Magic and Folklore in Rabbinic Literature.* Some contributions by Ithamar Gruenwald (Ramat-Gan: Bar-Ilan University Press, 1994).

Speyer, Wolfgang. *Frühes Christentum im antiken Strahlungsfeld: Ausgewählte Aufsätze.* Wissenschaftliche Untersuchungen zum Neuen Testament 50 (Tübingen: J. C. B. Mohr [Paul Siebeck], 1989).

Stewart, Charles. *Demons and the Devil: Moral Imagination in Modern Greek Culture* (Princeton: Princeton University Press, 1991).

Stockmeier, Peter. "Hermes," *RAC* 14 (1988), 772–80.

Stroumsa, Guy G. "Dreams and Magic among Pagans and Christians," (forthcoming).

———. "Dreams and Visions in Early Christian Discourse," (forthcoming).

Sullivan, Lawrence E., ed. *Hidden Truths: Magic, Alchemy and the Occult* (New York, London: Macmillan, 1987, 1989).

Swartz, Michael D. *Mystical Prayer in Ancient Judaism: An Analysis of Ma'aseh Merkavah.* Texte und Studien zum antiken Judentum 28 (Tübingen: J. C. B. Mohr [Paul Siebeck], 1991).

Tambiah, Stanley Jeyaraja. *Magic, Science, Religion and the Scope of Rationality* (New York: Cambridge University Press, 1990).

te Velde, H. "Some Remarks on the Mysterious Language of the Baboons," in J. H. Kamstra, ed., *Funerary Symbols and Religion. Essays Dedicated to Professor Heerma van Voss* (Kampen, 1988), 129–36.

Thee, Francis. *Julius Africanus and the Early Christian View of Magic.* Hermeneutische Untersuchungen zur Theologie 19 (Tübingen: J. C. B. Mohr [Paul Siebeck], 1984).

Thissen, Heinz-J. "Etymogeleien," *ZPE* 73 (1988), 303–5.

———. "Ägyptologische Beiträge zu den griechischen magischen Papyri," in E. Graefe and U. Verhoeven, eds., *Religion und Philosophie im alten Ägypten. Festgabe für Philippe Derchain.* Orientalia Lovaniensia Analecta 39 (1991), 293–302.

———. "Nubien in demotischen magischen Texten," in D. Mendel and U. Claudi, eds., *Ägypten im afro-orientalischen Kontext. Aufsätze zur Archäologie, Geschichte und Sprache eines unbegrenzten Raumes: Gedenkschrift Peter Behrens* (Köln: Institut für Afrikanistik an der Universität zu Köln, 1991), 369–76.

———. "'..... αἰγυπτιάζων τῇ φωνῇ .....' Zum Umgang mit der ägyptischen Sprache in der griechisch-römischen Antike," *ZPE* 97 (1993), 239–52.

Thraede, Klaus. "Hexe," *RAC* 14 (1988), 1269–75.

Thyen, Hartwig. "Ich-Bin-Worte," *RAC* 17 (1994), 147–213.

Toorn, Karel van der, Bob Becking, and Pieter W. van der Horst, eds. *Dictionary of Deities and Demons in the Bible* (Leiden: Brill, 1995).

Totti, Maria. "Βρεὶθ καὶ Μανδοῦλις (in den Pap. Graec. Mag. und einer Inschrift aus Talmis)," *ZPE* 67 (1987), 263–65.

———. "Der Traumgott Apollon-Helios-Harpokrates-Tithoes in zwei Gebeten der magischen Papyri," *ZPE* 73 (1988), 287–96.

Totti, Maria, ed. *Ausgewählte Texte der Isis- und Sarapisreligion.* Subsidia Epigraphica, Quellen und Abhandlungen zur griechischen Epigraphik XII (Hildesheim: Olms, 1985).

Turcan, Robert. *Les cultes orientaux dans le monde romain.* 2nd ed. (Paris: Les Belles Lettres, 1992).

Versnel, H. S. "'May He Not Be Able to Sacrifice . . .' Concerning a Curious Formula in Greek and Latin Curses," *ZPE* 58 (1985), 247–69.

———. "Beyond Cursing: The Appeal to Justice in Judicial Prayers," in Christopher A. Faraone and Dirk Obbink, *Magika Hiera: Ancient Greek Magic and Religion* (New York: Oxford University Press, 1991), 60–106.

———. "πεπυσμένος: The Cnidian Curse Tablets and Ordeals by Fire," in Robin Hägg, ed., *Ancient Greek Cult Practice from the Epigraphic Evidence: Proceedings of the Second International Seminar on Ancient Greek Cult* (Stockholm: Svenska institutet i Athen, P. Åströms Förlag, 1994), 145–54.

Winkler, John J. "The Constraints of Eros," in Christopher A. Faraone and Dirk Obbink, *Magika Hiera: Ancient Greek Magic and Religion* (New York: Oxford University Press, 1991), 214–43.

Zuntz, Günther. *AIΩN im Römerreich. Die archäologischen Zeugnisse.* Abhandlungen der Heidelberger Akademie der Wissenschaften. Philosophisch-historische Klasse 3 (Heidelberg: Carl Winter; Universitätsverlag, 1991).

Zwierlein-Diehl, Erika. *Magische Amulette und andere Gemmen des Instituts für Altertumskunde der Universität zu Köln.* Abhandlungen der Rheinisch-Westfälischen Akademie der Wissenschaften. Sonderreihe Papyrologica Coloniensia XX (Opladen: Westdeutscher Verlag, 1992).

III. Literature on specific passages of the PGM (for more extensive annotations see Brashear, William M., "The Greek Magical Papyri: An Introduction and Survey; Annotated Bibliography (1928–1994)," *ANRW* II, 18.5 [1995]: 3380–3684).

PGM I

Smith, Morton, "Pagan Dealings with Jewish Angels, P. Berlin 5025b, P. Louvre 2391," *Studii Clasice* 24 (1986), 175–79.

PGM I.203–207

Faraone, Christopher. "Notes on Three Greek Magical Texts," *ZPE* 100 (1994), 81–86.

PGM I.315–25, 341–42

Merkelbach and Totti, *Abrasax,* I.10–16.

PGM II.1–183

Merkelbach and Totti, *Abrasax,* I.35–64.

PGM II.81ff.

Mantziou, Mary. "Ὁ μαγικὸς ὕμνος στὸν Ἀπόλλωνα καὶ στὸν Ἥλιο (PGM II, ὕμνος 11 = P II, 81–102, 107–108, 132–140, 163–166," *Σύνδειπνον, Mel. in hon. Dimitrios Loukatos* (Ioannina, 1988), 117–56.

PGM III.1–164

Merkelbach and Totti, *Abrasax,* I.81–102.

PGM III.165–262

Merkelbach and Totti, *Abrasax,* II.62–76.

PGM III.494–609

Merkelbach and Totti, *Abrasax,* II.1–33.

PGM IV

Maltomini, Franco. "PGM IV 354–55 (e paralleli) e Fragmentum Grenfellianum 18–19," *ZPE* 78 (1989), 95–97.

Merkelbach, Reinhold. "Astrologie, Mechanik, Alchimie und Magie im griechisch-römischen Ägypten," in *Begegnung von Heidentum und Christentum im spätantiken Ägypten* (Riggisberg: Abegg-Stiftung, 1993), 49–62.

———. "Kosmogonie und Unsterblichkeitsritus. Zwei griechisch-ägyptische Weiherituale," in Erik Hornung and Tilo Schabert, eds., *Auferstehung und Unsterblichkeit* (Munich: Fink, 1993), 19–51.

PGM IV.94–153

Meyer, Marvin W. "The Love Spell of PGM IV, 94–153. Introduction and Structure," *Acts of the 2nd International Congress of Coptic Studies, Rome 22–26 sept. 1980* (Rome, 1985), 193–201.

PGM IV.296–466
   Martinez, David G. *P. Michigan XVI. A Greek Love Charm from Egypt (P. Mich. 757).*
   American Studies in Papyrology 30 (Atlanta: Scholars Press, 1991), 8ff.
PGM IV.436–61
   Merkelbach and Totti, *Abrasax,* I.10–16.
PGM IV.475–824
   Merkelbach, *Abrasax,* III.155–83
PGM IV.930-1114
   Merkelbach and Totti, *Abrasax,* I.2–10.
PGM IV.1115–1165
   Merkelbach and Totti, *Abrasax,* II.34–42.
PGM IV.1196–1199
   Faraone, Christopher. "Notes on Three Greek Magical Texts," *ZPE* 100 (1994), 81–86.
PGM IV.1596–1715
   Merkelbach and Totti, *Abrasax,* I.104–122.
PGM IV.1957–89
   Merkelbach and Totti, *Abrasax,* I.10–16.
PGM IV.2891–2942
   Merkelbach and Totti, *Abrasax,* II.113–21.
PGM IV.3040–60
   Sperber, Daniel. "Some Rabbinic Themes in Magical Papyri," *Journal for the Study of
   Judaism* 16 (1985), 95–99.
PGM V.70–122
   "Pap. Oxyr. 3835," *The Oxyrynchus Papyri* 56 (1989), 57–61.
PGM V.96–172
   Merkelbach and Totti, *Abrasax,* II.153–70.
PGM V.459–89
   Merkelbach and Totti, *Abrasax,* II.146–52.
PGM V.459–89
   Philonenko, M. "Une Prière magique au dieu créateur (PGM 5, 459–489)," *Comptes
   rendus des séances de l'Académie des Inscriptions et Belles Lettres* (1985), 433–52.
PGM VII
   Jordan, David R. "The Inscribed Gold Tablet from the Vigna Codini," *AJA* 89 (1985),
   162–67.
PGM VII.260–271
   Betz, Hans Dieter. "Jewish Magic in the Greek Magical Papyri (PGM VII.260–71),"
   Paper read at the International Symposium on Magic at the Institute for Advanced
   Study at Princeton, March 27–28, 1995 (forthcoming).
PGM VII.411–16
   Halleux, Robert. *Les Lapidaires grecs* (Paris: Les Belles Lettres, 1985), 288, no. lxvii.
   Reiner, Erica. "Nocturnal Talk," in Tzvi Abusch, John Huehergard, and Piotr Steinkeller,
   eds., *Lingering Over Words: Studies in Ancient Near Eastern Literature in Honor of Wil-
   liam L. Moran.* Harvard Semitic Studies 37 (Atlanta: Scholars Press, 1990), 421–24.
PGM VII.505–528
   Merkelbach and Totti, *Abrasax,* II.43–55.
PGM VII.491–504
   Merkelbach and Totti, *Abrasax,* II.97–102
PGM VII.701f.
   Daniel, Robert W. "Hekate's Peplos," *ZPE* 72 (1988), 278.
PGM VII.756–794
   Merkelbach and Totti, *Abrasax,* II.103–12.
PGM VIII.74–81
   Merkelbach and Totti, *Abrasax,* I.10–16.
PGM XIa
   Fauth, Wolfgang. "Aphrodites Pantoffel und die Sandale der Hekate," *Grazer Beiträge*
   12–13 (1985–1986), 193–211.

PGM XI.a.1–40

Speyer, Wolfgang. "Zum Bild des Apollonios von Tyana bei Heiden und Christen," in *Frühes Christentum im antiken Strahlungsfeld: Ausgewählte Aufsätze.* Wissenschaftliche Untersuchungen zum Neuen Testament 50 (Tübingen: J.C.B. Mohr [Paul Siebeck], 1989), 176–92, 496.

PGM XII, XIII

Daniel, Robert. *Two Greek Magical Papyri in the National Museum of Antiquities in Leiden. A Photographic Edition of J 384 and J 395 (= PGM XII and XIII).* Abhandlungen der Rheinisch-Westfälischen Akademie der Wissenschaften, Sonderreihe Papyrologica Coloniensia, vol.XIX (Opladen: Westdeutscher Verlag, 1991).

PGM XII.14–95

Merkelbach and Totti, *Abrasax,* I.65–80.

PGM XII.201–69

Merkelbach and Totti, *Abrasax,* I.155–78.

PGM XII.244–52

Merkelbach and Totti, *Abrasax,* I.16–19.

PGM XII.351–64

Maltomini, Franco. "Appunti magici," *ZPE* 66 (1986), 157–60.

PGM XIII

Smith, Morton. "P. Leid J 395 (PGM XIII) and Its Creation Legend," in A. Caquot, M. Hadas-Lebel, and J. Riaud, eds., *Hellenica et Judaica: Hommage à Valentin Nikiprowetzky* (Leuven: Peeters, 1986), 491–98.

PGM XIII.289

Edwards, M. J. "ΧΡΗΣΤΟΣ in a Magical Papyrus," *ZPE* 85 (1991), 232–36.

PGM XIII.732–1056

Merkelbach and Totti, *Abrasax,* I.179–222.

PGM XIII

Jordan, David R. "The Inscribed Gold Tablet from the Vigna Codini," *AJA* 89 (1985), 162–67.

Merkelbach, Reinhold. "Kosmogonie und Unsterblichkeitsritus. Zwei griechisch-ägyptische Weiherituale," in Erik Hornung and Tilo Schabert, eds., *Auferstehung und Unsterblichkeit* (Munich: Fink, 1993), 19–51.

PGM XIII.1–230 and 343–371

Merkelbach, *Abrasax,* III.92–153.

PGM XIII.971–74

Faraone, Christopher A. "Notes on Three Greek Magical Texts," *ZPE* 100 (1994), 81–86.

PDM xiv.448–51

Faraone, Christopher A. "Aphrodite's ΚΕΣΤΟΣ and Apples for Atalanta: Aphrodisias in Early Greek Myth and Ritual," *Phoenix* 44 (1990), 235n.35.

PGM XIVa

Merkelbach and Totti, *Abrasax,* II.77–82.

PGM XVI

Jordan, David R. "A New Reading of a Papyrus Love Charm in the Louvre," *ZPE* 74 (1988), 231–43.

PGM XX.1–2

Daniel, Robert W. "A Note on the Philinna Papyrus (PGM XX, 1–2)," *ZPE* 73 (1988), 306.

PGM XX.4–10

Faraone, Christopher A. "The Mystodokos and the Dark-Eyed Maidens: Multicultural Influences on a Late Hellenistic Incantation," in Marvin Meyer and Paul Mirecki, eds., *Ancient Magic and Ritual Power* (Leiden: Brill, 1995), 297–333.

PGM XX.15

Dickie, Matthew W. "The Identity of Philinna in the Philinna Papyrus (PGM² XX.15; SH 900.15)," *ZPE* 100 (1994), 119–22.

PGM XXI.1–28

Merkelbach and Totti, *Abrasax,* I.135–54.

PGM XXII

Brashear, William M. "Zwei Zauberformulare," *Archiv für Papyrusforschung und verwandte Gebiete* 38 (1992), 19–26.

Marcovich, Miroslav P. "The Isis with Seven Robes," *ZPE* 64 (1986), 295–96.

PGM XXIII

Terence DuQuesne, *Jackal at the Shaman's Gate: A Study of Anubis Lord of Ro-Setawe, with the Conjuration to Chthonic Deities (PGM XXIII; P Oxy 412)*. Text, translation, and commentary; and an annotated bibliography of the Anubis archetype. Oxfordshire Communications in Egyptology III (Thame, Oxon.: Darengo, 1991).

PGM XXXVI

Jordan, David R. "The Inscribed Gold Tablet from the Vigna Codini," *AJA* 89 (1985), 162–67.

PGM XXXVI.211–230

Merkelbach and Totti, *Abrasax,* II.56–61.

PGM XXXVII.1–26

Totti, Maria, ed. *Ausgewählte Texte der Isis- und Sarapisreligion*. Subsidia Epigraphica, Quellen und Abhandlungen zur griechischen Epigraphik XII (Hildesheim: Olms, 1985), nos. 9, 10.

PGM LVII

Merkelbach and Totti, *Abrasax,* II.83–96.

PGM LXII.12–16

Fauth, Wolfgang. "Dardaniel (PGM LXII 12–16)," *ZPE* 98 (1993), 57–75.

PGM LXX

Jordan, David R. "A Love Charm with Verses," *ZPE* 72 (1988), 245–59.

Betz, *Hellenismus und Urchristentum,* 147–55.

PGM LXXII

Merkelbach and Totti, *Abrasax,* II.83–96.

PGM LXXIX.1–7

Maltomini, Franco. "PGM LXXIX 2–4 (=PGM LXXX 1–3)," *Studi classici e orientali* 35 (1985), 313–14.

PGM LXXXII

Daniel, Robert W. "Unidentified Prose: *P. Vars* 4," *BASP* 22 (1985), 29–32.

PGM LXXXIII.1–20

Daniel and Maltomini, *Supplementum Magicum I,* no. 29.

PGM LXXXIV.1–21

Daniel and Maltomini, *Supplementum Magicum I,* no. 40.

PGM LXXXV.1–6

Parsons, Peter. *Times Literary Supplement,* Nov. 21, 1986, p. 1316.

PGM LXXXVII.1–11

Daniel and Maltomini, *Supplementum Magicum I,* no. 14.

PGM LXXXVIII.1–19

Daniel and Maltomini, *Supplementum Magicum I,* no. 11.

PGM LXXXIX.1–27

Daniel and Maltomini, *Supplementum Magicum I,* no. 13.

PGM XCI.1–14

Daniel and Maltomini, *Supplementum Magicum I,* no. 9.

PGM XCVI.1–8

Daniel and Maltomini, *Supplementum Magicum I,* no. 15.

PGM XCVIII.1–7

Daniel and Maltomini, *Supplementum Magicum I,* no.7.

PGM XCIX.1–3

Daniel and Maltomini, *Supplementum Magicum I,* no. 33.

PGM C. 1–7

Daniel and Maltomini, *Supplementum Magicum I,* no. 20.

PGM CI

Brashear, William M. "Ein neues Zauberensemble," *Studien zur altägyptischen Kultur* 19 (1992), 79–109.

PGM CI.1–53

Daniel and Maltomini, *Supplementum Magicum I*, no. 45.

PGM CIV.1–8

Daniel and Maltomini, *Supplementum Magicum I*, no. 4.

PGM CVI.1–10

Daniel and Maltomini, *Supplementum Magicum I*, no. 10.

PGM CVII.1–19

Daniel and Maltomini, *Supplementum Magicum I*, no. 44.

PGM CVIII.1–12

Daniel, Robert W. "It Started with Eve," *ZPE* 74 (1988), 249–51.

PGM CIX.1–8

Giangrande, Giuseppe. "Hermes and the Marrow, Once Again," *Museum Philologum Londiniense* 7 (1986), 39–42.

Faraone, Christopher A. "Hermes But No Marrow: Another Look at a Puzzling Magical Spell," *ZPE* 72 (1988), 279–86.

Versnel, H. S. "A Twisted Hermes. Another View of an Enigmatic Spell," *ZPE* 72 (1988), 287–92.

Daniel and Maltomini, *Supplementum Magicum II*, no. 56.

PGM CX

Packman, Zola M. "Instructions for the Use of Planet Markers on a Horoscope Board," *ZPE* 74 (1988), 85–95.

PGM CXII.1–5

Daniel and Maltomini, *Supplementum Magicum I*, no. 16.

PGM CXIII.1–4

Daniel and Maltomini, *Supplementum Magicum I*, no. 17.

PGM CXV.1–7

Daniel and Maltomini, *Supplementum Magicum I*, no. 12.

PGM CXX.1–13

Daniel and Maltomini, *Supplementum Magicum I*, no. 1.

PGM CXXII

Maltomini, Franco. "P. Berol. 21243 (formulario magico). Due nuove letture," *ZPE* 74 (1988), 247–48.

PGM CXXII.5ff.

Janko, Richard. "Berlin Magical Papyrus 21243. A Conjecture," *ZPE* 72 (1988), 293.

PGM CXXII.1–15

Faraone, Christopher A. "Aphrodite's ΚΕΣΤΟΣ and Apples for Atalanta: Aphrodisias in Early Greek Myth and Ritual," *Phoenix* 44 (1990), 219–43.

PGM CXXVIII.1–11

Daniel and Maltomini, *Supplementum Magicum I*, no. 28.

PGM CXXX

Daniel and Maltomini, *Supplementum Magicum I*, no. 3.